White County
Tennessee

Court Minutes
&
Court of Pleas *and* Quarter Sessions

1835-1841

By:

Work Projects Administration

Please direct all correspondence and orders to:

www.southernhistoricalpress.com
or
SOUTHERN HISTORICAL PRESS, Inc.
PO BOX 1267
375 West Broad Street
Greenville, SC 29601
southernhistoricalpress@gmail.com

ISBN #0-89308-454-9

Printed in the United States of America

WHITE COUNTY

COURT OF PLEAS AND QUARTER SESSIONS

1835-1841

Note: Page numbers in this index refer to those of the original volume from which this copy was made. These numbers are inserted within parenthesis throughout the copy.

State of Tennessee.

At a Court of Pleas and Quarter Session began and held for the County of White at the Court house in the Town of Sparta, before the Worshipful the Justices of said Court, on the second Monday being the Thirteenth day of July in the year of our Lord one thousand eight hundred and thirty five, and of the Independence of the United States of America the Sixtieth year

Present the Worshipful

Thomas Eastland, chairman	
David Snodgrass,	
John Jett	
John Bryan	
Charles Reeves	
Joseph Herd	
William Knowles	
David Hasting	
John Rose	Esqr
Joseph Cummings, Jr.,	
Jesse Scoggan	Justices
Dan Griffith	
Stephen Holland	
Saml A. Moore	
Thomas Barnes	
Thomas Cooper	
Edmund Cunningham	
Eli Sims	

Ordered. by Court, that David Snodgrass, John Jett, and Joseph Cummings, Jur Esquires be appointed commissioners to settle with Joseph Herd, Administrator of Benjamin Bowman Deceased and made report there of to the next term of this Court Isad.

Ordered by Court that Turner Lane, John Bryan and Jesse Scoggin be appointed commissioners to settle with Woodson P. White Executer of John Porter, Decd. And report to the present term of this Court Isad.

Ordered by Court unanmously that, William Glenn Merchants of Sparta, be allowed the sum of Twelve Dollars for furnishing this Blank Book as a record book for White County Court - that the Sheriff of White County pay for the same out of any monies in his hands of the Taxes of the year 1835. And that the same be good with him in the settlement of his account with the Trustee of White County.

Ordered by Court that John Kirkpatrick be appointed Overseer of the road from the Turnpike road East of Sparta, passing through the Wild-Cat-Cove, and intersecting the road from Sparta to Joseph Hunters, being a road of the third class. And keep the same in repair as the law requires, that all persons residing on the lands of John Rose Esqr. be assigned to work thereon. Isd.

Dan Griffeth Esqr. returned a list of Taxable property and polls in Capt. Dodsons Company for the year 1835.

This day William Curtlow produced in open Court four wolf scalps, under the the age of four months, and proved that they were killed in White County - where upon there being present five acting Justices of the peace, it is ordered to be Certifed to the Treasure of West Tennessee for payment, and that the sheriff of White County burn said Scalps, who being here in Court received said Scalps into his possession and acted according Isd.

Ordered by Court that the Sheriff of White County, take into his custody and produce here in Court, the body Mary Ann Dabney, an orphan girl living in the home and under the control of Samuel Denton of said county on the first day of the next term of this Court to be dealt with as required by law Isd.

Ordered by Court that Barnett K. Mitchell be appointed Overseer of the road from Capt. Whites to the mouth of Cane Creek at the ford of Caney Fork, being a road of the second class that D. Hasting Esqr. assign a list of hands to work thereon &c.

(P-2) Ordered by Court that James Roberts be appointed Overseer of the road from Sinking Creek to Gum Spring Mountain, being a road of the second class, and keep the same in repair as the law requires, and that the same hands which worked under Willis Kiethly late Overseer there of Isd.

Ordered by Court that Isham B. Hasting be appointed Overseer of the road from the forks of the road at or near the mouth of Cane Creek to the top of the Hill at Esquire Hastings being a road of the second class, and keep the same in repair as the law requires that David Hasting Esquire assign a list of hands to work there on Isd.

Ordered by Court that Cason Swindle, be appointed Overseer of the road, from Wallings Gum to Andrew Goodsons, being a road of the Second class, and keep the same in repair as the law requires with the hands, which worked under William Roberts former Overseer there of Isd.

Ordered by Court that William C. Bounds be appointed Overseer of the road from falling Water to Jackson County line, being a road of the second class, and keep the same in repair as the law requires with the hands which worked under John Bradford former Overseer there of Isd.

This day Jesse Allen Senr produced in open Court one large wolf Scalp over the age of four months and proved that the same was killed in White County, where upon there being present five acting Justices of the peace, it is ordered that the same be certified to the Treasure of West Tennessee for payment, and that the Sheriff of White

County burn said Scalps, who being here in Court received the same into his custody and agted accordingly Issd.

Ordered by Court that the road as laid off and marked by Commissioners from James H. Pass to Bunker Hill, be established as a road of the Second Class

Ordered by Court that Iredale W. Stone, be appointed Overseer of the road as laid off by Commissioners from James H. Pass's to Matthew England's, being a road of the Second Class and open and keep the same in repair as the law requires that John Pennington Esqr. Assign a list of hands to work there on Issd.

Ordered by Court that Matthew England be appointed Overseer of the road, from the house of Matthew England, to the Rock Island road as laid off by Commissioners being a road of the Second Class, and open and Keep the same in repaid as the law requires, and that John Pennington Esqr. assign a list of hands to work there on Issd.

Ordered by Court that John Dew be appointed Overseer of the road as laid off by Commissioners from Rock island to Bunker-Hill being a road of the Second class, and open and keep the same in repair as the law requires, that John Pennington Esqr. assign a list of hands to work there on Issd.

Ordered by Court that William Lisk, William Irwin, Isaac Taylor, James Russell, and Aaron Hutchings free holders, be appointed a Jury of view to lay off and mark a road from the mouth of falling water to some convenient point in Allen Ferry road and report there of to the next term of this Court Issd.

This day Wamon Leftwich Admr. of the estate of James Rowland Decd. returned on Oath an account of the sales of the Deceased, which is ordered to be recorded.

Ordered by Court that Daniel Martin Senr. be appointed Overseer of the road from the eight Mile post on the Cathage road to the bridge at Bunker Hill, and also to the ford of the creek above the bridge, being a road of the first class, and keep the same in repair with the hands which worked under the former Overseer there of Issd.

(P-3) Ordered by Court that the following Gentlemen be appointed as Jurors to hold the next General Election for members to Congress of the United States Govenor of the State of Tennessee and Members to the General Assembly Towit - At the Precinct at Sparta John Jett, Charles Reeves and William Bruster - at the Precinct at David Hastings, Spencer Mitchell, Daniel Dale and Jesse Scoggin, at the Precinct at Mr. Warrens on the Mountain Joseph Kerr, George Potts, and Steuart Warren at the Precinct at Revd Ozias Denton, Robert Anderson, Senr., John Fryer and Lewis Phillips, at the Precinct at Robert Cooke, William Glenn, Senr. Richard Crowder and George Pertle, at the Precinct at the mouth of Falling Water Samuel Strong, Levi Bozarth, and George Allen, at the Precinct at Bunker hill, Jose C. Dew, Jesse England and Samuel Brown, at the Precinct at Hunters Mills, Thomas Barnes, William Bartlett, and Jesse Williams, at the Precinct at Matthew G. Moore, Samuel Johnston, Patrick Potts, and Lewis Bohannon Issd.

Ordered by Court that William Turner Be appointed Overseer of the road from Mark Lowreys field to the Mills of David Snodgrass, Esqr. being a road of the Second class and that he keep the same in repair as the law requires with the hands which worked under Abraham Broyles former Overseer there of Issd.

Ordered by Court that David Snodgrass and Sims Dearing Esquire be appointed to apportion and assign hands betwen the Overseers on the Cherry Creek and Plumb Creek roads and report there of to the next term of this Court Issd.

Ordered by Court that Jeremiah Wilhite be appointed Overseer of the road from the mile post near Wisdoms field, to the mill post near Howards being a road of the second class, and keep the same in repair as the law requires with the hands which worked under John Mason the former Overseer there of Issd.

Ordered by Court that James Bohannon be appointed Overseer of the road from Hunters Mill to the Jackson County line being a road of the second class and keep the same in repair as the law requires, that Thomas Barnes Esqr. assign a list of hands to work there on Issd.

State
vs
Richard Turner } Bastardy

This day came the Defendant with William G. Sims Into Court and acknowledged them selves indebted to the State in the sum of two hundred and fifty dollars each, to be levied of their respective goods and chattle lands and tenaments, to the use of the State to be rendered - nevertheless to be void on condition, that the said Richard Turner, shall keep free indemnified and harmless the County of White, from any colar of cost or damage, for and towards the support of a Bastard Male child, called and known by the name of William Williams, begotton and born of the body of Polly Williams a single woman.

Ordered by Court that Indemon Lane, Alexander Dillon, James Hunter, John Frankland and George Woods, free holders be appointed a Jury of view to lay off and mark a road the nearest and best way leaving the Dillon ferry road, a small distance North of the Caney fork, and of the ferry crossing the caney fork at a ford just below the ferry, and intersecting the old road at some convenient point on the South side of the River and report to the next term of this court, it being a road of the second class. Issd.

(P-4)

Isaac Hasting one of the heirs at law of Joseph Hasting Decd
vs
Sarah Hasting widow of Joseph Hasting Decd. } Motion

On motion of Isaac Hasting and for

reasons appearing to the satisfaction of the Court process is awarded him directed to the Sheriff of White County commanding him to make know to the said Sarah Hasting that she produce in the Court on the first day of the next session there of a writing in her hands purporting to be the last will and testament of the said Joseph Hasting Dec'd so that the Court may upon inspection there of and proof had, do what of right and according to law ought to be done in the premises.

Ordered by Court that Alexander Cooper be released from the payment of the Taxes upon 200 acres of land in White County for the year 1834, he owning no such lands, that the Sheriff have credit with the Trustee of White County on his next settlement of account &c.

Ordered by Court that the following additional hands be assigned to work on the road of which William H. Baker is Overseer Towit - John Acuff, George Pertle, Aaron Hutchings, William Anderton, and Samuel Stover.

This day John Bryan, Jesse Scoggin and Turner Lane Commissioners appointed to settle with Woodson P. White, Admr. of William S. Longstreet, Decd. returned their report on oath which is ordered to be recorded.

Ordered by Court that Woodson P. White Exr. of John Porter Decd. and Admr. of Joshua Porter, Decd. be allowed the sum of three dollars for money by him paid the comrs. who made a settlement and report on said estate.

Ordered by Court that Alexander Irwin, William Glenn, Henry Lyda, John M. Little, and Asa Certain freholders be appointed a Jury of view to lay and mark a roard round a pond on the Kentucky road passing through William Lisks land report thereof to the next term of this Court Issd.

Ordered by the Court that James M. Johnston be appointed overseer of the road from the Ten mile tree to Johnston Mill road being a road of the second class and keep the same in repair with the hands assessed the former Overseer Issr.

Ordered that the respective Overseers of the Sundry roads in the neighborhood of Gus Simpson at the next term of this Court, bring in these crews of hands so that the Court may assign hands to them respectively, agreeably to the dignity of these roads.

This day the list of Taxable property and polls in Capt. Samuel Allens Company for the year 1835 was returned which was ordered to be recorded.

Ordered by Court that the Sheriff of White County colects and receives lists of Taxable property &c. from these who have failed to return the same for the year 1834 and collect thereon a Singl Tax only.

Ordered by court that Presley Holland be appointed overseer of the road from Simpsons Mill to the gum spring road at the widow Rodgers being a road of the second Class and keep the same in repair as the law requires and that David Mitchell Esq. assign a list of hands to work thereon Issr.

(P-5) This day Samuel Turney one of the commissoners heretofore appointed to settle with Nicholas Cook guardean to the heirs of George Keezee Dec. returned their report thereof which is ordered to be Recorded

Ordered by Court that Joseph Phifer, Zachariah Anderson, Dan Griffeth and Thomas Eastland freeholders be appointed a Jury of reason to lay off and mark a road of the second Class, the nearest and best way, varying the several gaps of the mountain from the big bottom on the caney fork to intersect the Ross road near William Rotans place east of Joseph Phifers and report thereof to the next term of this Court. Issr.

This day Micajah Taylor a constable appointed in Court and resigned his office as such which is recorded.

Ordered by court that the folowing persons be appointed as Jurors to the next County Court for White County To wit.

James Scarbrouh, James Anderson, William Yarbrouh, Geo. W. Jones, John W. Dearing, Elias Yeager, James Graham, Samuel Porter, William Dodson, Bryant Sparkman, Lewis Glenn, William Little, William J. Cole, Overton Chisum, James Knowles, Jr., Levi Jarvis, William Burden, Henderson McFarland, John Dew, Daniel Martin, Robert Brown, Jerry Gillentine, Wm. C. Medcalf, James Scott, Joseph W. Little, and Thomas Yates, and Archebald Conner, and James Russell Constables Issr.

Ordered by Court that the following persons be appointed as Jurors to the next Circuit Court towit: Robert Watkins, George W. Miller, William C. Brittain, Robert Watson, William Snodgrass, James Walker, Samuel Miller, John Dew, Nathan Earles, William Pettett, Jonas Turner, Mark Lowry, Woodson P. White, Turner Lane, Sr., Jesse Scoggin, Spence Mitchell, John Bryan, John Bradley, John H. Carmachael, George Price, Henry Collier, Eli Sims, Richard Crowder, William Glenn, Joseph Clark, Robert Smith, William Usrey, and John Jett, and Archibald Conner, and William M. Bryan Constables & Issr.

Ordered by Court that Jesse Scoggin, David Hasting, John White, Sr., Robert Gamble, and Spence Mitchell, freeholders be appointed a Jury of reason to lay off and mark a road from the Sequachee road passing James Simmons's intersecting the road leading to McMinnville being a road of the third class, and report thereof to the next term of this Court. Issr.

Ordered by Court that the Sheriff of White County bring him into Court on the first day of the next term of this Court, the infant children of Eleaner Moore to be dealt with as the Court shall and may deem proper consistant with law. Issr.

Ordered by Court, unanomously that the pleading for in the following causes, certified from the Circuit Court of White County, examined and approved by the Attorney General be allowed the following persons to be paid by the Trustee of White County out of any monies not otherwise appropriated Towit:

In the case the State vs George Bradshaw, Anthony Dibrell, Clerk $7.25 J. B. McCormack, Atty General $2.50, David L. Mitchell, Sheriff $2.00,

In the case the State vs Saskville McClure, Anthony Dibrell Clerk $4.50 David L. Mitchell Sheriff, 50 cents Jacob G. Mitchell, Dep. Sheriff $1 - In the case the State vs Wm. L. Adams, A. Dibrell Clerk $5.12½, David L. Mitchell, Sheriff $1.41½, Witness James Anderson, $2.50 Atty. Gen. I. B. McCormack $2.50 In the case the State vs Wm. L. Adams, Anthony Dibrell Clerk $5.12½, David L. Mitchell, Sheriff $1.91½ - Witness James Anderson, $2.50 Attorney General I. B. McCormack, $2.50 - In the case the State vs Thomas Underwood, Anthony Dibrell Clerk $5 - David L. Mitchell Sheriff $2.16½ Witness William Adair 50 cents Witness James Anderson $4 - Witness Robert Anderson $4 - Wit - Lewis Phillips $1.50

(P-6) John B. McCormack atto. General $2.50 The state Phillip Smith, Anthony Dibrell $8 J. B. McCormack, $2. 50, State . John Waller, 4.37½ Shff. Jabez G. Mitchell $1. witness J. B. Moore $1.50 - John Basco $2 - Jeremiah Denton $1.50 - Atto. gens. J. B. McCormack Tax fee $2.50 - State . Danel Penrod, Anthony Dibrell $3.37½ Shff. Thurman 62½ cents. Att Gnrl. J. B. McCormack Tax fee $2.50 - State . Larkin Yates, Anthony Dibrell, clerk $3.12½ D. L. Mitchell Sheriff 62½ cents - W. G. Sims $1. Atto. gnrl. J. B. McCormack Tax fee $3 - Witness W. Baker $1. - witness Wm. H. Baker $3 - Atto gnrl. J. B. McCormack. Tax fee $2.50 State . Susan Heath, Anthony Dibrell Clerk $2.62½ Attorney General. J. B. McCormack Tax fee $3 - witness John England $4 - Sheriff D. L. Mitchell , 16½c Jacob A. Lane Clerk $6.12½ William G. Sims $1.41½ - Attorney General J. B. McCormack Tax fee $2.50 - Constable John England, 25 cents.

Ordered by the court enamously that Jacob A. Lane clerk White Court be allowed the sum twenty dollars for working out the Tax lists &c. for the year 1835 - to be paid out of the Taxes of said year Issr.

The Court proceded to the appointment of a constable in Capt. Allens company for the next coming two years, and to that office appoint Robert H. McManus who thereupon took an oath to support the constitution of the United States the State of Tennessee and the several oaths prescribed by law.
and with Joseph Herd and William G. Sims, intered in to and acknowledged bond in the sum of one thousand dollars conditioned as the law devices.

Ordered that Court be adjoured untill to morrow
Morning 9 Oclock

David Snodgrass
Sims Dearing
Lewis Pettett

Tuesday morning 14th July A.D. 1835 Court met prusuant to adjournment
Present the Worshipful

David Snodgrass)
Sims Dearing) Justices
Lewis Pettett)

For reasons appearing to the satisfaction of the Court, it is ordered that Isaac Taylor, William Matlock and Joseph Kerr, James Scott, summonsed as Jurors to attend this Court at the present term of this Court, from further attendance or such be released and discharged &c.

The Sheriff of White County returned the writ of venire Facias to him directed To wit:-

George Ogden, William C. Bullard, William Matlock, James Scott, John H. McCully, Robert Denny, Andrew Bryan, Benjamin Lewis, Robert Anderson, Preston Chisum, Willis B. Hasting, William Plumley, Mickus Taylor, John Brown, Jr., Jesse Keithly, James Walling, Jr., William Lisk, Sr., Isaac Taylor, George W. Miller, Joseph Kerr, James Hudson, Benjamin Weaver, William Bounds, David Nicholds, Frances Johnston, and Thomas Miller Executed &c. -
on all except Ben. Weaver, Jas. Hudson, Willis B. Hasting, and Wm. Lisk, July 13, 1835 - David L. Mitchell Sheriff

Out of which venire was drawn by ballot the following names of good and lawful men Citizens and house holders and freeholders of the County of White To wit - William C. Brittain foreman, Robert Anderson, William Bounds, William Plumley, Andrew Bryan, Thomas Miller, John Brown, Jr., (P-7) James Walling, Jr., Preston Chisum, Benjamin Lewis, Mickus Taylor, Jesse Keithly, George Ogden good and lawful men Citizens and house and freeholders of the County of White who being elected unparrelled sworn and charged a Jury of grand inquest for the state of Tennessee in the body of the County of White and having received their charge, retired to consult of Indictements presentments &c.

Dudley Hunter
vs Issr.
Joseph Kerr

In debt

This day came the defendant in proper person and declaired that he could no further gainsay the plainaff action for the sum of thirty dollars thirty nine and one half cents the balance dew on the writing obligatory in the declaration in this cause mentioned besides cost - It is therefore considered by the Court, that the plainaff recover against the defendant the sum of thirty dollars thirty nine and one half cents the balance of the debt in the declaration mentioned assumed as aforesaid together with his cost by him about his suit in this behalf expended and said defendant may be imerced &c.

The grand Jury again returned into Court with the following Bill of Indictment Towit: The state against George Mitchell for an assault & Battery on the body of Stephen Hickman "A true Bill" and again returned to consult further of Indictments presentments &c.

State
vs
George Mitchell

Ind. for A.B.

Stephen Hickman
Prosicuter

On motion of the Attorney General a Capias is awarded the State against the body of the defendant returnable here in Court instantly.

George P. Shepherd Executor and
Nicy B. Shepherd Executor of
William H. Smith, Dec.

Issr.

Stephen Martin

In debt

This day the parties by their Attornies and thereupon came a Jury of good and lawful men Towit: Robert Denny, William Ward, Alfred Merrett, Peter Carter, John M. Carter, Daniel Martin, Alexander Moore, William Anderson, James M. Haggard, James Herd, William J. Lewis, & John McCullough, who being elected hired sworn the truth to speak upon the issue joined upon their oath do say that the defendant hath well and truly paid and settled the debt on the plainaff declaration as in pleading he hath alledged -

It is therefore considered by the Court that the plainaff take nothing by their bill but for their false claim be imerced &c. that the Defendant depart hence without delay and recover against the plainaff his cost by him about his defence on this behalf expended &c.

George Ogden

vs Issr.

Jesse Lincoln

In Debt

This day came the parties by their Attornies (P-8) and thereupon came a Jury of good and lawful men To wit - John Gailly, Henry Rutledge, Hiram Gist, Washington Staples, James Bradley, Richard Harris, Isaac Sharp, Charles Henseley, Benjamin Turner, Edward Gleeson, John Allen, and John Gracy who being elected tried and sworn the truth to speak upon the issue joined upon their oath do say that the defendant hath not well and truly paid the debt in the declaration mentioned but owes unto the plainaff the sum of one hundred dollars that the plainaff hath sustained damages by occasion of the detention thereof to the sum of one dollar and sixty cents as the plainaff in his declaration against him hath complained besides cost. It is therefore considered by the Court that the plainaff recover against the defendant the sum of one hundred dollars the debt in the declaration mentioned together with the further sum of one dollar and sixty cents the damages aforesaid in manner and form aforesaid assessed, together with his cost by his about his suit in this behalf expended and said defendant may be imerced &c.

Charles R. Sperry

vs Issr

Thomas Gist, Sen.

Debt on Fifa

This day came the plainaff by his attorney and it appearing to the States parties of the Court upon the production of all the papers and procedings had in this cause before the Justices of the peace for white County that the plainaff by the Judgement of William Bruster, late a Justic of the peace, recovered against said defendant on the 24th day Febuary A.D. 1834 the sum of seven dollars twenty three and three fourth cents debt, besides cost and that on execution issuing thereon the 3rd day of July A.D. 1835 came to the hands and possession of Micajah Taylor, constable who returned the same into this Court with the following endorsment thereon Towit: July 3rd 1835 No personal property found. - levied on one track of land containing seven acers situated in White County granted by the State of Tennessee to the said Thomas Gist Sen. by grant No 6507 dated 15th August 1827 and begining on the South East corner of a sixty five acers Survey of Archebald Conner, running thence as set forth in said grant also one other tract of land containing thirteen and three fourth Acers part of grant No 6388 issued by the State of Tennessee to Alexander Lowry, being the same land conveyed to said Thomas Gist S. by deed from Elaxnder Lowry, dated 19th July 1831 and regestered in the regestors office of White County in Book H. page 599 - July 3rd 1835 -

Therefore on motion of the plainaff by his attorney it is considered by the court that the aforesaid several tracts of land be considered in Satisfaction of the plainaff debt with cost of motion &c. and that the same or so much thereof as shall be of value sufficient be sold in satifaction thereof.

And it is further considered by the Court that the plainaff recover against said defendant his cost by him about his motion in the behalf expended and it is further ordered that a writ of vindinonexpenas be awarded the plainaff directed to the Sheriff of White County commanding &c. returnable &c.

Simpson & Nance)
vs Issr.) Debt on Fi - Fa
Thomas Gist, Sen.)

This day came the plainaff by his attorney and it appearing to the Satisfaction of the Court upon the production of all the papers and poceidings had in this cause before the Justic of the peace that the plainaff by the judgement of William Bruster Esquire late a Justice of the peace (P-9) for White County recover aganst said defendant the sum of three dollars sixty two and a half cents Debt on the 10th day of May A.D. 1834 besides cost and that an exoution issuing thereon the 3rd day of July A.D. 1835 came to the hands and possession of Micajah Taylor a constable in the County of White; who returned the same into this Court with the following endorsment thereon To wit. July 3rd 1835 no personal property found in any County. - Levied on one track of land containing seven acers estate in the County of White granted by the State of Tennessee to the said Thomas Gist Sen., by grant No 6507 dated 15th August 1827 and beginning on the North East Corner of a sixty five acer survey of Archebald Conner running thence as set forth in said grant Also one track of land containing thirteen and three fourth acers part of grant No 6388 issued by the State of Tennessee to Alexander Lowry being the same land conveyed to said Thomas Gist Sen. by deed from Alexander Lowry, dated 19th July 1831 and regestered on the Regesters office of White County in Book H. page 599. - July 3rd, 1835 -

Therefore on motion of the plainaff by his attorney, it is considered by the Court that the aforesaid several tracts of land be condemned in satisfaction of the plainaffs debt with cost of motion &c.

and that the same or so much thereof as shall be of value sufficent be sold in satisfaction thereof. - And it is further considered by the Court that the plainaff recover against said defendant his cost by him about his Motion in this behalf expended and it is further ordered by the Court that a writ of vindenonexpenas be awarded the plainaff directed to the Sheriff of White County commanding &c. Returnable &c.

William Curry
vs Issr.
Thomas Gist Sen.

Debt on Fi. Fa.

This day came the plainaff by his attorney and it appearing to the satisfaction of the Court upon the production of all the papers and proceedings had in this Cause before the Justices of the peace; that the plainaff by the judgement of William Bruster, Esq. late a Justie of the peace for the County of White on the 24th day of Febuary A.D. 1834 recovered against the Defendant the sum of fifty Six and a fourth cents debt, besides Cost and that an execution issuing thereon the 3rd day of July A.D. 1835, came to hands and possession of Micajah Taylor a constable in said County who returned the same into this Court with the following endorsement thereon Towit: July 3rd 1835 no personal property found in any county. - Levied on one track of land containing seven acers estate in White County granted by the State of Tennessee to the said Thomas Gist Sen. by grant No 6507 dated 15th August 1827 And begining on the North East corner of a sixty five acers survey of Archebald Conner running thence as set forth in said grant. Also one tract of land containing thirteen and three fourths acers part of grant No 6388 issued by the State of Tennessee to Alexander Lowry being the same land conveyed to said Thomas Gist Sen. by deed from Alexander Lowry dated 19th 1831 and regestered in the Regesters office of White County in Book H. page 599 July 3rd 1835 - Therefore on motion of the plainaff by his Attorney it is considered by the Court that the aforesaid several tracks of land be condemned in satisfaction of the plainaffs debt and cost of motion &c. and the same or so much thereof as shall be of value suffesent be sold in satisfaction thereof. - and it is further considered by the Court that the plainaff recover against the defendant his cost by him about his motion in this behalf expended &c. and it is further considered and so ordered by the Court that a writ of vindetion exponas be awarded the plainaff directed to the Sheriff of White County Commanding &c. returnable &c.

(P-10)

Charles Burgess
vs
William Bullock &
Edward Bullock

Motion

For reason appearing to the satisfaction of the Court it is ordered that the Cost on these causes severally be corrected in the taxation thereof by adding thereto the cost and Dudley Hunter, Constable and that execution for the collection thereof issued.

Be it rememberd that on this 14th day of July A.D. 1835, Personally appeared in open court Capt. James Herd to the Court known, and thereupon in presence of the Court took and subscribed the following affidavit To wit:- James Herd says that he is well acquainted with Micajah Rickets who is an applicant for a pension - and serve him at Fort Scott on Flink River whoreas he was in the service of the United States as a private Soldier does not recollect the Captains Company to which he belonged - he was then going upon his crutches had been wounded as affront understood whilst engaged against the enemy, being the Seminole Indians sworn to in open Court 14th July 1835

To wit: Jacob A. Lane Clerk, James Herd whereupon it is ordered to be certified by the Court, that it appears of the Court, that the said James Herd is a person of good name, fame and reputation and entitled to full faith and credit in a Court of Justic. - And it is further ordered to be certified that this Court, is a Court of record.

Ordered that Court be adjourned until

to morrow morning 9 Oclock

David Snodgrass
Sims Dearing
Lewis Pettett

Wednesday morning 15th July A.D. 1835 Court met pursuant to adjourment. Present the worshipful

David Snodgrass
Sims Dearing
Lewis Pettett } Esqs Justices

This day the Com. appointed at the last term of this Court to lay off and mark a road from Greenville Templetons to the Gum Spring near Mrs. Rodgers returned their report which is ordered to be recorded and said road established as a road of the third Class.

Ordered by Court that Greenville Templeton be appointed Overseer of the road as laid out and marked by Commissioners from Greenville Templetons intersecting the Gum Spring road between the widow Rodgers and Capt. Herds being a road of the third Class, and open and keep the same in repair as the law requires and that Joseph Herd Esq. assign a crew of hands to thereon.

State
vs } Ind. A.B.
Peter Carter } Grey Smallman Pros.

This day came the Attorney General (P-11) as well as the defendant by his attorney able and learned in the law and said defendant being arranged and charged upon the bill of Indictement pleaded not guilty thereto and for his trial put himself upon the County and the Attorney general doth the like - whereupon came a Jury of good and lawful men To wit: - John McCullough, Robert Denny, Smith Cambell, John C. Cantrell, Alexnder Moore, Edward M. Murray, Wm. Moore, John Gailly, Wm. Allen, George W. Isham, William Bruster, and George Cooley, who being elected tried and sworn the truth to speak upon the issue of traverse joined upon their oath do say that defendant is not guilty of the Assault and Batterey in manner and form as charged in the bill of Indictment as in pleading he hath alledged. It is therefore considered by the Court that the defendant from the allegation contained in the bill of Indictment be released and for on discharged that he depart hence without day and recover against the county of White all cost on part of the prosecution that Certificates issue to the Trustee of White County for the payment of the same.

This day John Harlowe a Citizen of the County of White appeared in the presence and hearing of the Court in a state of intoxecation to the great annoyance of the Court thereby impending the execution of the public commission which the Court was there engaged and setting for the trial thereof and the said John Harlowe being led to the bar of the Court in custody of the Sheriff of White County - It is therefore considered and so ordered by the Court that the said John Harlowe, for such contempt be imprisoned in the common jail of White County without bail or mainprise untill the going down of the sun on this day - And the Sheriff being here in Court received said John Harlowe into his custody and carried said sentence into execution accordingly

State)
vs) Ind for A.B.
Jonathan Simmons) Bramen Harden Pros.

This day came as well the Attorney General as the defendant in proper person aided by counsel learned in the law and the defendant being arraigned and charged upon the bill of Indictment pleaded not guilty thereto and for his trial put himself upon the County and the Attorney General dothe the like whereupon came a Jury of good and lawful men To wit: - Jeremiah Witt, William Ward, Charles P. Shockley, John M. Carter, George Broyles, Matthew Johnston, Peter Carter, William Wells, James Simpson, Ramon Penner, Osbourn Walker and John Cantrell, who being elected tried and sworn the truth to speak upon the issue of treverse joined and having heard the evidence and arguement of counsel thereon retired to consult their verdict and again returned into Court, and declaird that they could not agree thereon where upon by consent of the attorney general and the defendant and with the assent of the Court James Simpson, one of the Jurors is withdrawn and the rest of the Jurors from rendering their verdict released and discharged and this cause continued untill the next term of this court

State)
vs) Ind for A.B.
Jonathan Simmons) Bramen Harden Pros.

This day came John Medley into open Court

in proper person and acknowledged himself indebted to the State of Tennessee in the sum (P-12) of two hundred and fifty dollars to be levied of his proper goods and chattels lands and tenement to the end of the State never the less to be void in condition that the said John Medley, shall will and truly make his personal appearance in this court on the third day of the next term of of this Court there and then to give evidence in behalf of the State, against the defendant and attend from day to day and not depart thereof without leave of the Court first had and obtained

State)
vs) Ind for Rest
Josiah Wooldrige,)
William Wooldrige,)
Marshal Wooldrige &)
Isaac Adcock) Smith Cantrell Pros.

This day came Smith Cantrell and John Cantrell in proper person into open Court and acknowledged themselves indebted to the State in the sum of two hundred and fifty dollars each to the airs of the state their respective goods and chattels, lands and tenements never the less to be void on condition that the said Smith Cantrell and John Cantrell shall well and truly make their personal appearance in this Court on the third day of the next term of this Court then and there to give evidence and prosecute in behalf of the State against said Defendants and not depart thereof without leave of the Court first had and obtained &c.

State)
vs) Ind for Rest
The Same) Smith Cantrell Pros

On motion of the Attorney General on Alias Capias is awarded the State against the body of the defendant returnable at the next term of this Court

State)
vs) Ind for Gaiming
Samuel Scruggs &)
Edward Rudder) On motion of the Attorney General on Alias Capias is awarded the State against the defendant returnable here at the next term of this Court

State)
vs) Ind A.B.
Michael Moore) On motion of the Attorney General here at the

next term of this Court.

(P-13)

State }
vs } Ind for A.B.
William Simmons } On motion of the Attorney General on Capias is awarded the State against the body of the Defendant returnable here at the next term of this Court

State }
vs } Ind for gaiming
William Hitchcock } On motion of the Attorney General a Capias is awarded the State against the body of the defendant returnable here at the next term of this Court

State }
vs } Ind for A. B.
George Mitchell } On motion of the Attorney General a Capias awarded the State against the body of the defendant returnable here at the next term of this Court.

State }
vs } Ind for Gaiming
William Carland } On motion of the Attorney General a Capias is awarded the State against the body of the defendant returnable here at the next term of this Court.

State }
vs } Pars for Gaiming
Abraham Broyles } On motion of the Attorney General a Capias Instantm is awarded against the body of the defendant returnable here in Court Constantly.

William Ward }
vs } Debt fr.
Stephen Holland } This day came the parties by their Attornies and thereupon came a Jury of good and lawful men To wit: Robert Denny, John McCullough,

John Graey, John L. Price, James Hudgins, Alfred Merrett, John Brown, Jonathan T. Fairington, William Smith, Jonathan Simmons, Jonathan Scott and John Whitley, good and lawful men who being elected tried an sworn the truth to speak upon the premeses who having heard part of the evidence in said cause, when it appeared to the satisfaction of the Court during the progress of the trial of said cause that Jonathan Simmons, one of the Jurors impanneled for the trial of said cause whereupon the Court now providing for the trial of said cause being unanimously of the opinion that the said Jonathan Simmons, the juror aforesaid is too unwell and wholly unable to serve and set on the trial of said cause, it is ordered by the Court that Jonathan Simmons be permitted to retire, and it is further ordered and by the Court so directed that (P-14) the Sheriff summons instantm a Juror in the place of the said Jonathan Simmons, - whereupon the the Sheriff of White County summonsed and brought into Court Madison Johnston as a Juror, who being elected in due form of law, it is ordered and directed by the Court that the said Madison Johnston, be sworn as a Juror to set on the trial of said cause, in place of the said Jonathan Simmons and that the trial of said Cause be commenced Denovo. -
and the said Madison Johnston being sworn in due for of law as a Juror, for the trial of said cause took his seat in the Jury box with the other Jurors and the trial of said cause commenced Denovo.

Ordered that Court be adjourned untill to morrow morning 9 Oclock

David Snodgrass
Sims Dearing
Lewis Pettett

Thursday morning 16 July 1835 Court met pursuant to adjournment Present the worshipful

David Snodgrass
Sims Dearing
Lewis Pettett } Esqs Justices

Ordered by Court, that the order made on yesterday estableshing a road of the third Class from Greenville Templetons to the Gum Spring road near Wm. Rodgers and appointed as Overseer thereon be set aside and cancelled &c

The grand Jury again returned into Court with the following bills of Indictment To wit: the State vs Winkfield Hill for a nuesance "A true Bill" the State William A. Cook for a neusance a true Bill the State against William Carland for an affray "A true Bill" The State vs Robert Hewett not a true Bill the State vs William L. Adams for an assault & battery not a true bill and return to consult &c - whereupon it is considered by the Court that the said Robert Hewett and Willa L. Adams recover against the County of White all cost in their cases expended and that certificates issue to the trustee of White County for payment &c.

State
vs } Ind for Nuisance
Wenkfield Hill

On motion of the Attorney general a capias is

awarded the State against the defendant returnable here in Court instantly

State
vs
William A. Cook

Ind for nuisance

On motion of the Attorney General a capias is awarded the State against the body of the defendant returnable here in court instantly.

(P-15)

State
vs
William Carland

Ind for An Affray

On motion of the Attorney General a Capias awarded the State against the defendant returnable here in Court instantly

The grand jury again came into Court and declared they had nothing further to present it is ordered that they from further attendance as Grand Juror during this term be releasesed and discharged -

State
vs Iss.
William Carland

Ind for An Affray

This day came the Attorney Gensal as well as the Defendant in proper person who being aranged and charged upon the bill of Indictment pleadded guilty thereto and for his trial put himself upon the grase and mercy of the Court. - It is therefore considered by the Court that the defendant for such his offence make his fine by the payment of the sum of one dollar together with all cost in this behalf expended &c.

William Ward
Juror Acknl iss'd vs Issr
Stephen Holland

debt fre

This day came the parties by their attornies and thereupon also came the following Juror sworn in this cause on yesterday To wit: Robert Denny, John McCullough, John Gracy, John L. Price, Alfred Merrett, John Brown, Jonathan T. Fairington, William Smith, Jonathan Scott, John Whitley, Madison Johnston, and James Hudgins who being elected tried and sworn the truth to speak upon the primeses upon their oath do say that the defendant does not owe unto the plainaff the debt in this warrent in this cause mentioned or any part thereof but that upon a fair adjustment of the subsisting accounts between the parties, outstanding and existing at the time of serving out the warrant in this cause the plainaff owes unto said defendant the sum of nine dollars seven and three fourth cents the ballance of the debt due to the defendant from the plainaff as the defendant is pleading hath alledged besides cost -

Therefore on motion of the defendant by his attorney it is considered by the Court that the defendant recover against the plainaff and James Godard his Security the sum of nine dollars seven and three fourth cents, the debt aforesaid in manner and form aforesaid together with his cost by him about his defence in this behalf expended &c.

James Scott

vs Iesr. — Debt Cr.

Elam Sherrell
John Bussell
Jose C. Dew

This day came the parties by their attornies and thereupon came a jury of good and lawful men To wit: Daniel Bartlett, John Pennington; George W. Isham; Joshua Morris; Edward Gleeson; Sevier Evans, John Vincent; John Carter; Moses Netherton, Charles Denny; Turner B. Henley and (P-16) William Green; who being elected tried and sworn the truth to speak upon the primese and upon matters relating to the usurious transaction mingled with the contract and writing in the warrant in this cause mentioned upon their oath do say that all that portion an part of the debt in the warrant in this cause mentioned as above the sum of thirty five dollars and fifty cents is usurious as the defendants in their petition and plea in this cause set forth and pleaded hath alledged; and the Jurors aforesaid upon the oath aforesaid do further say that the defendants owe unto the plaintiff the sum of Seventy one cents, the balance of the debt, in the warrant in this cause mentioned, as the plaintiff hath alledged, besides cost - It is therefore considered by the court on motion of the plainaff by his attorney that he recover against the defendant and Leonard Sailors their security for the prosecution of the Certiorari the sum Seventy one cents the balance of the debt aforesaid in manner and form aforesaid assessed together with his cost by him about his suit in this behalf expended and said defendant may be amerced &c.

State

vs — Ind for A.B.

Jonathan Simmon — Bramon Harden Prosecutor

This day personally appeared in open Court Certaorari William G. Sims, Jabez G. Mitchell, and Jacob A. Lane, and acknowledged themselves indebted to the State of Tennessee in the sum of two hundred and fifty dollars each to the one of the State to be rendered to be levied off their goods and chattels lands and tenements - neverthe less to be void on condition that the said Jonathan Simmons the above names defendant shall well and truly make his personal appearance in this Court on the third day of the next Session thereof there and then to answer the State on the above charge and attend from day to day and not depart thereof without leave of the court first had and obtained &c.

Ordered that Court be adjourned untill to morrow morning at 9 oclock

David Snodgrass
Sims Dearing
Lewis Pettett

Friday morning 17 July 1835 Court met pursuant to adjournment Present the worshipful

David Snodgrass }
Sims Dearing } Esq Justices
Lewis Pettett }

State }
vs } Ind for A.B.
George Mitchell } Stephen Hickman Pros.

This day came as well the attorney general as the defendant in proper person who being arraigned, and charged upon the bill of Indictment pleaded guilty thereto and for his trial put himself upon the grace and mercy of the Court - It is therefore considered by the Court that the defendant for such his offence make his fine by the payment of the sum of one dollar together with all costs &c - whereupon it is agreed and so ordered by the court that the execution of the Judgment be stayed untill the second Monday of October next

(P-17)

Robert Burk }
vs } In Debt
Charles R. Sperry }
James H. Jenkins }

This day came the parties by their attornies and thereupon came a Jury of good and lawful men Towit: John A. Carrick, James Carrick, John W. Robert, Edward M. Murray, William Carland, John W. Williams, William C. Brittain, George Mitchell, William W. Wilkes, William Moore, Samuel Tucker, and Simon Doyle, who being elected tried and sworn the truth to speak upon the issues joined upon their oaths do say that they find issues for the plainaff that the defendants owe unto the plainaff the sum of one hundred dollars the debt in the Declaration mentioned that the plainaff hath sustained damages by occasion of the detintion thereof to the sum of two dollars and twenty five cents, besides cost It is therefore considered by the Court the plainaff recover against the defendant the sum of one hundred dollars the debt in the declaration mentioned together with the damages aforesaid in manner and form aforesaid assessed together with his cost by him about his suit in this behalf expended and said defendants may be amerced &c.

Anthony Dibreil }
John H. Anderson }
vs } Debt Motion

Leighton Ferrell Sheriff
of Warren County

This day came the plainaff by their Attorney and the defendant Att. be again solomely called to appear in Court and shew cause if anything he hath agan say why the judgment rendered in this Court rendered Ni Si at the last term should not be taken against him final came not but made defendant. And it appearing to the satisfaction of the Court, that a copy of the judgment Ni Si rendered in this Court against him at the last term, had been returned made known to said Defendant and he being called to appear and defend the above cause &c. Came not - Therefore on motion of the plainaff by his Attorney it is considered by the Court that the plainaff recover against the defendant the sum of ninety six dollars, being the amount of a Judgment obtained by the plainaffs against a certain Stephen D. Hill in this Court on the 12th, day of April 1832 with interest thereon up to this day a case having issued thereon against said Stephen D. Hill which came to the hands and possession of said defendant as Sheriff of Warren County - which he failed to return as required and as in said judgment is set forth together with their cost by them about their motion in this behalf expended &c.

George P. Shepherd, Executor and
Nicy B. Shepherd, executor of
William H. Smith, Deceased

vs

Jacob A. Lane

In Covenant

This day came the parties by their attornies and thereupon came a Jury of good (P-18) and lawful men, To wit: John A. Carrick, John W. Bearing, John W. Roberts, Edward M. Murray, William Carland, John W. Williams, William C. Brittain, George Mitchell, William W. Wilkes, William Moore, Samuel Tucker, and Simon Doyle, who being elected tried and sworn the truth to speak upon the issue joined

Eliza Pugsley &
Allen A. Hall
vs
Anthoney Dibrell &
Wamon Leftwich

In Assumpset

This day came the parties by their Attornies and thereupon came a Jury of good and lawful men Towit: Andrew Cope, Harrison Holland, Amos McGowen, Jack Lamb, Guffree G. Garner, Asa Certain, William Matlock, Avery Norris, Webster Hutchens, George W. Isham, John Vincent, and Charles R. Sperry, who being elected tried and Sworn the truth to speak upon the issue joined upon their oath do say that the defendant and assurance and take upon themselves in manner and form as the plainaffs in their declaration against them hath complained and they do assess the plainaffs damages by occasion of the nonperformance of said assumption to the sum of two hundred and fifty nine dollars sixty seven cents besides cost - It is therefore considered by the Court that the plainaffs recover against said defendant the sum of two hundred and fifty nine dollars sixty seven cents the damages ajoined in manner and form aforesaid assesses together with their cost by them about their suit in this behalf expended &c.

Anthony Dibrell,
Wamon Leftwich
vs Issr
John W. Ford

Debt motion

This day came the plainaff by their attornies and thereupon came a jury of good and lawful men To wit: Andrew Cope, Harrison Holland, Amos McGowen, Jack Lamb, Guffree G. Garner, Asa Certain, William Matlock, Avery Norris, Webster Hutchens, John Vincent, George W. Isham and Charles R. Sperry, who being elected tried and sworn the truth to speak and well and truly enquire whether the plainaffs were security for the defendant upon the endorsement of a certain note, upon which a certain Eliza Pugsley and Allen A. Hall by the judgment of this Court on this recovered against said plainaff for the sum of two hundred and fifty nine dollars sixty seven cents, upon their oath do say that said plainaffs were the security for said defendant upon the (P-19) endorsement of said note in the cause aforesaid Therefore on motion of the plainaff by their attorney it is considered by the Court that the plainaff recover against the said John W. Ford the sum of two hundred and fifty nine dollars sixty seven cents the debt aforesaid together with the amount of the costs on said suit of Pugsley and Hall against said plainaffs together with the costs of motion in this behalf expended

Trent C. Conner &
Crocket Harbert
Daniel Dale &
Pleasant White
Advrs of John Dale deceased

Case

On motion of the plainaff by their Attornies a rule is admitted to shew cause why an Alias Capias should be awarded them against Pleasant White one of the defendants to which the

Attorney of Daniel Dale one of the defendant objects on the grounds that no process had issued for more than two terms therefore said cause stood discontinued and abated

Same }

vs } Case

The same } This day came the parties by their Attornies and thereupon the motion of law arising cost of the double rules of plainaff and defendant to shew cause why a Capias should be awarded or this cause should stand abated being solomely argued, it seems to the Court upon the whole matter the law is for the plainaff it is therefore considered by the Court that said defendant will be discharged and it is further considered by the Court that one Alias be awarded the plainaff against the defendant Pleasant White returnable here at the next term of this Court to which the defendant doeth except

Robert Burk }

vs } In debt

Charles R. Sperry & }
James H. Jinkens } This day came the defendants and prayed for and obtained an appeal the next honorable circuit Court for White County and for the prosecution of the same entered into and acknowledged bond with John Warren security considered as the law requires.

Eliza Pugsley & }
Allen Hall }

vs } In assumpset

Anthony Dibrell & }
Wamon Leftwich } This day came the defendants by attoney and prayed for and obtained an appeal to the next honorable Circuit Court for the County of White to be held at Sparta on the third Monday of November next and for the faithful prosecution of the same entered into and acknowledged bond with John B. McCormack - their security considered as the law requires &c.

(P. 20)

State }

vs } Prose for gaiming

William Carland } This day came the defendant with Richard Nelson and Jacob A. Lane into open Court and acknowledged themselves endebted to the State in the sum of one thousand dollars To wit: the said William Carland in the sum of five hundred dollars and the said Richard Nelson and Jacob A. Lane in the sum of two hundred and fifty dollars each; to be bound of their respective goods and chattels lands and tenements to the law of the state - never the less to be void on condition that the said William Carland, shall well and truly make his personal appearance before the Justices of our next Court of pleas and quarter sessions to be held for the County of White at the Court house in the town of Sparta on the third day of the session then and there to answer the state on the above charge and not depart thereof without leave of the Court first had and obtained &c. the Attorney General agrees that deft. may appear by cause that in the Court same person enters his security for the payment of fine and costs.

Anthony Dibrell &
John H. Anderson
Lieghton Ferrell,
Shff Warren County

Debt detention

Ordered by Court that the judgement obtained by the plainaffs on this day be set aside for Erra in the same.

Anthony Dibrell &
John H. Anderson

vs

Lieghton Ferrell,
Sheriff of Warren County

Debt detention

This day came the plainaff by their Attornies and thereupon it appearing to the satisfaction of the Court that a judgement NiSi was obtained by the plainaff against said defendant at the last term of this Court for the sum of one hundred and twenty five dollars and that a copy of the same issued which was by the of Warren County returned in to this Court regularly made known to said defendant more than ten days before the settling of this cause and the said defendant on this day being solomly called to appear in Court and shew cause if any he hath or can only the judgement Nisi, taken in this cause at the last term of this Court against him should not be made final, came not but made default -

Therefore on motion of the plainaff by their Attorney it is considered by the Court that the plainaff recover against said defendant the sum of one hundred and twenty five dollars the amount of the judgement rendered at the last term of this Court as aforesaid it being for his neglect, failure and refusal as sheriff to make due return upon a writ of Capias.

(P-21) Friday Evening 17th July A.D. 1835 Ordered that Court be adjourned until Court in Course

Teste
J. A. Lane, Clk

David Snodgrass
Sims Dearing
Lewis Pettett

(P-22) State of Tennessee,

At a Court of pleas and quarter Session began and

held for the County of White at the Court house in the town of Sparta before the Worshipful the Justices of said Court, on the second Monday being the 12th day of October in the year of our Lord, One Thousand eight hundred and thirty five and of the Independence of the United States the sixtenth year

Present the Worshipful

Thomas Eastland, chairman

David Snodgrass
John Bryan
John Jett
Edward Cunningham
Joseph Cummings
Nathan Holland
John Rose
John Wallace
Samuel A. Moore
William Knowles
Dan Griffith
Edmund Stamps
George Welch
Joseph Herd
Isaac Buck
Sims Dearing
E. A. Sims
Thomas Barnes
H. Pass
Jesse Scoggin
William Irwin
Thomas Cooper
David Hasting

Esqrs

Ordered by Court that William Bruster be appointed Overseer of the Carthage, road from the West end of the Bridge at Sparta, to the two mile post, being a road of the first class and keep the same in repair as the law requires, and that the same boundry of hands which worked under Josiah Turner former Overseer be assigned to work there on &c.

Ordered by Court that Patterson E. McBride, be appointed Overseer of the road from Snodgrass Mills to the Mile post at Wisdoms field being a road of the second class, and keep the same in repair as the law requires with the hands which worked under Solomon Duncan former Overseer there of Issd -

Ordered by Court that the following persons be assigned to work under Berryman Holland Overseer of the road from Jesse Walling to John Smiths, being a road of the first class Towit: Charles Smith, Terry Walden, Senr., Terry Walden, Jr., Joseph Gooch, negro man, Renny Chaslean, William Kerr, John Pennington, James Dodson, David Patterson, Henderson Keithly and Jackson Downing, Issd.

Ordered by Court that John Fryer, Lewis Phillips, John Franklin,

Alexander Moore, and George Woods free holders, be appointed a Jury of view to lay off and mark a road from the road crossing Caney fork at Dillons ferry, Beginning at a point in said road, North of the river, thence crossing said river below the ferry intersecting the same, South of the river, and report there of to the present term of this Court or at next Court 'Issd -

Ordered by Court that Abraham Ditty, John Ditty, Jr., William Rhea, Thomas Whitefield and James Ellison free holders be appointed a Jury of View to lay off and mark a road on the West side of William Ellisons farm crossing the old road at Cane Creek, and intersecting the same at or near the Gentry Cabin and report there of to the next term of this Court Issd.

This day the Commissioners appointed at the last term of this Court to alter and change a portion of the Kentuckey road, passing through William Lisks lane returned their report there of, making the following changes on said road Towit - leaving the old road near William Lisks draw bars on the East side of said road - running parrellel with the old road at ten feet in side of the field of said Lisks, intersecting the old road at the top of the Hill, which is ordered to be established as a road of the first class, and that the same be laid out thirty feet wide, and that the same be kept in repair as the law requires with the hands which worked on the old road Issd.

(P-23) Ordered by Court that Thomas Lisks, James Davis, William Walker, James Smiths and Micajah Felts free holders be appointed a Jury of view to lay off and mark a road from the mouth of falling water to the Allen ferry road where Davis's road intersects the same and report there of to the present term of this Court. Issd. -

Ordered by Court that the Sheriff of White County bring here into Court on Monday next the bodies of Susannah Glenn, Montgomery Glenn, Jesse Glenn and Rebecca Glenn, minors and orphans to be dealt by agreeably to the law and as the Court in its sound discretion may deem right

Ordered by Court that Monroe Johnston bring here into Court at the next term of this Court the body of an orphan girl bound to him as an apprentice, then and there to satisfy before the Court the manner in which demeans himself toward said girl in the relation of servant Issd -

Ordered by Court that Robert Smith be appointed Overseer of the road from the West end of the bridge, at the Iron works to the widow Smiths gate, being a road of the first class and keep the same in repair as the law requires and that John Jett Esqr assign a list of hands to work there on

This day the Commissioners appointed here to fore to lay off and mark a road from Greenville Templeton, to the Gum Spring road near Colonel Herds returned their report there of which is ordered by the Court to be established as a road of the second class, and that Greenville Templeton be appointed Overseer there of and open and keep the same in repair as the law requires and that Joseph Herd, Esqr. assign a list of hands to work there on Issd.

Ordered by Court that Robert Anderson Senr., David Mitchell and Joseph Cummings Commissioners here to fore appointed to assign provisions out of the estate of Dempsey Penner Decd. to support his widow and children for one year be above the sum of one dollar and fifty cents each, to be paid out of the Estate of the said Dempsey Penner Decd and that the order making them an allowance at April term of this Court be set aside -

Ordered by Court that Samuel H. Keithly be released from the payment of the Taxes upon fifty one Acres of land for the year 1835; the same being improperly returned and that the Sheriff of White County have a credit with the Trustee of White County on the Settlement of his account Issd -

Ordered by Court that Monday next, be assigned and set apart for the exclusive transaction of County business

Ordered by Court that David Snodgrass, George Welch and William, Irwin, Esquires be appointed Commissioners to settle with Robert L. Mitchell, William Baker, Executers of Edward Holmes; Decd. - and report there of to the next term of Court Issd -

This day James Scals, produced in open Court three wolf scalps over the age of four months each, and proved that he killed the same in White County - where upon there being present five acting Justices of the peace it is ordered that the same certified to the treasure of West Tennessee for payment, and that the Sheriff of White County burn said scalps, who being here in Court recovered said scalps into his custody and acted accordingly Issd - J. A. Lane.

Ordered by Court that William Hill, Samuel Brown, Enoch Golden, be appointed Commissioners to assign to Palmer Roberts the widow of William Roberts Decd. provisions out of said estate for the support and maintainance of said widow and her family for one year and report thereof to the next term of this Court &c.

(P-24) This day the death of William Carroll, late of the County of White was suggested and that he departed this life intestate where upon Mary Jane Carroll widow and relict of the said William Carroll Deceased was appointed administratarix of all and singular, the goods and chattle rights and credits of the said William Carroll Deceased who there upon took the oath prescribed by law, and to geather with Charles Watson entered into and acknowledged bond in the sum of three thousand dollars conditioned as the law requires.

This day Mary Jane Carroll administratrix of all and singular the goods and chattles rights and credits of William Carroll Deceased - returned into open Court upon oath an Inventory of the estate of the Deceased which is ordered to be recorded -

This day the death of Jabaz Anderson late of the County of White was suggested and that he departed this life intestate - where upon Nancy Anderson widow and relict of Jabaz Anderson Deceased was appointed administratrix of all and singular the goods and chattle rights and credits of the Deceased, who there upon took the oath prescribed by law, and to geather with Thomas Jones entered into and acknowledged bond in the sum of three hundred dollars conditioned as the law requires.

This day Nancy Anderson administratrix of all and singular the goods and chattle rights and credits of Jabaz Anderson Decd - returned into Court on oath an Inventory of the estate of the Deceased which is ordered to be recorded -

This day the death of Zachariah Jones, late of the County of White was suggested and that he departed this life intestate where upon Rebecca Jones was appointed administratrix and Thomas Jones administrator of all and singular the goods and chattle rights and credits of the Deceased; who there upon took the oath prescribed by law; and to geather with Anthony Dibrell, Lee R. Taylor, and David Dean; entered into and acknowledged bond in the sum of Ten Thousand dollars conditioned as the law requires -

This day the death of William Jones was suggested and that he departed this life intestate where upon Rachel Jones was appointed administratrix of all singular the goods and chattle rights and credits of the said William Jones Deceased and took the oath prescribed by law, and to geather with William Bruster and Eli Sims entered into and acknowledged bond in the sum of three hundred and fifty dollars conditioned as the law requires.

This day Rachel Jones Administratrix of all and singular the goods and chattle rights and credits of William Jones Deceased returned into Court on oath an Inventory of the estate of the Deceased upon oath which is ordered to be recorded -

This day the death William Roberts; late of the County of White was suggested and that he departed this life intestate where upon Patience Roberts, was appointed administratrix and John Griffith administrator of all and singular the goods and chattle rights and credits of the said William Roberts Deceased who took the oath prescribed by law, and to geather with Jose C. Dew, entered into and acknowledged bond in the sum of four hundred dollars conditioned as the law requires.

This day the death of Robert Goad late of the County of White was suggested and that he departed this life intestate, where upon John Frankland was appointed administrator of all and singular the goods and chattle rights and credits of the said Robert Goad Deceased, who there upon took the oath prescribed by law and with William Shockley, entered into bond in the sum of three hundred dollars conditioned as the law requires -

(P-25) This day John Frankland administrator of all and singular the goods and chattle rights and credits of Robert Goad Deceased returned into Court upon oath an Inventory of the estate of the Deceased which is ordered to be recorded &c -

This day the death of Thomas Pane late of the County of White was suggested and that he departed this life intestate; where upon Jesse

Walling was appointed administrator of all and singular the following goods and chattle rights and credits of the Deceased, in the County of White, Towit: -

Four head of horses, 1 waggon, 1 pair of carriage harness, 1 shot gun, powder & horn, 2 pistoles, 1 watch, one small trunk with sundry articles in it, 1 large chest of clothing, 1 Bed and furniture, 1 clock, 1 mans saddle, 1 pair of saddle Bags, 2 boxes small articles bells &c., 1 pair candle moulds, 2 pairs of shoes, 1 pair of boots, 1 Bag of clothes, part of a bolt Osnalong ? cloth, 1 pail, 1 hat, 1 cap, 1 chain, 1 Bag, who there upon took the oath prescribed by law, and togeather with Joseph Herd entered into bond in the sum of one thousand dollars conditioned as the law requires.

This day Jesse Walling administrator of all and singular the goods and chattle rights and credits of Thomas R. Pane Deceased in the County of White returned on oath an Inventory of the estate of the Deceased in White County which is ordered to be recorded -

Ordered by Court that John Frankland Admr of the estate of Robert Goad Deceased advertise and sell the personal property of the Deceased giving twenty days notice of the time and place of said sale.

Ordered by Court unanimously present twenty one acting Justices of the peace that the County of White, pay all debt in this motion and motion made against Samuel Denton, who had in his Custody Mary Anne Abnor a minor and orphan from whose profession it was sought to discharge her by a former rule of this Court made at the last term, to be paid by the County Trustee out of any monies not other wise appropriated -

Ordered by Court that John Humphrey Jr., be appointed overseer of the old Carthage road from the fork of the Kentucky road, from the home of Robert Cook Esqr. being a road of the second class and keep the same in repair as the law requires and that William Womack, William Knowles, Esqr. assign a list of hands to work there on Issd.

Ordered by Court that Charles R. Sperry, Charles Meeks, John Overby, William R. Tucker, and William Bruster, free holders be appointed a Jury of view to lay off and mark a road, Beginning at the West end of N. Oldhams lane on the Allen ferry road, thence with the West boundry of N. Oldhams field, passing through a small field of J. A. Lane, Intersecting the road leading from the Carthage road to Lanes Mills at the corner of the Lot - including the present residence of said Jacob A. Lane, and report there of to the present term of this Court Issd -

This day William Steekly produced in open Court one large wolf scalp over the age of four months and proved that the same was killed in White County, where upon there being present five acting Justices of the peace, it is ordered that the same be certified to the Treasure of West Tennessee for payment, and that the Sheriff of White County burn said scalps, who being here in Court received the same into his possession and acted accordingly Issd J. A. Lane.

Ordered by Court that Isaac Taylor, William Lisk and Eli Sims be appointed Commissioners to assign and set a part provisions out of the estate of Zachariah Jones Decd. for the support of his widow and children for one year, and report there of to the next term of this Court.

(P-26) Ordered by Court that Isaac Taylor, Eli Sims, and William Lisk; be appointed Commissioners to assign and set a part to the widow of Jabaz Anderson Deceased a sufficient portion of provisions out of the estate of the Deceased for the support of said widow and her family for one year and report there of to the next term of this Court Issd -

Ordered by Court that Isaac Taylor, Eli Sims, and William Lisk, be appointed Commissioners to assign and set a part out of the estate of William Jones Decd. a sufficient quantity of provisions for the support of his widow and family for one year, and report there of to the next term of this Court - Issd

This day was produced in open Court a Writing purporting to be the last will and testement of Joseph Haston, Deceased, late of the County of White and the due execution and publication there of proven in open Court by the oath of William Denny, and John S. Parker, One of the subscribing witness there to for the purpose and things there in mentioned and that the said Joseph Haston was at the date of the execution and publication there of was of sound and disposing mind and memory, and that said Writing is the last Will and Testament of the said Joseph Haston Dec'd. which is ordered to be recorded. Issd -

This day was produced in open Court a Writing purporting to be the last Will and Testament of Joseph Henry Deceased, late of the County of White, and the due execution and publication there of as the last will and Testament of the said Joseph Henry Deceased, proven in open Court by the oath of Thomas Barnes, one of the subscribing witness there to for the purpose and things there in mentioned and that the said Joseph Henry was at the date of execution and publication there-of of sound and disposing mind and memory which is ordered to be so certified -

This day Mary Anne Abner an orphan girl aged eleven years, was bound to Samuel Denton to serve him after the manner of an apprentice untill she attains the full age of sixteen years, where upon the said Samuel Denton with Samuel Turney his security, entered into a covenant where he promises and agrees to be taught and instructed the said Mary Ann Abnor to read and write and at the expiration of her term of service to give her in addition to her wearing apparel to good suits of cloths wearing apparel suitable to appear in public, one feather bed and furniture of the value of thirty dollars and one cow & calf of the value of ten dollars which is ordered to be recorded -

On the Petition of Rebecca Jones administratrix and Thomas Jones, administrator of Zachariah Jones, Deceased late of the County of White setting forth that the said Zachariah Jones died possessed of eight Slaves there in stating that in their opinion it would be most consistant with the interests of the respective distributors of said estate, that said negro Slaves should be sold, and that a division there of cannot be consistantly made. - And it appearing to the satisfaction of the Court, from the facts set forth in said petition and from the examination of witness in support of the statements made there in, that said slaves mentioned in said petition cannot be equitably and properly divided and apportioned amongst those intitled to the distribution unless said slaves be sold, and that it would be to the advantage of them concerned to have said slaves sold -

It is there fore considered by the Court and so ordered and directed, that the said Rebecca Jones, Administratrix and Thomas Jones Administrator of Zachariah Jones, Deceased sell said eight slaves in said petition mentioned the property of said Zachariah Jones Deceased, in his life time on a credit of twelve months, giving twenty days notice of the time and place of (P-27) said sales taking from the purchaser bond with approved security, and the proceeds of the sale of said slaves to distribute amongst those entitled to the same as required by law Issd -

The Court proceeded to the appointment of a constable in the bounds of Capt. Mitchells Company and to that office do appoint James Sherly, for the next ensuing two years, who there upon took an oath to support the Constitution of the United States the State of Tennessee, and the several oaths prescribed by law, and togeather with James McCann, and Bartlett Belcher who entered into and acknowledged bond in the sum of one thousand dollars conditioned as the law requires

This day the Court proceeded to the appointment of a Constable in the bounds of Capt Allens Company and to that office do appoint Hays Arnold for the next ensuing two years, who there upon took an oath to support the constitution of the United States the State of Tennessee, and the several oaths prescribed by law and togeather with James Randols and William G. Sims entered into and acknowledged bond in the sum of one thousand dollars conditioned as the law requires -

This day the Court proceeded to the appointment of a Constable in Captain Hargis Company for the next ensuing two years, and to that office do appoint Joseph England, who took an oath to support the constitution of the United States the State of Tennessee and the several oaths prescribed by law, and togeather with John England, and George Henry, entered into and acknowledged bond in the sum of one thousand dollars conditioned as the law requires.

Ordered that Court be adjourned untill to morrow morning at 9 Oclock

Thos Eastland
Sims Dearing
David Snodgrass

Tuesday morning 13th October 1835 Court met pursuant to adjournment Present the worshipful

David Snodgrass } Esqrs
Sims Dearing }
Lewis Pettett } Justices

The Sheriff of White County returned the writ of Venire facias to him directed Towit - James Anderson, James Scarbrough, William

Yarbrough; George W. Jones, John W. Dearing, Elias Yeager; James Graham, Samuel Porter, William Dodson, Bryant Sparkman; Lewis Glenn; William Little, William J. Cole, Overton Chisum; James Knowles, Jr.; Levi Jarvis, William Burden, Henderson McFarland, John Dicus, Daniel Martin, Robert Brown, Terry Gillentine, William C. Metcalf, James Scott; Joseph W. Little & Thomas Yeates, Jurors Archd Conner; & James Russell Constable; Executer on all except Elias Yeager, James Scott, William Little, William C. Metcalf, G. W. Jones, Thomas Yeats, Joseph W. Little, James Scarbrough, out of which Venire was drawn by ballot the following names, good and lawful men, and house and free holders of the County of White who being elected unparrelled sworn and charged a Jury of Grand Inquest for the State of Tennessee in the body of the County of White (P-28) and having received their charge retired to consult of presentments Indictments &c.

State
vs
Winkfield Hill

Indt for Nuisance

This day came as well the Attorney General as the Defendant in proper person, who being arraigned and charged upon the bill of Indictment pleaded Guilty there to and for his trial put him self upon the grace and mercy of the Court It is there fore considered by the Court that the Defendant for such his offence make his fine by the payment of the sum of six and one fourth cents, and that the State of Tennessee, recover against said Defendant her cost by her about her prosecution in this behlf expended &c

State of Tennessee
vs Issd.
William A. Cooke

Indt. for Nuisance

This day came as well the attorney General as the Defendant in proper person, who being arraigned and charged upon the bill of Indictments pleaded guilty there to; and for his trial put himself upon the grace & mercy of the Court. It is there fore considered by the Court that the Defendant for such his offence, make his fine by the payment of six and one fourth cents, and the State of Tennessee also recover against said Defendant all cost by him about his prosecution in this behalf in this Court expended &c.

The Grand Jurors again returned into open Court with the following bill of Indictments Towit The State against Greenville Templeton for the disturbance of the public Worship of the Almighty God - A true Bill - And again retired to consult of Indictments and presentments &c.

State
vs
Greenville Templeton

Indt for the disturbance of public Worship

George Ailsworth Pros.

On motion of the attorney General a Capias

is awarded the State against the body of the Defendant returnable here in Court instantly

John Knight
vs
William Jones

Debt Cer

On motion of the plaintiff by his Attorney, a rule is admitted to shew cause why the supercedias should be dismissed in this cause -

John Knight
vs Issd
William Jones

Debt Supr

This day came the parties by their attornies and there upon the matters of law arising out of the rule to shew cause why the Supercedias in this cause should be dismissed, being solemnly argued and mature deliberation there on for it seems to the Court upon the whole matter that the law is for the plaintiff It is there fore considered by the Court that said rule be sustained and that the plaintiff recover against said Defendant his cost by him about his suit in this behalf expended.

(P-29)

Foster G. Crutcher & Alexander Allison partners trading under the style of Crutcher & Allen
vs
Jose C. Dew & John Dew

In Debt.

This day came the parties by their Attornies, and there upon came a Jury of good and lawful men Towit - Nathaniel C. Davis, James Simpson, Nathaniel Austin, Benjamin Vaughan, Richar Jay, John Dodson, Thomas Simpson, Isaac Sharp, Elisha Rogers, Abraham Saylors, William Jones, Thomas Jones, who being elected tried and sworn the truth to speak upon the issue joined upon their oath do say that the Defendant hath not well and truly paid the debt in the Declaration mentioned as in pleading they hath alledged, but owe unto the plaintiff the sum of one hundred and fifty eight dollars and forty six cents, the Debt in the Declaration mentioned, that the plaintiff hath sustained damages by occasion of the detention there of to the sum of fourteen dollars forty five cents besides cost, as the plaintiff in declaring hath alledged. It is there fore considered by the Court that the plaintiff recover against the Defendant the sum of one hundred and fifty eight dollars and forty six cents the debt in the declaration mentioned, togeather with the further some of fourteen dollars and fifty five cents, the damage afore said in manner and form afore said assessed togeather with their cost by them about their suit in this behalf expended, and said Defendant may be immerced &c -

Jesse Lincoln)
vs Issd) In Debt -
Robert Hewett)

This day came the parties by their attornies and there upon came a Jury of good and lawful men Towit - Nathaniel C. Davis; James Simpson; Nathaniel Austin; Benjamin Vaughan; Richard Jay; John Dodson; Thomas Simpson; Isaac Sharp, Elisha Rodgers, Abraham Saylors, William Jones, and Thomas Jones, who being elected tried and sworn the truth to speak upon the issue joined upon their oath do say that the Defendant hath not well and truly paid the Debt in the plaintiffs declaration as in pleading he hath alledged; but owes unto the plaintiff the sum of one hundred and seventy five dollars thirty eight cents the debt in the plaintiffs declaration, that the plaintiff hath sustained damages by occasion of the detention there of to the sum of two dollars and ninety cents besides cost as the plaintiff in declaring hath alledged. It is there fore considered by the Court that the plaintiff recover against said Defendant the sum of one hundred and seventy five dollars and thirty eight cents - the debt in the declaration mentioned togeather with the further sum of two dollars and ninety cents the damages afore said in manner and form afore said assessed togeather with his cost by him about his suit in this behalf expended; and said Defendant may be immerced -

Thomas J. Williams Assee)
vs Issd.) In Debt
William R. Tucker)

This day came the parties by their Attornies and there upon came a Jury of good and lawful men Towit - Nathaniel C. Davis, James Simpson; Nathaniel Austin, Benjamin Vaughan; Richard Jay, John Dodson, Thomas Simpson, Isaac Sharp, Elisha Rodgers; Abraham Saylors, (P-30) William Jones; Thomas Jones, who being elected tried and sworn the truth to speak upon the issue joined upon their oath do say that the Defendant hath not well and truly paid the debt in the declaration mentioned but owes unto the plaintiff one hundred and twenty two dollars, and seventy eight cents the balance of the debt in the declaration mentioned, that the plaintiff hath sustained damages of by occasion of the detention there of, to the sum of four dollars and ninety cents, besides cost as the plaintiff in his declaration against him hath complained. It is therefore considered by the Court that the plaintiff recover against the Defendant the sum of one hundred and twenty two dollars and seventy eight cents the balance of the debt in the Declaration mentioned togeather with the further sum of four dollars and ninety cents the damages a fore said in manner & form a fore said assessed to geather with his cost by him about his suit in this behalf expended; and said Defendant may be immerced - &c.

David Campbell Assignee)
vs) In Debt -
Nathan Haggard &
Alvin Cullom)

This day came the parties by their

Attornies and there upon came a Jury of good and lawful men Towit - Nathaniel C. Davis, James Simpson, Nathaniel Austin, Benjamin Vaughan, Richard Jay, John Dodson, Thomas Simpson, Isaac Sharp, Elisha Rodgers, Abraham Saylors, William Jones, Thomas Jones, who being elected tried and sworn the truth to speak upon the issue joined upon their oath do say that the Defendant hath not well and truly paid the debt in the Declaration mentioned as in pleading they hath alledged but owe unto the plaintiff the sum of five hundred dollars the debt in the Declaration mentioned that the plaintiff hath sustained damages by occasion of the detention there of to the some of ten dollars and seventy five cents besides cost as the plaintiff in his declaration there of against them hath complained -

It is there fore considered by the Court that the plaintiff recover against the Defendant the sum of five hundred dollars the debt in the declaration mentioned to geather with the further sum of ten dollars and seventy five cents the damages afore said in manner and form a fore said assessed togeather with his cost by him about his suit, in this behalf expended, and said Defendant may be amerced. &c.

Jesse Lincoln) vs) In Debt Nelson Hewett)

This day came the parties by their attornies and there upon came a Jury of good and lawful men Towit - Nathaniel C. Davis, James Simpson, Nathaniel Austin, Benjamin Vaughan, Richard Jay, James Dodson, Thomas Simpson, Elisha Rogers, Isaac Sharp, Abraham Saylors, William Jones, Thomas Jones, who being elected tried and sworn the truth to speak upon the issue joined upon their oath do say that the Defendant has not well and truly paid the debt in the Declaration mentioned, as in pleading he hath alledged, but owes unto the plaintiff the sum of one hundred and twenty four dollars, and forty cents the debt in the declaration mentioned that he hath sustained damages by occasion of the detention there of to the sum of three dollars seven and one half cents besides cost - as the plaintiff in his declaration there of against the Defendant hath complained

It is there fore considered by the Court that the plaintiff recover against the Defendant (P-31) the sum of one hundred and twenty five dollars and forty cents the Debt in Declaration mentioned, togeather with the further sum of three dollars thirty seven and one half cents the damages a fore said in manner and form a fore said and said Defendant may be Amerced &c.

Thomas J. Williams assee) vs) In Debt William R. Tucker)

This day came the Defendant by his Attorney and prayed for an appeal in the above cause to the next honorable Circuit Court for White County and to have it is granted on giving bond and security for the prosecution there of before the rise of this Court or on factum that execution issue &c.

Jesse Lincoln vs Robert Hewett } In Debt

This day came the Defendant by his Attorney and prayed for an appeal in the above cause to the next honorable Circuit Court - to be held for the County of White and to him it is granted on giving bond and security before the rise of this Court or on factum that execution issue

Jesse Lincoln vs Nelson Hewett } In Debt

This day came the Defendant by his Attorney and prayed for an appeal to the next Honorable .. Circuit Court for White County, and to him it is granted, on giving bond and security for the prosecution there of before the rise of the Court or on factum that execution issue

Foster G. Crutcher and Alexander Allison, partners trading under the Style of Crutcher & Allison vs Jose C. Dew, and John Dew } In Debt

This day came the Defendant by their attorney, and prayed for an appeal in the above Cause to the next honorable Circuit Court for White County, and to them it is granted giving bond and security before the rise of this Court or on factum that execution issue -

John Knight vs William Jones } Pet. for Certiorari

On Affidavit of the Defendant and for reasons disolved in his petition of said Defendant, it is ordered by the Court that Writs of Certiorari and superoedeas be awarded him directed &c. agreeably to the prayer of the petitioner - And said Defendant here in court took the oath prescribed by law, prescribing the mode of prosecuting suits at law, as a pauper, and it appearing to the Court that said Defendant had good cause of defence in this cause and that he is wholly unable to give security, to prosecute his Writs of Certiorari and Superoedeas in the above cause, it is ordered, by the Court that he be permitted to prosecute the same as a pauper &c.

Be it remembered, that on the 13th day of October A.D. 1835 appeared in open Court William Wilkinson to the Court House and made oath that the matters and things set forth in the within petition are true in substance and in fact - (P-32) and at the same time also appeared in open Court Jesse England and Daniel Hoffman citizen of the County of White to the Court satisfactorly known, as persons of good name, fame & reputation and entitled to full credit on oath in a Court of Justices who being sworn in due form of law upon their oath do say that they are well acquainted with William Wilkinson the aforesaid with in named petitioner that he is a person of good character and entitled to full credit upon his oath in a Court of Justices; that they believe the statement set forth in said petition to be true in substance and in fact - Where upon the Court are of opinion and so certify that the said William Wilkinson is a soldier of the revolution as in said petition set forth, and that the statements there in contained are true in substance and in fact and that the said Jesse England and Daniel Huffman are entitled to full credit on oath in a Court of Justices; And it is further ordered by the Court that the same be certified under the seal of this Court, and that the same is a Court of record -

Ordered that Court be adjourned untill to morrow morning 9 Oclock.

David Snodgrass
Sims Dearing
Lewis Pettett

Wednesday Morning 14' October 1835, Court met pursuant to adjournment. Present the worshipful

David Snodgrass
Sims Dearing
Lewis Pettett } Esqrs. Justices

State vs William Simmons } Indt for T.B.

On motion of the attorney General a capias is awarded the state against the body of the Defendant directed &c. returnable here in open Court, at the present term

State vs Elizabeth McCline } Forfd Regn

This day came the Attorney General and the Defendant altho again solemnly called to appear in Court and prosecute and give evidence in behalf of the State against a certain Pierce Cody on a charge for an assault Battery came not but made default where by she hath forefited to the use of the State the sum of two hundred and fifty dollars -

It is therefore considered by the Court that the State of Tennessee recover against the Defendant the sum of two hundred and fifty dollars agreeably to the tenor and effect of her said recognizance, unless sufficient cause of his inability to attend be shewn at the next term of this Court, - and on motion of the Attorney General a Writ of Scire facias is awarded the State against the Defendant directed to the Sheriff of White County, returnable here at the next term of this Court &c.

James Russell summoned as a Constable to attend on this Court at the present term is released and discharged from further attendance there on &c.

(P-33)

State)
vs) Forfd Recognizance
Eleanor McGuirk)

This day came the Attorney General and the Defendant, altho again Solemnly called to appear in Court and prosecute and give evidence in behalf of the State against a certain Pierce Cody on a charge for an Assault and Battery came not but made default - It is therefore considered by the Court that the State of Tennessee recover against said Defendant the sum of two hundred and fifty dollars agreeably to the tenor and effect of his said recognizance unless sufficient cause of his inability to attend be shewn at the next term of this Court and on motion of the Attorney General a Writ of Scire facias is awarded to the State against the Defendant directed &c. returnable here at the next term of this Court.

State)
vs) Motion for Attachment
Elizabeth McCline)

On motion of the Attorney General an attachment is awarded the State against the body of the Defendant to appear in Court at the present term there of to give evidence and prosecute in behalf of the State against a certain Pearce Cody for an Assault & Battery

State)
vs) Motion for Attachment.
Eleanor McGuirk)

On motion of the Attorney General an attachment is awarded the State against the body of the defendant, to appear in this Court at the present term there of to give evidence, and prosecute in behalf of the State against a certain Pearce Cody, for an assault and Battery.

State)
vs) Indt for Gaming -
William Carland)

This day came as well the Attorney General

as the Defendant in proper person aided by counsel able and learned by law who being arraigned and charged upon the bill of Indictments pleaded not guilty there to, and for his trial put himself upon the County, and the attorney general doth the like. Where upon came a Jury of good and lawful men Towit - Pleasant Waller, William Burden, Samuel Porter, Robert Brown, John W. Dearing, Bryant Sparkman, William Yarbrough, James Knowles, William J. Cole, Lewis Glenn, William Dodson, Levi Jarvis who being elected tried and sworn the truth to speak upon the issue of traverse joined upon their oath do say that the defendant is not guilty in manner and form as charged upon him in the bill of Indictments as in pleading he hath alledged -

It is there fore considered by the court that the Defendant from the allegation contained in the bill of Indictments be released and forever discharged and that he depart hence without day and recover against the County of White all cost in this behalf expended as part of the prosecution and that Certificate issue for the same directed to the Trustee for payment as required by law -

State
vs
Alexander Gettings
Anne Gettings Prosx

Peace Warrant

This day came Indemon B. Moore, who is bound for (P-34) appearance Bail for the Defendant, and surrendered said Defendant in discharge of him self, and he from his undertaking is released and forever discharged and he from his undertaking is released discharged and said Defendant prayed in custody of the Sheriff of White County who being here in Court received the body of said Defendant into his custody &c

State
vs
Jonathan Simmons

Indt for A.B.

Bemon Hardin prosecutor

This day came as well the Attorney General as the Defendant in proper person who being arraigned and charged upon the bill of Indictment pleaded not guilty there to and for his trial put him self upon the County and the Attorney General doth the like. Where upon came a Jury of good and lawful men Towit - Alfred Merrett, George DeFreese, Micajah Rickets, Jonas Turner, Smith Cantrell, Robert Anderson Jr., Thomas Simpson, Thomas Clements, James Randols, John Vincent, Alexander Lowrey and Jonas Turner, who being elected tried and sworn the truth to speak upon the issue of traverse joined upon their oath do say that the Defendant is not guilty in manner and form as charged upon him in the bill of Indictments as in pleading he hath alledged.

It is there fore considered by the Court that the Defendant from the allegation contained in the bill of Indictments be released and for ever discharged, and that he depart hence with out day and recover against the County of White all cost in this behalf expended on part of the prosecution and that Certificate issue directed to the Trustee of White for the payment of the same.

State
vs
Greenville Templeton

Indt for disturbanse of Public Worship
George Ailsworth, Pros.

This day came the Defendant into open court with Samuel Turny and William G. Sims and acknowledged themselves indebted to the State of Tennessee, in the sum of one thousand dollars Towit - the Defendant in the sum of five hundred dollars and the said Samuel Turny, William G. Sims in the sum of two hundred and fifty dollars each, to be levied of their respective goods and chattle, lands and tenements to the use of the State to be rendered. Never the less to be void on condition that the said Defendant shall well and truly make his personal appearance in this Court from day to day during the present term of this Court, and then and there answer the State on the above charge and not depart there of without leave of the Court first had and obtained.

State
vs
Greenville Templeton

Indt for disturbance of public Worship
George Ailsworth, Pros -

This day came as well the Attorney General as the Defendant in proper person who being arraigned and charged upon the bill of Indictment pleaded guilty there to and for his trial put him self upon the grace and mercy of the Court. It is therefore considered by the Court, that the Defendant for such his offence make his fine by the payment of the sum of one dollar and it is further considered by the Court that the State recover against said Defendant all cost in this behalf expended &c. and on motion of the Attorney General it is ordered that the Defendant stand on his recognizance untill the fine & cost are paid or security given for the same.

(P-35)

State
vs
Greenville Templeton

Indt. for disturbance of public Worship
George Ailsworth, Pros.

This day came Samuel Turny and Indemon B. Moore into open Court, and undertook and become security for the Defendant in the above cause, for the payment of the fine and cost - and agrees that execution may issue against their estate jointly with the Defendant for the collection there of.

State
vs

Peace Warrant

Alexander Gettings) Anne Gettings, Pros.

On motion of the Attorney General a rule is admitted to shew cause why the Defendant shall be further bound to keep the peace towards the citizens of the State of Tennessee, but more especially towards Anne Gettings the prosecutrix in the above cause.

State)
vs) Peace Warrent
Alexander Gettings) Anne Getting, Pros.

This day came the Attorney General as well as the Defendant in proper person aided by counsel able and learned in the case and there upon the matters of law out of the rule to shew cause why the Defendant should be further bound to keep the peace toward the citizens of the State of Tennessee but more especially towards Anne Gettings the prosecutrix, being solemnly agreed and mature deliberation there on had, it seems to the Court upon the whole matter, that the law is for the State - It is there fore considered by the Court that said rule be sustained -

State)
vs) Peace Warrant
Alexander Gettings) Anne Gettings, Pros.

This day came the Defendant with Indemon B. Moore, into open Court and acknowledged them selves indebted to the State of Temessee in the sum of seven hundred and fifty dollars Towit - the Defendant in the sum of five hundred dollars and the said Indemon B. Moore in the sum of two hundred and fifty dollars, to be levied of their goods and chattle lands and tenements to the use of the State, never the less, to be void on condition that the said Alexander Gettings shall well and truly keep the peace of the State toward the good citizens but most especially toward the said Anne Gettings for the full span and term of three months from the date here of and shall well and truly make his personal appearance before the Justices of our next Court of pleas and Quarter Session to be held for the County of White at the Court house in the town of Sparta on the second Monday of January next then and there to answer the State further upon the charge afore said, and not depart there of with out leave of the Court first had and obtained.

The grand Jury again returned into Court the following Bills of Indictments Towit: - The State vs William Bosarth for a Nousance "A true Bill", The State vs Pearce Cody for an Assault & Battery a true Bill also a presentment the State vs Arnold Moss a Newsance also a presentment the State vs Andrew Lowell for a Neusance also an (P-36) Indictment the State against John Cantrell and Abraham Cantrell for an assault & Battery a true Bill and having nothing further to present it is ordered by the Court that the Grand Jury from further attendance as such be released and discharged during the present term of this Court -

State

vs

Andrew Lowell

Presentment for a Neusance

On motion of the Attorney General a capias is awarded the State returnable here in Court instantly

State

vs

Arnold Moss

Presentment for a Neusance.

On motion of the Attorney General a capias is awarded the State against the Defendant returnable here in Court instantly

State

vs

William Bozarth

Indt for a neusance

Richd Crowder Prosecuter

On motion of the Attorney General a capias is awarded the State against the body of the Defendant returnable here in Court instantly.

State

vs

John Cantrell
and
Abraham Cantrell

Indt for an Affray

Shelby Kerby, Prosecutor

On motion of the Attorney General a capias is awarded the State against the body of the Defendant returnable here in Court instantly.

State

vs

William Bozarth

Indt for a Neusance

Richd Crowder, Prosr.

This day came Richard Crowder the above named prosecutor into open Court and acknowledged himself indebted to the State in the sum of two hundred and fifty dollars, to be levied of his goods and chattle lands and tenements to the use of the State to be rendered - never the less to be void on condition, that the said Richard Crowder shall well and truly make his personal appearance before the Justices of our next Court of pleas and quarter Session to be holden for the County of White at the Court house in the town of Sparta on the second Monday of January next on the third day of the term then and there to prosecute and give evidence in behalf of the State against the Defendant in the above cause and not depart without leave of the Court first had and obtained -

State)
vs) Indt for an Affray
John Cantrell) Shelby Kerby Prosecuter

This day came Shelby Kerby the above named prosecuter, in proper person into open Court and acknowledged him self indebted to the State in the sum of two hundred and fifty dollars to be levied of his goods and (P-37) chattle lands and tenements to the use of the State to be rendered never the less to be void on condition that the said Shelby Kerby shall well and truly make his personal appearance before the Justices of our next Court of pleas and quarter Session to be holden for the County of White, at the Court house in the town of Sparta on the second Monday of January next then and there to prosecute and give evidence in behalf of the State against said Defendant and attend from day to day and not depart there of without leave of the Court first had and obtained.

Ordered that Court be adjourned untill to morrow morning 9 Oclock

David Snodgrass
Sims Dearing
Lewis Pettett

Tuesday morning 15th October 1835 Court met pursuant to adjournment - Present the worshipful

David Snodgrass)
Sims Dearing) Esqr
David Pettett) Justices

Nathan Haggard to the use of Crocket Harbert & Trent C. Connor
vs) Case
Daniel Dale & Pleasant White Admr of John Dale, Deceased)

On motion of the plaintiff by their Attorney an alias pluras summons is awarded the plaintiff directed &c. against Pleasant White one of the Defendants returnable here at the next term of this Court.

State)
) Prest for Gaming
William Hitchcock)

This day came the Attorney General and declared that he could no further prosecute the above cause against said Defendant neither is the above further prosecuted. Therefore by consent of the Court, it is ordered that the Defendant depart hence with out day &c. and it is further considered by the Court that the Defendant depart hence and recover against the County of White all cost expended in part of the prosecution, and that Certificate issue directed to the trustee of White County for the payment of the same &c

State
vs
Eleanor Holderfield and
Louisa Holderfield

Prest for a Neusance

This day came the Attorney General and declared that he could no further prosecute the above cause against said Defendants neither is the same further prosecuted - Therefore by consent of the Attorney General and with the assent of the Court it is considered by the Court, that the defendant depart hence and recover against the County of White all cost in this behalf expended on part of the prosecution, and that Certificate issue to the trustee of White County for payment &c -

(P-38)

State
vs
Pearce Cody

Ind for an Assault & Battery
Elizabeth McCline, Prosecutor

This day came the Attorney General as well as the Defendant in proper person aided by Counsel abel and learned in the law who being assigned and charged upon the bill of Indictments pleaded not guilty there to, and for his trial put himself upon the County and the Attorney General doth the like where upon came a Jury of good and lawful men Towit - George Ailsworth, Joseph Rodgers, Jr., John Vincent, Spencer Holder, Senr., Thomas Simpson, John Gailly, Russell Gist, John Ramsey, William Green, John Williams, John Whitley and William M. Moore who being elected tried and sworn the truth to speak upon the issue of traverse joined upon their oath do say that the Defendant is guilty in manner and form as charged against him in the bill of Indictment - &c

State
vs
Pearce Cody

Indt for an Assault & Battery
Elizabeth McCline

This day came the Defendant by his Attorney and on motion a rule in asset of the judgement of this Court on the verdict of the Jury rendered in the above cause is admitted - the Defendant by his Counsel alleging that the said Elizabeth McCline the prosecutrix in this cause whose name is marked as such on the bill of Indictment against said Defendant is a married woman and therefore not liable for cost should said prosecution be frivolous or malicious and cannot agreeably to law be taken doemed compitent to prosecute &c

State
vs

Indt for an Assault and Battery

Pearce Cody) Elizabeth McCline, Pros -

This day came the Attorney General as the Defendant in proper person aided by his Counsel able and learned in the law, and there upon the matters of law arising out of the rule is assert of Judgement upon the Verdict of the Jury rendered in this cause being argued and mature deliberation by the Court there on had for it seems to the Court upon the whole matter that the law is for the States. It is there fore considered by the Court that said rule be discharged.

State)
vs) Indt for an Assault & Battery
Pearce Cody) Elizabeth McCline, Pros.

This day came the Attorney General as well as the Defendant in proper person, - Therefore on motion by the Attorney General it is considered by the Court that the Defendant for such, his offence in the Indictment in this cause mentioned and who stands guilty by the verdict of a Jury this day rendered in said cause make his fine by the payment of the sum of five dollars, and that the State of Tennessee recover against said Defendant all cost by her about her prosecution in this behalf expended and said Defendant may be taken, &c.

State)
vs) Indt for T. B.
Pearce Cody) Elizabeth McCline, Pros.

This day came the Defendant and prayed for and obtained an appeal to the next Honorable Circuit Court to be holden for the County of White at the Court house in the town of Sparta on the second Monday of November next &c

(P-39)

State)
vs) Indt for an Assault & Battery
Pearce Cody) Elizabeth McCline, Pros -

This day came the Defendant into open Court in proper person with Samuel Turney, and acknowledged them selves indebted to the State of Tennessee in the sum of seven hundred and fifty dollars Towit - The Defendant in the sum of five hundred dollars and the said Samuel Turney in the sum of two hundred and fifty dollars to be levied of their respective goods and chattle lands and tenements to the use of the State to be rendered never the less to be void on condition that the said Pearce Cody the above Defendant shall well and truly make his personal appearance before the Honorable the Judges of our next Circuit Court to be holden for the County of White at the Court house in the town of Sparta on the third Monday of November next, then and there to

Answer the State on the above charge and attend from day to day and not depart there of with out leave of the Court first had and obtained &c.

State
vs
Pearce Cody

Indt for an Assault & Battery
Elizabeth McCline, Pros.

This day came the Elizabeth McCline the prosecutor in the above cause and Eleanor McGuirk a witness and acknowledged them selves indebted to the State of Tennessee in the sum of two hundred and fifty dollars each, to be levied of their proper goods and chattle lands and tenements to the use of State to be rendered - Never the less to be void on condition, that the said Elizabeth McCline the above named prosecutrix, and Eleanor McGuirk a witness shall well and truly make their personal appearance before the Honorable the Judge of our next Circuit Court to be holden for the County of White at the Court house in the town of Sparta on the third Monday of November next, the said Elizabeth McCline to prosecute and give evidence against said Defendant and the said Eleanor McGuirk to give evidence against said Defendant in the above cause, and then and there attend from day to day during said term and not depart there of with out leave of the Court first had and obtained -

State
vs
Elizabeth McCline

Forft Recognizance

This day came the Attorney General as well as the Defendant in proper person and by consent of the Attorney General and with the assent of the Court, it is ordered by the Court that the forfeiture taken against said Defendant in the above cause at the present term of this Court be set aside, on the payment of the cost - It is there fore considered by the Court that the State of Tennessee recover against said all cost in this behalf expended and execution issue for the collection of the same.

(P-40)

State
vs
Elizabeth McCline

Attachment

This day came the Attorney General as well as the Defendant by her Attorney and by consent of the Attorney General and with the assent of the Court it is ordered that the attachment in this Cause against the Defendant the and all preceedings there on be set aside on the payment of the cost by said Defendant - It is there fore considered by the Court that the State of Tennessee recover against said Defendant all cost on part of the State, in suing forth and prosecuting the attachment in this cause and that execution issue for the collection, there of.

State) Attachment
vs)
Eleanor McGuirk)

This day the Attorney General as well as the Defendant by her attorney, and by consent of the Attorney General and with the assent of the Court it is ordered that the Attachment in this cause against the Defendant and all proceedings there on had be set aside payment of the cost by said Defendant, - It is there fore considered by the Court that the State of Tennessee recover against said Defendant all cost on part of the State in suing forth and prosecuting the attachment in this cause and that execution issue for the collection there of -

State) Indt for A.B.
vs)
Michall Moore)

On motion of the Attorney General a capias is awarded the State against the body of the Defendant, directed to the Sheriff of Jackson County returnable here at the next term of this Court.

State) Indt for A.B.
vs)
William Simpson) Bemon Hardin, Pros

On motion of the Attorney General a capias is awarded the State against the body of the Defendant returnable here at the next term of this Court -

State) Indt for Gaming
vs)
Abraham Broyles)

On motion of the Attorney General a capias is awarded the State against the Defendant returnable here at the next term of this Court -

State) Scifar
vs)
Chaplel Averett)

On motion of the Attorney General Alias Writ of Scire facias is awarded the State against the Defendant returnable here at the next term of this Court -

State) Gaming
vs)

Samuel Scruggs &
Edward Rudder)

On motion of the Attorny General an alias plures Capias is awarded the State against the body of the Defendant returnable here at the next term of this Court.

(P-41)

State

vs

Josiah Wooldridge
William Wooldridge
Marshall Wooldridge
Isaac Adcock

Indt for Riot
Smith Cantrell, Prosecutor

On motion of the Attorney General a capias is awarded the State against the Defendant, directed to the Sheriff of Warren County returnable here at the next term of this Court.

Ordered that Court be adjourned untill to morrow morning 10 Oclock

David Snodgrass
Sims Dearing
Lewis Pettett

Tuesday morning October 11th, 1835, Court met pursuant to adjournment. Present the Worshipful

David Snodgrass
Sims Dearing
Lewis Pettett) Esqrs Justices

Right Lane

vs Issd

Endymeon Lane

Debt on Fifar

This day came the plaintiff by his Attorney and it appearing to the satisfaction of the Court upon the production of all the papers and proceedings had in this Cause, that the plaintiff by the Judgement of Stephen Holland Esquire, one of the acting Justices of the peace for the County of White on the 21st day of Febuary A.D. 1835, recover against the Defendant the sum of fifty dollars and fifty cents for debt, besides fifty cents cost; and that an execution issuing there on the 9th day of October in the year 1835, come to the hands and possession of William B. Cummings a constable in the County of White, who delivered the same unto this Court with the following endorsement there on Towit: - No personal property of the Defendant found in any County, levied on the following tract of land situated in White County bounded as follows Towit - Beginning below Dillons ferry on the Caney fork on Cherry tree, running thence South to a black Oak, thence west to a hickory, thence North to the Caney fork, thence with Caney fork to the Beginning. Containing two hundred acres more or less levied on this 10th day October 1835 W. B. Cummings Const.

And now, on motion of the plaintiff by his Attorney it is considered by the Court, that the a fore said tract of land be condemed in satisfaction of the plaintiffs debt with cost, and that the same or so much there of as shall be of value sufficient be sold to satisfy the same, and it is further considered by the Court that the plaintiff recover against the Defendant his cost by him about his motion in this behalf expended &c - And it is further considered by the Court and so ordered that a Writ of Vinditioni exponas be awarded the plaintiff directed to the Sheriff of the County of White commanding &c returnable here &c

Right Lane
vs Issd — Debt on Fifar
Endymeon Lane

This day came the plaintiff by his Attorney and it appearing to the satisfaction of the Court upon the prosecution of all the papers and proceedings (P-42) here in said cause, that the plaintiff recover against said Defendant before Stephen Holland Esqr the 21st day of Febuary in the year 1835 the sum of fifty dollars and fifty cents debt and fifty cents cost, and that an execution issuing there on the 9th day of October A.D. 1835 come to the hands and possession of William B. Cumming, constable which was returned into this Court with the following endorsements there on Towit - come to hand the same day issued. No personal property of the defendant found in any County levied on the following tract of land, situated in White County, bounded as followith Towit - Beginning below Dillons ferry on the Caney fork on a Cherry tree, running thence South to a black Oak, thence West to a hickory, thence North to the Caney fork, thence with the Caney fork to the Beginning containing two hundred acres more or less levied by me 10th day of October 1835, W. B. Cummings Constable and now on motion of the plaintiff by his attorney it is considered by the Court that the a fore said tract of land be condemed in satisfaction of the plaintiffs demand for debt and cost and that said tract of land or so much there of as shall be of value sufficient be sold in satisfaction of said Debt and it is further considered by the Court that the plaintiff recover against said Defendant his cost of motion in this behalf expended &c and it is further considered by the Court and so ordered that a Writ of Venditioni exponas be awarded the plaintiff directed to the Sheriff of White County commanding &c returnable here &c

Right Lane
vs Issd — Debt on fifar
Endymeon Lane

This day came the plaintiff by his Attorney and it appearing to the satisfaction of the Court, upon the production of all the papers in this cause, that the plaintiff by the Judgement of Stephen Holland Esqr a Justice of the peace for White County on the 21st day of Febuary in the year 1835, recover against the Defendant the sum of sixty one dollars and fifty seven cents for debt, also fifty cents cost, and that execution issuing there on, come to the hand and possession of William B. Cummings Constable in White County. Which was returned into this Court with the following endorsements there on Towit -

Beginning below Dillons ferry, on the Caney fork on a cherry tree, running thence South to a black Oak, thence West to a hickory; thence North to the Caney fork, thence with the Caney fork to the Beginning, containing two hundred Acres more or less, levied by me the 10th day of October 1835, W. B. Cummings Const - and now on motion of the plaintiff by his Attorney, it is considered by the Court, that the afore said tract of land be condemed in satisfaction of the plaintiffs debt and cost; and that said tract of land or so much there of as shall be of value sufficient, be sold in satisfaction there of,

And it is further considered by the Court that the plaintiff recover against said Defendant his cost of motion in this behalf expended &c. And it is further considered by the Court that a Writ of Venditioni exponas issue directed to the Sheriff of White County, returnable here &c. // Be it remembered that on this day being the 16th day of October A.D. 1835 appeared in open Court Abel Pearson the foregoing and with in named petitioner to the Court known, and made oath that the matters and things set forth in the with in petition are true in substance and in fact - and at the same day also appeared in open Court Archebald Connor and Nicholas Cook, citizens of the County of White, in the State of Tennessee, to the Court known as persons of good name and reputation and entitled to full credit upon oath, in a Court of Justices who being sworn in due form of law upon their oath do say, that they are well acquainted (P-43) with Abel Pearson the a fore said and with in named petitioner that he is a person of good charectar, and entitled to full faith and credit upon oath in a Court of Justices, that they believe the statement set forth in said petition to be true in substance and infact. Where upon the Court is of opinion and so certify, that the said Abel Pearson is a Soldier in the late war as in said petition set forth and that the Statements there in contained are true, and further that the said Archebald Connor and Nicholas Cook are entitled to full faith and credit in a Court of Justices - And it is further ordered by the Court to be certified under the seal of this Court, and that this Court is a Court of record.

Ordered that Court be adjourned untill to morrow morning at 9 Oclock

David Snodgrass
Sims Dearing
Lewis Pettett

Saturday morning 17th October A. D. 1835 Court met pursuant to adjournment Present the Worshipful -

David Snodgrass Sims Dearing Lewis Pettett	Esquires Justices

State vs Rezia Jarvis	Bastardy Eleanor McGuirk, Pros.

This day came the Defendant in proper person who

stands charged upon the oath of Eleanor McGuirk single woman of the County of White with being the father of a Bastard female child, named Margaret Elizabeth aged about fifteen months old, begotton by the Defendant upon the body of the said Eleanor McGuirk, and that said Bastard child is likely to be chargeable to the County of White, - It is therefore considered by the Court that said Defendant is the reported Father of said Bastard child and liable for keep and save harmless the County of White from its support maintainance where upon it is ordered by the Court that said Defendant find to keep the County of White indemnified from any color of cost or damage for and towards the support of said Bastard child - Where upon came the Defendant into open Court with John Vincent and Jacob A. Lane, and entered into and acknowledged bond in the sum of one thousand dollars payable to the Justices of the Court of pleas and quarter session for White County conditioned to save free, harmless and indemnified the County of White from all color of cost or damage for and toward the support and maintainance of the aforesaid female Bastard child named Margaret Elizabeth McGuirk begotton by said Defendant upon the body of said Eleanor McGuirk, the above named prosecutrix, - Therefore it is considered by the Court that the State of Tennessee recover against said Defendant all cost by her in this behalf expended, and that execution issue for the collection there of

State)
vs) Pros for Neusance
Andrew Lowell)

On motion of the Attorney General an (P-44) alias Capias is awarded the State against the body of the Defendant directed to the Sheriff of White County, returnable here at the next term of this Court.

State)
vs) Prost for a Neusance
Arnold Moss)

On motion of the Attorney General a Capias is awarded the State against the body of the Defendant directed to the Sheriff of White County, returnable here at the next term of this Court -

State)
vs) Indt for Neusance
William Bozarth) Richd Crowder, Pros

On motion of the Attorney General an alias Capias is awarded the State against the body of the Defendant returnable here at the next term of this Court.

State)
vs) Indt for A.B.
John Cantrell &
Abraham Cantrell) Shelby Kerby, Pros

On motion of the Attorney General a Capias is awarded the State against the body of John Cantrell one of the defendants directed to the Sheriff of Warren County returnable here at the next term of this Court.

State vs John Cantrell & Abraham Cantrell	Indt for A.B. Shelby Kerby, Prosecutor

On motion of the Attorney General an Alias Capias is award the State against Abraham Cantrell one of the Defendants directed to the Sheriff of White County, returnable here at the next term of this Court.

Ordered that Court be adjourned untill to morrow morning next at 9 Oclock

David Snodgrass
Lewis Pettett
John Jett

Monday morning 19th October 1835, Court met pursuant to adjournment Present the Worshipful

David Snodgrass, Chairman
John Jett
Sims Dearing
Lewis Pettett
John Bryan
Eli Sims
William Irwin
Edmund Cunningham
Joseph Herd
Joseph Cummings
Elijah Frost
Stephen Holland and
John Rose

Esquires Justices

Ordered by Court that Joseph Clark, Jnr., be appointed Overseer of the road from the forks of the Kentucky road to the home of William Knowles Esqr being a road of the first class and keep the same in repair as the law requires and that William Knowles Esqr assign a list of hands to work there on Issd.

Ordered by Court that Robert Glenn, Jr., be appointed Overseer of the road from Richard Crowder, to the forks of the road, being a road of the second class, and keep the same in repair as the law requires, that Eli Sims Esqr assign a list of hands to work there on -

(P-45) Ordered by Court that John Jett, Esqr, assign a list of hands to work on the road of which Lewis Turner, is Overseer being a road of the first class

Ordered by Court that David L. Mitchell, Samuel Turney;

John Humphreys, John Massa, and (Cooper) Robert Glenn, free holders, be appointed a Jury of view to lay off and mark a road of the second class from the Shipping post road west of Sparta, passing David L. Mitchell, thence crossing the mountain, passing near Samuel Turneys residence thence toward Shipping post on the mouth of Barren Creek on Caney fork and report there of to the next term of this Court Issd.

Ordered by Court that Indemon B. Moore be appointed Overseer of the road from the top of Gum spring Mountain to James McGowens, being a road of the second class, and keep the same in repair as the law requires, and that Joseph Herd, Esqr assign a list of hands to work there on Issd.

Ordered by Court that Elijah Frost, John Austin, and Nathaniel Austin, be substituted a Jurors to the next Circuit Court of White County, in lieu of George W. Miller, John Bryan and Turner Lane, Senr. Issd.

Ordered by Court that Jacob A. Lane, be appointed Overseer of the road from the Shipping post road west of where the same crosses town Creek passing through Jacob A. Lane, corn field and leaving the same at the top of rising ground, near the North East Corner there of, thence along a ridge intersecting the road a small distance South of the top of a hill, on the old road formerly crossing town Creek at a place called Ricts-Mill and open and keep the same in repair as the law requires is established as a private way and keep the same in repair by said Lane

This day Micajah Frost produced in open Court one large wolf scalp over the age of four months, and proved that he killed the same in White County - Where upon there being present four acting Justices of the peace it is ordered that the same be certified to the Treasure of Middle Tennessee for payment and that the Sheriff of White County burn said scalps, who being here in Court, received the same into his custody and acted accordingly Issd to Wm. Glenn.

Ordered by Court that the road here to fore discontinued, leading from Sparta crossing the Calf Killer below Anderson Salt Well to the forks of the road near where Charles McGuire now resides be re-established as a road of the second class -

Ordered by Court that John Brown be appointed Overseer of the road from the ford of the Calf Killer below Anderson Salt Works to the forks of the road near Charles McGuire, being a road of the second class and keep the same in repair as the law requires, and that David Snodgrass and John Rose Esqr assign a list of hands to work there on.

Ordered by Court that John Kitchenside be appointed Overseer of the road from the town of Sparta to the ford on the Calf Killer below Anderson Salt Works being a road of the 2nd class, and keep the same in repair as the law requires, and that David Snodgrass and John Rose Esqr assign a list of hands to work there on.

Ordered by Court that Charles Denny be appointed Overseer of the road from William Dennys old place, to the top of the Mountain at John Frisbys being a road of the second class, and keep the same in repair as the law requires and that David Hasting, and Joseph Cummings Esqr assign a list of hands to work there on,

Ordered by Court that Joseph Cummings, Jr., Esqr be appointed commissioners of the poor house in the County of White to supply the vacancy occasioned by the removel of Coln. Charles Reeves from the County of White -

(P-46) This day Allen L. Mitchell Superentendant of the Poor House and the appurtenances there unto belonging in the County of White returned his report of the State and condition of the paupers there at, and the condition of said persons &c. which is ordered to be filed in the Clerks Office

Ordered by Court that the Trustee of White County pay over to John White, Senr., a Jury Ticket No 297 - here to fore filed in his Office on the 8th November 1830 for $2.50 cents, the same having been lost or mislaid, said John White to be chargeable there with should the same be produced at a further day Isd

This day John Fryer Executor of Charles Carter, Senr., Deceased, late of the County of White produced here in Court upon oath his account against said estate for the sum of fifty one dollars eighty cents for services by him rendered and preformed in attending to said estate as one of the Executors there of, which is deemed reasonable; and allowed by the Court to be by him retained out of the assets of his estate in his hands, and is ordered to be recorded Isd

On the Humble petition of Peter Buram and Thomas L. Clements they are permitted to erect a Grist Mill and other water machinery across the Caney fork above the Great Falls at a shoel called and known by the name of Luxton old Fish Dam Shoel they being the propritors and owners of the lands at said Site on both banks of said river.

For reasons appearing to the satisfaction of the Court, it is ordered that the precinct here to fore established at the home of David Hasting Esqr. be discontinued, and that a precinct for holding elections for Govenor &c be established at Kirklands Store, on the South side of Caney fork.

Ordered by Court that Joseph Cummings and Lewis Pettett, Esqr be appointed to apportion hands betwen Winkfield Hill, Sampson Witt and John Holder, Jr., Overseer paying due regard, to the class to which said roads respectively belong Isd

Ordered by Court that William King be released from the payment of the taxes upon one White poll and one town Lot in the County of White for the year 1835 the same being charged to him; and that the Sheriff of White County have a credit for the full amount there of, with the trustee of his County, in the settlement of his account for said year -

Ordered by Court that the road as reviewed by commissioners duly appointed passing by the home of James H. Jinkins be established as a road of the first class, as said Jinkins has opened the same, and that the old road be discontinued; and be permitted to enclose the same by a fience should he think fit so to do

This day the commissioners appointed at the present term of this Court to review lay off and mark a road leaving the Allens ferry road at the end of the lane, west of where Nicholas Oldham now lives; and running thence with the west boundry of his field, passing through a small corn field of Jacob A. Lane's and intersecting the Shipping Port road, near said Lanes present dwelling house, returned their report there of on oath taken before the Sheriff of White County, which is ordered by the Court to be established, and opened by Jacob A. Lane, as the law requires, and when opened, to be kept in repair by David L. Mitchell, Overseer with the hands assigned him, and all that part of the Shipping Port - road which lies betwen the intersections of said new road as laid off; and the forks near Oldhams Barn be discontinued, and when the new road is opened, that said Lane be permitted to enclose by a fience said old road then discontinued, annuled and set aside -

(P-47) This day the death of William Shropshire late of the County of White was suggested, and it being shewn that he departed this life interstate, - where upon Winkfield Hill, was appointed administrator of all and singular the goods and chattles, rights and credits of the Deceased; and took the oath prescribed by law and togeather with John Holder; Jr., intered into and acknowledged bond in the sum of five hundred dollars conditioned as the law requires

Ordered by Court that the road leading from Gum Spring road near Mrs. Rodgers to General Simpsons Mills, be reduced from a road of the second class; and established as a road of the third class; and that Joseph Herd Esqr. assign to the Overseer there of a list of hands to work there on Isad.

This day Joseph Herd administrator of the estate of Benjamin Bowman Decd. returned upon oath an additional Inventory of the estate of the Deceased, which is ordered to be recorded -

This day Ransom Geer Executor of the last will and testament of the estate of Samuel Usrey returnable here into Court; and Inventory of the property of the Deceased, upon oath, with the certificate and there to of Anthony Dibrell, Esqr. all of which is ordered to be recorded.

This day the Commissioners here to fore appointed to examine and inspect the condition of the Bridge across the Calf Killer at the West end of Turnpike Street in the town of Sparta; returned their report there of, that said Bridge was and is wholly out of repair and unsafe for the passing of carriages &c. Where upon appeared in open Court William Simpson the proprietor and undtaker there of and agrees that so soon as the water rises; that lumber can be had, that he will put the same in a state of good repair - and the Court there upon agrees, and so orders that further day be given him to put said Bridge in repair untill the rise of the water, that he can procure material to repair the same, that he then the law and they to report to Court.

Ordered by Court that Sims Dearing and Thomas Cooper Esqrs

be appointed to apportion hands betwen John Robertson, James M. Johnston, and Frederick Geer Overseers &c. Issd.

Ordered by Court that James M. Johnson be appointed Overseer of the road from the Ten Mile post to Johnsons Mill, - being a road of the second class, and keep the same in repair as the law requires; and that Thomas Cooper Esqr assign a list of hands to work there on Issd.

Ordered by Court that Joseph Kerr be appointed Overseer of the road from near his own house to Ross's Road, being a road of the third class, and Keep the same in repair as the law requires, with his own hands

This day the Commissioners here to fore appointed to settle with Joseph Herd Admr of the estate of Benjaman Bowman, Decd. returned their report there of which is ordered to be recorded.

Ordered by Court that David Snodgrass and John Jett comrs. appointed to settle with Joseph Herd Admr of the estate of Benjaman Bowman, Decd be allowed the sum of three dollars each, for two days service; and Joseph Cummings Comr for like service be allowed the sum of One dollar and fifty cents for One days service in said settlement, to be paid out of the estate of the Deceased by said Administrator

Ordered by Court that James Frisby and his two sons be assigned as hands to work on the road of which Frederick Lyda is Overseer from the farms of William Bruster to Merretts old field Issd.

(P-48) This day Nancy Anderson was appointed Guardian to Robert Anderson, James M. Anderson, Thomas Anderson, Rebecca Anderson, Francis Anderson, Archebald Anderson, Martela Anderson, minors and heirs of Jabez Anderson Decd who took the oath prescribed by law, and with Robert Anderson Jr., entered into and acknowledged bond in the sum of one thousand dollars, conditioned as the law requires.

This day William Bruster was appointed Guardian to Thomas Jones, and William T. Jones, Minor and heir of William Jones Deceased, who took the oath prescribed by law and togeather with Jacob A. Lane entered into and acknowledged bond in the sum of one thousand dollars conditioned as the law requires

This day Hugh Gracy was appointed Guardian to William Gracy Betsy Ann Gracy, Sarah Jane Gracy, John Gracy, Wamon Gracy, Lawson Gracy Mary Gracy and Margaret Gracy infant children of his deceased wife, one of the heirs of Zachariah Jones Deceased late of the County of White, who took the oath prescribed by law and togeather with Richard Crowder, entered into and acknowledged bond in the sum of one thousand dollars conditioned as the law requires

This day Richard Crowder, was chosen Guardian by John Jones, James Jones, Eliza Jones, Jefferson Jones, children and heirs of Zachariah Jones Deceased, and in like manner was appointed as such by the Court to the heirs a fore said, who took the oath prescribed by law and with Hugh Gracy entered into and acknowledged bond in the sum of five thousand dollars conditioned as the law requires

Ordered by Court that Samuel Turney Esqr. Gentleman Attorney at law be appointed attorney General protum during the present term of this Court.

Ordered by Court that Adam Hutchings be assigned as a hand to work on the road of which William Russell is Overseer Issd.

Ordered by Court that David L. Mitchell Sheriff of White County, take into his custody the children of Henry Glenn directed to be brought into this Court at a former day of the present term of this Court, and place them under the care and protection of such persons as he may think fit and bring them into this Court on the first day of the next Session there of, then and there to be dealt by agreeably to law. Issd -

Ordered by Court that John Jett, John Wallis, John Rose, David Snodgrass, Lewis Pettett, John Fryer, and Woodson P. White, free holders be appointed a Jury of View to examine the road leading from the plantation of William Bruster, passing William Lisks to Jones &c. to the pealed Chestnut, also the road leading from the same point passing Eli Sims Esqr. Capt Hutchings &c to the pealed chestnut also any intermediate routes betwen said roads, and report to the next term of this Court which is the best and most eligible site for a road of the first class, and which is most conderoive to the public interest

This day Palmer Roberts widow and relict of William Roberts Deceased, late of the County of White filed her petition on each for an agreement of Dower on the lands of which the said William Roberts Deceased died seized and possessed. Where upon it is ordered that a copy of the same with notices be served on the represenbive heirs at law of the said William Roberts Decd. and that said petition be continued over until the next term of this Court, for further proceedings to whom there on &c - that a Writ &c issue directed to the Sheriff of White County Commanding &c as required by law, returnable here at the next term of this Court.

(P-49) Ordered by Court that Nathanial Henric, who is the lawful Owner of a tract of land in White County containing 1250 acres part of an entry for 5000 reported in the name of Abner Duncan for double Tax for the year 1834 be permitted to pay the cash occuring there on in consequence there on of said report, and the amount of single Tax only for said year. And that the Sheriff only sell the residue of said tract of 5000 for the taxes there on - and it is further ordered by the Court that said Nathaniel Henric be released from the payment of all Taxes on said 1250 - acres of land for said year 1834 above the single Tax on the payment of the same, and the cost of making said report, and publication, also the cost occuring on the release and damages there of

This day William Moore the son of Eleanor Moore age six years and six months old was by the consent of said Eleanor Moore bound to William M. Young to serve him after the manner of an apprentice, untill he attains age of twenty one years where upon came the said William M. Young with David L. Mitchell his security, and entered into and acknowledged a covenant whereby he promises to teach and instruct said apprentice to read and write and Arithmetic to the single Rule of three inclusive, and at the end of the term to give him an extra suit of Jeans cloths and fifty dollars in cash, and during said Term to learn him the Farming business in all its various branches it being the trade or mystery which said William M. Young professeth

This day James Moore the son of Eleanor Moore, aged five years and six months old was by the consent of said Eleanor Moore bound to William M. Young, to serve him after the manner of an apprentice untill he attain the full age of twenty one years - where upon came the said William M. Young into open Court with David L. Mitchell his security and entered into and acknowledged a covenant, where in and where by he promises to teach or cause to be instructed the said James Moore to read write and Arithmetic as for as the single Rule of three inclusive to teach him the Farmer trade in all its various branches, it being the art or mystery which the said William M. Young professeth and at the expiration of said term to give said apprentice one extra suit of decent home spun Jeans cloths, and fifty dollars in cash.

Foster G. Crutcher &
Alexander Allison
partners trading under
the style of
Crutcher & Allison

vs — In Debt

Jose C. Dew & John Dew

This day came the Defendant and entered into and acknowledged bond for the prosecution of the appeal prayed in this cause to the next term of this Circuit Court for White County with Isaac Howard security conditioned as the law requires.

Ordered by Court that the following persons be appointed as Jurors to the next term of this Court Towit: William Usery, John A. Carrick, Thomas Broyles, Bartlett Belcher, John Fisher, William B. Hutson, James Woody, William Tabor, John Flatt, Samuel Lance, John H. Dale, Hartwell Wilson, George C. Howard, Alexander Brown, Thomas Frasher, Samuel Miller, Anderson S. Rogers, Joseph Gooch, Jacob Porter, William Earles, Samuel Johnston, Edward Elms, John Lollar, Sebird Rhea, John Bradford, John Cash, as Jurors and Archebald Connor and James Sherly as constables to attend there on.

(P-60) Ordered that the following Justices be appointed to recieve lists of Taxable property and polls in the following Captains companies for the year 1836 Towit - In Captain Allen company, John Jett, Esqr. In Capt Lewis Company John Bryan Esqr. In Captain Rodgers Company, Joseph Herd Esqr. In Capt Hyders Company Isaac Buck Esqr. In Captain Mitchell's company, David Snodgrass Esqr. In captain Hargis company, Edmund Stamps Esqr. In Captain Swift company, William Knowles Esqr. In Captain Sims Company, Eli Sims Esqr. In Captain Frasher Company, Jonathan T. Bradly Esqr. In Capt Stockleys Company David Hasting Esqr. In Captain Dodsons Company Dan Griffith Esqr. In Captain Warrens Company, Elijah Frost Esqr. in Captain Dunagans Company, George Welch Esqr. in Captain Saml Allen Company, William Irwin Esqr. in captain Bradfords

Company John Pennington Esqr. in Captain Flatts Company, John Rose Esqr. in Captain Coles Company, Lewis Pettett Esqr. in Captain Adams Company Joseph Cummings Esqr. and report to the next term of this Court.

This day John Griffith and Patience Roberts Administrator and Administratrix of William Roberts Deceased returned into Court upon oath an Inventory of part of the estate of the Deceased, which is ordered to be recorded.

This day the Death of Jeremiah Denton, late of the County of White was suggested, where upon was produced in open Court the last will and Testament of the said Jeremiah Denton Deceased by Ozias Denton, who is appointed sole Executor of said will by the Deceased - and now the due execution and publication there of was proven in open Court by the oath of Joseph Herd and Isaac Denton. Subscribing Witness there to, as the last Will and Testament of the said Jeremiah Denton, and that said Testator was at the date of the execution of said will, of sound and disposing mind and memory - where upon the Court being of opinion that said will was duly, properly and well proven to be the last will and Testament of the said Jeremiah Denton Deceased, it is ordered to be recorded, - Where upon in like manner came the said Ozias Denton, and took the oath prescribed by law, and to geather with John Fryer and Lewis Pettett, entered into and acknowledged bond, in the sum of three thousand dollars conditioned as the law requires &c Issd.

Ordered by the Court unanimously, present thirteen acting Justices of the peace for the County of White pay all cost on the following suits prosecuted for the use of the County by William Baker, Overseer of the road Towit - The suite against Aaron Hutchings $2. In the suit against Aaron Hutchings $2. In the suit against George Porter 75 cents, the suits against George Porter 50 cents - and it is ordered by the Court, that Certificates issue for the Cost in said Suits respectively directed to the trustee of White County for payment out of any funds in his hands not otherwise appropriated &c

Ordered that Court be adjourned untill to morrow morning 9 Oclock

David Snodgrass
Elijah Frost
Lewis Pettett
John Jett

(P-51) Tuesday morning October 20, 1835, Court met pursuant to adjournment Present the Worshipful

David Snodgrass
Elijah Frost
Lewis Pettett and
John Jett
} Esquires Justices

Be it remembered that on this day appeared in open Court Winkfield Hill, administrator of William Shropshire Deceased, late of the County of White and produced a pension Certificate bearing date the sixth day of October in the year One thousand eight hundred and twenty seven - allowing the said William Shropshire a pension from the seventeenth day of September one thousand eight hundred and twenty seven during his natural life, after the rate of eight dollar per month, for service rendered as a private in the Army of the Revolution inscribed on the pension art roll of West Tennessee and at the same time the said Winkfield Hill, with a certain Joab Hill and Thomas Underwood Citizens of the County of White to the Court known entitled to full faith and credit upon their oath in a Court of Justice being sworn in due form of law, proved to the satisfaction of the Court that the said William Shropshire, departed this life on the tenth day of August last past; And that the said William Shropshire is and was identical William Shropshire named in the foregoing and aforesaid Pension Certificate which came to the hands and possession of said Winkfield Hill, administrator after the decease of said William Shropshire - and that said William Shropshire was entitled to said pension from the fourth day of March in the year eighteen hundred and thirty five, to the tenth day of August in said year, being the day of his death, on account of services rendered as a private in the revolution, during the revolutionary war, and at the time of his dea th he resided in the County of White, in the State of Tennessee, and had resided there for almost the span of eight or ten years; and that previous there to had resided in Green County, State of Georgia; all of which is ordered by the Court to be Certified

signed David Snodgrass
Lewis Pettett
John Jett

Saturday August 20th 1835, Ordered that Court be adjourned till Court in Course

David Snodgrass
Lewis Pettett
John Jett

Test
Jacob A. Lane
Clerk

(P-52) State of Tennessee -

At a Court of Pleas and Quarter Session begin and held for the County of White at the Court house in the town of Sparta, before the Worshipful the Justices of said Court, on the second Monday being the eleventh day of January in the year of our Lord one thousand eight hundred thirty six, and of the Independence of the United States the sixtieth year

Present the Worshipful

Thomas Eastland, Chairman
David Snodgrass
John Jett
George Welch
John Rose
Lewis Pettett
William Knowles
Isaac Buck
David Hasting
Sims Dearing
Joseph Herd

Jesse Scoggin)
Edmund Cunningham)
John Wallis)
Dan Griffith)
Eli Sims) Esquires
William Irwin)
John Pennington) Justices
Edmund Stamps)
Thomas Cooper)
Jonathan J. Bradley)

Ordered by Court that John Detty, Senr., be released from the payment of Tax upon free poll for the year 1835 and that the Sheriff have a credit for the same in the settlement of his accounts -

Ordered by the Court that John F. Detty be released from the payment of the Taxes for the year 1835 on 98 acres of land and that the Sheriff have a credit for the same in the settlement of his accounts

Ordered by Court that Carter Whitefield be released from the payment of a poll Tax for 1835 - and that the Sheriff have a credit for the same in the payment of his

This day Patience Roberts Admrx and John Griffith Admr of William Roberts Dec'd returned a list of the sales of the property of the Deceased upon oath, which is ordered to be recorded -

This day Rachel Jones Admrx of William Jones Decd returned into Court upon oath an account of the property of the deceased upon oath, which is ordered to be recorded -

This day Rachel Jones Admrx of the estate of William Jones Decd appeared in Court and there upon in writing suggests that the estate of the said William Jones Decd is wholly insufficent to pay off and discharge the debts of the deceased, and that said estate is there fore insolvent which is ordered to be recorded -

This day Reubin Randolph produced in open Court one wolf scalp under the age of four months, and proved that the same was killed in the County of White, where upon, there being present five Acting Justices of the peace, it is ordered, that the same be Certified to the Treasure of Middle Tennessee for payment and that the Sheriff of White County burn said scalps, who being here in Court received the same into his possession and acted accordingly J. A. Lane Issd

This day John Brombelow produced in open Court three Wolf scalps, each under the age of four months and proved that he killed them in White County, where upon there being present five Acting Justices of the peace, it is ordered that the same Certified to the Treasure of Middle Tennessee for payment - and that the Sheriff of White County burn said scalps - who being here in Court received said scalps into his possession and acted accordingly - J. A. Lane Issd.

Ordered by Court that Thomas Stipe, William Prater, John Felkins, and William Griffey, be assigned to work on the road of which

Robert Gamble is Overseer from the mouth of Cane Creek to William Dennys old place being a road of the second class

(P-53) Ordered by Court that the road from the cross roads at Cocks to Wallings landing be and the same is hereby discontinued

Ordered by Court that William Whitefield, John Tacket, James Cooper, Jesse Perkins, Jonah Whitefield, Benjamin Hitchcock, and James Spears, be assigned as hands to work on the road of which Carter Whitefield, is Overseer from the Carthage road to where the Caney fork comes in as and keep tho same in repair as a road of the second class

Ordered by Court that Stephen Farley be appointed Overseer of the road from Glade Creek to Rum Creek, being a road of the second class, and that the same hands which worked under William Goodwin former Overseer there of be assigned to work there on -

Ordered by Court that James Dodson be appointed Overseer of the road from Jesse Wallings to John Smiths being a road of the first class and keep the same in repair, with the same hands which worked under Berryman Holland, former Overseer there of -

Ordered by Court that Claibourn Williams be released from the payment of taxes on 57½ acres of land for the year 1835 - and that the Sheriff have a credit for the same in the settlement of his account -

Ordered by Court that Lucy Claybrooks be released from the payment of tax on one slave for the year 1835, - and that the Sheriff have a credit for the same in the settlement of his account - Issd

This day Asa Certain Guardean to the minor children and heirs of Edward Holmes Decd returned his account on oath which is ordered to be recorded -

Ordered by Court that John Jett, Lewis Pettett, and Samuel A. Moore Esquires, be appointed Comr to settle with Daniel Walling Admr of William Fisher Decd and report there of to the next term of this Court

Ordered by Court that Caleb Mason, David L. Mitchell, Robert Glenn, Joshua Mason and John Humphrey freeholders be appointed Comr to lay off and mark a road from the West side of Town Creek being the shipping point road thence passing through Charles Sperrys land, by the house of David L. Mitchell crossing Gum spring Mountain - intersecting the old road near Robert Glenns being a road of the second class, and report there of to this Court at the present Session

This day the Comr appointed to lay off and mark a road from the Shipping point road West of Town Creek, passing David L. Mitchell intersecting the old road near Coopers, Robert Glenn returned their report on oath, that said road was laid out and marked where upon it is ordered that the same be established as a road/of the second class, and that D. L. Mitchell the Overseer there of open the same as required by law -

Ordered by Court that John J. Gammon, be released from the

payment of a poll Tax for the year 1835 - and that the Sheriff have a credit for the same in the settlement of his account Issd. -

This day Thomas Jones Admr of Zachariah Jones Decd returned on oath an Inventory of the estate of the Deceased which is ordered to be recorded -

This day Thomas Jones Administrator of Zachariah Jones Deceased, returned upon oath an account of the sales of the property of the Deceased which is ordered to be recorded -

Samuel Brown Guardean to the heirs of John Dyer, Deceased, returned his account on oath which is ordered to be recorded - &c

(P-54) This day John Pennington and Sarah Dyer Guardean to the minor heirs of John Dyer Deceased returned on oath their account which is ordered to be recorded -

This day John Pennington Esqr returnes a list of Taxable property and polls in Capt Bradfords Company, for the year 1836, which is ordered to be recorded -

Jan 5

Ordered by Court unanimously - that John Bryan Esqr be allowed the sum of five dollars for holding an Inquest over the body of William Gracy Decd. who came to his death by freezing, to be paid by the trustee of White County, out of Any Monies not otherwise appropriated -

This day John Jett, Joseph Herd and Joseph Cummings were appointed commissioners of the Poor house in White County who took the oath prescribed by law -

This day Allen L. Mitchell was appointed Superintendant of the poor house in White County for the year 1836, and took the oath prescribed by law -

This day the death of George W. Hawkins late of the County of White was suggested, and that he departed this life interstate - where upon John R. Glenn, was appointed administrator of all and singular, the goods & chattles, rights and credits of the said George W. Hawkins Decd. and took the oath prescribed by law and with Joseph W. Little entered into and acknowledged bond in the sum of two hundred dollars conditioned as the law requires -

This day was produced in open Court a writing purporting to be the last will and Testament of Isaac Plumlee Deceased - Where upon the due execution and publication there of was proven in open Court by the oath of Andrew K. Parker and John Gillentine, subscribing Witnesses there to for the purposes and things there in mentioned, that the said Isaac Plumlee, signed, sealed published and declared the same to be his last will and Testament in them present and subscribed their names as Witnesses there to at his request, and in his presence and that he was at the date of the execution, thereof of sound and disposing mind and memory - and on the same day appeared in open Court Margaret Plumlee who is appointed sole executrix of said last will and Testament and took upon him self the execution there of, and took the oath prescribed by law; and with John Plumlee and Gabriel Cummings entered into and acknowledged Bond in the sum of five thousand dollars conditioned as the law requires -

Ordered by Court that Joseph S. Ellison be appointed Overseer of the road, from George Cardwells to Felts branch being a road of the second class and keep the same in repair as the law requires, that George Welch Esqr assign a list of hands to work there on -

Ordered by Court that Joseph Cummings Jr., and Lewis Pettett be appointed Commissioners to settle with Thomas Hill Snr., Guardean to the heirs of James Hill Decd, and report there of to the next term of this Court.

Ordered by Court that Sandford Stamps be appointed Overseer of the road from the 19 mile post to the Standing Stone, being a road of the second class, and keep the same in repair as the law requires that Edward Stamps assign a list of hands to work there on

Ordered by Court that Patrick Givens, Joseph Givens and William Givens, children of Charlotte Givens to be dealt by according to law -

(P-55) Ordered by Court that Samuel Dunagan, Reubin Whitson, James C. Crawley, Welcher Cardwell and Jesse England free holders be appointed a Jury of View to lay off and mark a road from near where Benjamin Mackie now lives the nearest and best way to Bunker Hill near Dunagans Crock Kill being a road of the second class and report there of to the next term of this Court

This day the Jury of View appointed at the last term of this Court to lay off and mark a road from the mouth of falling water to Allens ferry road returned their report of the same, which is established as a road of the second class - that Frederick Davis be appointed Overseer there of, that all the hands residing on James Davis's lands near the mouth of falling Water be assigned to work there on - to open and keep the same in repair as the law requires -

Ordered that John Swindle be appointed Overseer of the road from Rock Island to the two mile post on the Kentuckey road, being a road of the first class, and keep the same in repair with the hands which worked under Madison L. Moore former overseer there of -

Ordered by Court that Asa Certain be appointed Overseer of the road from Rum Creek to the 13 mile post being a road of the second class, and keep the same in repair with the hands which worked under William Glenn, former Overseer there of -

Ordered by Court that Thomas C. Martin be appointed Overseer of the road from falling Water to the intersection of the Carthage road, being a road of the second class and that he keep the same in repair as the law requires with the hands which worked under James C. Crawley, former Overseer there of

Ordered by Court that John Austin, John Roland, William Green,

Woodson P. White and Solomon Dodson, free holders be appointed a jury of View to lay off and mark a road of the third class from the mouth of Andrew Bryans lane, thence the nearest and best way passing the house of Captain John Baker, Berry Wilsons to intersect the road at William Wallis Big Spring branch, and report there of to the next term of this Court -

Ordered by Court that William Wilson, be appointed Overseer of the road from the mouth of Bryans Lane at his cotton patch to Coopers shop on Ross's road, being a road of the second class - and keep the same in repair with the hands which worked under Andrew Lowell former Overseer there of -

George Welch Esqr returned a list of Taxable property and polls in Captain Dunagans Company for 1836 - which is ordered to be recorded -

Ordered by Court that Aaron Hutchings be appointed Overseer of the road from the peeled chestnut to the Shipping port road - being a road of the first class and keep the same in repair with the hands which worked under William Russell former Overseer there of -

Ordered by Court that the road of which Greenville Templeton is Overseer from the Gum Spring road near Mrs Rodgers to said Templetons be established as a road of the third class -

Ordered by Court that John Passons be appointed Overseer of the road from Jeremiah Webbs, passing Hollands Mill then to Jonathan Shorts being a road of the second class and keep the same in repair as the law requires, that William Womack assign a list of hands to work there on

(P-56) This day Jesse A. Bounds produced in open Court his stock mark Towit - A crop crop off of the left ear, and split in the right, which is ordered to be recorded -

This day Eliza Bounds produced in open Court her stock mark Towit - Crop and split in the left ear, which is ordered to be recorded -

David Nicholas produced his stock mark in open Court Towit - Crop off of the right ear and under bite in the left; which is ordered to be recorded -

William Simpson produced his stock mark in open Court Towit - A smooth crop and under bite of each ear, which is recorded -

For reasons appearing to the satisfaction of the Court, it is ordered that Samuel Thomas be released from the appraised value of eight hogs taken up by him as estray -

For reasons appearing to the satisfaction of the Court it is ordered that Eliza Ledbetter bound to James T. Officer as an apprentice be released and forever discharged from further service as such to said James Officer -

Ordered by Court that the Treasure of the Poor house Commissioners pay to William Glenn, merchant of Sparta fourteen dollars seventy five cents out of the poor Tax of the year 1836 - for the funeral expenses of Catharine Corbit of the town of Sparta who was casually burned to death

Ordered by Court unanimously, that the Trustee of White County pay over to James Eartham the sum of one hundred and seventy five dollars the consideration given for Lot No 70 purchased by White County from Joseph Kerr, the said debt having been transfered to said Eastham for a valuable consideration Issd.

This day John Franklin Admr. of Robert Goad Decd returned upon oath an account of the sales of the property of the deceased which is ordered to be recorded -

This day Eliza Ledbetter was bound to Joseph Anderson, being now twelve years of age to serve him after the manner of an apprentice untill she attains the age of eighteen years. Where upon the said Joseph Anderson, with Archebald Connor entered into a covenant with Archebald Connor conditioned as the law requires

This day the death of William Brown late of the County of White was suggested and that he departed this life interstate where upon James Thomas and John Brown were appointed Administrators of all and singular the goods and chattle rights and credits of William Brown Deceased, who took the oath prescribed by law and David Snodgrass and Jonathan T. Bradly entered into and acknowledged bond in the sum of three thousand dollars conditioned as the law requires

Ordered by Court that James H. Jinkens be appointed Overseer of the road from Sparta to the east end of Reeves ridge being a road of the first class and that the same hands which worked under the former be assigned to work there on -

This day Jesse Allen Glenn aged nine years on the 24th August next was bound to Andrew Lowell to serve him after the manner of an apprentice, untill he attains the age of twenty one years - Where upon the said Andrew Lowell with Archebald Connor entered into and acknowledged Covenant conditioned &c

This day the Commissioners of the Bridge at Sparta, returned their report of the state and condition of the Bridge a fore said, which is approved of by the Court -

(P-57) This day Nancy Ann Glenn aged Ten years on the 20th of March next, was bound to Archebald Conner, to serve him after the manner of an apprentice untill she attains the age of eighteen years &c Where upon the said Archebald Connor with Andrew Lowell entered into and acknowledged Covenant &c which is recorded -

Ordered by Court that the Sheriff of White County at the next term of this Court produced here in Court Nancy Mays, and her two infant children, John Mays & Thomas Mays to be dealt by according to law -

Ordered by Court that eleven tracts of land the property of

the heirs of William King Deceased, each be released from Double Taxes of the year 1836 - and that they pay the Cost of releasing each tract respectively as a fore said, and that said tracts severally be subject to only a single Tax -

Ordered by Court that all lands here to fore sold for taxes, which have had a double tax charged there on - when the owners there of offer to pay a single Tax, that the Sheriff is directed to recieve the single Tax only -

Ordered by Court that William Womack, and William Knowles Esqr. assign hands to work on the road of which John Humphrey is Overseer - and report there of to the next term of this Court -

Ordered by Court that Mark Lowry, Daniel Clark, and Anthony Dibrell be appointed Comr to ass ign and set a part to the widow of William Brown Decd a sufficient quantity of provisions for the support of said Widow and her children for one year, and report there of to the next term of this Court -

This day John H. Dale Guardean to the minor heirs of John Dale Decd. returned on oath an account of the estate of his wards which is ordered to be recorded -

Ordered by Court that Mary Bedwell be released from the payment of Tax on 91 Acres of land for the year 1835 and that the Sheriff have a credit for the same in the settlement of his account -

For reasons appearing to the Satisfaction of the Court it is ordered that further time untill the next term of this Court be given to return lists of Taxable property for the year 1836

This day the death of Edmund Godard was suggested, that he departed this life interstate Where upon George Sparkman was appointed Administrator of all and Singular the goods and chattle rights and credits of the said Edmund Godard Decd - who took the oath prescribed by law and to geather with Edmund Godard and Daniel Hollingsworth entered into and acknowledged bond in the sum of one thousand dollars conditioned as the law requires -

Ordered by Court that Jonathan Scott be appointed Overseer of the road from near William Prices to the middle of a slash where Isaac Howard lives being a road of the second class and keep the same in repair as the law requires, that J. T. Bradley Esqr assign a list of hands to work there on

Ordered by Court that Silas Cash be appointed Overseer of the road from the center of a slash where Isaac Howard lives to the road near Shady grove meeting house being a road of the second class and keep the same in repair as the law requires that John Pennington Esquire assign a list of hands to work there on

This day Jesse Walling Admr of Thomas H. Paul Decd returned on oath an account of the sales of the property of the Decd. which is ordered to be recorded.

(P-58) This day James W. Copeland administrator ~~to the heirs of~~ John Anderson deceased returned upon oath a report of his Guardianship which is ordered to be recorded -

This day Ozias Denton Administrator of the estate of Jeremiah Denton deceased returned an account of the sales of said estate upon oath which is ordered to be recorded -

This day Thomas Stipe was appointed Guardian to his daughter Glaphey Stipe a minor and for the faithful preformance of his Guardianship entered into and acknowledged bond with John Stipe and John Gillentine his securities in the sum of six hundred dollars conditioned as the law requires

William M. Bryan a Constable of White County this day appeared in open Court and took an oath to support the constitution of the United States and the State of Tennessee. And togeather with the several oaths prescribed by law, and with Eli Sims his security entered into and acknowledged bond in the sum of One thousand dollars conditioned as the law requires

This day appeared in open Court Robert G. Anderson Constable of White County and took and oath to support the constitution of the United States, and of the State of Tennessee. And the several oaths prescribed by law, and with William M. Bryan and Alexander B. Lane entered into and acknowledged bond in the sum of One thousand Dollars conditioned as the law requires -

This day James Russell a Constable of White County appeared in open Court and took an oath to support the constitution of the United States and of the State of Tennessee and the several oaths prescribed by law and with Lewis Pettett and Eli Sims entered into and acknowledged bond in the sum of One thousand dollars conditioned as the law requires -

Ordered by Court that the following persons be summonsed as Jurors to the next Honorable Circuit Court for White County to wit - James Scarbrough, Senr., Isaac Brogdon, Thomas Robertson, George Thomas, William McKinny, Patrick Potts, Jesse Scoggins, Spencer Mitchell, James Randals, Joseph Herd, Turner Lane, Jr., Andrew Lowell, David Snodgrass, William Snodgrass, William Dodson, George Sparkman, Robert Anderson, Lewis Phillips, Hartwell Wilson, John Baker, James Simpson, Senr., William C. Britthin, John Jett, James Hudgins, Abraham Ditty, and William P. Rhea, and Archebald Connor and Robert H. McManus, as Constables to attend there on.

This day John Fryer Guardian to the heirs of Charles Carter, Sr., deceased, returned his report upon oath-which is ordered to be recorded -

Ordered by Court that John Jett, Joseph Cummings and Joseph Herd, commissioners of the Poor house in White County for the year, 1835 - be allowed for their services for said year the sum of five dollars each to be paid by the Treasure of the poor house commissioners out of the Tax, 1835 -

Ordered by Court that John Jett, Joseph Cummings and Joseph

Herd, Esqr. be appointed Commissioners of the poor house in the County of White for the year 1836 - who being here present in open Court took the oath required by law.

This day John Jett Esqr. was appointed Treasure of the Commissioners of the poor house in White County for the year 1836 - and who being in open Court took the oath of Office -

Ordered by Court unanimously that William R. Tucker keeper of the common Jail of White County be allowed the sum of fifty dollars for building a platform for the common Jail of said County to be paid by the Trustee of White County out of the tax of 1836 -

(P-59) Ordered by Court unanimously that Allen L. Mitchell Superentendant of the poor house of White County for the year 1835 be allowed the sum of One hundred and fifty eight dollars thirty seven and a half cents for services rendered agreeable to his account, to be paid by the Treasure of the poor house Commissioners out of the poor Tax for the year 1835 - that he be released from seventeen dollars for rules 1835. Issd.

Where as some years ago a road was changed near where Jacob A. Lane then lived but now where Nicholas Oldham lives leaving the Allen ferry road a small distance West of Where said Oldham crib Stands Where there was formerly an old road then with said old road to the Carthage road being a distance of about One hundred and fifty or two hundred yards Now it is ordered that said Nicholas Oldham be permitted to open the same, and inclose the old part of the road which was discontinued by the former rules, establishing the new way, on the application of Jacob A. Lane.

Jacob A. Lane the clerk of this Court produced the receipts Which by law he was this day bound to produce. Which is ordered to be recorded -

Ordered by Court that Henry Kuhn be appointed Overseer of the road from Moores field Crossing near Doyles Mill passing near to where Melvins live, being a road of the second class and keep the same in repair as the law requires and that David Mitchell Esqr. assign a list of hands to work there on -

Ordered by Court that Thomas Snodgrass, John Rodgers, John Parker, Iredell Stone and Ransom Geer, free holders be appointed a Jury of review to examine the old road & new one passing near John Gooches and report at the next term of this Court -

Ordered by Court that the road as reviewed marked and laid out by Commissioners from W. M. Brusters plantation passing Eli Sims to the peeled chestnut be established as a road of the first class that the hands residing on William Irwin's farm and William Brusters farm be assigned to work there on in addition to the hands already assigned, and that the hands on the Shipping port road be assigned to work there on in opening said road only - This is a compromise - Issd.

This day appeared in open Court William Simpson and agrees

that he will reduce for keeping up the bridge at Sparta the sum of one hundred dollars annually, but should said bridge be swept away or other wise destroyed that during the time he is rebuilding the same, no pay shall be demanded or required during said time or during the time it may be impassable this is not to alter the former contract entered into betwen the Court and said Simpson

William H. Smith, Ex
vs
Jacob A. Lane

In Cov -

Ordered by the Court that the above cause be transfered to the next Honorable Circuit Court for White County as directed by act of the general assembly, to which day said cause is continued - done by Court of peals -

Samuel Turney
vs
Alexander Glenn

Original Attachment

Ordered by Court that the above cause be transfered to the next Circuit Court of White County as directed by act of the general Assembly to which day said cause is continued - done by Court of peals -

(P-60)

Washington Burgis
vs
Abraham Isbell

In Debt

Ordered by Court that the above cause be transfered to the next Circuit Court of White County by act of the General Assembly to which day said cause is continued - done by Court of peals -

H. & J. Hickman & Co
vs
John B. Rodgers

Debt -

Ordered by Court that the above cause be transfered to the next Circuit Court of White County by act of the general Assembly to which day said cause is continued - done by Court of peals -

Jesse Lincoln
vs
Joseph Kerr

In Cov -

Ordered by Court that the above cause be transfered to the next Circuit Court of White County by act of the General Assembly to which day said cause is continued - done by Court of peals

John Wright
vs
Wilborn Jones

Debt Cr -

Ordered by Court that the above cause be transfered to the next Circuit Court of White County by act of the General Assembly to which day said cause is continued - done by Court of peals.

Nathan Haggard
to the use of
Crocket Herbert &
T. C. Connor
vs
John Dales, Admrs.

Trespass

Ordered by the Court that the above cause be transfered to the next Circuit Court of White County by act of the General Assembly to which day the above cause is continued - done by Court of peals

Martha Crawley
by her next friend
vs
Henry Moore & wife

Trespass

Ordered by Court that the above cause be transfered to the next Circuit Court of White County by act of the General Assembly to which day said cause is continued - done by Court of peals -

Thomas Stevens Exr
vs
Robert Hewett

In Cov -

Ordered by the Court that the above cause be transfered to the next Circuit Court of White County by act of the General Assembly to which day said Cause is continued - done by Court of peals -

John Witt
vs
John Cain

Debt -

Ordered by the Court that the above cause be transfered to the next Circuit Court of White County by act of the General Assembly to which day said cause is continued - done by Court of peals -

(P-61)

The State
vs

Scifr.

Chapel Averett) Ordered by Court that the above cause be transfered to the next Circuit Court of White County by act of the general Assembly to which day said cause is continued - - by Court of appeal.

State
vs
Michael Moore

Ind. Ass. & Battery

Ordered by Court that the above cause be transfered to the next Circuit Court of White County by Act of the General Assembly to which day said cause is continued, - by Court of appeals

State
vs
William Simmons

Ind. Ass. & Battery

Ordered by the Court that the above cause be transfered to the next Circuit Court of White County by act of the General Assembly to which day said cause is continued. - by Court of appeals

State
vs
S. Scruggs &
E. Rudder

Pros for Gaming

Ordered by Court that the above cause be transfered to the next Circuit Court of White County by act of the General Assembly to which day said Cause is continued - by Court of Appeals

State
vs
J. Wooldrige & others

Ind. for a Riot

Ordered by Court that the above cause transfered to the next Circuit Court of White County by Act of the general Assembly to which day said cause is Continued, - by Court of Appeals -

State
vs
Abraham Broyles

Pros for Gaming

Ordered by Court that the above cause be transfered to the next Circuit Court of White County by Act of the general Assembly to which day said cause is Continued, - by Court of Appeals

State
vs
Arnold Moss

Present for Nuisance

Ordered by Court that the above cause be transfered to the next Circuit Court of White County by act of the General Assembly to which day said Cause is Continued, - by Court of Appeals -

State
vs
William Bozarth

Pres. for Nuisance

Ordered by Court that the above cause be transfered to the next Circuit Court of White County by Act of the general Assembly to which day said cause is continued, - by Court of Appeals

State
vs
John Cantrell &
A. Cantrell

Ind. Ass. and Battery

Ordered by Court the above cause be transfered to the next Circuit Court of White County by Act of the General Assembly to which day said Cause is Continued, - by Court of Appeals -

(P-62)

State
vs
Andrew Lowell

Prest. for a Nuisance

Ordered by Court that the above cause be transfered to the next Circuit Court of White County by act of the general assembly to which day said cause is Continued, - by Court of Appeals

For reason appearing to the satisfaction of the Court it is ordered that a writ issued returnable to the next term of this Court directed to the Sherriff of White County commanding him to summons according to law a jury of twelve freeholders of White County to ascertain according to law whether George Miller of said County is or is not an Idiot or Lunatic and in the event he is found to be such, then to ascertain what real and personal estate may belong to said George Miller and duly report and return the same to the next term of this Court isd.

Wamon Leftwich, Guardian to Malinda Rowland return upon oath an account of the State and condition of the estate of his ward in his hands which is recorded.

This day John Jett, Treasure of the poor house Commissions, Appeared in Court and entered into and Acknowledged bond with David L. Mitchell and William G. Sims in the sum of one thousand dollars condition as the law requires

State
vs

Bastardy

David Wilson) Matilda Tucker, Prosx.

This day came the defendant in proper person into open Court and there upon produced a receipt in writing signed by the prosecutrix Acknowledging the payment of the sum in full which by law she would be entitled to from said Defendant for begetting upon her body a bastard child, - where upon it is ordered by the Court and is considered that said Defendant find sureties to keep the County endemnified from all Cost and charges for and towards the support and maintenance of said Bastard Child. - And now came said defendant and Hartwell Wilson and Jacob A. Lane into open Court and acknowledged themselves endebted to the State in the sum of five hundred to the use of the County of White, void on condition that they keep free indemnified and harmless the County of White from the support and maintenance of the above Bastard Child, charged on oat by the said Matilda to be begotten on her body by said David Wilson, - where upon it is considered by the Court that the State of Tennessee - cover against said defendant all Cost in this behalf expended

Orderd that the Court be adjouned till Court in Course

Test

J. A. Lane
Clk.

David Snodgrass
George Welch
John Jett

(P-63)

RePorte of
Commissioners on Election
Districts in White County
Returned into this office
the 28th, January A.D. 1836

Survey of county into districts

State of Tennessee }
County White } %

We whose names are hereunto annexed having been appointed by the General Assembly as Commissioners to lay of the districts in the County aforesaidment and after being duly sworn according to the act of assembly by John Jett Esq. one of the acting Justices of the peace for said County of White proceeded to act in conformity of said act do lay off the following districts in the following manner

To Wit:

Sparta District No 1

Commincing at Christopher Hoffmans on the side of Cumberland Mountain east of Sparta running South with the bluff on top of said Mountain a short distance thence West round the head of James Hudgins

Cove and plantation thence to William Bakers ridge thence South west on side ridge to some Cabins called ONeeils Cabins; thence down side ridge between the lands of Pleasant Waller and Jesse Lincoln where Jonathan Clinny now lives leaving Waller out thence west to Harmon H. Mayborns including him thence to the mouth of a large spring branch on the Calf Killer on the west side, thence up side branch to its head; thence passing between the farm of Squire Jett and Charles Smith leaving Jett in this district, thence West to Hays Arnolds including him; thence to James Williams including him thence up the ridge to the top of said ridge; thence, north with the top of said ridge to Morrissons Gap. thence down the ridge between the lands of Moses Youngs and Henry Lyda to the four Mile tree east of said Lyda's on the road leading from Sparta to Allen's ferry, thence across said ridge to the lands of Mrs. Ussery thence East to Montgomery Dibrell's leaving him out, thence a east course a direct line to Mark Lowry's leaving him out; thence passing an old house on the top of the hill above the ford of the Calf Killer passing from Sparta to Cherry Creek, thence across the river and a direct line up a ridge thence with the top of said ridge between the Wild Cat Cove and Sparta to the Cumberland Mountain; thence South with the top of said Mountain to Christopher Hoffmans including said Hoffman. The Election to be held at Sparta in the above

Hickory Valley District No 2

Comnincing at the Calf Killer oposite of Jetts Spring branch thence down the river to the ford below S. R. Doyles Mills, thence withe the wagon road south east passing by a field of John Denton on the north of his house keeping said road to where a road turns off leaving Robert Loves plantation all on the right hand; thence a direct line eastwardly across the ridge to Rhodam Lewis's including him thence William Lewis's line between him and John Felton thence passing along the field of Spence Mitchell near the Union Meeting-house thence passing in a direct line between the farm of Jacob Anderson and John Scoggins Sr., thence to the old road leading from Sparta to Porter's ford thence crossing the Caney Fork at said Ford thence passing through the land of said Porter thence up the (P-64) ridge between Cain Creek and Caney Fork leaving John Yates out to the top of the Mountain thence a north course round with the brow of the Mountain so as to include all living on both sides of the Caney Fork as far up as Capt Dotsons Company of Malitia thence a cross the Caney Fork including all below the top of said Mountain, running thense with the brow of said Mountain passing Joseph Fifer's leaving him out thence Northwardly around said Mountain to where a wagon road leads down said Mountain to John Austin's including him thence down the ridge to William Bakers leaving him out thence Westwardly with said ridge to ONeeil's old Cabins thence passing between Jonathan Clinny and Pleasant Waller, thence to H. Mayborns leaving him out, thence to the Beginning.
The Election to be held at Mrs Dale's in the above district -

Fryer's. District No 3. -

Comnincing at the top of the ridge west of James William's thence a south cours on the top of said ridge, so as to include James Roberts farm thence to the top of the ridge between Mrs. Bowmans and Thomas Underwood thence along said ridge South crossing the Stage road

etween Lewis Phillips and Robert Anderson theno between the farms of James W. Copeland & Warrens to the old powder mill on the Caney Fork thence up the same to the mouth of the Calf Killer thence up the Calf Killer to the mouth of John Jotts Spring branch thence west leaving John Jett out thence to Hays Arnolds leaving him out, thence westwardly to James William leaving him out thence to the Beginning.
Election to be held at John Fryers.

Mrs Dillon's District No 4

Commincing at the top of the ridge between James Hembree now lives and William Templeton, thence westwardly passing the Mithodist Campground thence across the hickory nut mountain to widow Fisher including all her farm thence to the Caney Fork at Walling's at Wallings old gin thence up the Caney Fork to the mouth of Rocky thence with the dividing line between Warren County and White to Jesse Davis's thence Northwardly to an old road leading from the Arch Cove to Rosse's Ferry thence along said road to said ferry thence crossing the Caney Fork thence up the same to the old powder mill thence northwest between Robert Anderson and James W. Copeland to the point of the ridge north of Lewis Phillip's thence up the ridge between Thomas Underwood and Mrs. Bowmans, thence round on the top of said ridge westwardly to the beginning
Election to be held at

Mrs Dillon's

Joseph Clark District No 5

Commincing on the top of the ridge between where James Hembree now lives and William Templeton farm thence westwardly passing the Methodist Campground thence crossing the Hickory nut Mountain west course to the widow Fisher's leaving her farm out thence to the Caney Fork at Wallings Gin thence down the same to the mouth of Townsends Creek thence up said Creek to the head of the same thence eastwardly to Richard Crowders leaving him out thence to the point of the Mountain near the farm of William Glenn where Canada Rigsby now lives thence up said Mountain to the top of the same thence south with said Mountain to the beginning
Election to be held at Joseph Clark

(P-65)

James Russell's District No 6

Commincing at the 4 mile tree on the Sparta road east of Henry Lyda's thence west with said road passing Henry Lyda's to William Lisks thence north with the Kentucky road to a wagon road north of Stephen Farleys thence Westwardly with said wagon road to Coles lower Mill on the Falling Water thence south with the Rockisland road below the farm of James M. Nelson thence with a right hand path leading to Isaac Taylor Mill Creek crossing the same above the mill thence with said path to where it intersects the road leading from Sparta to Allen ferry at the Widow Jones including the same, thence with the road to Lincolns ferry so as to include James Hayes, thence up the Caney fork to the mouth of Townsends Mill Creek thence up said Creek to the head

passing Richard Crowders including the same thence to the point of the Mountain near the farm of William Glenn where Canada Rigsby now lives thence up said Mountain to the top of the same - thence North down a ridge between the land of Youngs and H. Lyda to the Begining.
Election to be held at James Russells

Mouth of Falling Water No 7

Commincing at the Jackson County line west John Ellison's thence southwardly to Whitefield's Mill leaving him out thence suth east to Coles lower mill on the Falling Water at the falls, thence with the said towards Rockisland below James M. Nelson's to where a road turns off to the right leading to Issac Taylor Mill Creek Crossing the same above said Mill running thence with a path to the widow Jone's leaving her out; thence with the road to Lincolns ferry leaving out James T. Hayes down the Caney Fork to the County line, thence round with said line to the Beginning.
Election to be held at the mouth of Falling Water

Milledgeville District No 8

Commincing at the line between White & Jackson Counties where the Kentuckey road crosses said line thence with said road south to Cross road between David Goodwin old place & Stephen Farleys; thence said cross road west to Coles lower mill; thence to Whitefield mill; thence to the County line near John Ellisons including the same; thence eastwardly with the County line to the beginning.
Election to be held at Milledgeville

William Matlock District No 9

Commincing at David Goodwins on the Kentucky road leaving him out thence eastwardly crossing the road near William Prices including him thence eastwardly to the lane between Scott & Anderson passing John Anderson leaving him out, thence passing Ignatius Howard leaving him out, thence to the top of the Mountain between the same and R. Howard thence with the top of said Mountain thence with the top of said Mountain, south passing Enoch Goldens leaving him out thence south west down the ridge to the Widow Browns leaving her place out; thence passing James Thomas leaving him out thence to Montgomery Dibrells including him, thence westwardly to the widow Usserys' leaving her out (P-66) thence southwest across the ridge to the 4 mile post east of H. Lyda's thence westwardly with the road to William Lisks including Henry Lyda, thence north with the Kentucky road to the beginning
Election to be held at
William Matlock's. -

Post Oak District No 10

Commincing at David Goodwins old place on the Kentucky road thence north with the said to County line, thence eastwardly passing William Bradford leaving him out passing H. G. Huddleston leaving him out, passing Thomas Nicholds leaving him out passing Samuels Queens leaving him out, thence a direct line to Benjamin Julens leaving him out, thence with the top of the ridge south to the Widow Ramseys leaving her out, thence down said ridge to Robert Howards including the same thence to the Gapp of the Mountain where the road crosses passing Ignatius Howards old place including the same, thence passing John Anderson including the same, thence passing through the land between Scott & Anderson to Wm. Price leaving him out, thence a direct line Northwestwardly leaving all the Linvills out to the beginning Election to be held at

Isham Farleys

John Bohannon District No. 11

Commincing at Julens on the Mountain including the same, thence down said ridge to Samuel Queens including him, thence to Thomas Nicholds including him, thence to H. G. Huddleston including him, thence to William Bradfords including him, thence a direct line to the County line where the Kentucky road crosses the same, thence with the County line eastwardly round to the standing - stone on the Walton road, thence south with a road leading towards the dry-valley including Robert Whitaker's, thence with the top of the ridge south to the beginning Election to be held at

John Bohannon's

Matthew G. Moore District No 12

Comminceing at the Standing-Stone on the County line, thence a south direction passing on near Robert Whitakers leaving him out, thence with said ridge to the head of Plumb Creek between Bartlett Belcher and Thomas Broyles, thence down the same to the Mouth crossing the Calf Killer on a strait line to Usserys Gapp of the Mountain, thence with the road towards Crooks to Rose's turnpike at Doe Creek, thence with said road to the County line, thence westwardly to the beginning Election to be held at

Matthew G. Moore's

Snodgrass' District No 13

Comminceing at the top of the Mountain at Usserys Gapp, thence down the Mountain on a direct line to the mouth of Plumb Creek thence up the same to the head between B. Belcher and Broyles, thence up the Mountain to the top, thence a North Course until we come opposite of the Widow Ramseys, thence to her hous including the same, thence down the ridge to Robert Howard leaving him out, thence to the gapp (P-67) of the Mountain where the path now passes, over towards the lands of William Hill, thence with the top of the ridge south including Enoch Golden, thence southwest to the Widow Browns including passing James Thomas' including the same to Montgomery Dibrell leaving him out, thence a eastwardly to Mark Lowreys including the same, thence passing the old Cabin near Anderson old salt-well thence crossing the Calf Killer to the point of the ridge between the wild Cat Cove and Sparta, thence on the top of said ridge to the top of the mountain - thence North with the various meanders of said Mountain top to the beginning Election to be held at David Snodgrass

Mrs Warren's District No 14

Commineing at the North east cornner of White County thence West the County line to Mrs Johnsons; thence south with Rose's Turnpike road to the meadows of Doe Creek thence; with Glenn's road to the top of the Mountain at Usserys gapp, thence a south course with the top of the Mountain to Christopher Hoffman's leaving him out Crossing the stage road leading from Sparta to Kingston, thence with the various meanders of said Mountain top to Joseph Fifers including him, thence crossing Rosses road, thence with said top of the Mountain crossing the Caney Fork above the big bottom, thence with the top of said Mountain to Kieths trace, thence eastwardly with said trace to the County line; thence North with the same to the beginning
Election to be held at

Mrs. Warrens

Andrew K. Parker District No 15

Commineing at Rosses ferry on the Caney fork on the south side of the same thence up said river to the mouth of the Calf Killer; thence said Calf Killer to the ford below S. R. Doyles Mills; thence eastwardly with said road passing John S. Dentons including him; thence eastwardly a direct line to William Lewis' lane between said Lewis and John Felton thence a direct line passing between Jacob Anderson and John Scoggins; thence to Porters ford on the Caney Fork; thence with a direct line to the top of the mountain including John Yates, thence southwardly with the top of said Mountain to Kieths old trace; thence eastwardly with same to the County line thence southwestwardly with the County line to Jesse Davis east of the Arch Cave thence northwest to an old road leading from said Cave to the beginning
Election to be held at

Andrew K. Parker's

Witness our hands and seals
This 26th day of January A.D. 1836

David L. Mitchell (Seal)
Joseph Cummings (Seal)
John England, Jr. (Seal)
Samuel Johnson (Seal)
Joseph Herd (Seal)

Commissioners

(P-68)

Only a map of the districts of the County

(P-69)

The State of Tennessee

At a Court of Please and Quarter Session began and held for the County of White at the Court house in the Town of Sparta before the Justices of said Court on the secondday Monday being the eleventh day of April in the year of our Lord one thousand eight hundred and thirty six and of the Independence of the United States the Sixtieth year

Present the worshipful

Thomas Eastland, Chairman
David Snodgrass
John Jett,
John Bryan;
John Rose;
William Knowls;
Eli Sims;
Joseph Herd;
Lewis Pettett,
John Wallis; Esqs
Isaac Buck;
Edmund Cunningham, Justices
Thos. Barns;
Joseph Cummings;
James Townsend; &
Edw'd Stamps

John Walker guardian to the minor heirs of Kindall Savage Deceased returned into open Court upon oath an account of the estate of his wards in his hand which is ordered to be recorded

State

vs paid Bastardy

William Turner Catharine Bowman Prosx

This day came the Defendant in proper person into open Court and thereupon produced a receipt in writings from the prosecutix in the above cause acknowleding the payment in full of the sum which by law she would be entitled to receve from said defendant for begetting upon the body of the said Catherine Bowman a bastard male child called and known by the name of John Vance Bowman. - where upon it is ordered and so considered by the Court that said defendant find sureties to keep the County of White; free and endempified from any color of Cost or damage for and towards the support and maintenance of said Bastard child; and now come here said defendant with David Snodgrass and Montgomery Dibrell into open Court and entered into and acknowledged bond inthe sum of five hundred dollars conditioned as the law requires to keep free and endimnified the County of White from all Cost and damage for and towards the support and maintenance of the Bastard Child aforesaid and it is further considered by the Court; that the State of Tennessee recover aganst said Defendant all Cost in this behalf in this Cause expended &c.

This day Anthony Dibrell, Mark Lowery and Daniel Clark Commissioners heretofore appointed to assign and set appart previsions for the support and maintenance of Catharine Brown widow of William Brown Deceased late of the County of White returned here in Court upon the oath of Anthony Dibrell and Mark Lowery said report which is confirmed by the Court and ordered to be recorded &c.

James Thomas on of the Administrators of William Brown, Dec'd returned into Court upon oath an Inventory of the estate of the deceased on oath which is ordered to be recorded &c.

(P-70) This day George Sparkman Administrator of Moses Godard Deceased, returned into Court upon oath, an Inventory of the estate of the Deceased, which is ordered to be recorded &c.

This day George Sparkman administrator of the estate of Moses Godard Deceased, returned into Court an account of the sales of the property of the Deceased upon oath, which is ordered to be recorded.

This day David L. Mitchell Sherriff of the County of White returned in open Court a list of taxes by him collected upon property and polls not returned for taxation for the year 1834 amounting to the sum of ninety dollars twenty five and one fourth cents.

This day David L. Mitchell Sherriff of White County returned in open Court a list of property and polls not returned for taxation for the year 1835 upon which he had collected the taxes, amounting to the sum of two hundred and seventy two dollars five and three fourth cents -

This day John Jett treasure of the Poor house in White County returned his report of the finances of the poor house establishment including the sums expended on building and improvements appropriations made for paying superentendant and maintaining the paupers &c. exhibiting thereon deficit, to the amount of about three hundred and twenty five dollars, for which no approppreation had been made for the payment thereof and recomends to the Court to make provisions for the extingueshment thereof -

It appearing to the satisfaction of the Court, that David L. Mitchell sherriff of White County, had collected, from sundry persons who had failed to return their property &c. for taxation for the years 1834 and 1835 the sum of three hundred and forty dollars fifty six and three fourth cents after deducting his commissions therefrom, for collection - whereupon it is ordered by the Court unanimously, that the sum of three hundred and twenty four dollars part there of be applied to the use of the poor house &c
for White County to meet the deficit set forth in the report of John Jett Treasure of the Poor house this day returned, and that the residue thereof bring sixteen dollars fifty six and three fourths cents. by said Sherriff paid over to the Trustee of White County and applied to the extinguishment of the County claims remaining due and unpaid so far as the same shall extend &c

(Issued seperately)

Ordered by Court that Isaac Buck, Thomas Cooper, Nathan Cooper, Jonathan Hyder, and Jacob Hyder, Sr., freeholders be appointed a jury of view to lay off and mark a road leaving the road from Whitakers Mills to the Walton road, so as to pass the house of John Hunter entersecting the road below the forks of the Creek, being a road of the same class, and report thereof to the next term of this Court. Iss'd.

Ordered by Court that Thomas Hawks be appointed overseer of the road from the Blue Spring branch to the falling water, being a road of the second class; and keep the same in repair as the law requires; with the hands which worked under John Taylor former overseer thereof. Issd -

Ordered by Court that Joseph Anderson be appointed overseer of the road from Lewis Phillips to John Haltermans being a road of the first Class, that the same hands which worked under John Holder

(P-71) This day Creasy Mays aged ten years, was bound to Joseph Kerr to serve him after the manner of an apprentice untill she attains the age of eighteen years - where upon the said Joseph Kerr with Anthony Dibrell his security entered into a Covenant conditioned, that said Joseph Kerr shall teach and instruct or cause to be taught and instructed said apprentice to read the scred scriptures distinctly and at the expiration of said term to give her one cow and calf, one bed an furniture and two suits of decent Callico dresses &c.

This day, the Jury summonsed to enquire into the sanety of George Miller of the County of White, return their report of his ensanity with the amount of the value of his estate - whereupon it is considered and so ordered by the Court that a guardian be appointed for said George Miller, to take into his care and custody the estate of said George of every discription and act thereon in all respects as guardians for minors by law and required to act in case of the estates of minors during his insanity or incapacity to control his property - whereupon, the Court thought fit, to appoint and accordingly did appoint Anthony Dibrell guardian to the said George Miller during his disability - whereupon appeared in open Court the said Anthony Dibrell and took the oath prescribed by law and together with Samuel V. Carrick, James Thomas, and John L. Price entered into and acknowledged bound in the sum of Ten thousand dollars conditioned as the law requires - whereupon it is considered and so ordered by the Court that said guardian pay all cost accuring in relation to the inquiry made as aforesaid, of the sanety of said George Miller out of the estate of said George Miller &c.

That the Sherriff deliver all he has unharmed

Be it remembered that on this being the 11th day of April A.D. 1836 appeared in open Court Thomas Hill who being first sworn in due form of law says that William Shropshire late of the County of White, a soldier of the revolution and a pensioner departed this life the 10th of August A.D. 1838 as he believes; that said William Shropshire once had a wife but that they seperated and remained seperate for about thirty years before the death of said William, that it is not known to affiant whether the wife of said William is living or dead; if living she would now be about seventy or seventy five years of age but if living she resides in parts unknown said William Shropshire had some Children by said wife but they also if living reside in parts unknown. -

Affiant further states that said William Shropshire wrote and made diligent enquirey after his children in his lifetime but could get no intelligence, where they resided or whether they were living. -

Winkfield Hill Administrator of said William Shropshire; Deceased, first being sworne upon his oath says the he has no knowledge of the residance of the Children of said William Shropshire nor of his wife or whether any of them are living, knows that said William Shropshire and his wife have been seperated at least thirty years that if his wife and Children are living they reside in parts unknown to this affiant. - Whereupon it is ordered by the Court to be certified that the said Thomas Hill and Winkfield Hill to the Court known are persons of good (P-72) name and repretation and entitled to full credit upon oath in a Court of Justic, that it is satisfaction proven that the wife and children of said William Shropshire Deceased, a revolutionary pensoner if living resides in parts unknown, - and it is further ordered to be certified that this Court is a Court of reason &c

This day Thomas Irwin was appointed guardian to James M. Irwin, Archebald T. Irwin, Elizabeth M. Irwin, Robert L. Irwin, and John H. Irwin minor heirs of __________ Irwin Deceased, who took the oath prescribed by law, and with William G. Sims entered into and acknowledged bond in the sum of two hundred dollars

Ordered by Court that Abraham Ditty, John Ditty, Jr., William Rhea, Thomas Whitefield and James Ellison free holders be appointed a jury of view to lay off and mark a road on the west side of William Ellisons farm leaving the old road at Cane Creek and intersecting the same at or near the Gentry Cabins and report thereof to the next term of this Court. - Iss'd.

Ordered by Court that James Kitchenside be appointed overseer of the road from the McKinney Cabins east of Clifty Post office to Scarbroughs Mills, being a road of the second class, and keep the same in repair as the law requires with the same hands which worked under the late Overseer thereof Iss'd.

Ordered by Court that Burrell Short be appointed overseer of the road from James McGowans to Franks's ferry being a road of the second Class, and keep the same in repair as the law requires that William Knowles Esq. assign a list of hands to work thereon. Iss'd.

Ordered by Court that William Robertson be appointed overseer of the road from the middle of falling water to the Allens ferry road being a road of the second Class that the following hands be assigned to work thereon To wit: Hiram Childress, Samuel Lafferty, William Lafferty, James McDaniel, Allen Green, Anthony Vincent, Samuel Stover, Henry Waddle and John Marshall. Iss'd

This day Ammon L. Kerr aged four on the 29th day of the present month April 1836 was bound to Thomas Green to serve him after the manner of an apprentice untill he attains the full age of twenty one years, who thereupon entered into a covenant Conditioned as the law requires to give said apprentice eighteen months schooling and decent clothes.

Ordered by Court that Joseph Cummings and Lewis Pettett Esq. - be appointed Commissioners to settle with Thomas Hill Guardian to the heirs of James Hill Deceased and report thereof to the next term of this Court. Issd.

For reasons appearing to the satisfaction of the Court it is ordered that the Trustee of White County pay to Spencer Holder a Jury Ticket of two.dollars and fifty cents No 69 filed 1st August 1829 the original being lost or mislaid.

This day John Franklin Adm'r of the estate of Robert Goad Dec'd returned in open Court on oath an account of the sales of the property of the deceased which is ordered to be recorded.

(P-73) Ordered by Court that George Potts be appointed overseer of the road from the Ross road to the Northern end of Sam'l Thomas's land being a road of the second Class and that all persons residing in the following bounds work thereon. - North of a line oposite Mrs. Flynns including Mrs. Flynns to Thomas's lane then to the mouth of Bee Creek and up Caney fork to where Calloway Davis lives including all hands residing on said road on both sides to the County line; thence to the beginning. Iss'd.

Ordered by Court that Thomas F. Barnett be appointed overseer of the road from the Northern end of Samuel Thomas's lane to the Bledsoe County line being a road of the second Class, that all hands residing between the boundry of George Potts district, Bee Creek, and to the County line be assigned to work thereon. Iss'd.

Ordered by Court that George Henry be appointed overseer of the road from the mouth of mill creek to the nineteen mile post being a road of the second class and keep the same in repair with the hands which worked under the former overseer thereof. Iss'd

On affidavit of Rachel Vincent a free woman of Color it is ordered by the Court that the Sherriff at the next term of this Court bring here the bodies of Bertha & Lucy Ann, persons of Color children of said Rachel Vincent to be dealt by according to law -

Ordered by Court that further time untill the next term of this Court, be given Nancy Mays to produce her children in this Court to be dealt by according to law.

Ordered by Court unanemiously that the Treasure of the poor house pay to Anthony Dibrell the sum of fifty dollars being the amount of an allowance here to fore made to James McPeak a pauper; said Dibrell having disbursed said Amount for the support of said McPeak and for his funeral expences; to be paid out of any money not otherwise appropriated and in the order of payment of said claim allowed James McPeak as it stand upon the docket of the Treasure of the poor house of White County.

Ordered by Court that Edmund Cunningham; Nathaniel Austin, John Austin, James M. Austin; Samuel Johnston, James Hudgins and William Green, freeholders, be appointed a jury of view to lay off and mark a road of the second Class; from John Austins, through the Bear Cove meandering the Mountain; not enterfering with James Hudgins good land and to entersect the turnpike road at conveniant point and report to the next term of this Court. Iss'd

Ordered by Court that John Jett, Lewis Pettett and Samuel A.

Moore be appointed Commissioners to settle with Isaac Taylor and Daniel Walling Admrs. of the estate of William Fisher Dec'd. and report thereof to the next term of this Court. Iss'd -

Ordered by Court that Samuel V. Carrick, Woodson P. White, Anthony Dibrell, William Green and Simon Doyle freeholders, be appointed a Jury of view to lay of and mark a road of the second Class, from Simpson Mills entersecting the gum Spring road near the foot of the mountain on the East side thereof and report thereof to the next term of this Court. Iss'd

(P-74) This day the death of James Young merchant late of the Town of Sparta was suggested - And at the same time a writing was produced purporting to be the unucupative will of said James Young, Dec'd. where upon the same in like manner was proven by the oath of William L. Young and Richard Crowder whose presence the statement made by said James Young covering the disposition of his property as he wised and they particularly called upon, and that the said James Young was at the time of making said statement and giving said direction was of sound and disposing mind and memory and that the said entructions and directions concerning the disposal of his effiets was by said William L. Young and Richard Crowder reduced to writing within three days after the death of said James Young and that said writing here produced Contains the whole of said instructions and directions given as aforesaid in his last illness, and shortly before his death which is deemed by the Court to be property and sufficently proven and ordered to be recorded. Issd.

This day William L. Young was appointed Administrator of all and singular the goods and Chattels, rights and credits of James Young the deceased, withe the unucupative will of the deceased annexed and took the oath presented by law and with Anthony Dibrell and James Eastland entered into and acknowledged bond in the sum of Ten thousand dollars conditioned as the law requires.

Ordered by Court that John Rose, Thomas Little, Joseph Hunter, James Hudgins and Washington P. Duncan free holders be appointed a jury of view to lay off and mark a road from the forks of the road above Sparta to entersect the road leading up Userys Gapp crossing Blue Spring Creek at Littles Bridge being a road of the second Class, and report there of to the next term of this Court. Issd.

This day Mary Jane Carroll, Adminestrator of William Carroll Dec'd. returned upon oath an Inventory of the estate of the deceased on oath which is ordered to be recorded.

This day Mary Jane Carroll Adminestrator of the estate of William Carroll deceased, returned in Court upon oath an account of the sales of the property of the Deceased, which is ordered to be recorded.

For reason appearing to the satisfaction of the Court it is ordered that the order directing the children of Rachel Jinkins to be brought here at the next term of this Court be set aside.

This day Joseph Cummings here to fore appointed Commissioner to the poor house in the County of White appeared in Court and took the oath presented by law -

Ordered by Court that the Sherriff of White County bring him into Court at the next term thereof the bodies of Henry Brewington and Ann Brewington persons of Color, minors to be dealt by according to law. Iss'd -

Ordered by Court James Thomas, John Walker, Montgomery C. Dibrell, Mark Lowery and John England freeholders be appointed a Jury of view to mark and lay of a road from Mrs. Browns intersecting the Carthage road near Montgomery C. Dibrell and report thereof to the next term of this Court. Iss'd.

Ordered by Court that David Snodgrass, John Waller, and Thomas Eastland be appointed Commissioners to assign and set apart to Mrs. Phebe Allen the widow of George Allen Deceased, provisions out of the estate of the disceased sufficent for the support of herself and family for one year. Iss'd.

(P-75) This day appeared in open Court Joseph Cummings a soldier of the Revolution to the Court known and thereupon filed his declaration upon oath explanitory of the preparing and submitting to the war department of the United States, his original Declaration in order to obtain a pension under the actof Congress, of the 7th of June, 1832 which is by the Court deemed sufficent, and orderd to be so certified under the seal of the Court, Iss'd -

Ordered by Court that Burrell Maynor, Joseph Brown, Shadrack Mooneyham, Daniel Walling and Vardsy Camp freeholders, be appointed a Jury of view to lay off and mark a road of the third Class, from the head waters of Cane Creek to John Walling's Mill and report thereof to the next term of this Court. Iss'd -

This day the death of George Allen Dec. late of the County of White was suggested and proven in due form of law,
that he departed this life in estate.

Whereupon Phebe Allen and Joseph Herd were appointed Adminestratox and Adminestrator of all and singular the goods and Chattels rights and credits of the said George Allen Dec'd. who took the oat prescribed by law and together with Anthony Dibrell, James Thomas, Samuel S. Allen and Jesse Allen, Jr., intered into and acknowledged bond in the sum of four thousand dollars Conditioned as the law requires.

For reasons appearing to the satisfaction of the Court it is ordered that a returnable to the next term of this Court directed to the Sherriff of White County, Commanding him to summons according to law a Jury of twelve men freeholders of White County to ascertain according to law whether Jane Hall of said County is insane or otherwise and in the event that she is found to be insane or idiot or lunatic then to ascertain what real and personal estate she has or is entitled to, and report the same with all the facts relative thereto, to the next term of this Court.

Ordered by Court that Jesse Allen, Jr., be permitted to keep a ferry on the Caney fork on his own lands at the crossing of the Caney Fork near Shipping port and be entitled to receive the following rates of toll Towit:

For each wagon and four or more horses mules or steers . . . . 50 cents
For each Carryall or big wagon with two horses or cart . . . . 25 cents
For each pleasure Carriage . . . . 25 cents
For each poolman . . . . $6\frac{1}{4}$ cents
For each led horse, mule, or Jack . . . . $6\frac{1}{4}$
For each head of Cattle or sheep . . . . 1 cent

This day Creasy Mays aged ten years was bound to Joseph Kerr to serve him after the manner of an apprentice untill she attains the age of eighteen years whereupon the said Joseph Kerr with Anthony Dibrell his Security entered into and acknowledged bond conditioned as the law requires &c.

Ordered that Court be adjourned untill Tomorrow morning at 9 o'clock

Thos. Eastland
John Jett
John Rose

Tuesday Morning, April 12th, 1836

Court met pursuant to adjournment
Present the Worshipful

Thomas Eastland
John Rose
John Jett
} Esq. Justices

Winkfield Hill Adm. of William Shropshire
vs
Matthew Watson
} Letter Atto.

Was this day acknowledged in open Court by Winkfield Hill Adm. of William Shropshire, Dec'd. for the purpose and things thereon mentioned and ordered to be recorded and so certified

Ordered that Court be adjourned untill Court in Course

Test.
J. A. Lane Clerk

Thos Eastland
John Rose
John Jett

(P-76) State of Tennessee

At a County Court began and held for the County of White at the Court house in the town of Sparta in said County and State before the Justices of our said Court on the first Monday being the second day of May in the year of our Lord One thousand eight hundred and thirty six and of the Independance of the United States the sixtieth year

Present,

Thomas Eastland, Chairman
John Jett,
William Knowles,
John Bryan,
David Snodgrass,
Joseph Cummings,
Edmund Stamps,
Elijah Frost,
Samuel A. Moore,
Joseph Herd,
Eli Sims,
George Welch,
Isaac Buck,
John Pennington,
and Jesse Scoggins

Esquires Justices

This day Joshua Mason, Jonathan Farrington, William Bruster, John Jett, John Wallis, John Bryan, Thomas Green, Jesse Walling, Matthias Hutson, Lewis Pettett, Wm. Knowles, William Glenn, Richard Crowder, Samuel Strong, Henry Benton, William Hitchcock, James Ellison, Montgomery C. Dibrell, Asa Certain, William C. Bounds, John Pennington, Isaac Buck, William Bartlett, Edmund Stamps, Elisha Camron, David Snodgrass, Thomas Eastland, Elijah Frost, John Gillentine, and William Steakley appeared in open Court, and produced commissioners from the Governer appointing them Justices of the peace under the amended constution of the state of Tennessee and thereupon respectively took the oath perscribed by act of assembly and thereupon entered upon the duties of their office and took their seats

There was then present the Worshipful -

Thomas Eastland,
Joshua Mason,
Jonathan Farrington,
William Bruster,
John Jett,
John Wallis,
John Bryan,
Thomas Green,
Jesse Walling,
Matthias Hutson,
Lewis Pettett,
William Knowles,
William Glenn,
Richard Crowder,
Samuel Strong,
Henry Benton,
William Hitchcock,
James Ellison,
Montgomery C. Dibrell

Asa Certain, William C. Bounds, John Pennington, Isaac Buck, William Bartlett, Edmund Stamps, Elisha Camron, David Snodgrass, Elijah Frost, John Gillentine, and William Steakly	Esquires Justices of the view Court.

The Court being organized proceeded to the appointment of a Chairman of said Court whereupon Thomas Eastland Esquire unanimously appointed and thereupon entered upon the duties thereto Annexed. -

This day Nicholas Oldham produced in Court the Certificate of the Coroner of White County shewing that he was duly and Constutionally elected Clerk of the County Court of White County for the four years next ensuring, whereupon the said Nicholas Oldham being in open Court and took an oath to support the Constution of the United States and of the State of Tennessee and the several oaths prescribed by Law and entered into and acknowledged bonds Conditioned as the law requires, being in the following words to wit:

Know all men by these presents that we Nicholas Oldham, William Glenn, Wamon Leftwich, William Bruster, John Warren, Mark Lowery (P-77) Samuel V. Carrick all of the County of White and State of Tennessee held and firmly bound unto his Excellency Newton Cannon Governer in and over the state of Tennessee for the time being or his successors in office in the sum of Five thousand dollars current money, which payment well an truly to be made and done we jointly and severally bind ourselves and each of our heirs, executors and Adminestrators firmly by their presents sealed with our seals and dated the 2nd day of May A.D. 1836

Where as it appearing to White County by the Certificate of the Coroner of White County that Nicholas Oldham was duly and Constitutionally elected clerk of the County Court of White County for the next ensuing four years from the 5th day of March 1836 Now the condition of the above obligation is such that if the above bound Nicholas Oldham shall earfully and safely keep all the records of the County Court of White County faithfully and truly discharge all the duties of his said office of Clerk, and shall well and truly in all things appertaining to his said office of Clerk demean himself according to law - then this obligation to be null and void otherwise be and remain in full force and virtue.

Test.
Thos. Eastland (Sea)
Chairman of White County Court

Nicholas Oldham (Seal)
William Glenn (Seal)
Wamon Leftwich (Seal)
William Bruster (Seal)
John Warren (Seal)
Mark Lowery (Seal)
Samuel V. Carrick (Seal)

Know all men by these present that we, Nicholas Oldham,

William Glenn, Wamon Leftwich, William Bruster, John Warren, Mark Lowery, Samuel V. Carrick, all of the County of White and State of Tennessee held and firmly bound unto Newton Cannon Esq. Governer in and over the State of Tennessee for his, succession in office in the sum of one thousand dollars which payment well and truly to be made and done we bind ourselves and each of our heirs, executors or Adminestrators jointly and severally firmly by these presents seald with our seals and dated the 2nd. day of May A.D. 1836.

The condition of the above obligation is such that whereas the said Nicholas Oldham hath been duly and Constitutionally elected Clerk of the County Court of White County - Now if the said Nicholas Oldham shall well and truly collect and pay over all fines and forfietures agreeablly to law, then shall the above obligation be null and void otherwise to be and remain in full force and vertue.

Test
Thos Eastland (Seal)
Chairman of White County Court

Nicholas Oldham (Seal)
William Glenn (Seal)
Wamon Leftwich (Seal)
William Bruster (Seal)
John Warren (Seal)
Mark Lowery (Seal)
Samuel V. Carrick (Seal)

Know all men by their presents that we Nicholas Oldham, William Glenn, Wamon Leftwich, William Bruster, John Warren, Mark Lowery, Samuel V. Carrick, are held and firmly bound unto Newton Cannon Esquire Governer is in and over the State of Tennessee for the being in his succession in office in the sum of one thousand dollars which payment well and truly to (P-78) be made we bind our selves and each of our heirs executors or adminestrators jointly and severally firmly by these presents sealed with our seals and dated the 2nd, day of May A. D. 1836

Now the condition of the above obligation is such that where as the said Nicholas Oldham hath been duly and Constitutionally elected Clerk of the County Court of White County. -

Now if the said Nicholas Oldham shall well and truly collect and pay over all monies that may come into his hands by virtue of his said office to the proper office entitled to receive the same. -

Then the above obligation to be null and void else remain in full force and vertue.

Test
Thos. Eastland (Seal)
Chairman of White County Court

Nicholas Oldham (Seal)
William Glenn (Seal)
Wamon Leftwich (Seal)
William Bruster (Seal)
Mark Lowery (Seal)
Samuel V. Carrick (Seal)

This day David L. Mitchell*exhibited in open Court all the receipts which he is required by law to produce.

This day David L. Mitchell produced in open Court the Coroners Certificate of his having been duly and Constitutionally elected Sherriff of the County of White for the next ensuing two years, and he the said David L. Mitchell being presents in open Court took an oath to support the Constitution of the United States and of the State of Tennessee and the several oaths presented by law, and together with, Thomas Roberts; James Randols; David Snodgrass; Spence Mitchell; John Jett; James Snodgrass; and Woodson P. White entered into and acknowledged bond in the sum of Twelve thousand five hundred Dollars conditioned as the law requires - And thereupon entered upon the duties of his office. -

Bond.

Know all men by these presents that we David L. Mitchell, Thomas Robertson; James Randols, David Snodgrass; Spence Mitchell; John Jett; James Snodgrass; Woodson P. White all of White County and State of Tennessee are held and firmly bound unto his execllency Newton Cannon Governer in and over the State of Tennessee for the time being or his successions in office in the sum of twelve thousand five hundred dollars current money well and truly to be made and done we bind ourselves and each of our heirs executors or adminestrator; jointly and severally firmly by these presents sealed with our seals the 2nd, day of May A.D. 1836.

Now the condition of the above obligation is such that where as the above bound David L. Mitchell has been duly and constitutionally elected Sherriff of White County as appears from the Certificate of the Coroners of White County dated the 7th day of March A.D. 1836.

If therefore the said David L. Mitchell shall well and truly executed and due return make, of all process and precepts to him directed and pay and satisfy all fees and sums of money by him received or levied by vertue of any process into the proper office by which the same by the law thereof ought to be paid or to the person or persons to whom the same shall be due his, her or their executors, Adminestrators; Attornies or Agents and in all other things well, truly and faithfully executed the said office of Sherriff so long as he shall Continue therein according to law

Then the obligation to be null and void otherwise be and remain if (P-79) in full force and vertue

Test
N. Oldham CK.

David L. Mitchell (Seal)
Thomas Robertson (Seal)
James Randols (Seal)
David Snodgrass (Seal)
Spence Mitchell (Seal)
John Jett (Seal)
James Snodgrass (Seal)
W. P. White (Seal)

* Sherriff of White County

This day appeared in open Court David L. Mitchell Sherriff of the County of White and appointed William R. Tucker keeper of the Common Jail of White County who being here in open Court took the several oaths prescribed by law and thereupon entered upon the duties of his office.

This day Robert Cox produced here in open Court the certificate of the Coroners of White County of his having been duly and Constitutionally elected Trustee for the County of White and who being here present in open Court took an oath to support the Constitution of the United States and of the State of Tennessee and the several oaths prescribed by law and together with William L. Young, Anthony Dibrell, James Eastland, and Richard Crowder, entered into and acknowledged bond in the sum of five thousand dollars Cond. as the law requires.

This day Joseph W. Roberts produced here in open Court the certificate of the Coroner of White County and it appearing that he was duly and Constitutionally elected Register for the County of White for next ensuing four years and he being present here in open Court took an oath to support the Constitution of the United States and of the State of Tennessee - and the several oaths prescribed by law and together with Anthony Dibrell, Thomas Roberts, Robert Anderson, Jesse Walling, and Joseph Herd, entered into and acknowledged bond in the sum of twelve thousand five hundred dollars Conditioned as the law requires. -

This day David L. Mitchell Sherriff of White County filed in Court a Certificate, certifying that Indemon B. Moore was duly and Constitutionally elected constable for the Civil District No 5 in White County.

This day Isaac Buck, Ex. Coroner of the County of White filed his Certificate of election of Constables in the County of White as follows;
To wit:

In Civil District No 1 Hays Arnold and Charles Meek.
In District No 2 Samuel Dotson
In District No 3 William Fryer -
In District No. 4 Alexander Moore
In District No. 5 Indemon B. Moore
In District No 6 Adam Clouse -
In District No. 7 William Bozarth - -
In District No 8 Zachariah Hitchcock
In District No 9 John Walker
In District No 10 James H. Isham
In District No 11 Joseph D. Hyder
In District No 12 Joseph England
In District No 13 Charles McGuire
In District No 14 Noah H. Bradley
In District No 15 Edward Moore

who were all duly and Constitutionally elected.

This day Charles Meek who was elected Constable in Civil District No 1 in White County appeared here in open Court and took an oath to support the Constitution of the United and of the State of Tennessee and the several oaths prescribed by law and together with

James Lowery and Charles McGuire entered into and acknowledged bond in the sum of one thousand dollars Conditioned as the law requires.

(P-80) This day Hayes Arnold who was elected constable in Civil District No.1 in the County of White appeared in open Court and took an oath to support the Constitution of the United States and of the State of Tennessee and the several oath prescribed by law and together with James Randols and Samuel D. Arnold Entered into and acknowledged bond in the sum of one thousand dollars Conditioned as the law requires. -

This day Samuel Dodson who was elected Constable in Civil District No. 2 in the County of White, appeared here in open Court and took an oath to support the Constitution of the United States and of the State of Tennessee and the several oaths prescribed by law and together with Solomon Dodson and Joseph Herd entered into and acknowledged bond in the sum of one thousand dollars conditioned as the law requires.

This day William Fryer who was elected Constable in Civil District No. 3 in the County of White appeared here in open Court and took an oath to support the Constitution of the United States and of the State of Tennessee and the several oaths prescribed by law and together with James H. Doyle and John Fryer entered into and acknowledged bond in the sum of one thousand Conditioned as the law requires.

This day Alexander Moore who was elected Constable in Civil District No. 4 in the County of White appeared here in open Court and took an oath to support the Constitution of the United States and of the State of Tennessee and the several oaths prescribed by law and together with Samuel A. Moore and William G. Sims entered into and acknowledged bond in the sum of One thousand dollars Conditioned as the law requires. -

This day Indemon B. Moore, who was elected Constable in Civil District No. 5 in the County of White appeared here in open Court and took an oath to support the Constitution of the United States of the State of Tennessee and the several oaths prescribed by law and together with Greenville Templeton and Lenias B. Farris entered into and acknowledge bond in the sum of One thousand dollars conditioned as the law requires.

This day Adam Clouse who was elected Constable in Civil district No. 6 in the County of White appeared in open Court and took an oath to support the Constitution of the United States and of the State of Tennessee and the several oaths prescribed by law and together with Aaron Hutchings and John Cantrell entered into and acknowledged bond in the sum of One thousand dollars Conditioned as the law requires.

This day William Bozarth who was elected Constable in Civil district No. 7 in the County of White appeared in open Court and took an oath to support the Constitution of the United States and of the State of Tennessee and the several oaths prescribed by law and together with Levi Bozarth and Henry Benton entered into and acknowledged bond in the sum of One thousand dollars Conditioned as the law requires.

This day Zachariah Hitchcock who was elected Constable in Civil district No. 8 in the County of White appeared in open Court and took the oat to support the Constitution of the United States and of the State of Tennessee and the several oaths prescribed by law and together with John England and Ezekiel Hitchcock entered into and acknowledged bond in the sum of One thousand dollars Conditioned as the law requires

(P-81) This day John Walker who was elected Constable in Civil District No. 9 in the County of White appearing here in open Court and took an oath to support the Constitution of the United States and of the State of Tennessee and the several oaths prescribed by law and together with Montgomery C. Dibrell and Daniel McClain entered into and acknowledged bond in the sum of One thousand dollars Conditioned as the law requires

This day James Isham who was elected Constable in Civil District No. 10 in White County appeared here in open Court took an oath to support the Constitution of the United States and of the State of Tennessee and the several oaths prescribed by law and together with John Gooch and Elisha Camron entered into and acknowledged bond in the sum of One thousand dollars Conditioned as the law requires.

This day Joseph D. Hyder who was elected Constable in Civil District No. 11 in the County of White appeared here in open Court and took an oath to support the Constitution of the United States and of the State of Tennessee and the several oaths prescribed by law and together with Isaac Buck and William Bartlett entered into and acknowledged bond in the sum of One thousand dollars Conditioned as the law requires

This day Joseph England who was elected Constable in Civil district No. 12 in the County of White appeared here in open Court and took an oath to support the Constitution of the United States and of the State of Tennessee and the several oaths prescribed by law and together with Richard England and Edmund Stamps entered into and acknowledged bond in the sum of one thousand dollars Conditioned as the law requires

This day Charles McGuire who was elected Constable in Civil District No. 13 in the County of White appeared here in open Court and took and oath to support the Constitution of the United States and of the State of Tennessee and the several oath prescribed by law and together with Charles Meeks and Elias Yeager entered into and acknowledged bond in the sum of one thousand dollars Conditioned as the law requires -

This day Noah H. Bradley, who was elected Constable in Civil District No. 14 in the County of White appeared in open Court and took an oath to support the Constitution of the United States and of the State of Tennessee and the several oaths prescribed by law and together with Richard England and James Thomas returned into and acknowledged bond in the sum of One thousand dollars conditioned as the requires. -

This day Edward Moore who was elected Constable in Civil District No. 15 in the County of White appeared in open Court and took an oath to support the Constitution of the United States and of the State of Tennessee and of the several oaths prescribed by law and together with James Moore and Shadrack Mooneyham entered into and acknowledged bond in the sum of one thousand dollars Conditioned as the law requires

Isaac Buck Esquire Coroner of White County appeared in open Court and resigned his Office as Coroner which is Ordered to be recorded. Issd.

Ordered by Court that John Ayers be released from the sum of fifty six and one fourth Cents of the tax for the year 1835 he being over charged that sum and that the Sherriff of White County have a Credit in his settlement with the Trustee of White County -

(P-82) The Court then proceeded to the appointment of an Entry Taker for the County of White for the next ensuing four years and to that office do unanimously appoint John H. Anderson Esq. who being present here in open Court took an oath to support the Constitution of the United States and of the State of Tennessee and the oath of office and together with William G. Sims, David L. Mitchell, Richard Nelson, and Joseph Herd entered into and acknowledged bond in the sum of Ten Thousand dollars Conditioned as the law requires

The Court then proceeded to the appointment of a Surveyor for the County of White for the next ensuing four years and to that office do unanimously appoint Jonathan C. Davis Esquire who being present in open Court took an oath to support the Constitution of the United States and of the State of Tennessee and the oath of office and to gether with Joseph Herd, David L. Mitchell and William G. Sims entered into and acknowledged bond in the sum of Ten Thousand dollars Conditioned as the law requires - -

This Court then proceeded to election of a Coroner for the County of White for the next ensuing two years and to that office do appoint Simon R. Doyle who being here in open Court took an oath to support the Constitution of the United States and of the State of Tennessee and the several oaths prescribed by law and together with John Wallis, William Simpson, John Fryer and Joseph Herd entered into and acknowledged bond in the sum of Two thousand Five hundred dollars Conditioned as the law requires. -

The Court then proceeded to the election of a Ranger for the County of White for the next ensuing two years and to that office do unanimously appoint John Bryan Esq. who being present in open Court took an oath to support the Constitution of the United States and of the State of Tennessee and the oath of office and together with William M. Bryan, David L. Mitchell, William G. Sims and Joseph Herd, entered into and acknowledged bond in the sum of Five Hundred dollars Conditioned as the law directs.

William Jay
to
Stephen Wilkerson } Letters of Attorny

Was this acknowledged in open Court by William Jay the Grantor for the purposes and things therein Contained which is ordered to be recorded and Certified under the seals of the Court - . (cert)

This day the death of William Duncan deceased late of the County of White was suggested - and that he departed this life intestate - Whereupon Susannah Duncan was appointed administrator of all and singular the goods and chattles, rights and credits of the said William Duncan deceased - who took the oath prescribed by law and together with Pleasant Farley and John Bussell entered into and acknowledged bond in the sum of Five hundred dollars Conditioned as the law requires

(Letters Iss'd)

This day the Commissioners appointed at the last term of this Court to settle with Daniel Walling and Isaac Taylor Executors of the estate of William Fisher deceased, returned their report which is received by the Court and ordered to be recorded - -

Ordered by Court that Daniel Walling one of the executors of the estate of William Fisher deceased be allowed the sum of twenty seven dollars to be by him retained out of said estate for services rendered said estate or Executor -

(P-83) Ordered by Court that John Jett, Samuel A. Moore and Lewis Pettett Commissioners appointed by this Court to settle with the executor of William Fisher deceased, be allowed the sum of one dollar and fifty cents per day each for two days service rendered in settling with said Executors, to be paid out of the estate of the deceased - . Iss'd -

This day the Commissioners appointed at the last term of this Court to settle with Thomas Hill Sr. Guardian of the heirs of James Hill deceased returned their report which is received by the Court and ordered to be recorded and said Commissioners hereby relinquish all claims for Compensation for services rendered in said settlement.

The Court then proceeded to the appointment of Commissioners of the Revinue for the County of White for the year 1836 to take in the list Polls and assessment of the taxable property in said County for said year and thereupon do appoint the following persons as Commissioners in their respective Civil District to wit,

In	Civil	District	No. 1	Jonathan Farrington, Esq.	Coms.
"	"	"	No. 2	John Bryan, "	"
"	"	"	No. 3	Thomas Green, "	"
"	"	"	No. 4	Matthias Hutson, "	"
"	"	"	No. 5	Joshua Mason, "	"
"	"	"	No. 6	William Glenn, "	"
"	"	"	No. 7	Henry Benton, "	"
"	"	"	No. 8	William Hitchcock "	"
"	"	"	No. 9	Montgomery C. Dibrell, "	"
"	"	"	No.10	William C. Bounds, "	"
"	"	"	No.11	Isaac Buck, "	"
"	"	"	No.12	Edmund Stamps, "	"
"	"	"	No.13	David Snodgrass, "	"
"	"	"	No.14	Elijah Frost, "	"
"	"	"	No.15	Willie Steakly "	"

Ordered by Court that Richard Nelson and John H. Anderson Esquires be appointed Commissioners to settle with Wamon Leftwich Esq. late Trustee of White County and report thereof to the next term of this Court. Issd

Ordered by Court that David Snodgrass and Edmund Stamps Esquires be appointed Commissioners to settle with Thomas Henry Adminestrator of William Parker deceased and report to the next term of this Court. -

Ordered by Court that William Bruster, David Snodgrass and John Jett Esquires be appointed Commissioners to settle with Robert L. Mitchell and William Baker executors of Edward Holmes deceased and report to the next term of this Court. (Issd)

Ordered by Court that David Snodgrass and Montgomery C. Dibrell Esquires be appointed Commissioners to settle with John Franklin Adminestrator of Robert Goard deceased and report tomorrow.

Ordered by Court that John Franklin admr. of Robert Goard deceased be allowed the sum of fifteen dollars for services rendered said estate as adminestrator to be by him retained out of said estate.

(P-84) Ordered by Court that William Hitchcock, Ebenezer Jones and William Kerr be appointed Commissioners to assign and set apart to Susannah Duncan and her family being the releet and Widow of William Duncan dec'd. a sufficcent allowance for one years support out of the estate of the deceased and report thereof the next term of this Court. - (Issd)

Ordered by Court that Lewis Phillips be appointed Overseer of the road from Hills branch to a point oposite Lewis Phillips being a road of the first class and keep the same in repair as the law requires and the same list of hands that worked under Winkfield Hill late overseer thereof. (Issd)

Ordered by Court that William Mills be appointed overseer of the road from the falling water to Abraham Dittys branch being a road of the frst Class and keep the same in repair as the law requires with the same hands that worked under Levi Lollar former overseer thereof. (Issd)

Ordered by Court that James Hudgins, Samuel V. Carrick, John Rose, Anthony Dibrell, Joseph Herd, Joseph Hunter and Thomas Little freeholders be appointed a Jury of review to examine lay off and mark a road of the first Class the nearest and best way from the West end of the Bridge at Sparta passing through the land of William Bruster, Nicholas Oldham and Jacob A. Lane Crossing town Creek at or near the mouth and intersecting the McMinnville Road at the forks where the road leading by the Harriet Iron Works turns off and report thereof to the next term of this Court -

Elizabeth Hargis, Widow of William Hargis, dec'd
to
Matthew Watson } Letter of Attorney

Was this acknowledged in open Court by Elizabeth Hargis widow of the said William Hargis deceased for the purpose and things therein Contained which is recorded and ordered to be Certified under the seal of the Court.

David L. Mitchell, Esq. Sherriff and Collecter of the taxes of the County of White for the years 1834-1835 returned in open Court a list of delenquents for the taxes of the year 1834 amounting to the sum of forty four dollars for which he is entitled to a Credit in the settlement of his accounts with the Trustee of his County (Iss'd)

David L. Mitchell, Sherriff and Collector of the taxes of the County of White for the year 1835 this day returned into open Court a list of the delenquents for the taxes of the year 1835 amounting to the sum of fifteen dollars and seventy five cents for which he is entitled to a credit in the settlement of his accounts with the Trustee of White County. (Issd)

Ordered by Court that Isaac Buck Esq. Coroner of White County be allowed the sum of six dollars being for six days service in holding the election for County offices in March last to be paid by the Trustee of White County out of any monies Not otherwise appropriated (set aside)

This day was produced in open Court a writing perporting to be the last will and testament of William Hargis deceased whereupon the due execution and publication thereof was proven in open Court by the oath of Samuel Johnson our subscribing witness thereto for the purpose and things therein set forth that the said William Hargis signed sealed published and declared the same to be his last will and testement in his presence and that he subscribed his name. (P-85) as witness thereto at his request and in his presence - and that he was at that date and execution thereof of sound disposing mind and memory which is ordered to be recorded

This day was produced in open Court a writing purporting to be a Codicil to the last will and testament of William Hargis late of White County deceased whereupon the due execution and publication thereof was proven in open Court by the oaths of Samuel Johnson and Washington G. Hargis subscribing thereto for the purpose and things therein mentioned that the said William Hargis signed sealed published and declared the same to be a Codicil to his last will and testament in their presecnce and that they subscribed their names as witnesses thereto at his request and in his presences - and that he was at the date and execution thereof of sound and disposing mind and memory - which is ordered to be recorded - -

Ordered by Court that Isaac Taylor one of executors of the estate of William Fisher deceased be allowed the sum of fifteen dollars for services rendered as executer to be retained out of the estate of the deceased -

Ordered that Court be adjourned untill tomorrow Morning 10 Oclock.

Thos. Eastland
David Snodgrass
John Bryan
John Jett

Tuesday Morning 3rd May A.D. 1836

Court met pursuant to adjournment
Present the Worshipful

Thomas Eastland, Chairman Esq.

John Jett,
David Snodgrass,
Richard Crowder,
John Bryan,
Elisha Cannon,
William Knowles,
Jesse Walling,
John Pennington,
Montgomery C. Dibrell,
Elijah Frost,
Henry Benton,
William C. Bounds, } Esq. Justices
William Bruster,
Asa Certain,
Thomas Green,
Samuel Strong,
Joshua Mason,
John Gillentine,
Jonathan Farrington,
Willie Steakley,
Matthias Hutson, and
William Glenn

Ordered by Court that the order entered up, by the Clerk on yesterday allowing Isaac Buck Esq. Coroner of White the sum of six dollars be set aside - .

Ordered by Court that Richard Crowder Esqr. be appointed a Commissioner instead of Thomas Eastland Esq. to assign and set apart one years provision to relect and widow of George Allen deceased -

For reasons appearing to the satisfaction of the Court it is ordered by the Court that Anthony Dibrell Guardian of George W. Miller surrendered to Noah H. Bradley a certain promisory note drawn by said and payable to said Miller for one hundred dollars dated the 13th Febuary 1836 and due Ten months thereafter -. because there were two notes given said Miller for the same Consideration.

(P-86) This day Henry Bruington a colored boy aged about fifteen next fall was this day bound to Joel Yeager to serve him after the manner of an apprentice untill he arrives at the age of twenty one years; where upon the said Joel Yeager with David Snodgrass and Elias Yeager his securities entered into Covenant Conditioned that the said Joel Yeager shall when he arrives at full age give him a horse, saddle and bridle with sixty dollars and two suits of homespun jeans Clothes -.

This day the death of Joseph Parker deceased late of the County of White suggested in open Court and that he departed this life entestate - whereupon John Parker was appointed adminestrator of all and singular the goods and chattles, rights and Credits of the said Joseph Parker deceased who took the oath prescribed by law - and with David Snodgrass, John Gillentine and John W. Dearing entered into and acknowledged bond in the sum of two thousand dollars conditioned as the law requires - .

(Issd) Ordered by Court that David L. Mitchell, Joseph Cummings, John England, Jr., Samuel Johnson, and Joseph Herd, Commissioners appointed by the Legeslature to lay off the County of White in Civil district be allowed the sum of one dollar and fifty cents per day each for six days services by them performed in laying off said Districts to paid out of the taxes of the year 1836.

This day William G. Sims Deputy sherriff of White County returned into Court a list of Delenquents for the taxes of the years 1834 and 1835 amounting in all to the sum of nineteen dollars twenty five - which David L. Mitchell sherriff and Collector of said County is entitled to have a credit in the settlement of his accounts with the Trustee of White County. (Issd)

(Issd) Ordered by Court that Joshua Mason, Elisha Swift, Robert Mason, John Humphrey and Henry C. Evans freeholders be appointed a Jury of view to lay off and mark road of the third Class, leaving the shipping ford road near Elijah Pertles, thence the nearest and best way to the Caney fork at David Fisher and report thereof to the next term of this Court.

This day the Commissioners appointed yesterday to settle with John Franklin adminestrator of Robert Goard deceased, returned upon oath their report of settlement which is recorded by the Court and ordered to be recorded - that the adminestrator is chargeable with one hundred and eleven dollars twelve and a half Cents - that he be entitled to a credit for seventy one dollars forty cents, leaving a balance in the hands of the adminestrator of the sum of Thirty nine dollars seventy two and a half cents with which he still stands chargeable - .

Issd

Ordered by Court that Anthony Dibrell, be released from the appraised value of two stray sows, one valued at one dollar seventy five cents and the other at one dollar fifty cents, one having -
and the other claimed by James Lowery.

Ordered by Court that William Glenn merchant be allowed the sum of eleven dollars for a blank record book for the Registers office of White County to paid by the Sherriff of White County out of the taxes for the year 1836

Ordered by Court that Jacob A. Lane be allowed the sum of thirty dollars being for two large pine presses furnished the clerks offices of White County Court for the safe keeping of the records thereof to be paid by the sherriff of White County out of the taxes of the year 1836

Ordered by Court that the sherriff of White County summons

Charles McGuire and John Walker Constables to attend on the next term of the Circuit Court for White County -

(P-87) Iss'd

Ordered by Court tha James Lowery be appointed overseer of the road from the West end of the bridge at the town of Sparta to the two mile post on the Carthage road being a road of the first class and keep the same in repair as the law requires and that the same boundary of hands which worked under William Bruster former overseer be appointed to work thereon -

Ordered by Court that the order appointing Commissioners at the last term of this Court appointing a Jury of view from the forks of the road above Sparta be disannulled and set aside - .

(Isd)

Ordered by Court that John Rose; Thomas Little; Joseph Hunter, Brice M. Little and Washington P. Duncan free holders be appointed a jury of view to lay off and mark a road of the second class from the forks of the road above Sparta; intersecting the road leading up Userys gap near Taylors crossing Blue Spring Creek at Littles bridge and report to the next term of this Court.

The Commissioners heretofore appointed by this Court to lay off and mark a road and change the road leading from Whitakers up the Hollow and by the house of John Hunters this day made their report which is by the Court required - .

(Isd)

Ordered by Court that Aaron England be appointed overseer of the road from Goodwins branch to Hardeys old Cabbins on the Kentucky road being a road of the first Class and keep the same in repair as the law requires with the same hands that worked thereon under William B. Jones former overseer thereof - .

This day the Commissioners heretofore appointed by this Court to lay off and mark a road on the west side of William Allisons farm leaving the old road at Cane Creek and intersecting the same at or near the Gentry Cabins made their report which is received by the Court - and said road is established and that the overseer of the old road work that part which is hereby established - - and keep the same in order as required by law.

This day appeared in open Court, Isaac Taylor and for reasons appearing to the satisfaction of the Court disclosed in his affedavit - that at the July term of said Court 1834 he resigned his appointment as one of the executors of the estate of William Fisher deceased; which the Clerk neglected to enter on record - .

It is now ordered by the Court that his resignation be entered and recorded now for them -

Ordered that Court be adjourned till Court in Course

list of hands to work thereon. Isd.

Ordered by Court that Isaac Lollar be appointed overseer of the road from the falling waters to Abraham Dittys branch being a road of the first Class and keep the same in repair as the law requires with the same hands that work under William Mills former overseer thereof be assigned to work thereon.

Ordered by Court that Wamon Leftwich Administrator of James M. Rowland deceased be allowed the sum of eighty four dollars and seventy one cents being for money advanced and services rendered in settling said estate to be by him retained out of the money in his hands of said estate.

This day John R. Glenn, Adminestrator of George W. Hawkins deceased.

Returned upon oath an acct. of the sales of said estate which is ordered to be recorded. Isd.

Ordered by Court that Avery Green be appointed Overseer of road from the forks of the road called the McMinnville road to sinking Creek being a road of the second Class and keep the same in repair as the law requires with the same hands that worked under Hayes Arnold former Overseer thereof.

This day the Commissioners appointed at the last term of this Court to settle with Robert L. Mitchell and William Baker executors of the estate of Edward Holmes deceased returned their settlement which is ordered to be recorded.

Ordered by Court that Robert L. Mitchell and William Baker executors of the estate of Edward Holmes deceased be allowed the sum of fifty dollars each for their services rendered in attending to and settling said estate to be by them (P-89) retained of of the monies in their hands belonging to said estate (Isd)

Ordered by Court that John Jett, David Snodgrass and William Bruster Esqs. be allowed the sum of one dollar and fifty cents per day each for two days services as commissioners in settling with Robert L. Mitchell and William Baker executors of Edward Holmes deceased to be paid by the said executors out of the money of said estate.

This day the Commissioners heretofore appointed by this Court to settle with Wamon Leftwich late trustee of White County returned their report which is ordered by the Court to be recorded.

Ordered by Court that Richard Nelson and John H. Anderson Esquires Commissioners appointed to settle with Wamon Leftwich late trustee of White County be allowed the sum of two dollars each for one days services rendered in making said settlement to be paid by the sherriff of White County out of the taxes for the year 1836.

Ordered by Court that Wamon Leftwich Esq. late Trustee of White County be allowed the sum of two hundred and sixty one dollars fifty seven and a half cents for monies advanced while Trustee, to be paid by the Trustee of White County out of the first monies that may come into

Test.
N. Oldham Ck.

Thos. Eastland
Richard Crowder
Willie Steakley

(P-88) State of Tennessee

At a County Court began and held for the County of White at the Court house in the town of Sparta before the Justices of said Court on the first Monday being the sixth day of June in the year of our Lord one thousand eight hundred and thirty six And of the Independance of the United States the sixtieth year

Present the Worshipful

Thomas Eastland, Esq. Chairman
William Knowles,) Esquires
John Bryan,)
Joshua Mason,)
Jonathan Farrington,)
William Glenn,)
David Snodgrass,)
Willie Steakley,)
Matthias Hutson,)
Elisha Camron,)
William C. Bounds,)
Jesse Walling,)
Asa Certain,) Justices
John Wallis,)
John Gillentine,)
Thomas Green,)
Montgomery C. Dibrell)
James Allison,)
Elijah Frost,)
John Jett,)
William Bruster,)
Richard Crowder,)
William Bartlett,)
and Lewis Pettett - .)

This day Susannah Duncan adminestratrix of the estate of William Duncan Deceased returned an Inventory of said estate upon oath which is ordered to be recorded.

Ordered by Court that the road as laid off and marked by Commissioners which was rejected at the last term of this Court be now received and established a road of the second Class.

(Issd).

Ordered by Court that Joseph Hunter be appointed overseer of the road from Littles bridge passing Murphy's and Veneents and intersecting the Ussery gap. road on the first bench below the flat rock being a road of the second Class and keep the same in repair as the law requires, and that David Snodgrass Esq be assigned to apportion a his hands with interest thereon from the 10th day of May 1836 at the rate of 6 per cents perannum untill paid.

This day the Commissioners heretofore appointed by this Court to assign and set apart a sufficency of provisions for the support of Rachel Jones widow of William Jones deceased returned their report which is ordered to be recorded -

This day the Commissioners heretofore appointed by this Court to assign and set apart a sufficency of provisions for the support of the widow of Jabez Anderson deceased returned their report which is ordered to be recorded.

This day the Commissioners heretofore appointed by this Court to assign and set apart a sufficency of provisions for the support of the Widow and family of Zachariah Jones deceased returned their report which is ordered to be recorded.

Ordered by Court that William Earles be released from the appraised value of seven stray hogs which have strayed from him (Issd)

Ordered by Court that Robert Anderson, James Copeland, John Sorrells, Alexander Brown and Thomas Adair be assigned as hands to work on the road of which Lewis Phillips is overseer.

This day John Plumlie produced in open Court one large wolf scalp over the age of four month and proved that it was killed in the County of White and there being present five acting Justices of the peace, whereupon it is ordered that it be certified to the Treasures of the state of Tennessee for payment and that the sherriff of White County burn said scalp, who being here in open Court received the same into his custody and acted accordingly (certified) (Issd)

Ordered by Court that David Snodgrass, Montgomery C. Dibrell and William C. Bounds Esquires be appointed Commissioners to assign and set apart a sufficent quantity of provisions for the support of the widow and family of Joseph Parker deceased, and report thereof to the next term of this Court. (Issd)

Ordered by Court that Joshua Mason Esq. be appointed to apportion list of hands between Robert Glenn and Indeman B. Moore overseer on the Kentucky road and report thereof to the next term of this Court.

This day John Mason Guardian to James Howard a minor returned upon oath his report which is ordered to be recorded.

(P-90) This day John Gillentine was appointed guardian to William F. Carter a minor heir of Charles Carter Sr. deceased and together with Jacob Stipe and Joseph Cummings Jr. entered into and acknowledged bond in the sum of Four thousand dollars conditioned as the law requires. (Issd)

Ordered by Court that Woodson P. White, Andrew Bryan, William M. Bryan, Sr. Benjamin Lewis, and Hartwell Wilson freeholders be appointed commissioners to lay off and mark a road of the 2nd class from the mouth of Andrew Bryans lane passing the house of L. R. Wilson to intersect the old river road at Wallis Spring branch and report thereof to the next term of this Court. Isd

Ordered by Court that William McGarr be appointed overseer of the road from the forks of the road at Wm. Brusters plantation to George W. Eastlands old place on the Sims road being a road of the first Class and keep the same in repair as the law requires with the same hands that worked under William G. Sims former overseer thereof and also the hands that belong to William Bruster, ward plantation - . (Isd)

Ordered by Court that Henry Rutledge be appointed overseer of the road from the Usery gap road to its intersection with the Calf killer road being a road of the second Class and keep the same in repair as the law requires, with the same hands that worked under James Bradley former overseer thereof - Iss'd

Ordered by Court that James Beckwith be appointed Overseer of the road from the Flat rock on Userys gap road to interesection of the Turnpike road east of Mrs. Vandavers being a road of the second Class and keep the same in repair as the law requires and Thomas Eastland Esq. Assign him a list of hands to work thereon. Iss'd

Ordered by Court that Richard Crowder, Jacob Firtle, Hiram Lewis, Charles Meek and John Shaw freeholders be appointed Commissioners to lay off and mark a road of the second Class from Lanes Mill passing Robert B. Glenn's to intersect the shipping port road at William Glenn Esq. and report thereof to the next term of this Court.

Ordered by Court that Christopher Swindle be appointed Overseer of the road from the two mile post to the house of John Knowles Sr. being a road of the first Class and keep the same in repair as the law requires with that same hands assigned to William Hutson former Overseer thereof -.

This day the Commissioners heretofore appointed by this Court to lay off and marked a road of the second Class from the forks of the road above Sparta and intersecting the road leading up Userys gap near Taylors Crossing Blue Spring Creek at Littles bridge returned their report which is recorded by the Court and said road as laid off and marked is established. Isd

Ordered by Court that Thomas Little be appointed Overseer of the road from the forks of the road above Sparta to Little's bridge being a road of the second Class and keep the same in repair as the law requires and that David Snodgrass Esq. assign a list of hands to work thereon. Iss'd

Ordered by Court that John A. Pass be appointed overseer of the road from Littles bridge to the intersection of the road leading up Userys gap near Taylors being a road of the second Class and keep the same in repair as the law requires and that David Snodgrass Esq. assign a list of hands to work thereon.

(P-81) Iss'd

Ordered by Court that Thomas Whitefield, John Whitefield, and William Barr be assigned to work on the road of which Joseph S. Ellison is Overseer -.

Ordered by Court that Cornelius Davis be released from the payment of the taxes on 500 acres of land for the year 1835 he being overcharged that much

And it is further ordered that Simon R. Doyle be charged with the taxes thereon for the year 1835 who being present in open Court assumes the payment thereof.

Ordered by Court that part of the Shipping port road which leaves the Allens ferry road at the North West Corner of N. Oldhams field passing along by Jacob A. Lanes house thence crossing town Creek below Lanes Mills; thence leaving the Shipping port road passing through Jacob A. Lanes cornfield (now wheat field) leaving the said field at the top of rising grends near the north east corner thereof thence along a ridge intersecting the road a small distance south of the top of a hill on the old road formerly crossing town creek at a place called Reels Mill be and the same is hereby declared and established a road of the first Class whereupon Jacob A. Lane is appointed overseer thereof who agrees to open said road; to build a bridge across Town Creek and to graduate said road so that it shall not exceed an elevation of more than six and one half degrees and that he keep the same in repair as the law requires at his own expence - .

The Commissioners hereto appointed by this Court to examine lay off and mark a road the nearest and best way from the west end of the bridge at Sparta passing thereof the lands of William Bruster; Nicholas Oldham and Jacob A. Lane Crossing Town Creek at or near the mouth and intersecting the McMinnville road at the forks where the road leading by the Harriet Iron Works turns off this day returned their report, which is by the Court rejected. Iss'd

Ordered by Court that James Hudgins, Samuel V. Carrick; John Rose; Woodson P. White; Joseph Herd, Joseph Hunter, Thomas Little, Asa Certain, Richard Crowder, Eli Sims, Henry Lyda and Charles Meek freeholders, be appointed Commissioners to lay off and mark and measure a road of the first Class the nearest and best way from the west end of the bridge at the town of Sparta passing through the lands of William Bruster, Nicholas Oldham and Jacob A. Lane crossing Town Creek at or near the mouth and intersecting the McMinnville road at the forks where the road leading by the Harriet Iron Works turns off also to examine and measure the road from the west end of said bridge passing said N. Oldhams dwelling house to the North west corner of his field, thence turn off with the Shipping port road and passing Jacob A. Lanes dwelling house and crossing Town Creek a short distance below Lanes Mill; thence leaving the shipping port road on the west side of said creek and passing through Jacob A. Lanes cornfield (now a wheatfield) leaving the said field at the top of rising ground near the North east Corner thereof thence along a ridge intersecting the old road a small distance south of the top of a hill in the old road formerly crossing town Creek at a place called Reels Mill - this rout leaving the Allens ferry road to old road beyond Reels old Mill ford having been this day established and declared a first Class road, and report to the next term of this Court as well the advantages and disadvantages that will result to the public or to individuals as the particular distance of each rout Respectively.

(P-62) Iss'd

Ordered by Court David L. Mitchell, Esq. Sherriff of White County be allowed the sum of thirty three dollars twenty five cents for money by him expended in the execution and burial of Bennet Dula and Jesse Mitchell for Capital offences and other incedental expences as per account exhibited to this Court to be paid out of the taxes for the year 1836 Iss'd

Ordered by Court that the following persons who were summonsed by the Sherriff of White County in obedience to an order of the Supreme Court of Errors an appeals for the state of Tennessee for the purpose of guarding the common Jail of White County for the better securing & safe keeping of Bennett Dula and Jesse Mitchell who were then under the sentence of death for Capital offinces be allowed the following Sums for the following services

To Wit.

John Smith for Eleven days guarding the Jail			$1.00	per d	$11.00
Robert Smith for 15 days guarding the Jail			@ $1.00	per day	$15.00
Samuel Tucker for 16 days	"	"	@ $1.00	do	16.00
Hayes Arnold	16 days	" "	@ $1.00	do	16.00
John Sprawls	15 days	" "	@ 1.00	do	15.00
Robert H. McManus	12 days	" "	@ 1.00	do	12.00
Sawyer Simpson	11 days	" "	@ 1.00	do	11.00
Henry Frasure	11 days	" "	@ 1.00	do	11.00
James Mays Jr.	14 days	" "	@ 1.00	do	14.00
James Mays Sr.	12 days	" "	@ 1.00	do	12.00
Charles Smith	12 days	" "	@ 1.00	do	12.00
Charles McGuire	9 days	" "	@ 1.00	do	9.00

Amounting in all to the sum of - - - - - - - - - - - 154.00

One hundred and fifty four dollars to be paid out of the taxes for the year 1836.

For reasons appearing to the satisfaction of the Court, it is ordered by the Court that Anthony Dibrell guardian for George W. Miller be and he is here by discharged from his said guardainship and that from all future and further liabilities relative to said guardianship released and discharged - -

the Court further order that the said Anthony Dibrell guardian as above pay over and possess the said George W. Miller of all such monies and papers and estate both real and personal as shall have come into his hands and possessions by vertue of his said guardianship -.

And it is further considered by the Court the said George W. Miller pay all the Cost which have occured relative to the proceedings herein had and that execution issued for the Collection thereof &c. -

Ordered by Court that John Jackson a pauper be sent to the poor house of White County by the sherriff of White County there to be kept and maintained at the proper Cost and charges of the County of White. Iss'd

Ordered by Court that the following list of hands be assigned to work on and assist in opening a road of the first Class from the Peeled Chestnut to George W. Eastland old place on the Sims road, on which

Aaron Hutchings is overseer
To wit.
William Bussell, Webster Hutchings, Bailey Angel, William Cantrell, [illegible] Bozarth, James Bozarth, Robert Townsend, Joseph Bozarth, Mary Bennet, Washington Irwin, Elijah Bussell, Zachariah Bussell, John James, John Clouse, Willie Julin, James Julin, Hiram Lewis, Andrew Campbell (P-93) William Singleton, James Redman, William Glenn, William Rigsby, John Hutchings and Barney Harlow, it is further ordered by the Court that all the hands that belong to the shipping port road be exempt from any further labor on this road after the same shall have been opened and put in order according to law. Iss'd

On the petition of Joseph Herd Administrator and Phebe Allen Administrator of George Allen deceased late of the County of White setting forth that the said George Allen died siezed and possessed of six slaves therein stated that in their opinion it would be most consistant with the interest of the respective distrobuters of said estate that said negro slaves shall be sold and that a division thereof cannot consistently be made - . And it appearing to the satisfaction of the Court from the facts set forth in said petition and from the examination of Witnesses in support of the statement made therein, that said slaves mentioned in said petition cannot be equitably and properly divided and apportioned mongst those entitled to the distribution thereof unless said slaves are sold and that it would be to the advantage of those concerned to have said slaves sold.

It is therefore considered by the Court and so ordered and directed that the said Joseph Herd administrator and Phebe Allen administration of George Allen deceased sell said six slaves in said petition mentioned the property of the said George Allen deceased, in his life time on a credit of twelve months from the tenth day of August next giving twenty days notice of the time and place of said sale taking from the purchase or purchasers bond with approved security and the procedings of the sale of said slaves to distribute amongst those entitled to receive the same as required by law.

Ordered that Court be adjourned till tomorrow 9 O'clock

Thos. Eastland
J. Farrington
Elijah Frost

Tuesday Morning 7th June A.D. 1836 Court met pursuant to adjournment Present the Worshipful

Thomas Eastland Esq Chairman
Jonathan Farrington
Elijah Frost
William Glenn
Richard Crowder
} Esquires Justices

This day David L. Mitchell Esq. Sherriff of White County appeared in open Court and appointed William R. Tucker Deputy sherriff of White County who being present in [illegible] took an oath to support the constitution of the United States and of the State of Tennessee and the several oaths required by law and thereupon entered upon the duties of his office -.

(P-24) Ordered that Court be adjourned untill Court in Course

Thos. Eastland
J. Farrington
Elijah Frost

(P-25) State of Tennessee

At a County Court began and held at the Court house in the town of Sparta for the County of White before the Justices of said Court on the first Monday being the 4th day of July in the year of our Lord one thousand eight hundred and thirty six and of the Independence of the United States the sixty first year

Present the Worshipful

John Jett Esq. Chairman pro-tem
Lewis Pettett,
William Knowles,
William Glenn,
Willie Steakley,
Matthias Hutson,
David Snodgrass,
Montgomery C. Dibrell, — Esquires
Richard Crowder,
Jonathan Farrington,
Thomas Green,
John Gillentine,
John Wallis,
James Allison, — Justices
William C. Bounds,
John Bryan,
William Bruster,
Jesse Walling,
Edmund Stamps,
Isaac Buck,
William Bartlett,
Elisha Camron and
Joshua Mason

Ordered by Court that Samuel Brown be apponted a Commissioners in stead of William C. Bounds Esq. to assist in assigning and setting apart one years provisions to the widow and family of Joseph Parker deceased and report to the present term of this Court Iss'd

This day the Commissioners appointed to assign and set apart one years provisions for the support and maintainace of the widow and family of Joseph Parker deceased returned their report which is ordered to be recorded - .

Ordered by Court that David Snodgrass Montgomery C. Dibrell and Samuel Brown Commissioners appointed to assign provisions to the widow of Joseph Parker deceased [illegible] the sum of one dollar fifty cents for one days service in making said assignment - .

Ordered by Court that William Glenn Esq. be appointed a Commissioner instead of John Wallis Esq. to assist in assigning one years provisions to the widow and family of George Allen deceased and report to the next term of this Court Iss'd

This day the Commissioners appointed by this Court to assign and set apart one years provisions for the support and maintainance of the widow and family of George Allen deceased returned their report which is ordered to be recorded - .

Ordered by Court that William Glenn, Richard Crowder and David Snodgrass, Commissioners appointed by this Court to set apart one years provisions to the widow of George Allen deceased be allowed each the sum of one doller fifty cents for two days services in making said assignment.

At the last term of this Court John Fryer Guadian to William F. Carter a minor heir of Charles Carter Sr. deceased appeared in open Court and renounced his guardianship and for reasons appearing to the satisfaction of the Court it was ordered by the Court that (P-96) the said John Fryer guardian as aforesaid from all future and further liabilities respecting said guardianship be released and discharged - .

And it appearing to the satisfaction of the Court that at the last term of this Court the aforesaid William F. Carter a minor heir of Charles Carter Sr. deceased appeared in open Court and he being of proper age chose John Gillentine Esq. to be his guardian who then being present in open Country entered into acknowledge bond with sufficent security conditioned as the law requires - and it is ordered by the Court that this order be made now for them - .

This day James Seals produced here in open Court four wolf scalps under the age of four months and proved that he killed them in the County of White whereupon there being present five acting Justices of the peace it is ordered by the Court that they be Certified to the Treasure of the state of Tennessee for payment and that the Sherriff of White County burn said scalps who being here present in Court received said scalps into his custody and acted accordingly - . Iss'd

Ordered by Court that David Haston, Robert Gamble, John Felkins, John Seals and John Yates freeholders be appointed a Jury of view to lay off and mark a road of the third Class from near William L. Mitchells fince, the nearest and best way to intersect the Pikeville road near where the same crosses Thomas Stypes spring branch and report thereof to the next term of this Court - .

This day the death of Azaciah Long late of the County of White was suggested and that he departed this life intestate whereupon George Cline is appointed adminestrator of all and singular the goods and Chattles, rights and credits of the deceased and took the oath required by law and with John Wallis and Richard Nelson intered into and acknowledged bond in the sum of five hundred dollars Conditioned as the law requires - .

For reasons appearing to the satisfaction of the Court that at April term 1835 of this Court an appointment of Forty dollars was made for the support of a Certain Vincent Ayers for one year and also that said Vincent Ayres departed this life on the 13th day July last - It is therefore Considered and so ordere by the Court that said order be re-[illegible] except the sum of Nine dollars thirty cents which is [illegible] to [illegible] John Ayres by the Treasures of the poor house Commissioners [illegible] any money not otherwise appropriated - . (Isad)

Ordered by Court that Burrel Manor, Willie B. Haston, Christopher [illegible], Daniel Walling and Charles Denny freeholders be appointed a Jury [illegible] to lay off and mark a road of the second Class turning off from [illegible] Cain Creek road near Mr. Galls, thense up the mountain between Cain Creek and the Dry Cove thence striking the Hoodin Pile trace when it Crosses town Creek and report thereof to the next term of this Court.

Ordered by Court that John Fryer guardian to William F. Carter be allowed the sum of nineteen dollars and forty six cents being for monies advanced and and services rendered agreeably to his account to be by him retained out of the estate of his said Ward - .

(P-97) Monday 4th July A.D. 1836

This day was produced in open Court the within writing purporting to be the last will and Testament of Joseph Henry deceased late of the County of White and the due execution and Publication thereof as the last will and Testament of the said Joseph Henry deceased was proven in open Court by the oath of William Bartlett one other witness thereto for the purposes and things therein mentioned, and that the said Joseph Henry was at the date of the execution and publication thereof of sound and disposing mind and memory which having been heretofore in like manner proven by the oath of Thomas Barnes the other subscribing witness thereto for the same purposes it is ordered to be recorded - . Iss'd

This day was produced in open Court a writing purporting to be the last will and testament of Thomas Curtis deceased late of the County of White and the due exeution and publication thereof as the last will and testament of the said Thomas Curtis deceased was proven in open Court by the oath of Barnett Kemp one of the subscribing witnesses thereto for the purposes and things therein Contained and that the said Thomas Curtis was at the date of the execution and publication thereof of sound and disposing mind and memory - . Iss'd

Ordered by Court that Theodorick B. Rice be released from the payment of taxes on 2600 acres of land for the year's 1833 and 1834 amounting in all to the sum of thirty four dollars twelve and one half cents he having been overcharged that amount and that the sherriff of White County have a credit thereof in the settlement of his accounts with the Trustee of White County for the Taxes of the year 1836 - . Iss'd

Ordered by Court that the order appointing Woodson P. White, Andrew Bryan, William M. Bryan Sr., Benjamin Lewis and Hartewell Wilson freeholders Commissioners to lay off and mark a road of the second Class from the mouth of Andrew Bryans lane passing the house of L. R. Wilson to intersect the old river road at Wallis's spring branch be renewed and report thereof to next term of this Court - Iss'd

Ordered by Court that the order appointing Richard Crowder, Jacob Pirtle, Hiram Lewis, Charles Meek and John Shaw freeholders

Commissioners to lay off and mark a road of the second Class from Lanes Mill passing Robert B. Glenns and to intersect the Shipping [illegible] at [illegible] Esq. be renewed and report thereof to the next term of this Court.

Ordered by Court that Samuel Johnson, David Snodgrass and Anthony Dibrell, Commissioners appointed by this Court to settle with the adms and admr. of Elijah England deceased be each allowed the sum of 1.50 for one days service each in addition to this former allowance for services rendered in said settlement to be paid out of the estate of the deceased -

Ordered by Court that Moses Goodard deceased late guardian to the heir of John Smallman deceased be allowed the sum of Forty dollars being for services rendered and money expended in transacting the business of his (P-98) said guardianship to be retained out of the estate of his wards - . Iss'd

Ordered by Court that Alexander Lowry Sr., James Hudgins, Nathaniel C. Davis, Samuel Lance and Henry Lance freeholders be appointed a Jury of view to lay off and mark a road of the 3rd Class leaving the turn pike road near Col. Lowrey's passing up the mountain and by Doct Spring's dwelling house and to intersect the Turn pike road again where the old and new road fork and report thereof to the next term of this Court.

This day Joseph Herd Adminestrator of the estate of George Allen deceased return upon oath an Inventory of the estate of the deceased which is ordered to be recorded - .

This day Joseph Herd adminestrator of the estate of [illegible] Allen deceased returned upon oath an account of the sales of the property of the deceased which is ordered to be recorded - . Iss'd

Ordered by Court that William Knowles and Joshua Mason Esq. be appointed to apportion and assign the bounds of hands between the diffrent overseers from Webbs to Parsons on the Kentucky road &c and report to the next term of this Court - . Iss'd

Ordered by Court that Matthias Hutson, Lewis Pettett and Thomas Green Esquire be appointed to assign and apportion hands between Sampson Witt Overseer on the Rosses ferry road a road of the 2nd Class and Lewis Philips overseer on the Rockisland road a road of the first Class and report to the next term of this Court.

Ordered by Court that Sally Robertson be released from the appraised Value of one estray steer appraised to the sum of three dollars - . Iss'd

Ordered by Court that John Smith and Sawyer Simpson be allowed the sum of four dollars each for four days service each in addition to the allowance made them at the last term of this Court to be paid out of the taxes for the year 1836 being for services rendered the County of White in guarding the Common Jail of said County. Issd.

Ordered by Court that Nicholas Cook guardian to the minor heirs of George Keesee be allowed the sum of sixteen Dollars and fifteen cents for services rendered and money expended for the benifit of his said wards which Anthony Dibrell Esq. Collected of said estate is required to pay or so much thereof as he may have means in his hands belonging to said Estate - .

Ordered by Court that Jesse Davis be appointed overseer of the road from the eight mile post to the Falling water being a road of the first Class and keep the same in repair as the law requires with the same hands which worked under Daniel Martin former overseer thereof to work thereon - Issd

Ordered by Court that William Bozarth be appointed Overseer of the road from the knotty oak to Allens ferry being a road of the first Class and keep the same in repair as the law requires with the same list of hands which have been heretofore assigned to work thereon Iss'd

Ordered by Court that John Wallis, John Gillentine and Willie Steakley Esquires be appointed Commissioners on Hales turnpike

(P-99) Monday 4th July A.D. 1836

Ordered by Court that the following persons be summonsed by the Sherriff of White County as Jurors for the October term of White Circuit Court 1836

To wit.

Moses Carrick, Daniel McLain, Rhodum Doyle, James Graham, Mark Lowery, William Wisdom, Jesse Walling, Edward Anderson, John Cash, Samuel Dyer, John Gillentine, Thomas Moore, John J. Whitfield, Eli Sims, Richard Crowder, Robert Anderson Sr. George D. Howard, Walker Bennett, Smith, Sims Dearing, Alexander Bohanon, Thomas Nicholas, Lewis [illegible], Joseph Clark and Jose C. Dew - And Hayes Arnold and Charles Mee[illegible] Constables to attend thereon - . Issd

Ordered by Court that Leonard Murry be appointed overseer of the road from Plumb Creek to the forks of the road at Thomas Cooper's being a road of the second Class and keep the same in repair as the law requires that the same hands that worked under Frederick Green former overseer be assigned to work thereon - .

Ordered by Court that William Buckner be appointed Overseer of the road from the forks of the road at Hunters Mill leading up the river to Jacob Hyders being a road of the second Class and keep the same in repair as the law requires and that William Bartlett and Isaac Buck Esquires assign a list of hands to work thereon - . Isaac Buck Esq. one of the Commissioners of the Revenue for the County of White returned upon oath a list of the taxable property and Polls in said County in District No 11

Ordered by Court that the following Tax be levied and raised for the year 1836

For County Tax

On each $100 Value of property	5 Cents
On each free poll	12½ cents

For Jury Tax

on each $100 worth property	½ 5 Cents

On each free poll $12\frac{1}{2}$ Cents

For Poor Tax

on each $100 worth property 6 cents

On each free poll $12\frac{1}{2}$ cents

For Bridge Tax at Sparta

On each $100 Value of property $1\frac{1}{4}$ cents

To be levied and collected by the sherriff of White County in manner and form as persoribed by law.

Ordered that Court be adjourned till tomorrow Morning 10 Oclock

John Jett
Jonathan Farrington
Thomas Green

(P-100) Tuesday Morning 5th July A.D. 1836

Court met pursuant to adjournment
Present the Worshipful

John Jett
Thomas Green
Jonathan Farrington } Esq. Justices

Ordered that Court be adjourned untill Court in Course

John Jett
Thomas Green
Jonathan Farrington

N. Oldham
Clerk

(P-101)

State of Tennessee

At a Court began and held for the County of White at the Court house in the town of Sparta before the Justices of said Court on the first Monday being the first day of August in the year of our Lord One thousand eight hundred and thirty six and of the Independence of the United States the sixty first year

Present the Worshipful

John Jett Esquire Chairman pro tem
Willie Steakley,
John Gillentine,
Elijah Frost,
Jonathan Farrington,
Jesse Walling,
Montgomery C. Dibrell,
John Bryan,
Joshua Mason,
John Wallis, } Esquires Justices

William Bartlett,
William Bruster,
Matthias Hutson,
William Hitchcock,
Edmund Stamps,
Henry Benton,
Thomas Green,)

William Little appearing in open Court and took an oath to support the Constitution of the United States and of the State of Tennessee and the oath prescribed by law for Justices of the peace and thereupon entered upon the duties of his office - .

This day Henry Benton exhibited his stock mark which is a swallow fork and an under bit in the right and a smooth crop off the left ear which is ordered to be recorded - . Iss'd

Ordered by Court that Burrel Manor, Willie B. Haston, Christopher Steakley, Daniel Walling and Charles Denny freeholders be appointed a Jury of view to lay off and mark a road of the second Class from Cain Creek road near Mrs Taylors thence up the Mountain between Cain Creek and Dry fork thence striking the Hoodenpile trace where it crosses Pine Creek and report thereof to the next term of this Court - . Iss'd

This day George Bohannon was appointed administrator of all and singular the goods and Chattles, rights and Credits of Joseph Henry late of White County with his will annexed and with William Bartlett entered into and acknowledged bond in the sum of two hundred dollars conditioned as the law requires. Issd

This day the Commissioners appointed at the last term of this Court to lay off and mark a road of the third Class from near William L. Mitchells fence to entersect the Pikeville road where the same crosses Thomas Stipes spring Branch returned their report which is received and ordered that the same be established - . And that William L. Mitchell be appointed overseer thereof and Keep the same in repair as the law requires and Willie Steakley and John Gillentine Esquires assign a list of hands to work thence -

Ordered by Court that the double tax on all property listed and already returned for taxation in the County of White for the year 1836 be released.

(P-102) Monday August 1st. A.D. 1836

Iss'd

Ordered by Court that John G. Allen be appointed Overseer of the road from the knotty oak to Allens ferry being a road of the first Class and keep the same in repair as the law requires with the same list of hands which was assigned to work under William Bosarth former Overseer thereof - .

This day the Commissioners heretofore appointed by this Court to lay off and mark a road of the second Class from the mouth of Bryan's lane to intersect the old river road near Wallis' spring branch returned their report which was by the Court rejected.

Ordered by Court that Turner Lane Jr., John White Jr.; William Denny, Robert Gamble, Jacob Anderson, William Lewis Sr.; and John White Sr., freeholders be appointed a jury of view to lay off and mark a road of the second Class from the mouth of Andrew Bryan's lane passing the house of L. R. Wilson to intersect the old river road at Wallis spring branch and report thereof to the next term of this Court - . Iss'd

Ordered by Court that Richard England be appointed Overseers of the road from the four to the six mile post on the Carthage road being a road of the first Class and keep the same in repair as the law requires that the same hands that worked under William Matlock former overseer be assigned to work thereon - . Iss'd

Ordered by Court that David Whitaker, John Bohannon; William Bartlett, Jacob Hyder Sr., and George Bohannon freeholders be appointed a jury of view to lay off and mark a road of the second Class from the forks of the Creek near Henry Bohannons passing up Hyders Creek to Whitakers Mill thence passing the head of said Creek so as to intersect the road leading up the Dry Valley near Goodman Madewill and report thereof to the next term of this Court.

Ordered by Court that Richard Crowder and William Glenn Esq. be appointed to assign and apportion the hands between Thomas Clouse and all the overseers on the Sims road having due regard to the dignity of said roads respectively and report thereof to the next term of this Court - . (Iss'd)

Ordered by Court that Richard Crowder, William Glenn, John M. Little, Joseph W. Little, and Thomas Jones freeholders be appointed a jury of view so to lay off and mark, as to straiten the Sims road; from near the dwelling house of Eli Sims and to intersect the road again something like a mile west of said Sims dwelling house being a road of the first Class and report thereof to the next term of this Court. Iss'd

Ordered by Court that the road from the forks above Sparta passing Littles bridge up to McKinnys being a second Class road, be reduced and that the same be established a road of the third Class and that David Snodgrass and William Little Esq. assign and apportions the hands between Thomas Little; Barlow Fisk, Henry Rutledge; James Walker and Joseph Hunter overseers according to the (P-103) dignety of these several roads respectively - And report to the next term of this Court. Iss'd

Ordered by Court that Edmund Stamps and Esha Camron Esquires be appointed to apportion lists of hands between Edward Elms and George Henry Overseers on the road and report to the next term of this Court. Iss'd

Ordered by Court that Benjamin Lewis, Canady Rigsby, Hyram Lewis, Charles Meek and John Cantrell freeholders be appointed a jury of view to lay of and mark a road of the second Class from Lanes Mill passing Robert Glenns and to intersect the shipping port road at William Glenn Esq. and report thereof to the next term of this Court.

This day the Commissioners appointed at the last term of this Court to apportion hands between Lewis Philips Overseer on the Rock Island road and Sampson Witt on Rosses Ferry road returned their report which is recorded and it is ordered by the Court that John Sorrels,

Alexander Brown, Joseph Rickman, Thomas Adair, and James Copeland be assigned to work under Lewis Philips, And that William Anderson and his negro boy be placed under Sampson Witt Overseer - . Iss'd

Ordered by Court that William Buckner be appointed overseer of the road from the forks of the road at William Hunters Mill leading up the river to John Bohannons being a road of the second class and keep same in repair as the law requires and that William Bartlett and Isaac Buck Esqr. assign a list of hands to work thereon - .

Ordered by Court that Moses Holland, Thomas Holland, Nathaniel Markham, Westley Markham, be assigned to work under John Parsons Overseer of the road from Webbs to Jonathan Shorts as apportioned by Commissioners appointed for that purpose -

Ordered by Court that Joshua Mason and Richard Crowder Esquires be appointed to apportion hands between Harmon Littles and Robert Glenn Overseer of the road and report to the next term of this Court - . Iss'd

Ordered by Court that Alfred Merret, James Knowles, Levi Jarvis, Samuel Turney, Eli Marlow, Leroy Helton, Joseph Franks, Joseph B. Glenn, Joseph H. McDaniel, John Jenkins, Stephen G. Buxton, William D. Glenn, John McDaniel, Robert Martin, Miss Randals, Sam - . And all within said bounds be assigned to work under Robert Glenn Jr. Overseer on the Kentucky road and that Indemon B. Moore retain his former list with the exception of John Jenkins and John McDaniel as appointed by Coms. appointed by Court to make apportionment between them - .

Ordered by Court that Jonathan Farrington, John Bryan, Thomas Green, Matthias Hutson, Joshua Mason, William Glenn, Henry Benton, William Hitchcock, Montgomery C. Dibrell, William C. Bounds, Isaac Buck, Edmund Stamps, David Snodgrass, Elijah Frost, and Willie Steakley Revenue Commissioners of White County be each allowed the sum of five dollars
(P-104) for services rendered in taking in lists of taxable property and polls in the County of White for the year 1836 to be paid by the Trustee of White County out of the taxes of the year 1836 - . Iss'd

Ordered by Court that James Turner be appointed Overseer of the road from the Corner of Mark Lowrys field to the forks of the road near Anthony Dibrell being a road of the second Class and keep the same in repair as the law requires and that [the hands that worked under Barger Lowery former overseer thereof be assigned to work thereon - .] Montgomery C. Dibrell and William Little Esquires be appointed to apportion hands between him and Lewis Turner, Overseer on the Carthage road having regard to the dignity of each road - .

This day John Gillentine and John Wallis Esquires who were at the last term of this Court appointed Commissioners on Hales turnpike road appeared in open Court and took the oath prescribed by law and thereupon entered upon the duties of their office - . Iss'd

Ordered by the Court unanimously that the following persons be allowed the following fees in the respective State Cases which have all been Certified down to this Court from White Circuit Court and having been according to law examined and Certified by the attorney general as being legally taxed and properly chargable to the County of White

To wit

In the Case of the State of Tennessee vs Smith Roberts, William R. Tucker, Jailor $26.87½ - . Clerk William G. Sims $1.25

In the Case the State vs John & Abraham Cantrell - Clerk Anthony Dibrell 1.62½ - . Clerk William G. Sims 3.50 Clerk Jacob A. Lane $1.37½ - . Shff. William G. Sims $1.12½ - Shff. David L. Mitchell $2.62½ - . Atto. general John B. McCormack 2.50 -

In the Case the State against William Bozarth - Clerk Jacob A. Lane 1.25. Clerk William G. Sims $4.00 - Shff. David L. Mitchell $1.41½ Shff William G. Sims 62½ Cents - . Atto. Genl. John B. McCormack $2.50 -

In the Case the State against James H. Lewis; Anthony Dibrell Clerk $3.62½ Clerk William G. Sims $3.25 - Shff David L. Mitchell $2.12½ - Shff Jabaz G. Mitchell 50 Cents - Atto General John B. McCormick $2.50 to be paid by the Trustee of White County out of any monies not otherwise appropriated.

This day Anderson Finley aged two years on the 8th day of July 1836 was bound to James H. Jenkins to serve him after the manner of an apprentice untill he arrives at the age of twenty one years and for the faithful performance of his Covenant intered into and acknowledged bond with Samuel V. Carrick his security as the law requires - .

This day the Commissioners who were appointed at a former term of this Court to assign and set apart one years provisions for the support of the widow and family of William Duncan deceased returned their report which is received by the Court and ordered to be recorded - .

(P-105) Monday August 1st A.D. 1836.

This day David L. Mitchell Esq. Sherriff and Collector of the Taxes in the County of White for the year 1836 appeared in open Court and took the oath required by law and with David Snodgrass Thomas Roberts, Robert Love, James Randols, John Mitchell and William Glenn entered into and acknowledged their several bonds Conditioned as the law requires which bonds are in the words and figures following to wit:

<u>Bond for State Tax.</u>

Know all men by these presents that we David L. Mitchell and David Snodgrass, Thomas Robertson, Robert Love, James Randols and John Mitchell, William Glenn all of the County of White and State of Tennessee are held and firmly bound unto his excellency Newton Cannon Govener in and over the State of Tennessee for the time being or his successors in offices in the sum of Two Thousand dollars Current money, which payment well and truly to be made and done we bind ourselves and each of us and each and every of our heirs, executive and adminestrators jointly and severally firmly by these presents sealed with our seals and dated the first day of August A.D. 1836.

bound Whereas the above David L. Mitchell hath been appointed Collector of the taxes in the County of White for the year 1836.

Now the Condition of the above obligation is such that if the above bound David L. Mitchell Collector as aforesaid, shall, will and truly Collect tha taxes which are levied in the County of White and State aforesaid on property and polls for the year 1836, for the use of the state of Tennessee and shall pay over and account for the same with the Treasure of the state of Tennessee according to law -

And in all things therein demean himself according to law -

Then this obligation to be null and void, else to be and remain in full force and vertue.

(Signd)

Test.
N. Oldham Clk.

David L. Mitchell (seal)
David Snodgrass (seal)
Thomas Robertson (seal)
Robert Love (seal)
John Mitchell (seal)
William Glenn (seal)

Bonds for Tax on School Lands.

Know all men by these presents that we David L. Mitchell and David Snodgrass, Thomas Robertson, Robert Love, James Randols, John Mitchell, William Glenn all of this County of White and State of Tennessee are held and firmly bound unto Robert H. McEwin Superintendant of Public Education in Tennessee in the sum of one thousand Dollars for the use of Common schools in the state of Tennessee which payment well and truly to be made and done we bind ourselves and each of our heirs executors,
(P-106) And adminestrator, jointly and severally, firmly by these presents sealed with our seal and dated the first day of August A.D. 1836

Whereas the above bound David L. Mitchell hath been appointed Collector of the taxes in the County of White for the year 1836.

Now the Condition of above obligation is such that if the said David L. Mitchell shall well and truly and faithfully Collect and pay over all the taxes arising on school lands in the County of White to the Superentendant of public Education in the state of Tennessee and in all things demean himself according to law - then the above obligation to be null and void else to be and remain in full force and virtue

(signed)

Test
N. Oldham Cl.

David L. Mitchell (seal)
David Snodgrass (seal)
Thomas Robertson (seal)
Robert Love (seal)
James Randols (seal)
John Mitchell (seal)
William Glenn (seal)

Bond for County, Jury, Poor and Bridge Taxes.

Know all men by these presents that we David L. Mitchell, David Snodgrass, Thomas Robertson, Robert Love, James Randols and John Mitchell, William Glenn all of the County of White and state of Tennessee are held and firmly bound unto Thomas Eastland Esquire Chairman of the

County Court of White County or his successors in office in the sum of five thousand dollars Current money for the use of the County of White which payment well and truly to be made and done; we bind ourselves and each and every of our heirs; executors or Administrators, jointly and severally firmly by these presents sealed with our seals and dated the first day of August A.D. 1836.

Where as the above bound David L. Mitchell hath been appointed Collector of the Taxes for the County of white for the year 1836 -

Now if the said David L. Mitchell Collector of the taxes aforesaid shall well and truly and faithfully Collect all the taxes which have been assessed for the benefit of the County of White aforesaid; Towit; the County Tax, Jury Tax, Poor Tax, and Bridge Tax and pay the Monies over to the proper offices in his County and in all things related thereto demean himself according to law - then this obligation to be null and void otherwise be and remain in full force and virtue.

(signed)

Test
N. Oldham Clk.

David L. Mitchell (seal)
David Snodgrass (seal)
Thomas Robertson (seal)
Robert Love (seal)
James Randols (seal)
John Mitchell (seal)
William Glenn (seal)

(P-107) Monday 1st August A.D 1836.

This day the following Revenue Commissioners for the County of White returned upon oath their lists of property and polls in their respective Districts for taxation for the year 1836.

Towit:
Jonathan Farrington, in District Number one -
John Bryan Esq. in District Number two -
Thomas Green, in District Number three -
Matthias Hutson, Esq., in District Number four -
Joshua Mason, Esq., in District Number five -
William Glenn, Esq., in District Number six -
Henry Benton, Esq., in District Number seven -
William Hitchcock, Esq., in District Number eight -
Montgomery C. Dibrell, in District Number nine -
William C. Bounds, in District Number Ten -
Edmund Stamps, in District Number twelve -
David Snodgrass, in District No. 13 -
Elijah Frost, in District No. 14 - and
Willie Steakley, in District Number fifteen.

This day Edward Gleeson administrator of the estate of John W. Gleeson deceased appeared in open Court and offered to give other security for the faithful performance of his adminestration of said estate in discharge of his former securities for said adminestration. Whereupon John Wallis and Hayes Arnold, two of his securities also appeared in open Court in proper person and objected thereto, which objection is by the Court sustained - . And said application overruled - .

For reasons appearing to the satisfaction of the Court, it is ordered that James Mayes Jr. to whom was bound by the Court a certain orphan girl named Creasy Mayes and who afterwards surrendered said girl to this Court and that she was then bound to Joseph Kerr - that he and his security William G. Sims from the performance of their Covenant be released and forever discharged - .

Ordered by Court that John W. Simpson be released from the payment of the Double tax on one tract of land in District No. 7 - . which he had failed to list for taxation for the year 1836. Iss'd

This day John R. Glenn adminestrator of the estate of George W. Hawkins deceased made in open Court a suggestion in writings that the estate of his entestate was insolvent - .

Where upon it is ordered by the Court that the said John R. Glenn adminestrator as aforesaid ensert in the Central Gazette, a news paper published in the town of McMinnville Tennessee an advertisement requiring all persons having claims against the estate of said George W. Hawkins (deceased) to appear and file their Claims according to law on or before the first Monday in November next and also that said John R. Glenn put up a notice at the Court house door in Sparta to the same effect.

Ordered that Court be adjourned untill tomorrow Morning 10 Oclock

John Jett
William Bruster
Jonathan Farrington.

(P-108) Monday Morning 2nd August A.D. 1836

Court met pursuant to adjournment
present the Worshipful,

John Jett) Esquires
William Bruster)
Jonathan Farrington) Justices

Ordered that Court be adjourned untill Court in Course

Test
N. Oldham Clk

John Jett
William Bruster
Jonathan Farrington

(P-109) State of Tennessee

At a County Court began and held for the County of White and state of aforesaid at the Court house in the town of Sparta before the Justices of said Court on the first Monday being the fifth day of September in the year of our Lord one thousand eight hundred and thirty six and of the Independence of the United States the sixty first year

present The worshipful

Thomas Eastland Esq. Chairman
and John Bryan,
Elisha Camron,
David Snodgrass,
Lewis Pettett
William Knowles,
Joshua Mason, } Esquires
William Glenn,
William Hitchcock,
Thomas Green,
Jesse Walling,
John Wallis,
Willie Steakley,
Asa Certain,
Johathan Farrington } Justices
Richard Crowder,
James Allison,
William Bartlett,
William Bruster,
John Pennington,
John Jett, and
John Gillentine

This day Richard Moore produced in open Court two large wolf scalps over the age of four months and proved that they were killed in the County of White whereupon there being present five acting Justices of the peace it is ordered that the same be Certified to the Treasure of the state of Tennessee for payment and that the Sherriff of White County burn said scalps, who being present in Court received said scalps into his Custody and acted accordingly - . Iss'd to D. L. Mitchell -

Ordered by Court that James Seals be released from the payment of the tax on one white poll for the year 1835 he being overcharged that much. And that the sherriff and Collector have a credit with the Trustee of White County in settlement of his accounts.

This day William G. Sims Esquire was appointed Deputy Clerk of White County Court and being in open Court took an oath to support the Constitution of the United States and of the state of Tennessee and the oath of office - . Iss'd

Ordered by Court that order appointing David Whitaker, John Bohannon, William Bartlett, Jacob Hyder Sr. and George Bohanon freeholders a jury of view to lay off and mark a road of the second Class from the forks of the Creek near Henry Bohanons passing up Hyders Creek to Whitakers Mill, thence passing the head of said Creek so as to intersect the road leading up the dry Valley near Goodman Madewells be renewed and report thereof to the next term of this Court.

(P-110) Monday Morning 5th, September 1836

Iss'd

Ordered by Court that Sims McCann be appointed overseer of the road from Littles bridge to the intersection of the old Calf Killer road near Potts school house in place of Henry Rutledge being a road of the third Class and keep the same in repair as the law requires. Iss'd

Ordered by Court that Henry Rutledge be appointed overseer of the road from the ford of the river at Glenns salt well to the entersection of the Joseph Hunter road near the top of the mountain being a road of the second Class and keep the same in repair as the law requires. Iss'd

Ordered by Court that James Walker be appointed Overseer of the road from the ford of the river at Glenns salt well to the Cherry Creek road being a road of the second Class and keep the same in repair as the law requires - .

Ordered by Court that David Snodgrass and Elisha Camron Esquires be appointed to assigns hands to, and designate the bounds of hands between the following overseers of roads to wit:

James Walker, Henry Rutledge and Sims McCann and report thereof to the next term of this Court. Iss'd

Ordered by Court that John H. Carmichael be appointed Overseer of the road from near his house to entersect Rose's Turnpike road on Cumberland Mountain being a road of the second Class and keep the same in repair as the law requires -

And that Elisha Camron Esq. assign a list of hands to work thereon Issd

Ordered by Court that Gabriel P. Cummings be appointed Overseer of the road from Thomas Jackson to the middle of the Dry hollow being a road of the second Class and keep the same in repair as the law requires

And that the same list of hands be assigned him to work thereon which was assigned to Daniel Hollinsworth former overseer thereof -

Ordered by Court that John Jett, Joseph Herd, and William Bruster Esquires be appointed commissioners to settle with John H. Anderson and John W. Roberts adminestrator of William Anderson deceased and report to the present term of this Court.

Ordered by Court that, that part of the Allens ferry road leading from the forks near William Bruster plantation by the way of William Lisks to the peeled Chestnut (known by the name of Lisk road) be reduced from a first Class road and the same is hereby declared and established a second Class road only

And that all the overseers thereof keep the same in repair as such. Iss'd

Ordered by Court that Tidence L. Denton be appointed overseer of the road from John Haltermans to the Kentucky road being a road of the first Class and keep the same in repair as the law requires, And that Lewis Pettett Esq. assign bounds of hands between him and William B. Hutson overseer on the Kentucky road to work thereon. Iss'd

Ordered by Court that Francis Simmons be appointed overseer of the road from the middle of the dry hollow to Rosses road (P-111) being a road of the second Class and keep the same in repair as the law requires and that the same list hands which worked under James Godard former overseer thereof be assigned to work thereof. Iss'd

Ordered by Court that Robert Whitaker be appointed Overseer of the road from the foot of Cumberland Mountain to its enterseotion with the Calfkiller road on the top of the same being a road of the second Class and keep same in repair as the law requires -

And that the same hands that worked under James Madewell former overseer be assigned to work thereon. Iss'd

This day the Commissioners heretofore appointed to lay off and mark a road of the second Class from the mouth of Andrew Bryans lane passing the house of L. R. Wilson to entersect the old river road at Wallis Spring branch returned their report which is by the court received and said road established as a road of the third Class only - . that L. R. Wilson be appointed overseer thereof and keep the same in repair as the law requires and that John Bryan Esq. assign a list of hands to work thereon. Iss'd

Ordered by Court that Anthony Dibrell, Turner Lane Sr., and William Bruster Esq. be appointed Commissioners to settle with Capt. John Walker Guardian to the heirs of Kindal Savage deceased and report thereof to the next term of this Court. Iss'd

Ordered by Court that David Whitaker, John Whitaker, Jacob Hyder, Jesse Rogers and Nathan Bartlett Jr. freeholders be appointed a jury of view to lay off and mark a road of the third Class with as little injury to plantations as possible the nearest and best route from the forks of the little Caney fork Crossing the little Creek passing the house of Joseph D. Hyder thence passing Jonathan Hyders thence up the Creek to Jesse Rogers, thence to Charles Madewells thence to the Burnt Stand on the Walton road and report thereof to the next term of this Court. Iss'd

Ordered by Court that William M. Young, Henderson McFarland and John Bryan be appointed Commissioners to Settle with George Cline adminestrator of Azariah Long deceased, and report thereof to the next term of this Court Iss'd

Ordered by Court that George Cline, John Jett, Laban Wallis, William M. Young, and Jonathan C. Davis surveyor be apponted Commissioners to mark partition and divisions of the real estate of which David H. Mayborn died siezed and possessed according to law between David H. Mayborn and Harmon H. Mayborn heir at law of the said David H. Mayborn deceased on the petition of David H. Mayborn by his guardian David Mitchell and report thereof to the next term of this Court. Iss'd

Ordered by Court that Cason Swindle Jr. be appointed overseer of the road from James McGowens to Franks old ferry being a road of the second Class and keep the same in repair as the law requires and that William Knowles Esq. assign a list of hands to work thereon - .

(P-112) Monday Morning 5th September 1836

This day Joseph Herd, guardian to Susannah Bryan miner heir of John Bryan deceased, returned upon oath a report of guardianship which is ordered to be recorded - .

Ordered by Court that Jesse B. Tusley be appointed a Juror in the room instead of Daniel Walling to view and mark a road from Cane Creek to the Hoodenpile trace - .

The Commissioners this day appointed, to settle with John H. Anderson and John W. Roberts administrator of William Anderson deceased returned upon oath their report which is ordered to be recorded.

Ordered by Court that John H. Anderson and John W. Roberts administrators of William Anderson deceased be allowed the sum of twenty five dollars each for services by them rendered in settling said estate to be by them retained out of the monies of said Estate - . Issd

Ordered by Court that John Jett, Joseph Herd, and William Bruster Esquires Commissioners appointed by this Court to settle with John H. Anderson and John W. Roberts administrators of William Anderson deceased be allowed each the sum of one dollar and fifty cents for one days each rendered in making said settlement to be paid by said administrators out of the said estate.

This day the death of Eliza Anderson late of the County of White was suggested and that she died intested, whereupon John H. Anderson was appointed administrator of all and singular, the goods and chattles, rights and credits of the said Eliza Anderson deceased and in open Court took the oath perscribed by law and with Jesse Lineon and John Jett entered into and acknowledged bond in the sum of Two thousand dollars conditioned as the law requires.

This day Caleb Mason was appointed guardian to Nancy Glenn, Allen Glenn, Caleb Glenn, Margarett Glenn and James Glenn miner heirs of Alexander Glenn Deceased and with Robert Mason entered into and acknowledge bond in the sum of one hundred dollars conditioned as the law requires.

This day was produced in open Court a writing purporting to be the last will and testament of Thomas Curtis deceased late of the County of White, and the due execution and publication thereof as the last will and testament of the said Thomas Curtis deceased was proven in open Court by the oath of Mary Kemp the other subscribing witness thereto for the same purpose and that the said Thomas Curtis was at the date of the execution and publication thereof of sound and desposing mind and memory whereupon it is Ordered to be recorded - . Iss'd

Ordered by Court that William Anderson be appointed overseer of the road from Ozias Dentons to William Rickmans on Ross's [illegible] being a road of the second Class and keep the same in repair as the law requires and that the following bounds of hands (P-113) To wit: Anderson & Boy, Robert Melloway, Willie Tindale, James W. Copeland, John M. Sorrell, and Eli Brown be assigned to work there on.

This day John H. Anderson guardian to Matthias Anderson, Mary Anderson and Reubin Anderson minor heirs of William Anderson deceased exhibited in open Court his account as guardian against his said wards to wit: against Matthias Anderson for boarding, washing &c one hundred and [illegible] dollars seventy cents - against Mary Anderson Three hundred and Twenty one dollars seventy cents and against Reubin Anderson the sum of two hundred and seventy one dollars four cents which is allowed by the Court and ordered to be recorded. Iss'd

Ordered by Court that the following boundry of hands be assigned to work on that portion of the Sims road from William Brusters plantation to George W. Easthams old place of which William McGarrah is now Overseer to wit, Larkin Yates, Andrew J. Sims, Eli Stover, Joseph W. Little, James Pirtle, Thomas Prince, Jonathan Davis, Maxfield Davis, Isaac Pirtle, William Earls. Iss'd

Jesse Vermillion, Jacob Pirtle and Lewis Sims a black man.

Ordered by Court that the following boundary of hands be assigned to work on that portion of the sims road from George W. Eastham old place to the peeled Chestnut of which Aaron Hutchings is now overseer to wit.

Washington Irwin, Lackart Irwin, Joseph Bozarth, John Jones, Webster Hutchings, Berney Harlow, John Harlow, Elijah Russell, Zachariah Russell, William Russell, James Bozarth, Bird Bozarth, Robert Towndsend, William Cantrell and William Sullivan - .

Ordered by Court that the following boundary of hands be assigned to work on that portion of the Allens ferry road known by the name of Lisk road, of which William Baker is overseer the same having been reduced to a second class road to wit:

Thomas Jones, John Jones, James Jones, Henry Atkinson, James Dildine, Richard Baker, Dabney C. Baker, William Frisby, John Acuff and Jesse Sullivan.

Ordered by Court that the following boundary of hands be assigned to work on that portion of the Allens ferry road (Known by the name of the Lisk) of which William Lisk is overseer the same having been reduced to a second class road to wit: Lee R. Taylor, Jarrett C. Puckett, Jonathan Prince, William Taylor, Lewis Taylor a black man, George, a slave, Jacob a slave Peter, a slave Alfred Shaw, Edward Lisk and John Cooley

Ordered by Court that the following boundary of hands be assigned to work on that portion of the Carthage road of which Thomas Clouse is now overseer to wit:

John Cantrell, Smith Cantrell, William Farley, Ephraim Cook, Hiram Cook and Charles Cook - . Issd

Ordered by Court that Henry Crawley be appointed overseer of the road from Ross's old ferry to Warren County line being a (Public) road of the second Class and Keep the same in repair as the law requires with the same list of hands to work thereon that worked under Andrew McElroy former overseer thereof. Issd

The Commissioners heretofore appointed to lay off and mark a road of the second Class from Cane Creek near Mrs. Taylor, thence up the mountain between Cain Creek and the dry fork, thence Striking the Hoodenpile trace where it crosses pine creek returned their report which is received and said road is established a road of the second Class.

And that Willie B. Haston be appointed overseer thereof and to open and keep the same in repair as the law requires and that Willie Steakley and John Gillentine Esquires assign a list of hands to work thereon -

Ordered by Court that Asa Certain be appointed a juror in the room and stead of Thomas Jones to examine and report with others at to straitening the Sims road at and beyond Eli Sims Dwelling house. Iss'd

Ordered by Court that Charles Denny be appointed Overseer of the road from Thomas Moore's old ferry on Caney fork to the fork of Brush Creek being a road of the second Class and open and keep the same in repair as the law requires and that Willie Steakley and John Gillentine Esq. assign a list of hands to work thereon. Iss'd

Ordered by Court that the order made heretofore appointing James Hudgins, Alexander Lowery Sr. Henry Lance, Samuel Lance and Nathaniel C. Davis freeholders a Jury of view to lay off and mark a road of the first Class from Col. Alexander Lowery's passing by the dwelling house of Doct. Spring and to entersect the turnpike road again near the place where the old road entersects the same be renewed and report thereof to the next term of this Court Iss'd

Ordered by Court that Elijah Burden be appointed overseer of the road from Pleasant Wallers to Lowery's old place on the Pikeville road being a road of the first Class and keep the same in repair as the law requires and that John Bryan Esquire assign a list of hands to work thereon - . Iss'd

Ordered by Court that the road as examined, straitened and marked by Commissioners appointed at the last term of this Court, leaving the present road near the dwelling house of Eli Sims, and entersecting the road again about three fourths of a mile beyond his house be established, and that Eli Sims Esquire open the same according to law as a first Class road at his own proper Cost and Charges.

This day the following persons were reported to this Court for not having listed their property and polls for taxation in White County for the year 1836 who for such failure are subject to a double for said year -
To wit: In District No 1. Thomas Quillon, one hundred and tweenty and one half acres of Warrented land of the Value of three hundred dollars

And Matthias Nichols one white poll

In District (P-115) No 9 John Smith one White poll - and fifty acres deeded land of the Value of four hundred dollars - .

William Smith one White poll - .

In District No. 15 Thomas Wilson one white poll Jesse Turley one hundred acres of school land of the value of one hundred and fifty dollars

Thomas H. King one hundred acres school land of the value of twenty five dollars.

In District No. 6 James Eastham forty acres warrented land of the value of forty dollars and also one hundred and Ninety Nine acres of school land of the Value of one hundred and sixty dollars - .

It is considered by the Court and so ordered that each of the above persons do report from the double tax on their property and polls for said year 1836 be released and discharged.

Whereas at some former term of this Court Louisa Jane Ledbetter alias Eliza Ledbetter an orphan girl, was bound by this Court to a certain Joseph Anderson by Indenture, and it appearing to the satisfaction of this Court that the mother of the said orphan girl has entermarried with a Certain Samuel Crabtree of Warren County Certified to be of reputable Character, the being desirous to have said Child and to maintain it and rais it themselves, and the said Joseph Anderson being willing that said Child should be permitted to return to her Mother and it is therefore considered by the Court and so ordered that the said Indenture be cancelled and rescinded out the said Joseph Anderson from performing the contract therein be released and forever discharged.

Ordered that Court be Adjourned untill tomorrow Morning 10 Oclock

Jonathan Farrington
John Bryan
John Jett

Tuesday morning 6th Sept. 1836 Court met Pursuant to adjournment Present the Worshipful

John Jett
John Bryan
Jonathan Farrington) Esquire Justices

This day John H. Anderson guardian to the minor heirs of William Anderson deceased returned upon oath a report of his guardianship which is ordered to be recorded.

Ordered that Court be adjourned untill Court in Course

Test
N. Oldham
Clerk

Jonathan Farrington
John Bryan
John Jett

(P-116) Monday the 3rd October 1836
State of Tennessee

At a County began and held for the County of White at the court house in the town of Sparta before the Justices of said Court on the first Monday being the third day of October in the year of our Lord one thousand eight hundred and thirty six and of the Independence of the United States the sixty first year.

Present The worshipful

Thomas Eastland Esq. Chairman

David Snodgras,	
John Bryan,	
William Hitchcock,	
Richard Crowder,	
Jonathan Farrington,	
William Knowles,	
Edmund Stamps,	Esquires
Jesse Walling,	
James Allison,	
Asa Certain,	
Joshua Mason,	
Matthias Hutson,	
William C. Bounds,	Justices
John Wallis,	
Lewis Pettett,	
John Gillentine,	
Willie Steakley,	
William Bruster,	
and Thos. Green	

This day Nicholas Oldham Clerk of White County Court produced and read in open Court the following reports to wit;

Nashville 22 Sept. 1836. No. 34 $335.79

Received of Nicholas Oldham three hundred and thirty five dollars and 79 Cents Credited to him by No. 34 and due on account of Revinue by him Collected as Clerk of White County Court 1st. of May to the 1st. September 1836

Signed

Duplicates

Millier Francis

Treasure of Tennessee Comptrollers office Nashville Tenn 22nd September 1836 Received of Nicholas Oldham a Duplicate of the Tax list of White County for the year 1836.

Daniel Graham
Comptroller of the Treasur

Comptroller office Nashville Tenn. 22nd Sept. 1836

Received of David L. Mitchell his bond as Sherriff of White County for the due Collection of the public tax of said County for the present year dated 1st. August 1836

Daniel Graham
Comptroller of the Treasure

Nashville 22nd Sept. 1836

Rec'd of N. Oldham Esq. Clerk of the County Court of White County seventy three 12/100 dollars monies Collected by him on Tipling house License under the act of 1835 on a/c of the Common school fund for which Duplicate receipts are given

Robert H. McEwin
Super'd of public
enstruction

(P-117)

Monday 3rd October A.D. 1836

Nashville 22nd Sept. 1836
Received of the Clerk of the County Court of White County the bond of David L. Mitchell of the Collection of Taxes on school lands and paying them over as the law directs

R. H. McEwin
Supt. of Public Instruction

Received of Nicholas Oldham Clerk of the County Court of White County an abstract Statement of the County Tax, Jury tax and Bridge tax for the year 1836 Amounting to the sum of Fourteen hundred and seventy nine dollars twenty eight Cents and five Mills which the Sherriff of said County is bound for by law.

This 15th day of Sept. 1836

Robert Cox Trustee
of White County

Received of Nicholas Oldham Clerk of the County Court of White County an abstract Statement of the poor tax in said County for the year 1836 Amounting to the sum of six hundred and seventy three Dollars seventy six cents and seven mills which the Sherriff of White County is bound for by law.

This 15th day of September 1836

John Jett
Treasure

This day David L. Mitchell Esq. Sherriff of White County produced in open Court a Certificate of the election of Robert Smith as constable in White County in District No. 3 to fill the vacancy in said District occasioned by the Resegnation of William Fryer -

And the said Robert Smith also appeared in open Court and took an oath to support the Constitution of the United States and of the State of Tennessee and the several oaths prescribed by law and together with John Smith and John Wallis entered into and acknowledged bond in the sum of one thousand dollars conditioned as the law requires.

This day David L. Mitchell Esq. Sherriff of White County produced in open Court a certificate of the election of Elam Sherrell as Constable in White County in District No. 8 to fill the vacancy in said District occasioned by the resignation of Zachariah Hitchcock.

And the said Elam Sharrell also appeared in open Court and took an oath to support the Constitution of the United States and of the State of Tennessee and the several oaths prescribed by law and together with Leonard Saylers and Jose C. Dew entered into and acknowledged bond in the sum of One thousand Dollars Conditioned as the law requires

Ordered by Court that the further time of four mounts be given to Joseph Hunter to open and put in Complete repair that portion of the road of which he is Overseer - Iss'd

Ordered by Court that William Farley be appointed Overseer of the road from Snodgrasses Mill to the mile post at the corner of William Wisdoms field being a road of the second Class and keep the same in repair as the (P-118) law requires with the same hands that worked under Patterson E. McBride former Overseer thereof.

Richard Porterfield
to (Cert) } Deed of Conveyance 10 acres land
Nathan Pierce

The due execution of the within Deed of Conveyance was this day proven in open Court by the oath of John Robertson one of the subscribing witnesses thereto for the purposes and things therein mentioned and who made oath at the same time that Alexander Steele the other subscribing witness thereto did subscribe his name thereto as witness in his presence and that he now resides beyond the limits of the State of Tennessee which is ordered to be recorded and certified for Regestration

Richard Porterfield
to (Cert) } Deed conveyance 4 140/160 acres Land
Nathan Pierce

The due execution of the within Deed of Conveyance was this day proven in open Court by the oath of John Robertson one of the subscribing witnesses thereto for the purposes and things therein mentioned and at the same time made oath that Andrew Steel the other Subscribing witness thereto did subscribe his name thereto as witness in his presence and that he now resides beyond the limits of the state of Tennessee which is ordered to be recorded and Certified for Regestration. Iss'd

Ordered by Court that Tennessee Hooper be appointed Overseer of the road from the peeled Chestnut to the Knotty oak being a road of the first Class and keep the same in repair as the law requires withe the same hands that worked under Samuel Hooper former Overseer thereof. Iss'd

Ordered by Court that Daniel Bartlett be appointed Overseer of the road from Post Oak Creek to Hunters Mill being a road of the second Class and keep same in repair as the law requires and that the same hands that worked under David Nicholas former Overseer thereof be assigned to work thereon. Iss'd

Ordered by Court that Joseph McDaniel be appointed overseer of the road from Richard Crowders to the forks of the road being a road of the second Class and keep the same in repair as the law requires and that the same bounds of hands be assigned that worked under Robert Glenn Jr. former Overseer thereof. Iss'd

Ordered by Court that Robert Anderson Jr. be appointed over seer of the road from the west end of the bridge at the Harriett Iron Works to the widow Smiths gate being a road of the first Class and keep the same in repair as the law requires and that the same boundary of hands be assigned him that worked under Robert Smith former Overseer thereof. Iss'd

Ordered by Court that Joseph Parris be appointed Overseer of the road from falling Water to Jackson County line (P-119) being a road of the second Class and keep the same in repair as the law requires and that the same hands that worked under William C. Bounds former Overseer be assigned to work thereon - . Iss'd

Ordered by Court that William White be appointed Overseer of the road from the town of Sparta to the ford of the river below Andersons old saltwell being a road of the second Class and keep the same in repair as the law requires and that the same list of hands that worked under John Kitchenside former overseer thereof be assigned to work thereon. Iss'd

Ordered by Court that James Kelly be appointed Overseer of the road (from) in the place of Frederick Lyda so far as where Cooper was overseer formerly and keep the same in repair as the law requires being a road of the first Class and list of hands that worked under F. Lyda late Overseer thereof be assigned to work thereon. Iss'd

Ordered by Court that Daniel Dale be appointed Overseer of the road from the Ten mile post to the foot of the Mountain being a road of the first Class and keep the same in repair as the law requires and that the same list of hands be assigned that worked under Solomon Reese former Overseer thereof - . Iss'd

Ordered by Court that John Kitchenside be appointed Overseer of the road from the corner of his field along the road intersecting the Sparta road passing the Deep ford being a road of the 3rd Class and keep the same in repair as the law requires and that David Snodgrass and William Little Esquires assign a list of hands to work thereon. Iss'd

Ordered by Court that Edward V. Pollard be appointed Overseer of the road from Thomas Robertsons to the mouth of Townsend Mill Creek being a road of the second Class and keep the same in repair as the law requires and that William Knowles and Joshua Mason Esquires assign a boundary of hands to work thereon. - Iss'd

Ordered by Court that Thomas Stipes be appointed Overseer of the road from the fork of the road at Cain Creek above Swains to Denny's old plantation being a road of the second Class and keep the same in repair as the law requires and that the same list of hands be assigned him that worked under Robert Gamble former overseer thereof Iss'd

Ordered by Court that Baler Holder be appointed Overseer of the road from Hills Branch to Jesse Walling being a road of the first Class and keep the same in repair as the law requires and that the same list of hands be assigned him that worked under the former Overseer thereof. Iss'd

Ordered by Court that William Nash be appointed Overseer of the road from Joseph Coplers to the entersection of the road with the Kentucky road being a road of the first Class and keep the same in repair as the law requires and John Pennington and William C. Bounds Esq. assign a boundary of hands to work thereon.

(P-120) Monday 3rd. day of October A.D. 1836

Iss'd

Ordered by Court that Spencer Holder be appointed Overseer of the road from Lewis Philips to John Haltermans being a road of the first Class and keep the same in repair as the law requires and that the same list of hands be assigned him that worked under the former Overseer thereof. Iss'd

Ordered by Court that George Henry be appointed Overseer of the road from the mouth of mill Creek to the 19 mile post being a road of the second Class and keep the same in repair as the law requires and that Edmund Stamps and Elisha Cunron Esquires assign a list of hands to work thereon. Iss'd

Ordered by Court that the road as laid off and marked by Commissioners appointed at the last term of this Court of the second Class from the forks of the Creek near Henry Bohanons passing up Hyders Creek to Whitakers mill, thence passing the head of said Creek so as to entersect the road leading up the Dry Valley near Goodman Madewells be and the same is established a road of the second Class and that Matthias Welch be appointed Overseer thereof to open and keep the same in repair as the law requires and that William Bartlett and William C. Bounds Esquires assign a list of hands to work thereon. Iss'd

Ordered by Court that Benjamin McLain be appointed Overseer of the road from the two mile post to the four mile post on the Carthage road being a road of the first Class and keep the same in repair as the law requires and that the same list of hands that worked under Lewis Turner former Overseer thereof be assigned to work thereon. Iss'd

Ordered by Court that Samuel Miller be appointed Overseer of the road from Frank Johnsons old place to John Millers being a road of the second Class and keep the same in repair as the law requires and that John Wallis and John Bryan Esquires assign a list of hands to work thereon. Iss'd

Ordered by Court that John Sorrells be assigned to work on that portion of the road of which Lewis Philips is overseer Iss'd

Ordered by Court that Limas B. Farris be appointed Overseer of the road from the forks of the Kentucky road to the house of William Knowles Esq. being a road of the first Class and keep the same in repair as the law requires and that the same hands that work under Joseph Clark Jr., former Overseer thereof be assigned to work thereon. Issd.

Ordered by Court that Joseph G. Mitchell be appointed Overseer of the road from Capt. Whites to the mouth of Cane Creek being a road of the second Class and keep the same in repair as the law requires and that the same hands that worked under Barnett K. Mitchell former overseer thereof be assigned to work thereon.

This day John H. Anderson Esq. Entry Taken in White County appeared in open Court and resigned his office which is ordered to be recorded.

(P-121) Monday 3rd day of October A. D. 1836.

Ordered by the Court that the road leading from William Taylors to Pine Creek reduced from a second to a third Class road.

Ordered by Court that William B. Cummings and William Anderson be appointed Commissioners to settle with John Witt administrator of the estate of Dimpsy Pinner deceased and report thereof to the next term of this Court.

This day Mary Jane Carroll was appointed guardian to Samuel Lafayette Carroll a minor heir of William Carroll deceased who being present in open Court and together with Anthony Dibrell and William Williams entered into and acknowledged bond in the sum of Fifteen hundred Dollars conditioned as the law requires. Iss'd.

Ordered by Court that John Wallis, Simon Doyle, Robert Love, John Felton and William Lewis freeholdrs be appointed a Jury of view to lay off and mark a road of the third Class from Union meeting house to Simon R. Doyles Mill and report thereof to the next term of this Court. Iss'd.

It appearing to the satisfaction of the Court that Henderson McFarlan late a constable of White County attended on the Jury thirteen days at August term 1828 of White Circuit Court and also thirteen days at Febuary term 1829 of said Court each time in the case the State against Robert E. Lowery making in all twenty six days and that he has never received any compensation thereof.

It is therefore considered by the Court and so ordered that he be allowed the sum of Twenty six dollars to be paid by the Trustee of White County out of any monies in his hands not otherwise appropriated.

This day the Commissioners heretofore appointed to settle with John Walker guardian to the heirs of Kindale Savage deceased returned their report upon oath which is by the Court received and confirmed in all its parts and ordered to be recorded.

Ordered by Court that the estate of Dempsy Pinner deceased be released from the payment of the taxes on 140 acres of land for the year 1834 being overcharged that much. (Iss'd)

This day John Parker administrator of Joseph Parker returned upon oath an Inventory of the estate of the deceased which is ordered to be recorded.

This day John Parker administrator of Joseph Parker deceased returned upon oath a list of sales of the property of the deceased which is ordered to be recorded.

This day George Griffeth was appointed guardian to Rebecca Roberts, George Henry Roberts, Joseph Roberts and Mary Ann Roberts minor heirs of William Roberts deceased and with Thomas Snodgrass and John Parker entered into and acknowledged bond in the sum of one thousand dollars conditioned as the law requires.

(P-122) Iss'd.

Ordered by Court that John Parker be appointed Overseer of the road from James H. Pass's to Matthew Englands being a road of the second Class and keep the same in repair as the law requires and that John Pennington Esq. assign a list of hands to work thereon.

Iss'd. This day Joel Mooneyham produced in open Court three wolf scalps under the age of four months and proved that they were killed in the county of White whereupon there being present five acting Justices of the peace for said County it is ordered that they be certified to the Treasure of Tennessee for payment and that the Sherriff of White County burn said scalps who being present in the Court received said scalps into his Custody and acted accordingly.

Iss'd. Ordered by Court that the following persons be allowed the following sums of money in the case of the state of Tennessee against Robert Dudley on an Indictment for malicias mischief in White Circuit Court which has been examined by the attorney General and by him certified to be correct and properly chargable to the County of White To wit:

William R. Tucker Jailor the sum of $59.50/100 William G. Sims Clerk $1.93¾ Justices Sims Dearing and David Snodgrass $0.50 -. Constable Joseph England $1.25 Witness Henry Nash $2.00 - Witness John Weaver $1.75 and Witness Jeremiah Williams $1.50/100 to be paid by the Trustee of White County out of any monies not otherwise appropriated.

Iss'd. Ordered by Court that William Glenn (Merchant) be allowed the sum of Thirty Dollars for Record books furnished by him for the Circuit Court of White County to be paid by the Sherriff of White County out of the Taxes of the year 1836.

The Court proceeded to appoint an Entry taken for the County of White to fill the vacancy occasioned by the resegnation of John H. Anderson Esq. and to that office do appoint Jacob A. Lane Esq. who being present in open Court took an oath to support the Constitution of the United States and of the State of Tennessee and the oath of office and together with William Bruster, Nicholas Oldham, and William G. Sims entered into and acknowledged bond in the sum of Ten thousand dollars conditioned as the law requires.

Iss'd. Ordered by Court that William Knowles, and Joshua Mason Esquires be appointed to divide and apportion list of hands between Harmon

Little and Joseph McDaniels Overseer of the road and report to the next term of this Court.

This day Susannah Duncan adminestrix of the estate of William Duncan deceased returned upon oath a list of sales of the property of the deceased which is ordered to be recorded.

Ordered by Court that William Erwin be released from the payment of the tax on One White poll for the year 1836 he being over age.

(P-123) This day Anthony Dibrell Esq. was appointed adminestrator Debonis - non - of all and singular, the goods and chattles rights and credits of Thomas Duncan deceased late of the County of White who took the oath prescribed by law and together with Jacob A. Lane and Walker Bennett entered into and acknowledged bond in the sum of One thousand dollars conditioned as the law requires.

Iss'd. Ordered by Court that James Williams, David L. Mitchell, Hayes Arnold, Joseph Herd and Robert Anderson Jr. freeholders be appointed a jury of view to lay off and mark a road of the third Class from the residence of James William to a meeting house on the road from Sparta to Gum Spring where Mrs Webb formerly lived and report thereof to the next term of this Court.

Iss'd. Ordered by Court that the order made at the last term of this Court appointed David Whitaker, Robert Whitaker, Jacob Hyder, Jesse Rogers and Joseph D. Hyder freeholders be appointed a Jury of view to lay off and mark a road of the third Class with as little injury to plantations as possible, the nearest and best route from the forks of the little Caney fork crossing the little Creek passing the house of Joseph D. Hyder, thence passing Jonathan Hyders thence up the creek to Jesse Rogers, thence to Charles Madewells thence to the Burnt Stand on the Walton road be renewed and report to the next term of this Court.

On the humble petition of Earl J. Cook and for reasons appearing to the satisfaction of the Court he is permitted to erect and establish water machinary on the main Caney fork in the horse shoe bend.

Ordered by Court that Anthony Dibrell guardian be allowed a credit in the settlement of his account for $141.50 for the following minor heirs of Matthias Anderson deceased, for boarding, washing, lodging &c. of Elizabeth Anderson from the 15th March 1831 to 1st of April 1832 Thomas Andeson the same from 15 March 1831 up to the 24th February 1834 William Anderson the same from 15th March 1831 up to 1st of May 1832 for Curtis Anderson from 15th March 1831 up to 1st April 1832 and for Nancy Anderson from the 15th March 1831 up to 1st February 1833, to be charged to said wards respectively in proportion to the time they have been severally supported &c.

This day Nathaniel C. Hopkins aged thirteen years in December last (1835) was bound to Robert B. Glenn to serve him after the manner of an apprentice to learn the Black Smith trade and for the faithful performance of his covenant with William Glenn entered into and acknowledged bond conditioned as the law requires.

Iss'd. Ordered by Court that the sherriff of White County at the next term of this Court bring the bodies of Mack George; Henry George, Patsy George and Caswell George minor and paupers to be dealt by according to law on the Information of Matthias Hutson Esquire.

(P-124) Iss'd. Ordered by Court that the order made at the last term of this Court appointing George Cline, William C. Brittain, Laban Wallis, William M. Young and Jonathan C. Davis surveyor Commissioners to make partition and division of the real estate of which David H. Mayborn late of the County of White died, siezed, and possessed according to law between David H. Mayborn and Harmon H. Mayborn heirs at law of the said David H. Mayborn deceased be renewed, and report thereon to the next term of this Court.

Iss'd. Ordered by Court that the lot of road of which Jacob Keener is now Overseer be extended from the Northern end of said road from the house of William L. Mitchell to the ford of the river below Dales Mill being a road of the first Class and keep the same in repair as the law requires with the hands already assigned him.

This day Thomas Meek was appointed guardian to Nancy Isham and Evaline Meek minors and heirs of James Isham deceased and together with Daniel Richards/and Edward Anderson entered into and acknowledged bond in the sum of Eight hundred dollars conditioned as the law requires.

Ordered by Court that William Burden be taken from the milk sick hills, and be assigned to work on that portion of the Pikeville road of which Elijah Burden is overseer.

This day Thomas Green Esq. to whom at a former term of this Court was bound an orphan boy named Ammon L. Kerr to serve as an apprentice appeared in open Court with said apprentice and for reasons appearing to the satisfaction of the Court the said Thomas Green; and his security from the preformance of their Covenant are released and forever discharged and the said orphan boy Ammon L. Kerr surrendered to the Court to be further dealt by according to law.

This day Ammon L. Kerr aged four years the 19th day of April 1836 an orphan boy was bound to Joseph Herd to serve him after the manner of an apprentice untill he arrives at the age of twenty one years and for the faithful performance of his Covenant intered into and acknowledged bond conditioned as the law requires.

The Revenue Commissioners of the County of White make the following report of property and polls in the County of White the same having not been returned within the time limited by law subject to double tax for the year 1836 To Wit:

In District No. 2 William Kale one white poll - No. 3 James Melvin one white poll - Dist. No. 4 Joseph Dunn 124 acres deeded land worth $400 - and one white poll - James Anderson 20 acres deeded land worth $25 -. Stephen Holland 33½ acres school land worth $300. - Dist. No. 5 George Pirtle one white poll - . Dist. No. 6 William Irwin 301 acres school land worth $300. - Thomas Williams one white poll - one slave worth $500 -. Dist. No. 7 John W. Simpson 200 acres school land worth

$50 - . Dist. No. 8 William Goodwin one white poll -

(P-125) In Dist. No. 9 Benjamin Mackey one white poll and 200 acres deeded land worth $300- In Dist. No. 10 The heirs of Enoch Murphree 100 acres school land valued at $50 - In Dist. No. 15 Larkin Tally 100 acres school land worth $50 - Isaac Drake 55 acres deeded land worth $25 - John White Sr. one acres deeded land worth $5.00 which for reasons appearing to the satisfaction of the Court. It is considered and so ordered that they severally be released and discharged from the payment of the double taxes - and only be charged with a single tax for the year 1836.

For reasons appearing to the satisfaction of the Court which are disclosed in the affidavit of Mary J. Correll who is adminestratix of William Correll deceased that she in making out her two Inventories of the effects &c. of the deceased has included in the second Inventory by mistake the same notes which are set forth in her first Inventory on the same persons and not other and different notes.

It is therefore considered by the Court and so ordered that said mistake be corrected so as that said adminestratix be charged with said notes Once - instead of twice.

Iss'd. This day Patience Roberts widow and relect of William Roberts deceased filed her petition for dower out of the estate of her deceased husband and George Griffith guardian to the minor heirs of the said William Roberts deceased accepts the notice thereof and agrees and it is so ordered by the Court that the sherriff of White County summons Five Citizens freeholders of the County of White related neither by consanguinity or affinity to either of the above named persons to go on the premises of which the said William Roberts died seized and possessed and according to law lay off her dower out of said Lands mentioned in said petition so as to include the late residence of her deceased husband distinctly setting it apart by butts and bounds and in all things act according to law and make report thereof to the next term of this Court.

This day George Bohanon Adminestrator with the will annexed of Joseph Henry deceased returned upon oath an Inventory of the estate of the deceased which is ordered to be recorded.

This day George Bohanon adminestrator with the will annexed of Joseph Henry deceased returned upon oath a list of sales of the estate of the deceased which is ordered to be recorded.

This day the Clerk of this Court exhibited in open Court certain records of this Court commincing with the orgainsation thereof up to the November term 1811 and it appearing to the satisfaction of the Court there being present two thirds of the acting Justices of the peace for said County that said records are in a bad state of preservation and are in a condition likely to be lost. It is therefore considered by the Court expedient and proper and so ordered that the records above mentioned be transcribed according to law into a well bound book in a fair legible hand writing and therefore do appoint Nicholas Oldham Clerk of this Court to transcribe said (P-126) Records who being present in open Court accepts said appointment &c.

Be it remembered that this day appeared in open Court Mary Curtis relect and widow of Thomas Curtis late of White County deceased a Revolutionary pensioner and also appeared in open Court James Allison and Barnett Kemp witnesses to the Court known upon oath proved to the Satisfaction of the Court that Mary Curtis is the widow of the said Thomas Curtis deceased and that her husband was the identical person named in the pension Certificate here exhibited in open Court all of which is recorded and ordered to be Certified under the seal of this Court.

Mary Curtis }
to } Letter of Attorney
Robert Gibson }

The due execution of the above letter of Attorney was this day acknowledged in open Court by Mary Curtis the grantor for the purposes therein contained which ordered to be recorded and certified under the seal of this Court.

Andrew Welch, Adminestrator of Reason Rickets deceased late a Revolutionary soldier in the army of the United States filed affidavit upon oath for balance of pay and bounty due said Ricketts deceased and also appeared in open Court Jesse England to the Court known and proved to the satisfaction of the Court that Andrew Welch, adminestrator as aforesaid in this case is entitled to full credit whereupon it is ordered by the Court that the same be so certified under the seal of this Court.

Ordered by Court that Court be adjourned untill tomorrow Morning 10 O'clock

Thos. Eastland
David Snodgrass
John Wallis

Court met pursuant to adjournment Tuesday Morning 4th Oct. 1836 Present the Worshipful

Thomas Eastland
David Snodgrass
& Jno Wallis Esq.

Ordered that Court be adjourned untill Court in Course

Test.
N. Oldham, Clerk

Thos. Eastland
David Snodgrass
John Gillentine

(P-127) State of Tennessee

At a County Court began and held for the County of White at the Court house in the town of Sparta before the Justices of our said Court on the first Monday being the seventh day of November in the year of our Lord One Thousand eight hundred and thirty six and of the Independance of the United States the sixty first year

Present the worshipful

Thomas Eastland Esq. Chairman
John Bryan, Matthias Hutson, }
David Snodgrass, Elisha Camron, }

Jonathan Farrington, William Bruster; Elijah Frost, William Knowles; Jesse Walling; Joshua Mason; John Gillentine; Richard Crowder; William Bartlett, James Allison; Thomas Green; Lewis Pettett; and John Jett.) Esquires) Justices

It appearing to the satisfaction of the Court that Nicholas Oldham Clerk of White County Court in produsing his receipts which he was bound by law to do these was a mistake in the Comptrollers receipt and the Court then granted him the opportunity of having said receipt corrected and the said Clerk this day produced in open Court a receipt of the Comptroller of even date with the other which is ordered by the Court to be recorded <u>Nunk protunk</u> which is as follows

Comptrollers office

22nd Sept. 1836

Received of Nicholas Oldham Clerk of the County Court of White County the bond of David L. Mitchell Sherriff and Collector of the public taxes for said County for the present year dated August 1st 1836

Daniel Graham Comptroller
Of the Treasure"

Issd. Ordered by Court that Canady Rigsby be appointed Overseer of the road from Samuel Turney to ceder creek being a road of the first Class and keep the same in repair as the law requires and that the same bounds of hands be assigned him that worked under William Glenn former Overseer thereof -

Iss'd. Ordered by Court that Thomas Leek be appointed Overseer of the road from the Knotty oak to Allens ferry being a road of the first Class and keep the same in repair as the law requires and that the same boundary of hands be assigned, that was assign to Samuel Allen late Overseer thereof.

Iss'd. Ordered by Court that part of the Pikeville road from Pleasan Wallers to the foot of the Mountain be reduced to a second Class road only and that James Malloy be appointed Overseer on said road from Mrs Dales to the middle of the river at the ford below Dales Mill and keep the same in repair as the law requires and that John Gillentine and Willie Steakley, Esquire apportion bounds of hands between James Malloy, Jacob Keener and Daniel Dales Overseers.

(P-128) Monday the 7th day of November A.D. 1836

Ordered by Court that John Bussell Sr. be released from the payment of the tax on One White poll for the year 1836 he being over age.

Iss'd. Ordered by Court that Samuel Parker be released from the payment of the tax on one White poll for the year 1836 he being under age.

Ordered by the Court that the road leading from Greenville Templetons to be discontinued and entirely abolished.

Ordered by Court that the following hands agreeably to report of Commissioners be assigned in addition to his former list to Harman Little Overseer To Wit.

William D. Glenn and
Greenville Templeton

Iss'd. Ordered by Court unanimously that Nicholas Oldham Clerk of White County Court be allowed the sum of twenty dollars as compensation for making out and recording the tax list of White County for the year 1836 to be paid by the Sherriff of White County out of the taxes of said year.

Iss'd. Ordered by Court that Nicholas Oldham Clerk of White County Court be allowed the sum of Nine dollars for a blank record Book for the use of the said Court labelled

"Transcribed records 1806 to 1811 W. C."

to be paid by the Sherriff of White out of the taxes of the year 1836.

This day David L. Mitchell Esquires Sherriff of White County appeared in open Court and appointed Jabez G. Mitchell Deputy sherriff in said County who being present in open Court took an oath to support the Constitution of the United States and of the State of Tennessee together with the several oaths prescribed by law and thereupon entered upon the discharge of the duties of his office.

This day John R. Glenn Administrator of the estate of George W. Hawkins deceased exhibited in open Court his account against said estate for services rendered and money expended amounting to the sum of Sixty two dollars fifty four and three fourth cents which is by the Court allowed said adminestrator to be by him retained by him out of said estate; and it is ordered to be recorded.

Iss'd. Ordered by Court that Richard Crowder, Joshua Mason and Eli Sims Esquires be appointed Commissioners to make distribution of the effects of the estate of George W. Hawkins deceased between the credetors of the deceased in a rateable proportion that one claim bears to another agreeably to act of the general assembly and that said commissioners also make settlement with John R. Glenn, Adminestrators of said estate and report thereof to the next term of this Court.

Iss'd. Ordered by Court that Andrew K. Parker be appointed Overseer of the road from the top of the hill on the south side of the Muddy branch to the intersection of the road near brush Creek being part of the same on which Charles Denny was appointed Overseer and to open and keep his part repaired as the law requires and that John Gillentine and Willie Steakley Esquire apportion list of hands between them.

(P-129) Iss'd. Ordered by Court that Thomas Green and Jesse Walling Esquires apportion the hands between Baler Holder, John W. Simpson and James Roberts, Overseers having due regard to the dignety of the roads on which they are respectively Overseers.

Iss'd. Ordered by Court that George Bohanon be appointed Overseer of the road from the forks of the road at William Hunters mill leading up the river to John Bohanons being a road of the second Class and keep the same in repair as the law requires and that the same hands that worked under William Buckner former Overseer thereof be assigned to work thereon.

This day Henry George an orphan boy aged fourteen years bound to William B. Hutson to serve him after the manner of an apprentice untill he attains the age of twenty one years and for the faithful performance of his Covenant entered into and acknowledged bond with Matthias Hutson and Abel Hutson his securities Conditioned as the law requires.

Iss'd. It is ordered by the Court that the order requiring the sherriff of White County to bring Mack George, Patsy George and Caswell George orphans and paupers into Court to be dealt by according to law be renewed returnable to the next term of this Court.

This day David L. Mitchell Sherriff of White County to whom was directed the Writ requiring him to summons Commissioners to lay off Dower of the lands of which William Roberts late of the County of White died seized and possessed to Patience Roberts relect and widow of the said William Roberts deceased, made their report upon oath which is by the Court received and ordered to be recorded and Registered in the registers office of White County.

Ordered by Court that Johathan C. Davis surveyor be allowed the sum of two dollars for one days service laying off Dower to the widow of William Roberts deceased and that George Price, Jose C. Dew, George Cardwell and Welcher Cardwell Commissioners be allowed one dollar and fifty cents each for one days service each in laying off and setting apart Dower to Patiense Roberts widow of the said William Roberts deceased and that the said Patience Roberts pay all the costs relative to said Dower and that an execution issue for the collection thereof &c.

John Bryan Esq - Commissioner of the Revenue for District No.2 reports William Frasure Sr. in said Dist. for one white poll for 1836, who is subject to a double tax for having failed to give in his list according to law and for reasons appearing to the satisfaction of the Court it is ordered that said William Frasure be released from the Double tax for said 1836 and that he only be charged with a single tax.

Iss'd. Ordered by Court that Eli Sims, Richard Crowder and William Bruster Esqs. be appointed Commissioners to assign and set apart provisions for one year to the widow and family of William Glenn deceased and report thereof to the next term of this Court.

(P-130) Iss'd. Ordered by Court that the following persons be appointed Jurors to the next Circuit Court being February term A. D. 1837 To Wit.

John Crook, Nathaniel C. Davis, John Brown, Henry Lance, Joseph Herd, James Randols, John R. Glenn, Joseph Glenn Sr., Samuel Johnson, Elisha Camron, Jacob Anderson, John Gillentine, Adam Massa, John Dew, Austin Webb, James Webb, Joseph Little, David Heffner, Alexander Lowery Sr., Anthony Dibrell, Dan Griffith, William Bruster, Isaiah Hutson, Spencer Holder, Woodson P. White and Turner Lane, Jr., and Hayes Arnold and Noah H. Bradley Constables to attend thereon.

Ordered by Court that George D. Howard be released from the payment of the tax on one white poll for the year 1836 he being over age.

Iss'd. This day Daniel Walling guardian to the minor heirs of William Fisher deceased appeared in open Court and resigned his appointment as guardian which is by the Court received and it is ordered that the said Daniel Walling and his securities be released and forever discharged from all further and future liabilities as guardian.

This day John Fisher was appointed Guardian to William Fisher, James Fisher, Ambrose Fisher, Alfred Fisher, Nancy Fisher, and George W. Fishers minor heirs of William Fisher deceased and together with Matthias Hutson and Jesse Franks entered into and acknowledged bond in the sum of one thousand dollars conditioned as the law requires.

Iss'd. This day the death of William Glenn was suggested in open Court and that he died intestate whereupon William Glenn was appointed adminestrator and Sarah Glenn adminestrator of all and singular the goods and chattles rights and credits of the said deceased and together with William G. Sims and William Bruster intered into and acknowledged bond in the sum of Twelve Thousand dollars conditioned as the law requires.

Iss'd. Ordered by Court that John Jett, Joseph Herd, and Matthias Hutson be appointed Commissioners to settle with Daniel Walling adminestrator of William Fisher deceased and report thereof to the next term of this Court.

For reasons appearing to the satisfaction of the Court Joseph Herd is permitted to surrender to the Court a certain Inducted apprentice by the name of Ammon L. Kerr and it is ordered by the Court that Joseph Herd and securities from the condition of his bond of Indenture be released and forever discharged.

This day Ammon L. Kerr aged four years the 19th of April 1835 an orphan boy was bound to John Vincents to serve him after the manner of an apprentice untill he arrives at the age of twenty one years and for the faithful performance of his Covenant with Charles R. Sperry intered into and acknowledged bond conditioned as the law requires.

(P-131) This day the Commissioners heretofore appointed to lay off and mark a road from the forks of the little Caney fork to the Burnt Stand on the Walton road made their report which is recorded and said road as laid off and marked is established a road of third Class

Iss'd. Ordered by the Court that Samuel Madewell be appointed Overseer of the road as laid off and marked by Commissioners from the forks of the little Caney fork to the Burnt Stand on the Walton road being a road of the third Class and open and keep the same in repair as the law requires and that William Bartlett and Isaac Buck Esquires assign a list of hands to work thereon.

Ordered by Court that Samuel D. Arnold be released from the payment of the taxes for the year 1836 on land to the value of Nine hundred dollars he having been overcharged that much and that the Sherriff credit &c.

Iss'd. It appearing to the satisfaction of the Court from the return of the account of sales of the Estate of Joseph Henry deceased that the bond of the administrator George Bohanon is insufficcent and does not cover the amount for which said estate was sold - It is therefore considered and so ordered by the Court that the said George Bohanon administrator with the will annexed of Joseph Henry deceased make his personal appearance at the next term of this Court and then and there enter into additional Bond and further security for the better security and faithful performance of the administrator of the estate of the said Joseph Henry deceased &c.

Iss'd. Ordered by Court that the Order appointing Elisha Camron and Edmund Stamps Esquires to apportion hands between Edward Elms and George Henry Overseer be renewed - returnable to next Court.

This day William Glenn Administrator of William Glenn deceased returned upon oath an Inventory of the estate of the deceased which is ordered to be recorded.

This day Joseph Herd Administrator of the estate of George Allen deceased returned upon oath an account of sales of the negroes of the estate of the deceased which is ordered to be recorded.

On motion of Kiziah Hopkins by her attorney Richard Nelson Esqr. and the Court after hearing evidence and arguments are of opinion and so order that Henderson Hopkins and James Hopkins be bound as apprentices until they become twenty one years of age - And Thomas Hopkins by his attorney John B. McCormick Esq also appearing in open Court except to the opinion of the Court ordering said children to be bound and prays to be made Defendant in this cause - whereupon the Court order that Kiziah Hopkins be made plaintiff and Thomas Hopkins be made Defendant.

Kiziah Hopkins
vs
Thomas Hopkins } Motion for appeal

This day came the Defendant by his attorney and (P-132) prayed an appeal in this cause to the next honorable Circuit Court to be held for the County of White at the Court house in the town of Sparta on the first Monday of February next and to him it is granted on giving bond and security according to law before the rise of this Court.

Ordered that Court be adjourned untill tomorrow 10 O'clock

William Bruster
John Jett
Jonathan Farrington

Tuesday Morning 8th of Nov. 1836 - Court met pursuant to adjournment
Present The Worshipful

John Jett
William Bruster and
Jonathan Farrington } Esquires Justices

Ordered that Court be adjourned untill Court in Course

Test
N. Oldham Ck

William Bruster
John Jett
Jonathan Farrington

(P-133) State of Tennessee

At a Court (of please and) began and held for the County of White at the Court house in the town of Sparta before the Justices of said Court on the first Monday being the fifth day of December in the year of our Lord one thousand eight hundred and thirty six, and of the Independance of the United States the sixty first year

Present The Worshipful

David Snodgrass Esq. Chr. pro tem

William Knowles, John Bryan, Henry Benton, Elisha Camron, John Jett, Matthias Hutson, William Little, James Allison, Joshua Mason, Willie Steakley, Asa Certain, Edmund Stamps, John Wallis, William Bruster, John Pennington, Richard Crowder, John Gillentine, Jonathan Farrington, } Esquires Justices

This day the following persons were reported for not having retained their tax list for the year 1836, and are subject to Double tax To Wit.

In Dist. No. 7 Cyrus R. Taylor 1 white poll -
John Taylor Jr. 1 white poll - and
Isham Cole 1 white poll and 25 acres of school land valued at twenty five dollars -
In Dist. No. 6 George Pirtle fifty acres of land worth fifty dollars -
Thomas Hawks 1 white poll

Iss'd. Ordered by Court that Darcus Clark be appointed Overseer of the road from Jeremiah Webbs to Jonathan Shorts being a road of the first Class and keep the same in repair as the law requires and the same list of hands which was formerly assigned be assigned to work thereon.

Ordered by the Court that Joseph Brown be released from the payment of the tax on one white poll for the year 1836 being overcharged that much.

Iss'd Ordered by Court that David Snodgrass Esq. one of the members of this Court be appointed Chairman protempord for the present term.

Ordered by Court that the following persons be appointed Commissioners of the Revenue for the County of White for the year 1837 to wit.

In Dist. No. 1 William Bruster Esq.
In Dist. No. 2 John Bryan.
In Dist. No. 3 Thomas Green Esq.
In Dist. No. 4 Matthias Hutson Esq.
In Dist. No. 5 Joshua Mason Esq.
In Dist. No. 6 Richard Crowder Esq.
In Dist. No. 7 Henry Benton Esq.
In Dist No. 8 James Allison Esq.
In Dist. No. 9 Asa Certain Esq.
In Dist. No. 10 John Pennington Esq.
In Dist. No. 11 William Bartlett Esq.

In Dist.No. 12 Elisha Camron Esq.
In Dist. No. 13 William Little Esq.
In Dist. No. 14 Thomas Eastland Esq.
In Dist. No. 15 John Gillentine Esq.

(P-134) This day Edward V. Pollard with James L. Glenn and Rachel Glenn minor heirs of William Glenn Sr. deceased came into open court and the said James L. and Rachel Glenn being of proper age to choose their guardian made choice of the said Edward V. Pollard who being present in open Court with William Glenn Jr. and William G. Sims entered into and acknowledged bond in the sum of Three Thousand two hundred dollars conditioned as the law requires.

This day William Glenn Jr. was appointed guardian to Patsy Glenn and John Wilson Glenn, Infant heirs of William Glenn Sr. deceased and with William R. Tucker and Samuel Brown entered into and acknowledged bond in the sum of Three Thousand two hundred dollars conditioned as the law requires.

Ordered by Court that the order made at the October term of this Court allowing Henderson McFarland twenty Six dollars out of any money not otherwise appropriated be so changed and altered as to be paid out of the taxes of the year 1836 and that a Certificate. Iss'd. &c.

Ordered by the Court that Jane Hall a pauper be kept and maintained at the poor house in White County untill the next term of this Court.

Ordered by the Court that the Commissioners of the poor house in the County of White contract for finishing the repairs necessary to render the keepers house comfortable.

This day the Commissioners heretofore appointed by this Court to lay off and set apart provisions for one year for the support of the widow and family of William Glenn Sr. deceased returned their report which is received and ordered to be recorded.

Ordered by Court that Eli Sims, Richard Crowder and William Bruster Esq. be each allowed the sum of one dollar for services rendered in assigning provisions to the widow and family of William Glenn Sr. deceased.

This day Adrian Owens an orphan boy aged fourteen years the 14th day of June last was bound unto Elisha Camron to serve him after the manner of an apprentice untill he arrives at the age of Twenty one years and for the faithful performance of his Covenant together with William McKenny entered into and acknowledged bond conditioned as the law requires.

This day appeared in open court Jacob Andeson to whom was bound a certain orphan boy named John L. Anderson, and surrendered said appointed to the Court and it ordered by the Court that the said Jacob Anderson and his securities from all future and further liabilities on his covenant be released and forever discharged.

This day John L. Anderson an orphan boy aged nine years the 15th of April last past was bound unto William Burden to serve him after the manner of an apprentice untill he attains the age of twenty one years and for the faithful performance of his Covenant together with William McKinny entered into and acknowledged bond Conditioned as the law requires.

(P-135) Monday 5th December 1836.

The Commissioners heretofore appointed by this Court to apportion the effects of the estate of George W. Hawkins deceased this day made their report together with settlement with John R. Glenn adminestrator of said estate which is ordered to be recorded.

Ordered by Court that Richard Crowder, Joshua Mason and Eli Sims Esquires be allowed the sum of one dollar each for one days services in apportioning the effects of the estate of George W. Hawkins deceased and for settling with the adminestrators of said estate to be paid out of the funds of said estate.

Ordered by Court that George Early be released from the payment of the taxes of the year 1836 on one white poll he being over age.

Ordered by Court that John E. Campbell be released from the payment of the tax on one white poll for the year 1836 he being under age.(Issd)

This day the Commissioners heretofore appointed to settle with Daniel Walling Executor of the estate of William Fisher deceased returned their report upon oath which is ordered to be recorded.

Ordered by Court that Daniel Walling Executor of the estate of William Fisher deceased be allowed the further sum of three dollars for his services since a former settlement to be by him retained out of the funds of said estate.

Ordered by Court that John Jett, Matthias Hutson and Joseph Herd Esqs. be allowed the sum of one dollar and fifty cents each for making settlement with Daniel Walling Executor of the estate of William Fisher deceased to be paid out of said estate.

This day Daniel Walling late Guardian to the minor heirs of William Fisher deceased returned into Court the receipt of John Fisher the present Guardian of said heirs which is ordered to be recorded.

Iss'd. Ordered by the Court that the road leading from James T. Officers intersecting Roses Turnpike road on the Cumberland Mountain be reduced to a road of the third Class -

And that James England be appointed Overseer of the road above and keep the same in repair as the law requires that Edmund Stamps assigns bounds of hands &c.

Iss'd. Ordered by Court that Samuel Johnson, Elisha Camron, James T. Officer, Edmund Stamps and Patrick Potts freeholders be appointed a Jury of view to lay off and mark a road of the ____ Class from the upper end of Carmichaels plantation to entersect the same road at Potts hill and report thereof to the next term of this Court.

Iss'd. Ordered by Court that Elisha Camron and Edmund Stamps

Esquires be appointed Commissioners to apportion bounds of hands between all the Overseers on the road leading from Plumb Creek to the Standing Stone and report thereof to the next term of this Court.

(P-136) Iss'd. Ordered by Court that John Stipe be appointed Overseer of the road from the end of John Stipe's land to the muddy branch being a road of the second Class and open and keep the same in repair as the law requires and that John Gillentine and Willie Steakley Esquires assign a list of hands to work thereon.

Iss'd. Ordered by Court that Willie Steakley, Jacob Stipe, Terry Gillentine, John Stipe and John Gillentine freeholder be appointed a Jury of view to lay off and mark a road from the forks of the road at Cain Creek passing between Thomas Moores new house and stable intersecting the Pikeville road near the bend of the Creek below the mill and report thereof to the next term of this Court.

This day the Commissioners heretofore appointed to apportion bounds of hands to the following Overseers to wit

Henry Rutledge; Overseer - Robert Denny, Albert Horn, William B. Dearing, Johnson Corben; John H. McCully and James Walker one hand -

And to James Walker, Overseer - John A. Pass two hands Richard Spears; John Hampton, Jeremiah Williams; Moses Williams, Seaton Taylor; Isaac Abshire, Anderson Abshire, James Pearson; Thompson, Johnson; William Johnson, Thomas Little one hand John Little - David Snodgrass two hands James Snodgrass; William McCully; Henry McCully and James Williams returned their report which is confirmed in all its parts.

Ordered that Court be adjourned untill tomorrow Morning 10 O'clock

William Bruster
John Jett
Jonathan Farrington

Tuesday Morning 6th December A. D. 1836

Court met pursuant to adjounment Present the Worshipful

William Bruster, John Jett and Jonathan Farrington } Esquires Justices

Court adjourned till Court in course

Test
N. Oldham Clk

Jonathan Farrington
John Jett
William Bruster

(P-137) Monday Morning 2nd January 1837

State of Tennessee

At a Court began and held for the County of White at the Court house in the town of Sparta before the Justices of said Court on the first Monday being the second day of January in the year of our Lord one thousand eight hundred and thirty seven, and of the Independence of the United States the sixty first year

present the Worshipful

John Jett Esq. Chairman protem.
Lewis Pettett, Thomas Green,) Esquires
James Allison, Henry Benton,)
Edmund Stamps, Matthias Hutson,)
Jesse Walling, John Gillentine,)
Asa Certain, William Knowles,)
Elijah Frost, Johathan Farrington,)
Joshua Mason, William Little,) Justices
William Bruster, Richard Crowder.)

It appearing to the satisfaction of the Court that Thomas Eastland Esq. who was appointed at the last term of this Court to take a list of the taxable property and polls in Dist. No.14 declines accepting said appointment and therefore Order and appoint Elijah Frost Esq. Commissioners of the revenue in said District for the year 1837 who being present in Court accepts said appointment.

Ordered by Court that Cyrus R. Taylor, John Taylor Jr. and Thomas Hawks be released from the payment of the Double tax one white poll each and Isham Cole one white poll and 25 acres school land valued at twenty five dollars and also George Pirtle fifty acres of land worth fifty dollars be released from the double tax of the year 1836

This day the following persons were reported for not having given the list of their taxable property for the year 1836 and are subject to the payment of Double tax To Wit:

In District No. 7 Thomas I. Pistol one Black poll valued $550 William Curiton one white poll Richard Reeves one white poll, John Lefevers one white poll, Rial Medley one white poll -.

In District No. 8 Susannah Duncan 100 acres of Deeded land worth $200 - .

In Dist. No. 14 Samuel Gill one white poll -

In Dist. 9 Nancy Holmes 30 acres land worth $200

This day John Gillentine guardian to William T. Carter minor of Charles Carter Sr. deceased returned upon oath report of the condition of estate of his ward which is ordered to be recorded.

This day Emery Bennett appeared in open Court and produced a Commission from the Governer of the state of Tennessee authorizing to act as a Justice of the peace in the County of White who took an oath to support the Constitution of the United States and of the State of Tennessee and the oath of Office and thereupon took his seat upon the Bench.

This day Asa Certain Guardian to Alphonzo and Maniza Holmes minor heirs of Edward Holmes deceased his report upon oath which is Ordered to be recorded.

(P-138) This day Wamon Leftwich guardian to Miss Malinda Rowland returned his report upon oath which is ordered to be recorded.

This day appeared in open Court Elizabeth Cooper who being of the proper age to choose her guardian made choice of John Oliver who also appeared in open Court and together with Jesse Davis and William Williams entered into and acknowledged bond in the sum of two hundred Dollars conditioned as the law requires.

This day William Glenn Jr. administrator of the estate of William Glenn deceased returned in open Court upon oath an Inventory of said Estate which is ordered to be recorded.

Iss'd. Ordered by Court that William Mills be released from the payment of the Taxes of one white poll and of $20. value of land for the year 1836, he being overcharged that much and that the sherriff have a credit thereof.

This day John Pennington and Sarah Dyer guardian to the four youngest heirs of John Dyer deceased returned upon oath their report which is ordered to be recorded.

Charles Burgis
vs
John Bullock } Debt Cert.

It appearing to the satisfaction of the Court that the Clerk in taxing the Costs in the above suit he failed to tax the fees of Dudley Hunter a constable. It is therefore considered and so ordered by the Court that the taxation of the Costs in said suit be corrected so as to include the Constables costs and that the Clerk issue execution &c.

Charles Burgis
vs
John Bullock } Debt Cert.

It appearing to the satisfaction of the Court that the Clerk in taxing the Costs in the above suit he failed to tax the fees of Dudley Hunter a constable. It is therefore considered and so ordered by the Court that the taxation of the Costs in said suit be corrected so as to include the Constables Costs and that the Clerk issue &c.

This day Thomas Stipe guardian to Glaphey Stipe returned upon oath a report of his guardianship which is so ordered to be recorded.

(P-139) Iss'd. Ordered by Court that Nicholas Oldham Clerk of White County Court be allowed the sum of Three Dollars for money advanced for the payment of a record book for recording the Probates of Deeds in the County of White for the use of the Clerks office to be paid by the Sherriff of White County out of the taxes of the year 1836.

For reasons appearing to the satisfaction of the Court it is ordered that Wamon Leftwich from so much of his Covenant as requires him to give to his apprentice Nancy Dungry a free girl of color be released and discharged from 12 months schooling and in consideration thereof agrees and the Court hereby requires him the said Wamon Leftwich to pay to said apprentice Nancy Dungry Twelve dollars in money when her said term of apprenticeship shall expire And further the said Wamon Leftwich in line of giving said apprentice at the end of her serveation a horse, saddle and bridle worth one hundred Dollars agrees that he will give said apprentice the amount of the value of such horse saddle and bridle in cash which agreement the Courts accepts and the Court orders that said Wamon Leftwich enter into bond and security as required by law.

This day Thomas Hill guardian to the heirs of James Hill deceased made his report upon oath which is ordered to be recorded.

This day Samuel Brown guardian,to Robertson Dyer, Claiborn Dyer, John C. Dyer, Alfred Dyer, and Louisa Dyer enfant children and minor heirs of John Dyer deceased returned upon oath his report which is ordered to be recorded.

Iss'd. This day was exhibited in open Court a writing purporting to be the last will and Testament of James T. Robertson late of the County of White deceased whereupon also appeared in open Court Samuel Johnson and Edmund Stamps Subscribing witnesses to said writing and proved on oath the due execution and publication of said writing, to be the last will and Testament of the said James T. Robinson for the purpose and things therein mentioned and that at the date of the execution and publication thereof the said James T. Robinson was of sound disposing mind and memory which with the authorization thereof is ordered to be recorded.

And the same day appeared in open Court Leah Robinson the widow of the said James T. Robinson deceased and was appointed by the Court adminestratrix with the will or the Testator annexed of all and singular the goods and chattles rights and credits of the deceased and took the oath required by law and together with John Robinson and Samuel Johnson entered into and acknowledged bond in the sum of Ten Thousand dollars conditioned as the law requires.

Iss'd. Ordered by Court that William Warmich be appointed Overseer of the road from James McGowen to Franks' old ferry being a road of the second Class and keep the same in repear as the law requires with the list of hands which was assigned by William Knowls Esq. to Cason Swindle late overseer thereof be assigned to work thereon.

(P-140). Ordered by Court that the Commissioners appointed at the last term of this Court to view lay off and mark a road from the mouth of Cain Creek &c. be permitted not to make their report untill the next term of this Court.

Iss'd. Ordered by Court that Alexander P. Irwin be appointed Overseer of the road from Rum Creek to the 13 mile post being a road of the first Class and keep the same in repair as the law requires and that Richard Crowder and Emery Bennett Esqs. apportion lists of hands between James Kelly and said Irwin Overseer.

Ordered by Court that the following list of hands be assigned to work on that portion of the road of which Isaac Lollar is Overseer To Wit:

Luther Clark, John Mills, Joseph Mills, Simon & Anthony Crook, Charles Crook, William Crook, Charles Burgis, Reubin Whitson, Jackson Campbell, Levi Lollar, Sebert Rhea, Spartan Rhea, John Campbell, James C. Mitchell, John Mitchell, Jesse Perkins, Reubin Perkins, William Nash.

Iss'd. Ordered of Court that James Knowles be appointed Overseer of the road from Richard Crowder to the forks of the road being a road of the second Class and keep the same in repair as the law requires and that Richard Crowder and Emery Bennett Esquires assign bounds of hands to work thereon.

Iss'd. This day William Irwin produced in open Court one large wolf scalp over the age of four months and proved that he killed the same in White County and there being present five acting Justices of the peace.

It is ordered that the same be certified to the Treasure of the State of Tennessee for the payment and that the Sherriff of White County burn said scalps who being present in Court received said scalp into his custody and acted accordingly.

Iss'd. Ordered by Court that Allen L. Mitchell keeper of the poor house of White County be allowed for the support and maintainance of Robert Hewatt, Elizabeth Miller and Jane Hale the sum of one hundred and twenty four dollars thirty seven and one half cents and also the further sum of thirty dollars for his services in superintending said poor house making in all the sum of one hundred and Fifty four dollars thirty seven and one half cents to be paid by the Treasure of the poor house Commissioners out of any monies not otherwise appropriated.

This day John Jett, Joseph Herd and Joseph Cummings were appointed by the Court Commissioners of the poor house in White County for the Current year to wit: 1837

Iss'd. This day John Jett Esq. one of the Commissioners of the poor house in White County was by the Court appointed Treasure to said board of poor house Commissioners for the year 1837

Iss'd. Ordered by Court that John Jett, Joseph Herd, and Joseph Cummings Commissioners of the poor house in the County of White for the year 1836 be allowed the sum of seven dollars and fifty cents each for services rendered by them in superintending the affairs of said poor house to be paid by the Treasure of the board of the poor house Commissioners (P-141) of the County of White out of any money not otherwise appropriated.

This day the Commissioners of the poor house of White County who were by an order of the last term of this Court directed to Contract for the repairs of building on the poor house farm in said County, This day made their report shewing they had let the same to the Lowest bidder Charles Smith a Citizen of White County for the sum of seventy five dollars to be finished by the first day of April next and with Joseph Herd entered into bond for the faithful performance thereof which bond in file here in Court which is by the Court confirmed in all its parts.

Iss'd. Ordered by Court that James Davis be released from the payment on the taxes on 4539 acres of land amounting to the sum of twenty eight dollars thirty six cents and eight mills he being overcharged that much being the tax for the year 1835 And that the sherriff and collector of the taxes for said year have a credit with the Trustee of said County for the said amount of $28.36.8 in settlement of taxes of 1836

It appearing to the satisfaction of the Court that James Davis in giving in the value of his land the revenue Commissioners of the district in which he lives made a mistake in entering the value of said land so that instead of being charged with the taxes on 5050 dollars worth of land he is only charged with the taxes of $550.

It is therefore Considered and so ordered by the Court that the mistake be corrected so as that he pay the taxes on $4500 which amounts to the sum of $9.54½ in addition for the year 1836.

And that the Sherriff of White County collect and account for the same as other taxes for said year. Iss'd.

Ordered that Court be adjourned untill tomorrow Morning 9 O'clock

John Jett
William Bruster
Jonathan Farrington

Tuesday Morning 3rd January A. D. 1837
Court met pursuant to adjournment
Present the Worshipful

John Jett
Wm Bruster
Jonathan Farrington } Esquires Justices

This day came John Jett Esq. who was on yesterday appointed Treasure of the board of Commissioners of the poor house into open Court and took the oath required by law and with David L. Mitchell and William Bruster entered into and acknowledged bond in the sum of one thousand dollars conditioned as the law requires.

This day came into open Court Wamon Leftwich with William Bruster and David L. Mitchell and entered into bond and security for the faithful performance of his Covenant relative to the Inventory of a certain apprentice named Nancy Dungry which was on yesterday charged satisfactory to the Court.

(P-142) Ordered that Court be adjourned untill Court in Course.
Test
N. Oldham Clerk

Jonathan Farrington
William Bruster
John Jett

State of Tennessee
At a Court began and held for the County of White at the Court house in the town of Sparta befor the Justices of said Court on the first Monday being the sixth day of February in the year of our Lord one Thousand eight

hundred and thirty seven and of the Independence of the United States the sixty first year.

Present the Worshipful

Thomas Eastland Esq. Chairman
David Snodgrass, John Wallis, Lewis Pettett, Jesse Walling, Matthias Hutson, Willie Steakley, James Allison, William Little, Jonathan Farrington, John Bryan, Elisha Camron, John Gillentine, William Knowles, William Bruster, John Jett, Edmund Stamps, William Bartlett, Thomas Green, Emery Bennett and Richard Crowder. } Esquires Justices

Ordered by Court that Washington P. Duncan be released from the payment of the taxes on one White poll for the year 1836 he being overcharged that much and that the Sherriff have a credit thereof in settlement of his accounts.

This day William Glenn, Jr., guardian to part of the minor heirs of William Glenn returned upon oath the condition of the estates of his wards which is ordered to be recorded.

(P-143) Monday 6th February A. D. 1837

This day Edward V. Pollard guardian to part of the minor heirs of William Glenn deceased reported upon oath the condition of the estate of his wards which is ordered to be recorded. Iss'd

Ordered by Court that the following persons be allowed the following fees in the following cases which have been Certified to this Court by the Clerk of the Circuit Court of White County and also certified by the Attorney General as being correctly taxed and properly chargeable to the County of White to wit. In the case the state of Tennessee against Josiah Martin Indicted for trading with negroes

Clerk Anthony Dibrell $2.87½ Clerk William G. Sims $6.12½ Deputy Sherriff W. G. Sims $0.62½ Sherriff David L. Mitchell $4.54 - witness John R. Glenn $4 - witness Lyman Saben $3.50 Witness Maville Marlow $1.00 witness Jesse Allen $9.40 witness Eli Marlow $1.00 Atto. Genl. John B. McCormack $2.50

In the case the state against Samuel Anderson on Scifa. Clerk A. Dibrell $1.75 Clerk William G. Sims 2.37½ Sherriff Eli Thurman $1.00. Atto. Genl. John B. McCormack $2.50 In the case the state against William M. Bryan, Harvey Lewis & others - Ind't for a Riot Tavern Keeper William Glenn $7.50 Sherriff David L. Mitchell $16.75 witness Dan Griffith $2.00 Wit: Samuel Miller $2.00 Wit William Burden 1.50 wit William Green $2.00 Wit Berry R. Wilson $2.00 Wit John Baker $1.50 Wit Lydia Haskett 1.50 witness Sally Haskett $1.50 witness Cornelius Davis $2.00 In the case the State vs. David Jenkins clerk A. Dibrell $1.25 Clerk William G. Sims $0.75 Sherriff David L. Mitchell $0.50 In the case the state against Matthew G. Mason Clerk William G. Sims $6.31¼ Sherriff David L. Mitchell

$4.16½ Atto. Genl. John B. McCormack $2.50 In the case the State against Salley Ingram clerk Anthony Dibrell $4.25 Clerk William G. Sims $10.43¾ Sherriff David L. Mitchell $8.91½ Sherriff William G. Sims $1.50 witness Robert Bean$2.50 Atto. Genl. J. B. McCormack $2.50 on the case the State against John Winfry. Clerk A. Dibrell $1.75 Clerk W. G. Sims $0.75 Sherriff W. G. Sims $0.50 Sherriff D. L. Mitchell $0.50 Atto Genl. John B. McCormack $2.50 In the case the State against Elenor McGuirt clerk A. Dibrell $0.75 clerk W. G. Sims $1.12½ Sherriff W. G. Sims - $1.00 Clerk J. A. Lane $0.75 Atto. Genl. John B. McCormack 2.50 In case the State against Chapel Averett - Clerk A. Dibrell $0.75 Clerk W. G. Sims $0.75 Clerk J. A. Lane $2.00 Sherriff David L. Mitchell $1.00 John B. McCormack Atto. Genl. 2.50 In case the State vs. Joel Hatley, Clerk A. Dibrell $1.75 Clerk W. G. Sims $0.75 Sherriff Eli Thurman $1.00 Atto Genl. John B. McCormack $2.50 In the case the state vs. Elizabeth McClure, A. Dibrell Clerk $0.75. Clerk William G. Sims $1.12½. Clerk J. A. Lane $0.75 Shff W. G. Sims $1.00 Atto Genl. John B. McCormack $2.50 and that certificates issue to each respectively to be paid by the Trustee of White County out of any monies not otherwise appropriated.

This day personally appeared in open Court Joseph Cummings and Joseph Herd two of the Commissioners of the poor house of White County for year 1837 who were appointed at the last term (P-144) of this Court and took the oath required by law and thereupon entered upon the discharge of their duties.

The Court then proceeded to the appointment of a Chairman to Preside over this Court for the present year and thereupon unanimously appoint Thomas Eastland Esquire who entered upon the discharge of the duties of office.

This day James Thomas was appointed guardian to Amy Brown and James Brown minor heirs of William Brown deceased and also appeared in open court Rachal Brown and Daniel Brown also minor of the said William Brown deceased being of proper age to choose their guardian made choice of the James Thomas who together with Richard England, William Little and David Snodgrass entered into and acknowledged bond in the sum of Five Thousand Dollars Conditioned as the law requires.

Ordered by Court that William Erwin be charged the amount of the taxes on 301 acres school land valued at 300 dollars for the year 1837 he being undercharged that amount and that the Sherriff account with the Trustee therefore as other taxes of said year.

John Dale
to Iss'd
John Yates } Title Bond

It appearing to the satisfaction of the Court that the above title bond cannot be authenticated by any subscribing witness and It further appearing to their satisfaction by the oaths of Daniel Dale and Richard Nelson that they believe the signiture to be the same to be in the proper hand writing of the said John Dale which is ordered to be recorded - Let it be Regestered. Iss'd

Ordered by Court that John Stipe be appointed overseer of the road leading from his lane to Brush Creek for the distance of Three miles for his lane and that Willie Steakley and John Gillentine be appointed to keep the balance of said road in repair as the law requires at their own proper costs and charges being a road of the 2nd Class and that John Bryan and John Wallis Esq. be appointed to apportion lists of hands between Thomas Stipes, Isham B. Haston, John Stipe; Samuel Shockly; Charles Denny and Daniel Steakley overseers of roads having due regard to the dignity of said roads respectively of which they are overseers and report thereof to the next term of this Court. Iss'd

Ordered by Court that James C. Mitchell be appointed overseer of the road from Dittys branch on the Carthage road to the Jackson County line being a road of the first Class and keep the same in repair as the law requires that the same hands that worked under John Ditty former overseer thereof be assigned to work thereon.

Iss'd. Ordered by Court that Simion R. Doyle be appointed Overseer of the road from Moores ford crossing near Dales Mill passing near where Melvilles lives being a road of the second Class and keep the same in repair as the law requires and that the same hands which (P-145) worked under Henry Kuhn late overseer thereof be assigned to work thereon

Iss'd Ordered by Court that Joshua Brown be appointed Overseer of the road from Goodwins branch to Hardys old Cabins on the Kentucky road being a road of the first Class and keep the same in repair as the law requires and that the same hands that worked under Aaron England former Overseer thereof assigned to work thereon.

Iss'd. Ordered by Court that Robert Anderson Jr. be appointed Overseer of the road from the west end of the Bridge across the Calf Killer at the Harriett Iron Works to the widow Smiths being a road of the first Class and keep the same in repair as the law requires and that the same list of hands be assigned to work thereon that were assigned to work under the late Overseer thereof.

This day appeared in open Court George Mitchell and proved by the oaths of Sims Dearing; John A. Pass, Alexander Robinson and James England to the satisfaction of the Court that the said George Mitchell in a certain affray with William Robinson he had the upper part of his left ear bitt off which is ordered to be entered of records and so certified under the seal of this Court. (Cert)

This day James T. Hayes appeared in open Court and produced a Commission appointing him a Justice of the peace for White County and took the oath to support the Constitution of the state of Tennessee and of the United States and the oath of office and thereupon took his seat upon the Bench.

Ordered by Court that Benjamin Marr be released from the payment of the tax on one hundred dollars value of land for the year 1836 he being over charged that amount and that the Sherriff have a credit thereof in his settlement with the Trustee of his County.

Ordered by Court that William B. Cummings and William Anderson be appointed Comrs. to settle with John Witt Admr. of Dempsy Pinner de'd and report thereof to the next term of this Court.

Iss'd This day was produced in open Court one wolf scalp under the age of four months by John Brumbalo who proved that he killed the same in White County and there being present Thomas Eastland; John Jett; William Bruster; Jonathan Farrington and David Snodgrass Esq. Acting Justices of the peace - It is ordered that the same be certified to the Treasures of the State of Tennessee for payment and that the said scalp be burned and the sherriff being present in Court received said scalp into his custody and acted accordingly.

Ordered by Court that David Dean be released from the appraised value of a certain Heifer taken up by him as an Estray the same having escaped from him appraised to $2.00

Iss'd Ordered by Court that David Snodgrass; Lewis Bohanon and Samuel Johnson be appointed Com'rs to settle with the administrators of Thomas William deceased and report to the next term of this Court.

(P-146) Ordered by Court that Jeremiah Whitson be released from the payment of the tax on one White poll for the year 1836 he being over age the Sherriff of White County is ordered to refund to him Fifty cents the amount of said tax and that the Sherriff have a credit thereof in the settlement of his accounts.

Ordered by Court that the following rate of Taxes be assised for the year 1837 For the following purposes to Wit:

For County tax
 On each White poll $12\frac{1}{2}$ cents
 On each $100. value of property 5 cents.
For Jury tax
 On each White poll $12\frac{1}{2}$ cents
 On each $100. value of property 5 cents.
For Poor tax
 On each White poll $12\frac{1}{2}$ cents
 On each $100. value of property 5 cents.
For Bridge Tax at Sparta
 On each $100. value of property $1\frac{1}{4}$ cents.

To be levied and collected by the Sherriff of White County in manner and form prescribed by law.

And it is further ordered by the Court that the Clerk of this Court wherever during the year 1837 he is required to issue Licences under the privisions of the acts of assembly taxing the priviliges in this State; shall demand and receive on each and every such Licences so issued as a County tax for the use of White County a sum of equal to one half the State Tax on each and every such privilige which sums so received he shall pay to and accounts with the Trustee of White County according to law.

Ordered by Court that David Snodgrass and William Little be appointed Commissioners of Robert Bucks Turnpike road leading from Sparta on the rout to Kingston who being present in Court took the oath prescribed by law.

This day Anthony Dibrell administrator with the will annexed of William Gracy deceased produced a writing purporting to be the receipt of John Roberts for the sum of two hundred and sixty seven dollars thirty three cents for which it is ordered by the Court he shall have a credit in the settlement of said estate for the sum aforesaid by him disbursed out of the hire of the negroes of said estate for the support and maintainances of the Children in the will of the deceased mentioned.

And it is further ordered that the said Anthony Dibrell Admr. aforesaid be allowed Ten percent on the above amount for securing and disbursing the same to be by him retained out of said estate.

Iss'd Ordered by Court that Samuel Dodson be appointed overseer of the road from John Dodsons lane to Benjamin Stuarts being a road of the second Class and keep the same in repair as the law requires and that the hands that worked under James Graham former Overseer (P-147) thereof be assigned to work thereon.

Iss'd For reasons appearing to the satisfaction of the Court disclosed in the petition of the heirs at law of William Glenn deceased late of White County it is ordered that Richard Crowder, James Y. Hayes, Adam Clouse, Eli Sims, and John M. Little be appointed Commissioners to make partitions and divisions of all the real estate of which the said William Glenn died seized and possessed between the heirs at law and legal representations of the said William Glenn deceased acording to law and report thereof to the next term of this Court.

Iss'd Ordered by Court that Sarah Hagan be allowed for keeping and maintaining a certain infant male child a pauper by the name of Earl J. Cook for the time she has already had said child and for twelve months from this day the sum of Fifty dollars to be paid quarterly by Treasures of Poor house Commissioners out of any Surplus money in his hands of the tax of the year 1836

Subject however to the following conditions to wit: should said child be taken from her or die or move out of this County before the expiration of one year from this day then she is only to receive a rateable proportion of the above sum comnincing from the date she first took said child into possession untill the time it shall have been taken away or removed - and Solomon Charles being present here in Court undertakes to see that the said money is properly and Judiciously applied to the maintainance of said Child &c said Charles to receive the money and disburse the same.

Iss'd Ordered by Court that the order made at November term 1836 requiring George Bohannon admr. with the will annexed of Joseph Henry deceased to give additional security for his faithful performance of his said administration - be renewed and that a Supeona issued requiring him personally to appear before the Justices of said Court at the next term thereof.

Iss'd. Ordered by Court that George Miller be appointed Overseer of the road from Porters ford up the river being a road of the second Class and keep the same in repair as the law requires with the hands that worked under John Dodson former overseer thereof be assigned to work thereon.

Iss'd Ordered by Court that Adrian Bryan be appointed Overseer of the road from the middle of the Dry hollow to the Rosses road being a road of the second Class and keep the same in repair as the law directs and that the same list of hands that worked under Francis Simmons former Overseer thereof be assigned to work thereon.

Iss'd Ordered by Court that Isaac Taylor, William Glenn, Alexander Irwin, William Lisk, and Henry Lyda be appointed a jury of view to lay off and mark a road of the third class turning out of the stage road a small distanse west of a Cabin belonging to Esquire Bruster at or where the present path turns off leading to Zion meeting house thence on by said meeting house crossing the Rockisland road at Alexander Irwins, thence on by Taylors Lick, thence on road a new ground finced by said Taylor so as to intersect the Falling water was on the west side of said new ground and report thereof to the next term of this Court.

(P-148) Iss'd Ordered by Court that Eli Sims, William Lisk, Henry Lyda, Richard Crowder and William Lyda freeholders be appointed commissioners to examine lay off mark and so alter and change the Rockisland road leading to Gainsborough &c on the land of Isaac Taylor turning out at Jaylors Creek and to intersect the old road at or near the branch south of John Jaylors and report thereof to the next term of this Court.

Iss'd Ordered by Court that the sherriff of White County bring John Roberts and Lucenda Roberts children of color into the next term of the Court to be dealt by according to law.

Iss'd Ordered by Court that Woodson Yates be appointed overseer of the road from the middle of the river below Dales mill to the Ten mile post being a road of the second Class and keep the same in repair as the law requires and that the following list of hands be assigned to work thereon to wit: Samuel Porter, Jacob Keener, Eli Yates, Levi Yates, Alfred Yates, Solomon Seals, William Seals, David Walker -.

The Commissioners heretofore appointed to apportion the list of hands between Daniel Dale, James Malloy &c make the following assignment to Wit: to James Malloy Ov. Thomas Wilson, John Grantham, Neal Grantham, Maclin Maxfield, Nelson Kirby, Jacob Scoggin, William Worley and Green H. Moss and Daniel Dale Ov. Solomon Reese, George Rollins, Thomas Walker, James Simmons, Abijah Crane one slave, Daniel Dale one slave - which is ordered to be recorded - .

This day the Commissioners heretofore appointed to apportion lists of hands between Sundry Overseers in White County make the following report to wit: Hands assigned to George Henry Ov. Thomas S. Elms, William Robinson, John J. Gammon, James McMullins, William Kirkland, Alexander Officer, Henry Swink, William Walker, Gibert Hudson, James Hudson, Jackson Hudson, Alexander Bohanon, Asa Graham, Officers Charles, Col. Robinsons Witt, Vinett Henry, Thomas Henry, Harrison Whitson, James Whitson, James Scarbrough John Morrison, Moses Netherton, Elijah Netherton, Isaac Bumbalow

Hands assigned to James S. England Overseer to wit: James Scott, Aaron G. England, A. C. Robison, Andrew McNabb, Mrs. Englands Isaac, Charles Graham and Henry Graham - Hands assigned to Edward Elms Ov. Henry Graham, Washington G. Hargis, Joseph Johnson, Thomas B. Johnson, Wm. C.

Johnson; John Johnson; Henry Johnson; James Corder, Francis Moore; Thomas C. Hill, John Elms, Elms Reubin, Richard G. Jay; James A. Jay, William Vandiver and Robert Buchanon - .

Hands assigned to James M. Johnson Ov. Samuel P. Pirtle, Thomas M Gear, Frederick Gear, Patrick Potts, G. W. H. Potts, John Weaver, Benjamin Weaver, Andrew G. Cooper, James M. Stice, (P-149) Randolph Ramsey; Joseph England, Joseph H. March, Silas Knowles, Davis Weaver; Thomas Cooper; James T. Officer; Charles Southard and Joshua Morris - .

Hands assigned to Leonard Murray Ov. - John Fox, William Fox, Sims Dearing; William Dearing, Thomas Williams, James Shirley; Daniel Broyles, James Broyles, Reubin Broyles, William C. Medcalf, William Medcalf; James Yager, Henry Yager, Wesley Yeager, Yeagers Aaron, Campbell Burrington; John Broyles, Noah Shirley -

Hands assigned to Standford Stamps Overseer Samuel H. Williams, Elijaha Stamps, William Hargis, William Stamps, John Bumbalow, Reubin Randolph, John Henry, George W. Henry, and Enoch Netherton - all of which is ordered to be recorded.

This day the Commissioners heretofore appointed to apportion lists of hands between Harmon Little and James Knowles report that to James Knowles they assign Alfred Merrett, Levi Jarvis, Robert Glenn, Jr., William Hall, Abner Cook; Stephen A. Baxton; Harrison Hall; John Jenkins, Mrs. Randol's Sam, William D. Glenn - and to Harmon Little the following to wit: Greenville Templeton, Simpson Little, Joseph Glenn, Jr., Cabb Mason, and John R. Glenn all of which is ordered to be recorded.

Ordered by Court that the following persons be released from the payment of Double taxes for the year 1836 and only be charged with a single tax to wit:

In Dist. No. 3. Robert Melloway 1 White poll - In Dist.No. 8 Susanah Duncan 100 acres land valued at $200. deeded - In Dist. No. 9 Nancy Holmes 30 acres land worth 200$ - In Dist. No. 14 Samuel Gill 1 White poll - In Dist. No. 7 Thomas J. Pistol 1 slave value 550$ - William Curiton 1 white poll - Richard Reeves 1 white poll - John Lefevers 1 white poll - Rial Medley 1 white poll - William Barr 1 white poll - George Elrod 1 white poll - Isaac Thomas 1 white poll - John H. Graham 1 white poll - No. 14

Ordered that Court be adjourned untill tomorrow morning 10 O'clock

Thos. Eastland
David Snodgrass
Wm. Little

(P-150) (Monday) Tuesday Mroning 7th February 1837

Court met pursuant to adjournment
Present The Worshipful

Thomas Eastland Esq. Chairman
David Snodgrass }
William Little and } Esquires
John Jett }

This day Nicholas Oldham who has been appointed Deputy Register of White County by Joseph M. Roberts, the Register thereof appeared in open Court and took the oath of office of Deputy Register and thereupon entered upon the duties thereof.

Ordered that Court be adjourned untill Court in Course
Test
N. Oldham Clk

Thos. Eastland
David Snodgrass
Wm. Little

State of Tennessee

At a Court began and held for the County of White in the State aforesaid at the Court house in the town of Sparta before the Justices of said Court on the first Monday being the sixth day of March in the year of our Lord one Thousand eight hundred and thirty seven and of the Independence of the United States of America the sixty first year

Present the Worshipful

Thomas Eastland, Esq. Chairman
John Gillentine, John Wallis,
John Bryan, William Knowles,
William Little, Asa Certain,
Elijah Frost, Jesse Walling,
Richard Crowder, Emory Bennett,) Esquire
Henry Benton, Elisha Camron,
Matthias Hutson, Joshua Mason,
John Jett, Lewis Pettett, John) Justices
Pennington, James Allison, David
Snodgrass, William Bartlett and
Jonathan Farrington. co

(P-151) Monday 6th March A. D. 1837

Ordered by Court that Robert Officer be released from the payment of the Taxes assessed against him in the County of White for the year 1836

And that the sherriff of White County have a credit thereof in the settlement of his accounts with the Trustee of the County aforesaid and it is further ordered that the said Robert Officers name be stricken from the List of Taxable property and polls returned for the year 1837 he having given in his property and paid taxes in the County of Overton.

Ordered by Court that Altazard Williams be released from the payment of the taxes assessed against her in the County of White for the year 1836 And that the Sherriff of White County have a credit thereof with the Trustee of White County aforesaid in the settlement of his accounts.

And it is further ordered that the said Altazard Williams name be stricken from the list of Taxable property and polls returned for the year 1837 she having given in her property and paid the taxes in the County of Overton -

For reasons appearing fully to the satisfaction of the Court it is ordered by the Court that all persons reported by the Commissioners of the Revenue for the year 1837 as being subject to Double tax for failing to give in lists of their property within the time prescribed by law be (forever) released therefrom and that they only be charged with a single tax for said year 1837.

This day the Commissioners heretofore appointed by this Court to settle with the adminestrator of the Estate of Thomas Williams deceased, made there report to wit: That Robert Officer was not ready to go into a settlement which was received and ordered to be recorded.

Iss'd. Ordered by Court that David Snodgrass, Lewis Bohanon and Samuel Johnson be allowed the sum of one dollar and fifty cents each per day for one days services in endeavoring to make settlement with the adminestrators of the estate of Thomas Williams deceased to be paid by the adminestrators out of said estate.

Ordered by Court that David Snodgrass, Elisha Camron and William Little be appointed Commissioners to settle with Edward Elms and Robert Officer adminestrator of the estate of Thomas Williams Dec'd and report thereof to the next term of this Court.

Iss'd This day Andrew Jackson Johnson produced in open Court one large wolf scalp over the age of four months and proved that he killed the same in the County of White and there being present Thomas Eastland, Asa Ceartin, William Knowles, Elisha Camron and David Snodgrass five of the acting Justices of the peace in and for said County it is thereupon ordered that the same be certified to the Treasure of the state of Tennessee for payment and that the Sherriff of White County burn said scalp who being present in open Court received said scalp into his Custody and acted accordingly.

(P-152) Iss'd Ordered by Court that the order made at last term of this Court requiring the sherriff of White County to bring John Roberts and Lucinda Roberts children of color into Court at the present term to be dealt by according to law, be renewed returnable to the next term of this Court.

This day William Allen, Hannah Allen and George H. Allen children and minor heirs of George Allen deceased came into open Court and being of proper age to choose their guardian each one selected and made choice of William H. Allen as their guardian who being present in open Court took the oath prescribed by law and together with James Eastland and John Young entered into and acknowledged bond in the sum of two Thousand five hundred Dollars conditioned as the law requires.

Iss'd Ordered by Court that the following Justices Commissioners of the Revenue for the year 1837 To Wit:

William Bruster, John Bryan, Thomas Green, Matthias Hutson, Joshua Mason, Richard Crowder, Henry Benton, James Allison, Asa Certain, John Pennington, William Bartlett, Elisha Camron, William Little, Elijah Frost and John Gillentine Esquires be each allowed the sum of Five dollars for taking in and returning lists of the taxable property and polls in White County for the year 1837 to be paid by the sherriff of White County out of the taxes of the year 1837.

Iss'd. Ordered by Court that Jonathan Farrington Esquire assign a list of hands to work on the road under William White Overseer from Sparta to the Deep ford of the Calf Killer River and report to the next term of this Court.

This day George Bohanon adminestrator of the estate of Joseph Henry deceased with his will annexed who was at a former term of this Court filed to appear to day and enter into additional bond and security for the faithful performance of his adminestration came into open court with Joseph Bartlett and Thomas Bohanon entered into and acknowledged bond in the sum of twenty one hundred dollars conditioned as the law requires and it is considered by Court that George Bohanon pay all costs incident thereto.

Iss'd. Ordered by Court that Howard Cash be appointed Overseer of the road from post oak creek to Robert Howards being a road of the second class and keep the same in repair as the law requires and that the same hands be assigned to work thereon that were assigned to Samuel Dyer late overseer thereof.

Iss'd. Ordered by Court that Joseph Cummings Jr. be appointed overseer of the road from William Dennys old place to the place where Grisby lived being a road of the second Class and keep the same in repair as the law requires.

Ordered by Court that the following hands be assigned to work on that portion of the road of which Joseph Hunter is Overseer to Wit: William Murphey, Joel McDaniel, Brice Little and all those who reside on William and Brice Littles lands -

(P-153) Iss'd. Ordered by Court that William Denny be released from the payment of the appraised value (½) of an Estray Heifer taken up by him the same having died.

This day the Commissioners heretofore appointed to apportion bounds and lists of hands to sundry Overseers in White returned their reports which was ordered to be recorded - to wit: hands assigned to Matthias Welsh Overseer - David Whitaker, William Whitaker, James Whitaker, Jacob Hyder, Jr., John Whitaker, William Bohanon, Campbell Bohanon - Moses Grant, M. Jackson, Washington Jackson, Hillsom Crendine, John Bohanon, Sr., William Buckner, David Adams and Jonathan Hyder.

Hands and bounds assigned to Barlow Fisk Overseer To Wit: James Hudgins and 2 hands Shelby Hudgins - Samuel Lance, Joseph Holderfield, Christopher Hoffman and Madison Hoffman -

Bounds and hands assigned to John Kitchersides Overseer to wit: Anthony Lance, Pierce Cody, Sampson Lamb, Henry Lance, Moses A. Springs, John Kilpatrick and Isaac Weaver ________ . ________ .

Bounds and hands assigned to Thomas Little Overseer to wit: William Carter, Thomas Ellet, Garman Manning and John Flatt, ________ .

Bounds and hands assigned to John Stipe Overseer to wit: Alexander Grissum, Isaac Haston, John S. Parker, Richard Woodson, Nathan . Trogdon, Isham Teter, William Teter, Charles Steakley, Charles Denny, Cornelius Harris, Andrew K. Parker, Abraham Trogden and Nicholas W. Gillentine ______________ .

Bounds and hands assigned to Samuel Shockley Overseer to wit: Terry Gillentine; Wilson Griffin, Jacob Stipe 3 slaves, William Stipe and Samuel Shockley one slave ________.

Bounds and hands assigned to Daniel Steakley Overseer to wit: William M. Felkins, Martin Feed, Arther Mitchell, Nathan Grantham, Isaiah Hodges, William Hodge and John Hodge ________. ________.

Bounds of hand assigned to Isham B. Haston Overseer to wit: Charles P. Shockley, Tilman Brown; John Kirkland; James Moore 1 slave Edward Moore, Thomas Moore ________.

Bound and hands assigned to Thomas Stipe Overseer to wit: Russel T. Crain, Clayton McCormack, Jesse Dodson; Robert Baker; Joseph Walker, Thomas C. Haston and William Denny ________.

Bounds and hands assigned to Joseph Cummings Jr. Overseer to wit: Joseph Webb; William Hopkins; James Hopkins, Isaac Hopkins; Daniel Vaughn, William B. Cummings; John Frisby, Lynch A. Shockley and Thomas Shockley.

For reasons appearing fully to the satisfaction of the Court by proof and at the request and by the consent of William B. Hutson to whom at a former term of this Court was bound as an apprentice a certain boy named Henry George it is ordered by the Court that the Indentures of said apprentice boy be cancelled rescinded and for nothing sustained and there William B. Hutson deliver said boy to his mother without delay and it is further ordered that the said William B. Hutson and his securities from the conditions of their Covenant be released and forever discharged.

(P-154) Iss'd. Ordered by Court that the order of the last term of this Court appointing Eli Sims; William Lisk; Henry Lyda, Richard Crowder, and William Lyda freeholders Commissioners to examine and make and so change the Rock Island road leading to Gainsborough &c. on the land of Isaac Taylor as to turn of said road at Taylors Creek and Intersect the old road again at or near the Branch south of John Taylors be renewed and report there of to the next term of this Court.

Iss'd. Ordered by Court that the following persons be appointed as Jurors to the next term of the Circuit Court for the County of White Vire Nathaniel C. Davis, John L. Smith; Jonas Turner; Thomas Little; Jacob Anderson; John Gillentine; Simon Doyle; John Austin; Sr.; William B. Hutson; John Witt; Daniel Martin; Andrew Mainard; John England; Isaac Hutson, Anthony Dibrell, George Ogden, John A. Carrick; William C. Medkitt; James Scott; Henry Collier, Isaac Lollar; Daniel Richards; Robert Anderson, Sr.; John Taylor; Eli Sims, and Solomon Bullock -

And Hayes Arnold and Charles McGuire as Constable and that Venire facius Issue directed &c.

Ordered that Court be adjourned untill tomorrow 9 O'clock

Wm. Little
Emery Bennett
Thomas Green

Tuesday Morning 7th day of March A.D. 1837
Present the Worshipful

William Little) Esquires
Thomas Green)
Emey Bennett) Justices

This day the Commissioners heretofore appointed by this Court to settle with John Witt adminestrator of Dempsy Penner dec'd made their report upon oath which was received and ordered to be recorded.

Ordered by the Court that William B. Cummings and William Anderson be each allowed one dollar and fifty cents per day for 2 days service each in settling with the adminestrator of Dempsy Penner dec'd to be paid by the Adm'r out of the estate of the dec'd - .

This day the Commissioners heretofore appointed to review lay off and mark a road from the Allens ferry road near William Bruster passing Zion meeting house &c. to Isaac Taylor &c. made their report which is received and said road established as a road of the third Class.

(P-155) Ordered that Court be adjourned untill Court In Course

Test
N. Oldham Clk

Wm. Little
Emery Bennett
Thomas Green

State of Tennessee

At a Court began and held for the County of White at the Court house in the town of Sparta before the Justices of said Court on the first Monday being the third day of April in the year of our Lord One Thousand eight hundred and thirty seven and of the Independence of the United States the Sixty first year

Present the worshipful

Thomas Eastland, Esquire Chairman
William Bruster, Edmund Stamps,
James T. Hayes, Elisha Camron,
Asa Certain, William Knowles,
Joshua Mason, Lewis Pettett,
Jesse Walling, Elijah Frost,
John Bryan, Emery Bennett,) Esquires
Richard Crowder, Johathan
Farrington, Isaac Buck,
Willie Steakley, John Jett,) Justices
William Bartlett, Matthias Hutson,
John Gillentine, William Hitchcock,
John Pennington, William C. Bounds,
John Wallis, James Allison, William
Little, and Thomas Green.

This day appeared in open Court Samuel Dodson Constable in District No. 2 and resigned his office as Constable which is ordered to be recorded.

(P-156) This day Leah Robinson adminestrator with the will annexed of James T. Robinson deceased returned upon oath an Inventory of part of the estate of the deceased which is ordered to be recorded.

Iss'd. Ordered by Court that the Sherriff of White County bring into Court at the next term Alexander Dalton to be dealt by according to law.

The Court then proceeded to the election of Sherriff for the County of White to fill the vacancy occasioned by the death of David L. Mitchell Esquire late Sherriff of White County and to that office do appoint Jonathan T. Bradley Esq. who being present in open Court took the oath to support the Constitution of the United States and of the State of Tennessee and the several oaths required by law and together with Anthony Dibrell, John England, Sr., Richard England, James Thomas and John L. Price entered into and acknowledged bond in the sum of twelve Thousand five hundred dollars conditioned as the law requires and thereupon the discharge of duties of his office.

BOND.

Know all men by these presents that we Jonathan T. Brady, Anthony Dibrell; John England, Sr.; Richard England, James Thomas; John L. Price all of the County of White and State of Tennessee are held and firmly bound unto Newton Cannon Esq Governor in and over the state of Tennessee for the time being or his successors in office in the sum of twelve Thousand Five hundred dollars Current money well and truly to be made and done; we being ourselves and each of our heirs execution or Adminestrator jointly and severally firmly by these presents sealed with our seals and dated the third day of April A.D. 1837 whereas this day Jonathan T. Bradley hath been duly appointed Sherriff of White County the justices of said County to fill the vacancy in said office of sherriff occasioned by the death of David L. Mitchell Esq. late Sherriff of said Court as provided for by the Constitution of the state of Tennessee - .

Now the Condition of the above obligation is such that if the said Jonathan T. Bradley shall well and truly execute and due return make of all process and precipts to him directed and pay and satisfy all fees and sums of money by him received or levied by vertue of any process into the proper office by which the same by the tenor thereof ought to be paid or to the person or persons to whom the same shall be due his, her, or their executors adminestrators Attorneys or agents and in all things, well and truly and faithfully execute the said office of sherriff so long as he shall continue therein according to law. Then this obligation to be null and void otherwise be and remain in full force an virtue

J. T. Bradley (seal)
Anthony Dibrell (seal)
John England (seal)
Richard England (seal)
James Thomas (seal)
John L. Price (seal)

(P-157)
Test
N. Oldham; Clerk

Bond for Collection of the State Tax -
Know all men by these presents that we Jonathan T. Bradley, Anthony Dibrell; John England, Sr.; Richard England, James Thomas, John L. Price, all of the County of White and State of Tennessee and held and firmly bound into his excelleney Newton Cannon Governer in and over the state of Tennessee for

the time being or his successors in office in the sum of two Thousand dollars current money which payment well and truly to oe made and done we bind ourselves and each of our heirs execution and adminestrators jointly and severally, firmly by these presents sealed with our seals and dated the third day of April A.D. 1837 whereas the above bound Jonathan T. Bradley hath this day been appointed Collector of the Taxes in the County of White for the year 1837

Now the Condition of the above obligation is such that if the above bound Jonathan T. Bradley collector aforesaid shall well and truly collect the taxes which are levied in the County of White and State of Tennessee on property and polls for the year 1837 for the use of the State of Tennessee and shall pay over and account for the same with the Treasure of the state of Tennessee according to law, and in all things therein demean thereof accordingly these the above obligation to be null and void else be and remain in full force and virtue

Test
N. Oldham, Clerk

J. T. Bradley (seal)
Anthony Dibrell (seal)
John England (seal)
Richard England (seal)
James Thomas (seal)
John L. Price (seal)

Bond for County, Jury, Poor and Bridge Tax.
Know all men by these presents that we Jonathan T. Bradley, Anthony Dibrell, John England, Sr., Richard England, James Thomas, John L. Price all of the County of White and State of Tennessee an held and firmly bound unto Thomas Eastland Esq. Chairman of the County Court of White County or his successors in office in the sum of Five thousand dollars Current money for the use of White County which payment well and truly to be made and done we bind our selves and each of us and each of our heirs executors and adminestrators, jointly and severally firmly by these presents sealed with our seals and dated the third day of April A.D. 1837

Whereas the above bound Jonathan T. Bradley hath been this day appointed Collectors of the Taxes for the County of White for the year 1837

Now if the above bound Jonathan T. Bradley collector of the taxes aforesaid shall well and truly and faithfully collect all the Taxes which have been assessed for the County of White for the year 1837 (P-158) To wit: the County tax, Jury Tax, poor tax and Bridge tax for the benefit of said County and shall pay the monies over to the proper office in said County of White who are authorised to receive the same according to law, then the above obligation to be null and void else be and remain in full force and virtue.

Test
N. Oldham, Clerk

J. T. Bradley (seal)
Anthony Dibrell (seal)
John England (seal)
Richard England (seal)
James Thomas (seal)
John L. Price (seal)

Bond for School Tax.
Know all men by these presents that we Jonathan T. Bradley, Anthony Dibrell,

John England, Sr., Richard England, James Thomas, John L. Price all of the County of White and State of Tennessee are held and firmly bound unto Robert H. McEwin, Esq., Superentendant of Public instruction in Tennessee in the sum of one thousand dollars current money for the use and benefit of Common schools in Tennessee which payment well and truly to be made and done we being ourselves and each of us and every one of our heirs executors and adminestrators jointly and severally firmly these presents sealed with our seals and dated the third day of April A.D. 1837.

Where as the above bound Jonathan T. Bradley hath been this day appointed Collector of the taxes in the County of White for the year 1837

Now the Condition of the above obligations is such that if the said Jonathan T. Bradley shall well and truly and faithfully collect and pay over all the taxes arising on school land in the County of White and State aforesaid to the superentendant of public instruction in the state aforesaid according to law then the above obligation to be null and void else be and remain in full force and virture.

Test
N. Oldham, Clerk

J. T. Bradley (seal)
Anthony Dibrell (seal)
John England (seal)
Richard England (seal)
James Thomas (seal)
John L. Price (seal)

Ordered by Court that John A. Copeland be released from the payment of the Tax of one white poll for the year 1836 he being under age and that the sherriff of White County have a credit thereof with the Trustee of White County in settlement of their accounts - .

This day the Commissioners of the poor house of White County report that the repairs on the building of poor house are completed which is received and ordered to be recorded.

(P-159) Iss'd Ordered by Court that Samuel H. Kiethley be appointed overseer of the road from sinking Creek to the top of Gumspring Mountain being a road of the second Class and keep the same in repair as the law requires and that the same list of hands which worked under James Roberts late Overseer be assigned to work thereon.

Iss'd. Ordered by Court that Jonathan Farrington, William Little, David Snodgrass be appointed Commissioners to apportion lists and bounds of hands between the different Overseers of the road leading from Sparta up the river passing the deep ford to D. Snodgrass, Esq. so as to give list of hands to all the overseers on said road and report thereof to the next term of this Court.

Iss'd. Ordered by Court that Andrew Jackson be appointed overseer of the road from Jacob Hyders to the valley near his house being a road of the second Class and keep the same in repair as the law requires and that Isaac Buck and William Bartlett, Esq. assign a list of hands to work thereon.

Iss'd. Ordered by Court that Sebird Rhea be appointed Overseer of the road from the falls of the Falling Water to intersect the Gainsborough road being a road of the third Class and keep the same in repair as the law requires at his own expence - .

Iss'd. Ordered by Court that Jabez G. Mitchell be appointed Overseer of the road from the West end of Oldhams lane on the shipping port road passing Lanes Mill to the top of the Mountain being a road of the second Class and keep the same in repair as the law requires and that the same list of hands that worked under D. L. Mitchell late overseer thereof be assigned to work thereon -

Iss'd. Ordered by Court that James Snodgrass, William Little, John Rose, James Walker and Samuel Lance freeholders be appointed Commissioners be appointed a jury of view to lay of and mark a road of the second Class from the north west corner of I. Hunters 300 Acres tract of land running Westwardly crossing the Creek twice thence down on the North east side of the creek and again crossing the creek twice not to enterfere with any persons finces and report thereof to the next term of this Court.

Iss'd. Ordered by Court that Jacob L. Pirtle, Jesse Allen, Isaac C. Pirtle, David Haffner and John Young freeholders be appointed a jury of view to lay off and mark a road from William Earles land running with Richard Crowder wood pastures fence North so as to straiten the road and report thereof at the next term of this Court.

Ordered by Court that the order of last Court appointing David Snodgrass up William Little and Elisha Camron Esq. Com't to settle with the adminestrators of Thomas Williams deceased be renewed and report thereof to the next term of this Court - .

(P-160) Ordered by Court that the order of last Court requiring the sherriff of White County to bring into Court John Roberts and Lucenda Roberts children of color to be dealt by according to the law be renewed returnable to the next term of this Court.

Ordered by Court that James Lowry, Mark Lowry, Nicholas Oldham, William Bruster, and Samuel V. Carrick freeholders be appointed a Jury of view to examine the alteration of the road leading from the Carthage road up the river to Snodgrass so as to place said road on the outside of Anthony Dibrells new ground and to be placed equally on the line between James Lowry and Dibrells and equally on the line between Jacob A. Lane and said Dibrell and report tomorrow morning - .

This day the death of John M. Rotan late of White County was suggested and that he died intestate whereupon Dan Griffith is appointed adminestrator of all and singular the goods and chattles rights and credits of the deceased.

Ordered that Court be adjourned untill tomorrow morning 9 O'clock

Thos. Eastland
Jonathan Farrington
John Jett

Tuesday morning 4th April A. D. 1837

Court met pursuant to adjournment
Present the Worshipful

Thomas Eastland, Esq. Chairman
John Jett, William Little) Esq.
Jonathan Farrington)
William Bruster) Justices

Iss'd This day Dan Griffith who was yesterday appointed adminestrator of John M. Rotan deceased appeared in open Court and took the oath required by law and together with Seiscio Evans entered into and acknowledged Bond in the sum of eight hundred dollars conditioned as the law requires.

Iss'd Ordered by Court that the following hands be assigned to work on the milk sick in White County over which John W. Simpson is Overseer to wit:

Daniel Brown, John W. Simpson, 1 Black man, Edward Anderson, John Anderson, Jr., James Melvan, Isham Richards, William Burden and Charles Anderson.

This day the Commissioners heretofore appointed to examine and so to change the road leading from the Carthage road passing (P-161) up the river so as to pass around Anthony Dibrells new ground and so as to place said proposed change equally on the lines between the said A. Dibrell and James Lowry and between Jacob A. Lane and A. Dibrell be received and said proposed change be established as a road of the second Class and that the said A. Dibrell open said road according to law at his own proper Costs and changes after the opening of which accordingly the old road passing through said Dibrells new ground shall be discontinued and further that after said road shall be opened according to law the present Overseer of the old road is hereby required to keep the new part with the old in repair as the law requires.

Ordered that Court be adjourned untill Court in Course.
Test
N. Oldham, Clerk

Thos. Eastland
William Little
John Jett

(P-162) State of Tennessee
At a Court began and held for the County of White and State aforesaid at the Court house in the town of Sparta on the first Monday being the first day of May in the year of our Lord one Thousand eight hundred and thirty seven and of the Independence of the United States the 61st year
Present the Worshipful

Thomas Eastland Esq. Chairman
John Jett, John Bryan,)
William Knowels, Jonathan Farrington,)
Asa Certain, Jame Y. Hayes,) Esquires
Emery Bennett, Jesse Walling,)
William Bruster, Matthias Hutson,)
Joshua Mason, David Snodgrass,)
William Little, Elisha Camron,)
James Allison, Elijah Frost,) Justices
Edmund Stamps.)

Iss'd Ordered by Court that Richard Nelson and Anthony Dibrells esquires be appointed Commissioners to settle with Wamon Leftwich administrator of James Rowland deceased and report thereof to the next term of this Court.

Iss'd Ordered by Court that the Overseers on each side of the Calf Killer at what is called Rices Bridge keep said Bridge in repair each one the half of said Bridge by stopping the holes in said Bridge and knocking up the planks closer together where ever necessary with the same hands which is already assigned them.

Iss'd Ordered by Court that the road leading from Blue Spring to falling Water over which Thomas Hawks is Overseer be divided so that Thomas Hawks shall work from the Blue Spring to the branch between James . Nelson and said Hawks and that Daniel Martin be appointed Overseer from said Branch to the falling water and keep the same in repair as the law requires and that Richard Crowder and James T. Hayes assign a list of hands between them to work thereon.

This day John Walker; Constable in District No.9 of White County appeared in open Court and tendered his resignation as Constable which is received and ordered to be recorded.

On the humble petition of Robert Officer and Edward Elms adminestraters of the estate of Thomas Williams deceased and for reasons appearing to the satisfaction of the Court disclose in their said petition it is ordered by Court that for the sum of $486.31½ cents as therein mentioned they be allowed in the settlement of their accounts.

Ordered by Court that Robert Officer and Edward Elms adminestrators of Thomas Williams deceased be each allowed the sum of fifty dollars for services rendered in settling said estate to be by them retained out of said estate.

Iss'd Ordered by Court that the order made at the last term requiring the sherriff to bring into Court John Roberts and (P-163) Eucenda Roberts children of Sally Roberts of White County to be dealt by according to law, be renewed and that Sally Roberts be notified thereof.

Iss'd Ordered by Court that James M. Nelson; William Baker, William Grisby, Daniel Martin and James Dildine freeholders be appointed a jury of view to examine a road turning off from Rockisland road leading to Sainesborough near Taylors Creek and to intersect the old road again at or near the branch south of John Taylors be renewed returnable to the next term of this Court.

Iss'd Ordered by Court that Jacob Pirtle be appointed Overseer of the road from Robert Cooks to the Blue Spring branch being a road of the 2nd Class and keep the same in repair as the law requires with the same List of hands that were assigned to the late overseer thereof be assigned to work thereon.

This day the Commissioners heretofore appointed to settle with Robert Officer and Edward Elms adminestrators of the estate of Thomas Williams deceased returned upon oath their report which is by the Court received and ordered to be recorded.

Ordered by Court that David Snodgras, William Little and Elisha Camron Esq. be allowed the sum of one dollar fifty cents each per day for two days service each rendered in settling with the adminestrators of Thomas Williams deceased to be paid by the adminestrators out of said estate.

Iss'd Ordered by Court that Randolph Jones be appointed Overseer of the road from Austins Still house to William Rottans branch being a road of the second Class and keep the same in repair as the law requires with the same list of hands to work thereon that were assigned to work under the late Overseer thereof.

Iss'd Ordered by Court that William Frasure be appointed overseer of the road from William Rottans branch to the foot of Cumberland Mountain being a road of the second Class and keep the same in repair as the law requires; And that the same lists of hands be assigned that worked under Joseph Fifer late overseer thereof.

This day the Commissioners heretofore appointed to apportion lists and bounds of hands to Sims McKamn Overseer of the road returned their report to wit:

Thomas Bradley, Richard Bradley, Obie Dyer; Sally Bradleys, Bob Clayburn Williams; Randolph Ramsey, Moses Turner, James Sparks; Jonathan Elms returned their report which is ordered to be recorded.

Iss'd Ordered by Court that Joshua Mason; Cabb Mason; Greenville Templeton; Hugh Cook and Levi Jarvis freeholders be appointed a Jury of view to examine and change the road leading to shipping port through Robert Glenn, Jr., land being a road of the second Class and make report thereof to the next term of this Court.

This day the Commissioners heretofore appointed to assign a list of hands to work on the road leading from Sparta to the deep (P-164) ford returned their report to wit:

Moses Carrick; John A. Carrick, Seth L. Carrick; James M. Carrick; James Vandaver, John L. Price and hands and Madison Fisk which is ordered to be recorded.

Ordered by Court that Edmund Cunningham; Thomas Wilson; Thomas Frasure, Sr., and Thomas Frasure, Jr., be appointed Commissioners to lay off and set apart one years provisions out of the estate of John M. Rottan deceased for the support and maintainance of his widow and family and report thereof to the next term of this Court.

Iss'd Ordered by Court that Samuel Scurlock be appointed Overseer of the road from the forks of the Kentucky road to the house of Robert Cook, Esq., being a road of the second Class and keep the same in repair as the law requires that the same list of hands be assigned to work under him that were assigned to John Humphreys, Jr., late Overseer thereof.

Iss'd

Ordered by Court that the order made at the last term of this Court requiring the Sherriff of White County to bring Alexander Dalton the son of Elizabeth Dalton into Court to be dealt by according to law be renewed returnable to the next term of this Court and that the Sherriff notify the said Elizabeth Dalton of this proceedings &c.

Iss'd Ordered by Court that the order of last term appointing James Snodgrass; William Little; John Rose; James Walker and Samuel Lanse freeholders a jury of view to lay off and mark a road of the second Class from the north west corner of Joseph Hunters 300 acre tract of land running westwardly by crossing the Creek twice thence down the creek on the north side again crossing the Creek twice not to intersect with any persons fences be renewed and report thereof to the next term of this Court.

Iss'd Ordered by Court that the road leading from Thomas Roberts to the mouth of Townsends Mill Creek be and the same is hereby declined to be discontinued and disannulled. And that William Knowles and Joshua Mason Esq. be appointed to apportion the hands that were assigned to work said road between the difrent Overseers in that vicenity having due regard to the dignity of the respective roads.

This day the death of David L. Mitchell late of the County of White was suggested and that he died intestate. Whereupon David Snodgrass is appointed administrators of all and singular the goods and Chattles right and credits of the deceased who being here in open Court took the oath required by law and with William Glenn and William Little entered into and acknowledged bond in the sum of two thousand dollars conditioned as the law requires.

(P-165) Iss'd This day was produced in open Court a writing purporting to be the last will and Testament of Sampson Godard late of White County deceased and the due execution and publication thereof as the last will and testament of Sampson Godard deceased was this day proven in open Court by the oaths of Joseph Cummings, Jr., and James Goddard subscribing witnesses thereto for the purposes and things therein contained and that at the date and publication thereof the said Sampson Goddard was of sound and disposing mind and memory; whereupon also appeared in open Court Catharine Goddard who is appointed sole executrix in said will and testament of her deceased Husband, Sampson Goddard and undertakes the burden and execution thereof and thereupon took the oath required by law and together with James Goddard, Joseph Cummings, Jr., and Elijah Hill entered into and acknowledged bond in the sum of three Hundred dollars Conditioned as the law requires.

Iss'd This day was produced in open Court a writing purporting to be the last will and testament of Berry Hamblett, late of the County of White deceased and the due execution and publication thereof as the last will and testament of Berry Hamblett deceased was this day proven in open Court by the oaths of Trent C. Conner and John Wallis subscribing witnesses thereto for the purposes and things therein mentioned and that at the date of the execution and publication thereof the said Berry Hamblett was of sound and disposing mind and memory whereupon also appeared in open Court Elizabeth Hamblett who is appointed executrix in said last will and testament her deceased husband Berry Hamblett and undertakes the burden and execution of said will and testament and thereupon took the oath required by law and together with James Randols, Sr., and Joseph Herd entered into and acknowledged bond in the sum of six Thousand dollars conditioned as the law requires.

For reasons appearing to the satisfaction of the Court it is ordered by the Court that the securities of David L. Mitchell, Esq. deceased late sherriff and Collector of the public taxes in White County for the year 1836 be allowed the further time of sixty days from this day for the collection of and paying over the taxes due the County of White for said year 1836.

Iss'd Ordered by Court that David Snodgrass and Edmund Stamps be appointed Commissioners to settle with Thomas Henry adminestrator of the estate of William Parker deceased and report thereof to the next term of this Court.

Iss'd Ordered by Court that Dan Griffith be allowed the sum of two dollars and twenty five cents for services of work and labor done on the Common Jail of White County by George W. Slucer and also that Robert H. McManus keeper of the common Jail of White County be allowed the sum of one dollar seventy five cents for nails furnished and labor done in repairing the Jail of White County to be paid by the Trustee of White County of any monies not otherwise appropiated.

(P-166) This day Jonathan T. Bradley Esq. sherriff of the County of White appeared in open Court and appointed Jabez G. Mitchell and John England, Jr., Deputy Sherriff in said County of White who being present in open Court took the oath to support the Constitution of the United States and of the State of Tennessee and the several oaths required by law and thereupon entered upon the discharge of the duties of their office respectively.

Iss'd This day James C. Baker produced in open Court one large wolf scalp over the age of four months and that he killed the same in White County whereupon there being present Thomas Eastland, John Jett, John Bryan, William Knowles and Jonathan Farrington, Esquires, five of the acting Justices of the peace in said County it is ordered that the same be certified to the Treasure of the state of Tennessee for payment and that said scalp be distroyed whereupon the sherriff of White County being here present in Court received said scalp into his Custody and acted accordingly

Iss'd Ordered by Court that John L. Price be appointed Overseer of the road from Sparta to the deep ford on the Calf Killer being a road of the second Class and keep the same in repair as the law requires with the lists of hands in the bounds made out by Com's for that purpose.

Ordered by Court that the Court be adjourned untill Court in Course
Test
W. Oldham, Clerk

William Bruster
Jonathan Farrington
Elijah Frost.

(P-167) Monday Morning June the 5th A.D. 1837

State of Tennessee

At a Court began and held for the County of White at the Court house in the town of Sparta on the first Monday being the fifth day of June A.D. 1837 and of the Independence of the United States the sixty year before the Justices of said Court

Present the Worshipful

Thomas Eastland Esq. Chairman
David Snodgrass; John Bryan;
Lewis Pettett; John Wallis; Esquires
William Knowles, John Gillentine,
John Jett; Emery Bennett;
Elisha Camron; James Allison;
Isaac Buck; Joshua Mason; Justices
Richard Crowder; William Bruster;
Asa Certain, Jonathan Farrington,
Jesse Walling, William Little,
James T. Hayes; Edmund Stamps;
Wm. Bartlett; Thomas Green;
Samuel Strong.

This day the Court proceeded to the appointment of an Attorney General for the County of White and to that office do unaniniously appoint Samuel Jurney Esq. who being present in Court accepted said appointment and entered upon the discharge of the duties thereof.

This day the Commissioners heretofore appointed to settle with Wamon Leftwich adminestrator of James Rowland returned their report upon oath which is ordered to be recorded.

Iss'd Ordered by Court that Anthony Dibrell, Daniel Clark and Thomas Robertson be appointed Commissioners to assign one years provisions out of the estate of David L. Mitchell deceased to the widow and family of the deceased and report thereof to the present term of this Court.

This day the Commissioners heretofore appointed to assign one years provisions for the support and maintainance of the widow and family of John Rottan deceased returned their report upon oath which is by the Court received which is ordered to be recorded.

This day John Roberts a free boy of color aged thirteen years on the 24th day of November 1837 was bound to James Scott to serve him after the manner of an apprentice untill he shall have arrived at the age of twenty one years and for the faithful purformance of his Covenant entered into bond with Mark Lowry and Samuel Turney his security conditioned as the law requires

This day Lucinda Roberts a free girl of color age eight years on the 20th day of March 1837 was bound to James Scott to serve him after the manner of an apprentice untill she shall have attained the age of twenty one years and for the faithful performance of his Covenant together with Mark Lowry and (P-168) Samuel Turney entered into bond conditioned as the law requires.

Iss'd This day was suggested in open Court that Nathan Bartlett, Sr., Sate of White County had died and that he died intestate whereupon William Bartlett was appointed administrator of all and singular the goods and chattles rights and credits of the deceased and thereupon took the oath required by law and together with Robert Officer and Isaac Buck entered unto bond and security in the sum of seven Thousand Dollars Conditioned as the law requires.

This day Dan Griffith adminestrator of the estate of John M. Rotan, deceased returned upon oath an Inventory of the estate of the deceased which order to be recorded.

This day Alexander Dalton an orphan boy aged Ten years on the 11th day of April 1837 was bound to George Griffith to serve him after the manner of an apprentice untill he shall have attained the age of twenty one years and for the faithful performance of his Covenant entered into and acknowledged bond with Samuel Brown and John Griffith his security conditioned as the law requires

Iss'd On the Humble petition of William Glenn and for reasons appearing to the satisfaction of the Court he is permitted to keep a house of public entertainment at his own house in the town of Sparta, he having entered into and acknowledged bond with Nicholas Oldham and Jabez G. Mitchell his securities in the sum of twenty five hundred dollars conditioned as the law requires.

Iss'd Ordered by Court that David Snodgrass and William Bruster be appointed Commissioners to settle with the adminestrators of William Jones deceased and apportion the effects of said estate agreeable to act of assembly in such Cases made and provided and report thereof to the next term of this Court.

Iss'd Ordered by Court that Thomas Green and Jesse Walling Esq. be appointed Commissioners to settle with the adminestrators of the estate of James Isham deceased and report thereof to the next term of this Court.

This day the sherriff of White County filed in open Court the Certificate of the election of Randolph Jones as Constable in District No. 2 in White County to fill the vacancy occasioned by the resignation of Samuel Dodson late Constable in said District and the said Randolph Jones being present in open Court took the oath support the Constitution of the United States and of the State of Tennessee and the several oaths prescribed by law and together with John Wallis and George W. Potts entered into and acknowledged bond in the sum of one thousand dollars conditioned as the Law requires.

Iss'd Ordered by Court that John Little and Thomas Little's negro man Jack be transfered from Rutledges list of hands and be put on the list of hands that work under Thomas Little Overseer.

P-169) This day the sherriff of White County filed in open Court Certificate of the election of James C. Kelly as a constable in District No. 9 to fill the vacancy occasioned by the resignation of Capt John Walker late constable thereof. And the said James C. Kelly being here present in open court took the oath to support the Constitution of the United States and of the state of Tennessee and the several oaths required by law and together with Asa Certain an William Bruster entered into and acknowledged bond in the sum of One thousand dollars conditioned as the law requires.

Iss'd For reasons appearing to the satisfaction of the Court that the order of the last term of this Court discontinuing the road from the Gum Spring to the mouth of Townsend Creek be set aside and for nothing esteemed and that said road be reestablished a third Class road and that Edward V. Pollard be appointed Overseer of said road and keep the same in repair as the law requires.

For reasons appearing to the satisfaction of the Court it is ordered that the road leading from the forks of the Little Caney fork to the Burnt Stand on the Walton road be and the same is discontinued.

Iss'd Ordered by Court that Smith J. Walling be appointed Overseer of the road from the Rockisland to the forks of the Kentucky road being a road of the first Class and from the forks of said road to the two mile post on the Kentucky road being a road of the second Class and keep the same in repair as the law requires with the same list of hands that were assigned to work thereon under the late overseer thereof.

Iss'd Ordered by Court that Terry Gillentine be appointed Overseer of the road from the mouth of Cain Creek on main Caney fork to the forks of the road in the direction of McMinnville being a road of the second Class and keep the same in repair as the law requires and that the same list of hands be assigned to work under him that workod under Samuel Shockley late Overseer thereof.

For reasons appearing fully to the satisfaction of the Court it is ordered that the Order allowing Sarah Hagan the sum of fifty dollars at the February term 1837 of this Court for maintaining Earl J. Cook and Constituting Solomon Charles Superentendant to the disbursment of said sum of Fifty dollars be and the same is hereby revoked rescended and set entirely aside and that the Treasure of the poor house is hereby required not to pay the sum as heretofore described.

Iss'd Ordered by Court that William Little; John Rose; Samuel Lance, Brice Little and Washington P. Duncan freeholders be appointed a Jury of view to lay off and mark a road of the second Class from the north west corner of Joseph Hunters 300 acre tract of land running Westwardly crossing the Creek twice thence down the Creek on the North side again crossing the Creek twice so as not to interfere with any persons fences and report thereof to the next term of this Court

(P-170) Iss'd Ordered by Court upon the information of Noah H. Bradley Constable that the sherriff of White County bring here into Court at the next term thereof Thursby Conley, Hannah Conley and Levi Preston Conley orphans and minor children Polly Conley to be dealt by according to law

Ordered by Court that the order of the last Court appointing David Snodgrass and Edmund Stamps Commissioners to settle with Thomas Henry administrator of the estate of William Parker deceased be renewed and report thereof to the next term of this Court.

Iss'd This day the Commissioners heretofore appointed to divide hands between Thomas Hawks and Daniel Martin Overseer of the road returned their apportionment to wit:

To Thomas Hawk the following list of hands - John Taylor; Samuel Stover; Anthony Veneent; John Elrod; Jacob Nelson; Albert Davis; Richard Harris; Stephen Cole and to Daniel Martin the following James McDole; Jesse Farley, John Farley, Thomas Massy, Elijah Hickey, Cornelius Hickey, Isham Cole; William Rice and Darius Martins boy which is received by the Court and ordered to be recorded.

Ordered that Court be adjourned untill tomorrow Morning 9 O'clock

Thos. Eastland
John Jett
Edmund Stamps
John Gillentine

Tuesday Morning the 6th June A.D. 1837

Court met pursuant to adjournment
Present the Worshipful

Thomas Eastland; Esq. Chairman
John Jett; David Snodgrass; Edmund Stamps; John Gillentine } Esq. Justices

This day Elizabeth Hamblett executrix of Berry Hamblett deceased returned upon oath an Inventory of part of the estate of the deceased which is ordered to be recorded.

This day the Commissioners appointed on yesterday to assign one years provisions out of the estate of David L. Mitchell. deceased for the support and maintainance of widow and family of the deceased returned upon oath their report which is received and ordered to be recorded.

This day David Snodgrass adminestrator of the estate of David L. Mitchell deceased returned upon oath a part of the Inventory of said estate and also an account of the sales of said estate which is ordered to be recorded.

(P-171) Iss'd On the humble petition of Thomas Eastland and for reasons appearing to the satisfaction of the Court he is permitted to keep a tavern house of public intertainment at his own house in the County of White acknowledged bond in the sum of twenty five hundred dollars conditioned as the law requires.

Iss'd On the humber pitition of John Jett and for reasons appearing to the satisfaction of the Court he is permitted to keep a tavern house of public intertainment at his own house in the County of White and together with Thomas Eastland and Nicholas Oldham entered into and acknowledged bond in the sum of twenty five hundred dollars conditioned as the law requires.

On the humble pitition of Jesse Walling and for reasons appearing to the satisfaction of the Court he is permitted to keep a public house of entertainment at his own house in White County and together with Nicholas

Oldham and Jabez G. Mitchell entered into and acknowledged bond in the sum of twenty five hundred dollars conditioned as the law requires.

This day the Commissioners heretofore appointed to examine and change the road leading to shipping port through Robert Glenn, Jr. land being a road of the second Class made their report which road as changed is Established as a road of the second Class.

Ordered by Court that John Jett, Anthony Dibrell and William Simpson be appointed Commissioners to settle with David Mitchell adminestrator of the estate of David H. Mayborn deceased and report thereof to the next term of this Court.

Ordered that Court be adjourned untill Court in Course
Test
N. Oldham, Clk.

Thos. Eastland
David Snodgrass
Edmund Stamps

(P-172) State of Tennessee

At a Court began and held for the County of White at the Court house in the town of Sparta before the Justices of said Court on the first Monday being the third day of July Anno Dominni One thousand eight hundred and thirty seven. And of the Independence of the United States the sixty first year. Present the Worshipful

Thomas Eastland, Esq. Chairman
John Jett, John Bryan,
Lewis Pettett, Matthias Hutson,
Jesse Walling, William Knowles, } Esquires
James T. Hayes, Joshua Mason,
James Allison, Emery Bennett,
John Gillentine, Asa Certain, } Justices
John Wallis, Thomas Green,
William Little, Richard Crowder,
William Bruster,

Iss'd Ordered by Court that the order made at the last term requiring the sherriff of White County to bring into Court at the next term of this Court Thursby Conly, Hannah Conly and Levi Preston Conly orphans and minor children of Polly Conly to be dealt by according to law and you hereby required to notify Polly Conly of this proceedings by - &c

Iss'd Ordered by Court that William Little, John Rose, Samuel Lance, Brice Little and Washington P. Duncan, freeholders be reappointed a Jury of view to lay off and mark a road of the second Class from the North West Corner of Joseph Hunter 300 acre tract of land running Westwardly Crossing the Creek twice thence down the Creek on the north side agan crossing the Creek twice so as not to interfere with any persons fences and report thereof to the next term of this Court.

Iss'd Ordered by Court that Lewis Phillips be released from the payment of the Tax on one slave of the value of six hundred dollars for the year 1837 he being over charged that amount and that the Sherriff of White

County have a credit therefore in the settlement of his accounts.

Iss'd On the humble pitition of Lewis Phillips he is permitted to keep a tavern house of public entertainment in White County and thereupon entered into and acknowledged bond in the sum of two thousand dollars with Jabez G. Mitchell his security conditioned as the law requires.

Ordered by Court that Cason Swindle be released from the payment of the tax on one white poll for the year 1835 he being under age and that the securities of the late shff of White County have a credit in the settlement of his accounts with the Trustee of White County

Iss'd Ordered by Court that William Knowles be released from the payment of the taxes on one white poll for the year 1837 he being over age and that the sherriff of White County have a credit for the same in settlement of his accounts.

(P-173) Ordered by Court that Thomas Parris be released from the payment of the taxes on one white poll for the year 1836 he not being a Citizen of White County and that the securities of David L. Mitchell late Sherriff of White County have a credit therefor in the settlement of his accounts with the Trustee of this County.

Iss'd Ordered by Court that Joseph Upchurch be released from the paying of the tax on one white poll for the year 1837 And that the Sherriff of White County have a credit therefor in the settlements of his accounts.

Iss'd Ordered by Court that the road leading from Sparta to the deep ford on the Calf Killer be reduced from a second to a third Class road only - . that the present overseer is required to work said road as such/ and the Court assign David Dean, Madison Fisk and all the hands that John L. Price may from time to time have living with him to work thereon.

Iss'd Ordered by the Court that the same bounds which was formerly assigned to work that portion of the road leading from Sparta to the middle of the Bridge at the Harriett iron works be reestablished so as to also include James Hudgins & his hands, William Hunter & hands and any person occupying the houses at the west end of said Bridge on the bluff so as not to interfere with the hands assigned to the milk sick hills.

Iss'd Ordered by Court that Thomas Green and Jesse Walling Esquires, be appointed to settle with the adm's of the estate of James Isham deceased and report thereof to the next term of this Court.

Iss'd Ordered by Court that Thomas Green and Jesse Walling Esquires be appointed Commissioners to settle with Ozias Denton Executor of the estate of Jeremiah Denton deceased, and report thereof to the next term of this Court.

Iss'd Ordered by Court that John Jett and Thomas Green, Esqs. be appointed Commissioners to settle with Jesse Walling adminestrator of the estate of Thomas Paul deceased and report thereof to the next term of this Court.

Ordered by Court that James Easthum be released from the payment of forty two and one half cents the tax on 139 acres of land for the year

1836 he being overcharged that amount and that the Securities of David L. Mitchell late Sherriff of White County have a credit therefor in settlement of his accounts with the Trustee of White County.

Ordered by the Court that the Commissioners appointed at the last term of this Court to settle with Rachel Jones administratrix of William Jones deceased be allowed untill the next term of this Court to bring the report of this settlement. -

Ordered by Court that so much of the order allowing Dan Griffith Esq. two dollars and twenty five cents and Robert H. McManus one dollar seventy five cents as says to be paid out of any monies not otherwise appropriated" shall be so altered and changed as to read out of the Tax of the year 1837

Iss'd Ordered by Court that George W. Pirtle be released from the payment of the tax on one white poll for the year 1836 and that the securities of David L. Mitchell late Shff have credit for the same.

(P-174) Iss'd This day Thomas Frasure produced in open Court six small wolf scalps under the age of four months and proved by the oath of William Frasure that he killed them all in White County and there being present five acting Justices of the peace to Wit:
Thomas Eastland, John Jett, David Snodgrass, Lewis Pettett and John Bryan who order the same to be certified to the Treasure of the state of Tennessee for payment and that the said scalps be destroyed by the Sherriff of White County, who being here in Court received said scalps into his Custody and destroyed them in the presence of the Court.

Iss'd Ordered by Court that the following fees in the following cases be allowed the following persons which have been examined and certified by the attorney general for the State and for the County which they think reasonable and right and properly chargeable to the County of White to Wit:
In the case the state against Joseph Kerr, Jr., Indit. for Riot - Clerk William G. Sims \$4.12½ late Shff David L. Mitchell \$1.25 - .
In the case the state vs Samuel Scruggs and Edward Rudder Prest. for gaming Clerk W. G. Sims Clerk \$2.25 Clerk A. Dibrell 1.50 Clerk J. A. Lane \$2.37½ State Shff David L. Mitchell, 2.00\$ D. Shff William G. Sims 0.50¢ - .
In the case the State vs William M. Bryan, Prest for Affray - Clerk W. G. Sims \$4.87½ late Shff D. L. Mitchell \$1.54½ - D. Sheriff Jabez G. Mitchell 0.75 Witness Hayes Arnold \$2.00 - Wit. Allen L. Mitchel \$1.50 Wit. Sevier Evans 0.50 -. In the case of the State vs. Andrew Manard Prest for affray Clerk A. Dibrell \$5.87½ Clerk W. G. Sims \$6. late Shff David L. Mitchell \$3.54 - D. Sheff W. G. Sims \$2.00 Witness James Eastham \$1.50 - In the case the State vs Sally Roberts and Jane Price Ind't for keeping Disorderly house Clerk W. G. Sims \$6.68¾ - late shff David L. Mitchell \$4.25 Witness Benjamin Hitchcock \$1.50 In the case the State vs William L. Adams Ind't for gaming clerk W. G. Sims \$8.50 Justice J. Farrinton \$1.50 Shff J. G. Mitchell \$1.00 Shff W. R. Tucker \$1.50 Witness Jesse Allen \$5.20 Witness Joel Whitley \$2.00 In the case the State vs Turner Lane, Jr. Clerk W. G. Sims \$5.00 shff J. G. Mitchell \$1.25 Shff D. L. Mitchell \$2.81½ witness John Whitley \$1. witness Elias W. Bryant 0.50¢ - . In the case the State vs James Kerby Ind't A.B. Clerk W. G. Sims \$1.75 Justice William Bruster \$1.00 - Shff W. R. Tucker \$1.00 - . to be paid by the Trustee of the County of White out of any monies not otherwise appropriated.

Iss'd Ordered by Court that the following persons be summoned to attend as Jurors at the next Circuit Court to be held for the County of White on the first Monday of October next to wit:

John Crook, Elish Frost, Jacob Anderson; Spence Mitchell; James Holland, Joshua Mason, Stephen Wallis; William M. Bryan; Sr.; Abraham Cantrell, Jesse H. Vermillion, James H. Doyle, Joshua Pennington ; Matthias Hutson, George W. Anderson; Birtis Walker; Asa Certain; (P-175) David Snodgrass; Samuel Lance; Moses Carrick; Hugh Gracy; James Hudgins; James C. Crawley, Joseph S. Allison and Elisha Camron and Charles Meek and Hayes Arnold Constables to attend thereon and that a writ of Venirefacias issue directed &c.

Iss'd Ordered by Court that the following persons be appointed Judges in the County of White to hold an Election in their several Districts in August next for electing Representative in Congress members of the Legislation &c. to wit:

For Dist. No. 1.Anthony Dibrell, John Jett and Samuel V. Carrick
For Dist. No. 2. Simon Doyle; Solomon Dodson & John Austin
For Dist. No. 3. Thomas Green, Andrew Cope & Robert Anderson, Sr.
For Dist. No. 4. Lewis Pettett, Matthias Hutson & Joseph Anderson; Jr.
For Dist. No. 5. Thomas Roberts, John Humphrey & George Pirtle; Jr.
For District No. 6. Richard Crowder, James T. Hayes; Eli Sims.
For No. 7. Henry Burton; Samuel Strong; & James Eastham
For Dist. No. 8. Samuel Brown; Jose C. Dew & James Allison.
For Dist. No. 9. Richard England; Johathan Scott & Isaac Hutson
For Dist. No. 10. William C. Bounds; Samuel Dyer & John Pennington.
For Dist No. 11. William Bartlett - Isaac Buck and Thomas Barnes
For Dist No. 12. Elisha Camron; Edmund Stamps & Wm McKinny
For Dist. No. 13. David Snodgrass; William Wisdom & John Rose.
For Dist. No. 14. John Gipson; Benjamin Marr & John A. Jenkins.
For the Dist. No. 15. Joseph Cummings Jr., David Haston & Spence Mitchell.

The polls to be opened and closed according to law at the places of holding elections in the respective Districts.

State
vs } Bastardy
Stephen Pistole } Polly Ann Wilhite Prose.

This day came the Defendant in proper person in open Court with Robert Officer and John England and acknowledge themselves to be indebted to the state of Tennessee in the sum of one thousand dollars to wit: the Defendant in the sum of five hundred dollars and Robert Officer and John England each in the sum of two hundred and fifty Dollars to the use of the County of White void on condition that the Defendant shall at the end of one year pay Forty Dollars and the end of two years thirty dollars and at the end of three years twenty dollars for the support and maintainance of a Bastard female child begotten by defendant on the body of Polly Ann Wilhite the Prosecutrix and that they will keep free endemnified and harmless the County of White from the support and maintainance of the above Bastard Child Charged on oath by the said Polly Ann to be begotten on her body by the said Stephen Pistol - .

Whereupon it is considered by the Court that the State recover against said Defendant all costs in this behalf expended &c.

Ordered by Court that David Snodgrass, John Jett and William Glenn Esquires be appointed Commissioners to make distribution of the money and affects of the estate of William Jones deceased which has been by the adminestratrix suggested as being insolvent, Pro rata - The adm't giving public notice thereof (P-176) according to the law regulating the distribution of ensolvent estates make report thereof according to law.

Ordered by Court that Nicholas Oldham be appointed Commissioners to Superentend the repairs of the Court house in the County of White to wit: the repairing of the windows by putting in glass and hanging such Shutters as are fallen down - repairing the sash where needed - put a new lock on the Door hang the doors up stairs and purchase a stove and pipes to be put up in the Court house in some suitable place - that when these repairs shall have been made the said Oldham is to take charge of the key of said Court house and keep it closed except at such times when it is necessary to be open - And the Court further order that said repairs of the Court house when done shall be paid by the Trustee of White County out of the tax of the year 1837.

Ordered that Court be adjourned till tomorrow Morning 9 O'clock

Thos. Eastland
Jonathan Farrington
John Jett

Tuesday Morning 4th July A. D. 1837

Court met pursuant to adjournment
Present the Worshful

Thomas Eastland
Jonathan Farrington } Esqs Justices
John Jett

Iss'd Ordered by Court that John Gillentine and Joseph Cummings, Jr. be appointed Commissioners to settle with the Adm's of the estate of John Dale Dec'd and report there of to the next term of this Court.

Ordered that Court be adjourned untill Court in Course
Test
N. Oldham Clk

Thos. Eastland
Jonathan Farrington
John Jett

(P-177) State of Tennessee
At a Court began and held for the County of White and state aforesaid at the Court house in the town of Sparta before the Justices of said Court on the first Monday being the seventh day of August in the year of our Lord one Thousand eight hundred and thirty seven and of the Independence of the United States of America the sixty second year

Present the Worshipful
Thomas Eastland, Esq. Chairman

Edmund Stamps, Lewis Pettet, John Bryan, Asa Certain, Isaac Buck, William Little, John Jett, Thomas Green, John Gillentine, Jesse Walling, William Bruster, Elisha Camron, John Wallis, James Allison, Emery Bennett, Richard Crowder, James T. Hays, William Bartlett,	Esquires Justices

For reasons appearing to the satisfaction of the Court it is ordered that the order made at the last term of this Court releasing James Eastham from the payment of the tax on 139 acres of land amounting to the sum of Forty two and one half cents for the year 1837 and giving D. L. Mitchell credit therefore be entirely set aside and for nothing esteemed and that the said Eastham stand charged with the same on the tax list of said year.

For reasons appearing to the satisfaction of the Court on the oaths Jesse Davis and William Williams its ordered by the Court that John Oliver guardian to Elizabeth Cooper a minor be removed from said guardianship - . And that the seccurities of the said John Oliver be from all future liabilities as such released and forever discharged.

Ordered by Court that Jesse Davis be appointed guardian to Elizabeth Cooper a minor heir of James Cooper deceased who together with William Irwin and Jonathan T. Bradley appeared in open Court and entered into and acknowledged bond in the sum of three hundred dollars Conditioned as the law requires.

This day William Hill was appointed guardian to James Hill, Margarett Hill, Thomas Hill and John Hill infant children of the said William Hill who with David Snodgrass and George Defrees appeared in open Court and entered into and acknowledged bond in the sum of two thousand Dollars Conditioned as the law requires.

This day appeared in open Court Samuel Turney who was at a former term of this Court appointed Solicitor for the County Court of White County and took the oath required by law and thereupon entered upon the duties of his office

Iss'd Ordered by Court that Thomas Meek be released from the payment of the tax on one White poll for the year 1837 he being over age and that the sherriff of White County have a credit therefor.

(P-178) Iss'd Ordered by Court that the order of the last term of this Court appointing Jesse Walling and Thomas Green Esquires Commissioners to settle with the adminestrators and adminestrix of James Isham deceased be renewed and report thereof to the next term of this Court.

This day the Commissioners heretofore appointed to settle with Jesse Walling administrator of Thomas R. Paul deceased made their report upon oath which is received and confirmed in all its parts and ordered to be recorded - .

This day appeared in open Court Nicholas Oldham who was at the October term 1836 appointed Transcribed of the records of this Court therein set forth, and took the oath perscribed by law and the Court being fully satisfied that it was an omission, order this entry to be made Nunk protunk.

Ordered by Court that Ozias Denton Executor of the estate of Jeremiah Denton deceased be allowed the sum of Seventy four dollars eighty seven cents for services rendered in settling said estate to be by him retained out of the estate of the decedent.

It appearing fully to the satisfaction of the Court that in the account of the sales of the estate of Jeremiah Denton deceased the executor had improperly charged himself with the sum of one hundred and Twenty four dollars and fifty six and one fourth cents - it is considered and so ordered by the Court that the said Executor have a credit therefore in the settlement of said estate.

This day the Commissioners heretofore appointed to settle with Ozias Denton Executor of Jeremiah Denton deceased returned upon oath their report of settlement which is received and ordered to be recorded.

Ordered by Court that the order heretofore made appointing John Jett, Anthony Dibrell and William Simpson Commissioners to settle with the administrator of David H. Maybern deceased be renewed and report thereof to the next term of this Court.

This day Elizabeth Hamblett executor of the estate of Berry Hamblett deceased returned upon oath an additional Inventory of the estate of the deceased which is ordered to be recorded -

This day Joseph D. Hyder Constable in District No. 11 appeared in open Court and resigned his office as Constable which is ordered to be recorded - .

Iss'd Ordered by Court that the order of last Court appointing Joseph Cummings, Jr. and John Gillentine, Commissioners to settle with the adminestrators of John Dale deceased be renewed and report thereof to the next term of this Court.

Iss'd Ordered by Court that James Hard be appointed Overseer of the road from Jesse Walling to John Smiths being a road of the first Class and keep the same in repair as the law requires with the same hand's that were assigned to and worked under James Dotson late Overseer thereof -

(P-179) Iss'd Ordered by Court that Nicholas Oldham Clerk of White County Court be allowed the sum of nine dollars and fifty cents for two tax books for Sherriffs list and one Blank book for recording of taxes of said County of White to be paid by the Trustee of White County out of the taxes of the year 1837.

Iss'd Ordered by Court that Nicholas Oldham Clerk of White County Court be allowed the sum of twenty dollars for his services in making and recording the taxes List of White County for the year 1837 to be paid by the Trustee of White County out of the taxes of 1837

This day Nicholas Oldham transcriber of Certain records of White

County Court towit: from 1806 to 1811 produced in open Court a Book containing said records Transcribed which the Court unanimously approve and received and order that said records be filed in the office of the Clerk of this Court all of which is ordered to be recorded - .

Iss'd Ordered by Court that Nicholas Oldham be allowed the sum of one hundred dollars for services rendered in transcribing the records of this Court from 1806 to 1811 to be paid by the Trustee of White County out of the taxes of the year 1837 after all the Special orders of 1837 of prior date Shall have been paid out of the taxes of said year but should there not be a sufficincy to pay said one hundred Dollars or whatever balance may be unpaid there in that event to be paid out of the tax of 1838 to be laid for that purpose.

Iss'd Ordered by Court that Josiah Prater be appointed overseer of the road from Clifty Creek to the intersection of the Loss Creek road with the Ross road being a road of the second Class and keep the same in repair as the law requires and that the same bounds of hands that worked under Thomas Eastland Esq. late overseer thereof be assigned to work thereon.

Iss'd Ordered by Court that Isaac Buck and Thomas Barnes be appointed Commissioners to apportion Lists and bounds of hands between the diferent overseers of roads in District No. 11 having due regard to the dignity of said roads respectively and report thereof to the next term of this Court.

Ordered by Court that the road leading from Robert Andersons to Rosses old ferry on Caney fork being a road of the second Class be reduced to a road of the third Class and as such esteemed and that the Overseer thereof keep it in order as such.

Iss'd Ordered by Court that Jesse Walling & Thomas Green Esqs. be appointed Commissioners to apportion hands between the different Overseers on the Rockisland road from Hill branch to John Haltermans taking the hands from the Ross road and report to the next term of this Court.

Ordered by Court that John Gillentine and Lewis Pettett be appointed to approtion hands between Adreant Bryan and Henry Crawley Overseers of the road and report to the next term of this Court.

(p-180) Ordered by Court that the order appointing Commissioners to settle with Rachel Jones adminestratrix of William Jones deceased at the last term of this Court be set Aside.

Iss'd Ordered by Court that the order made at September term 1836 of this Court appointing James Hudgins; Alexander Lowry; Samuel Lance; Henry Lance and Nathaniel C. Davis freeholders to lay off and mark a road of the third Class from Col. Alexander Lowrys passing the dwelling house formerly occupied Doct Springs and intersect the Turnpike road near where the old road intersects the same be'renewed and report thereof to the next term of this Court.

Iss'd Whereas at the July term A.D.1836 of this Court the Court ordered that Nicholas Cook guardian to the heirs of George Kezee deceased be allowed the sum of Sixteen Dollars fifteen cents for services rendered and money expended for the benefit of his said ward; which Anthony Dibrell late Clerk of White Circuit Court as receiver of the monies of the estate of George Kezee deceased was required to pay or so much thereof as he should have funds in his hands belonging to said estate.

And it being suggested to the Court that the said receiver aforesaid refuses to pay said sum of money above mentioned to the said Nicholas Cook guardian as aforesaid alledging that it had been previously paid.

Whereupon it is Considered and so ordered by the Court that the said Anthony Dibrell receiver as aforesaid make his appearance at the next term of this Court and shew cause by producing testimony why the aforesaid sum of sixteen dollars fifteen cents should not be paid out of said estate and that he be served with a copy of this order.

Ordered by Court that Thomas Green and Jesse Walling be each allowed the sum of one dollar fifty Cents for one days services in settling with Ozias Denton Exr., of Jeremiah Denton deceased to be paid out of the estate of the deceased.

Ordered that Court be adjourned untill tomorrow Morning 9 O'clock

John Jett
Wm. Bruster
Wm. Little

Tuesday Morning 8th August 1837 - Court met pursuant to adjournment
Present the Worshful

John Jett, William Bruster, William Little — Esquires Justices

Ordered that Court be adjourned untill Court in Course
Test
N. Oldham; Clk

John Jett
Wm. Bruster
Wm. Little

(P-181) State of Tennessee

At a Court began and held for the County of White and State aforesaid at the Court house in the town of Sparta before the Justices of said Court on the first Monday being the fourth day of September in the year of our Lord one thousand eight hundred and thirty Seven and of the Independence of the United States the Sixty second year.

Present the worshipful

John Jett; Lewis Pettett,
Emery Bennett, Elijah Frost,
Edmund Stamps; John Wallis,
Isaac Buck; Matthias Hutson,
William Bartlet; Wm. Knowles,
William C. Bounds; Elisha Camron,
James T. Hayes, John Bryan,
Thomas Green, Jesse Walling,
John Gillentine; Joshua Mason.
— Esquires Justices

Ordered by the Court that John Jett Esq. be appointed Chairman Pro-tempore of this Court for the present term.

This day the Sherriff of White County returned into open Court the Certificate of the election of Thomas Welch as Constable in the Eleventh District in White County to fill the vacancy occasioned by the resegnation of Joseph D. Hyder late Constable of said District.

This day appeared in open Court Thomas Welch who was duly elected Constable in the 11th district in White County to fill the vacancy occasioned by the resegnation of Joseph D. Hyder and took the oath to support the constitution of the United States and the State of Tennessee and the several oaths prescribed by law. And together with Jesse A. Bounds and Mark Whitaker entered into and acknowledged bond in the sum of one thousand dollars conditioned as the law requires.

Iss'd Ordered by Court that William Lafferty be appointed Overseer of the road from the falling water at Childresses to the intersection of the Allens ferry road at Lisks being a road of the second Class and keep the same in repair as the law requires and that Henry Benton and Samuel Strong Esquires assign a bounds of hands to work thereon.

Iss'd Ordered by Court that William Cook, Earl J. Cook, Thomas Robertson, Jeremiah Webb, and William Jackson freeholders be appointed a Jury of view to lay off and mark a road of the third Class from Wallings road to Cooks Mill at the mouth of Barron and report thereof to the next term of this Court.

Iss'd Ordered by Court that James A. Haston, William Wallis, Sr., and Joberry Felton be assigned to work on that part of the Milksick Hills of which John Wallis is Overseer. (P-182)

Iss'd This day the death of Webster Hutchings late of the County of White deceased was suggested and that he died intestate.

Whereupon Mary Hutchings and Benjamin Hutchings were appointed adminestratrix and adminestrator of all and singular the goods and chattles rights and credits of the deceased who being present in open Court and took the oath prescribed by law and together with Joseph Herd and Lee R. Taylor entered into and acknowledged bond in the sum of Five hundred dollars conditioned as the law requires.

This day Edward Watkins an orphan boy aged fourteen years was bound to Waman Leftwich to serve him after the manner of an apprentice to the Saddling business for the full space and term of five and one half years from this day and for the faithful performance of his Covenant entered into and acknowledged bond with Anthony Dibrell his Security conditioned as the law requires.

This day the Commissioners heretofore appointed by this Court to settle with the adminestrators of the estate of John Dale deceased returned their report upon oath which is received and ordered to be recorded.

Ordered by the Court that John Gillentine and Joseph Cummings, Jr., be each allowed one dollar for one day's services in settling with the admrs of John Dale deceased to be paid out of said estate.

Iss'd Ordered by Court that Eli Sims and William Irwin be appointed Commissioners to assign and set apart one years provisions out of the estate of Webster Hutchings deceased for the widow and family of the deceased and report thereof to the next term of this Court.

Iss'd This day William Hudson was appointed Guardian to William Dyrham and George Durham minor children of David Durham deceased and took the oath required by law and together with Richard Judson and Isaac Hutson entered into and acknowledged bond in the sum one thousand dollars conditioned as the law requires.

Ordered by Court that Nancy Bowman be allowed the sum of one hundred and eighty eight dollars; thirty three and one half cents, for boarding Cloathing and schooling the minor Children; heirs of Benjamin Bowman deceased to be paid by the guardian of said heirs - out of their estate.

Iss'd Ordered by Court that Jesse Franks be appointed Overseer of the road from John Haltermans to the Kentucky road being a road of the first Class and keep the same in repair as the law requires; and that the same list and bounds of hands that worked under Tidence L. Denton be assigned to work thereon.

(P-183) Ordered by Court that Madison Fisk; William M. Young; John Wallis and Wamon Leftwich be appointed Commissioners to settle the administrator of Azariah Long deceased and report thereof to the next term of this Court.

Andrew Welch, Admr. of Reason Ricketts, dec'd (Cert) William B. Campbell } Letter of Attorney

This day personally appeared in open Court Andrew Welch Admr of Reason Ricketts to the Court known and acknowledged the due execution of the forgoing Letter of Attorney to William B. Campbell to be his act and deed for the purposes therein mentioned which is ordered to be recorded and Certified under the seal of this Court.

This day John Mason guardian to James Howard a minor heir of James Howard dec'd returned his report upon oath which is ordered to be recorded.

This day William Bartlett adminestrator of the estate of Nathan Bartlett deceased returned upon oath an Inventory & account of the sales of said estate which is ordered to be recorded.

Iss'd Ordered by Court that Russell Gist one of the adminestrators of the estate of James Isham dec'd be allowed the sum of seventy five dollars for services rendered and money expended by him in aiding in the settlement of said Estate to be paid out of the estate of the Decedent.

This day the Commissioners heretofore appointed by this Court to settle with the admr. of James Isham deceased returned their report upon oath which is received and ordered to be recorded.

Ordered by Court that Thomas Green and Jesse Walling be each allowed the sum of one dollar fifty cents for two days services each in settling with the adminestrators of James Isham deceased to be paid out of the estate of the deceased.

This day Alexander A. Dillon was appointed guardian to Ann Cook; Polly Cook; Minerva Cook and George Cook minor heirs of George L. Cook; deceased - who appeared in open Court and took the oath required by law and together with James Dillon and Jacob A. Lane entered into and acknowledged bond in the sum of five hundred dollars conditioned as the law requires.

Iss'd This day the Commissioners heretofore appointed to lay off and mark a road from Colo. Lowery passing Doct Spring late residence on Cumberland Mountain and entersecting the turnpike road again beyond Hoffmans made their report verbally the solicitor assenting whereupon it is ordered by the Court that the same be established a road of the third Class and that Barlow Fisk be appointed overseer thereof and keep the same in repair as the law requires at his own expense.

(P-184) This day Joseph Herd guardian to the heirs of Benjamin Bowman deceased returned his report upon oath which is ordered to be recorded.

This day the death of Micajah Taylor late of the County of White was suggested and that he died entestate whereupon Creed A. Taylor was appointed adminestrator of all and singular the goods and chattles right and credits of the deceased who being in open Court took the oath prescribed by law and together with William Taylor and Jesse Walling entered into and acknowledged bond in the sum of three thousand Dollars Conditioned as the law requires.

Iss'd Ordered by Court that James T. Hayes Esq. be appointed to assign to Jacob Pirtle a list of hands to work on the road of which he is Overseer.

Iss'd Ordered by the Court that the order appointing Jesse Walling and Thomas Green Commissioners to apportion the hands from off the Rosses ferry road between the diffrent Overseers on Rockisland road from Hills branch to John Haltermans be renewed and report thereof to the next term of this Court.

Iss'd Ordered by court that the order appointing John Gillentine and Lewis Pettett Esqs to apportion lists of hands between Adrian Bryant and Henry Crowley Overseers of the road be renewed and report thereof to the next term of this Court.

Walter Hutson &
George Bradshaw
to Cert.
Henderson McFarlan } Title Bond

It appearing fully to the satisfaction of the Court that the subscribing Witnesses to the within Title bond to wit; Jacob Conner and John M. Rottan were both dead; and further the Court being fully satisfied upon the oaths of Richard Nelson and John Wallis to the Court known; that Walter Huston and George Bradshaw did execute said Bond for the purpose therein contained which is ordered to be received and certified for Regestration in the County of White.

The State
vs
William Green

Bastardy

Louisa Campbell Pros'x

This day came as well the Defendant as the prosecutrix Louisa Campbell in their proper persons into oupen Court; and thereupon the Prosecutrix acknowledged that she received in full; all Compensation to which by law she was entitled of the Defendant for the begotting upon her body a bastard female child whereupon it is considered by the Court that the Defendant find sureties to keep the County of White indemnified (P-185) from all costs and charges for and toward the support and maintenance of said Bastard child - whereupon it is considered by the Court that the State of Tennessee recover against the Defendant all Costs in this behalf expended. And now came William Bruster into open Court and agrees that execution may issue jointly with the Defendant against his goods and chattles for the collection of the Costs in the above cause - And the Defendant together with William Bruster intered into and acknowledged bond in the sum of five hundred Dollars conditioned to keep the County of White endemnified from all costs &c. as the law requires.

This day the Commissioners who were appointed to apportion bounds of hands to the diffrent Overseers in the 11th District in White County returned their report which is ordered to be recorded as follows - .

To James Bohanon - Overseer the following hands to wit - .
Thomas Barnes, Jr., David Norriss, David Buck, Aaron England, Jr., Solomon Bullock, John M. Bullock, Edward Bullock, Thomas J. Nicholas, Isaac L. Huddleston, Isaac A. Huddleston - .

To Austin Webb, Overseer to wit:
William Webb, Jr., Webbs Nathan, Wards Squire, Stephen Ward, William Martin, Thomas Cooper, John Hunter; David Wiser, Francis Alred, Daniel Adams, and Jesse Rogers - .

To Joseph Bartlett, Overseer; to wit:
Joseph Pryor; Thomas Bohanon, Dudley Hunter and hands; John Robertson, Thomas Welch; James Kennard, John Kennard, Andrew Townsend, William Creacy, Thomas Clouse; James Kirby, Pleasant Kirby, Samuel Ayers, Aaron Thomas; Theophelus McMillion; John Julin; Coleman Buckner; William Kinnard; Nathan Pryor.

To Robert Whitaker to wit:
William Whitaker, Sr., Goodman Madewell, James Jackson, William Phillips, James Robertson, Moses Robertson, David Robertson, William Robertson, Solomon Madewell, James Madewell, Samuel Madewell, & John Dixon.

To George Bohanon to wit:
John Hyder, Joseph D. Hyder, John Bohanon; Sr., William Bohanon; Henry Bohanon; James Bartlett; Jonathan Oxendine; William Daniel; Bartlett Jocob - .

To Andrew Jackson to wit:
Jonathan Hyder William Buckner; Isaiah Madewell; John Madewell; Jr.; John Maddis, Washington Jackson; Newell Jackson; Nelson Oxendine and Moses Grant.

To Matthias Welch to wit:
James Whitaker, William Whitaker, Jacob Hyder, Jr., John Whitak, John Bohanon, Jr., William Bohanon, Sr., Campbell Bohanon and John Jackson, Jr.

This day was produced in open Court an infant male child by the name of George Huffman and it appearing to the satisfaction of the Court that said child is a pauper in a very destitute and suffering Condition properly within the Jurisdiction of this Court.

(P-186) It is therefore considered and so ordered by the Court that the infant Pauper George Huffman be conveyed to the Poor House of White County and be by the keeper thereof maintained and supported at the expence of said County.

Iss'd Ordered by Court that the order made at July term of this Court requiring the Sherriff of White County to bring into This Court Thursby Conley, Hannah Conley and Levi Preston Conley, children of Polly Conley to be dealt by according to law and giving notice to the said Polly Conley of this proceeding be renewed returnable to the next term of this Court.

Ordered by Court that it be adjourned untill tomorrow morning 10 O'Clock

John Jett
Jonathan Farrington
John Bryan

Tuesday Morning 5th day of September A.D. 1837 Court met pursuant to adjournment. Present the Worshipful

John Jett
John Bryan and
Jonathan Farrington } Esquire Justice

Ordered that Court be adjourned untill Court in Course
Test
W. Oldham, Clk

John Jett
Jonathan Farrington
John Bryan

(P-187)

State of Tennessee
At a Court began and held for the County of White and State aforesaid at the Court house in the town of Sparta before the Justices of said Court on the first Monday being the second day of October in the year of our Lord One thousand eight hundred and thirty seven and of the Independence of the United States the sixty second year.
Present the Worshipful

David Snodgrass, Chairman, P.T.
John Jett, Jonathan Farrington
John Wallis, Wm. Knowles,
Joshua Mason, Elijah Frost,
Asa Certain, James Allison,
Elisha Camron, William Bruster,
James T. Hayes, Richard Crowder,
Isaac Buck, William Bartlett.

The Clerk of this Court produced and read in open Court the following receipts which were ordered to be recorded to wit:

"Received of N. Oldham Clerk of White County Court the Tax list of Property and Polls in White County Tenn's for the year 1837 made out at full length according to law Re'd the 8th day of April 1837

J. T. Bradley, Shff.
of White County"

'Sparta 2nd September 1837

Received of N. Oldham Clerk of White County Court an abstract Statement of the County, Jury and Bridge Taxes for White County for the year 1837 Amounting to the sum of Fifteen hundred and twenty five Dollars thirty one cents and two mills

Ro. Cox Trustee
of White County"

Sparta 2nd Sept. 1837

Received of N. Oldham Clerk of White County Court an abstract Statement of the Poor Tax in White County for the year 1837 amounting to Six hundred and Ninety five Dollars Sixteen Cents and two Mills.

John Jett, Treasure of Poorhouse
Com's of White County"

Sparta 4th Sept. 1837

Received of N. Oldham Clerk of White County Court an Abstract Statement of the school land tax in White County for the year 1837 Amounting to the sum of Seventy six Dollars twenty cents and four mills

R. H. McEwin, Superentendant
of public instruction in Tennessee
By John W. Simpson his
$76.20.4 Agent for White County.

(P-188) "Sparta 4th Sept. 1837

Received of N. Oldham Clerk of White County Court One hundred and twenty one Dollars eighty seven and one half cents in full for monies by him received on Tipling house Licence for the year ending the first September 1837 as shown by his Report thereof.

R.H.McEwin, Superentendant
of Public instruction in Tennessee
by J. W. Simpson his Agent
for White County"

Sparta 4th September 1837

Received of N. Oldham Clerk of White County Court the Bond of Jonathan T. Bradley Esq Sherriff of White County for the Collection of the school tax in White County according to law for the year 1837

R. H. McEwin, Superentendant
of Public instruction in Tennessee
By J. W. Simpson his agent in
White County.

Sparta Tenn. 28th September 1837

Received of N. Oldham Clerk of White County Court One hundred and seventy seven Dollars Sixty eight and three fourth cents being for County

Tax on Priviliges in White County for the year ending first September 1837 agreeable to his account thereof this day filed

Robert Cox Trustee
of White County."

Nashville Tennessee 25th Sept. 1837

Received of Nicholas Oldham his Statement of Public revenue collected as clerk of White County Court from 1 Sept 1836 to Sept 1 1837

Daniel Graham
Comptroller of the Treasure

Nashville 25 Sept. 1837 No. 360.

$845.68 - - Received of Nicholas Oldham Esq. eight hundred and forty five Dollars 68 cents audeted to him by No.360 and due on account of Revenue by him Collected as Clerk of the County Court of White County from the 1 Sept 1836 to 1 Sept. 1837

(Signed Duplicates)

Miller Francis
Treasures of Tennessee."

Comptroller offices 25th Sept. 1837

Received of Nicholas Oldham Clerk of White County Court the Bond of Jonathan T. Bradley Esq. Sherriff and Collector of the Public Taxes for the present year dated the third day of April 1837

Daniel Graham
Comptroller &c."

Comptrollers office 25 Sept. 1837

Received of Nicholas Oldham Clerk of White County Court a Duplicate of the Tax List of White County for the year 1837

Daniel Graham
Comptroller &c."

(P-189) Comptroller office 25 Sept 1837

Received of Nicholas Oldham Clerk of White County Court a Duplicate receipt of R. H. McEwin Esq. Superentendant of Public instruction dated 4th September 1837 for one hundred and twenty one Dollars eighty seven and one half cents which by law he is required to file in my office

Daniel Graham
Comptroller &c."

Iss'd Ordered by Court that Jonathan Elms be appointed Overseer of the road from Littles Bridge to the intersection of the old Calfkiller road near Potts school house being a road of the third Class and keep the same in repair as the law requires and that the same list and bounds of hands that worked under Sims McCann late Overseer thereof be assigned to work thereon.

Iss'd Ordered by Court that Daniel Simrell be appointed Overseer of the road from the middle of the Bridge at the Harrett Irons to the Widow Smiths gate being a road of the first Class and keep the same in repair as the law requires and that the same bounds of hands that worked under Robert Anderson late overseer thereof be assigned to work thereon.

Iss'd Ordered by Court that Henry C. Evans be appointed Overseer of the road from Robert Cooks to the forks of the Kentucky road being a road of the 2nd Class And keep the same in repair as the law requires. And that the same list of hands that worked under the late Overseer thereof be assigned to work thereon.

This day the Clerk of White County Court reported that Sundry persons in White County had failed and refused to pay the County tax imposed on Priviliges to wit: William Glenn $22.50 Buck & Barnes $10. Warren & Dibrell 22.50 S. V. & H. L. Carrick $10 - William Simpson $57.50 - which is ordered to be recorded whereupon it is considered and so directed by the Court that the Clerk of this Court make application to each of the above named persons for the payment of said several sums of monies above mentioned and if upon application as above all of said sums of money above mentioned or any one of them shall not have punctually paid the Court order the Clerk to make out a statement of such as still remain unpaid and place said Statement in the hands of the Sherriff of White County for Collection, to be Collected and paid to the Trustee of said County as other public Taxes.

Iss'd Ordered by Court that Washington Frasure be appointed Overseer of the road from Rottans to the foot of the mountain being a road of the second Class and keep the same in repair as the law requires And that the same list of hands that worked under Wm. Frasure late Overseer thereof be assigned to work thereon.

(P-190) Iss'd Ordered by Court that Joseph Hunter, William McKinney, Sims Dearing, Thomas Little, Charles McGuire and James Snodgrass freeholders be appointed a jury of view to examine lay off mark and change the road if expedient from the ford of the river at Glenn's old Salt wells and to intersect the Usrey Gap road near the Flat rock on the Mountain and report thereof to the next term of this Court.

Iss'd It appearing to the satisfaction of the Court that Sally Bradley had paid the sum of two Dollars twenty and one half cents being the Tax on three slaves for the year 1836 and it appearing to the satisfaction of this Court that her slaves were not taxable for said year 1836 It is therefore ordered by the Court that the Trustee of White County pay the said Sally Bradley the aforesaid sum of two Dollars twenty and one half cents out of the tax of the year 1836

Iss'd Ordered by Court that, that part of the Sims road of which William McGarrah and Aaron Hutchings are Overseers be remeasured and be equally divided into three lots and that Andrew J. Sims, Jesse H. Vermillion and William R. Tucker be appointed Overseers thereon being a road of the first and keep the same in repair as the law requires - And that Richard Crowder and Asa Certain Esquires be assigned to divide the hands that worked under McGarrah and Hutchings equally between the three new Overseers and assign to each Overseer his particular portion of said road. And report thereof to the next term of this Court.

Iss'd Ordered by Court that Samuel Stover be appointed Overseer of the road from the Blue Spring in the place of Thomas Hawks former Overseer being a road of the second Class and keep the same in repair as the law requires. And that the same bounds of hands that worked under the late Overseers be assigned to work thereon.

Iss'd Ordered by Court that Moses Cantrell be appointed Overseer of the road from the Peeled Chestnut to the Knotty oak being a road of the first Class and keep the same in repair as the law requires and that the same bounds of hands that worked under Tennessee Hooper late Overseer thereof be assigned to work thereon.

Iss'd This day was exhibited in open Court a writing purporting to be the last will and testament of David Robertson late of the County of White deceased. Whereupon the due execution and publication thereof to be the last will and testament of the said David Robertson was proven in open Court by the oath of John Madewell; and that at the date of the execution and publication thereof as such the said David Robertson was of sound and disposing mind and memory which is ordered to be recorded.

(P-191) Iss'd Ordered by Court that William Baker; Richard Baker; John Sullivan; William Frisby and Lee R. Taylor Freeholders be appointed a jury of view to examine and so change the road leading from Rock Island to Gainsborough as to turn of said road near Taylors Creek on the land of Isaac Taylor. And intersect the old road again at or near the branch south of John Taylors. And report thereof to the next term of this Court.

Iss'd Ordered by Court that James Randols; Hays Arnolds, Timothy Couch; Limas B. Farris and Samuel A. Moore, Jr.; freeholders be appointed a Jury of view to lay off and mark a road of the third Class from Sparta passing the Bridge at the Harriett Iron works the nearest and best rout to the place where John H. Jones now lives and report thereof to the next term of this Court.

Iss'd Ordered by Court that the order of last Court appointing Jesse Walling and Thomas Green Esquires to apportion the hands from off the Rosses Ferry road between the diffrent Overseer on Rock Island road from Hill branch to John Halterman be renewed and report thereof to the next term of this Court.

Ordered that Court be adjourned untill tomorrow Morning 10 O'clock

Thos. Eastland
David Snodgrass
Asa Certain

Tuesday Morning 3rd October A.D. 1837 Court met pursuant to adjournment
Present the Worshipful

Thomas Eastland, Esq.; Chairman
David Snodgrass, Elisha Camron; }
Asa Certain; William Bruster; } Esq.
Joshua Mason; Wm. Bartlett } Justices

Iss'd Ordered by Court that William Garland be appointed Overseer of the road from the two mile post to the four mile post on the Carthage road being a road of the first Class and keep the same in repair as the law requires and that the same list of hands that works under Benjamin McClain late Overseer thereof be assigned to work thereon.

Iss'd Ordered by Court that Josiah Turner be appointed Overseer of the road from the west end of the Bridge at the town of Sparta to the two mile post on the Carthage road being a road of the first class and keep the same in repair as the law requires and that the same hands that worked under James Lowry Overseer be assigned to work thereon.

(P-192) Iss'd Ordered by Court that Joshua Hickey be appointed Overseer of the road from the four to the 6 mile post on the Carthage road being a road of the first Class and keep the same in repair as the law requires and the same list of hands that worked under the late Overseer thereof be assigned to work thereon.

Iss'd Ordered by Court that Samuel Thomas be appointed Overseer of the road from the forks of the road near Scarbroughs mill on the Sequatchee Valley road to S. Thomas house being a road of the second Class and keep the same in repair as the law requires and that all the hands in the following bounds be assigned to work thereon to wit: Begining at Mrs. Flinns including all the hands there; thence a direct line to Samuel Thomas including all the hands there; thence to the mouth of Bee Creek; thence up the Caney fork to the Stage road; thence east with the same to the County line including the hands within 100 yards on both sides of said road; thence with the County line westwardly to Mrs. Flynns including all the hands in said boundry.

Iss'd Ordered by Court that Jonathan Farrington and Asa Certain Esquires be appointed to apportion and divide the hands if necessary between Josiah Turner Overseer on the Carthage road, Daniel Clark Overseer on the Lincolns ferry road and Jabez G. Mitchell Overseer on the Shipping port road; so that each Overseer may have a fair and equal division of hands according to the Condition and grades of the several roads and report thereof to the next term of this Court.

Ordered that Court be adjourned untill Court in Course
Test
N. Oldham, Clk.

Thos. Eastland.
David Snodgrass
Wm. Bartlett.

(P-193) State of Tennessee

At a Court began and held for the County of White and state aforesaid at the Court house in the town of Sparta before the Justices of said Court on the first Monday being the Sixth day of November in the year of our Lord One thousand eight hundred and thirty seven; and of the Independence of the United States the Sixty second year.

Present the Worshipful

Thomas Eastland, Esq., Chairman
David Snodgrass, Matthias Hutson,
Elisha Camron, Lewis Pettett,
John Bryan; William Knowles, } Esquires
Elijah Frost, James T. Hayes,
Jesse Walling, Joshua Mason,
Richard Crowder, William Bartlett,
Asa Certain, William Bruster,
John Gillentine; John Jett,
Edmund Stamps; Thomas Green; } Justices
Jonathan Farrington.

Iss'd Ordered by Court that James M. Nelson be released from the appraised value of twelve head of sheep posted by him as Estrays

Iss'd Ordered by Court that Joseph Hunter, William McKenny, Sims Dearing, Thomas Little, Charles McGuire and James Snodgrass, freeholders be appointed a jury of view to examine lay off and change the road if expedient at the ford of the river at Glenns old salt well and to intersect the Ussery Gap road near the flat rock on the Mountain and report thereof to the next term of this Court.

This day the Commissioners heretofore appointed by this Court to apportion hands from off the Ross's ferry road and to put them on the Rockisland road make their report which is by the Court received and affirmed and ordered to be recorded to wit: Report Lewis Phillips Overseer four hands to wit: William Anderson & Boy, James W. Copeland and William Rickman - To Spencer Holder, Overseer eight hands to wit: Milford Casy, James Harden, Jerry Logan, James McBride, Buman Harden, Jerry Witt, Henry Keithly, and Hugh Harden.

Iss'd Ordered by Court that Sevier Evans be appointed Overseer of the road leading from Robert Hewetts across the Mountain to the intersection of the Ross road near Bryans field being a road of the third Class and keep the same in repair as the law requires and that the same list of hands that worked under the late Overseer thereof be assigned to work thereon.

(P-194) Iss'd This day was produced in open Court a writing purporting to be the last will and testament of David Robertson late of the County of White deceased and the due execution and publication thereof as such was proven in open Court by the oath of Annis Madewell the other subscribing witness thereto for the purposes and things therein mentioned and that at the date of the execution and publication thereof the said David Robertson was of sound and disposing mind and memory, and the same having been the October term of this Court 1837 in like manner proven by the oath of John Madewell for the same purpose all of which is Ordered to be recorded.

This day was suggested in open Court the death of Andrew Hampton late of the County of White and that he departed this life intestate; Whereupon James Snodgrass appeared in open Court and is appointed administrator of all and singular the goods and Chattles, rights and Credits of the deceased and took the oath prescribed by law and together with John England Jr. and Samuel Brown entered into and acknowledged bond in the sum of three hundred Dollars Conditioned as the law requires.

Iss'd This day was produced in open Court writing purporting to be the last will and testament of James Madewell late of the County of White deceased and the due execution and publication thereof as such was proven in open Court by the oath of Annis Madewell one of the subscribing witness thereto for the purposes and things therein mentioned - And that the said James Madewell was at the date of the execution and publication thereof of sound and disposing mind and memory and at the same time made oath that David Robertson whose name is subscribed to said last will and testament as the other witness, did sign his name thereto as witness at the request and in the presence of the testators at the date of the execution and publication thereof And that the said David Robertson is now deceased which the Court deem sufficient and order the same to be recorded.

This day the Commissioners heretofore appointed to examine and change he road leading from Rockisland to Gainsborough turning off said road ear Taylors Creek made report; report wich is by the Court received and ffirmed and that said Taylor open said road at his own proper cost and harges.

Iss'd Ordered by Court that William Burden be appointed Overseer f the road from Lowery's old place to Pleasant Waller, being a road of the econd Class and keep the same in repair as the law requires and that the ame list of hands that worked under the late Overseer thereof be assigned o work thereon.

(P-195) This day personally appeared in open Court Anna Henry and John I. Henry two of the minor heirs of Joseph Henry deceased who being of proper age for choosing their Guardian did each in the presence of the Court select and choose George Bohanon to be their Guardian who being present in open Court and together with William Bartlett and Samuel Madewell entered into and acknowledged bond in the sum of seven hundred Dollars conditioned as the law requires.

This day George Bohanon was appointed Guardian to William Henry, Rebecca Henry, Eliza Jane Henry, and Wamon Henry four of the Minor heirs of Joseph Henry deceased who being present in open Court together with William Bartlett and Samuel Madewell intered and acknowledged bond in the sum of fourteen hundred Dollars condition as the law requires.

This day the death of John Massa, Sr., late of the County of White was suggested in open Court and that he departed this life intestate whereupon John Massa, Jr., was appointed administrator of all and singular the goods and chattles rights and credits lands and tenements of the said John Massa, Sr., deceased and took the oath prescribed by law and together with George W. Potts and Jesse Williams entered into and acknowledged bond in the sum of four hundred Dollars conditioned as the law requires.

This day John Massa administrator of the Estate of John Massa deceased returned upon oath an Inventory of said Estate which is ordered to be recorded.

Iss'd Ordered by Court that John England, Jr., be appointed Overseer of the road from the Caney fork to Thomas Pistoles being a road of the second Class and keep the same in repair as the law requires and that the same list of hands that worked under the late Overseer thereof be assigned to work thereon.

Iss'd This day the Commissioners heretofore appointed to examine and lay off a road from Sparta to John H. Jones returned their report and that part of said road as marked by the Commissioners leaving the Franks ferry road at a large White oak blazed, on the south side of the Mountain, thence as marked by Commissioners to said Jones be received and established as a road of the third Class - And that Timothy Couch be appointed Overseer thereof and open and keep the same in repair as required by law.

Iss'd Ordered by Court that Madison Fisk, William M. Young, John Wallis, and Wamon Leftwich be appointed Commissioners to settle with George Cline administrators of Azanah Long deceased and report thereof to the next term of this Court.

Iss'd Ordered by Court that Lewis Pettett and Joseph Cummings, Jr., be appointed Coms. to settle with Thomas Hill guardian to the heirs of James Hill deceased and report to the next term of this Court.

This day Creed A. Taylor adminestrator of Mecajah Taylor (P-196) Deceased returned upon oath an Inventory of said Estate in part which is Ordered to be recorded.

This day the Commissioners heretofore appointed to apportion lists and bounds of hands between Adrian Bryant and Henry Crawley Overseers of the road make the following report to wit: To Adrian Bryant Overseer - John M. Carter; Peter Carter; John Davis; William Moore; Thomas W. Williams; Reuben Davis and William Dodson and to Henry Crawley Overseer - George Wood; John Fisher, Solomon Charles, Sampson Smallman; Wright Lane and Duncan Harden, which is received and ordered to be recorded.

Ordered by Court that David Snodgrass and Anthony Dibrell be appointed Commissioners to settle with George Bohanon adminestrator of the Estate of Joseph Henry deceased and report thereof to the next term of this Court.

Iss'd This day the death of Mary Wallis late of the County of White was suggested in open Court and that she departed this life intestate whereupon John Wallis was appointed adminestrator of all and singular the goods and Chattles; rights and credits of the said Mary Wallis deceased and took the oath prescribed by law and together with John W. Simpson, William Simpson and Simon R. Doyle entered into and acknowledged bond in the sum of three thousand Dollars conditioned as the law requires.

Ordered by Court that John Jett and Thomas Green Esqs. be appointed Commissioners to settle with John W. Simpson guardian to the heirs of Abraham Conner deceased and report thereof to the next term of this Court.

This day the death of John Haily late of the County of White was suggested in open Court and that he departed this life intestate whereupon William Haily was appointed adminestrator of all and singular the goods and chattles rights and credits of the said John Haily deceased and took the oath prescribed by law and together with Samuel W. Moore and William L. Adams entered into and acknowledged bond in the sum of two hundred dollars conditioned as the law requires.

Iss'd Ordered by Court that Thomas Wilson be appointed Overseer of the road from the widow Dales to the middle of the Caney fork river below Dales Mill; being a road of the second Class and keep the same in repair as the law requires and that the same list of hands that worked under the late Overseer thereof be assigned to work thereon.

Iss'd Ordered by Court that David Snodgrass; James Snodgrass; Anthony Dibrell; Charles McGuire and John Brown freeholders be appointed a jury of view to examine; mark and so change the road leading from Sparta to Snodgrass's Mill via of Mark Lowry's as to turn off said road at a Brier field (P-197) at the Corner of Mark Lowrys field passing through Barger Lowry's land and to entersect the old road again at some convenient and eligible point and report thereof to the next term of this Court.

Iss'd Ordered by Court that Richard Crowder, John W. Simpson, John

Jett, Woodson P. White, Thomas Green, James H. Doyle and Samuel V. Carrick freeholders be appointed a jury of view to lay off and mark a road from near Andrew McElroys crossing the Cany fork at a new Bridge erected by W. & J. Payne and to entersect the Ross's ferry road again leading to Sparta at some suitable point and to specify in their report particularly as to the public utility of said road also what grade or importance ought to be attached to it as well as the properity or improperity of the opening said road and report thereof to the next term of this Court.

Ordered that Court be adjourned untill tomorrow Morning 9 O'clock

Thos Eastland
Wm. Bruster
Jonathan Farrington

Tuesday Morning 7th November A.D.1837 Court met pursuant to adjournment
Present the Worshipful

Thomas Eastland, Esq. Chairman
William Bruster,
Jonathan Farrington, Esqs.

Ordered that Court be adjourned untill Court in Course
Test
N. Oldham, Clk

Thos Eastland
Wm. Bruster
Jonathan Farrington

(P-198) State of Tennessee

At a Court began and held for the County of White and State aforesaid at the Court house in the Town of Sparta before the Justices of said Court on the first morning being the fourth day of December in the year of our Lord One thousand eight hundred and thirty seven And of the Independence of the United States of America the sixty second year.

Present the Worshipful

John Jett, Esq. Chairman Pro. tem
Isaac Buck, David Snodgrass,
John Gillentine, John Bryan,
James Allison, Matthias Hutson,
Jonathan Farrington, Joshua Mason, } Esq.
William Brtlett, Jesse Walling,
William Knowles, James T. Hayes,
John Wallis, William Little, } Justices
Asa Certain, Richard Crowder,
William Hitchcock, Elijah Frost,
Elisha Camron, John Pennington.

This day George Defreese a citizen of White County appeared in open Court and produced a Commission from the Governer of the State of Tennessee appointing him a Justice in and for said County and thereupon took the oath to support the Constitution of the United States and of the State of Tennessee and the oath of office and took his Seat upon the Bench.

This day George Cline adminestrator of the Estate of Azariah Long deceased returned upon oath an Inventory of said Estate which is ordered to be recorded.

This day George Cline adminestrator of the Estate of Azariah Long deceased returned upon oath an account of the sales of said Estate which is ordered to be recorded.

This day the Commissioners heretofore appointed to settle with George Cline adminestrator of the estate of Azariah Long decd. returned their report upon oath which is received and ordered to be recorded.

Ordered by Court that George Cline adminestrator of the Estate of Azariah Long Dec'd be allowed the sum of Twenty Dollars for Services rendered in the settlement of said estate to be by him retained out of said Estate.

This day John Wallis adminestrator of the estate of Mary Wallis deceased returned upon oath an Inventory of said estate which is ordered to be recorded.

Iss'd Ordered by Court that Lucenda George be allowed the sum of Five Dollars for taking care of and conveying a certain infant pauper child agreeable to order of Court to the poor house of White County to be paid by the Treasure of the poor house Commissioners out of the poor tax for the year 1837.

This day Creed A. Taylor admr. of the estate of Mecajah Taylor dece'd. returned upon oath an additional Inventory of said estate which is ordered to be recorded.

(P-199) This day Creed A. Taylor adminestrator of the estate of Micajah Taylor Dec'd returned upon oath an account of the sales of said estate which is ordered to be recorded.

This day Benjamin Hutchings adminestrator of the estate of Webster Hutchings Dec'd returned upon oath an account of the sales of said estate which is ordered to be recorded.

Iss'd Ordered by Court that James Allison, James M. Nelson and John Taylor be appointed commissioners to set apart one years provisions to the widow and family of John Massa Sr. dec'd out of said estate and report thereof to the next term of this Court.

Ordered by Court that the Clerks box in the Court house of White County be removed from its present situation and it is further ordered that Samuel Turney, William Simpson and Nicholas Oldham be appointed Commissioners to draft an improved plan for the Construction of a new Lawyers bar and Clerks box together with the probable Cost and submit it to the consideration of the Court at the next term.

Ordered by Court that John Witt, Sampson Witt, Elijah Hill, William Anderson, Joseph Cummings, Jr. and James Simpson freeholders be appointed a Jury of view to lay off and mark a road of the third Class from the corner of William Adairs field on Rosses ferry road thence crossing the Caney fork above Rosses old ferry, thence entersecting the old Pikeville road near Grief Smallmans and report thereof to day.

This day the Commissioners appointed today to vue lay off and mark a road of the third Class from the Corner of William Adairs field to the old Pikeville road passing the Caney fork above Rosses old ferry made their report wich is received and said road established.

Iss'd And that Sampson Witt be appointed Overseer thereof from Wm. Rickman to the Caney fork and keep the same in repair as the law requires and that John Witt, William L. Anderson, Jeremiah T. Witt and Henry Keithly be added to the list of hands to work thereon - . And that Elijah Hill be appointed Overseer thereof from the Caney fork River to the entersection with the old Pikeville road and keep the same in repair as the law requires.

And that Sampson Smallman and John M. Carter be assigned to work thereon

Iss'd Ordered by Court that Richard Crowder, John W. Simpson, John Jett, Woodson P. White, Thomas Green, James H. Doyle and Robert Anderson, Sr., freeholders be appointed a Jury to lay off and mark a road from near Andrew McElroys Crossing the Caney fork at the new Bridge erected by W. & J. Payne and intersecting the road again leading from Rosse's old ferry to Sparta at some suitable point and specify in their report particularly as to the public utility of said road also what grade or importance ought to be attached to it as well as the propriety or impropriety of opening said road and report thereof to the next term of this Court.

(P-200) Iss'd Ordered by Court that Benjamin Vaughn be appointed Overseer of the road from the forks of the McMinnville road to Sinking Creek being a road of the second Class and to keep the same in repair as the law requires and that the same list of hands that worked under Avery Green late Overseer thereof be assigned to work thereon.

Issd Ordered by Court that the order of last Court appointing David Snodgrass, James Snodgrass, Anthony Dibrell, Charles McGuire and John Brown freeholders a jury of view to lay off and change the road leading from Sparta to Snodgrasses Mill via of Mark Lowrys as to turn off said road at a brier field at the corner of said Lowry's field passing through Barger Lowrys land and entersect the old road again at some convenient and elegible point be renewed and report thereof to the next term of this Court.

Issd Ordered by Court that Reubin Perkins be appointed Overseer of the road from the Falling water to Abraham Dilly's branch being a road of the first Class and keep the same in repair as the law requires with the same list of hands and bounds that worked under Isaac Lollar late Overseer thereof.

This day the Commissioners heretofore appointed to lay off and mark a road from Glenns old salt well to the Flat Rock on the Mountain made their report unfavorable which is recieved and ordered to be recorded.

Issd Ordered by Court that John D. Mason be appointed Overseer of the road from the two mile post to the house of John Knowles Sr. being a road of the first Class and keep the same in repair as the law requires and that the same list and bounds of hands that worked under Christopher Swindle late Overseer thereof be assigned to work thereon.

Issd This day George Gardenhire produced in open Court one large

wolf scalp over the age of four months and proved that the same was killed in White County and there being present Five acting Justices of the peace of said County to wit:
John Jett; David Snodgrass; William Little, Jonathan Farrington and Isaac Buck Esq.

It is ordered that the same be certified to the Treasure of the State of Tennessee for payment and that the Sherriff of White County burn said scalps who being present in Court received said scalp into his custody and acted accordingly.

Isad Ordered by Court that Jonathan Farrington Esq. be allowed the sum of Twelve Dollars for work and labor done in repairing the Court house of White County to be paid by the Trustee of White County out of the tax of 1837.

This day John Massa Jr. Admr. of the estate of John Massa Sr. returned upon oath an account of sales of said estate which is ordered to be recorded.

(P-201) Isad Ordered by Court that Allen L. Mitchell keeper of the Poor house of the County of White be allowed the sum of one hundred sixteen Dollars two and three fourth cents being for boading and cloathing and washing for a woman & child paupers on the County of White for the year 1837 to be paid by the Treasure of the Poor house Commissioners out of any monies not otherwise appropriated.

Isad Ordered by Court that Allen L. Mitchell Superentendant of the poor house of White County be allowed the sum of Thirty Dollars for services rendered in Superentending the Paupers of the Poor house in said County to be paid by the Treasure of the poor house Commissioners out of any monies not otherwise appropriated.

Ordered by Court that William Little, David Snodgrass and Joseph Hunter be appointed Commissioners to assign and set apart to the widow of Andrew Hampton one years provisions out of his estate and report thereof to the next term of this Court.

This day Elijah Frost, Esq. reported to the Court that Eliza Haily is disirous and wishes Nathaniel C. Davis to be appointed her guardian which is ordered to be recorded.

Isad Ordered by Court that Calvin Brown be appointed Overseers of the road from the Carthage road near Joseph Cophers to the intersection with the Rockisland road leading towards Livingston being a road of the second Class and keep the same in repair as the law requires and that William C. Bounds and John Pennington Esqs. assign a list and bounds of hands to work thereon.

This day Jamison Bussy a minor but of suitable age appeared in open Court and volentairly selected and chose Tilman Brown to be his guardian - who also being present in Court and together with Joseph Cummings Jr. and John Gillentine entered into and acknowledged bond in the sum of three thousand two hundred dollars conditioned as the law requires.

This day the Commissioners heretofore appointed to settle with John W. Simpson; guardian to the heirs of Abraham Conner deceased returned their report upon oath which is ordered to be recorded.

Ordered by Court that John Jett and Thomas Green be allowed the sum of one dollar fifty cents each for one day's serving in making settlement with the guardian to the heirs of Abraham Conner and to be paid by said guardian.

Isd Ordered by Court that Jacob A. Lane late Clerk of White County Court produced at the next term of this Court receipts for all the stone hammers and Crow Bars that belong to the County of White and that a copy of this order be served upon him returnable to the next term of this Court.

Isd Ordered by Court that the following named persons Citizens of White County be summonsed to serve as jurors at the Febuary term of White Circuit Court A.D. 1838 to wit:
Daniel Hoffman; William White; Thomas Barnes; James Bartlett; William Knowles; James Holland; Benjamin Lewis; Samuel Miller; James Thomas; Joseph Hunter; Matthias Hutson; William B. Hutson; Spene Mitchell, (P-202)
Joseph Cummings; Jr.; William K. Bradford; Thomas Nicholas; Sims Dearing; Edward Elms; James Buck with Elijah Frost, Henry Lyda; James Scott; Jesse H. Vermillion, John Jaylor; Thomas Green & Jesse Walling - And Hayes Arnold and Charles McGuire Constables to attend thereon.

Ordered by the Court that the following named Justices be appointed Commissioners of the Revenue for the County of White for the year 1837 To wit:
In District No. 1 John Jett; Esq.
In District No. 2 John Wallis; Esq.
In District No. 3 Jesse Walling; Esq.
In District No. 4 Matthias Hutson; Esq.
In Dist. No. 5 Joshua Mason, Esq.
In Dist. No. 6 Richard Crowder; Esq.
In Dist No. 7 Henry Benton; Esq.
In Dist. No. 8 James Allison; Esq.
In Dist. No. 9 George Defrees, Esq.
In Dist. No. 10 John Pennington,Esq.
In Dist. No. 11 Isaac Buck; Esq.
In Dist. No. 12 Edmund Stamps; Esq.
In Dist. No. 13 David Snodgrass Esq.
In Dist.No. 14 Elijah Frost, Esq.
In Dist. No. 15 John Gillentine; Esq.

Ordered by Court that the following named persons in the following State cases be allowed the following sums which have been examined by Samuel Turny Esq. Atto. General for White County and by heirs reported verbally to the Court as being correctly taxed and properly chargeably to the County of White and the reading of said Bills of Cost before the Court is dispensed with - to wit: In the case the State against John Derryfield Clk W. G. Sims \$543¾ David L. Mitchell 75¢; J. T. Bradley 141⅔; witness John Gillentine \$5.00; In the case the State vs Duncan Harden and Elender Abbot; Clerk W. G. Sims \$5.25 Sherriff D. L. Mitchell 50¢. Sherrif J. T. Bradley 241⅔ -
In the case the State vs William Phillips - Clk. W. G. Sims \$5.50. Sherriff D. L. Mitchell 37½¢. Sherriff J. T. Bradley \$166⅔ - In the case vs John Phillips Clk W. G. Sims \$5.25 - D. L. Mitchell \$0.12½ - . J. G. Mitchell 50¢ J. T. Bradley \$1.50 - In the case the State vs Sharp R. Whitley; Clk.

W. G. Sims \$6.37½. Sherriff D. L. Mitchell \$2 - J. Bradley - 16½¢.
W. W. Crawford 50¢ Hugh Gracy \$2.50; George Slucer \$1.50
In the case the State vs. Jesse Kerby, Clerk W. G. Sims \$1.25. Justice
J. Farrington 50¢; Charles Meek \$2.00 In the case the State vs Eleanor
McGuire and Elizabeth McCline, W. G. Sims Clerk \$7.37½ D. L. Mitchell \$3.37½.
J. T. Bradley \$1.00, Richard Kerby \$1.50 George Slucer; 50¢
In the case the State vs Joseph Jones, Clk W. G. Sims 6.37½. Sherriff D.
L. Mitchell \$2.00. J. T. Bradley 16½¢ Witness John Gillentine \$4.00
In the case the State vs Isaac Dodson; Clk. W. G. Sims; 4.62½. Sherriff
D. L. Mitchell \$0.87½. J. G. Mitchell; Jr., \$1.25 to be paid by the Trustee
of White County out of any money not otherwise appropriat.

Ordered that Court be adjourned untill tomorrow 10 O'clock

William Little
George Defreese
John Jett.

(P-203) Tuesday Morning 5th December A.D. 1837
Court met pursuant to adjournment
Present the Worshipful

William Little } Esq.
George Defreese }
John Jett } Justices

Ordered that Court be adjourned untill Court in Course
Test
N. Oldham; Clk

William Little
George Defreese
John Jett.

State of Tennessee,

At a court began and held for the Court of White and State aforesaid at the Court house in the town of Sparta before the Justice of said Court on the first Monday being the first day of January in the year of our Lord one thousand eight hundred and thirty eight and of the Independence of the United States the Sixty Second year.

Present the Worshipful

John Jett Esq. Chairman P.T.
John Bryan, David Snodgrass,
Lewis Pettett, Matthias Hutson,
Richard Crowder, William Knowles,
Elisha Camron, James T. Hayes,
William Little, George Defreese,
William Bruster, Jonathan
Farrington, Asa Certain,
John Gillentine, Joshua Mason,
John Pennington, Jesse Wallington,
William Hitchcock,
James Allison, Elijah Frost.

On the application of Susannah Duncan, admr. of William Duncan dec'd and for reasons appearing to the satisfaction of the Court it is ordered that John Bussell one of her surities for the faithful adminestration of said Estate from all future and further liabilities as such be released and for ever discharged.

(P-204) This day appeared in open Court Susannah Duncan adminestrator of the estate of William Duncan Dec'd and together with Pleasant Farley and Jonathan T. Bradley entered into and acknowledged bond in the sum of five hundred Dollars conditioned as the law requires.

This day Allen L. Mitchell Superentendant of the Poor house of White County reported the condition thereof for the year 1837 which is ordered to be recorded.

This day the Commissioners of the poor house of White County reported that they had appointed Allen L. Mitchell keeper and superentendant of the poor house of said County for the year 1838 and also filed his bond for the discharge of duties which is by the Court received and affirmed in all its parts and ordered to be recorded.

Ordered by Court that John Jett, Joseph Cummings, Jr. and Joseph Herd Esq. be appointed Commissioners of the poor house in White County for the year 1838

Ordered by Court that John Jett Esq. one of the Commissioners of the poor house for White County be appointed Treasure of the board of said Poor house Commissioners for the year 1838

Isad Ordered by Court that John Jett, Joseph Cummings, Jr. and Joseph Herd, Esq. Commissioners of the poor house of White County for the year 1837 be each allowed the sum of Five dollars for services rendered as Coms. to be paid by the Treasurer of the poor house Coms. of said County out of any monies not otherwise appropriated Asa Certain guardian to Meniza & Alphonso Holmes minor heirs of Edward Holmes dec'd returned his report upon oath which is ordered to be recorded.

This day William Haily adminestrator of John Haily deceased returned upon oath an Inventory of said Estate which is ordered to be recorded.

This day John Pennington one of the guardians of part of the minor heirs of John Dyer deceased returned upon oath a report thereof which is ordered to be recorded.

This day William Hill Guardian to his own children returned upon oath his report thereof; and it is ordered by the Court that he be allowed the sum of fifty five dollars for expences to be by him retained - which is ordered to be recorded.

For reasons appearing to the satisfaction of the Court upon the production of a record under the seal of the Clerk of Hardiman County Court in the State of Tennessee releasing William Hill as guardian to his own children from making annual reports to the County Court of said County and extending to the County Court of his county the exclusive right to exercise authority over said guardian it is therefore ordered by the Court that said guardian make his annual reports to this Court.

This day John Gillentine Guardian to William F. Carter (P-205) returned upon oath report of his Guardianship which is ordered to be recorded.

This day Samuel Brown Guardian to part of the minor heirs of John Dyer deceased returned upon oath his report which is ordered to be recorded.

This day the Commissioners heretofore appointed to settle with Thomas Hill Guardian to the heirs of James Hill deceased returned upon oath their settlement which is received and ordered to be recorded.

This day the Commissioners heretofore appointed to set apart one years provisions to the widow and family of Webster Hutchings deceased made their report which is ordered to be recorded.

This day the Commissioners heretofore appointed to assign and set apart one years provisions to the widow and family of John Massa; Sr. made their report which is ordered to be recorded.

Ordered by Court that the orders of last Court appointing David Snodgrass and Anthony Dibrell Coms. to settle with George Bohanon admr. of Joseph Henry deceased be renewed and report thereof to the next term of this Court.

This day Joseph England a Constable in District No. 12 in White County appeared in open Court and resigned his office as Constable which is ordered to be recorded.

This day the death of Richard G. Jay late of this County of White was suggested in open Court and that he departed this life intestate.

Whereupon James A. Jay was appointed adminestrator of all and singular the goods and chattles, rights and credits of the said Richard G. Jay, deceased and took the oath required by law and together with William Jay and Edward Elms entered into and acknowledged bond in the sum of five hundred dollars conditioned as the law requires.

Issd Ordered by Court that Thomas C. Hutson be appointed Overseer of road from the fork of the road near the mouth of Caney fork to the top of the hill at David Haston being a road of the second Class and keep the same in repair as the law requires and that the same list and bounds of hands that were assigned to work under Isham B. Haston late Overseer thereof be assigned to work thereon.

Issd Ordered by Court that the order requiring that part of the Sims road of which William McGarrah and Aaron Hutchings are Overseers be remeasured and the same be equally divided into their lots and that Richard Crowder and Asa Certain Esqs. be assigned to divided the hands that worked under the above named Overseers equally between Andrew J. Sims, Jesse H. Vermillion and William R. Tucker, Overseer thereon - And assign to each his particular portion of said road be renewed and report thereof to the next term of this Court.

Issd Ordered by Court that James T. Hayes William R. Tucker and John Taylor be appointed Coms. to settle with the administrators and administratrix of the Estate of Zachariah Jones deceased and report thereof to the next term of this Court.

(P-206) Issd Ordered by Court that Thomas Walling, Indemon B.Moore, William Templeton, Matthias Hutson and Smith J. Walling freeholders be appointed a Jury of view to lay of and mark a road from Indemon B. Moore to intersect the Kentucky road near Cason Swindles being a road of the third Class and report thereof to the next term of this Court.

Issd Ordered by Court that John Humphreys, Robert Mason, Robert Glenn, Avery Norriss and Joshua Mason freeholders be appointed a Jury of view to lay of and mark a road of the third Class from the Shipping port road on the west side of the Gumspring Mountain extending the nearest and best way to David Fishers on the Caney fork and report thereof to the next term of this Court.

Issd Ordered by Court that Joshua Mason, Caleb Mason, Green Templeton, Levi Jarvis and James Knowles freeholders be appointed a Jury of view to lay off and mark a road of the second Class from the branch between Harmon Littles & Caleb Mason - And to intersect the road passing said Littles again and report thereof to the next term of this Court.

Ordered by Court that Samuel Brown, William Hill and James H. Pass be appointed Commissioners to settle John Griffeth and Patience Roberts Admrs and admrx. of the estate of William Roberts deceased and report thereof to the next term of this Court.

This day the Commissioners heretofore appointed by the Court to Draft an improved plan for the Lawyers bar, Jury & Clerks box in the Court house made their report which is received by the Court and adapted - Whereupon it is ordered that Samuel Turney, William Simpson, and Nicholas Oldham be appointed Commissioners to let out the Contracts of erecting the improvements adapted in said report publicly to the lowest bidder the undertaker to give bond and approved security for the faithful performance of the contract to be executed as soon as practicable to be executed under the superentendant of said Commissioners to be paid for out of the taxes of the year 1838 - And said Coms. to report thereof to the next term of this Court.

Isd Ordered by Court that John Jett and David Snodgrass Esq. be appointed Commissioners of White County for the year 1838 to settle with the Clerks of the Courts and with the County Trustee.

Isd Ordered by Court that David Snodgrass; James Snodgrass, Anthony Dibrell; Charles McGuire and George Broyles freeholders be appointed a Jury of view to lay off and change the road leading from Sparta to Snodgrasses Mill via of Mark Lowry so as to turn off said road at a brier field at the corner of his field passing through Barger Lowry's land and entersect the old road again at some convenient and eligible point and report thereof at the next term of this Court.

Isd Ordered by Court that Joseph Rogers be appointed Overseer of the road from Richard Crowders to the forks of the road being a road (P-207) of the second Class and keep the same in repair as the law requires and that the same list and bounds of hands that were assigned to work under James Knowles late Overseer thereof be assigned to work thereon.

Isd Ordered by Court that Richard Crowder; John W. Simpson; George O. Howard; Woodson P. White; Thomas Green; James H. Doyle and Robert Anderson, Sr. freeholders or any five of them be appointed a Jury of view to lay off and mark a road from near Andrew McElroy Crossing the Caney fork at the new bridge erected by W. & J. Payne; and entersecting the Rockisland road leading to Sparta at some suitable point and specify in their report particularly as to the public utility of said road also what grade or importance ought to be attached to it; as well as the propriety or impropriety opening the same and report thereof to the next term of this Court.

Ordered that Court be adjourned until Tomorrow Ten O'Clock

John Jett
Jonathan Farrington
William Little

Tuesday Morning 2nd January 1838 Court met pursuant to adjournment
Present the Worshipful

John Jett)
Jonathan Farrington) Esqs.
William Little)

This day James H. Isham a Constable in White County in District No.10 presented his resignation which is received and ordered to be recorded -

This day John Jett Esq. who was appointed one of the Commissioners of the poor house of White County appeared in open Court and took the oath required by law and together with Jonathan T. Bradley and John England entered into and acknowledged bond in the sum of one thousand dollars conditioned for the faithful discharge of the duties of his office as Tresure of the poorhouse Coms. of White County.

Ordered that Court be adjourned untill Court in Course
Test
N. Oldham, Clk.

John Jett
Jonathan Farrington
William Little

(P-208) State of Tennessee

At a Court began and held for the County of White at the Court house in the Town of Sparta before the Justices of said Court on the first Monday of February being the 5th day in the year of our Lord one thousand eight hundred and thirty eight and of the Independence of the United States the Sixty second year.

Present the worshipful

John Jett, Esq. Chairman Pro-tem
Thomas Green, John Bryan,
Jesse Walling, Joshua Mason,) Esq.
George Defrees, Asa Certain,
Elijah Frost, David Snodgrass,
William Little, William C. Bounds,
James Allison, Edmund Stamps,
Elisha Camron, John Gillentine,) Justices
Matthias Hutson, Lewis Pettet,
James T. Hayes, John Wallis,
William Knowles, and
Isaac Buck.

This day the Sherriff of White County filed in open Court the Certificate of Election of William K. Bradford as Constable in District No. 10 to fill the vacancy occasioned by the resignation of James H. Isham, late Constable therein and the said William K. Bradford being present in open Court took an oath to support the Constitution of the United States and of the State of Tennessee and the several oaths prescribed by law and together with William C. Bounds and Thomas Nicholas entered into and acknowledged bond in the sum of Four thousand dollars conditioned as the law requires.

This day the Sherriff of White County filed in open Court the Certificate of election of George W. H. Pott to the office of Constable in District No. 12 to fill the vacancy occasioned by the resignation of Joseph England late Constable thereof and the said George W. H. Potts being present in open Court took an oath to support the constitution of the United States and of the state of Tennessee and the several oaths prescribed by law and together with John England, Jr. and Elisha Camron entered into and acknowledged bond in the sum of Five thousand Dollars conditioned as the law requires.

Ordered by Court that the Order heretofore made releasing and exempting Absolum McCoy from the payment of a poll tax be rescinded and entirely set aside.

Ordered by Court that Wamon Leftwich, David Snodgrass, and Reubin Robertson be appointed Commissioners to settle with Anthony Dibrell and David Ames Executors of the estate of Jacob Robertson deceased and report thereof to the next term of this Court.

This day William Glenn, guardian to part of the heirs of Wm. Glenn deceased returned his report upon oath which is ordered to be recorded.

(P-209) This day Elsy England, Guardian to the heirs of Elijah England deceased returned her report upon oath which is ordered to be recorded.

This day James Snodgrass adminestrator of the estate of Andrew Hampton deceased returned upon oath an account of the sales of said estate which is ordered to be recorded.

This day Robert Cox Esq. Trustee of the County of White made his report of the finances of the County of White which is received and ordered to be recorded.

This day Edward V. Pollard, Guardian to part of the heirs of Wm. Glenn dec'd returned upon oath his report which is ordered to be recorded.

This day James A. Jay, adminestrator of Richard G. Jay deceased returned upon oath an account of the sales of said Estate which is ordered to be recorded.

This day the Commissioners heretofore appointed to settle with the admrs. and admx. of the estate of Zacharriah Jones deceased made their report upon oath which is ordered to be recorded.

Ordered by Court that the adminestrator and adminestratrix of the estate of Zacharriah Jones dec'd be allowed the sum of One hundred Dollars for services rendered in settling said estate.

Ordered by Court that James T. Hayes, John Taylor and William R. Tucker be each allowed the sum of one dollar pr day for two days services each rendered in settling with the admr. & admx. of the estate of Z. Jones dec'd to be paid out of the estate of the decedent.

This day William Templeton, Guardian to John Davis returned upon oath his report which is ordered to be recorded.

This day William K. Williams an orphan boy age six years on the 29th day of October 1837 was bound to John Young to serve him after the manner of an apprentice untill he arrives at the age of Twenty one years and for the faithful preformance of his Covenant entered into bond and security conditioned as the law requires.

This day Ephraim Dawson an orphan boy aged fifteen years on the 5th day of July 1837 was bound to William G. Green to serve him after the manner of an apprentice untill he arrives at the age of Twenty one years and for the faithful preformance of his Covenent entered into and acknowledged bond with Woodson P. White his security conditioned as the law requires.

For reasons appearing to the satisfaction of the Court at the request of Mary Jane Carrol who is guardian to Samuel L. Carrol it is ordered by the Court that Anthony Dibrell and William Williams her securities for her faithful performance of said guardianship from all future and further liabilities therein be released and for ever discharged.

This day Mary Jane Carroll who is guardian to Samuel Lafayett Carroll appeared in open Court and together with Anthony Dibrell and Samuel Turney entered into and (P-210) acknowledged bond in the sum of one thousand dollars conditioned as the law requires.

This day Thomas Robertson and Woodson P. White were appointed guardians to Mary Mitchell, Thomas R. Mitchell and James S. Mitchell minor heirs of David L. Mitchell deceased and together with David Snodgrass and Joseph Herd entered into and acknowledged bond in the sum of Four thousand dollars conditioned as the law requires.

Issd Ordered by Court that William Lewis, Andrew Bryan, Daniel M. Doyle, John Wallis and John White, Sr., freeholders be appointed a jury of view to lay off and mark a road of the third Class from Simon Doyles the nearest and best way to entersect the Pikeville road at some suitable and convenient place near the farms of John Dale and Stephen Wallis and report thereof to the next term of this Court.

Issd This day the Commissioners heretofore appointed by this Court to lay off and mark a road of the third Class from Wallings or the Franks ferry road to Cooks Mill on Barrows returned their report which is received and said road established and that William A. Cook be appointed Overseer thereof and keep the same in repair as the law requires with his own hands.

Issd Ordered by Court that Richard Broyles be appointed Overseer of the road from Snodgrass's Mill to the mile post near William Wisdoms field being a road of the second Class and keep the same in repair as the law requires and that the same list of hands that worked under William Farley late overseer thereof be assigned to work thereon.

Issd Ordered by Court that Absolum McCoy be appointed Overseer of the road from Pleasant Waller to the gap of the Mountain at Lowerys old place being a road of the Second Class and keep the same in repair as the law requires with the same list of hands that worked under the late overseer thereof.

Issd Ordered by Court that Thomas Prince be appointed Overseer of that part of Sims road that may be allotted to him by Richard Crowder and Asa Certain Esqs. being a road of the first Class and keep the same in repair as the law requires with the hands that may be assigned him by said Justices.

Issd Ordered by Court that the order of the last term requiring that part of the Sims road of which William McGarrah and Aaron Hutchings are Overseers be remeasured and the same be equally divided into their lots and that Richard Crowder and Asa Certain Esq. be assigned to divide the hands that worked under the above named overseers equally between Andrew J. Sims, William R. Tucker and Thomas Prince Overseers thereon and assign to each his particular portion of said road be renewed and report thereof to the next term of this Court.

(P-211) Ordered by Court that the road from the branch between Harmon Littles and Caleb Masons to entersect the road passing said Littles as laid off and marked by Commissioners be and the same is hereby established and that part of the old road which this is intended to change be discontinued.

Ordered by Court that the road as marked by Commissioners passing Mark Lowrys brier field through Barger Lowrys lane be and the same is hereby established and that part of the old road which is intended to change be discontinued.

Isd. Ordered by Court that John B. Bradley be appointed overseer of the road from the forks of the road north of Snodgrass's Mill to Plumb Creek being a road of the second Class and keep the same in repair as the law requires with the same list of hands that worked under Abraham Yeager late Overseer thereof.

Isd Ordered by Court that Venitt Henry, Jeremiah Whitson, Harrison Whitson, Ignatius Howard, and William Scarbrough freeholders be appointed a Jury of view to lay off and mark a road of the third Class leaving the Calf Killer road near William C. Medcalfs thence the nearest and best way through the board valley, thence to entersect the dry valley road near William Pryor and report thereof to the next term of this Court.

The Commissioners heretofore appointed by this Court to lay off and mark a road of the third Class from the shipping port road west of the Gumspring mountain extending the nearest and best way to David Fisher on the Caney fork this day made their report which was received and said road ordered to be established.

Isd Ordered by Court that the order of last Court appointing Thomas Walling, Indemon B. Moore, William Templeton, Matthias Hutson and Smith J. Walling freeholders to lay off and mark a road of third Class from Idemon B. Moore's to intersect the Kentucky road near Cason Swindles be renewed and report thereof to the next term of this Court.

Isd Ordered by Court that Mark Whitaker be appointed Overseers of the road from post oak Creek to Hunters Mill being a road of the second Class and keep the same in repair as the law requires And that the same hands that worked under Daniel Bartlett former overseer thereof be assigned to work thereon.

Isd Ordered by Court that William Hargis be appointed Overseer of the road from the nineteen mile post to the Standing Stone being a road of the second Class and keep the same in repair as the law requires and that the same hands that worked under Sandford Stamps former Overseer thereof be assigned to work thereon.

This day the Commissioners heretofore appointed by this Court to lay off and mark a road from near Andrew McElroy's Crossing the Caney fork at the new Bridge erected by W. & J. Payne and intersecting
(P-212) the Rockisland road leading to Sparta at some suitable point made their report which is recorded by the Court and said road Established a road of the second Class and that W. & J. Payne open and keep the same in repair as the law requires at their own proper Cost and expence.

Isd Ordered by Court that Matthias Hutson, Peter Burum, Alexander

Moore, Robert Mason & James Holland freeholders be appointed a jury of view to so change the Kentucky road at Wm. Knowles that it shall pass the nearest and best way through his plantation and intersect the same again and report thereof instantly.

The Commissioners this day appointed by the Court to view lay of and so change the Kentucky road passing Wm. Knowles as to run the nearest and best way through his plantation made their report and said road is established.

Issd Ordered by Court that William Knowles and Joshua Mason Esq. be appointed Coms. to apportion lists of hands between Harmon Little and the adjoining Overseer on the shipping port road and report thereof to the next term of this Court.

Issd Ordered by Court that Hugh Gracy, Jonathan C. Davis, Hampton Yarborough, Owen W. Bates and John Young freeholders be appointed a Jury of view to lay off and mark a road of the third Class from Jesse Lincolns Mills the nearest and best way passing Hugh Gracy intersecting the Allens ferry road again near Eli Sim's and report thereof to the next term of this Court.

Issd Ordered by Court that Andrew Lowell to whom was bound an orphan boy named Jesse Allen Glenn that he make his appearance at the next term of this Court with the said Jesse A. Glenn and show Cause why he should not surrender the said boy to the Court on account of ill treatment and misusage; and that said Lowell be served with a copy of this order on information of Caleb Mason.

Ordered by Court that James T. Godwin be allowed the sum of one hundred and twenty dollars for five years board of Nancy Anderson one of the minor heirs of Matthias Anderson deceased*guardian to the said Nancy Anderson aforesaid is hereby required to pay the same out of the estate of his ward.

Issd Ordered by Court that David Snodgrass, Anthony Dibrell and Richard Nelson, Esq. be appointed Commissioners to inspect the book of Entry Takers office of White County since the appointment of the present incumbant (J. A. Lane) who are directed to examine the original files of Locations and the Books in which they are recorded and to report especially upon any particular Locations filed in said office where they were made and recorded. &c. and which may be asked for by said Entry Taker at the making out of said report. And report thereof to the (P-213) next term of this Court.

Ordered by the Court that the following rate of Taxes be laid for the year 1838

To Wit:

For County Tax

On each one hundred dollars value of property Five Cents
On each White free poll Twelve and one half Cents.

For Jury Tax

On each one hundred dollars value of property Five Cents
On each White free poll Twelve and a half Cents

*and that Anthony Dibrell

For Poor Tax

On each One hundred dollar value of property Five Cents
On each white free poll Twelve and a half Cents.

For Bridge Tax at Sparta

On each one hundred dollars value of property one & one fourth Cents. To be levied and collected by the sherriff of White County in the manner and form prescribed by law.

And it is further ordered by the Court that the Clerk of this Court where ever during the year 1838 he is required to issue Licence under the provisions of the Act of the General Assembly taxing the priviliges in this State; he shall demand and receive to the use of the County of White on all shows or exhibitions of natural and artificial curiosities a sum equal to the full amount of the state tax thereon and on all other Licences for priviliges a sum equal to one half the state tax thereon respectively all of which sums so received shall be accounted for with the Trustee of said County according to law.

Ordered by Court that William Simpson be allowed and paid the sum of one hundred Dollars for keeping the Bridge across the Calf Killer at the town of Sparta in good repair during the year 1838, to be paid by the sherriff of White County out of the Taxes of 1838

Ordered by Court that the road leading from John W. Simpsons Mill to the intersection with the Gumspring road near the widow Rogers be increased to a second Class road that the several Overseers thence observe the same and keep the same in repair according to law.

Isd Ordered by Court that Archebald Conner, Harrison Holland, Joseph Herd, Andrew Cope, and Green Templeton freeholders be appointed a jury of view to lay off and mark a road from the Gumspring road passing Green Templeton to the Shipping port road near Harmon Littles of the second Class and report thereof to the next term of this Court.

(P-214) Ordered by Court that the road leading from Berry R. Wilson to the Rush Spring be discontinued and abolished and that the Overseer thereof be exempt from working thereon.

Ordered that Court be adjourned untill tomorrow morning 9 O'Clock

John Jett,
David Snodgrass,
Jesse Walling.

Tuesday Morning 6th day of February 1838 Court met pursuant to adjournment
Present the worshipful

John Jett } Esq.
David Snodgrass }
Jesse Walling } Justices

Ordered by Court that David Snodgrass and Anthony Dibrell be appointed Commissioners to settle with the adminestrators of Joseph Henry deceased and report thereof to the next term thereof of this Court.

Ordered that Court be adjourned untill Court in Course

Test

N. Oldham, Clk.

John Jett
Jesse Walling
James Allison

(P-215) State of Tennessee

At a Court began and held for the County of White in the State aforesaid at the court house in the town of Sparta before the Justices of said Court on the first Monday being the fifth day of March in the year of our Lord One thousand eight hundred and thirty eight and of the Independence of the United States the Sixty second year

Present the Worshipful

John Jett, Esquire Chairman Pro-tem.
David Snodgrass, William Little,
Matthias Hutson, John Bryan,
William Knowles, Elisha Camron,
Lewis Pettett, Elijah Frost,
James Allison, Jesse Walling,
Joshua Mason, Thomas Green,
George Defrees, William Bruster,
Asa Certain, John Gillentine
Richard Crowder, William Bartlett,
William C. Bounds.

Ordered by Court that all persons who have been or may here after be reported by the Commissioners of the Revenue of White for double tax for the year 1838 failing to give in lists of their taxable property and polls be released and discharged and only be subject to pay a single tax for said year 1838.

Isd Ordered by Court unammously that William Glenn merchant be allowed the sum of ninety four Dollars fifty six and one fourth cents the amount of his Bill for stove and other articles furnished for the repairs of the Court house of White County to be paid by the Sherriff of White County out of the taxes of the year 1837

Isd Ordered by Court that William Simpson be allowed the sum of two Dollars twenty seven and a half cents for his bill of Articles furnished for repairing the Court house of White County to be paid by the Sherriff of White County out of the taxes of the year 1837

Isd Ordered by Court that Messrs White & Young be allowed the sum of two dollars and sixty cents for his bill of articles furnished for the Court house of White County to be paid by the Sherriff of White County out of the taxes of the year 1837

Isd Ordered by Court that Nicholas Oldham be allowed the sum of twelve dollars for furnishing a Blank record Book for the use of the Regesters office of White County to be paid by the Sherriff of White County out of the taxes of the year 1838

Isd Ordered by Court that Obadiah Harlow be allowed the sum of one dollar for work and labor done on the Jail of White County and that Robert H. McManus be allowed the sum of one dollar and seventy five cents for furnishing brick to repair said Jail to be paid by the Trustee of White County out of the taxes of 1838.

(P-216) Isd Ordered by Court that the following Offices in the following State Cases be allowed the following fees for services which are certified from the Circuit Court of White and also examined and certified by the Attorney General for said County as correctly Taxed and properly

chargeable to the County of White To Wit;
In the Case the State vs. James Kerby Clerk W. G. Sims $1.87½
Sherriff Jabez G. Mitchell $1.25 -
The State vs McGuire & McClure, Witness Randolph Whitley $2.00
Mark Lowry $1.50, Barger Lowry $1.50 David Cook $1.50 The State vs
James Kerby Clerk W. G. Sims $2.06¼, Sherriff J. T. Bradley $0.62½
The State vs James Kerby Clerk W. G. Sims $2.06¼ Sherriff J. T. Bradley
0.62½ The State vs James Kerby clerk W. G. Sims $2.06¼
Sherriff J. T. Bradley $0.62½
The State vs. W. W. Crawford Clerk W. G. Sims $1.81¼
Sherriff J. T. Bradley $1.25
The State vs. W. W. Crawford Clerk W. G. Sims $1.81¼
Sherriff J. T. Bradley $1.25
The State vs W. W. Crawford Clk W. G. Sims $1.81¼
Sherriff J. T. Bradley $1.25
The State vs. W. W. Crawford Clk W. G. Sims $1.81¼
Sherriff J. T. Bradley $1.25
The State vs W. W. Crawford Clk W. G. Sims $1.81¼
Sherriff J. T. Bradley $1.25
The State vs. W. W. Crawford Clk. W. G. Sims $2.06¼
Sherriff J. T. Bradley $0.62½
The State vs W. W. Crawford Clk W. G. Sims $2.06¼
Sherriff J. T. Bradley $0.62½
The State vs W. W. Crawford-Clk W. G. Sims $2.06¼
Sherriff J. T. Bradley$0.62½
The State vs W. W. Crawford Clk W. G. Sims $2.06¼
Sherriff J. T. Bradley 0.62½
The State vs W. W. Crawford Clk W. G. Sims $2.06¼
Shff J. T. Bradley 0.62½
The State vs William Rottan Clk W. G. Sims $8.62½
Sherriff John England $4.00 Sherriff J. T. Bradley 0.16½ Sherriff Randolph
Jones 1.25 Witness Jacob Anderson $0.50 Wit William Green $2.93
The State vs Joshua Norris Clk W. G. Sims $5.93¾ Sherriff John England
$1.75 Sherriff David L. Mitchell 0.75
The State vs. Young Austin Clk W. G. Sims $2.00 Sherriff J. T. Bradley $1.00
The State of Tennessee vs John Wright Clerk W. G. Sims $4.25 Sherriff J. T.
Bradley $0.16½ Constable Alexander Moore $1.25 Justice William Knowles 0.50
The State vs Andrew Lowell and Telitha Baker Clk W. G. Sims $6.25
Sherriff J. T. Bradley $5.16½ Witness John Baker $0.50 Wit. Cynthia Baker
$0.50 Wit. Jacob Anderson $0.50 Witness Polly Frasure $0.50 Witness Byrum
Jones $0.50 Witness John Austin $0.50 to be paid by the Trustee of White
County out of any monies not otherwise appropriated.

Ordered by Court that Nicholas Oldham, William G. Sims, Jabez G. Mitchell, James Lowry and Hayes Arnold freeholders be appointed to examine and so alter and change the Shipping port road passing Charles Meeks plantation leaving the old road near where Charles Meek formerly lived keeping the ridge on the South side of the farm formerly owned by Charles R. Sperry thence round bearing northwardly intersecting the old road at or near where the road from Sinking Creek passes the same to Lincolns Mill and report thereof instantly whereupon the Jurors aforesaid made their report upon oath, and it is ordered by the Court that said change be established and that said Charles Meek open the same at his own expence and that when said road shall have been opened according to law the old road to be discontinued.

(P-217) For reasons appearing to the satisfaction of the Court from testimony that Christopher Bankman a Citizen of White County is in very destitute circumstances and is a proper subject for this Court to extend relief. It is therefore considered by the Court that said Christopher Bankman be conveyed to the poor house of said County there to be maintained and taken care of as other paupers at the expence of White County.

This day Dan Griffeth adminestrator of the estate of John M. Rottan dec'd returned upon oath an account of the sales of said estate which is ordered to be recorded.

Ordered by Court that the order of the last term of this Court appointing Vinett Henry; Jeremiah Whitson; Harrison Whitson; Ignatius Howard; and William Scarborough freeholders a Jury of view to lay off and mark a road of the third Class; leaving the Calf Killer road near William C. Medkitts; thence the nearest and best way through the board valley; thence to intersect the Dry valley road near William Pryors be renewed and report thereof to the next term of this Court.

Ordered by Court that the order of last term appointed David Snodgrass; Anthony Dibrell and Richard Nelson Esq. Coms. to inspect the Books of the Entry Takers office of White County Since the appointment of the present incumbent (J. A. Lane) who are directed to examine the original files of Locations and the books in which they are recorded - And to report especially upon any particular location filed in said office when they were made how recorded and so forth, and which may be ask for by said Entry Taker at the making of said report be renewed and report thereof to the next term of this Court.

Isd Ordered by Court that the order of the last term of this Court appointing Archebald Conner, Harrison Holland; Joseph Herd; Andrew Cope; and Green Templeton freeholders a Jury of view to lay off and mark a road of the second Class from the Gumspring road passing Green Templetons to the shipping port road near Harmon Littles be renewed and report thereof to the next term of this Court.

Ordered by Court that the orders of last term appointing William Lewis, Andrew Bryan, Daniel M. Doyle; William M. Bryan; Sr. and Hartwell Nelson freeholders a Jury of view to lay off and mark a road of the Third Class from Simon Doyles the nearest and best way to intersect the Pikeville road at some suitable and convenient point near the farms of John Dale and Stephen Wallis be renewed and report thereof to the next term of this Court.

Ordered by Court that the Order of the last term appointing Thomas Walling; Indemon B. Moore; William Templeton; Matthias Hutson, and Smith J. Walling freeholders a Jury of view to lay off and mark a road of the third Class from Indemin B. Moores to intersect the Kentucky road near Swindles be renewed and report thereof to the next term of this Court.

Isd Ordered by Court that the order of the last term appointing Hugh Gracy, (P-218) Jonathan C. Davis, Hampton Yarborough; Owen W. Bates; and John Young freeholders a Jury of view to lay off and mark a road of third Class from Jesse Lincolns Mill the nearest and best way passing the house of Hough Gracy intersecting the Allens ferry road near Eli Sims be renewed and report thereof to the next term of this Court.

Ordered by Court that the Orders of the last term appointing

William Knowles & Joshua Mason, Esqs. to apportion bounds and lists of hands between Harmon Little and the adjoining Overseers on the shipping port road be renewed and report thereof to the next term of this Court.

Issd Ordered by Court that Mark Lowry be appointed Overseer of the road from the Corner of Mark Lowrys brierfield to the forks of the road near Anthony Dibrells being a road of the second Class and keep the same in repair as the law requires and that the same list of hand that worked under James Turner late Overseer thereof be assigned to work thereon.

Ordered by Court that Daniel Kelly be appointed Overseer of the road from the ford of the Calf Killer below Andersons salt well to the forks of the road near Charles McGuire being a road of the second Class and keep the same in repair as the law requires and that the same list of hands that worked under John Brown late Overseer thereof be assigned to work thereon. -

Issd Ordered by Court that James McFee be appointed Overseer of the road from the mouth of John Bryans lane at his cotton patch to the Coopers Shop on Rosses road being a road of the second Class and keep the same in repair as the law requires. And that the same list of hands that worked under William Wilson late Overseer thereof be assigned to work theredn.

Issd Ordered by Court that George Howard be appointed Overseer of the road from the center of a slash near where Isaac Howard lives to the road near Shady grove meeting house being a road of the second Class and keep the same in repair as the law requires and that the same list of hands that worked under Silas Cash late overseer thereof be assigned to work thereon.

Issd Ordered by Court that John Payne be appointed Overseer of the road from McElroy's Crossing the Caney fork at W & J. Paynes Bridge to the intersection of the Rockisland road being a road of the second Class and keep the same in repair as the law requires and that Alexander Moore, John Wilson, Thomas Rawlings, David Rawlings, Peter Carter, Jr. Thomas Adair, Tulain Holder and Spencer Holder, Sr. be assigned to work thereon.

Ordered by Court that, that lot of road of which Adrian Bryant is overseer be extended as far as to the entersection of Paynes road near McElroy and keep the same in repair as the law requires with the same list of hands already assigned him.

Ordered by Court that the following list of hands be assigned
(P-219) to work under William M. Bryant, Jr., Overseer of the Milk sick fince to wit: David Moore, William L. Bryan, John Austin, Jr., Elijah P. Lewis, David G. Wilson, Jesse Kirby, Laban Wallis, Jr.

Ordered by Court that the following hands be assigned to work on that portion of the road of which William Anderson is Overseer to wit: Wm. Anderson's Slave, James W. Copeland and William Adair.

This day the death of William McConnel late of the County of White was suggested in open Court and that he departed this life intestate whereupon James A. McConnel is appointed administrator of all and singular the goods and chattles rights and credits of the said Wm. McConnell deceased and thereupon took the oath prescribed by law and together with Jesse A. Bounds and John England, Jr., entered into and acknowledged bond in the sum of four hundred Dollars conditioned as the law requires.

For reason appearing to the satisfaction of the Court it is ordered that the securities of Jesse A. Bounds administrator of Thomas Bounds deceased from all future and further liabilities therein be released and forever discharged.

Ordered by Court that Jesse A. Bounds be appointed administrator of Thomas Bounds dec'd also admr. Debonis-non of Thomas Bounds deceased who was executor to the last will and testament of Isaac Clark deceased and together with William C. Bounds, Thomas Stone, Jonathan T. Bradley and John England, Jr., entered into and acknowledged bond in the sum of Ten thousand Dollars conditioned as the law requires.

Issd This day was produced in open Court a writing preporting to be the last will and Testament of John Farley late of the County of White deceased, and the due execution and publication thereof as such was proven by the oath of James H. Pass and Simson Cash two of the subscribing witness thereto for the purposes and things therein contained and that the said John Farley at the day of the date of the last will and testament aforesaid and publication thereof was of sound and disposing mind and memory all of which is ordered to be recorded.

This day Charles Meek produced in open Court a certificate of Election from the Coroner of White County Certifying that said Charles Meek was elected on the first Saturday in March 1838, a Constable in Civil District No. 1 for the next ensuring two years there after who being present in open Court took an oath to support the Constitution of the United States and of the State of Tennessee and the several oaths prescribed by law and together with Benjamin McClain and Daniel Clark entered into and acknowledged bond in the sum of four thousand Dollars conditioned as the law requires.

This day Hayes Arnold produced in open Court a Certificate of his election from the Coroner of White County as Constable in Civil District No. 1 for the next ensuring two years from and after the first Saturday in March 1838 - who being present in open Court (P-220) took an oath to support the Constitution of the United States and of the State of Tennessee and the several oaths prescribed by law and together with Sevier Evans and Daniel Walling entered into and acknowledged bond in the sum of four thousand Dollars Conditioned as the law requires.

This day John H. Graham produced in open Court from the Coroner of White County a certificate of his Election to the office of Constable in Civil District No. 2 for the two years next ensuring from and after the 1st Saturday in March 1838 who being present in open Court took an oath to Support the Constitution of the United States and of the State of Tennessee and the several oaths prescribed by law and together with James Graham, John Dodson and John Graham entered into and acknowledged bond in the sum of four thousand dollars Conditioned as the law requires.

This day Robert Smith produced in open Court from the Coroner of White County a certificate of his election to the office of Constable in Civil District No. 3 for the two years next ensuring from and after the first Saturday in March 1838 who being present in open Court took the oath to support the Constitution of the United States and of the State of Tennessee and the several oaths prescribed by law and together with Joseph Herd and William Bruster entered into and acknowledged bond in the sum of four thousand dollars conditioned as the law requires.

This day Alexander Ward produced in open Court from the Coroner of White County the Certificate of his Election to the office of Constable in Civil District No. 4 for the next insuring two years from and after the first Saturday in March 1838 - who being present in open Court took an oath to support the Constitution of the United States and of the State of Tennessee and the several oaths prescribed by law and together with Andrew J. Sims and Idemon B. Moore entered into and acknowledged bond in the sum of four thousand Dollars Conditioned as the law requires.

This day Cornelius Jarvis produced in open Court from the Coroners of White County the Certificate of his election to the office of Constable in Civil District No. 5 for the next ensuring two years from and after the first Saturday in March 1838 - and who being present in open Court took the oath to support the Constitution of the United States and of the State of Tennessee and the several oaths prescribed by law and together with Joshua Mason, Robert Mason and Levi Jarvis entered into and acknowledged bond in the sum of four thousand dollars Conditioned as the law requires.

This day William H. Baker produced in open Court from (P-221) the Coroner of White County the Certificate of his Election to the office of Constable in Civil District No. 6 for the two years next ensuring from and after the first Saturday in March 1838 and who being present in open Court took an oath to support the Constitution of the United States and of the State of Tennessee and the several oaths prescribed by law and together with William White, John Taylor, Thomas Jones and James C. Baker entered into and acknowledged bond in the sum of four thousand Dollars Conditioned as the law requires.

This day Samuel Nolen produced in open Court from the Coroner of White County the Certificate of the Election of Samuel Nolen to the office of Constable in Civil District No. 8 for the two years next ensuring from and after the first Saturday in March 1838 and who being present in open Court took an oath to support the Constitution of the United States and of the State of Tennessee and the several oaths prescribed by law and together with Jose C. Dew, Eskiel Hitchcock and Jesse Davis entered into and acknowledged bond in the sum of four thousand Dollars Conditioned as the law requires.

This day William K. Bradford produced in open Court from the Coroners of White County the Certificate of the Election of William K. Bradford to the office of Constable in District No. 10 for the two years next ensuring from and after the first Saturday in March 1838 And who being present in open Court took an oath to support the Constitution of the United States and of the State of Tennessee and the several oaths prescribed by law and together with William C. Bounds and Thomas Stone entered into and acknowledged bond in the sum of four thousand dollars Conditioned as the law requires.

This day Thomas Welch produced in open Court from the Coroner of White County the Certificate of the Election of Thomas Welch to the office of Constable in Civil District No. 11 for the two years next ensuring from and after the first Saturday in March 1838 and who being present in open Court took an oath to support the Constitution of the United States and of the State of Tennessee and the several oaths prescribed by law and together with William Bartlett and Jesse A. Bounds entered into and acknowledged bond in the sum of four thousand Dollars Conditioned as the law requires.

This day George W. H. Potts produced in open Court from the Coroner of White County the Certificate of his Election to the office of Constable in District No. 12 for the two years next ensuring from and after the first Saturday in March 1838 and who being present in open Court took an oath to support the Constitution of the United States and of the State of Tennessee and the (P-222) several oaths prescribed by law and together with Jonathan T. Bradley, Elisha Camron, James Snodgrass and Thomas Snodgrass entered into and acknowledged Bond in the sum of four thousand Dollars conditioned as the law requires.

This day Thomas Snodgrass produced in open Court from the Coroner of White County the Certificate of his Election to the office of Constable in Civil District No. 13 for the two years next ensuring from and after the first Saturday in March 1838 and who being present in open Court took an oath to support the Constitution of the United States and of the State of Tennessee and the several oaths prescribed by law and together with James Snodgrass and William G. Sims entered into and acknowledged Bond in the sum of Four Thousand Dollars Conditioned as the law requires.

This day Isaac S. Brogden produced in open Court from the Coroner of White County the Certificate of his Election to the office of Constable in Civil District No. 14 for the two years next insuring the first Saturday in March 1838 and who being present in open Court took an oath to support the Constitution of the United States and of the State of Tennessee and the several oaths prescribed by law and together with John Warren and John Gipson entered into and acknowledged Bond in the sum of four thousand Dollars conditioned as the law requires.

This day William Sparkman produced in open Court from the Coroner of White County the Certificate of his election to the office of Constable in District No. 15 for the two years next ensuring from and after the first Saturday in March 1838 and who being present in open Court took an oath to support the Constitution of the United States and of the State of Tennessee and the several oaths required by law and together with Elijah Hill, Peter Burem and William L. Adams entered into and acknowledged bond in the sum of four thousand Dollars Conditioned as the law requires.

In obedience to an order made at the last term requiring Andrew Lowell to whom was bound a certain orphan boy named Jesse Allen Glenn to make his appearance in this Court with said apprentice and shew cause why he should not surrender said apprentice up to the Court for alledged misusage, bad treatment &c. by Caleb Mason, this day appeared in open Court and produced said boy and fer reasons appearing fully to the satisfaction of the Court from evidence produced by both parties It is ordered and considered by the Court that said Andrew Lowell is not guilty of the alleged misusage &c to said apprentice and that he from said allegations be released and discharged.

(P-223) Isd Ordered by Court that Robert Anderson, William Anderson, Joseph Anderson, Jr., Ozias Denton, George D. Howard, Sampson Witt, John Witt, Jeremiah Witt, James H. Doyle, Thomas Green, Christopher Kughn and James W. Copeland be appointed a jury of view to examine the new road opened by W. & J. Payne where it passes through the lands of Lewis Phillips and they are to hear evidence from both sides if produced before them and then determine as to what damages the said Lewis Phillips may have sustained if any by said road passing through the said Phillips farm &c. and report thereof to the next term of this Court.

Ordered that Court be adjourned till tomorrow 10 O'Clock

John Jett
John Bryan
William Little

Tuesday Morning the 6th March 1838 Court Met pursuant to adjournment
Present the Worshipful

John Jett
John Bryan and
William Little } Esqs. Justices

Ordered that Court be adjourned untill Court in Course

Test
N. Oldham, Clk.

John Jett
John Bryan
William Little

(P-224) State of Tennessee

At a Court began and held for the County of White at the Court house in the town of Sparta before the Justices of said Court on Monday the second day of April in the year of our Lord One Thousand eight hundred and thirty eight And of the Independence of the United States the 62nd year.

Present the Worshipful

Thomas Eastland Esq. Chairman
John Jett, David Snodgrass,
Isaac Buck, Lewis Pettett,
William Little, Matthias
Hutson, William Knowles,
Joshua Mason, John Wallis,
John Gillentine, Asa Certain,
Jesse Walling, John Bryan,
James Allison, Edmund Stamps,
Elisha Camron, Richard Crowder,
Thomas Green, William Bruster,
William Bartlett, George Defrees
and John Pennington. - } Esqs. Justices

This day Nathaniel C. Davis was appointed Guardian to Eliza Bailey an orphan girl who being present in open Court and together with Jacob A. Lane entered into and acknowledged bond in the sum of seventy Dollars conditioned as the law requires.

This day Simson Cash, Sr., who is appointed Executor in the last will and testament of John Farley deceased appeared in open Court and took upon himself the burden of the execution of said will and testament and took the oath prescribed by law and together with James H. Pass and John Gooch entered into and acknowledged bond in the sum of three Thousand Dollars conditioned as the law requires.

This day Joseph Cummings, Jr., and Joseph Herd two of the Commissioners of the poor house of White County and appeared in open Court and took the oath prescribed by law and thereupon entered upon the discharge of their duties.

This day the Commissioners heretofore appointed to apportion lists and bounds of hands between Harmon Little and other Overseers the shipping port road report as follows to wit:

To Harman Little Overseer the following hands Green Templeton, John W. Jenkins, Joseph Glenn, Sr., James Glenn, William D. Glenn, Robert Glenn, Jr., Simpson Little and John R. Glenn - and his bounds so to extend as to enclude the above named hands - To Joseph Glenn Overseer the following hands & bounds so to extend as to include where F. B. Smith now lives then with the mountain as before except Robert Glenns farm which shall be considered in said Littles bounds an then (P-225) from the point of the Mountain near Levi Jarvis to Crowders then to the west side of the Cypress pond and including where James Mayes now lives continuing as near the Center between the two between the two roads as practicable including James Knowles, Levi Jarvis, James J. Hembra, Alfred M. Merrett, Nathan Merrett, Abraham Cook, James Mayes, Henry M. Gibbs, Andrew Welch, William Hall, Harvey Hall, George A. Martin and Franklin B. Smith - And to

Canady Rigsby Overseer boundary so to extend as to include his former list of hands with the exception of James Maye's as follow Canady Rigsby, Jr., William Rigsby, James Glenn and his black boy Peter Hunter, Gilmore Wilson, Isham Cook, Elijah Pertle and Samuel D. Arnold which is by the Court received and ordered to be recorded.

Isad This day the Commissioners heretofore appointed to examine and lay off a road of the third Class from Simon Doyles the nearest and best way to entersect the Pikeville road at some suitable point near the farms of John Dale and Stephen Wallis made their report which is by the Court renewed and established a road of the third Class and at the same time appeared in open Court John H. Dale over a part of whose land the said road passes and objects to the establishment of said road and prays that Court will give him Damages in consequinces thereof It is thereupon ordered by the Court that Stephen Wallis, John White, Sr., William Burden, John Austin, John W. Simpson, Pleasant Waller, Jacob Stipe, David Hatson, Robert Love, Spence Mitchell, Jesse Scoggin and Samuel Parker, freeholders be appointed a Jury to examine the above road as laid off and marked by the Commissioners where it passes through the lands of John H. Dale and thereon to assess the amount of damages (if any) which the said John H. Dale hath sustained in consequinces of the establishment & opening of said road and report thereof at the next term of this Court.

This day David Moore, Thomas Moore and Richard Nelson appeared in open Court and acknowledged themselves indebted to the County of White in the sum of Two hundred and fifty dollars to be levied of their goods and chattles lands and tenements to the use of White County to be renewed nevertheless to be void on condition that they shall well and truly indemnify and keep harmless the County of White from the payment of any Cost or damages that may be awarded against the County of White in favor of John H. Dale in consequince of the establishing and opening a road of the third Class through his lands.

This day James C. Kelly produced in open Court a Certificate of the Sherriff of White County that he was constitutionally elected a Constable for the ensuring two years from the first Saturday in March last in Dist. No. 9, who being in open Court took an oath to support (P-226) the Constitution of the United States and of the State of Tennessee and the several oaths prescribed by law and together with William Bruster, Asa Certain and James Eastham entered into and acknowledged bond in the sum of four thousand dollars conditioned as the law requires.

Isad Ordered by Court that all taxes imposed by the Court on Privileges so far as they relate to merchants operating for the year 1836 be cancelled and set aside when the tax has been collected for said year it is ordered that the trustee of White County refund the same immediately to those persons entitled to the same and the sherriff of White County desist from the further collection thereof - . this is to operate on Merchants Licence so far as the County is concerned on Licence issuing previous to the 10th day of January A.D. 1837

This day Samuel Brown on the executions of John Crook deceased produced in open Court a writing purporting to be the last will and testament of John Crook, Sr., deceased late of the County of White and the due execution and publication thereof was proven in open Court by the oaths of William Mills and John W. Mills subscribing witnesses thereto for the purposes and things therein mentioned and that the said John Crook Sr. was at the date of the execution and publication thereof of sound and disposing mind and memory which deemed by the Court sufficently proved and ordered to be recorded.

And it is ordered that Samuel Brown and William Hill the executors named in said last will and testament who take upon themselves the burden of the execution thereof have leave untill the next term of this Court to qualify, give bond and security &c.

Ordered by Court that John Gillentine, Stephen Wallis; William Denny; Jacob Stipe and Jno. Stipe freeholders be appointed change the road near Robert L. Mitchells farm so as to pass round a hill and report thereof to the present term of this Court.

Ordered by Court that the old road passing Williams Knowles be discontinued and that he be permitted to close the same.

Isd Ordered by Court that George Potts; Cornelius Hickey; William Goodwin; Daniel Lundy and Jesse Davis freeholders be appointed a Jury of view to examine lay off and mark a road of the second Class from William Prices the nearest and best way passing where Jesse Davis use to live on the Rockisland road crossing said road and so on to Coles lower Mill on Falling water and report thereof to the next term of this Court.

Isd Ordered by Court that Lewis Bohanon; James Officer; John Suttles; James Hudson and William Sparks freeholders be appointed a Jury of view to lay off and mark a road of the third (P-227) Class; Beginning at or near John Suttles on the Calf Killer road; thence the nearest and best way to intersect the Walton road near the widow Johnson's stand and report thereof to the next term of this Court.

Isd Ordered by Court that Samuel Clenny; Joel Whitley and John M. Whitley be assigned on the milk sick of which Laban Wallis is Overseer in addition to the hands heretofore assigned him.

Isd Ordered by Court that John W. Mills be released from any charge on two stray steers posted by him, the same having been proven away being the property of James M. Tompkins of Rutherford County Tennessee.

Isd Ordered by Court that Samuel D. Arnold be released from the payment of one half the appraised value of an estray mare taken up by him which was give up by him.

Isd Ordered by Court that the following persons good and lawful Citizens of White County be appointed Jurors to the June term A.D. 1838 of White Circuit Court to Wit: John Jett, Dan Griffeth; William Burden; John Wallis, Jesse Walling, Thomas Green Matthias Hutson; Spencer Holder; Indemon B. Moore; Jesse H. Vermillon; Thomas Jones; Sr., James C. Hitchcock; William Mills, Sr., Asa Certain; George Defreese; Jacob Hyder; Sr., William Hunter; Sr., William C. Metcalf; James Officer; Thomas Little; William Snodgrass; John Gipson, Nathaniel C. Davis; Jesse Scoggin and Jacob Anderson and Hayes Arnold; and Charles Meek Constable to attend thereon and that a writ of venue facias issue directed &c.

This day the Commissioners heretofore appointed to lay off and mark a road of the third Class from Indemon B. Moores to intersect the Kentucky road near Cason Swindles made their report which is recieved and established.

Issd This day the Commissioners heretofore appointed to examine and mark a road of the 2nd Class from the Gum Spring road passing Green Templetons and to intersect the Shipping port road near Harmon Littles asked leave to report said road as a 3rd Class road which was granted; then made their report which is received and said road established a road of the third Class and that Green Templeton be appointed Overseer thereof and open and keep the same in repair as the law requires and that Joshua Mason and Jesse Walling, Esq. assign him a list of hands to work thereon.

Issd Ordered by Court that Andrew Rogers be appointed Overseer of the road from Lowerys old place to the widow Dales being a road of the first Class and keep the same in repair as the law requires and that the same list of hands that worked under Dyer White late Overseer thereof be assigned to work thereon.

(P-228) The Commissioners this day appointed to change the road passing the farm of Robert L. Mitchell make the following report to wit: turn off at the top of the bank of main Caney fork at the mouth of Cain Creek on the west side of said road continuing untill parallel with Robert L. Mitchells fence thence with the direction of his fence to the old road which is received and established.

Issd Ordered by Court that the Order appointing Henry Crawley Overseer of the road from the Warren County line be so amended as to extend to the Bridge erected by the Mr. Paynes across Caney fork and keep the whole in repair as the law requires with the list of hands already assigned him.

Issd. Ordered by Court that the order appointing Hugh Gracy, Jonathan C. Davis, Hampton Yarborough, Owen W. Bates and John Young freeholders a Jury of view to lay off and mark a road of the third Class from Jesse Lincolns Mills the nearest and best way passing the house of Hugh Gracys and intersecting the Lincolns ferry road near Eli Sims, Esq. be renewed and report thereof to the next term of this Court.

Issd This day Joseph Cummings, Jr. produced in open Court a writing purporting to be the last will and testament of James Goddard late of the County of White deceased and the due execution and publication thereof was proven in open Court by the oaths of Joseph Cummings, Jr. and Moses Hollinsworth subscribing witness thereto for the purpose therein contained and that the said James Goddard was at the date of the execution and publication thereof of sound and desposing mind and memory all of which is ordered to be recorded And at the same time appeared in open Court Daniel Hollinsworth who in said last will and testament is appointed Executor thereof and took upon himself the burden of the execution thereof and thereupon took the oath prescribed by law and together with Joseph Cummings, Jr. and William Pettet entered into and acknowledged bond in the sum of four hundred dollars conditioned as the law required - .

Issd Ordered by Court that John Jett, John Wallis, Jesse Walling, Matthias Hutson, Joshua Mason, Richard Crowder, Henry Burton, James Allison, George Defrees, John Pennington, Isaac Buck, Edmund Stamps, David Snodgrass, Elijah Frost, and John Gillentine Revenue Commissioners of the

County of White for the year 1838 be allowed the sum of five Dollars each for services rendered in taking the tax list for 1838 to be paid by the Trustee of White County out of the Taxes of the year 1838.

Ordered by the Court that in making the repairs in the Court house of White County the Bannesters in front of the Jurors boxes is not to be removed at all.

(P-229) This day the Court proceeded to the election of three Justices of the peace to hold Quorrem Court for the ensuing twelve months and for that purpose David Snodgrass, John Jett and John Bryan, Esqs. were duly elected.

Cabb Mason
vs Issd
Andrew Lowell

Complaint of mistreatment of Ind appmt
Jesse Allen Glenn

For reasons appearing to the satisfaction of the Court at the last term of this Court from the entroduction of evidence and argument of Counsel thereon discharged the defendant from the alligations of said complaints and now is considered by the Court and so ordered that the Defendant depart hence without day and recover against the Plaintiff all Costs in this behalf expended &c And that execution issue.

This day Jonathan T. Bradley Esq. Sherriff and collection of the public Taxes in the County of White for the year 1837 produced in open Court the following named receipts to wit: From Miller Francis Esq. Treasure of the State of Tennessee dated Nashville 1 October 1837 For the sum of five hundred and ninety six dollars fifty seven cents - Also Robert Cox Trustee of White County dated 2 Apriil 1838 for the sum of fourteen hundred and thirty three dollars eighty cents. Also From John W. Simpson agent for the school fund dated 5 Feb'y 1838 the sum of Seventy six dollars twenty and a half cents and also from John Jett, Esq. Treas. of the Poor house dated 2nd April 1838 the sum of six hundred and ninety five dollars seventy six and a half cents which are read and ordered to be recorded.

Issd Ordered by Court that the Treasures of the poor house of White be directed and is hereby required to pay to the Trustee of White County all the surplus funds in his hands arising from the poor tax of said County to be by him appropriated to the extenguishment of County Claims.

This day Robert Cox produced in open Court the Certificate of the Coroner of White County certifying that he was constitutionally elected Trustee of White County for the next ensuing two years from and after the first Saturday in March 1838 and thereupon took the oath required by law and together with Simon R. Doyle, Madison Fisk, John Young, William L. Young and Jesse Lincoln, entered into and acknowledged bond in the sum of Five thousand Dollars conditioned as the law requires.

Issd This day the death of William Sullivan late of the County of White deceased was suggested in open Courv am that he departed this life entestate whereupon John R. Jones is appointed admr. of all and singular the goods and chattles, rights & credits lands and tenaments of the said William Sullivan deceased and took the oath (P-230) required by law and together with Jacob A. Lane entered into and acknowledged bond in the sum of Five hundred dollars conditioned as the law requires.

Isd This day the death of James Sullivan late of the County of White deceased was suggested in open Court and that he departed this life entestate whereupon John R. Jones was appointed admr. of all and singular the goods and chattles, rights and credits of the said James Sullivan deceased and took the oath required by law and together with Jacob A. Lane entered into and acknowledged bond in the sum of five hundred dollars conditioned as the law requires.

This day John Massa admr of the estate of John Massa, Sr. returned upon oath an act of the sales of said estate which is ordered to be recorded.

This day Mary Baker widow and relect of the late Peter Baker deceased a soldier of the Revolution and later a United States Pensioner exhibited in open Court upon oath her Declaration for a pension under the several acts of Congress in such cases provided and also appeared in open Court Turner Lane, Sr. and John Austin to the Court favorably known, persons of good name fame and reputation and entitled to full credit in a Court of Justice proved to the satisfaction of the Court that Mary Baker was the lawful wife of the said Peter Baker which is by the Court signed and sealed all of which is ordered to be recorded and certified under the seal of this Court.

This day Jonathan T. Bradley Esquires produced in open Court from the Coroner of White County Certifying that he was duly and constitutionally elected sherriff in and for the County of White for the ensuing two years from and after the first Saturday March 1838 and thereupon being present in open Court took an oath to support the Constitution of the United States and of the State of Tennessee and the several oaths prescribed by law and together with James Thomas, John L. Price, Richard England, Samuel V. Carrick, Joseph Herd and John England, Sr., entered into and acknowledged the several following bonds for the faithful discharge of his office, and for the collection of the public Taxes in said County conditioned as the law requires which are in the words and figures following to wit:

BOND

Know all men by these presents that we Jonathan T. Bradley, James Thomas, John L. Price, Richard England, Samuel V. Carrick, Josep Herd, John England, Sr. All of the County of White and State of Tennessee and held and firmly bound unto Newton Cannon, Esq. Govener in and over the State of Tennessee for the time being or his successors in office in the sum of Twelve thousand dollars Current Money which payment to all and truly to be made and done we bind ourselves and each and every of our heirs executors and adminestrators jointly and severally firmly by these present sealed with our seals and (P-231) dated the second day of April A. D. 1838 Whereas it appearing to the satisfaction of the County Court of White County that Jonathan T. Bradley hath been duly and Constitutionally elected sherriff in and for the County of White for the next ensuing two years from the first Saturday in March 1838

Now the condition of the above obligation is such that if the above bound Jonathan T. Bradley shall well and truly execute and due return make of all process and precepts to him directed, and pay and satisfy all fees and sums of money by him received or levied by vertue of any process into the proper office by which the same by the tenor thereof ought to be paid or to the person or persons to whom the same shall be due, his, her or their executors adminestrators attornies or agents and all other things well and truly and faithfully execute the said office of sherriff so long as he shall continue therein according to law.

Then this obligation to be null and void else be and remain in full force and vertue.

Signed

Test
N. Oldham, Clk.

J. T. Bradley (seal)
James Thomas (seal)
John L. Price (seal)
Richard England (seal)
Sam V. Carrick (seal)
Joseph Herd (seal)
John England (seal)

Bond for the State Tax and School tax

State of Tennessee White County

Know all men by these present that we Jonathan T. Bradley, James Thomas, John L. Price, Richard England, Samuel V. Carrick, Joseph Herd, John England, Sr., all of the State and County aforesaid and held and firmly bound into Newton Cannon, Govener of the State of Tennessee for the time being and his successors in office for the use of the State in the sum of eight thousand dollars to the payment of which well and truly to be made we bind ourselves our heirs executors and adminestrator jointly and severally, firmly by these presents sealed with our seals and dated the second day of April 1838 the conditions of the above obligations are such that where as the above bound Jonathan T. Bradley has been only and Constitutionally elected sherriff and Collector of the public taxes of said County of White for two years from the first Saturday in March 1838 Now if the said Jonathan T. Bradley shall well and truly collect all State taxes and also all taxes on school lands within said County which by law he ought to collect and well and truly account for and pay over all taxes by him collected or which ought to be collected on the first day of December in the year 1838 and 1839 respectively then the above obligations to be void otherwise to remain in full force and virtue

Test
N. Oldham, Clk.

J. T. Bradley (seal)
James Thomas (seal)
John L. Price (seal)
Richard England (seal)
Sam V. Carrick (seal)
Joseph Herd (seal)
John England (seal)

(P-232) Bond for the County Taxes

Know all men by these presents that we Jonathan T. Bradley, James Thomas, John L. Price, Richard England, Samuel V. Carrick, Joseph Herd, John England, Sr., all of the County of White and State of Tennessee are held and firmly bound unto Thomas Eastland Esq. Chairman of the County Court of White or his successors in office in the sum of Five thousand dollars current money for the use of White County which payment will and truly to be made and done we bind ourselves and each and every of our heirs executors and adminestrators jointly and severally firmly by these presents sealed with our seals and dated the 2nd day of April A. D. 1838. Where as the above bound Jonathan T. Bradley has been certified to this White County Court as having been duly and constitutionally elected sherriff of the County of White aforesaid for the next ensuing two years from the first Saturday in March 1838. Now if the above bound Jonathan T. Bradley shall well and truly and faithfully collect all the Taxes which shall been assessed for the County of White for the year 1838 To wit: The County Tax, Jury Tax, poor and Bridge Tax for the benefit of said County and shall pay the monies over to the proper offices in said County of White who are authorised to receive the same according to law then the above obligation to be null and void else be and remained in full force and vertue.

Test
N. Oldham, Clk.

J. T. Bradley	(seal)
James Thomas	(seal)
John L. Price	(seal)
Richard England	(seal)
Sam'l V. Carrick	(seal)
Joseph Herd	(seal)
John England	(seal)

This day Jonathan T. Bradley appeared in open Court and appointed Smith J. Walling deputy Sherriff in and for the County of White who being present in open Court took an oath to support the Constitution of the United State and of the State of Tennessee and the several oaths prescribed by law and thereupon entered upon the discharge of the duties of his office.

Issd Be it remembered that on this day the 2nd April A. D. 1838 appeared in open Court, James Allison and John Barr Citizen of White County to the court known persons of good name fame and reputation who are entitled to full faith and credit in a Court of record who being duly sworn say upon their oath that Margarett Haslett, Polly Goodman and Jane Jones are all the heirs at law of James Sullivan and William Sullivan dec'd who died in the services of the United States during the late war between the United States and the Kingdom of great Brittain all of which is ordered to be recorded and Certified under the seal of this Court.

(P-233) Issd Be it remembered that on this day the 2nd day of April A. D. 1838 appeared in open Court Samuel Turney Esq. a citizen of the County of White to the Court known a person of good name, fame and reputation who is entitled to full faith and Credit in a Court of record who being sworn in due form of law says upon his oath that Madison Fisk, Nathaniel Fisk, Lucinda Denton, Triphona Whitley, Cella Ames and Catharine Gilpatrick are all the legal heirs of William Fisk deceased who died in the service of the United States during the late war between the United States and the Kingdom of Great Brittian all of which is ordered to be recorded and Certified under the seal of the Court.

Ordered by Court that the order appointing David Snodgrass, Anthony Dibrell and Richard Nelson Esquires, Commissioners to inspect the books of the entry takers office of White County since the appointment of the present incumbent J. A. who are directed to examine the original files of Locations and the book in which they are recorded - and to report especially upon any particular location filed in said office when they were made, how recorded and which may be asked for by said Entry Taker at the making of said report be renewed and report thereof to the next term of this Court.

Ordered that Court be adjourned untill tomorrow morning 9 O'Clock

Thos. Eastland
David Snodgrass
John Jett

Tuesday Morning 3rd day of April A. D. 1838 Court met pursuant to adjournment. Present the Worshipful

Thomas Eastland	)	Esquires
John Jett	)	
David Snodgrass &	)	Justices
John Bryan		

This day appeared Jonathan T. Bradley Esq. Shff of White County and appointed John England Jr. deputy Sherriff in and for the County of White and who being present in open Court took an oath to support the constitution of the United States and the several oaths prescribed by law and thereupon entered upon the discharge of the duties of his office.

Issd Ordered by court that the following list of hands be assigned to work on that part of the road of which John England, Jr. is Overseer to wit: Thomas Sherrel, Elijah England, Elijah L. Bryan, Williams Wells, James H. Isham, Samuel Brown's blackman, John W. Mills, James Mills, John Goodwin, (P-234) John Howard, Malinda Farley, one hand, Isham Farley, one, Reubin Wilhite, Christopher Slyger and Elam Sherrel.

This day Jonathan T. Bradley Esquire Sherriff in and for the County of White appeared in open Court and appointed Jabez G. Mitchell another of his deputies who being present in open Court took the oath to support the Constitution of the United States and of the State of Tennessee and the several oaths prescribed by law and thereupon entered upon the discharges of the duties of his office.

Ordered that Court be adjourned untill Court in Course

Test
N. Oldham, Clk.

Thos Eastland
David Snodgrass
John Jett
John Bryan

State of Tennessee

At a Court began and held for the County of White and State aforesaid in the town of Sparta at the Court house before the Justices of said Court on the first Monday being the seventh day of May in the year of our Lord One thousand eight hundred and thirty eight and of the Independence of the United States the sixty second year.

Present the Worshipful

John Jott John Bryan & David Snodgrass	Quoram Justices

This day Samuel Brown and William Hill appeared in open Court who were appointed by John Crook, Sr., deceased executors to his last will and testament and renounced all their rights and priviliges as granted them by said will provided Anthony Dibrell Esq. will act as adminestrator.

Isd Ordered by Court that Anthony Dibrell Esquires be appointed adminestrator with the will annexed of John Crook, Sr., deceased who being present in open Court and took the oath prescribed by law and together with William Hill, Jesse Lincoln and Samuel V. Carrick entered into and acknowledged (P-235) bond in the sum of Thirteen thousand dollars conditioned as the law requires.

This day James A. McConnell adminestrator of William McConnell deceased returned upon oath an Inventory of said deceased which is ordered to be recorded.

This day William C. Brittain Esq. produced a Commissioners from the govener authorising him to act a Justice of the peace in White County who being present in open Court and took the oath to support the Constitution of the United States and of the State of Tennessee and the several oaths prescribed by law and there upon entered upon the discharge of the duties of his office.

Isd Ordered by Court that William Hitchcock and James Allison Esq. be appointed commissioners to apportion list and bounds of hands between William P. Rhea and Reubin Perkins Overseer of the road having due regard to the diffrent grades of the road and report thereof to the next term of this Court.

Isd Ordered by Court Stephen C. Pistole be appointed Overseer of the road from Goodwins branch to Hardys old Cabins on the Kentucky road being a road of the first Class and keep the same in repair as the law requires and that the same hands that worked under Joshua Brown late overseer thereof be assigned to work thereon.

Isd Ordered by Court that Lewis Bohanon, James Officer, John Suttles, James Hudson and William Sparks freeholders be appointed a Jury of view to lay off and Mark a road of the third Class Begining at or near John Suttles on the Calf Killer road, thence the nearest and best way to entersect the Walton Road near the Widow Johnsons be renewed and report thereof to the next term of this Court.

Isd Ordered by Court that William McKinny, Patrick Potts, Elisha

Camron, William C. Medcalf and Sims Dearing freeholders be appointed a Jury of view to lay off and mark a road of the third Class leaving the Calf Killer road near William C. Medcalfs thence the nearest and best way through the board valley thence to entersect the Dry valley road near William Pryors and report thereof to the next term of this Court.

Issd Ordered by Court that the order appointing George W. Potts, Cornelius Hickey, William Goodwin, Daniel Lundy and Jesse Davis freehold a Jury of view to lay off and mark a road of the second Class from William Prices the nearest and best way passing where Jesse Davis used to live on the Rockisland road crossing said road and so on to Coles Lower Mill on Falling Water be renewed and report thereof to the next term of this Court.

Issd Ordered by Court that James Yeager, be appointed Overseer of the road from Plumb Creek to the Ten mile post being a road of the second Class and keep the same in repair as the law requires and that the same list of hands that worked under Leonard Massy late overseer thereof be assessed to work thereon.

(P-236) Issd Be it remembered that on this 7th day of May A. D. 1838 appeared in open Court Samuel Denton a Citizen of White County to the Court known of good name, fame and reputation who is entitled to full credit in a court of record who being sworn in due form of law, says upon his oath that MadisonFisk Nathaniel Fisk, Lucinda Denton, Triphona Whitley, Colla Ames and Catharine Gilpatrick are all the legal heirs of Willard Fisk deceased who was a soldier in the late war between the United States and the Kingdom of Great Brittian and has since departed this life all of which is ordered to be recorded and certified under the seal of this Court. For reasons appearing to the satisfaction of the Court by Anthony Dibrell adminestrator of John Crook, Sr., deceased with the will annexed (that is, that said estate is at present in a wasteful condition he is permitted and so directed to make return of the Inventory and account of sales of said estate at the next term of this Court.

This day Daniel Hollinsworth adminestrator of James Goddard deceased returned upon oath an Inventory of said estate which is ordered to be recorded.

Issd Ordered by Court that James A. Jay be appointed Overseer of the road from Johnsons Mill to the mouth of Mill Creek being a road of the second Class and keep the same in repair as the law requires and that the same list of hands that worked under Edward Elms late overseer thereof be assigned to work thereon.

Ordered by Court that Cornelius Davis be assigned to work on that portion of the Milk sick fence of which Laban Wallis is overseer.

Issd Ordered by Court that the order appointing Stephen Wallis, John White, Sr., William Burden, John Austin, John W. Simpson, Pleasant Waller, Jacob Stipe, David Haston, Robert Love, Spence Mitchell, Jesse Scoggins and Samuel Parker freeholders a Jury to examine the road as laid off and marked by Commissioners where it passes through the lands of John H. Dale and thereon to assess the amount of Damages (if any) which the said John H. Dale hath sustained in Consequences of the establishment and opening said road be renewed and report thereof to the next term of this Court.

Issd Ordered by Court that Stephen Farley be appointed Overseer of the road from Glade Creek to Rum Creek being a road of the second Class and keep the same in repair as the law requires And that the same list of hands that worked under William Goodwin late Overseer thereof be assigned to work thereon.

Monday the 7th May A. D. 1838 Present the Worshipful

John Jett, John Bryan James Allison, David Snodgrass, Elisha Camron, William C. Brittian, George Defrees, Asa Certain, Thomas Green, John Gillentine, Joshua Mason, John Wallis, Jesse Walling, William Knowles, Richard Crowder, Matthias Hutson, } Esqs. Justices

being a majority of the acting Justices of the peace in & for said County.

The Court then proceeded to the appointment of a Coroner in and for the County of White and to that office do appoint Simon Doyle to that office for the next insuing two years who being present in open Court took an oath to support the Constitution of the United States and of the State of Tennessee and the several oaths prescribed by law and together with Simon Doyle and John Wallis entered into and acknowledged bond in the sum of two Thousand five hundred dollars conditioned as the law requires.

The Court then proceeded to the appointment of a Ranger in and for the County of White for the next ensuing two years and to that office do appoint John Bryan, Esq. who being present in open Court took an oath to support the Constitution of the United States and of the State of Tennessee and the several oaths prescribed by law and together with John Wallis and William M. Bryan entered into and acknowledged in the sum of Five hundred Dollars conditioned as the law requires.

This day John Bryan Ranger of White County appeared in open Court and appointed Nicholas Oldham his Deputy in said office of Rangers.

Ordered that Court be adjourned untill tomorrow morning 10 O'clock

John Bryan
John Jett
David Snodgrass

Tuesday Morning 8th May A. D. 1838 Court met pursuant to adjournment Present the worshipful

John Jett
John Bryan
David Snodgrass } Esquires Quo. Justices

This day the Commissioners heretofore appointed to lay off and mark a road of the third Class from Lincolns Mill to the (P-237)

intersection of the Lincoln ferry road beyond Eli Sims Esquire returned their report which is by the Court received and ordered to be established a road of the third Class.

Ordered that Court be adjourned untill Court in Course

Test
N. Oldham, Clk.

John Bryan
John Jett
David Snodgrass

State of Tennessee

At a Court began and held for the County of White and State aforesaid at the Court house in the town of Sparta before the Justices of said Court on the first Monday being the fourth day of June A. D. 1838 And of the Independence of the United States the sixty second year.

Present the worshipful

John Jett	}	Esqrs.
David Snodgrass &	}	Quoram
John Bryan	}	
	}	Justices

This day James Arnold an Orphan boy aged eleven years on the 3rd day of June 1838 was bound unto John Humphreys Sr. to serve him after the manner of an apprentice untill he shall arrive at the age of twenty one years and for the faithful performance of his Covenant entered with Jesse H. Vermillion into and acknowledged bond conditioned as the law requires.

This day Amelia Ann Jeffers aged seven years and Amarrilla Jeffers aged five orphan children of Allen Jeffers were bound unto William L. Young to serve him after the manner of apprentices untill they arrive to the age of twenty one years and for the faithful performance of his Covenant with John Young entered into and acknowledged bond conditioned as the law requires.

This day Anthony Dibrell adminestrator with the will annexed of John Crook Sr. deceased returned upon oath an Inventory and account of sales of said estate which is ordered to be recorded.

This day Jesse A. Bounds, Admr. Debonis non with the will annexed of Isaac Clark deceased returned upon oath (P-238) an Inventory and Account of sales of the property of said Estate which is ordered to be recorded.

Isad Ordered by Court that Overton Chisum be appointed Overseer of the road from the Rockisland to Samuel A. Moore, Esq. being a road of first Class from the Island the forks of the road and second Class from thence to squire Moore on the Kentucky road and keep the same in repair as the law requires And that the same list and bounds of hands that worked under Smith J. Walling late Overseer thereof be assigned to work thereon.

David Moore }
vs } Jury of Damages
John H. Dale }

Ordered by Court that Anderson S. Rogers, William M. Bryan, Sr. Stephen Wallis, Thomas Wilson, Benjamin Lewis, Hartwell Wilson, Littleberry Wilson, John Baker, John Bryan, Esq., Laban Foster, Cornelius Brown, and John White, Jr. freeholders be appointed a Jury to examine the road as laid off and marked by Commissioners where it passes through the land of John H. Dale and thereon to assess what Damages the said John H. Dale shall have sustained by the establishment and the opening of said road and report thereof to the next term of this Court.

This day Joshua Mason and Margarett Mason were appointed adminestrator and administratrix of all and singular the goods and chattles, rights and credits of Cabb Mason deceased who took the oath prescribed by law (being present in open Court and together with Robert Mason; Cornelius Jarvis and Thomas Robertson entered into and acknowledged bond in the sum of one Thousand Dollars conditioned as the law requires.

This day the death of Coleman Brown late of the County of White was suggested in open Court and that he departed this life entestate where upon James Brown was appointed administrator of all and singular the goods and chattles, rights and credits of the deceased who being present in open Court took the oath prescribed by law and together with John Brown and James Thomas entered into and acknowledged bond in the sum of six hundred and twenty dollars conditioned as the law requires.

This day Daniel Hollinsworth Executor of the last will and testament of James Godard deceased returned upon oath an account of the sales of the estate of the deceased which is ordered to be recorded.

Issd Ordered by Court that the order appointing David Snodgrass; Anthony Dibrell and Richard Nelson; Esqrs Commissioners to inspect the Books of the Entry takers office of White County since the appointment of the present incumbent J. A. Lane (P-239) who are directed to examine the original files of locations and the Books in which they are recorded - And to report specially upon any particular location filed in said office when they were made; how recorded &c.
And which may be asked for by said Entry taker as to the making of said report be renewed and report thereof at the next term of this Court.

Ordered that Court be adjourned untill to morrow morning 9 O'clock

John Jett
David Snodgrass
John Bryan

Tuesday 5th day of June A. D. 1838 Court met pursuant to adjournment Present the Worshipful

John Jett) Esqrs.
David Snodgrass)
& John Bryan) Quoram
)
) Justices

Issd Ordered by Court that James Rundalls; Eli Sims and John Humphrey, Sr. be appointed Commissioners to lay off set apart One years provisions to the releot and widow and family of Cabb Mason deceased for the support and maintaince and report thereof to the next term of this Court.

Issd Ordered by Court that the order appointing William McKinny; Patrick Potts; Elisha Camron; William C. Medcalf; and Sims Dearing freeholders to be a Jury of view to lay off and mark a road of the third a Class leaving the Calf Killer road near William C. Medcalf thence the nearest and best way through the board valley thence to intersect the Dry valley road near William Pryors be renewed and report thereof to the next term of this Court.

Isad Ordered by Court that the order appointing George W. Pott; Cornelius Hickey; William Goodwin, Daniel Lundy; and Jesse Davis; freeholders a Jury of view to lay off and mark a road of the second Class from William Prices the nearest and best way passing where Jesse Davis used to live on the Rockisland road crossing said road and so on to Coles lower mill on Falling Watter be renewed and report thereof to the next term of this Court.

Isad Ordered by Court that the order appointing Lewis Bohanon, James Officer; John Suttles; James Hudson and William Sparks freeholders a Jury of view to lay off and mark a road of the third Class from at or near John Suttles on the Calf Killer road thence*to intersect the Walton road (P-240) near the widow Johnson be renewed and report thereof to the next term of this Court.

Isad This day Jacob Yount, personally appeared in open Court and moved the Court for leave to Contest the validity of the last will and testament of John Crook, Sr. deceased late of the county of White and to him it is granted on giving bond and security as required by law who with Elijah Hootten and William Goolsby entered into and acknowledged bond in the sum of five hundred Dollars conditioned as the law requires whereupon it is ordered by the Court that the record and proceeding had on said will in said Court be certified under the seal of this Court and transmitted together with the original last will & testament of the said Deceased to the Honorable the Circuit Court of White County for further proceedings to be had thereon.

Isad Ordered by Court that Thomas M. Flimming be appointed Overseer of the road from Moores old ford on Caney fork to the intersection of the McMinnville road being a road of the 2nd Class and keep the same in repair as the law requires and that the same list and bounds of hands that worked under Daniel Steakley late Overseer thereof be assigned to work thereon.

Ordered that Court be adjourned untill Court in Course.

Test
N. Oldham, Clk.

David Snodgrass
John Jett
John Bryan

*to the nearest and best way

(P-241) State of Tennessee

At a Quarteraly Court began and held for the County of White in the State aforesaid at the Court house in the town of Sparta before the Justices of the Justices of said Court on the first Monday being the second day of July in the year of our Lord one thousand eight hundred and thirty eight and of the Independence of the United States of America the 62nd

Present the Worshipful

John Jett Esqr. Chairman Pro tem
David Snodgrass; John Bryan;) Esqs.
Joshua Mason; John Gillentine;
George Defrees; William Bruster;
Elijah Frost, Jesse Walling;
Elisha Camron, William C. Brittain;
Edmund Stamps; Asa Certain,
William Bartlett; Thomas Green;) Justices.
Richard Crowder; James Allison.

Isd Ordered by Court that the order of last Court appointing Eli Sims; Esq. one of the Commissioners to assign One years provisions to the widow and family of Caleb Mason deceased be so changed that Levi Jarvis be appointed in the place of Eli Sims and have leave to report to the next term of this Court.

David Moore)
vs) Pitition for Jury
John H. Dale) to assess Damages

By Consent of the parties and with the assent of the court it is ordered that the order of the last term appointing Andrew S. Rogers; William M. Bryan; Sr., Stephen Wallis, Thomas Wilson; John Baker; John Bryan, Esq. Laban Foster; Cornelius Brown and John White, Jr. a jury to examine the road as laid off by commissioners where it passed through the land of John H. Dale and thereon to assess the amount of damages (if any) which the said John H. Dale hath sustained in consequence of the establishment and opening of said road be renewed and report thereof to the next term of this Court.

Ordered by Court that the order of last Court appointing William McKinney, Patrick Potts; Elisha Camron; William C. Metcalf and Sims Dearing freeholders a Jury of view to lay off and mark a road of the third Class leaving the Calf Killer road near William C. Medkiffs thence the nearest and best way through the board valley thence to entersect the Dry valley road near William Pryors be renewed and report thereof to the next term of this Court.

(P-242) Isd Ordered by Court that the order of the last term appointing Lewis Bohanon; James Officer; John Suttles; James Hudson; and James Sparks freeholders a Jury of view to lay off and mark a road of the third Class from at or near John Suttles on the Calf Killer road thence the nearest and best way to intersect the Walton road near the widow Johnsons be renewed and report thereof to the next term of this Court.

This day the Commissioners heretofore appointed by this Court to lay off and mark a road of the second Class from William Prices to Coles lower mill on Falling Water, made their report which is by the Court received and said road is Established a road of the second Class.

This day Joseph Phifer produced in open Court one large wolf scalp over the age of four months and proved that he killed the same in the County of White whereupon there being present five acting Justices of the peace in and for said County to wit: John Jett, David Snodgrass, John Bryan, Joshua Mason and George Defrees Esq. it is ordered by the Court that the same be certified to the Treasure of the State of Tennessee for payment and that the sherriff of White County destroy said scalp who being present in open Court received said scalp into his Custody and acted accordingly.

For reason appearing fully to the satisfaction of the Court it is ordered that Dan Griffeth be allowed the sum of Eleven dollars six and one fourth cents for furnishing Coffin and things as per Bill and burying a certain Polly Brinles a pauper late of White County deceased and that Hiram W. Rogers and William Lollis be each allowed one Dollar for Digging the grave of the deceased to be paid by the Treasure of the poor house of said County out of the poor tax of 1838.

. It appearing to the sale faction of the Court that at a former term of this Court John Bryan Esquire was allowed five dollars for holding an Inquest over the body of a certain William Gracy who came to his death casually to be paid by the Trustee of White County it is ordered that same be so amended, that the Treasure of the poor house of White County be required to pay the same out of the poor tax of the present year.

For reasons appearing to the satisfaction of the Court from the evidence of Nathaniel Austin and others that David C. Dempsy a citizen of White County from infirmity and old age is in a state of destitution and really suffering for want of the necessaries to support life -

It is therefore considered by the Court that said Dempsy be received by said Court as a pauper and be conveyed to the poorhouse of said County to be maintained at the proper cost and charges of said County and that Nathaniel Austin be appointed to convey the said Dempsy to the poor house of said County provided that the said Dempsy who has an annuity of Pension coming from the United States government sum annully of about $30. per annum (P-243) will deposit his Pension certificate with the Treasure of the poor house and at the time or times of arriving the monies thereon will give such authority as will enable the Treasure of the poor house to recive said monies and that the same as for as it will go shall be applied exclusivelly to the support of the said David C. Dempsy so long as he shall live and is under charge of the Court and resedue of said expences to be paid by the County of White.

Isad Ordered by Court that Nicholas Oldham Clerk of White County Court be allowed the sum of twenty two dollars and fifty cents for making out and recording the tax tests for the County of White for the year 1838

Also the furthur sum of five Dollars and twenty five cents for two Blank records Books furnished the County Court office - One for Regesters of marriges the other Common school Docket amounting in all to the sum of twenty seven Dollars seventy five cents to be paid by the sherriff of White County out of the tax of the year 1838.

Issd Ordered by Court that William G. Sims Esq. Clerk of White Circuit Court be allowed the sum of twelve dollars for a Blank record Book furnished by him for the use of the Circuit Court to be paid by the Sherriff of White County out of the taxes of the year 1838.

It appearing to the satisfaction of the Court that in running the line of DeKalb County it leaves a fraction of the 7 District in White County which is cut off and debanded from priviliges of other Districts in White County.

It is therefore Considered and so ordered that, that part of said fraction of the 7 District that lies south of Taylors Creek be and the same is hereby attached to the 6th District and that part of said fraction that lies north of Taylors Creek be and the same is hereby attached to the eight District to have priviliges in common with the Citizens of the District to which they are attached.

Whereas Stephen Farley a Citizen of the 6th District in the laying off the District of White County is called for as a liner and the said Farley representing to this Court that it is much more convenient for him to belong to the 9th District it is therefore considered by the Court that said District be so altered that the said Farley shall be included in the 9th District and that said Farley be entitled to all the priviliges thereof.

Issd Ordered by Court that John Howard be appointed Overseer of the road from the forks of the road at Joseph Kophers to the intersection of the Kentucky road at John Howards fence being a road of the third Class and keep the same in repair as the law requires and John Pennington and George Defrees Esquires assign list and bounds of hands between the difrent overseers of the road in the neighborhood thereof so as to apportion hands to work on said road.

This day John Jett; David Snodgrass and William Littles Esquires Commissioners of Robert Burks turnpike road for Sparta towards Kingston appeared in open Court and tendered their resignation which is received and ordered to be recorded.

(P-244) Ordered by Court that the order of last Court appointing David Snodgrass, Anthony Dibrell and Richard Nelson Esquires Commissioners to inspect the books of the Entry takers office of White County since the appointment of the present incumbent (J. A. Lane) who are directed to examine the original files of locations; and the Books in which they are recorded and to report specially upon any particular filed in said office when they were made; how recorded &c. and which may be asked for by said Entry taker at the making of said report be renewed and report thereof to the next term of this Court.

Ordered by Court that Thomas Stone be appointed Overseer of the road from Falling Water to Jackson County line being a road of the second Class and keep the same in repair as the law requires and that the same hands that worked under Joseph Farris late Overseer thereof be assigned to work thereon.

Ordered by Court that David Snodgrass; William Little and William Simpson be appointed Commissioners on Robert Burks turnpike road leading from Sparta towards Kingston, who being present in open Court & took the oath prescribed by law.

Issd Ordered by Court that John Gillentine, Jesse Walling and Thomas Moore be appointed Commissioners on Hales turnpike road leading from Sparta to Pikeville who being present in open Court took the oath required by law.

Ordered by Court that Elisha Camron Esquire be appointed an additional Commissioner on Robert Officers turnpike road who being present in open Court took the oath required by law.

This day Joshua Mason one of the adminestrators of Caleb Mason deceased returned upon oath an Inventory and account of sales of estate of the deceased which is ordered to be recorded.

On the humble petition of John R. Glenn signed by many Citisons of the County of White and for reason appearing to the satisfaction of the County he is permitted to erect a grist mill and other water Machinery where he has his saw mill on Ceder Creek and Townsend Mill Creek in said County.

Issd Ordered by Court that the following named persons good and lawful men, Citizens of the County of White be appointed Jurors to October term 1838 of the Circuit Court for the County aforesaid to wit: William C. Brittian, Daniel McClain, John Austin, David Moore, Andrew Cope, Winkfield Hill, Lewis Pettet, Thomas Hutson, Joseph Clark, James Holland, David Snodgrass, William Little, John Crook, Elijah Frost, Joseph Cummings, Spence Mitchell, Asa Certain, John England, Sr. James T. Hayes, Richard Crowder, Elisha Camron, Edmund Stamps, William C. Bound, John Pennington, James C. Hitchcock, James Allison and James C. Kelly and Thomas Snodgrass Constables to attend thereon and that a most Venerefacias issue directed to the sherriff of White County returnable &c.

(P-245) Issd On the information of George Defrees Esquire it is ordered by the Court the Sherriff of White County bring in to open Court at the next term the two orphan children of Sally Aldredge and one orphan child of Polly Aldredge to be dealt by as the law directs.

Where as William S. Parkman a Constable of White County has been legally notified Peter Buram and Elijah Hill his securities to appear at present term of this Court in order to give other and sufficient security for his office of Constable and to release the said P. Buram and Elijah Hill; and for reason appearing to the satisfaction of the Court the said Parkman and Hill being present in open Court it is Ordered by the Court that the said Peter Buram and Elijah Hill securities as aforesaid from all future and further liabilities as security for the said William S. Parkman be released and forever discharged where upon the said William S. Parkman together with Solomon S. Parkman, Gabriel P. Cummings, Francis Simmon and Zachariah Simmons entered into and acknowledged bond in the sum of four thousand dollars conditioned as the law requires.

The State) Bastardy
vs)
Lee R. Taylor) Sarah Nolen
) Prosecutrix

This day came the Defendant in proper person into open Court and thereupon produced a receipt in writing from the prosecutrix in the above cause acknowledging the payment in full of the sum which by law she would be entitled to receive from said defendant, for begetting upon the body of the said Sarah Nolen a bastard male child where upon it is ordered and considered by the Court that said defendant find securities to keep the County of White for and endimnified from any coler of cost or damage foresaid towards the support and maintainance of said Bastard child and now came here said defendant with William H. Baker and Jonathan T. Bradley into open Court and acknowledged themselves endebted to the County of White in the sum of five hundred Dollars to be levied of their respective Goods and Chattles, lands and tenaments to the use of the County of White to be rendered nevertheless to be void on conditioned that they keep free and indemnified the County of White from all costs and damages for and towards the support and maintaince of the Bastard child afore said and it is further considered by the Court that the state of Tennessee recover against the said defendant all costs in the behalf in this cause expended and that executed issue &c.

State) Bastardy
vs)
Lee R. Taylor) Sarah Nolen, Pros.

This day came the defendant in proper person into open Court and thereupon produced a receipt in writing from (P-246) The Prosecutrix in the above cause acknowledging the payment in full of the same which by law she would be entitled to receive from said defendant for begetting upon the body of the said Sarah Nolen a bastard female child; whereupon it is ordered and so considered by the Court that said Defendant find securities to keep the County of White for and indimnified from any color of cost or damages for and towards the support and maintaince of said Bastard child and now came here into open Court the said defendant, with William H. Baker and Jonathan T. Bradley and acknowledged themselves indebted to the County of White in the sum of Five hundred Dollars to be levied of their respective goods and Chattles, Lands and temmints to the use of White County to be rendered nevertheless to be void on condition that they keep free and indemnified the County of White from all Cost and damage for and towards the support and maintainee of the female Bastard child aforesaid and it is further considered by the Court that the State of Tennessee recover against the said defendant all costs in this behalf in this cause expended and that execution issue &c.

Isd Ordered by Court that the following persons be allowed the following sums of money in the following state cases which have been certified by the Clerk of the Circuit Court of White County from said Court and which have been examined and certified by the solicitor of White County as correctly taxed and properly chargeable to said County To Wit: the State vs James Kerby, William G. Sims \$2.12½ Shff J. G. Mitchell 1.25 - The State vs James Kerby, Clerk W. G. Sims 2.12½; Shff J. G. Mitchell 1.25 - The State vs James Kerby, Clerk W.G.Sims 2.12½, Shff J.G.Mitchell 1.25 - The State vs William Kerby, Clerk W.G.Sims \$4.93¾ Shff Bradley, 1.41½ - witness Joshua Mason, Jr. \$1.00 The State vs George W. Campbell Clerk W. G. Sims \$3.87½, Shff. Samuel Callahan 0.62½ - . The State vs Hall Oxendine Clerk W. G. Sims \$.6 cent. Shff D. L. Mitchell 0.62½ - . Shff John England 0.75 Shff J. T. Bradley 1.41½ - witness Lewis Bohanon \$2.11 - . The State

vs Michael Moon; Clerk W. G. Sims $6.87½ Sherriff W. G. Sims $2.75 Shff D. L. Mitchell $3.87½ Shff J. T. Bradley $.62½ Shff John England 1.75 Shff David Cox of Jackson County $1.00 - . Jacob A. Lane Clerk of County Court $12.25 The State vs Edward Gleeson Clerk W. G. Sims $3.87½ Shff J. T. Braddley 62½ - The State vs Randolph Ramsey Clerk W. G. Sims $5.18¾ Shff J. T. Bradley $2.12½ - - witness Thomas Price 0.75 - The State vs John Pennington Clerk W. G. Sims $7.43¾ - Shff D. L. Mitchell .75 Shff J. T. Bradley 1.00 Witness Willie W. Crawford 1.00 - The State vs William G. Martin Clerk W. G. Sims 5.18¾ Shff J. T. Bradley 2.12½ - Witness Thomas Price 75 The State vs Patrick H. Armstrong Clerk Sims 3.87½ Shff Samuel Callaham 62½ - The State vs. James England Clerk W. G. Sims $4.31¼ Shff J. T. Bradley 1.87½ witness Thomas Price 75 The State vs John C. Oram; Clerk W. G. Sims 4.68¾ Shff J. T. Bradley $2.00 Witness Thomas Price .75 The State vs. Robert S. Windle; W. G. Sims $3.87½ Shff Samuel Callaham 62½ - The State vs David Cook Clerk W. G. Sims 5.00 Shff J. T. Bradley $1.25 Shff John England 50 The State against (P-247) Jesse Allen; Jr. Clerk W. G. Sims $6.25 Shff J. T. Braddley 1.68½ Witness Joshua Mason 1.50 All of which to be paid by the Trustee of White County out of any monies not otherwise appropriated.

Ordered that Court be adjourned untill tomorrow Morning at 12 O'clock

John Jett
Wm. Bruster
W. C. Brittian

Tuesday Morning 3 July 1838 Court met pursuant to adjournment
Present the Worshipful

John Jett, William C.Brittain, William Bruster } Esqs Justices

Ordered that Court be adjourned untill Court in Course

Test
N. Oldham; Clk.

John Jett
Wm. Bruster
W. C. Brittian

(P-248)

State of Tennessee

At a Court began and held for the County of White and State aforesaid at the Court house in the town of Sparta before the Justice of said Court on the first Monday being the sixth day of August in the year of our Lord one Thousand eight hundred and thirty eight. And of the Independence of the United States of America the sixty third year.

Present the Worshipful

John Jett David Snodgrass & John Bryan	Esquires Quorum Justices

This day the Clerk of this exhibited in open Court a report of a settlement made with George Bohannon adminestrator with the will annexed of Joseph Henry deceased which is confirmed in all its parts and ordered to be recorded

David Moore
vs
John H. Dale) Damages on road

This day came the Jury heretofore appointed by this Court to assess damages consequent on the establishment and opening a certain road through the lands of John H. Dale returned their report as follows to wit: we whose names are hereunto subscribed having been appointed by the worshipful Court of pleas and Quarter Sessions to assess to John H. Dale the Damages he may sustain in consequence of a road passing over part of his lands in White County which road was ordered to be laid out on the application of David Moore; have carefully examined and according to law considered of the damages aforesaid do report that we believe has received damages by occasion of said road passing over his lands to the sum of seven dollars & 50 cents - And hereby assessed the same as the damages done to said Dale in the premises all of which is respectfully submitted this 4th day of August 1838

John Bryan (seal)
Stephen Wallis (seal)
Thomas Wilson (seal)
Benjamin Lewis (seal)
William M. Bryan (seal)
John White, Jr. (seal)
Laban Foster (seal)
John Baker (seal)
Bery R. Wilson (seal)
Hartwell Wilson (seal)
Cornelius Brown (seal)
Anderson S. Rogers (seal)

which is by the Court received and confirmed. It thereupon considered by the Court that the defendant recover against the plaintiff and Thomas Moore and Richard Nelson his securities the aforesaid sum of seven dollars and fifty cents the damages aforesaid by the Jury aforesaid assessed together with all costs by him in his defence in this behalf expended and that execution issue.

This day pearsonally appeared William B. Parkman a constable in the

15 District of White County and resigned his office as subh which is ordered to be recorded.

(P-249) Isad Ordered by Court that John Taylor be appointed Overseer of the road from the branch near James M. Nelson to the blue Spring branch towards Rockisland being a road of the second Class and keep the same in repair as the law requires and that Richard Crowder, James T. Hayes Esquires be appointed Commissioners to assign and apportion lists and bounds of hands to said Taylor, William Baker and William Lisk Overseer having due regard to the grades of the diffrent roads.

Isad This day Charles Denny produced in open Court one large wolf scalp over the age of four months and proved that he killed the same in White County. Whereupon there being present five acting Justices of the peace in and for said County to wit: John Jett, David Snodgrass; John Bryan, Edmund Stamps and Joshua Mason; ordered the same to be recorded and certified to the Treasures of the State of Tennessee for payment, and that the Sherriff of White County burn said scalps who being present in open Court received the same into his custody and acted accordingly.

Isad On the humble pitition of James Dillon; and for reasons appearing to the satisfaction of the Court by evidence that said Dillon has erected a Toll bridge across the Caney Fork at what is called Dillons ferry and that said Bridge is in sufficient forwardness of completion as to render safe passage to all wagons and other travelling vehicles &c.

And do establish and authorise the said James Dillon to ask, demanded and received the following sales of Toll at said bridge To wit for each wagon drawn by 4 horses or steers 50 cents

For each 4 wheel pleasure carriage	75 cents
For each 2 wheel " "	50 cents
For each Carryal	25 cents
For each Barouch and two horses	50 cents
For each Cart	25 cents
For each Gig	25 cents
For each man and horse	12½ cents
For each lead horse; mule of Jack	6¼ cents
For each Footman	6¼ cents
For each head of hogs, cattle or sheep	1 cent

Isad Ordered by Court that so much of the order heretofore made that assigning hands to William A. Cook Overseer of a third Class road be set aside except as to one slave and that the balance of the hands which worked with him from time assigne to that portion of the road of whitch Overton Chisum is overseer.

This day William Pryor a minor being of sufficent age appeared in open court and chose his father Joseph Pryor as his Guardian who being present in open Court together with William Bartlett and Joseph Bartlett entered into bond and security in the sum of Two hundred dollars conditioned as the law requires.

(P-250) The State of Tennessee vs William C. Johnson } Bastardy Elly Whitson, Proex.

This day came the Defendant into open Court and with Charles McGuire and James Hennessee acknowledged themselves indebted to the State of Tennessee to the use of White County in the sum of One thousand dollars to wit: the Defendant in $5.00 and each security $2.50 - to be levied of their respective goods and chattles lands and tenements to the use of White County to be rendered to be void on conditioned that the said Defendant William C. Johnson shall pay or cause to be paid to the said Polly Whitson the above named prosecutrix at the end of One year forty Dollars at the end of two years Thirty Dollars and at the end of Three years twenty dollars for the support and maintaince of a certain Bastard male child begotten by the defendant upon the body of the said Polly Whitson the prosecutrix and that they will keep free and indemnified and harmless the County of White from all cost and damages towards the support and maintaince of the aforesaid Bastard male child charged upon oath of the said Polly Whitson the above named prosecutrix to have been begotten on her body by the said William C. Johnson. Whereupon it is considered by the Court that the State of Tennessee recover against the defendant and his securities all costs in this behalf expended &c. and that execution issue &c.

This day personally appeared in open Court Eliza Bartlett and William Bartlett minor but of suffisent age to chose their guardian did in open Court chose and select their father Joseph Bartlett to be their guardian and at the same time the Court appointed the said Joseph Bartlett graudian to his three other minor children to wit: Nathan Bartlett, Betty Bartlett and Margrett Bartlett who being present in open court together with David Snodgrass and Jesse A. Bounds entered into and acknowledged bond in the sum of one thousand dollars conditioned as the law requires.

Isad Ordered by Court that Wamon Leftwich, William Simpson, William M. Young, Samuel V. Carrick, John Warren, William G. Sims and Frank C. Conner Esquires be appointed and hereby Constituted Commissioners of the Corporation of the town of Sparta in the County of White and State of Tennessee with full authority to possess hold and enjoy all such powers priviliges and immunities and to make ordain, enact and enforce such rules, regulations or Bye laws as are contemplated in and granted by the several acts of the General Assembly incorperating the said town of Sparta with full power to enter for which upon the preformance of their duties.

(P-251) This day the Commissioners heretofore appointed to assign and set apart one years provisions for the support and maintaince of the widow and family of Cabb Mason deceased out of his Estate made their report which is ordered to be recorded.

This day James A. McConnell adminestrator of William McConnell deceased returned upon oath an account of the sales of the property of the deceased which is ordered to be recorded. -

Ordered that Court be adjourned untill tomorrow morning at 10 O'clock

John Jett
John Bryan
David Snodgrass

Tuesday Morning 7th August 1838 Court met pursuant to adjournment

Present the Worshipful

John Jett
David Snodgrass
John Bryan and
Wm. Bruster

Esq.

Justices

Issd Ordered by Court that the Commissioners appointed on yesterday for the Town of Sparta be respectfully requested forthwith to organise their board by the appointment of a present and such other offices as may be deemed by them necessary and proper under the existing laws for the Regulation of said Town and that through their president and Clerk they report to the next term of this Court whether they have appointed an Overseer of the Streets or not and what regulations they may have made for the presevation of the enclosure of the Court house and such other information as they may think proper to communicate to said Court and that the Sherriff of said County served said Commissioners with a copy of this order.

Ordered that Court be adjourned untill Court in Course

Test
N. Oldham, Clk.

John Jett
David Snodgrass
John Bryan

(P-252) State of Tennessee

At a Court began and held for the County of White at the Court house in the town of Sparta before the Quorum Justices of said Court on the first Monday being the third day of September in the year of our Lord One thousand eight hundred and thirty eight and of the Independence of the United States of America the sixty third year

Present the Worshipful

John Jett	)	Esquires
David Snodgrass	)	Quorum
John Bryan	)	Justices

Ordered by Court that report of Wm. Hitchcock and James Allison; Esq. assign hands to William P. Rhea to wit William P. Campbell; John Campbell and Bird S. Rhea be received and ordered to be recorded-.

This day Sevier Evans exhibited in open Court his stock mark to wit a hole in each ear which is ordered to be recorded - .

This day Nicholas Oldham exhibeted in open Court his stock mark to wit: a swollow fork and under bit in the right ear and an under bit and smoth crop off the left ear which is ordered to be recorded.

This day Jacob A. Lane exhibited in open Court his stock mark to wit to wit: a hole in the right ear and a crop off the left ear which is ordered to be recorded.

This day the sherriff of White County produced in open Court a Certificate of the election of Henry Kuhn Constable in the 15th District of said County to fill the vacancy occasioned by the resegnation of William Sparkman late Constable therein who being present in open Court took an oath to support the constitution of the United States and of the State of Tennessee and the several oaths prescribed by law and together with Terry Gillentine and Samuel Parker entered into and acknowledged bond in the sum of four thousand Dollars Conditioned as the law requires.

This day John Young to whom was bound a certain orphan by name William K. Williams as an apprentice - . Came and surrendered to the Court the said orphan boy and prayed that said bond of Indenture may be cancelled and entirely set aside and for sufficent reasons appearing to the satisfaction of the Court the said John Young is released from all future and further liabilities therein.

This day William K. Williams an orphan boy aged six years on the 29th October 1837 was bound to John Warren to serve him after the manner of an apprentice untill he arrives at the age of twenty one years and for the faithful performance (P-253) of his Covenant entered into and acknowledged bond with Charles Meeks his security conditioned as the law requires.

This dey Susannah Duncan appeared in open Court and was appointed guardian to Polly Duncan, Jesusha Duncan; John T. Duncan; James W. Duncan and Tilman C. Duncan minor heirs of William Duncan dec'd and took the oath prescribed by law and together with George W. Potts and Pleasant Farley entered into and acknowledged Bond in the sum of Fifteen hundered Dollars conditioned as the law requires.

Issd For reasons appearing fully to the satisfaction of the Court it is ordered by the Court that Sevier Evans be allowed the sum of Thirty Dollars being the amount by him paid to R. Nelson Esquires as a fee for prosecution John M. Anderson for killing John M. Rottan to be paid by Dan Griffith adminestrator of said Rottan out of the Estate of the deceased.

Ordered by Court that the Commissioners of the town of Sparta have leav untill the next term to make their report.

This day Anthony Dibrell one of the executors of Jacob Robinson deceased returned upon oath an additional sale of said estate which is ordered to be recorded.

This day the Clerk of White County Court produced in open Court the report of a settlement with Anthony Dibrell one of the executors of Jacob Robinson deceased which is confirmed in all its parts and ordered to be recorded.

And it is further considered by the Court that Anthony Dibrell Executor as aforesaid be allowed lawful entemest on the six hundred and one dollars sixty seven and a half cents the amount due him from said estate from the 3rd day of September 1835 until paid to be paid out of said Estate.

Issd This day was exhibited in open Court a writing purporting to be the last will and testament of Stephen Farley late of the County of White deceased and the due execution and publication thereof as the last will and testament of the said Stephen Farley Deceased was provided in open Court by the oaths of William Goodwin and Pleasant Lynnville two of the subscribing witnesses thereto for the purposes and things therein contained and that the said Stephen Farley at the date of the execution and publication thereof as such was of sound and disposing mind and memory all of which is ordered to be recorded and at the same time appeared in open Court Thomas Tallent and Jeremiah Farley the Executors nominated and appointed by the said Stephen Farley in said last will and Testament who agree to take upon themselves the further of the execution (P-254) of the said last will and Testament and thereupon took the oath required by law and together with William Goodwin, Pleasant Lynnville and Pleasant Farley entered into and acknowledged bond in the sum of One thousand Dollars conditioned as the law requires.

This day was exhibited in open Court a writing purporting to be the last will and testament of William Lewis late of the County of White deceased, and the due execution and publication thereof as the last will and testament of the said William Lewis Deceased was proved in open Court by the oaths of Edward V. Pollard and John R. Glenn subscribing witness theretofore the purposes and things therein mentioned and that the said William Lewis was at the date of the execution and publication of said last will and Testament of sound and disposing mind and memory all of which is ordered to be recorded.

And there being no execution provided or appointed by said last will and testament whereupon it is ordered by the Court that Benjamin Lewis be appointed adminestrator of all and singular the goods and chattles, rights and credits of the said William Lewis deceased with his last will and testament annexed who being present in open Court took the oath required by law and together with William H. Baker, Thomas Robertson and Joseph Herd entered into and acknowledged bond in the sum of nineteen hundred dollars conditioned as the law requires.

This day Benjamin Lewis adminestrator with the will annexed of William Lewis deceased returned upon oath an Inventory of the said deceased in part which is ordered to be recorded.

State vs William E. Camp } Bastardy

Sarah Sanders Prosecutrix

This day came the Defendant in proper person into open Court and thereupon produced a receipt in writing signed by the prosecutrix acknowledging the payment of the sum in full which by law she would be entitled to from said defendant for begetting upon her body a Bastard male child whereupon it is ordered by the Court and so considered that said Defendant find securities to keep the County of White endimnified from all Cost and charges for and towards the support and maintaince of said bastard male child; and now came the said Defendant and Vardesy Camp and Joseph Kuhn into open Court and acknowledged themselves indebted to the State of Tennessee in the sum of five hundred dollars to the use of the County of White void on conditioned that they keep free and endemnified and harmless the County of White from the support and maintainance of the above bastard male child charged on oath by the said Sarah to be begotten on her body by the said William E. Camp. Whereupon it is ordered by the Court that the State of Tennessee recover against said Defendant all Cost in this behalf expended &c.

(P-255) This day the Clerk of this Court reported a settlement made with Susannah Duncan adminestratrix of the estate of William Duncan deseased which received and confirmed in all its parts and ordered to be recorded.

Ordered by Court that John A. Pass be appointed Overseer of the road from the ford of the river at Glenns old salt well to the entersection of the Jo. Hunter road on the mountain being a road of the second class and keep the same in repair as the law requires and that the same list of hands that worked under Henry Rutledge late overseer thereof be assigned to work thereon.

Issd Ordered by Court that Indamon B. Moore be appointed Overseer of the road as laid off by Commissioners from his house to the intersection of the Kentucky road at Cason Swindles being a road of the 3rd Class and that Matthias Hutson Esq. assign a list of hands to work thereon.

Issd Ordered by Court that Lewis Pettet Esq. be appointed to assign a list of hands to Timothy Couch Overseers of a third Class road and report thereof to the next term of this Court.

Ordered that Court be adjourned untill tomorrow morning at 9 O'clock

John Jett
John Wallis
John Bryan

Tuesday Morning 4th September A.D. 1838 Court met pursuant to adjournment
Present the Worshipful

John Jett ⎫
John Bryan & ⎬ Esquires Justices
John Wallis ⎭

Issd Ordered by Court that the superentendant of the poor house of White County bring into Court at the next term a certain child which is now a pauper upon said County to be further dealt by as may seem right and proper by said court and according to law.

This day John Jett squires exhibited his stock mark in open Court to wit; a smooth crop off each ear and an under bit in the right ear which is ordered to be recorded.

This day John Wallis Esq. exhibited in open Court his Stock mark to wit; a smooth crop and split in the left ear and a swallow fork in the right ear which is ordered to be recorded.

State
vs Issd
William C. Johnson

Bastardy

Polly Whitson; Prosx.

It is ordered by Court that the (P-256) Defendant William C. Johnson be summoned to appear at the next term of this Court and to abide such further action of the Court as may seem proper and right and according to law.

Ordered that Court be adjourned untill Court in Course

Test
N. Oldham; Clk.

John Jett
John Bryan
John Wallis

State of Tennessee

At a County Court began and held for the County of White and State aforesaid in the Court house in the town of Sparta before the Justices of said Court on the first Monday being the first day of October in the year of our Lord one thousand eight hundred and thirty eight. And of the Independence of the United States the Sixty third year.

Present the worshipful

Thomas Eastland, Esq. Chairman
John Jett, Elijah Frost,
Thomas Green, David Snodgrass, } Esquires
John Bryan, William Little,
William Knowles, Edmund Stamps,
George Defrees, Asa Certain,
Jesse Walling, Elisha Camron,
Matthias Hutson, Richard Crowder,
John Gillentine, William Bartlett, } Justices
James T. Hayes, Lewis Pettett - .

This day John Wallis and Willie Steakley Esquire appeared in open Court and resigned their respective offices as Justices of the peace in for said County which is ordered to be recorded.

This day the Clerk of this Court produced in open Court all the receipt which by law he is hound to do which is ordered by the Court to be spread upon the minutes of this Court Towit - . $617.10 Nashville 13 Sept 1838 No. 579 Received of Nicholas Oldham Six hundred and seventeen dollars 10 cents audited to him by No.579 and due on account of Revenue by him collected as clerk of the County Court of White County from the 1st Sept 1837 to 1 Sept 1838

signed Duplicates Miller Francis
Treasure of Tennessee

Comptrollers office Nashville 12 Sept 1838
Received of N. Oldham his Statement of Revenue collected as clerk of White County Court from 1 Sept 1837 to 1 Sept. 1838 amount collected 622.10 pay commissioners
Daniel Graham & Snodgrass $500 - .
Warrent No 579 for $617.10

(P-257) Comptrollers Office Nashville, Tenn., 12 Sept. 1838
Received of N. Oldham the Revenue bond of Jon T. Bradley Sherriff of White County dated 2nd April 1838 with penalty of 1000 for collection of the State taxes for the years 1838 & 1839

Daniel Graham
Comptroller of the Treasurey

Received of N. Oldham Clerk of White County Court two hundred and fifty Dollars eighty three cents which by law he has collected on priviliges in the County of White for the year ending 1 Sept 1838 as pr his Statement this day filed
this 20th Sept 1838

Ro. Cox Trustee of
White County

Received of N. Oldham Clerk of White County Court the Tax list for the County of White for the year 1838

J. T. Bradley Shff.

Sparta 29th Sept. 1838

Received of Nicholas Oldham Clerk of White County Court an abstract Statement of the poor tax in White County for the year 1838 amounting to the sum of Six hundred and eighty three Dollars Ten Cents and one mill this date above $683.10.1

John Jett Treasurer
of the poor house Comrs.
of White County

Sparta 28th Sept. 1838

Received of Nicholas Oldham Clerk of White County Court an abstract Statement of the County Tax, Jury Tax and Bridge tax of White County for the year 1838 amounting in all to the sum of Fourteen hundred and ninty eight dollars fifty cents and eight mills - this date above

$1498.50.8

Ro. Cox Trustee of
White County

Isd For reasons appearing to the satisfaction of the Court it is ordered by the Court that Benjamin Hutchings one of the admrs. of Webster Hutchings de'd settle with Mary Hutchings the widow of said Webster Hutchings dec'd for 1 Bl salt 50.00 sugar & 25.00 Coffee deducting from the value of said provisions the amount of a certain note which she held and collected from her father and take her receipt for the amount of said provisions above mentioned. -

Isd Ordered by Court that the order of the last term requiring William C. Johnson to appear at this term be renewed returnable to the next term of this Court.

Isd Ordered by Court that Washington Webb be appointed Overseer of the road from the middle of the Bridge at the Harriett Iron Works to the widow Smith's gate being a road of the first Class and keep the same in repair as the law requires. And that the same bounds of hands that worked under Daniel Simrell late Overseer thereof be assigned to work thereon.

(P-258) This day the death of Samuel Jackson late of the County of White deceased was suggested in open Court and that he departed this life intestate where upon Zachariah Anderson appeared in open Court and produced and swore to his account against the said Jackson amounting to the sum of Sixty three Dollars and forty six cents - Therefore for reasons appearing to the satisfaction of the Court that the said Zachariah Anderson being a creditor of said Jackson Dec'd he is permitted to administrator on all and singular the goods and chattles, rights and credits of the aforesaid Samuel Jackson deceased and took the oath required by law and together with Anthony Dibrell and Joseph Herd entered into and acknowledged Bond in the sum of Twenty six hundred dollars conditioned as the law requires.

This day Benjamin Lewis, Executor of the last will and testament of

William Lewis deceased returned upon oath an additional Inventory of said Estate which is ordered to be recorded.

This day Benjamin Lewis Executor of the last will and testament of William Lewis deceased returned upon oath an account of the sales of said Estate which is ordered to be recorded.

Issd Ordered by Court that John D. Walker be appointed Overseer of the road from the west end of the Bridge at Sparta to the two mile post on the Carthage road being a road of the first Class and keep the same in repair as the law requires and that the same list and bounds of hands that worked under Josiah Turner late Overseer thereof be assigned to work thereon.

This day the Superentendant of the poor house produced in open Court a certain pauper male child named George Walker and after deliberation of the Court it is ordered by the Court that said pauper child be taken back to the poor house of White County to be taken care of untill the further direction of this.

Issd Ordered by Court that Thomas Roberts be appointed Overseer of the road from Sinking Creek to the top of Gum Spring Mountain being a road of the 2nd Class and keep the same in repair as the law requires. And that the same list of hands which worked under Samuel H. Kiethley late Overseer thereof be assigned to work therein.

Ordered by Court that the Sherriff of White County refund unto Mrs. Leah Robinson the sum of Two dollars twelve and a half cents she having been Overcharged $10.00 in the value of two negroes and that the sherriff of White County have a credit thereof in the settlement of his account - .

For reason appearing to the satisfaction of the Court it is ordered that Hiram Lewis be released from the appraised value of a bay horse taken up by him some time in the year 1838.

Issd Ordere by Court that Thomas S. Elms be appointed overseer of the road from the mouth of Mill Creek to the 19 mile post (P-259) being a road of the second Class and keep the same in repair as the law requires and that the same list of hands that worked under George Henry late overseer thereof be assigned to work thereon.

Issd Ordered by Court that Edmund Stamps and Elisha Camron Esquires be appointed to assign bounds of hands between James A. Jay and other neighboring overseers of the road and report thereof to the next term of this Court.

Issd Ordered by Court that Osburn Walker be appointed Overseer of the road from the two mile post to the four mile post on the Carthage road being a road of the first Class and keep the same in repair as the law requires. And that the same list of hands that worked under William Carland late Overseer thereof be assigned to work thereon.

Issd Ordered by Court that the Plott and certificate of Survey of the dividing line between White & Bledsoe Counties - made by Aaron Schoolfield and Jonathan C. Davis Surveyor on the 15th day of December 1828 be

Regestered in the Registers office of White County and that the Sherriff of White County pay to Register of said County one dollar for Registering the same out of the taxes of the year 1838.

Issd Ordered by Court that the order appointing Lewis Bohanon; James Officer; John Suttles, James Hutson and James Sparks freeholders a Jury of view to lay off and mark a road of third Class from at or near John Suttles; on the Calf Killor road; thence the nearest and best way to entersect the Walton road near the widow Johnson be renewed and report thereof to the next term of this Court.

Issd Ordered by Court that the order appointing William McKenny; Elisha Camron; Harrison Whitson and Sims Dearing freeholders a Jury of view to lay off and mark a road of the third Class leaving the Calf Killer road near William C. Metcalfs thence the nearest and best way through the board valley to intersect the Dry Valley road Wm. Pryors be renewed and report thereof to the next term of this Court.

Ordered by Court that the revenue arising on the tax on Priviges for the year 1838 which has been paid into the Trustee office of White County by the Clerk of this Court be appropriated to the extinguishment of Jury claims in said County exclusively.

Ordered by Court that John Rogers (Cherry Creek) be appointed Overseer of the road from post oak Creek to Robert Howards being a road of the second Class and keep the same in repair as the law requires and that the same list of hands that worked under Howard Cash late Overseer thereof be assigned to work thereon - .

(P-260) Issd Ordered by Court that Richard Crowder and James T. Hayes be appointed to divide and apportion list of hands between John Taylor and William Lisk &c. be renewed returnable to the next term of this Court.

For reasons appearing to the satisfaction of the Court it is ordered by Court that Anthony Dibrell administrator of John Crook Sr. deceased with his will annexed pay unto Isaac Crook the sum of Fifty one Dollars being the amount of his account allowed by the Court for taking care of the property of said estate &c to be paid by said adminestrator out of said Estate.

Issd Ordered by Court that William Hitchcock Esq. and James Allison Esquire be appointed to apportion and divide the hands between Daniel Martin and the other Overseer in that neighborhood having due regard to grades of the diffrent roads and report thereof to the next term of this Court.

Issd Ordered by Court that the lot of road from Austins Still house to the foot Cumberland Mountain be extended so that the same extended to the north East side of Little Laurel Bridge 2nd Class and that George Washington Frasure be appointed Overseer thereof and keep the same in repair as the law requires and that James Dodson; Daniel Wilson; Michael Henderson; John Miller; Archebald Welch & Isaac Davis added to the list of hands that formerally worked that lot of road from Austins still house to the foot of the Mountain.

Issd Ordered by Court that portion or lot of road of which the Overseer from Clifty is bound to keep up be so altered as to extend to the Bridge on Little Laurell and that he keep the same in repair as the law requires with the hands already assigned thereon - .

Issd Ordered by Court that Hiram Lewis be appointed Overseer of the road from DeKalb County line to Ceder Creek being a road of the second Class and keep the same in repair as the law requires with the same hands that belong to that lot or road which now remains in White County.

Issd Ordered by Court that Brice Little be appointed Overseer of the road from Little's Bridge passing Murphys & Vencents and entersecting the Usery Gap road on the first bench below the Flat rock; thence to the flat rock being a road of the second Class and keep the same in repair as the law requires and that the same list of hands that worked under Joseph Hunter late Overseer thereof be assigned to work thereon.

Issd Ordered by Court that William Lisk surrender to Andrew Jr Sims Overseer of the road the sledge hammer and Crowbar belonging to the roads in that Company for the purpose of keeping them in repair.

(P-261) Issd Ordered by Court unanimously that the following persons be allowed the following fees in the following State Cases which have been examined by the solicitors for White County and reported as correctly taxed and properly chargeable to the County of White To wit:
In the case the State of Tennessee vs Solomon Roberts Clerk W. G. Sims $7.56 Shff J. T. Bradley $2.50 Shff D. L. Mitchell 0.75 witness Hugh Gracy 0.50
In the case of the State vs Pleasant Lawson - Clerk W. G. Sims 6.37½ Shff D. L. Mitchell 1.25 Shff J. T. Bradley 1.00 Shff John England 0.50
In the case the State vs Anderson Britt Clerk W. G. Sims 7.75 Shff D. L. Mitchell 1.25 Shff J. T. Bradley 2.00
In the case the State vs David Little Clerk W. G. Sims 6.00 Shff J. G. Mitchell 2.75 Shff J. T. Bradley 0.66⅔ Shff John England 0.50 witness Joseph Cummings 1.50 witness William B. Hutson 2.46 -
In the case the State vs Andrew Welch Clk W. G. Sims 2.00 Justice Joshua Mason 50 - Constable Cornelius Jarvis 1.75
In the case the State vs William Hall Clerk W. G. Sims 5.12½ Shff J. T. Bradley 62½ Shff J. G. Mitchell 1.75 Shff Smith J. Walling 25.
State vs Elisha Camron Clerk W. G. Sims 7.12½ Shff John England 50 Shff J. G. Mitchell 50 - Witness W. C. Metcalf 5.75 Campbell Brewington 1.25 James Shirley 4.00 William McKinny 5.75 Charles McGuire 3.00 Justice David Snodgrass 50. Constable C. McGuire 2.00 -
In the case the State vs Josiah Wooldridge; William Wooldridge & Marshall Wooldridge Clerk W. G. Sims 5.93¾ clk J. A. Lane 2.50 Shff D. L. Mitchell 4.87½ Shff W. G. Sims 1.50 Witness John Cantrell 3.00
In the Case the state vs G. W. H. Potts Clerk W. G. Sims 1.31¼
In the Case the State vs Elvis Taylor Clerk A. Dibrell 2.25 Clk W. G. Sims Shff J. T. Bradley .75 Merlin Young 1.25 Witness William Garland 75.
In the Case the State vs Jesse Allen Clerk W. G. Sims 7.06¼ Shff D. L. Mitchell 75 J. T. Bradley 2.00 Witness Hugh Gracy 50 - amounting in all to the sum of One hundred and thirty dollars eighty seven and a half cents to be paid by the trustee of White County out of any monies not otherwise appropriated.

Issd On the humble petition of Sunday Citizen of the County of

White and for reasons appearing fully to the satisfaction of the Court that the Com's of the County of Dekalb in running the divisional line between the County of White and DeKalb have run said line within a less distance than 12 miles from the Court house of the County of White in direct violation of the Constitution of the State in such cases provided.

It is therefore considered and so ordered by the Court that Jacob A. Lane Esquire be appointed to survey and distinctly mark the boundry line between the County of White & Dekalb in such a manner that no portion of said Boundary shall approach main to the Court house in the town of Sparta, than twelve mile according to the provisions of the Constitution of the State and report thereof to the January term of this Court.

Ordered by Court that Nicholas Oldham be appointed receiver for the County of White to receive from the offices appointed (P-262) for the purpose of distributing the Internal improvement fund of the State of Tennessee, that portion of money which may be apportioned to the County of White and that before receiving the fund aforesaid enter into bond and Security as required by law.

Ordered that Court be adjourned untill tomorrow morning 9 O'clock

Thos Eastland
John Bryan
John Jett

Tuesday morning 2nd October A.D. 1838 Court met pursuant to adjournment
Present the worshipful

Thomas Eastland) Esquires
John Jett and)
John Bryan) Justices

Issd Ordered by Court that Charles Graham be appointed Overseer of the road from the corner of the fince at the mouth of Bryan's lane to the forks of the road at Joseph Williams Cooper shop being a road of the second Class and keep the same in repair as the law requires and that John Bryan Esq. be appointed to assign a list of hands to work thereon.

Isd. Ordered by Court that Jesse Lincoln be appointed Overseer of the road from the forks of the road at Oldhams to Andrew Gambles School House being a road of the first Class and keep the same in repair as the law requires - And that the same list of hands that worked under Daniel Clark late Overseer thereof be assigned to work thereon.

Isd. For reasons appearing to the satisfaction of the Court upon the affidavit of Jacob Yount it is ordered by Court that the probate of the last will and testament of John Crook, Sr. Deceased at a former term of this Court and also the appointment of Anthony Dibrell as adminestrator of the said John Crook, Sr., deceased with his last will and testament annexed be set aside and from henceforth for nothing esteemed and it is therefore also ordered by the Court that Anthony Dibrell Esquire be appointed adminestrator Pendentelite of all and singular the goods and chattles, rights and credits of the said John Crook, Sr. deceased and being present in open Court took the oath required by law and together with Samuel V. Carrick, William Hill and Jonathan T. Bradley entered into and acknowledged bond in the sum of Thirteen Thousand Dollars conditioned as the law requires and it is ordered by the Court that the proceeding this day had in this Court relative to said will and appointments of adminestra aforesaid be certified to the Honorable the Circuit Court of White County now in session under the seal of this Court.

(P-263) Ordered that Court be adjourned untill Court in Course

Test
N. Oldham, Clk

Thos Eastland
John Bryan
John Jett

State of Tennessee

At a Quorum Court began and held for the County of White in the Court house in the town of Sparta before the Justices of said Court on the first Monday being the fifth day of November in the year of our Lord One thousand eight hundred and thirty eight and of the Independance of the United States the sixty third year.

Present the Worshipful

John Jett	)	Esqs.
David Snodgrass	)	Quorum
& John Bryan	)	Justices

For reasons appearing to the satisfaction of the Court upon the evidence of Samuel Brown

It is ordered that Sarah Dyer be allowed the sum of One hundred and twenty five Dollars and thirteen and one half cents which is to operate as a credit to the said Sarah Dyer in the settlement of her accts which has already been paid him.

Issd Ordered by Court that John Hunter be appointed Overseer of the road from Whitakers Mill intersecting the Walton road at the head of road hollow being a road of the second Class and keep the same in repair as the law requires and that Isaac Buck Esq. furnish him with a list of hands to work thereon.

Issd Ordered by Court that the Order appointing William McKinny, Vinett Henry, Elisha Camron, Harrison Whitson and James A. Jay, freeholders a Jury of view to lay off and mark a road of the third Class leaving the Calf killer road near William C. Metcalf thence the nearest and best way through the board valley to entersect the Dry valley road near William Pryors be renewed and report thereof to the next term of this Court.

Issd Ordered by Court that the following persons freeholders Citizens of (P-264) County of White be appointed as Jurors to the February term A. D. 1838 of White Circuit Court to wit: Jesse Lincoln, John Young, William M. Bryan, Sr., Siever Evans, Joshua Pennington, Christopher Kuhn, John Halteman, Jesse Franks, Joshua Mason, Robert Glenn, Eli Sims, William Lisk, John Lollar, Jesse Davis, Isaac Hutson, William Lyda, John Anderson, William Hill, William Webb, Jr., John Hunter, William McKinny, Thomas Broyles, John Rose, John W. Dearing, John Gibson, George Sparkman and William K. Bradford and Hayes Arnold Constables to attend thereon and that a writ of Venirifacias issue directed &c.

Issd This day the Clerk of White Circuit Court filed in this Court a record from said Court showing that an issue of Devisanet Vel now had been made in said Court upon the writing purporting to be the last will and testament of John Crook, Sr., Deceased - And it appeared from said record that said writing was decided and proved to be the last will and testament of the said John Crook, Sr. Deceased that the same was duly published and proclaimed as such and that the Testator at the time of executing the same was of sound and desposing mind and memory. It is therefore considered by this Court and so ordered that the above mentioned last will and Testament be recorded. And it is further considered and so ordered that Anthony Dibrell be appointed adminestrator of all and singular the goods and chattles rights and credits of the said John Crook, Sr. Deceased with his will annexed, who being present in open Court took the oath required by law and together with Wanon Leftwich, Jacob A. Lane, Jonathan T. Bradley, Samuel V. Carrick and Smith J. Walling entered into and acknowledged bond in the sum of thirteen thousand dollars conditioned as the law requires.

This day the death of Adam Clouse late of the County of White Deceased was suggested in open Court and that he departed this life entestate. Whereupon Richard Crowder Esq. was appointed adminestrator of all and singular the goods and chattles rights and credits of the said Adam Clouse deceased who being present in open court took the oath prescribed by law and together with John Taylor and Aaron Hutchings entered into and acknowledged bond in the sum of six hundred dollars conditioned as the law requires.

Isd Ordered by Court that Lee R. Taylor be appointed Overseer of the road from the Forks of the Allens ferry road at Brusters Farm to the poll Bridge at William Erwins being a road of the second Class and keep the same in reqair as the law requires. And that the same list of hands that worked under Wm Lisk late Overseer thereof be assigned to work thereon.

(P-265) Isd Ordered by Court that William A. Cook, David Cummings, Henry H. McClendon, Levi Robinson and William Jackson freeholders be appointed a Jury of view to lay off and mark a road of the second Class from William A. Cooks to Franks ferry road and report thereof to the next term of this Court.

Isd Ordered by Court that Joseph Bozarth be released from one half the appraised value of an Estray filly posted by him in the year 1837 he having failed to return the probate in the proper time.

Isd Ordered by Court that Lecil Smith be appointed Overseer of the road from the top of Gum Spring Mountain to McGowens old place being a road of the second Class and keep the same in repair as the law requires. And that William Knowles and Joshua Mason Esq. assign a list and bounds of hands to work thereon.

Isd For reasons appearing fully to the satisfaction of the Court it is ordered that the Lot of road Community at John Austins still house running up the mountain to the East side of Little Laurel Bridge on which George W. Frasure is now Overseer be divided into three district Lots to wit: it is ordered that John Austin be appointed Overseer from his still house to the branch West of old Capt Rottans that William Green be appointe Overseer from the branch west of Capt. Rottans to the foot of the mountain and that George W. Frasure continue as Overseer from that point to the East side of Little Laurel Bridge being a road of the second Class and keep the same in repair as the law requires and that John Bryan Esq. assign to each Overseer a proper list of hands belonging to said road between the three Overseers taking into consideration the lot of road attached to each overseer to work thereon respectively - .

This day the Clerk of this Court produced in open Court the report of a settlement made by him with the Admr. and Amx of George Allen deceased which is by the Court received and confirmed in all its parts and ordered to be recorded.

This day James McCamm to whom was bound on 14th day of July 1834 a certain orphan boy named Chaney N. Williams to serve as an apprentice and surrendered to the Court the said apprentice Boy and for reasons appearing to the satisfaction of the Court it is ordered that the Indentures of the said apprentice be set aside; cancelled and for nothing esteemed.

This day Chancy N. Williams aged thirteen years on the 7th day of January last was bound to John Warren to serve him after the manner of an apprentice untill he arrives at the age of Twenty one years and for the faithful preformanes of his covenant entered into and acknowledged Bond with Nicholas Oldham his security conditioned as the law requires.

(p-266) The State vs William C. Johnson } Bastardy Polly Whitson

This day the Defendant by his attorney Samuel Turney Esquire came into open Court together with David Snodgrass and Thomas B. Johnson and agree that they will pay the sum of Forty Dollars within thirty days from this time and thirty Dollars twelve months from this time and also twenty Dollars within two years from this time to the Trustee yet to be appointed to receive and disburse the same for the support and maintainace of the said Polly Whitson the prosecutrix and the Bastard child charged to be begotten on the body of the said Prosecutrix - .

And the said David Snodgrass and Thomas B. Johnson bind themselves to keep and render the County of White free harmless and endemnified from any charge or cost towards the support and maintainanse of the Bastard child aforesaid charged as aforesaid and that Defendant pay the cost &c.

The State vs William C. Johnson } Bastardy Polly Whitson Prosx.

For reasons appearing to the satisfaction of the Court it is ordered that William C. Metcalf be appointed Special Trustee to receive of the Defendant such Sums of money as he is required to pay towards the support and maintainanse of the said Polly Whitson, Prosecutrix and her Bastard child charged to have been begotten on her body by the Defendant at such times as the Defendant is required to pay the same, and the same to disburse toward the support and maintainanse of the said Polly and her bastard child in a frugal an economical manner - .

Issd Ordered by Court that Edmund Cunningham be appointed Overseer of the road from Rottans lane to a stoney point oposite to McDonalds mill being a road of the 3rd Class and keep the same in repair as the law requires and that John Bryan Esquire assign lists of hands between him and the diffrent Overseer of the roads in that neighborhood according to the grades of the diffrent roads.

This day Benj. Lewis adminestrator of William Lewis deceased returned upon oath an account of the sales of said estate which is recorded.

Ordered that Court be adjourned untill tomorrow 10 O'clock

John Jett
David Snodgrass
John Bryan

(P-267) Tuesday Morning 6th November 1838 Court met pursuant to adjournment Present the Worshipful

John Jett	}	Esquires
David Snodgrass	}	Quorum
John Bryan	}	Justices

This day the Commissioners heretofore appointed to lay off and mark a road of the third Class from near John Suttles on the Calf killer road, then the nearest and best way to entersect the Walton road near the widow Johnsons made their report which received by the Court and the same established a road of the third Class.

Issd Ordered by the Court that Alexander Bohanon be appointed Overseer of the road as laid off and marked by commissioners from near John Suttles on the Calf killer road to the Walton road being a road of the third Class and open and keep the same in repair as the law requires and that Edmund Stamps Esq. assign a list of hands to work thereon.

Issd Ordered by Court that Robert Anderson, James W. Copeland, George D. Howard, James Adair, and Thomas Green freeholders be appointed a Jury of view to lay off and mark a road of the second Class from Robert Anderson to entersect the road leading across the Caney fork at Payne's Bridge at some suitable point and report thereof to the next term of this Court -

Ordered that Court be adjourned untill Court in Course

Test
N. Oldham, Clk.

John Jett
David Snodgrass
John Bryan

(P-268) State of Tennessee

At a Quorum Court began and held for the County of White in the Court house in the town of Sparta before the justices of said Court on the first Monday being the third day of December in the year of our Lord One thousand eight hundred and thirty eight and of the Independance of the United States the 63rd year.

Present the Worshipful

John Jett	)	Esquires
David Snodgrass	)	Quorum
John Bryan	)	Justices

For reasons appearing to the satisfaction of the Court from testimony.

It is ordered by Court that Isaac Pirtle a citizen of White County by entirely exempt from working on any of the roads in said County.

This day John Felton exhibited in open Court his stock mark which is a smooth crop off the right ear and underbit in the left, which is ordered to be recorded.

Isad This day the death of Samuel Brock late a Citizen of the County of White was suggested in open Court and that he departed this life entestate whereupon John Walling was appointed adminestrator of all and singular the goods and chattles rights and credits of the deceased who being present in open Court took the oath prescribed by law and together with Jesse Walling and Smith J. Walling entered into and acknowledged bond in the sum of two hundred dollars conditioned as the law requires.

Isad Ordered by Court that Burrel Manor, W. B. Haston and Abijah Crane be appointed commissioners to assign and apart to the widow and family of Samuel Brock deceased one years provisions for their support and maintainance out of the estate of the deceased and report to the next term of this Court.

This day John Walling adminestrator of Samuel Brock deceased returned into open Court upon oath an Inventory of the estate of the deceased which is ordered to be recorded.

This day John Jett and David Snodgrass Esquires, Commissioners of the Revenue for White County for the year 1838 returned their report of settlement with the Trustee of White County which is received and ordered to be recorded.

Isad Ordered by Court that John Jett Esq. one of the Commissioners of the Revenue of White County be allowed the sum of Ten dollars for four days services in settling with the Trustee of White County to be paid out of the taxes of the year 1838.

(P-269) Isad Ordered by Court that David Snodgrass one of the Commissioners of the Revenue for White County be allowed the sum of seven dollars and fifty cents for Three days services in settling with the Trustee of White County to be paid by the Trustee of said County out of the taxes of the year 1838.

This day Anderson S. Rogers and Tilman Brown produced in open Court commissioners from the Governer under the season of the State appointing the said Anderson S. Rogers a Magestrate in the 2nd District and the said Tilman Brown a magestrate in the 15th District who being present in open Court took the oath to support the Constitution of the United States and of the State of Tennessee and the several oaths required by law and thereupon entered upon the discharge of their duties respectively.

Ordered by Court that the following Justices be appointed Commissioners of the Revinue for the year 1839 To wit:

In District No. 1. William C. Brittain Esq.
In District No. 2 John Bryan, Esq.
In District No. 3 Thomas Green, Esq.
In District No. 4 Matthias Hutson, Esq.
In District No. 5 Joshua Mason, Esq.
In District No. 6 James T. Hayes, Esq.
In District No. 7 - - - - - - - -
In District No. 8 James Allison, Esq.
In District No. 9 Asa Certain, Esq.
In District No. 10 William C. Bounds, Esq.
In District No. 11 Isaac Buck, Esq.
In District No. 12 Elisha Camron, Esq.
In District No. 13 William Little, Esq.
In District No. 14 Elijah Frost, Esq.
In District No. 15 John Gillentine, Esq.

Isd Ordered by Court that Jesse Franks, Felix A. Badger, Samuel A. Moore, William Knowles, William Templeton and Hiram Knowles freeholders be appointed a Jury of view to lay off a road of the second Class from William A. Cook to Frank ferry road and report thereof to the next term of this Court.

Isd Ordered by Court that Robert Anderson, James W. Copeland, George D. Howard, James Adair and Thomas Green freeholders be appointed a Jury of view to lay off and mark a road of the second Class from Robert Anderson to intersect the road leading across the Caney fork at Paynes Bridge at some suitable point and report thereof to the next term of this Court.

Isd Ordered by Court that Samuel V. Carrick, William Simpson and Lewis Fletcher be appointed Commissioners of the Common Jail in the County of White for the next ensuing twelve months.

Isd Ordered by Court that the order of the last term of this Court, (P-270) appointing William McKinny, Vinett Henry, Elisha Camron, Harrison Whitson and James A. Jay freeholders a Jury of view to lay off and mark a road of the third Class leaving the Calf killer road near William C. Metcalfs thence the nearest and best way through the Board Valley to intersect the Dry Valley road near William Pryors be renewed and report thereof to the next term of this Court.

It appearing to the satisfaction of the Court that Thomas Frasure is over the age of fifty years.

It is ordered by the Court that he be released from the payment of a Pole tax for the year 1838. And that the Sherriff of White County have a credit therefore in the settlement of his accounts.

Issd This day the death of Lenias B. Farris late of the County of White was suggested in open Court and that he departed this life intestate. Whereupon Eli Sims was appointed administrator of all and singular the goods and chattles, right and credits of the deceased and thereupon took the oath prescribed by law and together with Thomas Walling and John W. Dearing entered into and acknowledged Bond in the sum of two Thousand Dollars conditioned as the law requires.

Issd. Ordered by Court that Thomas Robinson, Joseph Clark and Alexander McDaniel be appointed Commissioners to assign and set apart to the widow and family of Lenias B. Farris One years provisions for their support and maintainance out of the estate of the deceased. And report thereof to the next term of this Court.

This day Aaron Hutching was appointed Guardian to Eliza Clouse minor heir of Adam Clouse deceased who appeared in open Court and took the oath required by law and together with Benjamin Hutchings and John Taylor entered into bond and security in the sum of two hundred dollars conditioned as the law requires.

This day Zachariah Anderson adminestrator of Samuel Jackson dec'd returned upon oath in open Court an Inventory of the estate of the dec'd which is ordered to be recorded.

Issd Ordered by Court that Joseph H. McDaniel be appointed Overseer of the road from William Knowles to the forks of the road being a road of the second Class and keep the same in repair as the law requires and that the same list and bounds of hands that worked under Lenias B. Farris, late Overseer thereof be assigned to work thereon.

(P-271) This day Addison A. Dillon, guardian to the minor heirs of George L. Cook Deceased appeared in open Court and surrendered his guardianship to the heirs aforesaid which is received by the Court and it is ordered by the Court the said Addison A. Dillon be released and forever discharged from all future and further liabilities relative to said guardianship.

This day Nancy Cook was appointed guardian to Ann Cook, Polly Cook, Minerva Cook and George Alexander Cook infant children of George L. Cook deceased and thereupon took the oath required by law and together with James Dillon and Addison A. Dillon entered into and acknowledged bond in the sum of Five hundred Dollars conditioned as the law requires.

Issd Ordered by Court that William Templeton, Samuel A. Moore, Jr., Joseph Anderson, Alexander Dillon, and Joel Smith freeholders be appointed a Jury of view to lay off and mark a road of the second class from William Knowle's to Dillons Bridge across Caney fork and report thereof to the next term of this Court.

This day Thomas Moore aged 73 years on the 2nd day of February last a Citizen of the County of White pearsonally appeared in open Court and filed his Declaration upon oath for a Pension under the act of Congress of the United States of the 7th June 1832, together with his vouchers

Robert L. Mitchell a clergiman and Abel Pearson both Citizens of the County of White in like manner sworn and to the Court known to be persons of good name, fame and reputation and entitled to credit upon their oath in a Court of Justice, which is signed by the Court and ordered to be certified under the seal of this Court.

Be it remembered that this day Mary Baker the relect and widow of Peter Baker deceased late a Revolutionary Pensioner of White County in the State of Tennessee personally appeared in open Court and filed upon oath her Declaration for a Pension from the United States under the provisions of the act of Congress of the 7th, July 1838 Granting half pay and pensions to certain widow and also appeared in open Court Thomas Crawley to the Court known and made oath in due form of law that he saw the said Mary Baker and Peter Baker married according to the laws of the State of North Carolina - And also appeared in open Court Turner Lane, Jr., and Jacob A. Lane also to the Court known who being in like manner sworn proved to the Court that the said (P-272) Peter Baker mentioned in said Declaration is the Identical Peter Baker referred to in said Pension Certificate therein mentioned that she is the widow of said Peter Baker deceased, that she still is a widow and remaining single and unmarried and resides in the County of White aforesaid whereupon It is ordered by the Court to be certified, that the foregoing persons whose names are subscribed to the foregoing affidavits are persons of good name, fame and reputation and are entitled to full faith and credit upon their oaths in a Court of Justices and that the said Mary Baker is the widow of the said Peter Baker Deceased in said Declaration mentioned and it is further ordered to be certified that this is a court of Record all of which is signed by the said Court and ordered to be recorded.

Ordered that Court be adjourned untill tomorrow morning 10 O'clock

John Jett
David Snodgrass
John Bryan

Tuesday morning 4th December 1838 Court met pursuant to adjournment
Present

John Jett } Quorum
David Snodgrass }
John Bryan } Justices

This day the Clerk of White County Court produced in open Court the report of a settlement with Zachariah Anderson administrator of Samuel Jackson, Deceased which is received and confirmed and ordered to be recorded.

Ordered by Court that Zachariah Anderson administrator of Samuel Jackson, Deceased hand over to David D. Turner adminestrator of the said Samuel Jackson, deceased in Maringo County State of Alabama or his legally authorised agent on application all such estate which is in the possession of the said Zachariah Anderson aforesaid adminestrator aforesaid belonging to the aforesaid Samuel Jackson deceased -

Ordered that Court be adjourned untill Court in Cour

est
. Oldham, Clk.

John Jett
David Snodgrass
John Bryan

(p-273) State of Tennessee

At a County Court began and held for the County of White and State aforesaid in the Court house in the Town of Sparta before the Justices of said Court On the first Monday being the seventh day of January in the year of our Lord One thousand eight hundred and thirty nine and of the Independence of the United States the sixty third year

Present the Worshipful

Thomas Eastland, Esquire Chairman
John Bryan, William Knowles,
John Jett, Isaac Buck, David
Snodgrass, William Bruster, Esquires
Asa Certain, Elijah Frost,
James Allison, Richard Crowder,
John Gillentine, Edmund Stamps,
Tilman Brown, Anderson S. Rogers,
Matthias Hutson, Thomas Green, Justices
George Defreese, J. T. Hayes,
Jesse Walling, William Little,
John Pennington, Elisha Camron.

Ordered by Court that William Knowles in District No. 6 and Richard Crowder in District No. 6 be appointed to take lists of Taxable property in their respective Districts as Revinue Commissioners for the year 1839.

Ordered by Court unanimously that the following rates of Taxes be laid for the year 1839 to wit:

For County Tax
On each One hundred dollars value of Property Five Cents
On each free White Poll twelve and one half Cents

For Jury Tax
On each One hundred dollars value property five cents
On each free White poll twelve and one half Cents

For Poor Tax
On each one hundred dollars value of property five cents
On each free white poll twelve and one half cents

For Bridge Tax at Sparta
On each one hundred dollars value of property One & one fourth cents to be levied and collected by the Sherriff of White in the manner and form prescribed by law. And it is further ordered by the Court that the Clerk of this Court where-ever during the year 1839 he shall be required to issue licinces under the provisions of the act of the general assembly taxing priviliges in this State, shall demand and receive for the use of White County on all shows or exhibitions of natural or artificial cureosities a sum equal to the full (p-274) amount of the State tax thereon; and on all other Licences on Priviliges a sum equal to one half the state tax thereon respectively, all of which sums so received shall be accounted for by said Clerk according to law.

This day the Clerk of this Court produced the report of a settlement made with John Griffith administrator and Patience Roberts administratrix of William Roberts deceased which is recieved confirmed in all its parts and ordered to be recorded.

For reasons appearing to the satisfaction of the Court it is ordered that the receiptor R. H. McEwin; Superentendant of Public instruction of the State of Tennessee be spread upon the minutes of this Court at full length which is in the following words and figures.

Nashville 5 Nov. 1838

Nicholas Oldham Esq.
Clk. Cty Court White Cty - .

The report made by you in complainer with the 27 sec of an act to establish a systum of common schools passed 24 Jan 1838; has been rec'd should a 7th District in your County be established as contemplated please inform me Yours with much Respect

R. H. McEwin Supt. &c.

This day the Commissioners heretofore appointed to lay off and set apart one years provisions to the widow and family of Samuel Brook deceased out of the estate of the deceased made their report which is received and orderod to be recorded - -

This day the Commissioners heretofore appointed to lay off and set apart one years provisions to the widow and family of Lenias B. Farris deceased out of the estate of the deceased made their report which is received and ordered to be recorded.

This day Francis Marion Dyer aged nine years on the 18th day of February 1839 was bound to Stuart Warren to serve him after the manner of an apprentice untill he shall have arrived at the age of Twenty one years and for the faithful performance of Covenant intered into and acknowledged bond conditioned as the law requires.

This day John Gillentine, guardian to William F. Carter made his report upon oath which is ordered to be recorded.

This day William Hill, guardian to his own children made his report upon oath which is ordered to be recorded.

(P-275) Isd. Ordered by Court unanimously that Allen L. Mitchell Superentendant of the poor house of White County be allowed the sum of two hundred and seventy seven Dollars ninety two Cents being the amount of his account for money expended for cloathing, washing and board as enumerated in his account for the support and maintainance of all the paupers in the poor house of said County for the year ending the 31st day of December 1838 to be paid by the Treasure of the poor house Commissioners out of any monies not otherwise appropriated.

Isd Ordered by Court that Nathan Earles be released from the pay of a Poll tax for the year 1837 he being over the age of fifty years that the Sherriff of White County refund said money that the Sherriff of White County have a credit for the same in the settlement of his account.

Isd Ordered by Court that William Little; Charles McGuire and William Snodgrass be appointed Commissioners to lay off and set apart one years provisions to the widow and family of James Brown deceased out of his estate and report thereof to the next term of this Court.

Isd This day the death of James Brown late of the County of White deceased was suggested in open Court and that he departed this life intestate; whereupon John Brown was appointed administrator of all and singular the goods and chattles rights and credits of the Deceased and also administrator De - bonis - non of Coleman Brown Deceased who being present in open Court and took the oath required by law and together with David Snodgrass and Jonathan T. Bradley entered into and acknowledged bond in the sum of two Thousand Dollars conditioned as the law requires.

Isd Ordered by Court that John W. Simpson; John Jett and John Bryan Esquires be appointed Commissioners to settle with the several clerks and Trustees of this County for the year 1839.

This day John Jett; David Snodgrass and John Bryan; exquires were appointed to hold the Courts of Q uorum for the year 1839.

This day Asa Certain; guardian to the heirs of Edward Holmes dec'd made his report upon oath which is received and ordered to be recorded.

(P-276) This day Ann Hutchings and Jane Hutchings two of the heirs of Webster Hutchings deceased being over the age of fourteen years appeared in open Court and chose James T. Hayes for their guardian and on the day James T. Hayes was appointed guardian to other minor heirs of the said Webster Hutchings deceased namely Polly Hutchings; Thomas Jackson Hutchings; Pleasant Justice Hutchings; Nancy Hutchings; Charles Dillard Hutchings and Albert Gillentine Love Hutchings who being present in open Court and together with Richard Crowder and John Taylor entered into and acknowledged bond in the sum of two thousand Dollars conditioned as the law requires.

This day John Walling administrator of Samuel Brook deceased returned upon oath an account of the sales of the property of said Estate which is ordered to be recorded.

This day George Griffith, guardian to the infant heirs of William Roberts deceased returned his report upon oath which is ordered to be recorded.

This day Samuel Brown; guardian to four of the infant children of John Dyer deceased returned upon oath his report which is ordered to be recorded.

This day John Pennington; guardian to the balance of the minor heirs of John Dyer deceased made his report upon oath which is recorded.

Isd Ordered by Court that Patience Roberts be allowed the sum of Seventy five dollars the amount of her accounts for boarding her four children for two years to be paid by George Griffith guardian to said children.

Isd Ordered by Court unanimously that William Simpson; David Snodgrass and William Little Commissioners on Robert Burks turnpike road be each allowed the sum of two dollars and fifty cents per day for three days services each on said road to be paid by the said Robert Burks

Ordered by Court that Mary Jane Carroll be allowed the sum of One hundred and fifty Dollars the amount of her acct. for Boarding Lodging and Cloathing Samuel Lafayett Carroll to be paid out of the estate of William Carroll deceased.

This day Woodson P. White and Thomas Robertson guardian to the infant heirs of David L. Mitchell deceased made their report upon oath which was ordered to be recorded.

(P-277) Isd Ordered by Court unanimously that John Jett; David Snodgrass and John Bryan Esquires Justices of the Quprum Court for the year 1838; be allowed each the sum of two dollars per day for their services as Quorum Justices for the year aforesaid to be paid by the Trustee of White County out of the taxes for the year 1838.

This day the Commissioners of the poor house for White County produced in open Court the bond of Allen L. Mitchell Superentendant of the poor house for said County for the year 1839 which is received by the Court and ordered to be recorded.

Ordered by Court that John Jett; Joseph Herd and Joseph Cummings; Jr. be appointed commissioners of the poor house of White County for the year 1839 and that John Jett Esq. be appointed Treasure to the Board of Commissioners of the said poor house; And the said John Jett and Joseph Cummings Jr. being present in open Court took the oath prescribed by law and thereupon entered upon the discharge of their duties.

Isd Ordered by Court unanimously that John Jett; Joseph Herd and Joseph Cummings; Jr., Commissioners of the poor house for the year 1838 be each allowed the sum of Ten dollars for services rendered to be paid by the Treasure of the poor house Commissioners out of any monies not otherwise appropriated.

Isd This day the death of Abner Hodges late of the County of White was suggested in open Court and that he died entestate whereupon Joseph Cummings Jr. is appointed adminestrator of all and singular the goods and chattles; rights and credits of the deceased; who being present in open Court took the oath prescribed by law and together with Gabriel P. Cummings and John Gillentine entered into and acknowledged bond in the sum of five hundred dollars conditioned as the law requires.

Isd Ordered by Court that Jesse Walling; John Gillentine and Thomas Moore Commissioners of Isham Hales Turnpike road be each allowed the sum of two dollars and fifty cents per day for three days services each to be paid them by Isham Hale - And that Thomas Moore and Jesse Walling be each allowed the sum of two dollars and fifty cents per day for two days services each to be paid by Mr. Griffith.

(P-278) Ordered by the Court unanimously that Thomas Eastland Esquire a member of this Court be appointed Chairman thereof for and during the year 1839.

Isd Ordered by Court that John Fisher be appointed Overseer of the road from Paynes Bridge to Warren County line being a road of the second Class and keep the same in repair as the law requires and that the same list and bounds of hands that worked under Henry Crawley late Overseer thereof be assigned to work thereon.

Isd Ordered by Court that Charles Burgess be appointed Overseer of the road from Lollars branch to Dittys branch being a road of the first Class and keep the same in repair as the law requires and that the same hands that worked under the late Overseer thereof be assigned to work thereon.

Ordered by Court that Joseph Cummings, Jr., John Witt, Sampson Witt, Ozias Denton and Spencer Holder freeholders be appointed a Jury of view to lay off and mark a road of the 2nd Class from Kuhns old field to Ozias Dentons and report thereof today.

Isd The Commissioners this day appointed to lay off and mark a road of the second Class from Kuhns old field to Ozias Dentons returned their report which is received and said road established and it is ordered that, that portion of the road leading from Kuhns old field to Robert Anderson be discontinued, And it is further ordered that, that portion just established be attached to the lot of road of which John W. Simpson is Overseer and that he open and keep the same in repair as the law requires with the hands already assigned him.

Isd Ordered by Court that order of the last term of this Court appointing a Jury to lay off and mark a road of the 2nd Class from Robert Anderson to intersect the road leading to Paynes Bridge across the Caney fork be set aside - .

Isd Ordered by Court that John Frisby be appointed Overseer of the road from Moore's old ferry across Caney fork to the forks of the road being a road of the second Class and keep the same in repair as the law requires and that the same list and bounds of hands that worked under Thomas M. Fleming late, Overseer thereof be assigned to work thereon.

(P-279) Isd Ordered by Court that Solomon Dodson, John Dodson, James Graham, Samuel Miller and John Graham be appointed a Jury of view to lay off and change the end of the Loss Creek road so that the same shall entersect the road above Noah Dodson plantation and report thereof to the next term of this Court.

Ordered that Court be adjourned untill tomorrow 10 O'Clock

John Jett
John Bryan
Elijah Frost

Tuesday Morning 8th Jan. A. D. 1839 Court met pursuant to adjournment
Present the worshipful

John Jett, John Bryan, Asa Certain, Elijah Frost, and William Bruster } Esqs. Justices

Isd Ordered by Court that William Simpson be allowed the sum of one hundred Dollars out of the taxes laid for the year 1839 upon the said Simpson keeping the Sparta Bridge in good repair for the year 1839 to be paid by the Trustee of White County out of the taxes of said year 1839.

Isad This day Benjamin Rains produced in open Court one large wolf scalp over the age of four months and also seven wolf scalps under the age of four months and proved that they were all killed in White County whereupon there being present five acting Justices of the peace for said County to wit: John Jett, John Bryan, Asa Certain, Elijah Frost and William Bruster Esquires it is ordered by the Court that the same be certified to the Treasure of the State of Tennessee for payment to the use and benefit of David Snodgrass and that said Scalps be burned and the Sherriff of White County being present in open Court received said scalps into his custody and acted accordingly.

This day John Jett, Esq. who was on yesterday appointed Treasure to the board of Poor house Commissioners in White County appeared in open Court together with John Bryan and Asa Certain entered into and acknowledged bond in the sum of One thousand Dollars conditioned as the law requires.

Ordered by Court that John Jett Treasure of the poor house of White deliver to David C. Dempsy his pension Certificate he being about to remove from White County.

(P-280) Isad This day Benjamin Rains produced in open Court one large wolf scalp over the age of four months and proved that the same was killed in White County whereupon there being present five acting Justices of the peace in and for the said County to wit: John Jett, John Bryan, Asa Certain, Elijah Frost and William Bruster, Esq. it is ordered by Court that the same be certified to the Treasure of the State of Tennessee for payment to the use and benefit of James M. Johnson, and it is ordered by Court that said Scalp be burned - And the sherriff of White County being present in open Court received said scalp into his costudy and acted accordingly.

This day Joseph Herd Esq. who was appointed on yesterday one of the Commissioners of the poor house of White County appeared in open Court and took the oath required by law and entered upon the discharge of his duties.

Isad Ordered by Court that the order of last term appointing William McKinny, Vinett Henry, Elisha Camron, Harrison Whitson and James A. Jay freeholders a Jury of view to lay off and mark a road of the third Class leaving the Calf killer road near William C. Metcalf, thence the nearest and best way through the board Valley to entersect the dry valley road near William Pryors be renewed and report thereof to the next term of this Court.

Ordered that Court be adjourned untill Court in Course

Test
N. Oldham, Clk.

John Jett
John Bryan
Wm. Bruster

(P-281) State of Tennessee

At a County Court began and held for the County of White and State aforesaid in the Court house in the town of Sparta before the Justices of said Court on the first Monday being the 4th day of February in the year of our Lord One Thousand eight hundred and thirty nine and of the Independence of the United States of America the sixty third year.

Present the worshipful

John Jett	)	Esquire
David Snodgrass	)	Quorum
& John Bryan	)	Justices

This day the Clerk of this County produced in open Court the report of a settlement made with Mary Jane Kelly (late Mary Jane Carroll adminestratrix of William Carroll deceased which is received by the Court and confirmed in all its parts which is ordered to be recorded.

Ordered by Court that the report of the Jury appointed to lay off and mark a road from William Knowles to Dillons bridge be rejected and that the order of appointment of commissioners be set aside.

Ordered by Court that John Brown be appointed Overseer of the road from the ford of the Calf Killer below Andersons old Salt well to the forks of the road near Charles McGuire being around the second Class and keep the same in repair as the law requires And that the same list and bounds of hands that worked under Daniel Kelly late Overseer thereof be assigned to work thereon.

Issd. This day was exhibited in open Court a writing purporting to be the last will and testament of Andrew Black deceased late of the County of White whereupon the due execution and publication thereof as such was proven in open Court by the oaths of Madison Fisk and John Gilpatrick two of the subscribing witnesses thereto for the purposes and things therein mentioned and also made oath that the said Andrew Black at the date of the execution and publication thereof as such was of sound and disposing mind and memory which is ordered to be recorded.

Issd Ordered by Court that Hiram Knowles, George Swindle, Stephen K. Charles, Jesse Franks and Samuel A. Moore, Jr., freeholders be appointed a Jury of view to lay off and mark a road from the stage road at Jesse Franks to Indemon B. Moore the nearest and best way so as not to entrude on individual rights and report thereof to the next term of this Court.

(P-282) This day Matilda Lowrey aged six the 15th day of March 1839 was bound to Joseph J. Cummings to serve him after the manner of an apprentice untill she arrives at the age of twenty one years and for the faithful purformance of Covenant entered into and acknowledged bond with Hayes Arnold his security conditioned as the law requires.

Issd Ordered by Court that Felix A. Badger, Jesse Franks, William A. Cook, John Swindle, Stephen K. Charles and Samuel A. Moore freeholders be appointed a Jury of view to examine and designate what alteration and improvement can or ought to be made in the road from Felix A. Badgers to Rock Island and report thereof to the next rerm of this Court.

Isad It appearing to the satisfaction of the Court that Samuel Oliver and his wife Clara Oliver Citizens of White County are in very indigent circumstances, from infirmity and old age and are in a condition likely to suffer for the necessaries of life it is therefore ordered by Court that William Williams transmit them to the poor house of White County there to be supported at the public charge and it is further ordered that the Treasure of the poor house of White County pay to William Williams the sum of one Dollars for his service in taking the aforesaid paupers to the poorhouse to be paid out of any monies not otherwise appropriated.

This day Mary Jane Kelly (late Mary Jane Carroll Guardian to Samuel Lafayett Carroll minor heir of William dec'd appeared in open Court and surrendered her guardianship aforesaid which is by the Court received and ordered to be recorded.

This day James C. Kelly appeared in open Court and was appointed guardian to Samuel Lafayett Carroll minor heir of William Carroll deceased and took the oath prescribed by law and together with Asa Certain and William G. Sims entered into and acknowledged bond in the sum of Five hundred dollars conditioned as the law requires.

Ordered by Court that William G. Sims be appointed guardian to Harriett R. Farris; William J. Farris; Mary Jane Farris and Amaranda S. Farris infant heirs of Lenias B. Farris Deceased and took the oath prescribed by law and together with Eli Sims and James C. Kelly entered into and acknowledged bond in the sum of two thousand Dollars conditioned as the law requires.

Ordered by Court that William Knowles and Lewis Pettett Esqs. be appointed to assign a list of hands to Timothy Couch Overseer of the road and report thereof to the next term of this Court.

(P-283) Isad Ordered by Court that William Templeton; Joel Smith; Alexander Dillon; Samuel A. Moore; Jr.; and Addison Dillon freeholders be appointed a Jury of view to lay off and mark a road of second Class from William Knowles to Dillons Bridge in such a manner as not to pass through the lands of Hiram Knowles and report thereof to the next term of this Court.

This day appeared in open Court Thomas Moore; and filed upon oath his affidavet as an amendment to his Declaration heretofore filed for a Pension of the United States agreeable to act of Congress; which is Ordered to be Certified under the seal of this Court.

This day the Commissioners heretofore appointed to lay off and set apart one years provision for the support and maintainance and support of the widow and family of James Brown deceased made their report which is ordered to be recorded.

Isad Ordered by Court that Robert Anderson; James W. Copeland; Thomas Green; John Mitchell and Solomon Sparkman freeholders be appointed a Jury of view to lay off and mark a road of the 2nd Class from the widow Fitzgerald old field to entersect Paynes road near John Philips and report thereof to the next term of this Court.

Ordered by Court that Anthony Dibrell be allowed the sum of Fifty dollars the amount of his account against the estate of Zachariah Jones deceased for services rendered to be paid by the administrator out of the real Estate of the Decedent.

James Townsend }
to Issd } Deed of Conveyance for 100 acres Land
William White }

It appearing fully to the satisfaction of the Court that the Conveyor James Townsend was dead, and that one of the witnesses Aaron Hutchings had proved in due form of law that James Townsend did executed the within Deed to William White and said witness not being able to prove the hand writing of Thomas Mayes the other subscribing witness thereto, that the said Mayes is dead or lives beyond the limits of this State whereupon appeared in open Court Eli Sims and William G. Sims who are entitled to full faith in a Court of Justices who were well acquainted with the said James Townsend in his lifetime and both familure with his hand writing being sworn in due form of law upon their oath do say that the signiture of James Townsend as well as the body of said Deed is in the proper (P-284) hand writing of said James Townsend the conveyor therein all of which is ordered to be recorded - and Registered.

This day William Glenn guardian to part of the minor heirs of William Glenn deceased made his report upon oath which is ordered to be recorded.

This day Edward V. Pollard guardian to part of the heirs of William Glenn dec'd made his report upon oath which is ordered to be recorded.

Issd Ordered by Court that Cornelius Hickey be appointed Overseer of the road from the branch between James M. Nelson and Thomas Hawks to the Falling Water being a road of the 2nd Class and keep the same in repair as the law requires and that William Hitchcock and James Allison Esquires divide the hands between Joshua Brown and said Hickey.

Ordered by Court that the following articles be set apart out of the estate of Abner Hodges dec'd as provisions for one years support for the widow and family of the deceased to wit; Thirty Bushels of corn, two hundred and fifty pounds of pickled pork, One Cow and calf and five dollars in money to buy sugar and coffee to be paid her out of the sales of the property of said Estate.

This day Joseph Cummings, Jr., adminestrator of Abner Hodges deceased returned upon oath an Inventory of said estate which is ordered to be recorded.

Issd Ordered by Court that the Sherriff of White County produced here in open Court at the next term of this Court a certain ellegetemate boy by the name of Lawson Holland alias Herd the child of the late Elisabeth Herd, now Elisabeth Martin, that the Court may do what may seem right and proper and according to law in relation to the present condition and future benefit of said boy.

Issd Ordered by Court Solomon Yeager, Sr., William Farley, William Wisdom, Elias Yeager, and Robert Denny freeholders be appointed a Jury of view to lay off and mark a road of the 2nd Class from John W. Dearing across the mountain to Glenns old salt well and report thereof to the next term of this Court.

This day William Templeton guardian to John Davis made his report upon oath which is ordered to be recorded.

(P-285) Isd Ordered by Court that William L. Mitchell; John Yates; John Graham, Sr., John Dodson, Sr., and Samuel Miller freeholders be appointed a Jury of view to lay off and make a road of the second Class from William L. Mitchells the nearest and best way to Michael Hendersons so as to injure no persons and report thereof to the next term of this Court.

Isd Ordered by Court that Nathan Earles be appointed Overseer of the road from near Joseph Cummings to Meeks Mill being a road of the 2nd Class and keep the same in repair as the law requires and that the same list and bounds of hands that worked under Joseph Ray late Overseer thereof be assigned to work thereon.

Ordered by Court that the same lists and bounds of hands that worked under Reubin Perkins late Overseer of the road be assigned to work under Charles Burges the present Overseer thereof.

This day Jacob A. Lane Esquire who was appointed by this Court at the October term 1838 to Survey the line between the County of White and the County of DeKalb agreeable to the Constitution of the State of Tennessee and to mark the same plainly and distinctly made his report which is by the Court received and affirmed and ordered to be recorded - And it is further ordered by the Court that said Report be Regestered in the Regester in the Regesters Office of White County.

Isd Ordered by Court that James Cooper be appointed Overseer of the road from the Carthage road to where the Caney fork road comes in and keep the same in repair as the law requires being a road of the second Class and that the same list and bounds of hands that worked under Carter Whitefield late Overseer thereof be assigned to work thereon.

Isd Ordered by the Court that John Broyles be released from the payment of a Poll tax for the year 1837 he being Over age and that the Sherriff of White County have a credit therefore in the settlement of his accounts.

Isd Ordered by Court that James C. Hitchcock be appointed Overseer of the road from the Falling water to the branch beyond John Lollars being a road of the first Class and keep the same in repair as the law requires and that the same list of hands that worked under Welcher Cardwell be assigned to work thereon.

(P-286) Ordered by Court that James Randalls; Thomas Walling, Daniel Walling, Thomas Robertson and Henderson Keithley freeholders be appointed a Jury of view to examine and so change the Gumspring road as to leave the same at or near Isham Rogers and entersect the same again near Joseph Herds and report to day. And all of the aforesaid Jurors being here present in open Court and all being duly sworn in due form of law make a favorable report verbally and the Court hereby establishes said change on condition that John Rogers open the same and puts it in good repair at his own proper expense. -

Ordered by Court that John H. Miller be released from the payment of a poll tax for the year 1838 he being over age and that the Sherriff of White County have a credit thereof in the settlement of his accounts.

Ordered that Court be adjourned untill tomorrow morning 10 O'clock.

John Jett
John Bryan
Matthias Hutson

Tuesday Morning 5th February 1839 Court met pursuant to adjournment
Present the worshipful

John Jett
David Snodgrass
John Bryan and
Matthias Hutson

Ordered by Court upon testamony of W. L. Adams and S. J. Walling that the sherriff of White County bring into open Court at the next term of this Court a certain orphan girl named Alvira Roberts daughter of Sally Roberts and also four certain orphans named Polly Adair, William Adair, Sally Adair, Hiram Adair, and Thomas Adair, children of Polly Adair to be dealt by according to law.

Isd Ordered that the order of last term appointing William McKenny, Vinete Henry, Elisha Camron, Harrison Whitson and James A. Jay freeholders a Jury of view to lay off and mark a road of the third Class leaving the Calf Killer road near William C. Metcalfs thence the nearest and best way through the board valley road* near William Pryors be renewed and report thereof to the next term of this Court.

(P-287) Isd Ordered by Court that the order appointing Solomon Dodson, John Dodson, James Graham, Samuel Miller and John Graham freeholders a jury of view to lay off and mark the road and so change the end of the Loss Creek road so that the same shall entersect the road above Noah Dodsons Plantation be renewed and report thereof to the next term of this Court.

This day Jonathan T. Bradly Esquire Sherriff of the County of White appointed Avery Norris Deputy Sherriff of White County who being present in open Court took the oath required by law and thereupon entered upon the discharge of the duties of his Office.

Ordered that Court be adjourned untill Court in Course

Test
N. Oldham, Clk.

David Snodgrass
John Jett
John Bryan

*to intersect the dry Valley road

(P-288) State of Tennessee

At a Quorum Court began and held for the County of White in the State aforesaid in the Court house in the town of Sparta before the Justices of said Court on the first Monday being the fourth day of March in the year of our Lord One thousand eight hundred and thirty nine. And of the Independence of the United States of America the sixty third year

Present the Worshipful

John Jett David Snodgrass & John Bryan	Esquires Justices

This day William Bartlett administrator of Nathan Bartlett deceased returned upon oath an additional account of sales of said estate which is ordered to be recorded.

This day William Bartlett Esquire in District No. 11 and Elisha Camron Esquire in District No. 12 appeared in open Court and resigned their offices as Justices of the peace for White County which is ordered to be recorded.

This day Thomas Welch a Constable in the 11th District appeared in open Court and resigned his office of Constable of the County of White which is ordered to be recorded.

Ordered by Court that John Witt; James Dillon; Smith J. Walling; William H. Phillips and Winkfield Hill be appointed a Jury of view to examine and change the road through Lewis Phillips plantation from Wm. Rickmans to the meeting house being a road of the third Class and report thereof immediately.

And the Jurors aforesaid being present in open Court and being duly sworn report favorably as to the change proposed in said road whereupon it is ordered by the Court that the change in said road be established and that said Lewis Phillips open and put the same in good order at his own expence that when said new road shall be opened; the old part to be disannulled and that the overseer thereon shall thereafter keep the same in repair as though no change had been made.

This day the Clerk of this Court produced the report of a settlement made with William Bartlett admr. of Nathan Bartlett deceased which is received and confirmed in all its parts and ordered to be recorded.

This day William Bartlett admr. of Nathan Bartlett dec'd returned upon oath an additional account sales made under a decree of the Court which is ordered to be recorded. set aside

(P-289) Ordered by Court that William Bartlett administrator of Nathan Bartlett deceased be allowed the sum of Twenty five dollars for supporting and taking care of an old and helpless negro woman named Clitty untill her death to be paid him out of said Estate.

This day the Clerk of this Court produced in open Court a report of a settlement with William Shockley who was the security of John Franklin administrator of Robert Goard deceased which is by the Court received and confirmed and ordered to be recorded.

This day the Clerk of this Court produced in open Court a report of a settlement made with John Parker administrator of Joseph Parker deceased which is confirmed in all its parts and ordered to be recorded.

Issd Ordered by Court that Thomas Eastland be appointed Overseer of the road from the McKenny Cabins East of Cilfty to Scarboroughs Mills being a road of the second Class and the same in repair as the law requires and that the same list of hands that worked under James Kitchensides late Overseer thereof be assigned to work thereon.

Issd Ordered by Court that William Moore be appointed Overseer of the road from James McGownes to Franks's old ferry being a road of the second Class and keep the same in repair as the law requires and that the same list and bounds of hands that worked under William Wammack late Overseer thereof be assigned to work thereon.

This day Richard Crowder administrator of Adam Clouse deceased returned upon oath an Inventory of said Estate which is ordered to be recorded

Issd Ordered by Court that James H. Pass, John Rogers, John Gooch, Benjamin Wilhite and Abraham McGhee freeholders be appointed a Jury of view to examine lay off and mark a road of the 2nd Class from the mouth of Benjamin Wilhites land passing John Gooches store and entersect the old road again at some convenient point and report thereof to the next term of this Court.

On the humble petition of Isaac Buck Esquire one of (P-290) the securities of William Bartlett for the administrators of the estate of Nathan Bartlett deceased and for reasons appearing to the satisfaction of the Court it is ordered by the Court that the said William Bartlett be notified and required to appear at the next term of this Court and release the said Isaac Buck by giving other good and sufficient security and the said Bartlett acknowledged the notice thereof in open Court and agrees to comply fully with the requirements of this order.

It appearing to the satisfaction of the Court that the Common Jail of White County needs some repairs in order to render said Prison more secure whereupon it is ordered by the Court that the Superintendant or Commissioners of said Common Jail contract to have such repairs as is necessary to be done thereon immediately and report thereof to the next term of this Court.

This day John T. Bradley Sherriff of White County appeared in open Court and appointed Archebald Conner Special Deputy sheriff for White County to collect, arrange Taxes in said County for the securities of David L. Mitchell late Sherriff of said County up to 1st January 1837 And to transact buisness before Justices of the peace and no further who being present in open court took the several oaths required by law and entered upon the duties of his Office - .

Issd This day the Sherriff of White County produced in open Court the body of Lawson Holland the child of Elizabeth Herd now Elizabeth Martin, and on the application of Robert Martin the Husband to the Childs mother it is ordered that the further consideration of the matter be continued untill the next term of this Court that evidence may be produced fairly before the Court for a hearing thereon and that the said Robert Martin and Elizabeth his mother produce the said boy before the Court at the next term to be dealt with by said Court as may seem to them right and proper and that the sherriff of White County produced said boy at the next term of this Court.

Ordered by Court that Andrew Lowell, Stephen Wallis, Anderson S. Rogers, John H. Dale, and John Baker freeholders be appointed a Jury of view to examine the road as opened by John Baker on the river road passing John Bakers house and entersecting the old road again near the top of the mountain and thereof to report instantly. And the Jurors aforesaid being present in open Court and duly sworn report favorably thereof whereupon the Court orders the same to be established and disannull the old road and require the Overseer to keep the same in repair as though said change has not been made.

(P-291) Isd Ordered by Court that Alfred Wilson be appointed Overseer of the road from the mouth of Anderson S. Rogers lane to where the same entersect the Loss Creek road being a road of the third Class and keep the same in repair as the law requires and that Mumford Wilson, James A. Baker be assigned to work thereon.

Ordered by Court that William C. Bounds, William K. Bradford, Jonathan C. Davis, Shadrack Price and John England freeholders be appointed a Jury of view to Examine and change the road from the top of the Caney fork hill passing Shadrack Prices house and entersecting the old road again near the line between John R. Barnett and said Price and report thereof enstantly. And the Jurors aforesaid being all present in open Court and duly sworn report favorably of said change, whereupon it is ordered by Court that said road be established that said Price open the same according to law at his own expence that when the same shall be properly opened, the old road to be disannulled and the Overseer on said road to keep the same in repair as though said change had not been made thereon.

Isd Ordered by Court that the order of the last term appointing William L. Mitchell, John Yates, John Graham, Sr., John Dodson, Sr., and Samuel Miller freeholders a Jury of view to lay off and mark a road of the 2nd Class from William L. Mitchell the nearest and best way to Michael Henderson and from thence up the mountain the nearest and best way to Thomas Eastlands Mills on Big Laurell be renewed and report thereof to the next term of this Court.

Isd Ordered by Court that the order appointing William McKenny, Venett Henry, Eliaha Camron, Harrison Whitson and James A. Way freeholders a jury of view to lay off and mark a road of the third Class leaving the Calf Killer road near William C. Metcalfs thence the nearest and best way through the board valley to entersect the dry valley road near William Pryors be renewed and report thereof to the next term of this Court.

Isd Ordered by Court that the order of last term appointing William Templeton, Joel Smith, Alexander Dillon, Samuel A. Moore, Jr. and Addison A. Dillon freeholders a Jury of view to lay off and mark a road of the second Class from William Knowles's to Dillons Bridge in such a manner
(P-292) as not to pass through the lands of Hirman Knowles be renewed

and report thereof to the next term of this Court.

Isd Ordered by Court that the order of the last term appointing Felix A. Badger, Jesse Franks, William A. Cook, John Swindle, Stephen K. Charles and Samuel A. Moore freeholders a Jury of view to examine and designate what alteration and improvement can or ought to be made in the road from Felix A. Badger to the Rockisland be renewed and report thereof to the next term of this Court.

Ordered by Court that the order of last term appointing Robert Anderson, James W. Copeland, Thomas Green, John Mitchell and Soloman Sparkman freeholders a Jury of view to lay off and mark a road of the second Class from the widow Fitzgeralds old field to entersect Paynes road near John Phillips be renewed and report thereof to the next term of this Court.

Isd Ordered by Court that the order of last term appointing Soloman Yeager, Sr., William Farley, William Wisdom, Elias Yeager and Robert Denny freeholders a Jury of view to lay off and mark a road of the 2nd Class from John W. Dearing across the mountain to Glenns old salt well be renewed and report thereof to the next term of this Court.

Isd Ordered by Court that the order of last term appointing Soloman Dodson, John Dodson, James Graham, Samuel Miller and John Graham freeholders a Jury of view to lay off and mark and change the end of the Loss Creek road as that the same shall entersect the road above Noah Dodson plantation be renewed and report thereof to the next term of this Court.

Isd Ordered by Court that the order of last term appointing Hirman Knowles, George Swindle, Jeremiah Denton, Sr., Jesse Franks and Samuel A. Moore, Jr., freeholders a Jury of view to lay off and mark a road from the stage road at Jesse Franks the nearest and best way to Indemon B. Moores so as not to intrude upon indevidual rights be renewed and report thereof at the next term of this Court.

Isd Ordered by Court that the order of last term requiring the Sherriff of White County to bring into this Court at the present (P-293) term certain orphan children namely Alzira Roberts daughter of Sally Roberts also Polly, William, Sally, Hiram and Thomas Adair children of Polly Adair to be dealt by according to law be renewed returnable to the next term of this Court.

Ordered that Court be adjourned untill tomorrow morning 10 O'Clock

John Jett
David Snodgrass
John Bryan

Tuesday Morning 5th March 1839 Court met pursuant to adjournment
Present the worshipful

John Jett
David Snodgrass
& John Bryan } Esquires Justices

Ordered that Court be adjourned untill Court in Course

John Jett
David Snodgrass
John Bryan

Test
N. Oldham, Clk.

(P-294) State of Tennessee

At a County Court began and held for the County of White and State aforesaid in the Court house in the Town of Sparta before the Justices of said Court on the first Monday being the first day of April in the year of our Lord One thousand eight hundred and thirty nine. And of the Independance of the United States of America the Sixty third year

Present the worshipful

John Jett, John Bryan, David Snodgrass, Matthias Hutson, Lewis Pettatt, William Bruster, George Defreese, William Knowles, Jesse Walling, Thomas Green, Anderson S. Rogers, Tilman Brown, John Gillentine, James Allison, William Little, Richard Crowder, and Asa Certain.	Esquire Justice

This day James Knowles appeared in open Court and produced a commission signed by the Covenor appointing a Justice of the peace in White County in the 5th District and took the oath to support the Constitution of the United States and of the States of Tennessee and the several oaths prescribed by law and thereupon took his seat upon the Bench.

Ordered by Court that the appointment of John W. Simpson as one of the Com's to settle with the Trustee & Clerk of the Courts of said County be set aside.

This day the sherriff of White County filed in open Court the certified of the Election of John L. Hyder to fill the vacancy of Constable in the 11th District occasioned by the resignation of Thomas Welch and the said John L. Hyder being present in open Court took an oath to support the Constitution of the United States and of the state of Tennessee and the several oaths prescribed by law and together with Joseph Bartlett and William Hudgins entered into and acknowledged bond in the sum of four thousand dollars conditioned as the law requires.

This day John L. Goodall Esquire late of the State of Kentucky produced in open Court a License of practising attorney and thereupon took the oaths required by law and entered upon the discharge of his duties.

For reasons appearing fully to the satisfaction of the Court it is ordered that the application of David Snodgrass admr. of David L. Mitchell deceased for allowance out of the estate of James Isham deceased as one of the adm'r of said Isham be continued untill the next term.

(P-295) This day was exhibition in open Court a writing purporting to be the last will and testament of Cason Swindle late of the County of White deceased and thereupon the due execution and publication thereof as the last will and testament of the said Cason Swindle deceased was this day proved in open Court by the oaths of Samuel A. Moore, Sr. and Samuel A. Moore, Jr., subscribing witness thereto for the purposes and things therein mentioned and that at the date of the execution and publication thereof as such was of sound and disposing mind and memory all of which is ordered to be recorded.

This day the Commissioners heretofore appointed to examine and mark a road from Fitzgerald old field to entersect Paynes road near John Phillips made their report which is rejected.

And it is further considered that the order appointing the Commissioners aforesaid to wit: Robert Anderson; James W. Copeland; Thomas Green; John Mitchell and Solomon Sparkman freeholders to lay off and mark a road of the 2nd Class from the widow Fitzgeralds old field to entersect Paynes road near John Phillips be renewed and report thereof to the next term of this Court.

This day the Commissioners heretofore appointed to lay off and mark a road from William Knowles to Dillons Bridge made their report which is rejected.

This day the Commissioners heretofore appointed to lay off and mark a road from the stage road at Jesse Franks to Indemon B. Moore made their report which is rejected.

Issd Ordered by Court that Robert Anderson, Sr., James Randolls, Sr., Joseph Clarks, Sr., John Witt and Sampson Witt freeholders be appointed a jury of view to lay off and mark a road of the 2nd Class from Wm. Knowles To Dillions Bridge in such a manner as not to pass through the land of Hiram Knowles and report thereof to the next term of this Court.

Ordered by Court that Thomas Meek be released from the payment of one white Poll for the year 1833 and 1834 he being over age and that the securities of David L. Mitchell late sherriff of White County Deceased have a credit for the sum of one dollar eighteen cents in their settlement with the Trustee of White County.

For reasons appearing to the satisfaction of the Court it is ordered that Jacob Stipe one of the security of John Gillentine guardian to William F. Carter be released and forever discharged. (P-296) from all further and future liabilities therein.

And the said John Gillentine guardian aforesaid being present in open Court and together with Joseph Cummings, Jr. and Tilman Brown entered into and acknowledged bond in the sum of four thousand dollars conditioned as the law requires.

This day Joseph Hunter minor over the age of fourteen years appeared in open Court and chose his father Dudley Hunter his guardian and whereupon the said Dudley Hunter being present in open Court took the oath prescribed by law and together with Joseph Bartlett and Robert Office entered into and acknowledged bond in the sum of Five Hundred Dollars conditioned as the law requires.

This day Joseph Cummings administrator of Abner Hogg deceased returned upon oath an acct. of the sales of said estate which is ordered to be recorded.

This day Thomas Snodgrass a Constable in the 13th District appeared in open Court and resigned his office which is ordered to be recorded.

This day William Little, Esq. a Justice of the peace in the 15th District of White County appeared in open Court and resigned his office; which is ordered to be recorded.

This day the death of Robert Glenn late of the County of White deceased was suggested in open Court and that he departed this life intestate whereupon Joseph Gleen was appointed administrator of all and singular the goods and chattles; rights and credits of the deceased who being present in open court took the oath prescribed by law and together with Edward Gleeson and Indemon B. Moore entered into and acknowledged bond in the sum of eight hundred Dollars conditioned as the law requires.

Issd Ordered by a majority of the Court that the Com's of the Revinue of the County of White for the year 1839 To wit: William C. Brittain; John Bryan, Thomas Green; Matthias Hutson; William Knowles, Richard Crowder, James Allison; Asa Certain, William C. Bounds; Elisha Camron; Isaac Buck; William Little; Elijah Frost and John Gillentine; Esquires, be each allowed the sum of Ten dollars for taking in and returning the tax list of their respective District for said year to be paid by the Trustee of White County out of the Taxes of the year 1839.

For reasons appearing to satisfa ction of the Court it is ordered that Isaac Buck one of the securities of William Bartlett admr. of Nathan Bartlett dec'd from all future and further liabilities therein be released and forever discharged.

(P-297) This day appeared in open Court William Bartlett adminestrator of Nathan Bartlett deceased and together with Robert Officer and Joseph Bartlett entered into and acknowledged bond in the sum of seven thousand dollars conditioned as the law requires.

Issd Ordered by Court that William P. Campbell be appointed Overseer of the road from the forks of the Gainesborough road to the Jackson County line being a road of the second Class and keep the same in repair as the law requires and that Jackson Campbell; and Henry Campbell be assigned to work thereon.

Issd Ordered by Court Robert H. McManus be allowed the sum of four dollars and fifty cents the amount of his account for money expended in cleaning the well belonging to White County attached to the Common Jail of said County to be paid by the Trustee of White County out of the taxes of 1839.

Issd Ordered by Court that Barnett K. Mitchell be appointed Overseer of the road from the top of the hill at Lowerys old place to the widow Dales being a road of the second Class and keep the same in repair as the law requires and that the same list and bounds of hands that worked under Anderson S. Rogers be assigned to work thereon.

Ordered by Court that for satisfactory reasons to the Court shown the Sherriff and Collector of the public taxes of the County of White is hereby authorised and required to enforce the collection of the public taxes and to exercise and enter all the duties of his office as Sherriff of White County fully and completely to the dividing line between the County of White and County of DeKalb as surveyed and marked and designated; particlarly as the line run*by this Court for that purpose.

*by Jacob A. Lane appointed

Isd Ordered by Court that Abijah Crane, James Malloy, Willie B. Easton, Isham B. Easton and Burrel Manor freeholders be appointed a Jury of view to examine the change in the road from said Manor to the Bridge below his house and report thereof to the next term of this Court.

(P-298) This day was produced in open court a writing purporting to be the last will and testament of John A. Shaw late of the County of White deceased and the due execution and publication thereof as such was proved in open Court by the oaths of James T. Hayes and Asa Certain subscribing witness thereto for the purposes therein contained and that the said John A. Shaw was at the date of the execution and publication thereof as such, of sound and disposing mind and memory which is ordered to be recorded whereupon Alford L. Shaw the executor mentioned in said last will and testament appeared in open Court and undertook the further of the execution of said last will and testament and took the oath prescribed by law and together with William H. Baker and James C. Kelly entered into and acknowledged bond in the sum of Two thousand dollars conditioned as the law requires.

Isd Ordered by Court that the Treasure of board of Commissioners of the Poor house of White County pay to Allen L. Mitchell the Keeper of the poor house to meet the Current expences of the year 1839 the sum of fifty dollars at the end of each quarter of said year comminoing the first day of January 1839 to be paid out of any monies in his hands not otherwise appropriated.

Isd Ordered by Court that Washington Williams be appointed Overseer of the road from post oak Creek to Hunters Mill being a road of the second Class and keep the same in repair as the law requires and that the same list of hands that worked under Mark Whitaker former Overseer thereof be assigned to work thereon.

Ordered by Court that all persons who have been reported by the Commissioners of the Revinue for White County for the year 1839 for double tax for failure to list their taxable property and polls within the time required by law be released from the payment of Double tax and required to pay single tax only.

For reasons appearing to the satisfaction of the Court it is ordered by Court that Polly Adair and her children who were required by an order of this Court to appear at the present term be entirely released from the requirement of said order.

Ordered by Court that Robert Anderson, Sampson Witt, John Witt, James W. Copeland and George Sparkman freeholders be appointed a Jury of view to lay off and mark a road of the third Class from Cummings ford on Caney fork to entersect the Rock island road at some suitable point and report thereof to the next term of this Court.

(P-299) Isd Ordered by Court that the following named persons be appointed to serve as Jurors at the June term of White Circuit Court next Towit: Steuart Warren, John Crook, Spence Mitchell, Jesse Scoggins, Berry R. Wilson, Benjamin Lewis, George Price, William Goodwin, Mark Lowry, John Brown, Sr., William Webb, James Jackson, Asa Certain, George Defrees, Matthias Hutson, Spencer Holder, James Hudgins, William M. Young, John H. Jones, George Purtle, Jr., William Bruster, Daniel Clark, James Herd,

Edward Anderson, Samuel Brown and William C. Bounds, good and lawful men and also Charles Meek and Hayes Arnold Constables to attend thereon and that a writ of Venire facias issue directed &c.

This day was produced in open Court Lawson Herd alias Holland as required by an order of a former term of this Court and upon the entroduction of abundant testimony in the case it appears fully to the satisfaction of the Court that said boy does not need the enterposition of this Court it is therefore ordered by the Court that the said boy Lawson and his mother Elizabeth Martin be released and discharged from the requisitions of said order.

This day Mary Baker exhibited in open Court the affidavet of Thomas Crawley and Margarett Crawley as an amendment to her declaration heretofore filed in this Court for a Pension under the late act of Congress providing for the widows of Revolutionary Pensions and the said Thomas Crawley and Margarett Crawley being to the Court Known, whereupon it is signed by the Court and ordered to be Certified under the seal of this Court.

Issd Ordered by Court that the order appointing William McKinney, Vinett Henry, Elisha Camron, Harrison Whitson and James A. Jay freeholders a Jury of view to lay off and mark a road of the third Class (from) leaving the Calf Killer road near William C. Metcalfs, thence the nearest and best way through the board vally to entersect the Dry Vally road near Wm. Pryors be renewed and report thereof to the next term of this Court.

Issd Ordered by Court that the order of last Court appointing Solomon Yeager Sr., William Farley, William Wisdom, Elias Yeager and Robert Denny freeholders a Jury of view to lay off and mark a road of the 2nd Class from John W. Dearing across the mountain to Glenns old salt well be renewed and report thereof to the next term of this Court.

Issd Ordered by Court that this order of last Court appointing
(P-300) James H. Pass, John Rogers, John Gooch, Benjamin Wilhite and Abraham McGhee freeholders a Jury of view to examine lay off and mark a road of the second Class from the mouth of Benj. Wilhites lane passing John Gooches Store and entersect the old road again at some convenient point be renewed and report thereof to the next term of this Court.

Issd Ordered by a majority of the Court that the following persons be allowed the sum of Fifty two Dollars for surveying, carrying the chain and marking the line between the Counties of White and DeKalb to wit; Jacob A. Lane surveyor twenty five Dollars for services, Plott and report, Jesse Allen, Jr., for marking said line five days five Dollars, John A. Crowder for three days marking said line, three dollars, William S. Lafferty three days marking said line three dollars and Isham Cook and William Curiton eight days each as chain Carriers eight dollars each agreeable to their account exhibited to be paid by the Trustee of White County out of the taxes of the year 1839.

Issd Ordered by Court that Nicholas Oldham be allowed the sum of one dollar for Regestering the Plott of the line between the Counties of White & DeKalb and the report of Jacob A. Lane the surveyor to be paid by the Trustee of White County out of the tax of the year 1839.

Issd Ordered by Court that the following persons be allowed the following sums of money as fees in the following State Cases which have been examined by the Attorney General for White County and reported as Correctly taxed and properly chargeable to White County towit:

In the Case the State vs Elijah Burden W. G. Sims 13.68¾ J. T. Bradley $2.75, John England 125 Randolph Jones $14.50 - John Jett 0.50 James Graham 25; Eliza J. Bryan 3.75; Patsey Gracy 25; William L. Bryan 50; Leah Bryan 25; John Austin $.6- Hartwell Wilson $5.25; Nathaniel Austin $.6- Stephen Wallis 4.50 Benjamin Lewis $4.50 David Moore $2.25; John Baker 1.50 S. R. Doyle 1.50; Laban Wallis $1.50 William Wallis 1.50
The State vs Patrick Potts - William G. Sims 4.12½ J. T. Bradley 1.91½ -
The State vs Alexander Gettings - William G. Sims 1.31¼
The State vs John Cook; W. G. Sims $6.81¼; D. L. Mitchell .62½J.T.Bradley 1.68½ witness James Kerby $2.50
The State vs Hampton Davis; W. G. Sims 7.81¼ John England 3.75 witness Thomas Price .75 - Amounting in all to the sum of one hundred and one dollar forty five and a half cents to be paid by the trustee of White County out of any money not otherwise appropriated.

(P-301) Issd Ordered by Court that the order of last Court appointing William L. Mitchell; John Yates; John Graham; Sr.; John Dodson; Sr.; and Samuel Miller freeholders a Jury of view to lay off and mark a road of the second Class from William L. Mitchell the nearest and best way to Michael Hendersons and from thence up the mountain the nearest and best way to Thomas Eastlands Mills on Big Laurel be renewed and report thereof to the next term of this Court.

Issd On the Humble petition of James H. Jenkins; S. & H. Carrick; Edward M. Murray; Wamon Leftwich; William L. Young & Brothers and Warren & Dibrell and for reasons appearing fully to the satisfaction of the Court from arguments upon the merits contained in said petition and the several exhibits therein referred to it is ordered by the Court that Jonathan G. Davis; James Hudgins; Daniel Clark; Madison Fisk and John Bryan freeholders be appointed a Jury of view to lay off and mark a road of the first Class commencing on the east boundary of the town of Sparta at a point in said East boundary line which will be in a direct line with the brick house now occupied by Wamon Leftwich and also the frame house now occupied by Thomas Walling and son as the southern boundary of said road running Eastwardly through part of the land owned by William Simpson & which are claimed by the said James H. Jenkins as a reseiver and the said James H. Jenkins and others and to entersect the Turnpike road leading from Sparta to Kingston at a point near the residence of William Hunter in the vicenity of Sparta - and said Jury are hereby enstructed by the Court to enquire also as to the necessity of opening said road and after a careful examination of both roads whether the road proposed will be of public utility and if a good road can be had where now proposed and report also which will be the nearest and best road and report fully upon all these matters at the next term of this Court.

Issd Ordered by Court that James Baker be released from the payment of the appraised value of Eleven head of stray hogs appraised to eight Dollars the same having been proved away from him in the time required by law.

On motion of the petition by their Counsel; the Court were required specially to enstrust the Jury of view ordered on the Petition of James H. Jenkins and others leading eastwardly from the public square of the town of Sparta to a point near the residence of William Hunter as follows; to report whether the proposed road will or will not increase the value of property where it passes; and be of conveniense to a considerable number of the Citizens of the town of Sparta and the County of White which enstructions the Court refused to give to which refusal petitions by their Counsel except.

(P-302) For reasons appearing to the satisfaction of the Court it is ordered that the last order made on the petition of James H. Jenkins and others be annulled; cancelled and entirely set aside. -

Ordered that Court be adjourned untill tomorrow morning 10 O'Clock

John Jett
David Snodgrass
Wm. Bruster
John Bryan

Tuesday Morning 2nd day of April A.D. 1839 Court met pursuant to adjournment
Present the worshipful

John Jett
David Snodgrass } Esqs. Justices
John Bryan

This day John T. Bradley Esqs. Sherriff of the County of White appeared in open Court and was appointed Collector of the public taxes of White County for the year 1839 and took the oath required by law and together with John Warren, Samuel V. Carrick; William G. Sims; Thomas Walling; John Brown; Sr., Joseph Herd and Richard Nelson entered into and acknowledged bond in the sum of Five thousand dollars conditioned as the law requires.

Bond.

Know all men by these presents that we Jonathan T. Bradley, John Warren; Samuel V. Carrick; William G. Sims; Thomas Walling; John Brown; Sr., Joseph Herd and Richard Nelson all of the County of White and State of Tennessee are held and firmly bound unto Thomas Eastland; Esq. Chairman of White County Court or his successors in office in the sum of Five thousand dollars Current money which payment will and truly to be made and done we and each and every one of us bind ourselves and each and every of our heirs executors and adminestrators jointly and severally firmly by these presents sealed with our seals and dated the 2nd day of April A.D. 1839. The conditioned of the above obligation is such that whereas the above bound Jonathan T. Bradley Sherriff of White County hath been this day appointed collector of the public taxes in White County for the year 1839.

Now if the above bound Jonathan T. Bradley shall well and truly and faithfully collect the taxes for said County for said year 1839 to wit: the tax levied for County purposes; the Jury tax and Bridge tax and poor tax of said County and shall well and truly pay all taxes by him collected over to the Trustee of White County and to the Treasure of the poor house Com's of said County according (P-303) to law. Then shall the above obligation be void else be and remain in full force and effect.

Test
N. Oldham; Clk.

Jonathan T. Bradley (seal)
John Warren (seal)
Saml. V. Carrick (seal)
William G. Sims (seal)
Thomas Walling (seal)
John Brown (seal)
Joseph Herd (seal)
R. Nelson (seal)

Ordered that Court be adjourned till Court in Course

John Jett
David Snodgrass
John Bryan

Test
N. Oldham; Clk.

State of Tennessee

At a Quorum Court began and held for the County of White and State aforesaid in the Court house in the town of Sparta before the Justices of said Court on the first Monday being the sixth day of May in the year of our Lord one thousand eight hundred and thirty nine And of the Independence of the United States of America the sixty third year.

Present the worshipful

John Jett
David Snodgrass } Esquire
and John Bryan } Quorum Justices

This day the Jury of view appointed at the last term of this Court to lay off mark a road &c. from the Corporation of the town of Sparta Eastwardly returned their report which is received by the Court and the further action and consideration thereof continued untill the July term of this Court. -

This day Joseph Glenn adminestrator of Robert Glenn deceased returned upon oath an Inventory and account of sales of the deceased which is ordered to be recorded - .

For reasons appearing to the satisfaction of the Court that an order should have been made appointing Commissioners (P-304) to lay off and set apart One years provisions to the widow and family of Robert Glenn dec'd last term and that James Knowles, Green Templeton and Levi Jarvis should have been appointed for that purpose. It is ordered by Court that the same be entered Nune-Pro-tune.

This day the Commissioners appointed to assign and set apart one years provisions out of the estate of Robert Glenn deceased to the widow and family of the deceased made their report which is ordered to be recorded -

Issd. Ordered by Court that William Hargis be appointed Overseer of the road from the 19 mile post to the Standing Stone being a road of the second Class and keep the same in repair as the law requires And that the same list of hands that worked under Stanford Stamps late, overseer of the road be assigned to work thereon.

Issd Ordered by Court that Daniel Clark be appointed Overseer of the Lincolns ferry road from the forks of the Carthage in Oldhams lane to Andrew Gambles School house being a road of the first Class and keep the same in repair as the law requires and that the same list and bounds of hands that were assigned to work under Jesse Lincoln late Overseer be assigned to work thereon - .

This day James Bartlett of the 11th District Sims Dearing of the 12th District and William R. Tucker of the 13th Dist. each appearing in open Court and produced a Commission from the Governer appointing them Justices of the peace in and for the County of White and thereupon each of them took the oath to support the Constitution of United States and of the State of Tennessee and the several oaths prescribed by law and entered upon the discharge of their duties - .

Ordered by Court that Robert Officer be released from the payment of the sum of five dollars and twenty five cents of the tax of 1838 And that the securities of David L. Mitchell late Sherriff of White County have a credit thereof in their settlement with the Trustee of said County.

Issd Ordered by Court that Hugh Gracy be appointed Overseer of the road from (his house) from the forks of the road at the corner of Youngs field to Lincolns and Clarks Mills passing the residence of Robert Nelsons Esq. and keep the same in repair as the law requires being a road of the 3rd Class.

(P-305)

This day the Sherriff of White County filed in open Court the Certificate of the election of David Little in 13th District as constable to fill the vacancy occasioned by the resignation of Thomas Snodgrass who appeared in open Court and thereupon took an oath to support the Constitution of the United States and of the State of Tennessee and the several oaths prescribed by law and together with William Little; William Sondgrass and James Snodgrass entered into and acknowledged bond in the sum of Four Thousand dollars conditioned as the law requires.

This day the Commissioners heretofore appointed to lay off and mark a road of the 2nd Class from the mouth of Benj. Wilhites lane passing Gooches store and to entersect the old road again made their report which is received and said road established a road of the 2nd Class.

Issd Ordered by Court that Spencer Anderson be assigned to work on that portion of the milk sick of which John W. Simpson is Overseer.

Ordered by Court that the application of the adminestrator of David L. Mitchell dec'd late one of the adminestrators of James Isham Dec'd for an allowance out of said Estate be continued and laid over untill the July term of this Court.

This day Robert Cox Trustee of White County personally appeared in open Court and together with John W. Simpson; Richard Nelson; Hugh Gracy and Isaac Buck entered into and acknowledged bond in the sum of Three thousand five hundred and ninty six dollars eighty two cents condition for the faithful receiving and disbursing the common school monies appointed to the County of White for the year 1839.

"Bond"

Know all men by their presents that we Robert Cox and John W. Simpson; Richard Nelson; Hugh Gracy, Isaac Buck; all of the County of White and State of Tennessee are held and firmly bound unto Robert H. McEwin; Esquire Superentendant of public enstruction & his successions in office in the sum of three Thousand five hundred and ninety six dollars eighty two cents current money which payment well and truly to be made and done; we and each of us bind ourselves, our heirs, Executors and adminestrator; jointly and severally firmly by these presents sealed with our seals and dated the 8th day of May A. D. 1839

Now the condition of the above obligation (P-306) is such that if the above bound Robert Cox Trustee of White County shall well and truly and faithfully pay over according to law all moneys which may come into his hands on account of Common schools for the County of White in the manner prescribed by law then the above obligation to be null and void else be and remain in full force and vertue.

Test - .
N. Oldham, Clk.

Ro. Cox (seal)
Jno. W. Simpson (seal)
Rich'd Nelson (seal)
Hugh Gracy (seal)
Isaac Buck (seal)

Isd Ordered by Court that the order heretofore made appointing Solomon Yeager, William Farley, William Wisdom, Elias Yeager and Robert Denny freeholders a jury of view to lay off and mark a road of the 2nd Class from John W. Dearings across the mountain to Glenns old salt well be renewed and report thereof to the next term of this Court.

Isd Ordered by Court that the order heretofore made appointing William McKenny, Venitt Henry, Elisha Camron, Harrison Whitson and James A. Jay freeholders a jury of view to lay off and mark a road of the third leaving the Calf Killer road near William C. Metcalfs thence the nearest and best way through the board valley to entersect the Dry Valley road near William Pryors be renewed and report thereof to the next term of this Court.

Isd Ordered by Court that Isaac Buck and James Bartlett Esqs. be appointed to approtion lists and bounds of hands between the diffrent Overseers in the Neighborhood of Hunters mills so as to give James Bohanon an additional supply of hands.

Ordered that Court be adjourned untill tomorrow morning 10 O'Clock

Thos Eastland
John Jett
John Bryan

Tuesday morning 7th May A. D. 1839 Court met pursuant to adjournment
Present the worshipful

Thomas Eastland, Esq. Chr.
John Jett
John Bryan &
William Bruster } Esqrs.

Isd Ordered by Court that the Order of last term appointing (P-307)
William L. Mitchell, John Yates, John Graham, Sr., John Dodson, Sr., and Samuel Miller freeholders a Jury of view to lay off and mark a road of the second Class from Wm. L. Mitchells the nearest and best way to Michael Henderson, thence the nearest and best way up the Mountain to Thomas Eastland Mills on Big Laurell be renewed and report thereof to the next term of this Court.

Isd Ordered by Court that the order of last term appointing Robert Anderson, Sr., James Randolls, Sr., Joseph Clark, Sr., John Witt and Sampson Witt freeholders a jury of view to lay off and mark a road of the second Class from William Knowles to Dillons Bridge in such a manner as not to pass through the land of Hiram Knowles be renewed and report thereof at the next term of this Court.

Isd Ordered by Court that the order heretofore made appointing Robert Anderson, Sampson Witt, John Witt, James W. Copeland and George Sparkman freeholders a jury of view to lay off and mark a road of the third

Class from Cummings ford on Caney fork to entersect the Rockisland road at some suitable point be renewed and report thereof to the next term of this Court.

Isad Ordered by Court that the order of last term appointing Robert Anderson; James W. Copeland; Thomas Green; John Mitchell; Solomon Sparkman freeholders a jury of view to lay off and mark a road of the 2nd Class from the widow Fitzgeralds old place to entersect Paynes road near John Phillips be renewed and report thereof to the next term of this Court.

Isad Ordered by Court that the order of the last term appointing Abijah Crane; James Malley; Willie B. Haston; Isham B. Haston and Burrel Manor a jury of view to examine the change of the road from said Manors to the Bridge below his house be renewed and report thereof to the next term of this Court.

Ordered that Court be adjourned until Court in Course

Test
N. Oldham, Clk.

John Jett
John Bryan
Wm. Bruster

(P-308) State of Tennessee

At a quorum Court began and held for the County of White in the Court house in the town of Sparta before the Justices of said Court on the first Monday being the third day of June in the year of our Lord One thousand eight hundred thirty nine and of the Independence of the United States of America the sixty third year

Present the worshipful

John Jett		
David Snodgrass		Esquires
and John Bryan		Justices

Isd Ordered by Court that Levi Kerr be appointed Overseer of the road from Hills branch to a post oposite Lewis Phillips being a road of the first Class and keep the same in repair as the law requires and that the same bounds of hands that worked under Lewis Phillips late Overseer thereof be assigned to work thereon.

This day Elizabeth Hill late Elizabeth Pinner being over the age of fourteen years appeared in open Court and made chose of Winkfield Hill to act as her Guardian whereupon the said Winkfield being present in open Court took the oath required by law and together with Elijah Hill and Lewis Pettet entered into and acknowledged bond in the sum of one thousand dollars conditioned as the law requires.

This day Richard Crowder administrator of the estate of Adam Clouse Deceased returned upon oath an account of the sales of the property of the deceased which is ordered to be recorded.

Ordered by Court that Daniel Hollingsworth adminestrator of the estate of James Goddard deceased be allowed the sum of thirty five dollars the amount of his account for services rendered (P-309) the deceased in his last sickness to be by him retained out of said estate.

Ordered by Court that William Harley adminestrator of John Hailey, Sr. des'd be allowed the sum of seventy five Dollars the amount of his account for board &c of the deceased before his death to be by him retained out of the estate of the Decedent.

Isd Ordered by Court that Sevier Evans be appointed Overseer of the public square and all the public streets and alleys with in the bounds of the Corporation of the town of Sparta and keep them in repair as the law requires And that all the hands within the bounds of the Corporation of the town aforesaid be assigned to work thereon.

Ordered by Court that John Taylor be released from the payment of the sum of four dollars and seven mills of the tax of the year 1836, he being overcharged 19 dollars in the value of his land and that the securities of David L. Mitchell late sherriff have a credit therefore in their settlement with the Trustee of White County.

This day Eli Sims adminestrator of Lenias B. Farris deceased returned upon oath an account of the sales of said estate which ordered to be recorded.

Ordered by Court that any persons who shall be guilty or whittling and cutting the late improvement made in the Court house or any part of the Court house itself for each and every offence shall be find at the desgidion of the Court a sum not less than five dollars and it shall be the duty of the Sherriff and his deputies to give information to the Court of each and every offinee aforesaid that may come within his or their knowledged. And it is further ordered that the Clerk of this Court is required to post up at the Court house Door the substance of this Order.

Ordered that Court be adjourned till tomorrow morning 10 O'Clock

John Jett
David Snodgrass
John Bryan

(P-310) Tuesday Morning 4th June 1839 Court met pursuant to adjournment Present the worshipful

John Jett } Esqrs.
David Snodgrass }
and John Bryan } Justices

For reasons appearing to the satisfaction of the Court it is ordered by the Court that John Witt guardian to Elizabeth Hill late Elizabeth Pinner, and his securities from all future and further liabilities therein be released and forever discharged.

Ordered that Court be adjourned untill Court in Course

Test
N. Oldham, Clk.

John Jett
David Snodgrass
John Bryan

State of Tennessee

At a Quarterly Court began and held for the County of White in the Court house in the town of Sparta before the Justices of said Court on the first Monday being the first day of July in the year of our Lord one thousand eight hundred and thirty nine And of the Independence of the United States the 63rd year.

Present the worshipful

Thomas Eastland, Esqr. Chairm.
John Jett, David Snodgrass,
John Bryan, Anderson S. Rogers,
William Knowles, William C. Brittain,
William C. Bounds, Jesse Walling,
Sims Dearing, Matthias Hutson,
James Allison, James Knowles,
William R. Tucker, Isaac Busk,
James Bartlett, John Gillentine,
James T. Hayes, Thomas Green,
Elijah Frost, Asa Certain,
Richard Crowder, George Defrees.

Richard Nelson Esquire this day tendered his resignation as Trustee of Prustly Academy which is ordered to be recorded.

(P-311) Issd Ordered by Court that Joseph Marinor, Esqr. be appointed a Trustee of Prustly Academy in the County of White.

This day the Clerk of this Court exhibited in open Court the report of a settlement made with John Witt late guardian to Elizabeth Hill late Elizabeth Pinner which is received and confirmed in all its parts and ordered to be recorded.

Issd Ordered by Court that the order of the last term of this Court appointing Solomon Yeager, Sr., William Farley, William Wisdom, Elias Yeager, and Robert Denny freeholders a jury of view to lay off and mark a road of the 2nd Class from John W. Dearings across the mountain to Glenns old salt wells be renewed and report thereof to the October term of this Court.

Issd Ordered by Court that the order of last term appoining Robert Anderson, James Randalls, Sr., Joseph Clark, Sr., John Witt, and Sampson Witt, freeholders a jury of view to lay off and mark a road of the second Class from William Knowles to Dillons Bridge in such a manner as not to pass through the land of Hiram Knowles be renewed and report thereof to the next Quarterly term of this Court.

Issd Ordered by Court that the order of the last term appointing William L. Mitchell, John Yates, John Graham, Sr., John Dodson, Sr., and Samuel Miller, freeholders a jury of view to lay off and mark a road of the second Class from William L. Mitchells the nearest and best way to Michael Hendersons and from thence the nearest and best way up the mountain to Thomas Eastlands Mills on Big Laurell Creek be renewed and report thereof to the next quarterly term of this Court.

Ordered by Court that Barger Lowry be appointed overseer of the road from the forks of the Carthage road oposite A. Dibrell to the intersection of the river road being a road of the second class and keep the same in repair as the law requires. And that the same list and bounds of hands that worked under the late Overseer thereof be assigned to work thereon.

Isd Ordered by Court that Isham Cook be appointed Overseer of the road from Hugh Cooks to Ceder Creek being a road of the third Class and keep the same in repair as the law requires and that the same list and bounds of hands that worked under Canada Rigsby late Overseer thereof be assigned to work thereon.

(P-312) Ordered by Court that the following persons be appointed Judges to Superentendant and hold the Election in their respective Districts in White County on the first Thursday in August next to elect one Governer of the state of Tennessee also one member to the Congress of the United States and also a senator and Representative to the general assembly of the State of Tennessee to wit:
In the first District; William C. Brittian; Jonathan C. Davis and Dan Griffith.
In the second District John Bryan; John Austin; John H. Dale -
In the third District Robert Anderson, Thomas Green & Jesse Walling -
In the fourth District Isaiah Hutson; Elijah Denton and Matthias Hutson
In the fifth District William Knowles; Thomas Robertson, John Humphrey, Sr.;
In the Sixth District James T. Hayes; Eli Sims; Henry Camron.
In the Seventh District Henry Burton; James Davis and James Eartham.
In the eight District John Lollar; Ebenezer Jones; Sr.; Abraham Ditty -
In the Ninth District George Defrees, Asa Certain and Richard England.
In the Tenth District Andrew Robinson; William Hill; William C. Bounds -
In the Eleventh District; William Pryor, Jacob Ryder; Thomas Barnes -
In the twelth District; William Glenn Joshua Fox; Davis Weaver.
In the thirteenth District Mark Lowery; John Rose and William Wisdom.
In the fourteenth District Nathaniel C. Davis; John Crook; Elijah Frost, and in District fifteen John Gillentine, Robert Gamble and Jesse Scoggin.

Isd Ordered by Court that the following named persons To Wit: Nathaniel C. Davis; Noah H. Bradley; Samuel V. Carrick; William Simpson and William C. Brittian; Mark Lowery; William Wisdom; Terry Waldon; Jesse Walling, Isham Farley; John Cash; Sr.; Anderson S. Rogers; William Green; Preston A. Chisum; Isaiah Hutson; Joseph Glenn; Jonathan Short; Reuben Broyles; Chisum Randolph; Joseph Pryor; William Rogers; Spense Mitchell; John Gillentine; John Taylor; William Irwin; Sr.; and James Scott freeholders good and lawful men citizens of the County of White be appointed Jurors to attend at the next October term A. D. 1839 of the Honorable Circuit Court for White County and that Hayes Arnold and Charles Meek Constables be appointed to attend on said court and that a writ of Venerifacias issue &c.

This day the Commissioners of the Revinue for White County appointed to Settle with the Trustee &c of White County returned upon oath their report of settlement with the Trustee of White County for the year 1838 which is received by the Court and ordered to be recorded.

(P-313) Isd Ordered by Court unanimously that John Jett one of the Commissioners of the Revinue of White County be allowed the sum of two dollars and fifty cents pr day for four days services in settling with the Trustee of White County and that John Bryan the other Commissioners be allowed two dollars and fifty cents per day for three days services in the settlement aforesaid to be paid by the Trustee of White County out of the taxes of the year 1839.

Isd Ordered by Court that William G. Sims Esqr. Clerk of White Circuit Court be allowed the sum of Ten dollars and fifty cents for a Blank execution Docket Book furnished by him for said Court to be paid by the Trustee of White County out of the tax of the year 1839.

Isd Ordered by Court that Nicholas Oldham Clerk of White County Court be allowed the sum of twenty nine dollars twenty five cents the amount of his act for furnishing two Sherriffs tax Books one for 1838 and one for 1839 - One Commissioners Docket making out the tax list for 1839 and for whitewashing the walls of the Court room to be paid by the Trustee of White County out of the taxes of the year 1839.

Isd Ordered by Court that Jesse Lincoln undertaker of the improvements inside of the Court house of White County to the use of Daniel Clark and Jesse Lincoln be allowed as per contract the sum of one hundred and twenty five dollars also the sum of Twelve dollars for six Benches in the Jury rooms also sixteen dollars for long table Benches in the Court room and extra painting and also the further sum of Ten dollars for steps to the Common Jail of White County as per account this day rendered amounting in all to the sum of one hundred and sixty three dollars to be paid by the Trustee of White County out of the taxes of the year 1839.

Isd Ordered by Court that William Simpson be allowed the sum of Fourteen dollars two cents being the amount of his account for materials furnished the Court house money expended on the trees & Court yards and for materials and work on the Common Jail of said White County to be paid by the Trustee of White County out of the tax of 1839.

Isd It appearing to the satisfaction of the Court that Andrew Cope is entitled to the benifit of a Certain Jury ticket regularly filed in his own name by No. 160 for two dollars in the Trustees office of White County that the same is lost or mislaid and cannot be found and that the same has not been transfered - It is considered and so ordered by the Court; (P-314) that the Trustee pay to the said Andrew Cope the aforesaid sum of Two dollars the amount of said Jury ticket No. 160 filed as aforesaid, and his receipt shall be good in settlement of his accounts.

State) Bastardy
vs Isd) Polly Whitson
William C. Johnson) Pro'x

On motion of the prosecutrix by her attorney and for reasons appearing to the satisfaction of the Court is ordered by the Court that the order made at the Nov. term of this Court 1838 appointing William C. Metcalf Trustee to receive the money from the Defendent to which the prosecutrix in this cause is entitled; be annulled set aside and for nothing esteemed - and it is further ordered that an execution be awarded her for the collection of the forty dollars against said Defendant and David Snodgrass and Thomas B. Johnson his securities returnable &c.

Ordered by Court that the further consideration of the report of the Jury of view from the widow Fitzgeralds old field to entersect Paynes road near John Phillips be laid over untill the next quarterly term of this Court.

This day the Court took into consideration of the report of the Jury of view made at the last term on the road from Cummings ford on Caney fork to entersect the Rockisland at Dentons Store and it is ordered by the Court that the same be established a road of the third Class. And it is further ordered that James W. Copeland be appointed Overseer of said road and open the same as laid off and mark by Com's as a third Class road and keep the same in repair as the law requires - And that Matthias Hutson and Lewis Pettet Esquires assigned a list of hands to work thereon having due regards to the other road in the vicinity.

This day the Commissioners heretofore appointed to lay off and mark a road leaving the Calf Killer road near Wm. C. Metcalf thence the nearest and best way through the board valley to entersect the dry valley road near William Pryor returned their report and it is ordered that the same be established a third Class road and that Venitt Henry be appointed to open the same as marked by the Com's and keep the same in repair as a third Class road and that Sims Dearing and Edmund Stamps Esquire be appointed to assigned a list of hands to work thereon.

(P-315) This day the Jury heretofore appointed to lay off and change the road passing Burrel Manors intersecting again at the Bridge below his house made their report and it is ordered that said road as changed be established and that part of the old road which this order changes be discontinued and that the overseer of the old road be required to keep the same in repair by law.

Ordered by Court that on the application and petition of James H. Jenkins and others for the opening of a road from the south east corner of lot No. 8 in the Corporation of the town of Sparta Eastwardly to intersect the Turnpike road near William Hunters near said town; that an issue be made between James H. Jenkins plaintiff and William Simpson Defendant for the purpose of trying said Case

James H. Jenkins
vs
William Simpson } Petition for Road &c.

This day came the parties by their attornies and upon the production of the report of the Jury of view heretofore filed upon oath in this Cause together with the petition of the plaintiff and after Solomn argument and mature deliberation of the Court thereon had, it seems to the Court and is so considered and so ordered that the report of the Jury of view in this case be set aside and refuse to open & establish said road

James H. Jinkens
vs
William Simpson } Petition for Road &c.

This day came the plaintiff by his attorney and prayed an appeal in the above cause the honorable Circuit Court of White County to be held in the town of Sparta on the first Monday of October next and to him it is granted by his giving bond and security as required by law before the rise of this Court.

Issd Ordered by Court that Elijah Frost be released from the appraised value of an Estray Cow posted by him appraised to Eight dollars the same having died.

Ordered by Court from satisfactory reasons to the Court shown that George Price and Joshua Brown who are liners in their respective districts be hereafter attached and included in the 8th District of White County and are hereby made entitled to all of the privilliges of the Citizens of the Eighth District of said County.

(P-316) This day was exhibited in open Court a writing purporting to be the last will and testament of Thomas Little late of the County of White deceased; Whereupon the due execution and publication thereof as such was proved in open Court by the oath of William G. Sims and Lewis Bohanon, subscribing witness is thereto for the purpose and things therein mentioned and they also made oath that the said Thomas Little was at the date of the execution, declaration and publication thereof as such of sound and disposing mind and memory all of which is ordered to be recorded where upon also Brice Little, David Little and William Snodgrass the executors appointed by the said last will and testament of said Thomas Little deceased appeared in open Court and undertook the burden of the execution of the last will and testament of the aforesaid Thomas Little deceased and thereupon took the oath required by law and together with David Snodgrass, James Snodgrass and William Little entered into and acknowledged bond in the sum of Five Thousand Dollars conditioned as the law requires.

Ordered by Court unanimously that the following described furniture and repairs be furnished and made in the Court house and upon the plank fence in closing the Court house to wit: four substantial poplar table to measure two and half feet by two feet with a drawer and brass knob to each table of the ordenary height for writing tables to be decently painted. Also two dozen strong substantial splitt bottom chairs also to be painted and lettered on the back of each chair with W. C. C. (White County Court) of diffrent color to the other painting. Also that what is now called the Jury box shall be removed entirely and a new floor to be extended of equal height with the new platt form of the bar up to the Justices Bench; also that the Banestering at each ends of said box be extended to correspond with the new banestering around said Bar fully to and be substantially fastened to the Justices bench and also that such painting shall be done thereon and upon said furniture as shall cause the same to correspond with the painting already done therein; and that the posts of the plank fence enclosing the court yard be sawed off in a sloping manner down to the second plank from the top of said fence to be newly capped with first rate thick white oak plank. The gates to be taken away and in place thereof at each opening in said fence erect strong substantial Stiles of first rate white oak timber of such deminsions and height as shall be suitable and fully approved of by the Commissioners of said repairs and such other repairs on said fence as shall be necessary to be done in order to promote the durability and stability of the same; and the whole of the items mentioned in said order be let to the lowest bider on the first Monday of August next bond and security to be required of the undertaker that said work shall be done in a reasonable time to be set by the Commissioners to be paid for out of the taxes of the year 1840.

And it is further ordered that William Simpson, William G. Sims (P-317) & N. Oldham be appointed commissioners to Superentend the letting out and erecting of the repairs and making of the furniture contained in this order and that public notice thereof be posted on the court house door in the town of Sparta emmediately after the rise of this court.

Ordered that Court be adjourned untill tomorrow morning 10 O'Clock

Thos Eastland
David Snodgrass
John Jett

Tuesday Morning July the 2nd 1839 Court met pursuant to adjournment
Present the worshipful

Thomas Eastland }
David Snodgrass } Esquire
and John Jett } Justices.

James H. Jinkens
vs } Petition &c for road
William Simpson

This day came James H. Jinkens the plaintiff in the above cause and together with James R. Herd and John L. Price into open Court and entered into bond and security in the sum of Five hundred dollars conditioned for the prosecution of the appeal prayed in this cause to the next honorable Circuit Court on yesterday.

James H. Jinkens
vs } Petition &c for Road
William Simpson

This day came William Simpson the above defendant into open Court and objects to being made defendant or a party in this cause in the appeal prayed in this cause to the next Circuit Court and the further consideration of the said objection is laid over untill the October term of this Court.

Isd Ordered by Court that William Overby be appointed Overseer of the road from the top of the mountain on the Shipping port road to the entersection of the Lincoln ferry road at the mouth of Oldhams lane being a road of the second Class and keep the same in repair as the law requires and that the same list and bounds of hands that worked (P-318) under Jabez G. Mitchell late Overseer thereof be assigned to work thereon.

Ordered that Court be adjourned untill Court in Course

Test
N. Oldham, Clk.

Thos Eastland
David Snodgrass
John Jett

State of Tennessee

At a Quorum Court began and held for the County of White in the Court house in the town of Sparta before the Justices of said Court on the first Monday being the fifth day of August in the year of our Lord one thousand eight hundred and thirty nine. And of the Independence of the United States of America the sixty fourth year

Present the worshipful

John Jett	)	Esqrs. Quorum
David Snodgrass	)	
& John Bryan	)	Justices

This day was suggested in open Court thet death of George W. Miller late of the County of White and that he departed this life entestate whereupon John L. Price was appointed adminestrator of all and singular the goods and chattles, rights and credits of the Deceased, who being present in open Court took the oath required by law and together with Jonathan T. Bradley and Richard England entered into and acknowledged bond in the sum of two thousand five hundred dollars conditioned as the law requires.

Issd Ordered by Court that Thomas Eastland, John Gipson and Isaac S. Brogdon be appointed Commissioners to assign and set apart one years provision to widow and family of George W. Miller deceased out of his estate and report thereof at the next term of this Court.

(P-319)	The State of Tennessee	)	
	vs	)	Bastardy
	John R. Glenn	)	Clara Cook Prosecutrix

This day came the Defendant John R. Glenn into open court and together with Richard Nelson and Samuel Turney and acknowledged themselves indebted to the County of White in the sum of five hundred dollars to be levied of their respective goods and chattles, lands and tenements to the use of said County to be rendered nevertheless to be void on condition, that the above defendant John R. Glenn shall keep free indemnified and harmless the County of White for any and all costs and changes towards the support of a Bastard child charged to have been begotten on the body of the said Clara Cook the Prosecutrix in this cause.

It is therefore considered by the Court and so ordered that the State of Tennessee to the use of Clara Cook the Prosecutrix recover against the defendant the sum of Ninety dollars to be paid as follows to wit: Forty dollars on or before the expiration of three months from this day, Thirty dollars on or before the fifth day of November 1840, and Twenty dollars on or before the fifth day of November 1841, and it is further considered by the Court that the State recover against said defendant all costs in this behalf expended. And that execution issue &c.

Issd Ordered by Court that Alfred Shaw be appointed Overseer of the Lincoln ferry road from the cross road between Aaron Hutchens and John Shaw to the middle of the Carter old field being a road of the first Class and keep the same in repair as the law requires and that the same bounds of hands that worked under Thomas Prince late Overseer thereof be assigned to work thereon.

Issd Ordered by Court that Joseph Bozarth be appointed Overseer of the Lincoln ferry road from the Peeled Chestnut to the Cross road between Aaron Hutchens and John Shaw being a road of the first Class and keep the same in repair as the law requires and that the same boundary of hands that worked under William R. Tucker late overseer thereof be assigned to work thereon -

Isd Ordered by Court that Jonathan Prince be appointed Overseer of the road from Milton Groces to the middle of the Carter old field on the Lincoln ferry road being a road of the first Class and keep the same in repair as the law requires and that the same boundary of hands that worked under Andrew J. Sims be assigned to work thereon and that Richard Crowder (P-320) and James T. Hayes, Esquire be appointed to establish the old boundary of hands between the different Overseer on the Sims road.

This day John Crook was appointed guardian to Hannah K. Miller and George W. Miller infant children of George W. Miller deceased with permission to appear before the Clerk of this Court at any time between now and the next term of this Court and take the oath and enter into bond and security in the sum of Three Thousand four hundred dollars. And on failure to do so to be void and of no effect.

This day appeared in open Court John W. McGhee over the age of fourteen years and chose for his guardian his father Abraham McGhee whereupon the said Abraham McGhee being present in open Court took the oath prescribed by law and together with Andrew Robinson and David Snodgrass entered into and acknowledged bond in the sum of two hundred dollars conditioned as the law requires.

For reason appearing to the satisfaction of the Court it is Ordered that James Snodgrass, William Wisdom and Thomas Snodgrass be appointed Commissioners to make partition divisions and settlement of the estate of Benjamin Hickman dec'd between the heirs of the Deceased and agreeable to an instrument drawn up and signed by the parties interested and report thereof at the present or next term of this Court.

It appearing to the satisfaction of the Court that William Bartlett one of the security of George Bohanon guardian to the minor heirs of Joseph Henry deceased has removed beyond the limits of the State of Tennessee it is therefore considered by the Court and so ordered that the said William Bartlett be released from all future liability therein and that the said George Bohanon guardian as aforesaid be ruled to give new security for said guardianship.

And the said George Bohanon guardian as aforesaid being present in open Court and with Thomas Welch, Daniel Bartlett and James Snodgrass entered into and acknowledged bond in the sum of Two thousand one hundred Dollars conditioned as the law requires.

Isd Ordered by Court that William R. Doyle be assigned to work on that portion of the milk sick of which Laban Wallis is overseer.

Isd Ordered by Court that John Chisum, Jr., be appointed (P-321) Overseer of the road from the Rockisland to Samuel Moore Esq. being a road of the first Class from the Island to the forks of the road and from thence to moores a second Class and keep the same in repair as the law requires and that the same list and bounds of hands that worked under

Overton Chisum late Overseer thereof be assigned to work thereon.

Issd Ordered by Court that William J. Malloy be appointed Overseer of the road from the middle of the Caney fork at Dales ford to the 10 mile post on the Pikeville road being a road of the second Class and keep the same in repair as the law requires and that the same bounds of hands that worked under the late Overseer thereof be assigned to work thereon.

Issd Ordered by Court that James Simmons be appointed Overseer of the road from the 10 mile post on the Pikeville road to the foot of the mountain being a road of the 2nd Class and keep the same in repair as the law requires and that the same bounds of hands that worked under the late Overseer thereof be assigned to work thereon.

Issd Ordered by Court that Thomas Moore be appointed Overseer of the road from the mouth of Cain Creek to the fork of the McMinnville road being a road of the second Class and keep the same in repair as the law requires.

And that the same bounds of hands that worked under the late Overseer thereof be assigned to work thereon - .

Issd Ordered by Court that John Frisby be appointed Overseer of the road from Moores Old Ford to the forks of the road being a road of the second Class and keep the same in repair as the law requires and that the same bounds of hands heretofore assigned him be assigned to work thereon - .

This day Montgomery Lowry an orphan boy aged 9 years the 20th day of November 1839 was bound to mark Lowry to serve him after the manner of an apprentice untill he attains the age of twenty one years and for the faithful performance of his covenant together with Nicholas Oldham entered into and acknowledged bond conditioned as the law requires.

Ordered that Court be adjourned nutill tomorrow morning at 10 O'clock

John Jett
David Snodgrass
John Bryan

(P-322) Tuesday Morning 6th day of August 1839 Court met pursuant to adjournment Present the worshipful

John Jett
David Snodgrass
and John Bryan
} Esquires
} Justices

This day the Commissioners of the Court house in White County appointed to let out sundry repairs &c made their report which is received and ordered to be recorded.

This day the Commissioners appointed on yesterday to make partition division and settlement between the heirs of Benjamin Hickman, deceased made their report upon oath which is received and ordered to be recorded.

Issd For reasons appearing to the satisfaction of the Court it is ordered that no person white or black or free persons of color shall be permitted to wash clothes or make a fire for the purpose of washing clothes or spread them out for the purpose of Drying at a shorter distance than fifty yards from the abutment of the Bridge at the town of Sparta both up and down the river and on each side of the river or under the bridge and that the Sherriff of White County shall correctly measure the distance of fifty yards above and below the abutments of the bridge on both sides of the river and shall distinctly mark the place by setting a stake substancially in the ground at each place and also he is hereby required to totify the heads of all families in the town of Sparta and on the west side of the river as far as William Brusters that for every contempt and violation of this order by the head of each family or by their permission or neglect shall be fined in a sum of not less than five dollars to be enforced from and after the seventh day of August 1839. And it shall be the imperitive duty of the Sherriff of White County and all his Deputies and also Charles Meek and Hayes Arnolds constables of said County in the first district to return and make known to the County Court of said County for each and every violation of this order at the term next succeeding the offence.

Ordered that Court be adjourned untill Court in Course

John Jett
David Snodgrass
John Bryan

(P-323) State of Tennessee

At a Quorum Court began and held for the County of White in the Court house in the town of Sparta before the Justices of said Court on the first Monday being the second day of September in the year of our Lord One thousand eight hundred and thirty nine and of the Independence of the United States of America the sixty fourth year

Present the worshipful

John Jett,	}	Esq. Quorum
David Snodgrass	}	
and John Bryan	}	Justices

Issd Ordered by Court David McClain be appointed Overseer of the road from the west end of the bridge at the town of Sparta to the ten mile post on the Carthage road being a road of the first Class and keep the same in repair as the law requires and that the same list and bounds of hands that worked under James Lowry late Overseer thereof be assigned to work thereon.

Issd Ordered by Court that Levi Jarvis be appointed Overseer of the road from Richard Crowder to the forks of the Rockisland road being a road of the second Class and keep the same in repair as the law requires and that the same list and bounds of hands that worked under Joseph Rogers late Overseer thereof be assigned to work thereon.

This day the Commissioners heretofore appointed to assign and set apart one years provisions to the widow and family of George W. Miller deceased made their report upon oath which is ordered to be recorded.

This day the death of Nicholas Bennett late of the County of White was suggested in open Court and that he departed this life intestate whereupon James C. Kelly was appointed administrator of all and singular the goods and chattles, rights and credits of the said Nicholas Bennett, Deceased who being present in open Court took the oath required by law and together with Jonathan T. Bradley and John England, Jr., entered into and acknowledged bond in the sum of Five hundred dollars conditioned as the law requires - .

This day Mary Baker and William Baker filed their affidavets to their amended Declarations for a Pension from the United States to the Court known and made oath in due form of law that the contents of the foregoing affidavets are ture which is signed by the Court and ordered to be certified under the seal of this Court.

Issd Ordered by Court that Meridith Baker be appointed Overseer of the road from the town of Sparta to the middle of the Bridge at the Harriett Iron works being a road of the first Class and keep the same in repair as the law requires and that the same list and bounds of hands that worked under J. H. Jenkins late Overseer thereof be assigned to work thereon.

(P-324) Issd Ordered by Court that Jesse A. Bounds be appointed Overseer of the road from Sinking Creek to the forks of the McMinnville road near the iron works being a road of the second Class and keep the same in repair as the law requires and that the same list and bounds of hands that worked under Benjamin Vaughn late Overseer thereof be assigned to work thereon.

Isd Ordered by Court that Isham Rogers be appointed Overseer of the road from Sinking Creek to the top of Gum Spring Mountain being a road of the second Class and keep the same in repair as the law requires and that the same list and bounds of hands that worked under Thomas Roberts late Overseer thereof be assigned to work thereon - .

Ordered by Court that Thomas Broyles; James Yeager; Brice Little, Alexander Office & John Brown freeholders be appointed a Jury of view to lay off, change the Calf Killer road so that the same shall leave the old road about 350 yds on this side of Plumb Creek crossing the Creek below the old ford and entersect the old road again at about 1250 yards the other side of the Creek and report thereof instantly.

This day the Commissioners appointed this day to examine the change proposed in the Calf Killer road crossing Plumb Creek made their report which is received and confirmed and said change or new road established a road of the second Class that William Glenn Esquire open and put same in repair as the law requires at his own proper cost and change and the Overseer of the old road after the new part is put in order keep it in repair as the old road - And the old road to be discontinued -

This day the death of John A. Barron late of the County of White was suggested in open Court and that he departed this life entestate whereupon James H. Jenkins appeared in open Court and was appointed adminestrator of all and singular the goods and chattles; rights and credits of the deceased and took the oath prescribed by law and together with Hugh L. Carrick and John L. Price entered into and acknowledged bond conditioned as the law requires in the sum of Twelve hundred dollars.

For reasons appearing to the satisfaction of the Court it is ordered by the Court that James H. Jenkins adminestrator of the estate of John A. Barron deceased surrender the wearing clothes of the deceased to the father of the deceased.

Ordered by Court that the order of last term appointing John Crook guardian to the heirs of George W. Miller dec'd set aside and for nothing esteemed.

(P-325) Isd Ordered by Court that Thomas Green; James H. Doyle; William Austin; Creed A. Taylor and Joshua Pennington freeholders be appointed a Jury of view to examine and lay off and mark the change proposed by Jesse Walling in the road leading from Doyles Mills to the Gum Spring road and report thereof to the next Quarterly term of this County Court.

This day the death of John A. Fryer late of the County of White was suggested in open Court and that he departed this life intestate whereupon; William Green being present in open Court was appointed adminestrator of all and singular the goods and chattles; rights and credits of the deceased who took the oath required by law and together with Thomas Green, James H. Doyle & William Simpson entered into and acknowledged bond in the sum of four thousand dollars conditioned as the law requires.

This day Joshua Mason adminestrator of Caleb Mason deceased returned upon oath with an additional account of sales of the property of said estate which is ordered to be recorded.

Issd For reasons appearing to the satisfaction of the Court from the statement of John R. Glenn that a certain female by the name of Elizabeth Lansdale a citezen of the County of White being aged and infirm and in a destitute condition and likely to suffer for the necessaries to support life - whereupon it is ordered that the aforesaid Ekizabeth Lansdale be conveyed to the poor house of White County to be there supported and maintained at the proper cost and charges of White County and that Robert B. Glenn convey the said Elizabeth to said poor house at his own cost and charge.

Issd This day was exhibited in open Court a writing purporting to be the last will and testament and codicil of Robert Mitchell, Sr., deceased late of the County of White and thereupon the due execution and publication of said writing as the last will and testament and Codicil of the said Robert Mitchell, Sr., was proved in open Court by the oath of James William one of the subscribing witness thereto for the purposes, things therein mentioned and at the same time made oath that the said Robert Mitchell, Sr., was at the date of the execution and publication of said last will and testament and Codicil of sound and disposing mind and memory all of which is ordered to be recorded.

It appearing fully to the satisfaction of the Court that Jabez G. Mitchell the other subscribing witness to the last will and testament and Codicil of Robert Mitchell, Sr., late of the County of White deceased is so wounded and otherwise disabled by sickness that he cannot with safety appear in open court for the purpose of authenticating the will and testament aforesaid and in all likelihood will be absent from the County of White at the next term of this Court and it further appearing to (P-326) this Court that the provisions of the will and the interest of the estate of the Deceased required active operation therein. It is therefore considered and so ordered that Nicholas Oldham, Clerk of this Court shall proceed to go to the house of Jabez G. Mitchell the witness aforesaid and swear him in due form of law, touching the due execution and publication of the aforesaid last will and testament and Codicil of the said Robert Mitchell, Sr., dec'd and also as to his soundness of mind and memory and report thereof tomorrow at the setting of the Court.

Ordered that Court be adjourned untill tomorrow 10 O'Clock

John Jett
David Snodgrass
John Bryan

Tuesday Morning 3rd September A. D. 1839 Court met pursuant to adjournment Present the worshipful

John Jett
David Snodgrass } Esquires
John Bryan } Justices

This day Nicholas Oldham Clerk of White County Court in obedience to an order of the worshipful County Court on yesterday proceeded to the house of Jabez G. Mitchell in White County who is a subscribing witness to the will and Codicil of Robert Mitchell, Sr. late of White County Deceased on the 3rd day of September in the year 1839 and the aforesaid Clerk did then and there cause the aforesaid Jabez G. Mitchell to swear upon the holy Evangelist of Almighty touching the execution of the said last will and testament of the said Robert Mitchell Deceased and who upon oath deposed that he the said Robert Mitchell, Sr., did sign seal execution and publish the said writing as his last will and testament and codicil for the purpose and things therein mentioned - And also made oath that the said Robert Mitchell, Sr. was at the date of the execution and publication of the said last will and testament and codicil of sound and disposing mind and memory which is ordered to be recorded whereupon personally appeared in open Court Spince Mitchell and David Mitchell, Sr., Executors appointed by the last will and testament and codicil of the said Robert Mitchell, Sr., and agreed and thereupon undertook upon themselves the burden of the execution of the said last will and testament of said Deceased and severally took the oath required by law and together with David Snodgrass and John Jett entered into and acknowledged Bond in the sum of Three thousand dollars conditioned as the law required.

(P-327) Issd Ordered by Court that Sevier Evans Overseer of the streets, square, alleys in the town of Sparta be and he is hereby required to work on that portion of the Allens ferry road from the west end of the bridge at the town of Sparta to the forks of the Carthage road at Oldhams being a road of the first Class and keep the same in repair as the law requires - And that William Bruster and all his hands and all the hand within the limits of the Corporation of Sparta except George Ogden, John Cook, Nicholas Cook and David Cook, Simon Bramblett, Isaac Rogers, Curtis P. Anderson, William G. Sims, William B. Hall, Mr. Drake, Nat Bramblett, Jeremiah Franklin be assigned to work on that portion or lot of road which is by this order added to the said Sevier Evans and it is further ordered that Daniel McClains order only commence at the forks of the Carthage road - Bruster and his hands to be excepted in his list.

Issd Ordered by Court that the road leading from the town of Sparta up the river to the ford below Andersons old salt well be raised from a third to a second Class road and that William G. Sims Esquire be appointed Overseer from the public square in the town of Sparta to said ford and keep the same in repair as the law requires and that the following list and bounds of hands be assigned to work therein to wit:

George Ogden, Nicholas Cook, John Cook, David Cook, Simon Bramblett, Isaac Rogers, Curtis P. Anderson, David Dean, William B. Hall, Mr. Drake, Nat Bramblett, Jeremiah Franklin be assigned to work thereon.

Issd Ordered by Court that David Snodgrass and Sims Dearing, Esqs. be appointed to apportion lists and bounds of hands between James Yeager and Phillip Bradly Overseers having due regard to the grades of the different roads.

For reasons appearing to the satisfaction of the Court it is ordered that Nathaniel C. Hopkins who was some years since bound to Robert B. Glenn as an apprentice be released from his Indenture and the said Robert B. Glenn from the performance of his covenant be released and forever discharged, provided however the said Glenn shall pay unto the said N. C. Hopkins the sum of Eight dollars in money and give him also one new suit of homespun wearing apparel.

Ordered that Court be adjourned untill Court in Course.

John Jett
David Snodgrass
John Bryan

Test
N. Oldham, Clk.

(P-328) State of Tennessee

At a County Court began and held for the County of White and state aforesaid in the Court house in the town of Sparta before the Justices of said Court on the first day being the seventh day of October in the year One thousand eight hundred and thirty nine And of the Independence of the United States of America the sixty fourth.

Present the worshipful

Thomas Eastland, Esquire Chairman
John Bryan; David Snodgrass; Elijah Frost; Anderson S. Rogers; Jesse Walling; William Knowles; Lewis Pettett; William C. Bounds; William C. Brittian, George Defrees; Asa Certain; James Allison; James Knowles; Matthias Hutson; Isaac Buck; Richard Crowder, Thomas Green; James Bartlett; John Gillentine; William R. Tucker. } Esquire Justice

This day Nicholas Oldham Clerk of White County Court produced in open Court all the receipts which he was required by law to do; which the Court ordered to be recorded as follows:

Comptrollers office 23 September 1839

Received of N. Oldham his Statement of Revinue Collected as Clerk of White County Court from 1st Sept. 1838 to 1st Sept. 1839

Amount Collected		563.92
Commissions	14.05	
Paid Jett & Bryan	5.-	19.05

Warrent No 866 this day for 544.83

Daniel Graham
Comptroller of the Treasure

Nashville 23 Sept 1839 No. 866 . . . . $544.83

Received of N. Oldham; Esq Five hundred and forty four dollars 83 cents audited to him by No. 866 and due on accounts of Revinue by him collected as clerk of White County Court from the 1st Sept 1838 to 1st Sept. 1839

Signed Duplicates

M. Francis
Treasure of Tennessee

Received of Nicholas Oldham Clerk of White County Court the abstract Statement of the County tax; Jury Tax, and Bridge tax of said County for the year 1839 amounting to the sum of Fourteen hundred and fourteen dollars twenty four cents and one mill (1414.24.1) this 16th day of September A. D. 1839

Ro. Cox Trustee of White County Received of Nicholas Oldham Clerk of White County Court (P-329) the sum of Five hundred and fifty four dollars seventy three cents ($254.73) being the amount of his account this day rendered for monies by him received by value of his office; as tax on priviliges in said County to use of said County for the year ending the 1st day of September 1839 - This 17th day of September A. D. 1839

Ro. Cox; Trustee
of White County

Received of Nicholas Oldham Clerk of White County Court the abstract Statement of the poor tax of said County for the year 1839 amounting to the sum of six hundred and forty three dollars; seventy eight cents and eight mills ($643.78.8)
This 11th Sept 1839

John Jett Treasure of
the Poor house Commission of White Cty.

Isd Ordered by Court that Elias Yeager be appointed Overseer of the road from the foot of the hill at James Snodgrass to the corner of Wisdoms field being a road of the 2nd Class and keep the same in repair as the law requires and that the same bounds of hands that worked under the former Overseer thereof be assigned to work thereon.

This day Anthony Dibrell was appointed guardian to Edward Watkins alias Edward P. Garrett who being present in open Court took the oath required by law and together with John W. Simpson and Richard Nelson entered into and acknowledged bond in the sum of four hundred Dollars conditioned as the law requires.

Ordered by Court that the road leading from Joseph Hunter to the top of the mountain be disannulled.

Isd Ordered by Court that the lot of road over which John A. Ross is Overseer be extended to the Flatt Rock and the hands of Joseph Hunter and William Murphy be added to said Pass's list of hands - And that all the hands on Brice Littles plantation be assigned to work on the road under that portion of which John Littles is overseer.

Isd Ordered by Court that the hands from Doe Creek and Alexander Lowry Eastwardly be assigned to work that portion of the road of which James Beckwith is Overseer.

Isd Ordered by Court that Reubin Broyles be appointed Overseer of the road from the fork of the road north of Snodgrass Mill to Plumb Creek being a road of the second Class and keep the same in repair as the law requires and that the same bounds of hands that worked under John B. Bradly late; Overseer thereof be assigned to work thereon.

(P-330) This day Vashti Glenn was appointed guardian to her infant children namly Robert S. Glenn, Joseph W. Glenn; William F. Glenn and Sarah Jane Glenn and being present in open Court took the oath required by law and together with Joseph Glenn and James Knowles entered into and acknowledged bond in the sum of eight hundred dollars conditioned as the law requires.

Isd Ordered by Court that William Metcalf be appointed Overseer of the road from Plumb Creek to the 10 mile post being a road of the second Class and keep the same in repair as the law requires and that the same bounds of hands that worked under James Yeager late Overseer thereof be assigned to work thereon.

Isd Ordered by Court that Jesse Walling and John Jett; Esqs. be appointed Commissioners to apportion bounds and list of hands between Jesse A. Bounds and William Overby Overseer of the Shipping Port road having due regard to the grades of the two roads - And report to next Quarterly term.

Issd by Court that James H. Doyle be appointed Overseer of the road from Hills Branch to Jesse Wallings being a road of the first Class and keep the same in repair as the law requires and that the same bounds of hands that worked under Baler Holder late Overseer thereof be assigned to work thereon.

Issd Ordered by Court that Simon R. Doyle Coroner of White County be allowed the sum of five dollars for holding an Inquest over the body of a certain Judith Frasure a Citizen of White County to be paid by the Treasure of the poor house out of any monies not otherwise appropriated. The report of the Jury of Inquest being received by the Court and ordered to be recorded.

Issd Ordered by Court that William G. Martin be appointed Overseer of the road from Dews Mill to the two mile post east of Bunkers hill being a road of the first and keep the same in repair as the law requires and that the same bounds of hands that worked under the late Overseer thereof be assigned to work thereon.

Issd Ordered by Court that James Allison and William Hitchcock Esquires be appointed commissioners to apportion list and bounds of hands between W. G. Martin and the Overseer of the Rockisland road and report to next 1/4ly Court.

This day the Clerk of this Court reported a settlement made with Wm. Haily, admr. of John Haily deceased which is confirmed and ordered to be recorded.

(P-331) This day the Clerk of this Court reported a settlement made with Creed A. Taylor, adminestrator of Micajah Taylor deceased which is confirmed and ordered to be recorded.

Ordered by Court that Creed A. Taylor adminestrator of the Estate of Micajah Taylor deceased be allowed the sum of Two hundred and three dollars 96½ cents the amount of his account for mony expended in settling said estate and for loss in exchange of mony to be by him retained out of the Estate of the deceased - .

Issd Ordered by Court that the order of July term last appointing Robert Anderson, James Randalls, Sr., Joseph Clark, Sr., John Witt and Sampson Witt freeholders a Jury of view to lay off and mark a road of the second Class from William Knowles to Dillons Bridge in such a manner as not to pass through the land of Hiram Knowles be renewed and report thereof to the next quarterly term of this Court.

Issd This day was produced in open Court a writing purporting to be the last will and testament of Zebidee Seals late of the County of White deceased and the due execution and publication thereof as such was proved in open Court by the oaths of William Denny, David Worley and J. S. Parker the subscribing witnesses thereto for the purposes therein contained and at the same time made oath that the said Zebedee Seals was at the date of the execution and publication thereof of sound and disposing mind and memory which is ordered to be recorded.

Ordered by Court that the further consideration of the report of the Jury of view on the road from Fitzgerolds old field to entersect Paynes road be continued untill the next quarterly term of this Court.

Ordered by Court that Susannah Duncan adminestratrix of the estate of William Duncan deceased be allowed the sum of Two hundred and fifty dollars the amount of her account for the support and amintainance of her five infant children and for schooling some of them to be by her retained out of the estate of the deceased.

This day Susannah Duncan guardian to the heirs of William Duncan deceased made her report upon oath which is ordered to be recorded.

This day William Green admr. of John A. Fryer deceased returned upon oath an Inventory and acct. of sales of said estate which is ordered to be recorded.

(P-332) This day the death of Benjamin Vaughn late of the County of White was suggested in open Court and that he departed this life entestate whereupon Nancy Vaughn appeared in open Court and was appointed adminestratrix of all and singular the goods and Chattles, rights and credits of the deceased and took the oath prescribed by law and together with Joseph Herd and Anderson S. Rogers entered into and acknowledged bond in the sum of four hundred dollars conditioned as the law requires - .

Isd Ordered by Court that, that portion of the road from the middle of the Carter old field to the DeKalb County line be equally divided between Joseph Bozarth and Alfred Shaw and that they respectively keep the same in repair as the law requires. And that James Knowles, James T. Hayes and Richard Crowder, Esqrs. apportion lists and bounds of hands between them and the Overseer of the Shipping port road - .

Ordered by Court that what is Called the Shipping port road leading from the mouth of Oldhams land across the mountain to Shipping port be reduced from a second to a third Class road.

Isd Ordered by Court that William Burden be appointed Overseer of the road from Pleasant Wallers to the Gap of the Mountain at Lowrys old place being a road of the second Class and keep the same in repair as the law requires. And that the same bounds of hands that worked under Absalum McCoy late Overseer thereof be assigned to work thereon.

This day Richard Crowder and James T. Hayes Esquires returned a list of hands assigned to Jonathan Prince Overseer of the road as follows towit: Melton Grose, Larkin Stuart, Larkin Yates, E. P. Sims, John Simpson, Benjamin F. Moore, Alexander Irwin, John W. Cope, Lockheart Irwin, Eli Sims's Lewis, James Pirtle, Hirm Vermillion and Foster Pirtle which is ordered to be recorded.

For reasons appearing to the satisfaction of the Court it is ordered by Court that John Jett, Joseph Herd and Joseph Cummings Esquires Commissioners of the poor house of the County of White are hereby required to employ Jonathan C. Davis, Esq. the principal surveyor of said County to measure and distinctly mark the lines of the several tracts which compose the tract of land upon which the poor house of said County is situated and report thereof to the next quarterly term of this Court.

Ordered by Court that Asa Certain the guardian to the minor heirs of Edward Holmes deceased who this day appeared in open Court and resigned said guardianship together with his securities be released and forever discharged from all future liabilities therein.

(P-333) Isd Ordered by Court that Solomon Wilhite be appointed Overseer of the road from Glades Creek to Rum Creek being a road of the second Class and keep the same in repair as the law requires and that the same bounds of hands that worked under Stephen Farley late Overseer thereof be assigned to work thereon -.

Ordered by Court that George McGhee be released from the payment of the poll tax on one Black poll for the year 1833 & 1834 and also from the tax on 97½ acres land for the year 1831 he being overcharged and that the securities of David L. Mitchell late Sherriff of White County have a credit thereof in the settlement of their accounts - .

This day Nancy Holmes and William J. Bennett appeared in open Court and were appointed guardian to Alphonso and Maniza Holmes infant heirs of Edward Holmes deceased and took the oath required by law and together with George Defrees and Anthony Dibrell entered into and acknowledged bond of three Thousand Dollars conditioned as the law requires - .

Ordered by Court that William McKinny be allowed the sum of Ten dollars being the amount of his account against the Estate of George W. Miller Deceased to be paid by the adminestrater out of the Estate of the deceased.

Isd Ordered by Court that Finis E. Plumlie and William McGuire be assigned to work on that portion of the road of which Thomas Moore is Overseer.

Isd Ordered by Court that John Lisk be appointed Overseer of the road from the two mile post to the four mile post being a road of the first Class and keep the same in repair as the law requires and that the same bounds of hands that worked under Osburn Walker late Overseer thereof be assigned to work thereon -

This day John Knowles and Caroline C. Knowles late; Caroline C. Gibbs appeared in open Court and both being over the age of fourteen years selected and made choice of Isaiah Hutson as their guardian who also being present in open court took the oath required by law and together with Stephen G. Buxton and Smith J. Walling entered into and acknowledged bond in the sum of eight hundred dollars conditioned as the law requires.

This day Stephen G. Buxton appearing in open Court and was appointed guardian to Sylvester C. Gibbs and took the oath prescribed by law and together with Thomas T. Crowder and Isaiah Hutson entered into and acknowledged bond in the sum of Eight hundred dollars conditioned as the law requires.

(P-334) Isd Ordered by Court that Preston Anderson be appointed Overseer of the road from near William Prices to the middle of slash where Isaac Howard now lives being a road of the second class and keep the same in repair as the law requires and that the same bounds of hands that worked under Jonathan Scott late Overseer thereof be assigned to work thereon.

This day Noah H. Bradley appeared in open Court and was appointed Guardian to Hannah Miller and George Miller infant heirs of George W. Miller deceased who took the oath prescribed by law and together with Jonathan T. Bradley, Richard England and John England, Jr., entered into and acknowledged bond in the sum of Three Thousand Dollars conditioned as the law requires.

This day James Allison appeared in open Court and was appointed guardian to Andrew Jackson Massa, and took the oath prescribed by law and together with Jose C. Dew and Henry Colier entered into and acknowledged bond in the sum of four hundred Dollars conditioned as the law requires.

Issd Ordered by Court that William Frisby be appointed Overseer of the road from the pole bridge to the fork of the road at Stuarts being a road of the second Class and keep the same in repair as the law requires and that the same bounds of hands that worked under the late Overseer thereof be assigned to work thereon.

Issd Ordered by Court that that part of the order of July term last appointing William L. Mitchell, John Yates - John Graham Sr., John Dodson, Sr., and Samuel Miller, freeholders a Jury of view to lay off and mark a road from the ford of the river next above Samuel Millers the nearest and best way up the mountain to Eastland Mill on Big laurel passing Michael Hendersons be renewed and report thereon to the next quarterly term of this Court - .

Issd Ordered by Court that the road leading from the forks at William L. Mitchell up the Caney fork to the ford across the river next above Samuel Millers be established a road of the second Class. And that Samuel Miller be appointed Overseer from the ford next above his house to the first ford below John Dodsons. And that James Graham be appointed Overseer from that point to the fork at William L. Mitchells and keep the same in repair as the law requires and that Anderson S. Rogers and John Bryan Esqs. apportion bounds of hands to each Overseer chosen.

Issd Ordered by Court that Joshua Stansbury be appointed Overseer of the road from the middle of the Bridge at the Harriett Iron Works to the widow Smiths gate being a road of the first Class and keep the same in repair as the law requires and that the same bounds of hands that worked under Washington Webb late Overseer thereof be assigned to work thereon.

(P-335) Issd Ordered by Court that the order of last term appointing Thomas Green, James H. Doyle, William Austin, Creed Taylor and Joshua Pennington freeholders a Jury of view to lay off and examine and mark the change proposed by Jesse Walling in the road leading from Doyles mills to the Gum Spring road be renewed and report thereof to the next quarterly term of this Court.

Ordered by Court that Isaac Buck, James Bartlett, William Bohanon, John L. Hyder and Goodman Madewell freeholders be appointed a Jury of view to change the road commincing on the Hill the other side of the widow Doyles passing Charles Penningtons and entersect the old road again at the lower end of the widow Doyles lane and report thereof.

And the Jurors aforesaid being present in open Court after being sworn made their report which is received by the Court and said change established.

Isd Ordered by Court that Jesse Walling and Thomas Green Esqs. be appointed to apportion lists and bounds of hands between John Holder, Jr. and James W. Copeland Overseers having due regard to the dignity of their respective roads - .

This day John L. Price administrator of George W. Miller deceased returned upon oath an Inventory and accounts of sales of the property of the estate of the deceased which is ordered to be recorded.

Ordered by Court that the following named persons be appointed commissioners of the Revinue in White County for the year 1840 To wit:
In the first District John Jett, Esq.
In the second District John Bryan, Esq.
In the third District Thomas Green, Esq.
In the fourth District Lewis Pettett, Esq.
In the fifth District James Knowles, Esq.
In the sixth District James T. Hayes, Esq.
In the 8th District Wm. Hitchcock, Esq.
In the 9th District George Defreese, Esq.
In the 10th District William C. Bounds, Esq.
In the 11th District Isaac Buck, Esq.
In the 12th District Sims Dearing, Esq.
In the 13th District William R. Tucker, Esq.
In the 14th District Elijah Frost, Esq., and
In the 15th District John Gillentine, Esq.

Isd Ordered by Court that Amasa Jones be appointed Overseer of the road from the Flatt Rock to the Stage road being a road of the 2nd Class and keep the same in repair as the law requires and that the same list of hands that worked under James Beckwith late Overseer thereof be assigned to work thereon - , together with those this day assigned.

Isd Ordered by Court that Samuel Lance Be appointed (P-336) Overseer of the road from Dentons Mills to the Turnpike road at A. Lowrys being a road of the second Class and keep the same in repair as the law requires and that the same bounds of hands that worked under the late Overseer thereof be assigned to work thereon.

Isd Ordered by Court unanimously that the follow/ing persons be allowed the following sums for fees in the following State cases which have been examined by the attorney general for White County and certified by him as correctly taxed and properly chargeable to said County of White To wit: In the case the State against John Wallis for gaming, Clerk W. G. Sims 5.50 Sherriff John England 1.62½ In case the State vs Robert Burk Clerk W. G. Sims 1.48¾, Sherriff P. R. Grissom of Bledsoe County 62½ cents In the case the State vs James C. Baker Clerk Sims $4.12½ Sherriff J. T. Bradley 62½ cents. The State vs Presby Holland for A. B. Clerk W. G. Sims 2.56¼ Shff. S. J. Walling 275 Justice Thomas Green 50 cents Andrew Cope 1.50 witness Jesse Walling 1.50 Wit. Isaac Denton 1.50 witness W. B. Taylor 1.50, witness Cornelius Jarvis 1.50, witness Thomas Hawks 1.50 The State against John C. Lincoln clerk W. G. Sims 6.12½ John England 1.25 Sheff. S. J. Walling 37½ Shff. J. G. Mitchell 0.25 cents witness William

Garland 2.25. The State against William Rigsby clerk W. G. Sims 8.62½ Shff John England 1.25 Sherriff J. G. Mitchell 2.12½ Shff William H. Baker 25 cents Sherriff J. T. Bradley 37½ cents witness Stephen Cole 75; witness Lee R. Taylor 75; witness Jesse Allen 1.50. The State vs Thomas Stipe Clerk W. G. Sims 6.00 Shff J. T. Bradley 1.25. Shff. S. J. Walling 87½ cents The State vs John A. Pass clerk W. G. Sims 3.56¼. Shff J. T. Bradley 93¾ cents. The State against Robert Hewett Clerk W. G. Sims 4.50 D. Shff John England 1.25 cents The State vs John Lamb clerk W. G. Sims 3.56½ Shff J. T. Bradley 93¾. The State vs Walker Harrison clerk W. G. Sims 6.18¾ Shff S. J. Walling 1.12½. Shff John England 50 cents - Shff John H. Graham 75 cents Shff John Baker 25 cents - Jailor Robert H. McManus 7.37½ witness William Jones 1.75. Mary Jones 1.75. Sharp R. Whitley 1.75. James P. Ford 1.50 Jesse Kerby 1.75. The State vs Lewis Fletcher clerk W. G. Sims 6.75. Shff. John England 2.00 Shff S. J. Walling 2.00 witness Jesse A. Bounds 75 cents witness W. Simpson 3.00. The State vs George and Abraham Broyles Clerk W. G. Sims 1.06¼ Shff J. T. Bradley 50 cents Shff S. J. Walling 25 cents. The State against Robert Hewett Clerk W. G. Sims 5.75. Shff J. T. Bradley 1.57½. Shff J. G. Mitchell 25 cents. The State vs William Matlock clerk W. G. Sims 5.12½ cents D. Shff John England $1.37½ amounting in all to the sum of one hundred and thirty five dollars thirty seven and a half cents to be paid by the Trustee of White County out of any monies not otherwise appropriated.

Issd Ordered by Court that Albert Davis be appointed Overseer of the road from Blue Spring branch to a branch south of James W. Nelson being a road of the second Class and keep the same in repair as the law requires and that the same bounds of hands that worked under John Taylor late overseer thereof be assigned to work thereon.

(P-337) Issd This day the death of Miles A. Camp late of the County of White Deceased was suggested in open Court and at the same time a writing was produced purporting to be the nuncupative will of the said Miles A. Camp dec'd whereupon the same in like manner was proved by the oath of Willis Steakley and Jane Camp in whose presence the statement made by said Miles A. Camp, concerning the disposition of his property as he wished; and they particularly called upon and that the said Miles A. Camp was at the time of making said Statement and giving said direction was of sound and disposing mind and memory, and that said enstructions and directions concerning the disposal of his effects was by said Willis Steakley and Jane Camp reduced to writing within six days after making said directions and also after the death of the testator and that said writing here produced contains the whole of said enstructions and directions given as aforesaid in his last illness and shortly before his death which is deemed by the Court to be properly and sufficiently proved and ordered to be recorded.

Ordered by Court that it be adjourned untill tomorrow 10 O'clock

Thos Eastland
David Snodgrass
John Bryan

uesday Morning 8th day of October A. D. 1839 Court met pursuant to adjournment Present the Worshipful

Thomas Eastland, Esq. Chairman
David Snodgrass }
John Bryan } Esq. Justices

Ordered that Court be adjourned until Court in Course

Thos. Eastland
David Snodgrass
John Bryan

Test
N. Oldham

(P-338) State of Tennessee

At a County Court began and held for the County of White in the State aforesaid in the Count house in the town of Sparta before the Justices of said Court on the first Monday being the fourth day of November in the year of our Lord One Thousand eight hundred and thirty nine. And of the Independence of the United States of America the Sixty fourth year

Present the Worshipful

John Jett, David Snodgrass } Esq
John Bryan, Lewis Pettett } Justices
James Allison and Jesse Walling }

This day James H. Jenkins exhibited in open Court his stock mark to wit: A smooth crop off each ear and two Splitts in the right which is ordered to be recorded.

This day David Snodgrass exhibited in open Court his Stock mark to wit: A crop off the left and crop and under half crop off the right ear which is ordered to be recorded - .

This day William Hitchcock exhibited in open Court his stock mark to wit: A crop and split in the left ear which is ordered to be recorded. -

This day the Clerk of this Court produced a settlement made with Benjamin Hutchins one of the administrators of Webster Hutchens Deceased which is received by the Court confirmed in all its parts and ordered to be recorded - .

This day Benjamin Hutchens was appointed guardian to John Clouse and Adam Clouse minor heirs of William Clouse deceased being under the age of fourteen years and also appeared in open Court John F. Clouse Minor heir of Adam Clouse deceased being over the age of fourteen years and made choice of the said Benjamin Hutchens as his guardian who also being present in open Court took the oath required by law and together with William H. Baker and William G. Sims entered into and acknowledged bond in the sum of four hundred dollars conditioned as the law requires.

This day the death of William W. Crawford late of the County of White was suggested in open Court and that he departed this life intestate whereupon William D. Crawford was appointed administrator of all and singular the goods and chattles, rights and credits of the deceased who took the oath required by law and together with Richard Nelson and Anthony Dibrell entered into and acknowledged bond in the sum of five thousand dollars conditioned as the law required.

(P-339) Issd Ordered by Court that the Sherriff of White County bring into open Court at the next term thereof a certain orphan boy named William P. Worley to be dealt by as the law directs.

This day Washington Gibbs Little a minor heir of Thomas Little deceased being over the age of fourteen years came into open Court and made choice of Brice Little as his guardian who being present in open Court took the oath prescribed by law and together with William Little and David Little entered into and acknowledged bond in the sum of Fifteen Hundred dollars conditioned as the law requires - .

Ordered by Court that Simon R. Doyle be released from the appraised value of an estray cow posted in the year 1838 which escaped from him.

This day William Hitchcock exhibited in open Court his Declaration for a Pension from the government of the United States together with Levi Perkins a Clergyman to the Court known and also Jacob Anderson and John Bryan Citizens of the County of White in like manner known who being duly sworn in open Court to the facts contained in their respective affidavits which is also signed by the Court and ordered to be certified under the seal of this Court.

This day the Commissioners heretofore appointed to assign a list and bounds of hands to Venett Henry Overseer of the road made their report which is ordered to be recorded towit: William Searbrough; James Searbrough; Preston Bowman, John Slaten, Jonathan Vincent; Harrison Whitson; William Bowman; John Brumbalow; James Whitson, William Carder; William Jay; James A. Jay; Harry McCamish, William Lowry and Andrew Henry.

Isd Ordered by Court that Anthony Dibrell; John Bryan and Thomas Robertson be appointed commissioners to assign and set apart One years provisions to the widow and family of Woodson P. White Deceased out of the estate of the deceased, and report thereof to the next term of this Court.

This day the death of Woodson P. White late of the County of White was suggested in open Court and that he departed this life entestate whereupon William M. Young was appointed adminestrator of all and singular the goods and chattles; rights and credits of the deceased and it being suggested to the Court that owing to the ill health of the said William M. Young he is unable to appear in open Court to be sworn and enter into Bond it is therefore ordered that the Clerk of this Court proceed to the dwelling house of the said William M. Young which is in the town (P-340) of Sparta and procure his signature to the Bond for the faithful performance of his adminestration and to adminester the oath required by law which said clerk done accordingly and thereupon appeared in open Court John Jett; John Warren; Anthony Dibrell; William M. Bryan; John Mitchell; Edward M. Murry and Joseph Herd entered into and acknowledged with the said William M. Young in the sum of forty thousand Dollars conditioned as the law requires.

Isd Ordered by Court that John A. Bradford be released from the payment of the tax on one hundred dollars value of school land for the year 1839 amounting to the sum of twenty one and one fourth cents - And that the Sherriff of White County have a credit thereof in the settlement of his accounts.

Ordered that Court be adjourned till tomorrow Morning at 9 O'clock

John Jett
John Bryan

Tuesday Morning 5th day of November A.D. 1839 Court met pursuant to adjournment Present the worshipful

John Jett } Esqrs.
John Bryan } Justices.

Ordered that Court be adjourned untill Court in Course

Test — John Jett
N. Oldham; Clk. — John Bryan

(P-341) State of Tennessee

At a Court began and held for the County of White in the Court house in the town of Sparta before the Justices of said Court on the first Monday being the second day of December in the year of our Lord one thousand eight hundred and thirty nine and of the Independence of the United States of America the Sixty fourth year.

Present the worshipful

John Jett
David Snodgrass
John Bryan

Esquires

Justices

This day the Clerk of this Court produced in open Court a report of a settlement made with John Massa administrator of John Massa, Sr. deceased which is received and confirmed by the Court and which is ordered to be recorded.

This day the Commissioners heretofore appointed to set apart and assign One years provisions to the widow and family of Woodson P. White deceased made their report which is ordered to be recorded.

This day was produced in open Court a writing purporting to be the last will and testament of Marshall Duncan late of the County of White Deceased, and the due execution and publication thereof as such was proved in open Court by oath of Andrew McBride and Elijah L. Golden subscribing witness thereto for the purposes therein contained and that the said Marshall Duncan was at the date of the execution and publication thereof of sound and desposing mind and memory which is ordered to be recorded and the same day Solomon Duncan the executor mentioned in that last will and testament of the deceased appeared in open Court and agreed to take upon himself the burden of the execution thereof and thereupon took the oath prescribed by law and together with Andrew McBride and James Snodgrass entered into and acknowledged bond in the sum of twelve hundred dollars conditioned as the law requires.

Ordered by Court that Jacob Anderson, Sr. be appointed guardian to Mary C. Brittain, Joseph L. Brittain and Thomas L. Brittain infant children of William C. Brittain deceased who being present in open Court and took the oath required by law and together with William Hitchcock and James Snodgrass entered into and acknowledged bond in the sum of two hundred Dollars conditioned as the law requires.

This day George Bohanon guardian to the minor heirs of Joseph Henry deceased returned his report upon oath which is ordered to be recorded.

(P-342) This day the death of Jeremiah T. Witt late of the County of White was suggested in open Court and that he departed this life intestate whereupon William Hailey appeared in open Court and was appointed administrator of all and singular the goods and chattles, rights and credits of the Deceased and took the oath prescribed by law and together with William Pettett and James Frisby entered into and acknowledged bond in the sum of six hundred Dollars conditioned as the law requires.

Ised Ordered by Court that Robert Anderson, Sr., James W. Copeland and James Adair be appointed Commissioners to assign and set apart out of the Estate of Jeremiah T. Witt, Deceased one years provisions for the support and maintainance of the widow and family of the Deceased and report thereof to the next term of this Court.

This day William Preston Worley aged Ten years on the 26th day of May 1839 was bound to James T. Glenny to serve him after the manner of an apprentice to learn the Saddlers trade untill he shall arrive at the age of twenty one years and for the faithful performance of his covenant entered into and acknowledged bond as the law requires.

William Snodgrass appeared in open Court and exhibited his Stock mark to wit: a smooth crop of the left ear and a slope of the under side of the right ear which is ordered to be recorded.

This day James H. Jenkins administrator of John A. Barron Deceased returned upon oath an Inventory and account of sales of the Estate of the Deceased which is ordered to be recorded.

Ordered that Court be adjourned untill tomorrow Morning 11 O'clock

John Jett
David Snodgrass
John Bryan

Tuesday morning 3rd December A.D. 1839
Present the worshipful

John Jett)
David Snodgrass) Esquires
John Bryan) Justices

Issd Ordered by Court that Hugh L. Carrick be appointed Overseer of the Corporation of the town of Sparta (except main Street from the north boundary line of the public square in said town northward) and also to extend across the bridge at Sparta westward as far as the forks of the Carthage road at Oldhams and keep the whole in repair as a road of the first Class agreeable to law and that the same list and bounds of hands that were assigned to Sevier Evans late Overseer be assigned to work thereon - .

Ordered that Court be adjourned (P-343) untill tomorrow morning 11 O'clock

John Jett
David Snodgrass
John Bryan

Wednesday Morning 4th December A. D. 1839 Court met pursuant to adjournment Present the worshipful

John Jett)
David Snodgrass) Esqrs
John Bryan) Justices

Ordered that Court be adjourned untill Court in Course

Test
N. Oldham; Clk.

John Jett
David Snodgrass
John Bryan

State of Tennessee

At a County Court began and held for the County of White and State aforesaid in the Court house in the town of Sparta before the Justices of said Court on the first Monday being the sixth day of January in the year of our Lord one thousand eight hundred and forty - And of the Independence of the United States of America the Sixty fourth year

Present the worshipful

Thomas Eastland, Esq. Chairman
John Jett; Asa Certain,
David Snodgrass; James Knowles;
Matthias Hutson; Wm. Knowles;
John Bryan, Anderson S. Rogers; Esquires
John Gillentine, William R.
Tucker; Jesse Walling; George
Defrees; Richard Crowder;
Sims Dearing; James Allison; Justices
Lewis Pettett, Tilman Brown;
Thomas Green; William Bruster;
John Pennington; Edmund Stamps.

Issd Ordered by Court that Stephen Hickman be released from the payment of the tax on one white Poll for the year 1839 he being over age and that (P-344) the Sherriff of White County have a credit therefore in the settlement of his accounts - .

Issd Ordered by Court unanimously that Nicholas Oldham Clerk of White County Court be allowed the sum of seven dollars and fifty cents for furnishing one blank record Book for the purpose of recording the probate of Deeds - to be paid by the Trustee of White County out of the tax of the year 1840 - .

Issd Ordered by Court that Isaiah Hutson, Samuel A. Moore; Sr.; Felix A. Badger; Jesse Franks and Preston Chisum freeholders be appointed a Jury of view to view and change the road from Felix A. Badgers to the Rockisland being a road of the first Class and report thereof to the April term of this Court.

This day William Little produced in open Court a Commission signed by the Governer of the State of Tennessee appointing him a Justice of the peace in White County who took an oath to support the Constitution of the United States and of the State of Tennessee and the oath of office and thereupon took his seat upon the Bench and entered upon the discharge of his duties.

This day Thomas Robertson, guardian to the minor heirs of David L. Mitchell, Dec'd returned his report upon oath which is ordered to be recorded.

Ordered by Court that Richard Crowder Esq. be appointed Commissioner in the 6th District for the year 1840 vice James T. Hayes, deceased.

This day James C. Kelly, adminestrator of Nicholas Bennett, Deceased returned upon oath an Inventory of the estate of the deceased which is ordered to be recorded.

This day the poor house Commissioners for White County in obediance to an order of this Court heretofore made requiring them to cause the lands belonging to the poor house of the said County to be surveyed made their report which is received by the Court and ordered to be recorded.

Ordered by the Court that Jonathan C. Davis Esquire Surveyor of White County be allowed the sum of Five dollars for making survey and plott of the lands belonging to the poor house establishedment in White County to be paid by the Treasure of the poor house of said County out of any monies not otherwise appropriated.

This day William D. Crawford admr of Willie W. Crawford deceased returned upon an Inventory and account of sales of the decased which is ordered to be recorded.

(P-345) It appearing to the satisfaction of the Court that in surveying out the lands belonging to the poor house establishment of White County, there is an enterferance with the claims of a certain Hayes Arnold some where between five and Ten acres and said Court being desirous to quest the title to said enterferance agrees to give the said Hayes Arnold the sum of Ten dollars And the said Arnold being present in open Court agrees that for the aforesaid sum of Ten dollars to be paid out of the poor tax for said County for the year 1839 he will Convey by deed to the Commissioners of the poor house for said County the lands above alluded to - And the aforesaid Commissioners are hereby directed to carry out and fully comply on their part with the requirements of the above contract.

This day the death of James T. Hayes Esquire late of the County of White was suggested in open Court and that he departed this life intestate - whereupon Richard Crowder was appointed adminestrator of all and singular the goods and chattles rights and credits of the deceased and took the oath required by law and together with Joseph Herd and John Taylor entered into and acknowledged bond in the sum of one thousand dollars conditioned as the law requires

For reasons appearing to the satisfaction of the Court it is ordered by the Court that Samuel Brown Guardian to Robert Dyer and Alfred Dyer two of the minor heirs of John Dyer deceased be allowed the sum of forty five dollars for services rendered in managing the estate of said Wards to wit Robertson Dyer the sum of twenty Dollars and Alfred Dyer the sum of twenty five dollars to beby him retained out of the estate of said wards respectively.

Ordered by Court unanimously that Josep Cummings, Jr., one of the commissioners of the poorhouse in White County for the year 1839 be allowed the sum of Ten dollars and that John Jett and Joseph Herd the other two Commissioners aforesaid be each allowed the sum of twelve dollars for services rendered as such and also for services in surveying poor house lands to be paid by the Treasure of the poor house out of any monies not otherwise appropriated.

Ordered by Court unanimously that John Jett, Joseph Herd and Joseph Cummings, Jr., esquires be appointed Commissioners of the poor house in White County for the year 1840 and thereupon appeared in open Court and took the oath required by law

Ordered by Court that John Jett Esquire one of the Commissioners of the Poor house of White County be appointed Treasure of said board of Commissioners for the year 1840

(P-346) Isd Ordered by Court that Anderson Keithly be appointed Overseer of the road from the top of Gum Spring Mountain to sinking Creek being a road of the second Class and keep the same in repair as the law requires And that the same bounds of hands that worked under the late Overseer thereof be assigned to work thereon.

Isd Ordered by Court that Jacob Stipe be allowed the sum of thirty seven dollars twenty seven and one half cents being the balance of his account for board for William F. Carter and his horse per account to be paid by John Gillentine guardian to said Carter out of the funds of said Carter.

Isd Ordered by Court that Doctor Robert Cox be allowed the sum of Forty Dollars for medical services rendered the prisoners in the common Jail of White County during the year 1839 to be paid by the Treasure of the poor house Coms. of White County out of the poor tax of 1840

Isd Ordered by Court that Simon R. Doyle coroner of White County be allowed the sum of one dollar per day for eight days services in advertising and holding elections in the year 1837 amounting to eight dollars to be paid by the Trustee of White County out of the tax of the year 1840.

Ordered by Court that Henry Lyda; William Glenn and Bertis Walker be appointed Commissioners to assign and set apart one years provisions to the widow and family of Nicholas Bennett Deceased out of the estate of the deceased and report thereof to the next term of this Court.

Isd Ordered by Court that James Allison and William C. Bounds Esquires be appointed to apportion lists and bounds of hands between Thomas Stone and Charles Burges Overseer of the road having due regard to their respective Classes - .

Isd Ordered by Court that Thomas Jones, Jr.; Joseph Bozarth and Jesse H. Vermillion be appointed Commission to assign and set apart one years provision out of the estate of James T. Hayes Deceased to the widow and family of the deceased and report thereof to the next term of this Court.

This day Samuel Brown guardian to part of the minor heirs of John Dyer deceased returned upon oath his report which is ordered to be recorded.

This day Alford L. Shaw Ex. of John A. Shaw Dec'd returned upon oath an Inventory of the Estate of the deceased which is ordered to be recorded.

(P-347) This day Alford L. Shaw Ex. of John A. Shaw Dec'd returned upon oath an account of the sales of the property of the deceased which is ordered to be recorded.

Isd Ordered by Court that the following persons good and lawful men Citizens of the County of White be appointed and summonds as Jurors to attend and serve as such at the February term 1840 of White Circuit Court to wit: Stuart Warren; Nathaniel C. Davis; Richard England; James Scott, Spence Mitchell; John Gillentine, Wm Farley; Solomon Yeager, Jr., Green Templeton; William D. Glenn; William Lewis; Zachariah Anderson; Joseph Herd; Charles Smith; Preston A. Chisum; Isaiah Hutson; Elisha Camron; Joshua Fox; John Taylor; Alexander P. Irwin; Wm. Mills; George Welch; Dan Griffeth; James Hudgins, John Bohanon and Thomas Barnes - And also Hayes Arnold and Charles Meek Constables to attend thereon And that a writ of venirefacias issue directed &c.

This day Allen L. Mitchell Superentendant of the Poor house for the year 1840 appeared in open Court and took the oath required by law and together with Jonathan T. Bradley entered into and acknowledged bond in the sum of five hundred dollars conditioned as the law requires - .

Isd Ordered by Court that Allen L. Mitchell Keeper and Superentendant of the poor house in White County for the year 1839 be allowed for the support and maintainance of six paupers in said Poor house the following sums to wit: for Elizabeth Miller seventy five dollars and fifty cents - Elizabeth Hutchens seventy four dollars eight and 1/3 cents George Shelton Sixty five dollars seventy five cents - .

Samuel Oliver forty Three dollars sixty two and a half cents Clara Oliver sixty dollars seventy five cents Elizabeth Lansdale twenty five dollars fifty cents and for tobacco for said paupers four dollars ninety three and 1/3 cents making all the sum of Three hundred and fifty dollars fourteen and one half cents being the amount of his acct. for the year 1839 to be paid by Treasure of the poor house Commissioners out of any money not otherwise appropriated.

Isd Ordered by Court that the road as laid off and marked by Commissioners heretofore returned leading from the widow Fitzgerald old field to entersect Paynes road near John Philips be established as a road of the third Class and that Forrister Fifer be appointed Overseer thereof and keep the same in repair as the law requires that Thomas Green and Lewis Pettett Esquires assign a list of hands to work thereon - .

Isd Ordered by Court that William Hargis be appointed Overseer
(P-348) of the road from the 19 mile post to the standing Stone being a road of the second Class and keep the same in repair as the law requires and that the same list and bounds of hands that worked under Sandford Stamps late Overseer thereof be assigned to work thereon.

Isd For reasons appearing to the Satisfaction of the Court it is ordered by the Court that John Gillentine guardian to William F. Carter a minor pay to Mrs. J. Herd and son the sum of seventy dollars and seventy six cents being the amount of the aforesaid Heirs account against said Carter to be paid out of the estate of said Wards.

This day the death of James Walling, Jr., late of the County of White was suggested in open Court and that he departed this life entestate whereupon Jesse Walling was appointed adminestrator of all and singular the goods and chattles rights and credits of the deceased and thereupon took the oath prescribed by law and together with Daniel Walling and Andrew S. Rogers entered into and acknowledged bond in the sum of One thousand dollars conditioned as the law requires - .

Ordered by Court that Andrew K. Parker, Joseph Cummings, Jr., John Gillentine, George Sparkman and Robert S. Mitchell freeholders be appointed a Jury of view to lay off and mark a road of the third Class from the top of Little Mountain near Squire Cummings to the Warren County line and report thereof instantly - .

This day the commissioners aforesaid made their report which is received by the Court and said road established a road of the third Class.

And it is ordered by Court that Robert S. Mitchell be appointed Overseer thereof and keep the same in repair as the law requires and that John Gillentine and Tilman Brown Esquire assign list and bounds of hands to work thereon of those who live on the mountain.

The Commissioners heretofore appointed to lay off and change the road leading from Doyles Mill to the Gum Spring road returned their report and said change as marked out is ordered to be established.

Ordered by Court that the order of October term appointing John Jett and Jesse Walling Esquire to apportion lists and bounds of hands between Jesse A. Bounds and William Overby Overseer on the Shipping port road having regard to the grades of the two roads be renewed and report thereof to the next quarterly term of this

Ordered by Court that Berman Harden, Milford Cary (P-349) James Harden, James McBride and Jerry Loggin, be assigned to work on that portion of the road over which John Holder is Overseer agreeable to the report of Commissioners - .

This day the Court proceeded to the appointment of three Justices to hold the Querum Court of White County for the year 1840 and to that office do appoint David Snodgrass, John Bryan and Sims Dearing Esquire - .

This day John Gillentine guardian to William F. Carter returned upon oath his report which is ordered to be recorded.

This day the Court proceeded to the appointment of one Notary Public for the County of White and to that office do appoint Jabas G. Mitchell Esquire for the next ensuing four years.

This day Solomon Duncan Exr. of Marshall Duncan Deceased returned upon oath an Inventory and account of the sales of said Estate which is ordered to be recorded - .

Issd Ordered by Court that John Jett and John Bryan Esquires be appointed Commissioners to settle with the County Trustee and several Clerks in White County for the year 1840

Woodson P. White
to Issd
William L. Mitchell
} Title Bond for 90 acres Land

It appearing to the satisfaction of the Court that the above obligor was dead and also that there was no subscribing witness to said Bond to attest the execution thereof whereupon appeared in open Court Richard Nelson and John Jett to the Court known and after being sworn in due form of law deposed and said that they were intemately acquanted with the said Woodson P. White the above named obligor in his life time and were also well acquanted with his handwritting - And that they verily beleive his signiture thereto is the genuine signiture and proper hand writing of the said Woodson P. White which is deemed by the Court sufficently authenticaled and ordered to be recorded.

This day John Pennington one of the guardians to the balance of the minor heirs of John Dyer deceased returned upon oath his report which is ordered to be recorded - .

Issd Ordered by Court that John Jett, David Snodgrass and John Bryan Esquires Justices of the Quorum Court be each allowed the sum of (P-350) One dollar and fifty per day for sixteen days services in holding the Quorum Court for White County for the year 1839 to be paid by the Trustee of White County out of the taxes of the year 1839

On the humble petition of John Gillentine Esquire and for reasons appearing to the satisfaction of the Court the said John Gillentine is permitted to build and erect a dam across the Caney fork river for the purposes of erecting Mills and other Machinery at any point across said river upon an Entry of 50 acres of Land which he has this day made in the Entry takers office of White County which is numbered 3189 - .

Ordered that Court be adjourned untill tomorrow Morning at 10 O'Clock

Thos Eastland
John Jett
John Bryan

Tuesday Morning 7th January A.D. 1840 Court met pursuant to adjournment Present the Worshipful

Thos Eastland Esq. Chairman
John Jett &
John Bryan } Esq. Justices

This day William G. Sims guardian to the minor heirs of Lenias B. Farris Deceased returned upon oath his report which is ordered to be recorded.

Issd Ordered by Court that the order of last term appointing Robert Anderson, James Randols, Sr., Joseph Clark, Sr., John Witt, and Sampson Witt freeholders a Jury of view to lay off and mark a road of the second Class from William Knowles to Dillons bridge in such a manner as not to pass through the land of Hiram Knowles be renewed and report thereof to the next April term of this Court.

This day John Jett Esquire Treasure of the poor house of White County appeared in open Court and took the oath prescribed by law and together with John Bryan and William G. Sims entered into and acknowledged bond in the sum of fifteen hundred dollars conditioned as the law requires - .

This day Henry Breakbell an orphan boy of the age of sixteen years on the 2nd day of May 1840 appeared in open Court (P-351) and was bound unto James M. Carrick to serve him after the manner of an apprentise untill he arrives at the age of twenty one years and for the performance of his Covenant entered into and acknowledged bond with John L. Price his security conditioned &c.

This day William Breadbell of the age of fourteen years on the 5th day of July 1840 appeared in open Court and was bound unto John L. Price to serve him after the manner of an apprentice untill he arrives at the age of Twenty one years and for the performance of his Covenant entered into and acknowledged bond with James H. Carrick his security Conditioned &c.

Ordered that Court be adjourned untill Court in Course

Thos Eastland
John Jett
John Bryan

Test
N. Oldham; Clk.

State of Tennessee

At a Court began and held for the County of White in the town of Sparta before the Justices of said Court on the first Monday of February in the year of our Lord One thousand eight hundred and forty and of the Independence of the United States the Sixty fourth year

Present the worshipful

David Snodgrass	}	Esq. Justices
John Bryan		
Sims Dearing		

This day Thomas Jones produced in open Court a Commissioners from the Govener of the State of Tennessee of his appointment of a Justices of the peace in and for the County of White and thereupon took an oath to support the Constitution of the United States and of the State of Tennessee and the oath prescribed by law and then entered upon the discharge of his duties - .

This day the Clerk of this Court produced in open Court the report of a settlement made by heirs with William Glenn one of the admrs. of William Glenn dec'd which is received by the Court and Confirmed and Ordered to be recorded.

(P-352) Monday February the 3rd A.D. 1840
This day the Clerk of this Court prodused in open Court the report of a settlement made by him with Asa Certain late Guardian to Alphonso Holmes and Maniza Holmes infant heirs of Edward Holmes Dec'd which is received by the Court and confirmed in all its parts and ordered to be recorded.

State	}	Bastardy
Issd vs		
Elias Wilhite		Martha Ann Broyles Prox

This day came the above Defendant in proper person and produced in open Court a receipt in writing from the prosecutrix in the above cause acknowledging the payment in full of the same which by law she would be entitle to receive from the said Defendant for begetting upon the body of the said Martha Ann Broyles a bastard male child whereupon it is ordered and so considered by the Court that said Defendant find surities to keep free and indimnified the County of white from any color of cost or damage for and towards the support and maintainance of said Bastard Child - And now came here said Defendant and David Snodgrass and Jeremiah Wilhite into open Court and acknowledged themselves endebted to the County of White in the sum of five hundred Dollars to be levied of their respective goods and Chattles lands and tenements to the use of the County of White to be rendered void on condition that said Bastard male child shall not in anywise become chargeable to the County and the Court further consider that execution issue against said defendant for collection of the costs -

This day Anderson S. Rogers was appointed by the Court guardian to Phebe Walling; Ruth Walling; Elizabeth Walling; Joseph Walling; Sally Walling; Nancy Walling and Isham Walling seven of the minor heirs of

James Walling Deceased and thereupon took the oath prescribed by law and together with Jesse Walling and Joseph Herd entered into and acknowledged bond in the sum of nine hundred dollars conditioned as the law requires.

This day Thomas R. Walling; Jesse Walling; Mary Russel late Mary Walling and Osias D. Walling being over the age of fourteen years selected and made chose of Joseph Herd as their guardian and the said Joseph Herd being present in open Court took the oath prescribed by law and together with James Randols and Anderson S. Rogers entered into and acknowledged bond in the sum of $500 conditioned as the law requires.

Isd Ordered by Court that Hayes Arnold be appointed Overseer of the road from the middle of the Bridge at the Harriett Iron Works to the widow Smiths gate being a road of the first Class and keep the same in repair as the law requires and that the same list and bounds of hands that worked under the late Overseer thereof be assigned to work thereon -

(P-353) Isd Ordered by Court that Osburn Walker; George Elmore; Cornelius Hickey; Henry Colier and William Williams freeholders be appointed a Jury of view to lay off and mark a road of the third Class from Dunagans Iron Works on Cain Creek passing Henry Colliers to Falling Water at the mouth of Glade Creek thence the nearest and best way to John Bussells still house thence the nearest and best way to entersect the Sparta road at or near John Walkers and report thereof to the next Quarterly term of this.

Isd Ordered by Court that Robert Wadkins be appointed Overseer of the road from the Corperation of the town of Sparta to the middle of the Bridge at the Harriett Iron Works being a road of the first Class and keep the same in repair as the law requires and that the same list and bounds of hands that worked under Merideth Baker late Overseer thereof be assigned to work thereon.

Isd Ordered by Court that Benjamin Wilhite be appointed Overseer of the road from Post Oak Creek to Robert Howards being a road of the second Class and keep the same in repair as the law requires and that the same list and bounds of hands that worked under John Rogers late Overseer thereof be assigned to work thereon.

Present the worshipful

David Snodgrass;
John Bryan;
Sims Dearing;
Anderson S. Rogers
and Matthias Hutson

} Esqs. Justices

Isd This day John Mason produced in open Court one large wolf scalp over the age of four months and proved by the oath of John Sliger that he killed the same in White County in the State of Tennessee and there being present David Snodgrass; John Bryan; Sims Dearing; Anderson S. Rogers and Matthias Hutson; Esqs five of the Justices of the peace for said County thereupon this ordered that the same be certified to the Treasure of the State of Tennessee for payment; And that the Sherriff of White County burn said scalp and who being here present, in open Court received said scalp into his Custody and acted accordingly.

Isad This day Asa Graham produced in open Court one large wolf scalp over the age of four months and proved by his own oath that he killed the same in White County Tennessee and there being present David Snodgrass John Bryan, Sims Dearing, Anderson S. Rogers and Matthias Hutson Esqs. five of the acting Justices of the peace in and for said County whereupon it is ordered by the Court that the same be certified to the Treasure of Tennessee for payment and that the Sherriff of White (P-354) County burn said scalp and who being present in open Court received said Scalps into his Custody and acted accordingly.

This day William Glenn guardian to part of the heirs of William Glenn Deceased returned upon oath his report which is ordered to be recorded - .

Ordered by Court that Elisha Camron, George G. Broyles, John Robinson, Alexander Officer and Davis Weaver freeholders be appointed a Jury of view to review and change the road of the second Class leaving the Calf Killer road at the foot of Potts hill and entersect the Calf Killer road at or near Mr. Carmichaels and report thereof to the present term of this Court. And the aforesaid Commissioners being present in open Court and after being sworn in due form of law made their report which is received by the Court and said proposed change established - And that James Officer, Sr., being appointed Overseer thereof to open said road as the law requires and that Sims Dearing Esquire assign a list and bounds of hands to work thereon.

This day Nancy Vaughn adminestratrix of Benjamin Dec'd Vaughn returned upon oath an Inventory and account of sales of the property of the Deceased - which is ordered to be recorded -

Ordered that Court be adjourned untill tomorrow 9 OClock

David Snodgrass
John Bryan
Sims Dearing

Tuesday Morning the 4th day of February A.D. 1840
Present the worshipful

David Snodgrass
John Bryan and
Sims Dearing } Esqs. Justices

This day Isaac Buck Esqr. one of the Justices of the peace in and for the County of White filed his resegnation as Justices of the Peace in the 11th District which is ordered to be recorded.

This day William M. Young Administrator of Woodson P. White deceased returned upon oath an Inventory and account of the sales of said estate which is ordered to be recorded

Isad Ordered by Court that Jesse M. Sullivan be appointed Overseer of the road from the Blue Spring branch to the crossing of the branch near James M. Nelson being a road of the second Class and keep the same in repair as the law requires and that Thomas Jones Esquire be appointed to assign a list of hands to work thereon.

This day Bird C. Deatherage an orphan boy aged sixteen years (P-355) on the 4th day of July 1839 was bound unto James T. Clenny to learn the trade of a saddler to serve him after the manner of an apprentice untill he shall attain the age of twenty one years and for the faithful performance of the Covenant entered into bond and with Smith J. Walling his security conditioned &c.

William Baker } to } Allen L. Mitchell } Deed of Conveyance for 50 acres of land

This day John Jett, William M. Young and Jabez G. Mitchell to the Court known appeared in open Court and after being sworn in due form of law deposed and said they were entimately acquanted with Woodson P. White whose Name is subscribed to the within Deed as a witness that they are acquanted with his hand writing and veribly believe it to be his genuine signature and that he has since departed this life; and the said Jabez G. Mitchell deposes and says he was well acquanted with John Hickey the other subscribing witness to the same; that he veribly believes his signature to be genuine and that he is also dead - which is deemed by the Court sufficently proved and ordered to be recorded -.

This day James T. Clenny appeared in open Court and moved the Court to rescind his covenant in the Indenture of William P. Worley bound to him at the December term 1839 and for reasons appearing fully to the satisfaction of the Court it is ordered and so considered by the Court that said Indenture be entirely cancelled and the said James T. Clenny released and forever discharged thereof - .

This day William Preston Worley and orphan boy aged Ten years on the 26th day of May 1839 was bound to William M. Bryan Jr. to serve him after the manner of an apprentice untill he arrives at the age of twenty one years and together with John H. Graham entered into acknowledged for the faithful performance of his Covenant

Ordered that Court be adjourned untill Court in Course

Test
N. Oldham, Clk.

David Snodgrass
Sims Dearing
John Bryan

(P-356) Monday Morning 2nd March A. D. 1840

State of Tennessee

At a quorum Court began and held for the County of White at the Court house in the town of Sparta before the Justices of said Court on the first Monday being the second day of March in the year of our Lord One thousand eight hundred and forty. And of the Independence of the United States the sixty fourth year

Present the worshipful

David Snodgrass } Esquires
John Bryan }
Sims Dearing } Quorum Justices

This day the clerk of this Court prodused in open Court the report of a settlement with Elizabeth Hamblett executrix of the last will and testament of Berry Hamblett Deceased which being unexcepted is confirmed by said Court and ordered to be recorded.

This day Jabez G. Mitchell Esquire who was elected at a former term of this Court Notary Public of White County produced in open Court his Commission signed by the govener of the state of Tennessee; and thereupon took an oath to support the constitution of the United States and of the State of Tennessee And the oath prescribed by law and together with William M. Young, Spencer Mitchell and Joseph G. Mitchell entered into and acknowledged Bond in the sum of Five thousand Dollars conditioned as the law requires

Commission

James K. Polk Govener of the State of Tennessee

To all who shall see these presents Greeting:

Whereas it has been certified to me that at the January term of the county Court for the County of White Jabez G. Mitchell was duly elected Notary Public for said County for the term of four years.

Now thereupon I James K. Polk govener as aforesaid do hereby Commission the said Jabez G. Mitchell Notary public as aforesaid for the term aforesaid conferring upon him all the powers priviliges and emoluments thereto belonging.

In testimony whereof I have hereto set my hand and caused the great seal of the State to be affixed at the City of Nashville on the 18th day of February 1840

By the Govener James K. Polk

Jon. S. Young; Secretary of State (L S)

(P-357) This day Brice Little one of the Executors of the last will and testament of Thomas Little Deceased returned upon oath an Inventory of the Estate of the Deceased which is ordered to be recorded.

This day Brice Little One of the Executors of the last will and Testament of Thomas Little deceased returned upon oath an account of the sales of the property of the deceased which is ordered to be recorded - .

Isd Ordered by Court that, that portion of the 15th District in White County that belongs to the County of White after running the dividing line between the Counties of White and Van Buren shall be and is hereby attached to the 2nd District of White County, with the right to enjoy all the powers and privileges as citizens of the 2nd District in voting for all Offices &c. which the Citizens of the 2nd District are entitled to.

This day Robert Cook one of the adminestrators of the estate of Elijah Sawyers Deceased filed his receipts in the final settlement and destribution of said Estate which is ordered to be recorded.

Isd Ordered by Court that William Bruster Esquire be appointed to assign a list of hands to Hugh Gracy overseer of the road having due regard to the dignity of his road and the diffrent roads in its neighbourhood.

Isd Ordered by Court that Cannon Quarles and Dennis Foster be appointed to work on that portion of the milk Sick hills &c. of which William M. Bryan Jr. is Overseer.

Isd Ordered by Court that William W. Knowles be appointed Overseer of the road from James McGowens to Franks old ferry being a road of the second Class and keep the same in repair as the law requires and that the same bounds of hands that worked under William Moore late Overseer thereof be assigned to work thereon.

Isd Ordered by Court that John Henry be appointed Overseer of the road from the 19 mile post to the Standing Stone being a road of the second Class and keep the same in repair as the law requires and that the same bounds of hands that worked under the late Overseer thereof be assigned to work thereon.

This day Joshua Mason was appointed guardian to (P-358) Nancy Glenn, Jesse Allen Glenn, Caleb Glenn, Margrett Glenn and James Glenn minor heirs of Alexander Glenn Deceased and thereupon took the oath prescribed by law and together with Smith J. Walling and Robert Mason entered into and acknowludged bond in the sum of two hundred Dollars conditioned as the law requires - .

This day Spence Mitchell one of the Executors of the last will and testament of Robert Mitchell Sr. Deceased returned upon oath an Inventory and account of the sales of the property of the deceased which is ordered to be recorded.

Isd Ordered by Court that William Hitchcock and William C. Bounds Esquires be appointed to devide the hands between Thomas Stone and Charles Burges Overseer of the road, having due regard to grades of the two roads and the distances of each road.

Ordered that Court be adjourned untill tomorrow Morning 9 O'Clock

Sims Dearing
William Little
John Bryan

Tuesday morning 3rd day of March A. D. 1840 Court met pursuant to adjournment Present the worshipful

John Bryan) Esquires
Sims Dearing }
William Little) Justices

State of Tennessee)
vs) Bastardy
James Scott) Elizabeth Savage Pros'x

This day came the Defendant with Nicholas Oldham into open Court and acknowledged themselves indebted to the State of Tennessee in the sum of seven hundred and fifty dollars to wit; the Defendant in the sum of five hundred dollars and the said Nicholas Oldham in the sum of two hundred and fifty Dollars to be levied of their respective goods and chattles lands and tenaments to the use of the State to be rendered - nevertheless to be void on conditioned that the above named defendant shall make his personal appearance before the Justices of our said Court to be held in the Court house in the town of Sparta on the first Monday in April next then and there to answer the State on the above charge and not depart hence without leave of the Court first had and obtained.

(P-359) Ordered that Court be adjourned untill Court in Course

Test
N. Oldham

Sims Dearing
William Little
John Bryan

State of Tennessee

At a county Court began and held for the County of White in the Court house in the town of Sparta before the Justices of said Court on the first Monday being the sixth day of April in the year of our Lord one thousand eight hundred and forty and of the Independence of the United States of America the sixty fourth year

Present the Worshipful

Thomas Eastland Esquire Chairman
Elijah Frost, William Little,
John Jett, William Bruster, — Esquires
John Bryan, Anderson S. Rogers,
Thomas Green, Jesse Walling,
Matthias Hutson, Lewis Pettett,
William Knowles, James Knowles,
Richard Crowder, Thomas Jones,
James Allison, William C. Bounds,
John Pennington, Sims Dearing,
James Bartlett, Asa Certain, and — Justices
George Defreese

This day William Huigins produced a Commission signed by Governer of the State of Tennessee appointing him Justice of the peace in White, who being present in open Court took an oath to support the constitution of the United States and of the State of Tennessee and the several oaths prescribed by law and thereupon took his seat upon the bench.

This day Nicholas Oldham produced in open Court the certificate of the Coroner of White County of his election of Clerk of the County Court of White County for the next succeeding four years who being present in open Court took an oath to support the Constitution of the United States and of the States of Tennessee and the several oaths presceibed by law and (P-360) together with Mark Lowry, Wamon Leftwich, Samuel V. Carrick, John Warren and Anthony Dibrell entered into and acknowledged bond conditioned as the law requires.

Bonds.

Know all men by these presents that we Nicholas Oldham, Mark Lowry, Wamon Leftwich, Samuel V. Carrick, Anthony Dibrell, John Warren all of the County of White and State of Tennessee are held and firmly bound unto his Excellency James K. Polk Esquire Governor in and over the State aforesaid for the time being or his successors in office in the sum of five Thousand dollars current money which payment well and truly to be made and done we bind ourselves and each and every of our heirs execution or adminestrators jointly and severally, firmly by these presents sealed with our seals and dated the 6th day of April A.D. 1840 whereas it is certified to the County Court of said County that Nicholas Oldham hath been duly and Constitutionally elected Clerk of the County Court of White County for the four years next insuing the first saturday in March A. D. 1840
Now the condition of the above obligation is such that if the above bound Nicholas Oldham shall carefully and savely keep all the records of the County Court of White County faithfully and truly discharge all the duties of his said Office of Clerk of said Court and shall well and truly in all things appertaining to his said Office of Clerk demean himself according to law then this obligation to be null and void otherwise be and remain

in full force and vertue

Test
Thos Eastland
Chairman of White County Court

N. Oldham (seal)
Mark Lowry (seal)
Wamon Leftwich (seal)
John Warren (seal)
Anthony Dibrell (seal)
Sam V. Carrick (seal)

Know all men by these presents that we Nicholas Oldham, Mark Lowry, Wamon Leftwich, Samuel V. Carrick, John Warren, A. Dibrell all of the County of White and State of Tennessee are held and firmly bound unto his Excellency James K. Polk Esq. Governor in and over the State for the time being or his sucessors in office in the sum of one thousand Dollars which payment well and truly to be made and done we bind ourselves and each and every of our heirs executors and adminestrators jointly and severally firmly by these presents, sealed with our seals and dated the 6th day of April A. D. 1840

Whereas the above bound Nicholas Oldham hath been duly and Constitutionally elected Clerk of the County Court of White County for the four years next succeeding the first Satuday in March 1840. Now if the above bound Nicholas Oldham shall well and truly collect and pay over all monies that shall come into his hands by verture of his office to these persons entitled by law to receive the same then shall the above obligation be null and void else be and (P-361) remain in full force and vertue

Test
Thos. Eastlend
Chairman of White County Court

N. Oldham (seal)
Mark Lowry (seal)
Wamon Leftwich (seal)
John Warren (seal)
Anthony Dibrell (seal)
Sam. V. Carrick (seal)

Know all men by these presents that we Nicholas Oldham, Mark Lowry, Wamon Leftwich, Samuel V. Carrick, Anthony Dibrell, John Warren all of the County of White and State of Tennessee are held and firmly bound unto his Excellency James K. Polk Esqs. Governer in and over the state of Tennessee for the time being or his successors in office in the sum of one thousand dollars which payment well and truly to be made and done we bind ourselves and each and every of our heirs executors and adminestrators jointly and severally, firmly by these presents sealed with our seals and dated the 6th day of April A. D. 1840

The condition of the above obligation is such that whereas N. Oldham hath been duly and constitutionally elected Clerk of White County Court for the four years next succeeding from and after the first Saturday in March 1840. Now if the above bound Nicholas Oldham shall well and truly collect and pay over all fines forfeitures agreeably to law, then the above obligation to be null and void else be and remain in full force and virtue

Test
Thos Eastland
Chairman of White County Court

N. Oldham (seal)
Mark Lowry (seal)
Wamon Leftwich (seal)
John Warren (seal)
Anthony Dibrell (seal)
Sam. V. Carrick (seal)

This day Robert Cox produced in open Court a certificate of his election to the office of Trustee of White County for the next ensuing two years who being present in open Court took an oath to support the Constitution of the United States and of the States of Tennessee and the several oaths prescribed by law and together with Anthony Dibrell, William Irwin and George Defreese entered into and acknowledged bond in the sum of Five Thousand Dollars conditioned as the law requires - .

This day Robert Smith produced in open Court certified of his election to the office of Regester of White County for the next ensuing four years, who being present in open Court took an oath to support the constitution of the United States and of the State of Tennessee and the several oaths prescribed by law and together with Charles Smith, John Smith, James Randols, Sr., Terry Walden, Thomas Green, and Anderson S. Rogers entered into and acknowledged bond in the sum of Twelve Thousand five hundred dollars conditioned as the law requires.

(p-362) This day Edward M. Murray was appointed Guardian to William L. White, Mary White, Frances M. White, Mariah White and John R. White minor heirs of Woodson P. White Deceased who being present in open Court took the oath prescribed by law and together with John Warren, William M. Young, John Jett and Jesse Walling entered into and acknowledged bond in the sum of twenty thousand dollars conditioned as the law requires.

This day Charles Meek produced in open Court a Certificate of his election as Constable in District No 1 who being present in open Court took an oath to support the Constitution of the United States and of the State of Tennessee and the several oaths prescribed by law and together with James Lowry and James Randols, Sr., entered into and acknowledged bond in the sum of Eight Thousand Dollars conditioned as the law requires.

This day Hayes Arnold produced in open Court a certificate of his election as Constable in District No 1 who being present in open Court took an oath to support the Constitution of the United States and of the State of Tennessee and the several oaths prescribed by law and together with William Little and Sevier Evans entered into and acknowledged bond in the sum of eight thousand dollars conditioned as the law requires.

This day James Graham produced in open Court a certificate of his Election as constable in District No 2 who being present in open Court took an oath to support the Constitution of the United States and of the State of Tennessee and the several oaths prescribed by law and together with John H. Graham, John Graham and Samuel V. Carrick entered into and acknowledged bond in the sum of six Thousand dollars conditioned as the law requires.

This day Creed A. Taylor produced in open Court a Certificate of his election as Constable in District No 3 who being present in open Court took an oath to support the Constitution of the United States and of the State of Tennessee and the several oaths prescribed by law and together with Jesse Walling and Spencer Holder, Jr., entered into and acknowledged bond in the sum of six Thousand dollars conditioned as the law requires.

This day Alexander Moore produced in open Court a Certificate of his election as Constable in District No 4 who being present in open Court took an oath to support the Constitution of the United States and of the State of Tennessee and the several oaths prescribed by law and together with Jesse Walling and William Templeton entered into and acknowledged bond in the sum of six Thousand dollars conditioned as the law requires.

This day Cornelious Jarvis produced in open Court a Certificate (P-363) of his election as constable in District No 5 and who being present in open Court took an oath to support the Constitution of the United States and of the State of Tennessee and the several oaths prescribed by law and together with, Green Templeton, Joshua Mason, Robert Mason & Levi Jarvis entered into and acknowledged bond in the sum of six Thousand Dollars Conditioned as the law requires.

This day William H. Baker produced in open Court a certificate of his election as Constable in District No 6 and who being present in open Court thereupon took an oath to support the constitution of the United States and of the State of Tennessee and the several oaths prescribed by law and together with Richard Baker, Green H. Baker, Thomas Jones and Alfred L. Shaw entered into and acknowledged bond in the sum of six thousand dollars conditioned as the law requires.

This day Isaac Lollar produced in open Court a certificate of his election as constable in Dist No 8 and who being present in open Court thereupon took an oath to support the constitution of the United States and of the State of Tennessee and the several oaths prescribed by law and together with William P. Rhea, Charles Burges and Joseph S. Allison entered into and acknowledged Bond in the sum of six Thousand dollars conditioned as the law requires.

This day James C. Kelly produced in open Court a certificate of his election as Constable in District No 9 and who being present in open Court thereupon took an oath to support the Constitution of the United States and of the State of Tennessee and the several oaths prescribed by law and together with Asa Certain and Robert Smith entered into and acknowledged bond in the sum of six Thousand dollars conditioned as the law requires.

This day William K. Bradford produced in open Court certificate of his election as Constable for District No 10 and who being present in open Court thereupon took an oath to support the constitution of the United State and of the State of Tennessee and the several oaths prescribed by law and together with John Pennington and William C. Bounds entered into and acknowledged bond in the sum of six Thousand Dollars conditioned as the law requires.

This day John Madewell produced in open Court a certificate of his election as Constable in District No 11 and who being present in open Court thereupon took an oath to support the Constitution of the United States and of the State of Tennessee and the several oaths prescribed by law and together with James Bartlett, (P-364) Samuel Madewell and Isaac Buck entered into and acknowledged bond in the sum of six Thousand dollars conditioned as the law requires.

This day James A. Jay produced in open Court a certificate of his election as Constable in District No 12 and who being present in open Court thereupon took an oath to support the Constitution of the united States and of the State of Tennessee and the several oaths prescribed by law and together with Richard Bradley, Daniel Bartlett and Harrison Whitson entered into and acknowledged bond in the sum of six Thousand Dollars conditioned as the law requires.

This day David Little produced in open Court a Certificate of his election as Constable in District No 13 and who being present in open Court thereupon took an oath to support the Constitution of the United State and of the State of Tennessee and the several oaths prescribed by law and together with William Little, Thomas Snodgrass and John England, Jr., entered into and acknowledged bond in the sum of six thousand dollars conditioned as the law requires.

This day Isaac S. Brogdon produced in open court a certificate of his election as Constable in District No. 14 and who being present in open Court thereupon took an oath to support the constitution of the United States and of the State of Tennessee and the several oaths prescribed by law and together with John Gipson and John Warren entered into and acknowledged bond in the sum of six Thousand Dollars Conditioned as the law requires.

This day the Commissioners appointed to suppentend the repairs &c to the Court house and fence around the same made their report which is received by the court and ordered to be recorded -

Isd Ordered by Court that Daniel Clark be allowed the sum of One hundred Dollars agreeable to his contract for repairs &c. on the Court house and Court yard fence to be paid by the Trustee of White County out of the taxes of the year 1840

Ordered by Court that the sum of Four hundred dollars be appropriated and applied to assist the Citizens of White County in Grading and Macadamising the public square in the town of Sparta and it is further ordered that a Special tax be levied and collected in the present year 1840 for that exclusive purpose

Isd Ordered by Court that Joseph Campbell be appointed Overseer of the road from Scarboroughs bridge to the dividing line between White and Bledsoe Countys being a road of the second Class and keep the same in repair as the law requires and that the same list and bounds of hands that worked under Samuel Thomas late Overseer thereof be assigned to work thereon.

(P-365) This day John Jett & John Bryan Esquire Commissioners for the year 1840 to settle with the Trustee &c of White County made their report upon oath as to their settlement with the Trustee of White County which is received and ordered to be recorded.

Isd Ordered by Court that Moses Grissom be appointed Overseer of the road from the forks to William Knowles on the Kentucky road being a road of the 2nd Class and keep the same in repair as the law requires and that the same list and bounds of hands that worked under Joseph H. McDaniel late Overseer thereof be assigned to work thereon

Ordered by Court that Mary Hutchings releot and widow of Webster Hutchens Deceased be allowed the sum of Eighty Dollars for supporting and maintaining eight minor children of the deceased for one year and eight months to be paid out of the estate of the deceased .

Issd. Ordered by Court that William Glenn be appointed Overseer of the road from Plumb Creek to the forks of the road being a road of the second class and keep the same in repair as the law requires and that the list and bounds of hands that worked under the late Overseer thereof be assigned to work thereon.

Ordered by Court unanimously that the following rates of Taxes be assigned for the year 1840 To Wit;

FOR COUNTY TAX

On each one hundred dollars value of property five cents
On each free Poll twelve and one half cents

FOR JURY TAX

On each $100 value of property five cents
On each free Poll twelve and one half cents

FOR POOR TAX

On each $100 value of property five cents
On each free Poll twelve and one half cents

FOR SPARTA BRIDGE TAX

On each $100 value of property one & one fourth cents

FOR PAVING SPARTA PUBLIC SQUARE
On each $100 value of property Three cents
On each free Poll twelve and one half cents

To be levied and collected by the Sherriff of White County in the manner and form as prescribed by law.

And it is further considered by the Court that the Clerk of this Court for every License he shall issue for the exhibition of natural or artificial curiosities for the year 1840 shall demand and receive for the use and benifit of the County of White a sum equal to the full amount of the State tax and for all other priviliges for purposes aforesaid a sum equal to one half of the State (P-368) tax thereon all of which money shall be accounted for with the Trustee of White County according to law.

Ordered by Court that William Simpson be allowed the sum of one Hundred dollars for keeping the Bridge across the Calf-killer at the town of Sparta in repair during the year 1839 to be paid by the Trustee of White County out of the tax of 1839 Levied for that purpose.

Ordered by Court that William Simpson be allowed the sum of One hundred dollars for keeping the bridge across the Calf-killer at the town of Sparta in repair during the year 1836 to be paid by the Trustee of White County out of the tax laid for that purpose in the year 1836.

This day William Haily administrator of Jeremiah T. Witt dec'd returned upon oath in open Court an account of the sales of the estate of the deceased which is ordered to be recorded.

This day Jesse Walling administrator of James Walling, Jr., Deceased returned upon oath in open Court an Inventory and account of the sales of the estate of the Deceased which is ordered to be recorded.

Issd Ordered by Court that James Baker be appointed Overseer of the road from the mouth of Anderson S. Rogers lane to where the same intersects the loss Creek road, being a road of the second Class and keep the same in repair as the law requires and that the same list and bounds of hands that worked under Alfred Wilson be assigned to work thereon.

This day James C. Kelly administrator of Nicholas Bennett Deceased returned upon oath into open Court an account of the sales of the estate of the Deceased which is ordered to be recorded.

On the humble petition of Thomas Roberts and for satisfactory reasons to the Court shown, he the said Thomas Roberts is hereby permitted and fully authorized, to build erect and establish a Dam across Sinking Creek and to erect Mills and other water Machinery on and across said Creek on the Land situated thereon in the name of Francis A. Roberts, without molestation or hinderance thereon.

This day the Commissioners heretofore appointed to lay off assign and set apart One years provisions out of the estate of Nicholas Bennett deceased; for the support and maintainance of the widow and family of the deceased made their report which is received by the Court and ordered to be recorded.

Ordered by Court that Larkin Stuart be appointed Overseer (P-367) from Melton Groses to the middle of the Carter old field being a road of the first Class and keep the same in repair as the law requires and that the same bounds of hands that worked under Jon. Prince be assigned to work thereon.

Issd Ordered by Court that Charles Pennington, Washington Williams, Matthew England, James H. Isham, Reubin Brown, Samuel Dyer and David Nicholas freeholders be appointed a Jury of view to lay off and examine the change in the road leading from Cherry Creek to White plains, leaving the road at John Ishams and intersecting the same again in about two or three hundred yards and report thereof to the next term of this Court.

Issd Ordered by Court that Isaac Lollar be appointed Overseer of the road from Lollars Branch to Dittys Branch being a road of the first Class and keep the same in repair as the law requires and that the list and bounds of hands that worked under Charles Burgess late Overseer thereof be assigned to work thereon.

This day the Commissioners heretofore appointed to lay off and examine a change in the McMinnville road from Felix A. Badgers to Rockisland made a report which is by the Court rejected.

Woodson P. White
to
Henry C. Evans } Title Bond

This day John Jett and Jabez G. Mitchell appeared in open Court and to the Court known and after being sworn in due form of Law depose and say they were intimately acquanted with Woodson P. White whose name is subscribed to the within Bond; that they had seen him often write his name and are well acquanted with his hand writting; that they veribly believe his signature to the within bond is his proper hand writing and genuine and that the said Woodson P. White has departed this life; whereupon it is Ordered by the Court that the same be recorded and Regestered.

It is Ordered by the Court that the petition of Sundry persons this day filed to raise the Shipping port road from a third Class road to a second Class road be laid over and continued untill the next term of this Court.

This day Jonathan T. Bradley Sherriff of White County produced in open Court a certificate from the Treasure of the state of Tennessee which is received by the Court (P-368) and ordered to be put upon the minutes of this Court; which is in the word and figures following to wit:

Nashville 1st April 1840

$630- . I certify that John England has deposited with me six hundred and thirty Dollars for Jonathan T. Bradley Sherriff of White County for Revenue due from him for the year 1839 The Comptroller being from home; I could not give him a regular receipt for want of a Warrent to receive said Revenue for said year But the amount above State exceeds the revenue for 1838 to some small extent which the Deputy sherriff Mr. England prefered doing so as to have a small excess in his favor
To Thomas Eastland Esq.
Chairman W. C. Court

M. Frances Treas. of
Tennessee

Ordered that Court be adjourned untill tomorrow morning 10 O'Clock

Thos. Eastland
Lewis Pettett
John Bryan

Tuesday Morning the 7th day of April A.D. 1840 Court met pursuant to adjournment Present the worshipful

Thomas Eastland Esq Chairman
Lewis Pettett, Asa Certain;
John Jett, Jesse Walling;
John Bryan; Anderson S. Rogers
Elijah Frost, Thomas Green,
William Little, William
Bruster, and George Defreese.

This day William G. Sims appeared in open Court as was appointed and sworn Deputy Clerk of White County Court.

This day Robert Smith Regester of White County appeared in open Court and Nicholas Oldham Deputy Regester of White County and took an oath for the faithful discharge of his duties as such.

Ordered by Court that the order made at the August Term 1838 of this Court appointing Commissioners for the Corporate limits of the town of Sparta be and the same is hereby rescinded.

Isd Ordered by Court that Anthony Dibrell, Wamon Leftwich, William M. Young, William Usery, Edward M. Murray, Lewis Fletcher and William Simpson be appointed and they are (P-369) hereby constituted Commissioners of the Corporation of the town of Sparta in the County of White in the State of Tennessee with full power and Authority to hold posess and enjoy all such powers priviliges and immunities and to make, ordain, enact and enforce such Rules, Regulations and bye laws as are contemplated in and granted by the several acts of the General Assembly of said State in incorporating the said town of Sparta with full power to enter forthwith upon the discharge of their duties.

Isd Ordered by Court that the following named persons be appointed and summoned as jurors to the June term 1840 of White Circuit Court To Wit: John Crook, Calloway Davis, Alexander McDaniel, William Knowles, Sr., William C. Bounds, John Pennington, Spencer Holder, Matthias Hutson, Richard England, Joshua Hickey, Isaac Buck, James Bartlett, Joshua Mason, James William, William Bruster, Daniel McClain, John Austen, Samuel Miller, Jesse Walling, Robert Anderson, Thomas Jones, William Irwin, Sr., George Price, Samuel Brown, William Snodgrass and John Brown good and lawful men citizens of the County of White and Charles Meeks and Hayes Arnold, constable to attend thereon and that a writ of venirefacias issue directed &c.

The State vs James Scott } Bastardy Elizabeth Savago Pros'x.

On motion of the Defendant by his attorney and upon the affidavit of the Defendant it is ordered by the Court that an issue be made up to try the truth of the charge in the contained Warrent in this case It is further ordered that this cause be continued untill the next term of this Court and that the said Elizabeth Savage the prosecutrix in the above cause be served with notice of this order.

Isd Ordered by Court that Charles Denny and John Kerby be assigned to work on that portion of the milk sick fence of which William M. Bryan, Jr., is Overseer - .

Isd Ordered by Court that Laban Foster be appointed Overseer of the road from John Bryans field to entersect the road leading from Sparta to Simpsons Mill at the Coopers Shop being a road of the second Class and keep the same in repair as the law requires and that the same list and bounds of hands that worked under Charles Graham late Overseer thereof be assigned to work thereon.

Ordered by Court that, that portion of the Shipping port road and that portion of the Herd Mill and that part of the Simpson road

(P-370) which passes over the lands of Jacob A. Lane on the west side of town Creek be discontinued so far as they pass over the lands of the said Lane; that the Herd road; and Shippingport road be so arranged and laid off as to run upon the line between Jacob A. Lane and Richard Nelson and Daniel Clark so as to cross town Creek at Daniel Clarks Mills, the Simpson road to entersect the same; the road to be opened by Jacob A. Lane on his own Land on said lines at his own proper Cost and charges And the said Jacob A. Lane agrees that on or before the first day of November next that he will run a lane through said Lane or field which will be made and enclosed by the permission of this order crossing town Creek where the Shippingport road now crosses said Creek to be of equal grade with the Shipping port road whatever that may be at the time of opening said lane -

Ordered by Court that Benjamin Flynn be appointed overseer of the road from Little Laurell Creek to Clifty being a road of the 2nd Class and keep the same in repair as the law requires and that the same bounds of hands that worked under Josiah Prator be assigned to work thereon.

Isd Ordered by Court that John Jett, John Bryan, Thomas Green, Lewis Pettett James Knowles, Richard Crowder, William Hitchcock, George Defreese, John Pennington, Isaac Buck, Sims Dearing, William R. Tucker, Elijah Frost Esquires Commission of the Revenue of White County for the year 1840 be allowed Ten dollars each for taking lists of the taxable property and poles in said County for said year to be paid by the Trustee of said County out of the tax of the year 1840

Isd It appearing to the satisfaction of the Court that owing to the unsettled conditioned of the disputed territory between the counties of White & DeKalb, it is enexpedient for the sherriff of White County to enforce the collection of the taxes in said disputed territory due and owing to the County of White - It is therefore considered and so ordered that the sherriff of White County desist from the collection of said taxes to the amount of $122.00½ until the further directed of this Court, and that the Sherriff of White County have a credit therefore in the settlement of his accounts for the year 1839

Isd This day Jonathan T. Bradley Esquire Sherriff and Collector of the public Taxes in White County returned upon oath a list of Delinquents for the taxes of the year 1837 and 1838 amounting to the sum of One hundred and twenty one dollars twelve and one half cents and ordered that the sherriff of White County have a Credit thereof in the settlement of his accounts for the year 1839

(P-371) Isd It appearing to the satisfaction of the Court from the settlement of John Jett, Esq. Treas. of the poor house of White County; that after satisfying all the claims against the poor house tax, to the present time there remains a surplus in his hands of the poor tax amounting to the sum of Three hundred and seventy three dollars ninety three and one half cents.

It therefore considered by the Court and so ordered, that the above sum of 373.93½ shall be applied to the extenguishment of County claims against the County of White.

And the Treasure of poor house is directed to settle with Jonathan

T. Bradley the sum of two hundred and forty three dollars thirteen cents the amount this day allowed him for delinquents and for taxes due in the disputed territory of White & DeKalb being a County claim and also to settle with said Bradley the sum of $130.00 for two County claims filed in the Trustees office in the year 1831 one in favor of Anthony Dibrell for $106.25 and one in the name of B. L. Ridley for $23.75 and when so settled the treasures of the poor house shall have over said vouchers to the Trustee of White County and shall be deemed as that much of the surplus of $373.93½ directed to be paid over to him as above, and the balance of said surplus amounting to eighty and one half cents to be paid over to the Trustee of said County for the purposes aforesaid.

Isd Ordered by Court unanimously that John Jett and John Bryan Esquires Com'rs to settle with Trustee, Clerks &c be each allowed the sum of two dollars pr. day for three days services in settling with Robert Cox Trustee of White County and for making out report amounting to the sum of seven dollars fifty cents each to be paid by the Trustee of White County out of the tax of the year 1840

Isd Ordered by Court unanimously that Robert Smith Esq be allowed the sum of nine dollars fifty cents for money expended in buying a Blank Book for the Regesters office of White County to be paid by the Trustee of White County out of the tax of 1840.

Isd Ordered by Court that William Glenn be allowed the sum of Four dollars fifty cents for furnishing one Blank record Book for the office of the Circuit Court of White County to be paid by the Trustee of White County out of the tax of 1840.

Isd Ordered by Court unanimously that Simon R. Doyle Corner of White County be allowed the sum of Ten dollars for holding two Inquests.- One over the dead body of a certain Duncan Harden who came to his death by Drunkeness and being out all night on the cold ground - and the other over the dead body of a certain John Hutchens who came to his death by murder - both being Citizens of the County of White to be paid by the Treasure of the poor house out of any monies not otherwise appropriated.

(P-372) Isd Ordered by Court that William Simpson be allowed the sum of one hundred dollars as compensation for keeping the Bridge across the Calf Killer at Sparta in repair during the year 1840 to be paid out of the tax of the year 1840 laid exclusively for that purpose.

This day Jonathan T. Bradley Esquire Sherriff and Collector of the public Taxes in White County for the years 1838 and 1839; prodused in open Court the receipts of Robert Cox Trustee and John Jett Treasure of the poor house of White County which are received by the Court and ordered to be recorded. To wit:

Received of Jonathan T. Bradley after Deducting the amount of Sherriff and Trustee Commissions the full amount of the taxes for the years 1838 and 1839 for which I now have the vouchers Received 7th day of April 1840

Ro. Cox
Trustee"

Received of Jonathan T. Bradley Sherriff of White County the whole amount of money due for the poor tax for the year 1838 and 1839 This 7th

April 1840

John Jett
Treasure of Poor house"

Issd Ordered by Court unanimously that the following persons be allowed the following sums of money for fees in the case of the State against Larkin Stewart certified from the Supreme Court of Tennessee at Nashville to wit: James P. Clark Clerk $9.25 Anthony Dibrell Clerk 3.75 J. A. Lane Clerk $6.75 Shff W. G. Sims $2.25 Shff D. L. Mitchell $1.00 Justice J. Rose $1.00 Court M. Taylor 0.50 Attorney General John B. McCormick 2.50 amounting in all to the sum of Twenty seven dollars to be paid by the Trustee of White County Court out of any monies not otherwise appropriated - .

This day Jonathan T. Bradley produced in open Court a certificate of his Election of Sherriff of White County for the next two years and having also produced all the receipts into open Court which by law he was bound to do and thereupon being present in open Court took an oath to support the constitution of the United States and of the State of Tennessee and the several oaths required by law and an oath for the faithful collection of the public taxes and together with James Randols, Sr., Thomas Walling, Richard Bradley, Hugh Gracy, Samuel V. Carrick, Richard England, Anthony Dibrell, William Glenn, Jr., and Zachariah Anderson entered into and acknowledged three bonds in the sum of thirty five Thousand dollars conditioned as the law requires which bonds are in the words and figures following to wit:

Bond

State of Tennessee White County
Know all men by (P-373) these presents that we Jonathan T. Bradley, James Randols, Sr., Thomas Walling, Richard Bradley, Hugh Gracy, Samuel V. Carrick, Richard England, Anthony Dibrell, William Glenn, Jr., John L. Price, Zachariah Anderson are held and firmly bound unto his Excellency James K. Polk, Esquire Govenor in and over the State aforesaid or his successors in office in the sum of Twenty Thousand dollars Current money which payment well and truly to be made and done, we bind ourselves and each and every of our heirs executors and adminestrators jointly and severally firmly these presents sealed with our seals and dated the 6th day of April A.D. 1840 where as it appearing to the satisfaction of the Court that Jonathan T. Bradley hath been duly and Constitutionally elected Sherriff in and for the County of White for the two years next ensuing

Now the condition of the above obligation is such that if the bound Jonathan T. Bradley shall well and truly execute and due return make of all process and precepts to him directed and pay and satisfy all fees and sums of mony by him received or levied by verture of process into the proper office which the same by the tenor thereof ought to be paid or to the person or persons to whom the same shall be due his, her or their executors, adminestrators agents and all others things well and truly and faithfully execute the said office of Sherriff so long as he shall continue therein according to law then this obligation to be void else be and remain in full force and virtue
Test
W. Oldham, Clk.

J. T. Bradley	(seal)
James Randols	(seal)
Thomas Walling	(seal)
Rich'd Bradley	(seal)
Hugh Gracy	(seal)
Sam. V. Carrick	(seal)
Richard England	(seal)
A. Dibrell	(seal)
William Glenn, Jr.	(seal)
John L. Price	(seal)
Zachariah Anderson	(seal)

State of Tennessee White County

Know all men by their presents that we Jonathan T. Bradley, James Randols, Sr., Thomas Walling, Richard Bradley, Hugh Gracy, Samuel V. Carrick, Richard England, A. Dibrell, William Glenn, Jr., John L. Price and Zachariah Anderson all of the County of White and State of Tennessee are held and firmly bound unto his excellency James K. Polk Esquire Govenor in and over the State aforesaid for the time being or his successors in office in the sum of Five Thousand Dollars to the payment of which well and truly to be made we bind ourselves our heirs executors and adminestrators jointly and severally, firmly by their presents, sealed with our seals and dated the 6th day of April A.D. 1840

The condition of the above obligation is such that whereas the above bound Jonathan T. Bradley has been duly and constitutionally elected sherriff and collector of the public taxes of said County of White for two years from the first Saturday in March (P-374) 1840 Now if the said Jonathan T. Bradley shall well and truly collect all State taxes and also all taxes on school lands within said County which by law he ought to collect and well and truly account for and pay over all taxes by him collected or which ought to be collected on the first day of December in the year 1840 and 1841 Respectively these the above obligation to be void otherwise to be and remain in full force and virtue

Test
N. Oldham, Clk.

J. T. Bradley	(seal)
James Randols	(seal)
Thomas Walling	(seal)
Richard Bradley	(seal)
Hugh Gracy	(seal)
Samuel V. Carrick	(seal)
Richard England	(seal)
A. Dibrell	(seal)
William Glenn, Jr.	(seal)
John L. Price	(seal)
Zachariah Anderson	(seal)

Know all men by these presents that we Jonathan T. Bradley, James Randols, Sr., Thomas Walling, Richard Bradley, Hugh Gracy, Samuel V. Carrick, Richard England, A. Dibrell, William Glenn, Jr., John L. Price & Zachariah Anderson, all of the County of White and State of Tennessee are held and firmly bound unto Thomas Eastland, Esquire Chairman of the County Court of said County and his successors in office in the sum of five thousand dollars current money for the use of White County payment well and truly to be made and done we bind ourselves and each and ever of our heirs executors and adminestrators jointly and severally firmly by these presents sealed with our seals and dated the 6th day of April A.D. 1840 whereas the above bound Jonathan T. Bradley has been certified to the County Court of said County as duly and constitutionally elected Sherriff of said County for the next ensuing two years and is also appointed collector of the public Taxes for the County aforesaid for the year 1840.

Now if the above bound Jonathan T. Bradley shall well and truly and faithfully collect all the taxes which shall be levied and assessed for the County of White for the year 1840 To wit: the County tax, Jury tax, poor tax and Bridge Tax and tax for paving the square in Sparta for the use of said County of White and shall pay the monies so collected over to the proper offices in said County who are autherised to received the same according to law then the above obligation to be null and void else be and remain in full force and vertue

Test
N. Oldham, Clk.

J. T. Bradley (seal)
James Randols (seal)
Thomas Walling (seal)
Rich'd Bradley (seal)
Hugh Gracy (seal)
Sam V. Carrick (seal)
Richard England (seal)
A. Dibrell (seal)
William Glenn, Jr. (seal)
John L. Price (seal)
Zachariah Anderson (seal)

(P-375) Tuesday 6th April A.D. 1840

This day Jonathan T. Bradley Esquire Sherriff of White County appeared in open Court and appointed John England, Jr., and Smith J. Walling to act as Deputy Sherriffs in the County of White who both being present in open Court were sworn to discharge their duties as such.

Ordered that Court be adjourned untill tomorrow at 2 Oclock P.M.

John Jett
Wm. Bruster
William Little

Wednesday 8th April A.D. 1840 Court met pursuant to adjournment Present the worshipful

John Jett } Esquires
William Bruster }
William Little } Justices

This day Jonathan T. Bradley Sherriff of White County and appointed Archibald Conner Special Deputy Sherriff to collect the arrears of Taxes in said County for the securities of David L. Mitchell late Sherriff of said County up to 1 January 1837. And to transact business before Justices of the peace and no further - who being present in open Court to the oath prescribed by law. And entered upon the discharge of his duties.

Ordered by Court that, that portion of road which leaves the Shippingport road near the foot of the mountain in Green's Cove & entersecting the Simpson road at the corner of Col. Richard Nelsons field be established a road of the third Class.

Issd Ordered by Court that Ozburn Walker; George Elmore; Cornelius Hickey; Henry Collier and William Williams freeholders be appointed a Jury of view to lay off and mark a road of the third Class from the Carthage road near John Walkers passing Henry Colliers to the DeKalb County line and report thereof to the next term of this court

Ordered that Court be adjourned untill Court in Course

Test
N. Oldham; Clk.

John Jett
Wm. Bruster
William Little

(P-376) State of Tennessee

At a Court began and held for the County of White and State aforesaid in the Court house in the town of Sparta before the Justices of said Court on the first Monday being the fourth day of May A.D. 1840 And of the Independence of the United States the sixty fourth year

Present the Worshipful

David Snodgrass, John Bryan
Sims Dearing, Edmund Stamps, } Esquires
Asa Certain, Thomas Green,
Wm. Knowles, William Little,
James Knowles, William Bruster, } Justices
John Jett.

This day the death of John R. Glenn late of the County of White was suggested in open Court and that he departed this life entestate thereupon William Glenn and Samuel Ramsey were appointed administrators of all and singular the goods and chattles lands and tenements of the said John R. Glenn Dec'd and who being present in open Court took the oath prescribed by law and together with Jonathan T. Bradley and Robert B. Glenn entered into and acknowledged bond in the sum of two Thousand five hundred dollars conditioned as the law requires.

This day George Pertle was appointed guardian to Caroline Hooper and David H. Hooper two of the infant heirs of Edward E. Hooper Deceased who being present in open Court took the oath prescribed by law and together with Joshua Mason and James Knowles entered into and acknowledged bond in the sum of two Thousand five hundred dollars conditioned as the law requires.

Isd Ordered by Court that William Austin be appointed Overseer of the road from Jesse Wallings to John Smiths being a road of the first Class and keep the same in repair as the law requires and that the same list and bounds of hands that worked under James Herd late Overseer thereof be assigned to work thereon.

Isd On the humble Petition of Sundry Citizens of White County it is ordered by Court that William McKinny, Richard Bradley, Sims Dearing, Benjamin Weaver and Thomas Broyles freeholders be appointed a Jury of view to examine lay off and mark a road of the third Class from the marked Chesnut on the mountain passing over the lands of B. Weaver, Thos Bradley, R. Bradley, and Thomas Broyles, to entersect the Calf Killer road near Thomas Broyles and report thereof to the next term of this Court.

This day Joshua Mason guardian to the heirs of Alexander Glenn dec'd made his report upon oath which is ordered to be recorded.

(P-377) Monday the 4th day of May A.D. 1840

This day the Court proceeded to the election of Surveyor for the County of White for the next ensuing four years, and to that office do appoint Jonathan C. Davis Esquire, who being present in open Court took an oath to support the Constitution of the United States and of the State of Tennessee and the oath of office and together with Samuel V. Carrick, William M. Young, John Jett, John Bryan and Thomas Green entered into and acknowledged bond in the sum of Ten Thousand Dollars conditioned as the law requires - .

This day the Court proceeded to the election of Coroner for the County of White for the next ensuing two years and to that office do appoint Simon R. Doyle Esquire who being present in open Court took an oath to support the constitution of the United States and the several oaths prescribed by law and together with John White; William Simpson; John Jett; Samuel V. Carrick and William Lewis; entered into and acknowledged bond in the sum of Five Thousand Dollars conditioned as the law requires.

This day the Court proceeded to the appointment of Ranger for White County for the two years next ensuing; and to that office do appoint John Bryan Esquire who being present in open Court took an oath to support the constitution of the United States and of the State of Tennessee and the oath of office and together with John Jett and Jabez G. Mitchell entered into bond in the sum of Five hundred dollars conditioned as the law requires - .

Issd Ordered by Court that Smith J. Walling; Samuel Jones; Robert Smith; Thomas Quillon and Hugh Gracy freeholders be appointed a Jury of view to lay off and mark a road of the second Class from Hugh Gracy's passing on in the direction to General Simpson Mills not to interfere with plantations and report thereof to the next term of this Court.

Issd Ordered by Court Frances Simmons be appointed Overseer of the road from Meeks Mill to VanBuren County line being a road of the second Class and keep the same in repair as the law requires and that the same list of hands that worked under Nathan Earles (in White County) late Overseer thereof be assigned to work thereon.

State of Tennessee) Bastardy
vs)
Stephen Pistole) Polly Ann Wilhite; Prosecutrix

On motion of the Prosecutrix by her attorney Richard Nelson Esquire and for reasons appearing to the satisfaction of the Court it is ordered by the Court that the Clerk of this Court issue executions on the amt. of that part of the Judgment which may have become due rendered in the above cause at the July term 1837 of this Court to the use and benefit of the Prosecutrix in this case & also pay the cost of this motion.

(P-378) Monday the 4th day of May A.D. 1840
Present Thos Green; D. Snodgrass, Jno. Bryan & Wm. Little Esquires

State of Tennessee)
vs) Bastardy
James Scott) Elizabeth Savage; Prox.

This day Came as well the Prosecutrix as the Defendant by their attornies and having heard the evidence and arguments of counsel on the issue made in this Cause; and after mature deliberation by the Court thereon had it is the openion of the Court that the Defendant is guilty of the begetting of the Bastard child upon the body of the said Elizabeth Savage the prosecutrix in this cause as charged against him in the warrent in this cause mentioned.

It is therefore considered by the Court and so ordered that the Defendant James Scott, pay unto the above Prosecutrix the sum of Ninety Dollars to wit: the sum of Forty dollars within Twelve months from this date; the sum of Thirty dollars with in two years from this date and also the sum of twenty dollars within Three years from this date that said Defendant find sureties to endemnify the County of White from all Costs and damages consequent in the support and maintainance of the said Bastard child begotten as aforesaid And further that the State of Tennessee recover against the said Defendant all Costs in this behalf expended &c.

From which Judgment of the Court the Defendant prayed an appeal to the next honorable Circuit Court to be held for the County of White on the first Monday of June next and to him it is granted.

State of Tennessee vs James Scott } Bastardy Elizabeth Savage; Prox.

This day came the Defendant with Nicholas Oldham into open Court and acknowledged themselves indebted to the State of Tennessee in the sum of seven hundred and fifty Dollars towit: the Defendant in the sum of five hundred dollars and the said Nicholas Oldham in the sum of two hundred and fifty dollars to be levied of their respective goods and chattles lands and tenements to the use of the State to be rendered nevertheless to be void on condition that the Defendant shall well and truly make his personally appearanse befor the Judge of our next Circuit Court to be held for the County of White in the Court house in the town of Sparta on the first Monday of June next on the 4th day of the term thereof, then and there to answer the above charge and attend from day to day and not depart thereof with out leave of the Court first had and obtained - .

Ordered that Court be adjourned (P-379) until tomorrow morning 10 O'Clock

John Bryan
Sims Dearing
William Little

Tuesday Morning 5th May A.D. 1840 Court met pursuant to adjournment Present the worshipful

John Bryan, Sims Dearing, William Little } Esquire Justices

This day Jonathan T. Bradley Esquire Sherriff of White County appointed Avery Norris one of his Deputy for said County who appeared in open Court and took the oaths prescribed by law and entered upon the discharge of his duties

This day Nicholas Oldham appeared in open Court and was appointed and qualified as Deputy Ranger of White County

Ordered that Court be adjourned until Court in Course

Test
N. Oldham, Clk.

John Bryan
Sims Dearing
William Little

State of Tennessee

At a Quorum Court began and held in and for the County of White in the Court house in the town of Sparta on the first Monday in June before the Justices of said Court being the first day of June in the year of our Lord One thousand eight hundred and forty and of the Independence of the United States of America the sixty fourth year

Present the Worshipful

David Snodgrass } Esqrs.
John Bryan }
Sims Dearing } Justices

Issd Ordered by Court that John White, Jacob Anderson, William Lewis,
(P-380) John Felton and Spence Mitchell, Jr., freeholders be appointed a Jury of view to lay off and mark a road of the third Class from Doyles Mills to entersect the hickory valley road near the union meeting house and report thereof to the next term of this Court - .

Issd Ordered by Court that Spencer Holder, Jr., be appointed Overseer of the road from John Haltermans to Lewis Phillips being a road of the first Class and keep the same in repair as the law requires and that the same list and bounds of hands that worked under John Holder late Overseer thereof be assigned to work thereon.

Issd Ordered by Court that Abraham Saylors be appointed Overseer of the road from Goodwins branch to Hardys old Cabbins on the Kentucky road being a road of the first Class and keep the same in repair as the law requires and that the same list and bounds of hands that worked under Stephen C. Pistole late Overseer thereof be assigned to work thereon.

This day Isaiah Hutson guardian to John W. Knowles filed in open Court said Knowles Receipt which is ordered to be recorded.

This day Dosia Lay, late Dosia Hooper one of the heirs of Edward E. Hooper Dec'd being over the age of fourteen years appeared in open Court and selected and made choice of George Pertle, Sr., as her guardian who also being present in open Court took the oath required by law and together with Asa Certain and William Cantrell entered into and acknowledged bond in the sum of eight hundred dollars conditioned as the law requires.

Isad Ordered by Court that, that portion of road over which Forrester Fifer is overseer be so extended as to run to Paynes Bridge being a road of the second Class and keep this as well as the other part in repair as the law requires - and that Thomas Green and Jesse Walling Esqrs assign a list and bounds of hands to work thereon -

State of Tennessee) Bastardy
vs)
James Scott) Elizabeth Savage, Prosx.

On motion of the Defendant by his Attorney he is permitted to withdraw the appeal granted him in the above cause at last term of this Court and it is orderd that he find securitits to endemnify the County of White as required by the Judgment of this Court at the last term thereof

State) Bastardy
vs)
James Scott) Elizabeth Savage, Prosx

This day Came the defendant with Smith J. Walling
(P-381) And Nicholas Oldham into open Court and became securities for the fine and cost in this cause rendered at the last term of this Court; and also bind themselves to keep harmless and free from any cost and damage the County of White as to the support and maintainance of the Bastard Child begotten upon the body of the Prosecutrix as charged in the warrent in this cause and that the State recover all costs; in this behalf expended &c and that execution issue for the collection of the same.

This day Mary Farley a Citizen of the County of White appeared in open Court and filed her Declaration for a Pension under the act of the Congress of the United States of America of the of the 7th July 1838 who with Judith Farley and Isham Farley to the Court known and made oath to the contents of their affidavits and it is ordered that the same be entered of record and that the Clerk of this Court certify the same under the seal of this Court.

Ordered that Court be adjourned untill tomorrow morning 10 Oclock

David Snodgrass
John Bryan
Elijah Frost

Tuesday morning the 2nd June A.D. 1840 Court met pursuant to adjournment
Present the Worshipful

David Snodgrass) Esqr
John Bryan)
Elijah Frost) Justice

State of Tennessee) Bastardy
vs Isad)
John R. Glenn) Clara Cock, Prosx

On motion of the Prosecutrix and for reasons appearing to the satisfaction of the Court it is ordered by the Court that the Clerk of this Court issue an execution on the judgment in this cause rendered at the August term 1839 of this Court for the collection of the sum of Forty dollars with enterest thereon from the time it fell due until paid agreeable to said judgment to the use and benefit of the above name prosecutrix - And that the state of Tennessee recover against said Defendant and her securities the cost of this motion.

Isad Ordered by Court that Gatleff McGuire be appointed overseer of the road from the ford of the Calf Killer to the foot of the hill at James Snodgrass being a road of the second Class and keep the same in repair as the law requires and that (P-382) the same list and bounds of hands that worked under Daniel Kelly late Overseer thereof be assigned to work thereon.

This day Elizabeth Hargis a Citizen of the County of White filed in open Court her Declaration under the act of Congress of the United States of the 7th July 1838 for a Pension and also appeared in open Court Larkin Wisdom to the Court known; and made oath to the contents of his affidavet which is signed by the Court and ordered by the Court that the Clerk of this Court certify the same under the seal of said Court.

Ordered that Court be adjourned until Court in Course

Test
N. Oldham; Clk.

David Snodgrass
John Bryan
Elijah Frost

State of Tennessee

At a County Court began and held for the County of White in the State aforesaid in the Court house in the town of Sparta before the Justices of said Court on the first Monday being the sixth day of July in the year of our Lord One thousand eight hundred and forty and of the Independence of the United States the 65th year

Present the Worshipful

John Jett; Esq Chr. Pro-tem
David Snodgrass; John Bryan;
Sims Dearing; Elijah Frost;
James Knowles; William Knowles;
Anderson S. Rogers; Lewis Pettett;
Jesse Walling, William Bruster;
Thomas Jones, John Pennington,
Asa Certain, William Little;
William Hudgins; George Defreese;
Richard Crowder; Thomas Green;

This day the Clerk of this Court produced in open Court the report of a settlement made with John Mason guardian to James Howard one of the heirs of James Howard Deceased which being unexcepted to; is received by the Court and affirmed in all its parts and is ordered to be recorded.

Isd This day the death of John Hutchens late of the County of White (P-383) was suggested in open Court and that he departed this life intestate, whereupon Aaron Hutchens was appointed administrator of all and singular the goods and chattles rights and credits of the deceased who being present in open Court took the oath prescribed by law and together with William G. Sims and William H. Baker entered into and acknowledged bond in the sum of six hundred Dollars conditioned as the law requires.

Isd Ordered by Court that Thomas Jones, Eli Sims and Joseph Bozarth be appointed Commissioners to assign and set apart to the widow and family of John Hutchens deceased one years support out of his estate and report thereof to the next term of this Court

This day Oliver P. Sims appeared in open Court and was appointed and sworn as Deputy Clerk of White County Court.

This day Susannah Walling the relect and widow of James Walling, Jr. deceased produced in open Court her account against the heirs and legal Representative of the deceased amounting to the sum of one hundred and sixty dollars and also appeared in open Court Joseph Herd and Anderson S. Rogers guardian to the minor heirs of the said Deceased and also Jesse Walling administrator of the estate of the deceased and the matters and things contained in said account being fully understood by the parties

It is agreed upon by consent of the guardians aforesaid and the administrator aforesaid and with the assent of the Court that the administrator allow a credit on the note of Susannah Walling due to the administrator thereof for the sum of one hundred and forty six dollars sixty six and three fourth cents being the Eleven twelths of the $160. which is properly chargeable to the children of the Deceased for their support and maintainance; and the credit so given shall operate as a legal voucher for the said Jesse Walling administrator aforesaid in the final settlement of his

accounts as adminestrator and it is ordered by the Court accordingly-.
(set aside page 435)

For reasons appearing to the satisfaction of the Court by the production of a record from the County Court of Van Buren County. It is Ordered by the Court that the Indenture of John Kelly as an apprentice to Sandford Medley be cancelled and for for nothing esteemed and that Sandford Medley and Joseph Cummings, Jr., and Charles Reeves his securities from the penalties of said bond be released and forever discharged - .

This day Samuel Lance appeared in open Court and produced a Commission from the Govenor appointing him a Justice of the (P-384) peace for White County and thereupon took an oath to support the Constitution of the United States and of the State of Tennessee and the oath prescribed by law and thereupon entered up the discharge of his duties by taking his seat upon the bench - .

On the humble Petition of Sundry Citizens of White County and for reasons appearing fully to the satisfaction of the Court it is ordered by the Court that the District line between the 8th and tenth District shall be as follows that from the crossing of the Rockisland road which is the line between the two Districts and post oak Creek down said Creek thence up the Caney Fork to the mouth of Hutchens Creek thence up said Creek to the Jackson County line thence with said line to Rockisland road, so as to make said Hutchens Creek on the west and post oak on the East sides of the Caney Fork the line between the two District - . which is established as the dividing lines thereof.

Issd Ordered by Court that Sarah Dyer be allowed the sum of Seventy Dollars for supporting and cloathing three of the minor heirs of John Dyer Deceased to wit: Louisa Dyer the sum of twenty five dollars, Claiborn Dyer the sum of twenty dollars and John C. Dyer the sum of twenty five dollars to be paid by Samuel Brown their guardian out of the estate of his wards - And it is further ordered that the said Sarah Dyer be allowed the further sum of One hundred and fifteen dollars for supporting and cloathing four other of the minor heirs of the said John Dyer Dec'd to wit: Nelson Dyer the sum of twenty five dollars, William A. Dyer the sum of Thirty dollars, Alzira Dyer the sum of Thirty dollars and Margrett Dyer the sum of Thirty dollars to be paid by John Pennington their guardian out of their estate being the amount of her account against said wards from the 17 July 1835 up to this date - .

Issd On the humble application of Spencer Holder a Citizen of the County of White and for reasons appearing to the satisfaction of the Court he is permitted to build a dam across the Caney Fork and erect a Grist Mill and other water machinery thereon at any place on his own land or on Grant No 7328 in the name of Spencer & Joseph Holder for twenty two acres provided the erection of the same shall not enterfere with any privilige heretofore given or be injurious to the property of other persons - .

Issd On the humble petition of sundry Citizens of White County and for reasons appearing fully to the satisfaction of the Court that something like thirty years since certain grist mills and other water machinery have been erected on the little Caney Fork commonly called the falling water which mills have heretofore been known as Hunters mills but now as Hiram

Browns and it appearing that said (P-385) Mills had not been established by this Court It is now ordered by the Court that those mills possess and enjoy the same priviliges and advantages as though they had been at first erected by the permission of this Court.

Ordered by Court (a majority of all the Justices present) that Simon R. Doyle Coroner of White County be allowed the sum of Thirteen dollars and fifty cents for nine days services and expances in open and holding the election for County officers in March in the year 1840 to be paid by the Trustee of White County - . out of the tax of year 1840.

Issd Ordered by Court that John W. Cope be appointed Overseer of the road from Milton Groces to the middle of the Carter Old field being a road of the first Class and keep the same in repair as the law requires and that Richard Crowder and Thomas Jones Esquires apportion the lands belonging on said road from Groces to the Peeled Chesnut between the overseers to work thereon - .

Issd Ordered by Court that Abel C. Hutson be appointed Overseer of the road from the two mile post to the house of John Knowles, Sr., being a road of the first Class and keep the same in repair as the law requires and that Matthias Hutson, Lewis Pettett and William Knowles apportion the hands between him and Jesse Franks to work thereon - .

For reasons appearing to the satisfaction of the Court from the petition of Sundry Citizens of White County that road commonly called the Shipping port road now a third Class road is ordered by the Court to be changed from a third to a second Class road and established as such. And that the diffrent overseer thereof are required to keep the same in repair as a 2nd Class road - .

Issd This day the Commissioners heretofore appointed to lay off and mark a road of the 3rd Class from Doyles mills to entersect the Hickory Valley road near the Union Meeting house made their report which is received and said road established a road of the third Class. And that Simon R. Doyle be appointed Overseer thereof and open and keep the same in repair as the law requires and that Anderson S. Rogers and John Bryan assign a list of hands to open and work on the same - .

This day the clerk of this Court produced in open Court the report of a settlement with Daniel Hollensworth executor of the last will and testament of James Goddard dec'd (P-386) which is received by the Court being unexcepted to, and affirmed in all its parts and ordered to be recorded.

This day the Clerk of this Court produced in open Court the report of a settlement with Joshua Mason Admr. of Caleb Mason dec'd which being unexcepted to, is received and affirmed in all its parts by the Court and ordered to be recorded.

This day the Clerk of this Court produced in open Court the report of a settlement with James Snodgrass admr. of Andrew Hampton Deceased which being unexcepted is received and affirmed in all its parts by the Court and ordered to be recorded - .

Issd Ordered by Court unanimously that Nicholas Oldham Clerk of

White County Court be allowed the following fees for the following service to wit: to issuing one hundred and seventy four Jury tickets at six and one fourth cents each - . To issuing seventy seven overseers orders at twelve and a half cents each issuing twenty Juries of view at twenty five cents each - . issuing four venirifacias to Circuit Court at fifty cents each to the case of pauperism fifty cents each - recording two settlements with the clerks of White County $1.00 each as per act exhibited up to 1st July 1840 amounting to the sum of Thirty One dollars to be paid by the Trustee of White County out of any monies not otherwise appropriated - .

Ordered by Court unanimously that William G. Sims Clerk of White Circuit Court be allowed the sum of Twelve dollars for furnishing a Blank record book for his office agreeable to his account to be paid by the Trustee of White County out of the taxes of 1840.

Isad Ordered by Court that James Hudgins, John Rose, Charles McGuire, Samuel Lance and William Simpson freeholders be appointed a Jury of view to lay off and mark a road of the third Class from James Hudgins passing John Rose's to Gibbs Mill and report thereof to the next term of this Court.

It appearing to the satisfaction of the Court that the clerk of this Court in making the order of allowance to the Justices of the Quorum Court for the year 1839 had made an error therein it ordered by the Court that the Clerk be permitted to correct said order and to make said order from the proper number of days to which they are entitled

This day Joshua Mason was appointed Guardian to Benjamin Mason, Amanda Mason and America A. Mason minor heirs of Gabb Mason deceased and thereupon took the oath required by law and together with Cornelius Jarvis and Indemon B. Moore (P-387) entered into and acknowledged bond in the sum of seven hundred Dollars conditioned as the law requires - .

Isad Ordered by Court that the following named persons Citizens of the County of White be appointed Jurors to the October term next of White Circuit Court to wit: Lewis Fletcher, Hugh Gracy, Samuel Lance, David Snodgrass, Benjamin Lewis, John White, Jr., Noah H. Bradley, Elijah Frost, Benjamin Hutchens, James M. Nelson, William Templeton, Tidence L. Denton, Joseph Herd, Terry Walden, Sr., George Defreese, Asa Certain, James Knowles, John Rasco, William Hudgins, Daniel Bartlett, Adam Massa, John Stuart, John Pennington, William C. Bounds and Sims Dearing as Jurors and David Little and Isaac Brogden constable to attend thereon and that a writ of Venirifacias issue directed to the Sherriff.

The State of Tennessee } Bastardy
vs }
Stephen Pistole } Polly Ann Wilhite, Prosx.

On motion of the Defendent by his Attorney and for reasons appearing to the satisfaction of the Court the Bastard Child charged to have been begotten by the Defendant on the body of the prosecutrix had departed this life at the age of one year and seven months that the Defendant had paid & satisfied the first payment of forty Dollars, that he was ready to pay the second payment of Thirty dollars but in as much as the Bastard Child had died the Defondant by his Counsel moved the Court to be released from the payment of the last payment of Twenty dollars and also Ten dollars of the second payment. It is therefore considered by the Court and so ordered that the above defendant be released from the payment of the sum of twenty dollars and that the Clerk refund unto the said Defendant the sum of ten dollars collected by scierifacias of the second payment that the Judgment of this Court as relates to the last payment be cancelled and entirely set aside.

Issd Ordered by Court that Jonathan C. Davis Esquire Surveyor of White County be appointed survey and distinctly mark and designate the line between the County of White and the County of Van Buren agreeably to the law and constitution of the State of Tennessee so as the said line shall not approach nearer to the Court house of the County of White than Twelve miles and report thereof at the next term of this Court.

Issd Ordered by Court unanimously that the following persons be allowed the following sums of money as fees for services in the following State cases which have been examined by the County solicitor and reported to said Court as correctly taxed and properly (P-368) changeable to White County to wit: In the case the state vs Joseph Simmons Clerk W. G. Sims $11.62½ - Shff. J. T. Bradley $3.54 Shff John England 1.50; Shff J. G. Mitchell 0.75, Shff S. J. Walling .25, Shff John H. Graham 0.50 Shff James Graham 0.25. In the case the State vs Dennis Foster - Clerk Sims 7.06¼ Shff J. T. Bradley 2.16½ Shff Jno England 1.25 Shff S. J. Walling 0.75 The State vs May Sparkman, Tabetha Guidal Clerk W. G. Sims 6.50 Shff S. J. Walling $4.62½ Shff Jno England 1.37½ The State vs Archebald Miller Clerk W. G. Sims 9.43¾. Shff D. L. Mitchell 0.62½ Shff J. G. Mitchell 0.62½, Shff J. T. Bradley $4.50 The State vs George W. Julin clerk W. G. Sims 0.56¼ - The State vs Jesse Allen and John Allen clerk W. G. Sims $7.68¾ Shff J. T. Bradley $6.00 Shff Jno England $1.00 Shff Wm. Bozarth $1.00 State vs Jesse Allen Clerk W. G. Sims $11.87½ Shff D. L. Mitchell $3.00. Shff J. G. Mitchell 0.50 Shff. Jno England 0.62½ Shff J. T. Bradley 2.50 Shff Wm. Bozarth 0.50 - State vs William Norwood Clerk W. G. Sims 8.81¼ Shff D. L. Mitchell 0.75 Shff J. T. Bradley $3.00 Shff Jno England $1.00 Witness W. G. Crawford for State $2.00 - State vs James M. Nelson Clerk Sims $8.06¼ Shff S. J. Walling 0.50 Shff J. England 1.91¼ Witness for State Joseph Herd 4.50 witness William Goodwin $3.75 Witness W. R. Hitchcock 2.25 witness Emory Bennett 2.25 State vs Griffin G. Gamer, clerk W. G. Sims 8.81¼ Shff. D. L. Mitchell .75 Shff J. T. Bradley 4.00 Shff Jno England .50 witness for State Hugh Gracy .50 State vs William Swift clerk Sims $7.50 Shff J. T. Bradley $3.12½ Shff Jno England 1.50 - State vs Joseph Franks Clerk W. G. Sims $8.81¼ Shff D. L. Mitchell $0.75 Shff J. T. Bradley 3.00 Shff J. S. Walling $1.12½ Shff Jno England 50 witness William B. Hutson $2.00 State vs Nicholas H. McLemore clerk, W. G. Sims 8.56¼ Shff J. T. Bradley $4.00 Shff D. L. Mitchell $.75, Shff Jno England 0.50 witness for State Hugh Gracy 0.50 State vs John Anderson Clerk W. G. Sims $8.81¼ Shff D. L. Mitchell 0.75 Shff J. T. Bradley 3.50 Shff Jno England 1.00 witness for State Hugh Gracy .50 State vs Riley Woods Clerk W. G. Sims 6.81¼ Shff J. T. Bradley 2.87½ Shff Jno England $1.00 witness for the State Thomas Price 0.50 State vs John Dew Clerk W. G. Sims 6.12½ Shff J. England 3.25 witness for State William Goodwin 5.25 witness Wm. Hitchcock $5.25 - . State vs Richard Frasure Clerk W. G. Sims $8.62½ Shff D. L. Mitchell .50 Shff J. G. Mitchell 0.50 Shff J. T. Bradley 4.50 - State vs Riley Woods Clerk W. G. Sims 4.87½ Shff J. T. Bradley 2.00 Shff Jno. England 0.50 - - State vs William Swift Clerk W. G. Sims $8.31¼. Shff J. T. Bradley 3.12½ Shff Jno England 1.75 witness for State Thomas Price 0.50 being cases decided in the Circuit Court of White County amounting in all to the sum of two hundred and sixty eight dollars forty three cents to be paid by the Trustee of White County out of any monies not otherwise appropriated.

Isad this day Isiah Hutson one of the securities of Stephen G. Burton who is guardian for a certain Sylvester C. Gibbs appeared in open Court and showed to the Court he had notified in writing the said Stephen G. Burton guardian in as aforesaid to appear before the Justices of the present term of this Court to given other and sufficent securities ship for said guardianship but the said Burton failing so to do

Therefore on motion of the said (P-389) Isaiah Hutson a summons is awarded him requiring the said Stephen B. Burton personally to appear at the next term of this Court and give sufficent other or Counter security to be approved by said Court and abide such order of the Court as it may seem to them of right and proper to make and that Subpoena issue directed to the sherriff of White County &c

Ordered that Court be adjourned until tomorrow morning 10 O'clock

John Jett
John Bryan
Elijah Frost

Tuesday Morning 7th July A.D. 1840 Court met pursuant to adjournment
Present the Worshipful

John Jett
John Bryan
Elijah Frost
William Little
} Esquire Justices

This day Elizabeth Arnold produced in open Court her Declaration for a Pension under the act of the Congress of the 7th July 1838 providing for Widows &c and by the oaths of Joseph Herd and Jabez G. Mitchell proved that she was of good name fame and reputation and entitled to full credit on her oath in any Court of record. Which is ordered by the Court to be certified under the seal of this Court.

Ordered that Court be adjourned until Court in Course

John Jett
Elijah Frost
William Little

(P-390) State of Tennessee

At a Quorum Court began and held for the County of White and State aforesaid in the Courthouse in the town of Sparta before the Justices of said Court on the first Monday being the third day of August in the year of our Lord One Thousand eight hundred and Forty and of the Independence of the United States of America the Sixty fifth year

Present the worshipful

David Snodgrass } Esquires
John Bryan }
Sims Dearing } Justices

Isd Ordered by Court that the order of the last term appointing James Hudgins; John Rose; Charles McGuire; Samuel Lance and William Simpson freeholders a jury of view to lay off and mark a road of the third Class from James Hudgins passing John Rose's to Gibbs Mills be renewed and report thereof to the next term of this Court.

Isd Ordered by Court that the orders of last Court appointing William McKinney, Richard Bradley; Sims Dearing, Benjamin Weaver and Thomas Broyles freeholders a jury to lay off and mark a road of the third class from the marked Chesnut on the mountain near Benjamin Weavers passing over the lands of Benjamin Weaver, Thomas Bradley; R. Bradley and Thomas Broyles to enterseet the Calf Killer road near Thomas Broyles be renewed and report thereof to the next term of this Court.

Isd Ordered by Court that the order of the last term of this Court appointing Smith J. Walling; Samuel Jones; Robert Smith; Thomas Quillon and Hugh Gracy a jury of view to lay off and mark a road of the second Class from Hugh Gracy's passing on in the direction to General Simpson's mills be renewed and report thereof to the next term of this Court.

Isd Ordered by Court that Joseph Herd; James Randols; Hayes Arnold; Jesse A. Bounds and Washington Webb freeholders be appointed a Jury of view to examine; change and alter the Gumspring road that the same shall leave the McMinnville road and enterseet the old Gumspring road again near Hayes Arnold so as to shorten the distance about 300 yards and report thereof to the next term of this Court.

Isd Ordered by Court that John H. Jones be appointed (P-391) Overseer of the road from the top of Gumspring mountain to McGowen old place being a road of the secon Class and keep the same in repair as the law requires and that the same list and bounds of hands that worked under Lecil Smith be assigned to work thereon.

This day Robert Cox Esquire Trustee for the County of White appeared in open Court and together with Mark Lowry, Anthony Dibrell and Eli Sims entered into and acknowledged Bond in the sum of Three thousand five hundred and thirty one dollars two cents contained for the faithful disbursment of the Common school fund in the County aforesaid as the law requires

BOND

Know all men by these presents that we Robert Cox; Anthony Dibrell; Mark Lowry and Eli Sims all of the County of White and State of Tennessee are held and firmly bound unto Robert P. Currin Esquire Superintendant of public instruction in the State of Tennessee and his successors in office in the pinal sum of three Thousand five hundred and thirty one dollars two cents

current money which payment well and truly to be made and done we bind ourselves and each and every of our heirs executors or adminestrators jointly and severally firmly by these presents sealed with our seals and dated the 3rd day of August A.D. 1840 void on condition that the said Robert Cox shall faithfully pay over according to law all monies which may come into his hands on account of common schools in White County else be in full force and virtue.
Test
N. Oldham, Clk.

Ro. Cox (seal)
Mark Lowry (seal)
Eli Sims (seal)
Anthony Dibrell (seal)

This day Stephen G. Burton guardian to Sylvester C. Gibbs a minor in obediance to an order of the late term of this Court appeared in open Court and surrendered to the Court his appointment of guardian to the aforesaid Gibbs which is received by the Court and the aforesaid Stephen G. Burton and his securities therein from all future and further liabilities released and for ever discharged.

This day Sylvester C. Gibbs a minor over the age of fourteen years appeared in open Court and made choice of his Brother Anson Gibbs as his Guardian who being present in open Court took the oath prescribed by law and together with Indemon B. Moore and Cornelius Jarvis entered into and acknowledged bond in the sum of $800. conditioned &c.

(P-392) Monday 3rd August A. D. 1840.

This day John Lewis a minor over the age of fourteen years appeared in open Court and made choice of and selected William M. Bryan, Jr., as his Guardian who also being present in open Court took the oath required by law and together with Charles Denny and Samuel Turney entered into and acknowledged bond in the sum of six hundred dollars conditioned as the law requires.

This day Joshua Mason Guardian to the minor heirs of Cabb Mason Deceased returned his report upon oath which is ordered to be recorded - .

Woodson P. White
to
John Baker & assynee of
Richard Kerby

Title Bond for 5 acres land

This day John Jett and William M. Bryan, Jr. personally appeared in open Court and after being sworn in due form of law deposeth and saith - that they were intimately acquainted with the above named obligor Woodson P. White in his lifetime - that they saw him often write and sign his name, that they veribly believe the signature to the within title Bond to John Baker and him assignee of Richard Kerby purporting to be his is his own proper hand writing and his genuine signature that he has since departed this life and there being no subscribing witness to said Title Bond it is deemed by the Court to be sufficently proved and ordered to be Registered in the Registers office of White County - .

Ised Ordered by Court that Sims Dearing and Edmund Stamps Esquires be appointed Commissioners to apportion lists and bounds of hands between Thomas S. Elms Overseer and the Overseers of the diffrent roads in that neighborhood.

This day William Glenn adminestrator of the Estate of John R. Glenn Deceased returned upon oath an Inventory and account of sales of said Estate which is ordered to be recorded - .

Ordered by Court that Simon Bramblett, Edward M. Murray, John L. Price, Jabez G. Mitchell and Moses Carrick be and they are hereby appointed Trustees of Prustley Academy to serve until the first Monday in April 1842

This day Aaron Hutchens adminestrator of John Hutchens dec'd returned upon oath an Inventory and account of sales of the Estate of the deceased which is ordered to be recorded -.

(P-393) Monday 3rd day of August A.D. 1840

Issd Ordered by Court that John Swindle, Samuel A. Moore, Sr., Rowland Blankenship, Isaiah Hutson and Jesse Franks freeholders be appointed a Jury of view to lay off and mark a road of the third Class from Browns Mills the nearest and best way to entersect the Kentucky road and report thereof to the next term of this Court.

This day the Commissioners heretofore appointed by this Court to lay off assign and set apart one years provisions for the support and maintainance of the widow and family of John Hutchens deceased made their report which is received and ordered to be recorded.

This day Mary Farley to the Court known appeared in open Court and filed upon oath her amended Declaration for a Pension from the United States together with her vouchers Thomas Tallent and Jeremiah Farley also to the Court known which is signed by the Court and ordered to be certified by the Clerk of this Court under the seal of this Court.

Ordered that Court be adjourned until tomorrow morning 10 O'clock

Sims Dearing
John Jett
John Bryan

Tuesday Morning 4th August A. D. 1840 Court met pursuant to adjournment
Present the worshipful

John Jett
John Bryan
Sims Dearing } Esqrs Justices

This day Anna Hutchens and James Hutchens being over the age of fourteen years minor heirs of Webster Hutchens deceased appeared in open Court and made choice of and selected Joseph Herd as their Guardian and the Court also appoint the said Joseph Guardian to Mary Hutchens, Thomas J. Hutchens, Pleasant J. Hutchens, Nancy Hutchens, Charles D. Hutchens and Albert G. Hutchens the balance of the minor heirs of the said Webster Hutchens Deceased who not being present in Court it is ordered that he appear at the next term of this Court and enter into bond and security and be sworn as the law requires.

This day Edward M. Murray, John L. Price, Jabez G. Mitchell, (P-394) Moses Carrick and Simon Bramblett who were on yesterday appointed Trustees of Prustley Academy came into open Court and took the oath required by law.

This day Asa G. Lamb aged fourteen years this day appeared in open Court and was bound to Richard G. Roberts Esquire to serve him after the manner of an apprentice to the trade of Taylor until he shall arrive at the full age of twenty one years - and for his faithful performance of his Covenant entered into and acknowledged bond with Anthony Dibrell his securities as the law requires.

Ordered that Court be adjourned until Court in Course

Test
N. Oldham, Clk.

John Jett
John Bryan
Sims Dearing

State of Tennessee

At a quorum Court began and held for the County of White in the Courthouse in the town of Sparta before the Justices of said Court on the first Monday being the seventh day of September in the year of our Lord One thousand eight hundred and of the Independence of the United States of America the sixty fifth year

Present the worshipful

David Snodgrass
Sims Dearing — Esquire
Lewis Pettett
William Little — Justices
Jesse Walling

Ordered by Court that Hamon Leftwich Esquire be appointed Commissioners of the Revenue of White County to settle with the diffrent Clerks in said County for the year 1840 to fill the vacancy caused by the death of John Jett Esqr.

This day the death of Edith Robertson late of the County of White was suggested in open Court and that she departed this life intestate whereupon Andrew Robertson was appointed adminestrator of all and singular the goods and Chattles rights and credits of the said Edith Robertson deceased who appeared in open Court and took the oath prescribed (P-395) by law and together with Samuel Dyer and Samuel Brown entered into and acknowledged bond in the sum of seven thousand Dollars conditioned as the law requires.

This day the death of Alsten Holland late of the County of White was suggested and proved in open Court and that he departed this life entestate. Whereupon Harrison Holland was appointed adminestrator of all and singular the goods and chattles rights and credits of the said Alsten Holland Deceased who also being present in open Court took the oath prescribed by law and together with Berryman Holland and Washington Webb entered into and acknowledged bond conditioned as the law requires.

This day was produced in open Court a writing purporting the last will and testament of George Defreese Esq late of the County of White and his death and also proved whereupon the due execution and publication of said writing as the last will and testament of the said George Defreese was proved in open Court by the oath of Jonathan Scoggins one of the subscribing witnesses thereto for the purposes therein contained and at the same time made oath that said George Defreese was at the date of the execution and publication thereof, of sound and disposing mind and memory.

This day Turner Lane Jr. produced in open Court a writing perporting to be the last will and testament of Turner Lane Sr. late of the County of White deceased whose death was proved in due form of law by the oath Andrew Lowell and the due execution and publication of said writing as the last will and testament of the deceased was proved in open Court by Hugh L. Carrick and Seth L. Carrick subscribing witness thereto for the purposes and things therein mentioned and who at the same time made oath that the said Turner Lane Sr. was at the date of the Execution and publication thereof as such, was of sound and disposing mind and memory which is ordered to be recorded.

Whereupon Jacob A. Lane and Turner Lane Jr., the executors appointed in the said last will and testament of the said Deceased appeared in open Court and undertook the further of the due execution of said last will and testament and thereupon took the oath required by law and together with John Wallis and Anthony Dibrell entered into acknowledged bond in the sum of one thousand dollars conditioned as the law requires

Isd Ordered by Court that James Arnold be appointed Overseer of the road from sinking Creek to the fork of the McMinnville road (P-396) near the Harriet iron works being a road of the second Class and keep the same in repair as the law requires and that the same list of hands that worked under Jesse A. Bounds late overseer thereof be assigned to work thereon.

Woodson P. White)
to) Title bond for 20 acres land
John Miller issue)

It appearing to the Court that W. P. White on the 7th day January 1835 executed his title Bond to John Miller Sr. for twenty acres of land to which there are no subscribing witnesses to prove the execution thereof whereupon personally appeared in open Court Jabez G. Mitchell and William G. Sims to the Court known and after being sworn in due form of law depose and say they were acquanted with Woodson P. White in his lifetime the within named obligor and also with his hand writing, having often seen him write and subscribe his name, and that they veribly believe that the name subscribed to the within Bond is the proper hand writing and genuine signature of the aforesaid Woodson P. White and that he has since the date thereof departed this life which is deemed by the Court sufficently proved and ordered to be recorded

Woodson P. White)
to) Title Bond for 25 acres land
Noah Dodson)

It appearing to the Court that on the 3rd day of April 1835 W. P. White executed his title Bond to Noah Dodson for 25 acres of land - to which there are no subscribing witnesses to prove the execution thereof whereupon personally appeared in open Court Jabez G. Mitchell and William G. Sims to the Court known and who after being sworn in due form of law depose and say they were (P-397) well acquanted with Woodson P. White the within obligor in his life time and also with his handwriting having often seen him write and subscribe his name and they veribly believe that his name subscribed to the within Bond is the proper hand writing and genuine signature of the said Woodson P. White and that since the date thereof he has departed this life which is deemed by the Court sufficently proved and ordered to be recorded.

This day Joseph Bartlett Guardian to part of the minor heirs of Nathan Bartlett deceased made his report upon oath which is ordered to be recorded. This day Joseph Pryor Guardian to William Pryor minor heir of Nathan Bartlett deceased made his report upon oath which is to be recorded - .

For reasons appearing to the satisfaction of the Court upon the application of Harrison Whitson one of the securities of James A. Jay one of the Constables of White County for a release from future liabilities - It is ordered by Court that the said James A. Jay personally appear at the next term of this Court and then enter into Bond with other and sufficent securities for the faithful performance of his duties as constable so as to release the said H. Whitson And that subpoena issue directed to the Sherriff &c.

This day Tandy A. Lane a minor heir of Turner Lane Sr Deceased being over the age of fourteen years appeared in open Court and made choice of and selected Turner Lane Jr. for his Guardian who being also present in open Court took the oath required by law and together with Joseph Herd and John H. Robinson entered into and acknowledged bond in the sum of five hundred dollars conditioned as the law requires. Whereas the last will and testament of George Defreese deceased late of the County of White was this day produced in open Court and proved in due form of law by the oath of Jonathan Scoggins one of the subscribing witness thereto and upon the application of the widow of the deceased and it being made appear that Jonathan T. Bradley Esq. the other subscribing witness to the said will was confined at home by sickness so that he could not personally appear before this Court at the present term in order to prove said will and it also being made appear to the Court that it manifestily to the interest of the estate of the deceased, that the will should be established and all executors qualified. It is therefore considered by the Court and so ordered that Nicholas Oldham Clerk of (P-398) This Court shall produce to the dwelling house of the said Jonathan T. Bradley in the County of White the other witness to the will aforesaid and swear him upon the holy Evangelist of Almighty God in due form of law touching the due execution and publication of the aforesaid writing purporting to be the last will and testament of the Deceased and also as to the state of mind as to making disposition of his estate and report thereof tomorrow morning at the settling of this Court.

Ordered that Court be adjourned until tomorrow morning 9 O'clock

David Snodgrass
Sims Dearing
William Little

Tuesday morning 8th day of September A.D. 1840 Court met pursuant to adjournment Present the worshipful

David Snodgrass } Esquires
Sims Dearing }
William Little } Justices

Issd This day Nicholas Oldham Clerk of White County Court came into open Court and made in obedience to an order made on him by the County Court requiring him to take the proff of Jonathan T. Bradley a subscribing witness to the last will and testament of George Defreese Deceased - report that I produced on Monday evening the 7th day of September 1840 to the residence of Jonathan T. Bradley that I did there and then swear the said Jonathan T. Bradley the other subscribing witnesses to the aforesaid will and testament of the said George Defreese deceased in due form of law upon the holy Evangelist of Almighty God touching the due execution and publication of the aforesaid will and as to his soundness of mind and who upon his oath deposed and said he was well acquanted with the said George Defreese that he did sign seal publish proclaim and declare the will aforesaid to be his last will and testament for the purposes therein expressed and also that at the date of the execution and publication thereof as such was of sound and disposing mind and memory which is deemed by the Court to be sufficiently proved and the same is ordered to be recorded - whereupon John England who is appointed by said will of the deceased the sole Executor thereof appeared in open Court and assign to take upon himself the burden of the execution of the said last will and testament of the said deceased and took the oath prescribed by law and together with William Lyda and Hugh L. Carrick entered into and acknowledged in the sum of six thousand dollars conditioned as the law requires

On the humble petition of Joseph Hunter it is ordered by the (P-399) Court that Joseph Hunter be permitted to open a road from the Bridge at the mouth of the Blue Spring Creek following the old road to entersect the river road on the bench of the mountain at the Usery Gap be established a road of the third Class and that said Joseph Hunter open and keep the same in repair as the law requires at his own proper Cost and charges which is not to operate to him so as to release his hands from working on other roads

Ordered that Court be adjourned until Court in Course

Test
N. Oldham, Clk.

David Snodgrass
Sims Dearing
William Little

(P-400) State of Tennessee

At a County Court began and held for the County of White in the State aforesaid in the Court house in the town of Sparta before the Justice of said Court on the first Monday being the fifth day of October A. D. 1840 and of the Independence of the United States of America the sixty fifth year

Present the Worshipful

Thomas Eastland, Esq. Chairman	
David Snodgrass, Lewis Pettett,	
William Knowles, Elijah Frost,	
John Pennington, James Knowles,	Esquire
Samuel Lance, Matthias Hutson,	
Jesse Walling, Thomas Green,	Justices
William Little, Sims Dearing,	
Richard Crowder, James Allison	
Edmund Stamps, Asa Certain,	
William Bruster and William Hudgins	

This day Nicholas Oldham Clerk of this Court exhibited and read the receipts which he is bound by law to produce which are ordered to be spread upon the minutes of this Court as follows to wit Comptrollers Office Nashville Tenn 16th Sept 1840 Received of N. Oldham his statement of Revenue Collectors Clerk of White County Court from 1st Sept 1839 - to 1st Sept. 1840

Amount Collected		535.40
	13.38	15.88
	2.50	519.50

Commissioners
Paid Coms. Leftwich
Warrent No 1102 this day for

Daniel Graham Comptroller

519.50 Nashville 16 September 1840 No 1102
Received of N. Oldham five hundred nineteen Dollars fifty cents audited to him by 1102 and due on account of Revenue by him collected as Clerk of White County Court from 1 Sept. 1839 to 1 Sept. 1840

Signed Duplicates M. Francis

Treasure of Tennessee

Comptrollers office Nashville Tennessee

21 Aug 1840 Received of N. Oldham his bond as clerk of White County Court to collect and pay over fines and forfitures dated 6th April 1840 with penalty of $1000 -

Daniel Graham Comptroller of the treasure

Comptrollers office Nashville Tennessee

5 May 1840 Received of Nicholas Oldham Clerk of White County Court the Bond of Jonathan T. Bradley as Sherriff of White County dated 6th April 1840 with penalty of 10.000

Daniel Graham

Comptroller

Received of N. Oldham Clerk of White County Court the tax list for the year 1840 the 25 April 1840 J. T. Bradley Shff Received of Nicholas Oldham Clerk of White County Court our Abstract Statements of the County, Jury, Sparta Bridge and public Square tax for the year 1840 amounting in the aggregate to the sum of one thousand seven hundred and five dollars thirteen cents and five mills, which he is bound by law to furnish to the Trustee of said County shewing the amount for which the Sheriff and collected of said County is bound to collect and (P-401) account Received this 28th day of September 1840

Robert Cox Trustee
White County

Received of N. Oldham Clerk of White County Court Two hundred and seventy seven dollars sixty four cents the amount of Revenue by him collected on Privilliges for the year ending the 1st day of September 1840 agreeable to his Statement this day filed this 17th day of September 1840

Ro Cox Trustee White County

This day Robert H. McManus appeared in open Court and produced a commissioner from the Govenor of the State of Tennessee as Justice of the peace for the County of White and thereupon took an oath to support the constitution of the United States and of the State of Tennessee and the oaths prescribed by law and took his seat upon the bench - .

This day William J. Bennett one of the guardians to the minor heirs of Edward Holms Deceased made his report upon oath which is ordered to be recorded - .

Issd Ordered by Court that William D. Glenn be appointed Overseer of the road from Richard Crowders to the forks of the Rockisland road being a road of the second Class and keep the same in repair as the law requires and that the same list and bounds of hands that worked under Levi Jarvis late Overseer thereof be assigned to work thereon - .

Issd Ordered by Court that Jesse Worley be appointed overseer of the road from the mouth of John Bryans lane to the Coopers shop in the direction of General Simpsons Mill being a road of the 2nd class and keep the same in repair as the law requires and that the same boundary of hands that were assigned to the late Overseer thereof be assigned to work thereon - .

Issd Ordered by Court that Western Watterman be appointed Overseer of the road from John Austins Still house to the branch west of Capt Rottans being a road of the 2nd Class and keep the same in repair as the law requires and that the same bounds of hands that worked under John Austin late Overseer thereof be assigned to work thereon - .

Issd Ordered by Court that John L. Smith be appointed Overseer of the road from the flat rock to the entersection of the Stage road being a road of the second Class and keep the same in repair as the law requires and that the same bounds of hands that worked under the late Overseer be assigned to work thereon - .

(P-402) Monday 5th October 1840

This day the death of William Hill late of the County of White was suggested in open Court and that he departed this life intestate whereupon John Parker and James Snodgrass were appointed adminestrators of all and singular, the goods and chattles, rights and credits of the deceased and who being present in open Court took the oath prescribed by law and together with William Snodgrass, Brice Little Samuel Brown, Elisha Camron, Samuel Dyer and Andrew Robinson entered into and acknowledged bond in the sum of Twelve thousand Dollars conditioned as the law requires.

This day the death of Rebecca Crook late of the County of White was suggested in open Court and that she departed this life entestate whereupon John Parker and James Snodgrass were appointed administrators of all and singular the goods and Chattles rights and credits of the Deceased and thereupon took the oath prescribed by law and together with William Snodgrass, Brice Little, Samuel Brown, Elisha Camron, Samuel Dyer, and Andrew Robinson entered into and acknowledged bond in the sum of Four thousand dollars conditioned as the law requires.

Isd Ordered by Court that David Snodgrass, Samuel Dyer and Andrew Robinson be appointed Commissioners to set apart one years provisions to the widow and family of William Hill deceased out of his Estate and report thereof to the next term of this Court.

Isd Ordered by Court that Stuart Warren be appointed Overseer of the road from the fork of the road at McKenny's old place to Scarboroughs mill being a road of the second Class keep the same in repair as the law requires with the same boundary of hands that worked under the late Overseer thereof be assigned to work thereon.

Upon the application of Jonathan T. Bradley Esq. Sherriff of White County Avery Norris one of his Deputies is displaced from office and that Noah H. Bradley be appointed Deputy Sherriff of said County who being present in open Court took the several oaths prescribed by law and thereupon entered upon the duties of his office - .

This day Margarett Hill and Thomas Hill two of the minor heirs of William Hill deceased being over the age of fourteen years appeared in open Court and chose James Snodgrass to be their guardian and on the same day the Court appointed the said James Snodgrass guardian to John Hill another of the minor heirs of the said Deceased he being under the age of 14 years who being present in open Court took the oath prescribed by law and together with William Snodgrass, Samuel V. Carrick, Samuel Brown, Brice Little, Elisha Camron and John Brown entered into and acknowledged bond in the sum of Ten Thousand dollars conditioned as the law requires.

(P-403) Monday 5th October 1840

This day William C. Bounds adminestrator with the will annexed of John Terry deceased returned upon oath an additional Inventory and account of the sales of said Estate which is ordered to be recorded. -

This day the death of James Turner late of the County of White was suggested in open Court and that he departed this life intestate. Whereupon Anna Turner and William Lyda were appointed adminestratrix and adminestrator of all and singular the goods and chattles rights and credits of the deceased and the said Anna being present in open Court took the oath prescribed by law and together with Anthony Dibrell and William Glenn entered into and acknowledged bond in the sum of Three thousand Dollars conditioned as the law requires and the said William Lyda on account of indesposition is unable to attend the present term of this Court is permitted to apply to the Clerk of this Court at anytime, and subscribe his name to said Bond with the adminestratrix and securities already given and be sworn-by said Clerk according to law before he shall enter upon the duties of said administration - .

Isd Ordered by Court that Samuel V. Carrick, John Lisk and Daniel Clark be appointed Commissioners to assign and set apart one years provisions for the support and maintainance of the widow and family of James Turner Deceased out of the estate of the deceased and report to the next term of this Court.

Isd Ordered by Court that Anthony Dibrell, William Matlock and Richard England be appointed Commissioners to assign and set apart one years support for the widow and family of George Defreese Deceased out of his Estate of the deceased and report thereof to the next term of this Court.

Isd Ordered by Court unanimously that Nicholas Oldham Clerk of White County Court be allowed the sum of twenty One dollars for making and recording the tax list for said County for the year 1840 also one dollar fifty cents for a Sherriffs tax book and one dollar for recording the settlement of the Clerk of White Circuit Court making in all the sum of twenty three dollars fifty to be paid by the Trustee of White County out of the taxes for the year 1840

Isd Upon the application of Anthony Dibrell and James M. Scott two of the securities of Elsa England who was guardian to the minor heirs of Elijah England Deceased and for reasons appearing to the satisfaction of the Court It is ordered that Elsa England guardian aforesaid be summoned to appear at the next term of this Court and then and there enter into bond with other and sufficent security in order that the said Dibrell and Scott may be released from the liability as her securities as aforesaid and that a Subponea issue directed &c.

(P-404) Monday 5th October 1840

Isd Ordered by Court that Hayes Arnold, Jesse A. Bounds, James Randols, Washington Webb and Joseph Herd freeholders be appointed a Jury of view to lay off and mark a change in the Gumspring road from the McMinnville road to entersect the old road again near Hayes Arnolds and report thereof to the next term of this Court.

Ordered by Court that Thomas Green Esq. and Charles Smith be and they are hereby appointed Commissioners of the poor house of White County to fill the vacancy occasioned by death of John Jett Esquire and that occasioned by Joseph Cummings Esq. falling into what is called VanBuren County who being present in open Court took the oath prescribed by law.

Ordered by Court unanimously that Thomas Green Esq. one of the Commissioners of the poor house of White County be appointed Treasure of said Board to fill the vacancy occasioned by the death of John Jett, Esq. late Treasure thereof.

This day Nicholas Oldham Clerk of this Court produced in open Court a report of a settlement made with Dan Griffith adminsstrator of John M. Rottan Dec'd which is recorded and confirmed in all its parts and ordered to be recorded.

Isd Ordered by Court that Meredith Carter be appointed Overseer of the road from the Rockisland to Samuel A. Moores Esq. be a road of the first Class from the Island to the fork and thence 2nd Class to Moores and keep the same in repair as the law requires and that the same bounds of hands that worked under John Chisum late Overseer thereof be assigned to work thereon - .

Isd Ordered by Court that Lucius Foster be appointed Overseer of the road from the widow Dales to the middle of the Caney Fork below Dales Mill being a road of the second Class and keep the same in repair as the law requires and that the same bounds of hands that worked under Thomas Wilson late Overseer thereof be assigned to work thereon - .

Isd Ordered by Court that Allen L. Mitchell Superintendant and keeper of the poor house for White County be allowed the sum of two hundred dollars for services allready rendered and yet to be rendered during the year 1840 in said poor house to be paid in quarterly installments of fifty dollars each by the Treasure of the poor house Commissioners of said County the quarterage commencing on the first day of January 1840 out of any monies not otherwise appropriated - .

(P-405) Monday 5th October 1840

Isd This day the death of John Jett Esquire late of the County of White was suggested in open Court and that he died intestate whereupon William Jared was appointed administrator of all and singular the goods and chattles rights and credits of the deceased who took the oath required by law and together with John White and William M. Young entered into and acknowledged bond in the sum of Three Thousand dollars conditioned as the law requires - .

This day Joseph Herd who was at a former term of this Court appointed guardian to the minor heirs of Webster Hutchens deceased appeared in open Court and took the oath prescribed by law and together with Simon R. Doyle and Benjamin Hutchens entered into and acknowledged bond in the sum of seven hundred dollars conditioned as the law requires - .

Isd Ordered by Court that the following named persons be appointed Judges of the Election to be held in the several Districts of White County on Tuesday the third day of November next for the purpose of Electing fifteen Electors in the State of Tennessee to vote for one President and one Vice President of the United States of America for the four years next ensuing the 4th day of March 1841 to wit:
In the 1st District Anthony Dibrell, William Bruster & James Hudgins
In the 2nd District John Wallis, Simon R. Doyle and John Austin, Sr.
In 3rd District Thomas Green, Joseph Herd, and Robert Anderson
In 4th District Joseph Anderson, Sr., Matthias Hutson and John Swindle
In 5th District Thomas Robertson, James Knowles, Jr. and John Humphreys
In 6th District Thomas Jones, Eli Sims, & Henry Camron
In District No William H. Allen, Henry Burton and Geo. W. Eartham
In District No 8 Joseph S. Allison, Geo. Welch and Samuel Usrey
In District No 9 William Glenn, Burtis Walker and James Frisby

In 10 District Indell Stone, Andrew Robinson and Washington F. Williams
In the 11 District William Pryor, Jacob Hyder and Thomas Barnes
In the 12 District Spencer Holeman, Elisha Camron and Ed Stamps
In 13th District John Rose, John Brown, Sr., and Wm. Snodgrass
In the 14 District John Crook, John L. Smith, John Gipson
In the District Joseph Cummings Jr., Spencer Mitchell & John Gillentine -; Election to be opened and held at the place in each district as designated for holding Elections for members of Congress and members to the Legislature &c.

Isd Ordered by Court that Asa Certain, Eli Sims and Thomas Jones Esqrs be appointed Commissioners to assign and set apart one years provisions for the widow and family of Jesse Vermillion deceased out of his Estate and report thereof at the next term of this Court. -

(P-406) Monday 5th October A. D. 1840

Isd Ordered by Court that Asa Certain, Eli Sims and Thomas Jones Esqs. be appointed Commissioners to assign and set apart a sufficiency of provisions to the widow and family of John Cantrell Deceased for their support for one year out of his Estate and report thereof to the next term of this Court

Isd Ordered by Court that Joseph Bozarth be appointed Overseer of the road from the branch at Aaron Hutchens to the DeKalb County line being a road of the first Class and keep the same in repair as the law requires and that Richard Crowder and Thomas Jones Esquires apportion lists and Bounds of hands between said Bozarth and Alfred Shaw to work thereon - .

Isd It appearing fully to the satisfaction of the Court by the Statement of the Trustee of White County that the 8th day of October 1830 these was filed in his office a county claim for one hundred and sixty dollars designated in his office and on his books by its No 171 filed in the name of John Gorden and it further appearing to the court by the oath of the said John Gorden to the Court known that said Claim No 171 for $160 filed as aforesaid is lost or so mislaid that it cannot be found; that he never has assigned or transfered the aforesaid Claim, but that the same is his own right and property.

It is therefore considered by the Court and so ordered that the Trustee of White County pay unto the said John Gorden the aforesaid sum of one hundred and sixty dollars filed as aforesaid and his receipt shall be good and a proper voucher in the settlement of his accounts - .

Isd Ordered by Court that Anthony Dibrell, David Snodgrass and William M. Young be appointed Commissioners to assign and set apart one years provision for the support of the widow and family of John Jett Deceased out of the Estate of the Deceased and report thereof to the next term of this Court

It appearing to the satisfaction of the Court that Daniel Clark who undertook the macadamizing of the public square in the town of Sparta has completed the same and also that the Commissioners thereof had received the same as fully completed. It is therefore considered and so ordered by the

Court the Trustee of White County pay unto the said Daniel Clark the sum of four hundred dollars out of the tax of the year 1840 which was laid for that exclusive purpose (Styled the public Square tax)

This day James A. Jay a constable in District No 12 of White County appeared in open Court and resigned his office as such which is ordered to be recorded. -

(P-407) Monday 5th October A. D. 1840

Isd Ordered by Court that Jesse Walling and Thomas Green, Esqs be appointed to apportion lists and bounds of hands between Levi Kerr and other Overseers of the road in the neighborhood having due regard to the dignity of the diffrent roads.

Ordered by Court that Allen L. Mitchell keeper of the poor house bring before the Court tomorrow when setting a certain orphan boy named George Shelton now in his charge to be dealt by as to said Court may seem right and proper and according to law -

Isd Upon the application and suggestion of Anthony Dibrell Esquire it is ordered by the Court that the Sherriff of White County bring Elen E. Parsons, Sarah Ann Parsons, Francis Marion Parsons and Major Parsons children of - - - - - - - - - - Parsons, instantly before this Court to be dealt by as may to this Court seem right and according to law shall be done.

This day Major Parsons aged five years on the 15 February 1841 was bound to Daniel Clark to serve him after the manner of an apprentice until he shall arrive at the age of twenty one years and with Nicholas Oldham his securities entered into and acknowledged bond for the faithful performance of his Covenant.

This day Francis Marion Parsons an orphan boy aged nine years on the 6th day of February 1841 was bound unto Thomas Green to serve him after the manner of an apprentice untill he shall arrive at the full age of twenty one years and together with Jesse Walling entered into and acknowledged bond for the faithful performance of his Covenant.

This day Sarah Ann Parsons an orphan girl aged ten years on the 21st day of October 1840 was bound to Joseph Anderson to serve him after the manner of an apprentice until she shall arrive the age of twenty one years and together with Spencer Holder his security entered into and acknowledged bond for the faithful performance of his covenant.

This day Elen E. Parsons an orphan girl aged twelve years on the 13h day of April 1841 was bound to Joab Hill to serve him after the manner of an apprentice untill she arrives to the age of twenty one years and together with Thomas Green his security entered into and acknowledged bond for the faithful performance of his Covenant.

Isd Ordered by Court that the order of a former term of this Court appointing (P-408) Samuel A. Moore, Sr., Isaiah Hutson, John Swindle, Jesse Franks and Rowland Blankenship freeholders a Jury of view to lay off and mark a road of the second Class the nearest and best way from Browns Mills to intersect the Kentucky road at some suitable point be renewed and report thereof to the next term of this Court.

Issd Ordered by Court unanimously that a commissioner of the Revenue be appointed to take in and list the balance of the property and polls in the 15th District of White County for the year 1840 which John Gillentine late Commissioner failed to return to this Court for taxation in said year that he forthwith proceed to take said list and make return thereof to the next ~~thereof to the next~~ term of this Court and that Simon R. Doyle be appointed Commissioner for that purpose - .

Issd This day appeared in open Court Henry W. Lyda a Citizen of the County of White a Student at law under Samuel Turney Esq. one of the Attornies in said County. And asked the Court for a certificate of Character &c. and it appearing to the satisfaction of the Court that he is a citizen of said County and that they believe him to be a young gentleman of good reputation and of respectable parentage and it is ordered that the same be certified by the clerk of this Court under the seal of this Court.

For reasons appearing to the satisfaction of this Court it is ordered that John Cooley be detached from the 6th and be attached to the 9th district of White County and that he be entitled to all and every privilige in the 9th District as the other citizens thereof - .

Ordered that Court be adjourned untill tomorrow 10 O'Clock

Thos. Eastland
Robt. H. McManus
Samuel Lance

Tuesday Morning 6th day of October A.D. 1840 Court met pursuant to adjournment Present the worshipful

Thomas Eastland, Esq. Chairman
Thomas Green
Robert H. McManus — Esquires
Samuel Lance
Richard Crowder & — Justices
James Knowles

This day Nicholas Oldham Clerk of White County court entered into and acknowledged Bond for the faithful collection and payment of (P-409) the Revenue arising on Priviliges in the sum of five thousand dollars conditioned as the law requires which is as follows to wit:

Bond

Know all men by these presents that we Nicholas Oldham, Jacob A. Lane, Anthony Dibrell, John Warren and William Glenn all of the County of White and State of Tennessee are held and firmly bound unto his Excellency James K. Polk Esquire Govenor in and over the state of Tennessee for the time being and his successors in office in the sum of Five thousand Dollars Current money which payment well and truly to be made and done we bind ourselves and each and every of our heirs executors and administrators jointly and severally firmly by these presents sealed with our seals and dated the 6th day of October A.D. 1840 the condition of the above obligation is such that whereas Nicholas Oldham hath been duly and constitutionally elected clerk of the County Court of White County from the first Saturday in March 1840 for the four years thence ensuing. Now if the said Nicholas Oldham Clerk as aforesaid shall well and truly and faithfully account for and pay over all monies which he shall collect by vertue of his office as State tax on priviliges in the County of White according to law unto the proper Office entitled to recover the same, then this obligation to be null and void else be and remain in full force and vertue - .

Test.

Thos. Eastland Chairman of White County Court

N. Oldham (seal)
J. A. Lane (seal)
Anthony Dibrell (seal)
John Warren (seal)
William Glenn (seal)

This day Thomas Green Esq. who was on yesterday appointed Treasure of the Commissioners of the poor house of White County appeared in open Court and took the oath prescribed by law and together with Nicholas Oldham and Robert H. McManus entered into and acknowledged Bond in the sum of Two thousand Dollars conditioned as the law requires - .

This day Moses Carrick, Simon Bramblett, John L. Price and Jabez G. Mitchell and Edward N. Murray Trustees of Prustley Academy in the County of White appointed at the August term 1840 of this Court appeared in open Court and together Wamon Leftwich, William G. Green, Sammel V. Carrick and John England, Jr., entered into and acknowledged bond in the sum of fifteen hundred dollars conditioned as the law requires - .

This day Allen L. Mitchell keeper of the Poor house of White County produced in open Court agreeable to an order of this Court made on yesterday a certain orphan boy named George Shelton aged five years and six months who the Court bound to William R. Tucker to serve him after the manner of an apprentice to the Blacksmiths trade untill he arrives the age of twenty one years and together with Allen L. Mitchell entered into and acknowledged bond (P-410) for the faithful performance of his Covenant.

Ordered that Court be adjourned untill Court in Course

Test

N. Oldham, Clk.

Thos. Eastland
Richard Crowder
Robt. H. McManus

State of Tennessee

At a quorum Court began and held for the County of White in the Court house in the town of Sparta before the Justices of said Court on the first Monday being the Second day of November in the year of our Lord One thousand eight hundred and forty. And of the Independence of the United States of America the sixty fifth year. Present the worshipful

Elijah Frost	)	Esquires
William Little &	)	
Sims Dearing	)	Justices

This day William Glenn, Jr., produced in open Court his Commission of appointment of Justices of the peace in and for the County of White to fill the vacancey in the 9th Dist. occasioned by the death of George Defreese, Esq. who being present in open Court took an oath to support the Constitution of the United States & of the State of Tennessee and the several oaths prescribed by law and thereupon entered upon the discharge of the duties of his office.

For reasons appearing to the satisfaction of the Court it is ordered by the Court that the Indenture of an orphan boy named Major Parsons who was at the last term of this Court bound as an apprentice to Daniel Clark, be cancelled and for nothing esteemed and the said Daniel Clark from the performance of his covenant therein be released and forever discharged.

This day Major Parsons an orphan boy aged five years on the 15th February 1841 was bound unto Andrew Gamble to serve him after the manner of an apprentice untill he arrives at the age of twenty one years and for the faithful performance of his covenant entered into and acknowledged bond conditioned as the law requires.

(P-411) Monday 2nd November A.D. 1840

This day Anna Turner Executrix of James Turner Deceased returned upon oath an Inventory and account of sales of the Estate of the Deceased, which is ordered to be recorded.

This day William Jared adminestrator of John Jett Deceased returned upon oath an Inventory in part of the effects of the estate of the Dec'd which is ordered to be recorded.

Isd This day the death of John Griffith late of the County of White Deceased was suggested in open Court and that he departed this life intestate. Whereupon James Dalton appeared in open Court and was appointed adminestrator of all and singular the goods and chattles rights and credits of the Deceased and thereupon took the oath prescribed by law and together with John Pennington and James H. Pass entered into and acknowledged bond in the sum of two hundred dollars conditioned as the law requires.

This day James Dalton adminestrator of John Griffith deceased returned upon oath an Inventory of the estate of the deceased which is ordered to be recorded.

Issd Ordered by Court that Simpson Cash, John Anderson and John Pennington be appointed Commissioners to lay off and set apart one years provision for the support of the widow and family of John Griffith deceased out of his estate and report thereof to the next term of this Court.

This day the death of William Lyda late of the County of White was suggested in open Court and that he departed this life intestate whereupon Anthony Dibrell and Richard Lyda were appointed adminestrator and adminestratrix of all and singular the goods and chattles rights and credits of the deceased and the said Anthony Dibrell appeared in open Court and took the oath prescribed by law and together with Richard Nelson, Samuel V. Carrick, Montgomery C. Dibrell and Joseph Herd entered into and acknowledged bond in the sum of Twenty thousand dollars conditioned as the law requires And the Court being satisfied that the said Rebecca Lyda from indesposition is unable to attend the present term of this Court, she is permitted to appear before the Clerk of this Court at any time during the recess of Court and subscribe her name to said bond with said adminestrator and securities already given and be sworn by said clerk according to law, before she shall enter upon the discharge of the duties of said adminestration

Issd Ordered by Court that Andrew Gamble, Daniel Clark and Asa Certain be appointed Commissioners to lay of and set apart to Rachel Lyda and children provisions for their support for one year out of the estate of the deceased and report thereof to the next term of this Court.

This day Vashti Glenn guardian to the minor heirs of Robert Glenn (P-412) deceased made report upon oath which is ordered to be recorded - .

This day Andrew Robinson adminestrator of Edith Robinson deceased returned upon oath an Inventory and account of the sales of said Estate which is ordered to be recorded.

It appearing to the satisfaction of the Court from the return of the account of the sales of the estate of Edith Robinson deceased that the bond of the adminestrator was too small It is therefore considered by the court that Andrew Robinson the adminestrator of said Estate be ruled forthwith to give a new bond in the sum of Twelve thousand dollars with additional or sufficent surity and the said Andrew Robinson being present in open Court and together with Anthony Dibrell, William Snodgrass, Samuel Brown and Samuel V. Carrick entered into and acknowledged bond in the sum of twelve thousand dollars conditioned as the law requires.

This day the Commissioners heretofore appointed by this Court to lay off and set apart to the widow and family of John Jett Deceased one years support made their report which is recorded and ordered to be recorded - .

This day the Commissioners heretofore appointed by this Court to lay off and set apart one years provisions for the support of the widow and family of George Defreese Deceased made their report which is received and ordered to be recorded. -

Issd Ordered by Court that Nathan Earls, Green Carroll, Harrison Earles, Drury Simmons and Simon R. Doyle freeholders be appointed a Jury of view to lay off and mark a road of the 3rd Class from Doyles Mill to intersect the road near Cumming's old ford on Caney fork and report thereof to the next term of this Court.

Ordered by Court that Asa Certain be appointed guardian to Caroline Hooper, David H. Hooper two of the minor heirs of Edward E. Hooper Deceased who being present in open Court took the oath required by law and together with John Young and Smith J. Walling entered into and acknowledged bond in the sum of sixteen hundred dollars conditioned as the law requires. -

Issd This day the death of George Pertle late of the County of White was suggested in open Court and that he departed this life intestate whereupon James Knowles appeared in open Court and was appointed administrator of all and singular the goods and chattles rights and credits of the said Deceased and thereupon took the oath required by law and together with Archebald Cannon, Alexander McDonald and Cornelius Jarvis entered into and acknowledged bond in the sum of Three Thousand Dollars conditioned as the law requires - .

For reasons appearing to the satisfaction of the Court it is ordered that two of Joseph Hunters hands be assigned to work on the road of which he is overseer and his other hands to remain on the road to which they are already assigned to work - .

(P-413) Monday 2nd November A.D. 1840

Issd Ordered by Court that Eleanor Moore and her two children paupers be retained in the poor house of White County where they have already been conveyed, there to be supported and maintained at the public expence untill the next term of this Court and that at the next term of this Court Allen L. Mitchell Esq. Keeper of said Poor house bring into open Court the oldest of the two children of the said Eleanor who are in his custody as keeper aforesaid, to be dealt with as may seem to the Court right and according to law should be done.

This day Joseph Cummings, Jr., guardian to the minor heirs of Eli Dodson Deceased returned upon oath his report which is ordered to be recorded.

Issd Ordered by Court that Green H. Wilson be appointed Overseer of the road from the top of the hill at Lowrys old place to the widow Dales being a road of the second Class and keep the same in repair as the law requires and that the same list and bounds of hands that worked under Barnett K. Mitchell late Overseer thereof be assigned to work thereon.

This day George Bohanon guardian to the minor heirs of Joseph Henry Dec'd made his report upon oath which is ordered to be recorded.

This day James S. England produced in open Court a Certificate of the Sherriff of White County of his being constitutionally elected constable of White County for the 12th District of said County to fill the vacancy occasioned by the resignation of James A. Jay and thereupon took an oath to support the Constitution of the United States and of the State of Tennessee and the several oaths prescribed by law and together with John Robinson, Thomas B. Johnson and John England, Jr., entered into and acknowledged bond conditioned as the law requires in the sum of six thousand dollars.

Isd Ordered by Court that John Mitchell, Thomas Green, Christopher Kuhn, Solomon Sparkman and Clenborn Gooch, freeholders be appointed a Jury of view to lay off and mark a road of the third Class the nearest and best way from the ford of the Caney fork at Sparkmans to James Randols mill so as to do as little injury to farms and individuals as possible and report thereof to the next term of this Court.

Ordered by Court that John Humphrey, Edward V. Pollard and Hugh Cock be appointed Commissioners to assign and set apart one years provisions for the support and maintainance of the widow and family of George Pertle Deceased out of his Estate and report thereof to the next term of this Court.

Ordered that Court be (P-414) adjourned untill tomorrow morning at 8 O'Clock.

Wm. Bruster
William Little
Robt. H. McManus
Elijah Frost

Tuesday Morning 3rd day of November A.D. 1840 Court met pursuant to adjournment Present the worshipful

William Bruster)
William Little) Esquires.
Robert H. McManus)
Elijah Frost) Justices

Ordered by Court that the order of this Court made at July term appointing Jonathan C. Davis, Esquire Surveyor of White County to survey and distinctly mark and designate the line between the County of White and the County of VanBuren agreeably to the Constitution and laws of the state of Tennessee as that said line shall not approach the Court house of White County near than twelve miles be renewed and report thereof at the next term of this Court.

This day the death of Theodorie B. Rice late of the County of White was suggested in open Court and that he departed this life intestate whereupon James H. Jinkens and Anthony Dibrell were appointed special administrators or adminestrators Pendente lite or during the pendency of a certain suit at Nashville - and thereupon took the oath required by law and together with Nicholas Oldham and Smith J. Walling entered into and acknowledged Bond in the sum of six thousand dollars conditioned as the law requires - . the said adminestration is limited to the Whastors heirs against Theodorick B. Rice and said adminestrators is to receive no other of further responsibilities therein.

Ordered that Court be adjourned until Court in Course

Test
N. Oldham, Clk.

Wm. Bruster
William Little
Robt. H. McManus

(P-415) State of Tennessee

At a Quorum Court began and held for the County of White in the State aforesaid in the Court in the town of Sparta before the Justices of said Court on the first Monday being the seventh day of December in the year of our Lord one thousand eight hundred and forty and of the Independance of the United States of America the sixty fifth year

Present the worshipful

David Snodgrass } Esquires
Sims Dearing }
John Pennington } Justices

Isd Ordered by Court that George Ogden be appointed Overseer of the road from the edge of the public square along main Street Northwardly to the limits of the Corporation of the town of Sparta this being a road of the first Class and thence to the ford of the Calf Killer below Andersons old salt well this being a road of the second Class and keep the same in repair as the law requires

And that Robert H. McManus and Wm. Little Esquires assign him a list and bounds of hands to work thereon.

Ordered by Court that the sherriff of White bring before this Court on tomorrow the 8th Instant two boys and one girl, orphan children of a certain Rebecca Lee of White County they being represented by Sharp R. Whitley as being in very destitute of the means of subsistence, to be dealt with by said Court as shall seem to them right and according to law - .

Ordered by Court that William Sprawles be released from the one half the appraised value of a certain stray heifer taken up by him appraised to $3.00 the same having died soon after - .

Ordered by Court that the following named Justices be appointed Commissioners of the Revenue for the year 1841 to take in lists of property and polls in White County for the year 1841 To Wit:

Robert H. McManus Esq. for the first District;
Anderson S. Rogers for the second District;
Jesse Walling Esq., for the Third District;
Matthias Hutson, Esq., for the Fourth District;
William Knowles, Esq., for the fifth District;
Thomas Jones, Esq., for the Sixth District;
William Hitchcock, Esq., for the eight District;
William Glenn, Esq., for the ninth District;
John Pennington, Esq., for the tenth District;

James Bartlett, Esq., for the eleventh District;
Sims Dearing, Esq., for the 12th District;
Samuel Lance, Esq., for the 13th District;
Elijah Frost, Esqr., for the 14th District to make and return their lists within the time prescribed by law - .

(P-416) Monday 7th December A. D. 1840

Isd Ordered by Court that Richard Bradley be appointed Overseer of the road from Littles Bridge to the entersection of the old Calf Killer road near Potts being a road of the third Class and Keep the same in repair as the law requires and that the same list and bounds of hands that worked under Jonathan Elms late overseer thereof be assigned to work thereon - .

This day William Bruster Esq. a Justice of the peace for White County presented to the worshipful Court his resignation of said office which was read and ordered to be recorded.

Isd Ordered by Court that George Broyles be appointed Overseer of the road from the forks of the Carthage road near Dibrells to the entersection of the river road being a road of the second Class and keep the same in repair as the law requires and that the same list and bounds of hands that worked under Barger Lowry late overseer thereof be assigned to work thereon.

It appearing to the satisfaction of the Court it is ordered by the Court that the order of the last term of this Court appointing G. H. Wilson Overseer of the road be set aside - .

Isd Ordered by Court that John Wallis, Jr., be appointed Overseer of the road from the Gap of the mountain at Lowrys old place to Mrs. Dales gate being a road of the second Class and keep the same in repair as the law requires and that the same list and bounds of hands that worked under Barnett X. Mitchell late Overseer thereof be assigned to work thereon - .

This day William Jared, Adminestrator of John Jett Deceased returned upon oath an additional Inventory of the Estate of the Deceased which is ordered to be recorded.

This day William Jared adminestrator of John Jett Deceased returned upon oath an account of the sales of the property of the Estate of the Deceased which is ordered to be recorded.

This day John Parker and James Snodgrass adminestrators of Rebecca Crook Deceased returned upon oath an Inventory of the Estate of the Deceased which is ordered to be recorded.

This day John Parker and James Snodgrass adminestrators of Rebecca Crook Deceased returned upon oath an account of the sales of the property of the deceased which is ordered to be recorded.

For reasons appearing to the satisfaction of the Court leave is given to the adminestrator of the estate of William Hill Deceased to make their return of the Inventory and account of the sales of the property of the Deceased at the next January term of this Court.

Upon the application of James Dalton adminestrator of John Griffith Deceased and for reasons appearing to the satisfaction of the Court, leave is given him to return his account of the sales of the property of the said deceased at the next term of this Court.

(P-417) Monday 7 December A.D. 1840

Issd Ordered by Court that William Knowles and James Knowles be appointed commissioners to apportion lists of and bounds of hands between William D. Glenn, John H. Jones and Harmon Little Overseers of the roads having due regard to grades of the diffrent roads and the distance each overseer has to work.

Ordered by Court that Samuel Brown be constituted and appointed guardian to Mary Hill, Lucy Hill and Richard Hill three of the minor heirs of William Hill Deceased they being under the age of fourteen years who being present in open Court took an oath prescribed by law and together with Andrew Robinson, James Snodgrass and John Parker entered into and acknowledged Bond in the sum of Ten thousand Dollars conditioned as the law requires.

Issd Ordered by Court that the order of this Court made at February term last appointing Osburn Walker, George Elmore, Cornelius Hickey, Henry Collier and Wm. Williams freeholders a jury of view to lay off and mark a road of third Class from Dunagans Iron works on Cain Creek passing Henry Colliers to the mouth of Glade Creek thence the nearest and best way to John Bussell still house thence the nearest and best way to entersect the Sparta road near Capt John Walkers be renewed and report thereof to the next term of this Court.

Ordered by Court that John Pennington, Charles Pennington, James H. Isom, Samuel Dyer and David Nicholas freeholders be appointed a Jury of view to examine and mark a change in the Cherry Creek road passing Charles Ishams and report thereof at the next term of this Court. -

This day James Adams a citizen of the County of White appointed in open Court and it being fully proved to the satisfaction of the Court that said Adams is wholly destitute of the means of subsestence, that from his peculiar situation he is unable to procure the means of maintaining himself and that he is a suitable object for the Court to extend relief. It is therefore considered by the Court that the said James Adams be conveyed to the poorhouse of White County, and put in the care of the Superentendant of said poorhouse thereto be supported and maintained at the public expences. And Sharp R. Whitley being present in open Court agrees to convey the said James Adams to the said poorhouse without cost or charge to White County and that an order issue directed &c.

This day James Knowles adminestrator of George Pertle deceased appeared in open Court and upon his motion leave is given him until the next term of this Court to return his Inventory of the property of the estate of the deceased.

(P-418) Monday 7 December A.D. 1840

Issd Ordered by Court that George Elmore be appointed overseer of the road from William Prices to the little mill being a road of the third Class and open and keep the same in repair as the law requires And that Asa Certain Esq assign a list of hands to work thereon - .

This day the death of James McGowen late of the County of White was suggested and proved in open Court and that he departed this life intestate whereupon Amos McGowen appeared in open Court and is appointed adminestrator of all and singular the goods and chattles rights and credits of the said Deceased and thereupon took the oath prescribed by law and together with Joseph Herd and Thomas Robertson entered into and acknowledged bond in the sum of six hundred dollars conditioned as the law requires and it is ordered that letters of adminestrations issue &c.

This day the death of Jesse Vermillion late of the County of White was suggested and proved in open Court and that he departed this life intestate whereupon Elizabeth Vermillion appeared in open Court and is appointed adminestratrix of all and singular the goods and chattles rights and credits of the Deceased and thereupon took the oath prescribed by law and together with Asa Certain and Jonathan T. Bradley entered into and acknowledged bond in the sum of two hundred dollars conditioned as the law requires and it is ordered that letters of adminestration issue &c.

Iesd Ordered by Court that Thomas Robertson, Joseph Herd and Peter Burum be appointed commissioners to assign and set apart one years provisions for the support and maintainance of the widow and family of James McGowen Deceased out of the Estate of the deceased and report thereof at thenext term of this Court.

This day the Commissioners heretofore appointed to assign and set apart one years provisions for the support and maintainance of the widow and family of William Hill Deceased made their report upon oath which is ordered to be recorded.

This day the Commissioners heretofore appointed to assign and set apart one years provisions to the widow and family of George Pertle deceased appeared in open Court and exhibited their report and by inspection thereof the Court are of opinion that the Commissioners aforesaid did not make a sufficent allowance - It is therefore considered and so ordered by the Court that said report be recommitted and that said commissioners be instructed to make such further additions of provisions to the widow and family of the Deceased as shall be a plentiful support for one year out of the estate of the said Deceased and report thereof to the next term of this Court.

Monday evening 7 Dec 1840 Ordered that (P-419) Court be adjourned untill 10 O'clock tomorrow morning

David Snodgrass
William Little
Robt. H. McManus

Tuesday the 8th day of December A.D. 1840 Court met pursuant to adjournment Present the worshipful

David Snodgrass) Esq.
William Little }
Robert H. McManus) Justices

Isd Ordered by Court that the order of yesterday requiring the sherriff of White County to bring two boys and one girl children of Rebecca Lee into Court to be dealt by as may seem right and according to law, be removed returnable to the next term of this Court.

Isd Ordered by Court that John England, Sr., John Smith, James Scott, William Snodgrass and Solomon Duncan freeholders be appointed a Jury of view to lay off and mark a road of the third Class from Snodgrass mill the nearest and best way passing John England, Sr., to entersect the Carthage road at some suitable point and report thereof to the next term of this Court.

This day Dosia Lay late Dosia Hooper appeared in open Court and made choice of and selected Thomas Walling to be her lawful guardian, who being also in open Court took the oath presceibed by law and together with Smith J. Walling and Thomas Green entered into and acknowledged bond in the sum of eight hundred dollars conditioned as the law requires.

Ordered by Court that Court be adjourned untill court in course

Test
N. Oldham, Clk.

David Snodgrass
Thomas Green
Robt. H. McManus

(P-420)
State of Tennessee

At a County Court began and held for this County of White and State aforesaid in the Court house in the Town of Sparta before the Justices of said Court, on the first Monday being the fourth day of January in the year of our Lord one thousand eight hundred and forty one and of the Independance of the United States of America the sixty fifth year. Present the worshipful

Thomas Eastland, Esq., Chairman of said Court
and David Snodgrass,
Samuel Lance,
Jesse Walling,
Sims Dearing, Asa Certain,
William Knowles, William
Little, William Glenn,
Robert H. McManus,
Anderson S. Rogers,
James Knowles, Thomas Jones,
Lewis Pettett, James Bartlett,
Matthias Hutson, Thomas Green
and Richard Crowder
} Esquires, Justices

This day appeared in open Court Jacob A. Lane duly appointed Deputy Clerk of this Court by Nicholas Oldham, Esq., Clerk thereof who thereupon took an oath to support the Constitution of the United States and the State of Tennessee and the oath of Deputy clerk of this Court as prescribed by law and by permission of the worshipful Court, entered upon the execution of the duties in Court of a Deputy Clerk.

This day Abraham Ditty produced in Court his stock mark as follows to wit: a hole in the right ear and under bit in the left ear which is ordered to be recorded.

Ordered by Court that Stewart Warren be appointed Overseer of the road from the west end of the Bridge over the Caney fork at Scarbroughs Mills to the intersection of said road with the Turnpike road at the McKinney Cabins being a road of the second Class and keep the same in repair as the law requires with the hands residing within the District assigned to Thomas Eastland, Esq, former overseer thereof.

This day Harmon Holland administrator of the estate of Alston Holland Deceased returned into Court upon oath an account of the sale of the property of the Deceased which is ordered to be recorded.

Thomas Little
To
Elisha Camron } Title Bond for 100 acres land more or less

It appearing to the satisfaction of the Court that Thomas Little the obligor hath departed this life whereupon appeared in open Court William G. Sims, William Little and Richard Nelson who being first sworn in due form of law upon their oath severally say that they are well (P-421) acquanted with the handwriting of Thomas Little Dec'd the obligor and that the signature to said bond is the proper handwriting of the said Thomas Little - .

Whereupon it is considered by the Court that the execution of said Bond is properly and well proven and that the same is the act and deed of said Thomas Little Dec'd which is ordered to be recorded that it be Registered in the Registers office of White County

Ordered by the Court unanimously that the following Bills of Cost of prosecution on part of the State of Tennessee against Sundry Defendants in the Honorable Circuit Court of White County, duly Certified by the Clerk of said Court directed to this Court for allowance examined by the Solicitor of this Court and deemed properly and legally taxed Towit:
In the case the State of Tennessee against William Burden - William G. Sims Clerk $4.37½ cents Dep. Shff S. J. Walling $1.50 cents
In the case the State of Tennessee against William Swift, William G. Sims clerk 9.25 - Shff J. T. Bradley $3.- Dep Shff John England $1.75 cents -
In the case the State against Mary Hutchens, William G. Sims clerk $4.37½ cents Dep Shff S. J. Walling $2.25 cents witness Reubin P. Hays .25 cents William J. Russell .25 cents Perry Russell .25 cents Lucy Hays .25 cents, James C. Baker .25 cents Justice Thomas Jones .50 cents
In the case the State against Alexander Moore, William G. Sims clerk seven dollars 54¼ cents. Dep Shff W. B. Cummings $1.25 - Dep Shff Jno. England 50 cents Shff J. T. Bradley $1.- D. Shff S. J. Walling .75 cents.
In the case the State against Ross Webb, William G. Sims Clerk $1.87½ Court Alexander Moore $2.25 witness Daniel T. Brown $3.11 - James Jones 25 cents. Helen Slatton .25 cents Edmund Blankinship 25 cents Justice Matthias Hutson 50 cents
In the case the state against Lewis Sparkman and Amanda Sparkman, William G. Sims clerk $6.12½ - D. Shff S. J. Walling $2.91½ cents -
In the case the State against Marmaduke Williamson and James Williamson William G. Sims clerk 7.56¼ cents Shff J. T. Bradley $4.29 cents D. Shff Jno. England .75 cents D. Shff Avery Norris 25 cents witness Moses Cantrell $1.50 cents whereupon it is ordered by the Court that the foregoing Bills of cost in said cases be paid by the County Trustee of White County out of any monies in the County Treasure not otherwise appropriated, and that the same be certified by the clerk of this court as the law requires.

Ordered by Court that Washington a Mulatto a slave the property of Capt John Gibson be permitted to cary a gun and hunt agreeably to the provisions of an act of assembly on such cases made and provided and that a certified issue as directed by law.

Edward M. Murray guardian to the heirs of Woodson P. White, Dec'd this day returned his account as guardian of said wards on oath which is ordered to be recorded &c

Ordered by Court that the District of road of which Hayes Arnold is Overseer commence at the west end of the Bridge across the Calf Killer at Rices Iron works instead of the middle of said Bridge heretofore

(P-422) Monday 4th January 1841

Ordered by Court that John Pennington, Charles Pennington, James H. Isham, Samuel Dyer and David Nicholas freeholders be appointed a Jury of view to examine and mark a change in the Cherry Creek road passing Charles Pennington and report thereof to the next term of this Court being a road of the second Class.

Ordered by Court that Osburn Walker, George Elmore, Cornelius Hickey, Henry Collier and William Williams freeholders, be appointed a Jury of view to lay off and mark a road of the third Class from Dunagans Iron-works on Cane Creek passing Henry Colliers to the mouth of Glade Creek thence the nearest and best way to John Bussells still house thence the nearest and best way to entersect the Sparta road near Capt John Walkers and report thereof to the next term of this Court.

Ordered by Court that John D. Clouse be appointed Overseer of the road from the DeKalb County line to Ceder Creek being a road of the second Class and keep the same in repair as the law requires with the hands which worked under Hiram Lewis former Overseer thereof

Ordered by Court that Joseph Upchurch and Solomon Dodson be released from the payment of a poll tax each, for the year 1840 they being over age and not subject to said tax and that a copy of this order be good with the Sherriff in the settlement of his accounts for the tax of said year for the amount of said poll Tax.

This day Anthony Dibrell admr of the estate of William Lyda Dec'd returned upon oath an Inventory, and an account of sales of the property of the Dec'd which is ordered to be recorded.

This day the Commissioners heretofore appointed to assign and set apart to the widow one years support and maintainance out of the estate of William Lyda Dec'd returned their report agreeably to law which is conformed by the Court and ordered to be recorded.

This day Jacob A. Lane Deputy Surveyor returned his report with a plott annexed of the line run between the counties of White and VanBuren, which is confirmed by the Court in all its parts, and ordered to be Received and Regestered in the Regestors office of White County.

Isd Ordered by the Court unanimously that the following sums be allowed the surveyor chaincarriers and markers; for services rendered in runing and marking the line between the Counties of White and VanBuren towit:
To Jacob A. Lane Deputy surveyor for eight days service and making out the plott and Report Twenty eight dollars. -
To John Overby for eight days carrying the chain eight dollars -
To Charles Hamlin for eight days carrying the chain eight dollars -
To Isaac Rogers for marking &c eight days eight dollars (P-423)
To William Lewis two days marking two dollars
To Thomas Moore for piloting on Rige way two days two dollars to the use of Jacob A. Lane he having paid said Moore that amount in all amounting to fifty six dollars to be paid out of the Tax of the year 1841 by the Sherriff of White County out of the first Taxes he collected for said year and that the receipt of the aforesaid persons for the amount due them respectively shall be good with said sherriff in the settlement of his accounts with the Trustee of White County for the year 1841

This day John England Executor of George Defreese Dec'd returned into Court upon oath an Inventory and account of the sale of the property of the Deceased which is ordered to be recorded.

This day John Pennington guardian to the heirs of John Dyer Dec'd returned upon oath an account of the condition of the estate of his ward in his hands which is ordered to be recorded &c.

This day Samuel Brown guardian to the heirs of John Dyer Dec'd returned upon oath an account of the condition of the estate of his wards in his hands which is ordered to be recorded.

For reasons appearing to the satisfaction of the Court it is ordered unanimously the payment of the sum of four hundred dollars or any part there of be withheld and suspended untill the further order of this Court be made, touching the manner of the execution of the contract entered into by Daniel Clark for McAdamizing the public square in the town of Sparta.

This day appeared in open Court William G. Jett, Mary Jett and Fordman Jett heirs of John Jett Dec'd over the age of fourteen years and severally choose and selected Mary Jett widow of said John Jett, Dec'd their guardian and in like manner the Court think fit to appoint and accordingly do appoint the said Mary Jett guardian to A. W. O. Jett, Woodson Jett, Sarah Jett and Thomas Jett infants and minors under the age of fourteen years, heirs of said John Jett Dec'd whereupon the said Mary Jett for the faithful execution of her guardianship entered into and acknowledged bond, with Anthony Dibrell, Turner Lane and Simon R. Doyle in the sum of five thousand dollars conditioned as the law requires.

Amos McGowen Admr. of the estate of James McGowen Dec'd returned into Court upon oath an account of the sales of the property of the Deceased which is ordered

Ordered by Court that William G. Sims be appointed guardian ad. Letters to all and singular the minor heirs of John Jett Dec'd pending the application of Mary Jett to be endowed with the lands of which John Jett her deceased seized and possessed.

(P-424) Monday 4th January 1841

Ordered that the following persons freeholders and house holders and Citizens of the County of White be appointed as Jurors to the next Honorable Circuit Court to be holden for the County of White on the first Monday of February next Towit:
Dan Griffith, Joshu Mason, Simon R. Doyle, John Austen, Jesse Walling, James Randols, Sr., Jesse Franks, Matthias Hutson, Jesse Allen, Harmon Little, Eli Sims, Thomas Jones, Jr., John T. Graham, David Bradford, William Glenn, Walker Bennett, John Parker, Samuel Brown, Dudley Hudgins, Sims Dearing, James Officer, Sr., Barlow Fisk, Barger Lowry, Robert M. Eastland, Steuart Warren, Hays Arnold and Charles Meek Constables &c.

This day James Dalton administrator of the estate of John Griffith dec'd returned upon oath an Inventory of the estate of the property of the Deceased which is ordered to be recorded

This day James Dalton administrator of the estate of John Griffith Dec'd returned an account of the sales of the property of the deceased upon oath which is ordered to be recorded.

This day the Commissioners heretofore appointed by a rule of this

Court to assign and set apart out of the estate of John Griffith Dec'd provisions for the support and maintainanee of his widow for one year returned their report of said assignment agreeably to law which the Court thinks reasonable and conforms which is ordered to be recorded.

Ordered by Court that William Irwin Sr., William Cantrell and Richard Crowder be appointed commissioners to assign and set apart out of the estate of Jesse H. Vermillion Dec'd one years provision for the support and maintainance of his widow &c. and report thereof to the next term of this Court.

Ordered by Court that the County of White be laid off into fifteen Civil Districts by changing and altering the present Districts as may seem most consistant with the spirit and true intent and meaning of the several acts of assembly directing the same and that David Snodgrass, Isaac Taylor, John W. Simpson, James Bartlett and Jacob A. Lane be appointed Commissioners who in conjunction with the Sherriff of White County are directed to carry this order into execution, and report thereof at the next term of this court according to law. -

Ordered by Court that further time untill the next term of this Court be given James Knowles Admr. of the estate of George Pertles, Sr., Dec'd to make out and return an Inventory of the property of the deceased

The Court proceeded to the appointment of a commissioner to take the census of White County for the year 1841 And to that office appoint John F. Vass Esq who took the oath prescribed by law

(P-425) Monday 4th January 1841

This day was produced in open Court a writing purporting to be the last will and testament of John Bryan Dec'd and his death being suggested and proven whereupon appeared in open Court William M. Bryan, Sr., and Alvin Foster whose names are subscribed as witnesses thereto who being sworn in due form of law upon their oath do say, that said writing is the last will and testament of the said John Bryan Dec'd that said John Bryan Subscribed and published the same as such in their presence, and that they subscribed the same as witnesses thereto and that the said John Bryan was at the date of the signing and publication of said last will and testament of sound and disposing mind and memory which is ordered to be recorded.

This day the Court produced to the appointment of an Entry Taker for land Claims in the County of White and to that Office Do appoint Jacob A. Lane for the next ensuing four years

Issd Ordered by Court that Wamon Leftwich and William Little Esquires be appointed Commissioners to settle with the Clerks and County Trustee of the County of White for the year 1841

Ordered by Court that Joseph Hord and Charles Smith be appointed Commissioners of the Poorhouse in White County for the year 1841

Ordered by Court that Thomas Green be appointed Treasure to the poorhouse for the year 1841

The Court proceeded to the appointment of a Ranger for the County of White and to that office do appoint Robert H. McManus for the next ensuing two years.

Ordered by Court that John Watson, Jr., be appointed Overseer of the road from a point near Esquire Bartletts to entersect the Cherry Creek road near Esq. Barnes being a road of the second Class and keep the same in repair as the law requires and that James Bartlett Esq. assign a list of hands to work thereon.

Ordered by Court that John Smith be appointed Overseer of the road from the Carthage road to the double chesnut on the mountain being a road of the third Class and keep the same in repair as the law requires and that William Glenn Esquire assign a list of hands to work thereon ordered by court that Solomon Duncan be appointed Overseer of the road from the double chesnut on the mountain to the entersection of the road with the Cherry Creek road near McKennys being a road of the third Class and keep the same in repair as the law requires And that David Snodgrass Esquire assign a list of hands to work thereon.

(P-426) Monday 4th January 1841

Ordered by Court that John R. Bartlett be appointed Overseer of the road from Falling Water to the Jackson County line being a road of the second class and keep the same in repair as the law directs with the hands assigned to work under Thomas Stone late Overseer thereof -

This day the Commissioners heretofore appointed by a rule of this Court to assign and set apart to Nancy McGowen widow of James McGowen, Dec'd one years provisions for her support and maintainance out of said estate returned their report thereof which is confirmed by the Court and ordered to be recorded.

Isd Ordered by Court that Joseph Herd and Charles Smith Comr. of the poor house be allowed the sum of Ten dollars each for their services for the year 1840. And that the Admr. of John Jett, Dec'd former Treasure of the poor house and Thomas Green Esq. the present Treasure be allowed the sum of Ten dollars for their services for said year to be allowed in proportion to the time that said John Jett served and the time that said Thomas Green, Esq. served in said capacity to be paid out of the poor Tax for the year 1840

Isd This day Allen L. Mitchell Superintendant for the poorhouse in the County of White produced his account for the year 1840 amounting to the sum of four hundred and thirty dollars nine and one half cents for expences, for Sundry purposes placed in said poor house which is allowed and confirmed in all its parts to be paid by the Treasure of said poor house, out of the tax of 1840 levied and raised for the support of the poor

The Court proceeded to the appointment of three Justices of Quorum and thereupon appoint David Snodgrass, Sims Dearing and Robert H. McManus Esquires Justices for the year 1841 in the County of White

Isd Ordered by Court that the Justices of the quorum court in the County of White be allowed the sum of one dollar and fifty cents each per day for each day they have served in that capacity in the year 1840 to be paid out of the Tax of the year 1840

On the petition of Jesse Pendigrass he is permitted to erect a grist and sawmill and other water machinery upon his own lands on the Calf Killer fork so as not to flood the lands of others to their prejudice.

Ordered by Court that William Simpson, William Little and Robert H. McManus Esq; be appointed Comrs. to let and superintend the repairs of the Jail of White County to the lowest bidder and report thereof to the next term of this Court.

(P-427) Monday 4th January 1841

Ordered by Court that William Simpson, Samuel V. Carrick, Anthony Dibrell, John Warren and William Usrey freeholders be appointed a Jury of view to lay off examine and mark a road of the second Class from the ford of town creek just below Lanes old mill running with and near an old road, entersecting Clarks mill road at some convenient point west of the west end of Oldhams lane and report thereof to the next term of this Court.

Ordered by court that Campbell Bohannon be appointed Overseer of the road from the forks of Caney fork, passing by John Bohannons still house, entersecting the dry Valley road near Goodman Madewells being a road of the second Class and keep the same in repair as the law requires and that James Bartlett esq. assign a list of hands to work thereon.

This day the death of Robert Hewett was suggested and proven and thereupon, John Hewett and Lewis Hewett were appointed adminestrators of all and singular the goods and chattles rights and credits of the deceased.

This day Joseph Herd was appointed guardian to Robert C. Pertle one of the minor heirs of George Pertle, Sr., Dec'd and took the oath prescribed by law, and with Thomas Green entered into and acknowledged bond in the sum of one thousand dollars conditioned as the law requires.

This day Richard Crowder Adm. of the estate of James T. Hays Dec'd returned into Court upon oath an Inventory of the estate of the Dec'd which is ordered to be recorded -

This day Richard Crowder adminestrator of the estate of James T. Hays Dec'd returned into Court upon oath an account of the sales of the property of the Dec'd which is ordered to be recorded.

The Commissioners appointed by a rule of the Court at a former session to assign and set apart to Lucy Hays order of James T. Hays Dec'd a sufficent quantity of provisions for her maintainance for one year, returned their report which is confirmed by the Court and ordered to be recorded.

Ordered by Court that the road as laid off and marked by Comr. heretofore appointed by this Court, leaving the Franks ferry road near Hayes Arnolds and entersecting the old road near the forks below the ironworks be confirmed and established, and that the Overseer of the old road open and keep in repair the new road as changed with his usual hands it being a road of the second Class.

Ordered by Court that the road as viewed, laid off and marked leading from Snodgrass's mill the nearest and best way, passing the residence of John England, Sr., intersecting the Carthage road near Wm. Minifee's (P-428) be established as a road of the third class having been laid out by Commissioners appointed by a rule of this Court made at a former day &c.

Ordered by Court unanimously that the following tax be levied and raised upon property in White County subject to taxables for the year 1841 To wit:

For County Tax:
On each one hundred dollars value of property five cents
On each Free White Poll, twelve and one half cents.

For Jury Tax:
On each one hundred dollars value of property five cents
On each Free White Poll, twelve and one half cents.

For Poor tax:
On each one hundred doller value of property five cents
On each Free White Poll twelve & one half cents

For Sparta Bridge Tax:
On each one hundred dollars value of property one and one fourth cents to be collected and levied by the Sherriff of White County as required by law - And it is further ordered by the Court, that the Clerk of this Court upon each Licence he may issue for the exhibition of natural or artificial curiosities for the year 1841 shall demand, collect and receive for the use of the County of White a sum equal to the full amount of the State tax, and for all other privilidges, for purposes aforesaid a sum equal to one half of the State Tax thence, all of which money he shall pay over, and account with the Trustee of the County of White agreeable to law.

Ordered by Court that John L. Smith be appointed Overseer of the road from the flat Rock to the entersection of said Road with the Stage Road being a road of the second Class and keep the same in repair as the law requires, and that the hands residing within the District under the former Overseer be assigned to work thereon -

Ordered that Court be adjourned untill tomorrow morning 10 O'clock

Thos. Eastland
Thomas Green
Robert H. McManus
Anderson S. Rogers

Tuesday Morning 5th January 1841; Court met pursuant to adjournment Present the worshipful

Thomas Eastland) Esquires
Thomas Green
Robert H. McManus
Anderson S. Rogers) Justices

(P-429) Monday 5th January 1841

This day Jacob A. Lane appointed Entry Taker of land claims in the County of White on yesterday appeared in Court with Anthony Dibrell and James Snodgrass and entered into and acknowledged bond in the sum of Ten thousand dollars; conditioned as the law requires and took the oath prescribed by law.

This day appeared in open Court Robert H. McManus appointed Ranger of the County of White on yesterday, and with William Usrey and Smith J. Walling entered into and acknowledged bond in the sum of five hundred dollars conditioned as the law requires, and took the oath prescribed by law.

This day James Snodgrass Adm. of the estate of William Hill Dec'd returned in open Court upon oath an Inventory of the estate of the Dec'd which is ordered to be recorded.

This day James Snodgrass Adm. of the estate of William Hill Dec'd returned in Court upon oath an account of the sales of the property of the Dec'd which is ordered to be recorded.

This day James Snodgrass guardian to the heirs of William Hill Dec'd returned upon oath an account of condition of the estate of his wards in his hands which is ordered to be recorded.

This day Noah H. Bradley guardian to the heirs of George W. Miller Dec'd returned into Court upon oath an account of the estate and condition thereof in his hands &c.

This day Asa Certain guardian to the heirs of Edward Hooper Dec'd returned into Court upon oath an account of the condition of the estate of his wards in his hands which is ordered to be recorded.

Ordered by Court that the rule made at the last session of this Court directing the Sherriff of White County to bring into Court Angeline Moon now at the poor house at the present term, be renewed; and that said pauper be brought up at the next term of this Court.

For reasons appearing to the satisfaction of the Court founded on the information of Hiram Rogers and John James, it is ordered that the Sherriff of White County forthwith take into his custody and bring into Court William Jones Jonathan Jones, Arnold Jones, Bluford Jones and Mary Jones, children of the widow Jones of Sparta who are represented to be in a suffering condition to the end that the Court may have such action thereon as the nature of the case may seem to demand according to law, and that process issue, to bring said children instantly before the Court.

(P-430) Tuesday 5th January 1841

This day appeared in open Court John Hewett and Lewis Hewett, appointed on yesterday adminestrators of Robert Hewett Dec'd and took the oath prescribed by law and with Anthony Dibrell and William Simpson entered into and acknowledged bond in the sum of three thousand dollars conditioned as the law directs.

This day John Gillentine guardian to William F. Carter returned into Court upon oath an account of the State and Condition of the estate of his ward in his hands which is ordered to be recorded &c.

For reasons appearing to the satisfaction of the Court it is ordered that all further proceedings touching the children of Nancy Jones of Sparta, be continued untill April Session A.D. 1841

Ordered by Court that the rule of this Court made at a former Session appointing a Jury of view upon a road of the second class runing from the ford on the Caney fork near Mr. Sparkmans passing Major Rendols mill intersecting the road leading to General Simpsons mill be renewed and that the same stand rated as a road of the third Class and report thereof to the next term of this Court &c.

Tuesday 5th January 1841 Ordered that court be adjourned untill Court in course

Test
Jacob A. Lane, D.Clk.

Thomas Eastland
Robert H. McManus
Thomas Green

(P-431) State of Tennessee

At a County Court began and held for the County of White and State aforesaid in the Court house in the town of Sparta before the Justices of said Court on the first Monday being the first day of February in the year of our Lord One thousand eight hundred forty one and of the Independence of the United States of America the sixty fifth year

Present the Worshipful,

David Snodgrass) Esquires
Robert H. McManus)
Sims Dearing &)
William Glenn, Jr.) Justices

This day David Snodgrass adminestrator of the Estate of David L. Mitchell Dec'd returned upon oath an additional Inventory and account of sales of the property of said estate which is ordered to be recorded - .

Issd Ordered by Court that John Smith be appointed Overseer of the road from the Bridge at the Harriet Irons to the widow Smiths gate being a road of the first Class and keep the same in repair as the law requires and that the same list and bounds of hands that worked under Hayes Arnold late Overseer thereof be assigned to work thereon -

This day William Glenn, guardian to the minor heirs of William Glenn Dec'd return his report upon oath is ordered to be recorded.

Issd Ordered by Court that Thomas T. Crowder be appointed Overseer of the road from the 10 mile post to the 15 mile post on the Kentucky road being a road of the second class and keep the same in repair as the law requires and that the same list and bounds of hands that worked under Richard Crowder late Overseer thereof be assigned to work thereon - .

This day the death of John M. Little late of the County of White was suggested in open Court and that he departed this life intestate - whereupon Harmon Little and William J. Russell are appointed adminestrators of all and singular the goods and Chattles, rights and credits of the said deceased and being present in open Court took the oath prescribed by law and together with Richard Nelson, Thomas Robertson and Richard Crowder entered into and acknowledged Bond in the sum of four Thousand Dollars conditioned as the law requires, and for reasons appearing to the satisfaction of the Court leave is given the adminestrators aforesaid to return their Inventory of said Estate at the May term 1841 of this Court.

(P-432) Monday 1 February A.D. 1841

Issd Ordered by Court that Joseph Glenn be appointed Overseer of the road from the top of the Gum Spring Mountain to Alexander Glenns be a road of the second class and keep the same in repair as the law requires and that the same list and bounds of hands that worked under Harmon Little be assigned to work thereon.

This day the death of William Usrey late of the County of White was suggested and proved in open Court - and that he departed this life intestate whereupon Samuel Usrey is appointed adminestrator of all and singular the goods and chattles, rights and credits of the said Deceased who being present in open Court took the oath prescribed by law and together with Daniel McClain & William Hitchcock entered into and acknowledged bond in the sum of four hundred dollars conditioned as the law requires.

Isd Ordered by Court that William C. Johnson be appointed Overseer of the road from the fork north of Snodgrass's mill to Plumb Creek being a road of the second class and keep the same in repair as the law requires, and that the same list and bounds of hands that worked under Reubin Broyles late Overseer thereof be assigned to work thereon.

This day James Knowles administrator of the estate of George Pertle Dec'd returned upon oath an Inventory and account of Sales of the Estate of the said Dec'd which is ordered to be recorded.

Isd Ordered by Court that James C. Crawley be appointed Overseer of the road from the Falling water to the branch beyond Lollar's being a road of the first class and keep the same in repair as the law requires and that the same list and bounds of hands that worked under James C. Hitchcock late Overseer thereof be assigned to work thereon - .

. This day Berryman Harden aged fifteen years on the 26th day of June 1840 an orphan boy was bound unto Jacob A. Lane to serve him after the manner of an apprentice untill he shall arrive at the age of Twenty one years and for the faithful performance of his covenant entered into Bond and with Turner Lane his surity as the law requires - .

This day Henry Harden an orphan boy aged fourteen years on the 1st day of January 1841 was bound to Turner Lane to serve him after the manner of an apprentice untill he shall attain the age of twenty one years and for the faithful performance entered into and acknowledged Bond Jacob A. Lane his surity as required by law.

(P-433) Monday 1st February A.D. 1841

This day Jefferson Harden an orphan boy aged six years on the 22nd day of March 1841 and Nelly Harden an orphan girl aged nine years on the 15th September 1840 were bound unto Thomas Jones to serve him after the manner of apprentices until they arrive at the age of twenty one years Respectively and for the faithful performance of his Covenant entered into and acknowledged bond with Smith J. Walling his security as required by law.

This day Elizabeth Harden an orphan girl aged eight years on the 5th day of April next was bound unto James Bartlett to serve him after the manner of an apprentice untill she arrives at the age of twenty one years, and for the faithful performance of his covenant entered into and acknowledged bond as the law requires with David Snodgrass his security - .

This day James Anderson appeared in open Court and was appointed guardian to two of his own children towit: William Anderson and James Anderson minor heirs of William Hill deceased and took the oath prescribed by law and together with William Snodgrass and William M. Bryant, Jr. entered into and acknowledged bond in the sum of twenty five hundred dollars conditioned as the law requires. -

This day Jacob A. Lane and Turner Lane Executors of the last will and Testament of Turner Lane Deceased returned upon oath an Inventory of the estate of the Deceased which is ordered to be recorded - .

Issd Ordered by Court that Samuel Jones be appointed Overseer of the road from the top of the mountain on the Shipping port road to its intersection of Lincolns ferry road between Oldham's and Clarks being a road of the second class and keep the same in repair as the law requires, and that the same list and bounds of hands that worked under William Overby late Overseer thereof be assigned to work thereon. -

This day William Green, Esq. produced in open court a commission appointing him one of the Justices of the peace in the 2nd District of White County - and thereupon took an oath to support the constitution of the United States and of the State of Tennessee and the several oaths prescribed by law and thereupon took his seat upon the bench - .

This day Margarett Dempsey and Sarah Dempsey two orphan twin girls aged two years on the 26 January 1841 were bound unto William Green to serve him after the manner of apprentice untill they respectively become twenty one years old; and for the faithful performance (P-434) of his Covenant entered into and acknowledged bond with Thomas Green his security as required by law.

Issd There as it appears fully to the satisfaction of this Court that a certain female pauper named Margarett Rose a citizen of the County of White is Insane, without suitable protection or support perfectly in a destitute condition and running at large, much to the annoyance of the people and the good morals of society and that suitable provisions should be made for her better protection and support. It is therefore considered by the Court and so ordered that the aforesaid Margarett Rose be conveyed to the Lunatic Hospital of the State of Tennessee there to remain untill her mind shall become fully restored to its right exercise - And it is further ordered by the Court that the Sherriff of White County take the said Margarett Rose into his custody and her safely keep and as soon as practicable deliver her to the Office of the Lunatic Hospital of the State of Tennessee in the City of Nashville in said State agreeable to law. And after hearing the testament upon oath of Jacob A. Lane, Esq. and Doctor Robert Cox Citizens of the County of White of good name, fame and reputation upon which we can fully rely - we certify that the aforesaid Margarett Rose has no real or personal estate or other means by which she can possibly support herself but is wholly dependent on cold charity - all of which is signed by the Court and ordered to be certified under the seal of this Court.

David Snodgrass (Seal)
Sims Dearing (Seal)
Robt H. McManus (Seal)

Present the worshipful

David Snodgrass, Robert H. McManus, William G. Glenn, Jr., Sims Dearing, William Green, William Hutchens, Thomas Jones, Thomas Green, Matthias Hutson, Lewis Pettett, Anderson S. Rogers, Jesse Walling, James Knowles, William Hudgins, William Little, Richard Crowder. } Esquires Justices

This day the Commissioners heretofore appointed by this Court to lay off mark a change in the shipping port road commincing at the ford of Town Creek below Lanes mill and entersect the Lincoln ferry road between Oldhams & Clarks mill made their report favorable which is received and said change established - And that the Overseer of the old road keep the same in repair as though no change had been made and that the old road from said creek to the corner of Oldhams fence be discontinued so soon as the new route is opened - .

This day the Commissioners heretofore appointed by this Court to lay off and mark a road of the 2nd class from Browns Mill to (P-435) intersect the Kentucky road made their report favorable which is received and said road established and it is ordered that Daniel T. Brown be appointed Overseer thereof and keep the same in repair as the law requires, and that Matthias Hutson, Esq., assign list and bounds of hands to work thereon - .

Isad Ordered by Court that William Glenn, Bartlett Belcher, John P. Bradley, William Wisdom, and Reubin Broyles freeholders be appointed a Jury of view to lay off and mark a road of the third class from Jeremiah Wilhites, the nearest and best way passing John P. Bradleys and Bartlett Belchers to entersect the Calf Killer road near Col. E. Camrons and report thereof to the next term of this Court.

For reasons appearing to the satisfaction of the Court it is ordered by the Court that the ordere of this Court at the July term 1840 making an allowance to Susannah Walling widow and relect of James Walling, Jr., deceased be set a side and for nothing esteemed - .

Whereas it appearing fully to the satisfaction of this Court that at the July term 1840 of this Court Susannah Walling the widow of James Walling, Jr., deceased appeared in open Court and produced her account of Statement of debts which were then due and owing by her which were contracted by her after the death of her husband James Walling, Jr., and before the estate of the deceased was adminestrated on, for necessaries for the comfortable support for herself and children to the amount of one hundred and sixty dollars which debts were owing to Joseph Herd & Son - Thomas Walling & Son and to William B. Taylor, as in said account set forth and it also appearing that said debts should be paid out of the effects of the Estate of the deceased - .

It is therefore considered by the Court and so directed and ordered that Jesse Walling the adminestrator of the Estate of the said Deceased pay the debts to J. Herd & Son, T. Walling & Son and William B. Taylor to the amount of one hundred and sixty dollars as mentioned in said account together with such interests as shall have legally accrued thereon at the payment thereof - And the same Debts and interest when paid by the said adminestrator receipts thereof shall constitute good and valid vouchers to his credits in the final settlements of the adminestrations of the estate of the said James Walling, Jr. Deceased.

Ordered that Court be adjourned till tomorrow 9 O'clock

Robert H. McManus
Sims Dearing
David Snodgrass

(P-436) Tuesday Morning 2nd February A.D. 1841

Court met pursuant to adjournment
Present the worshipful

David Snodgrass } Esqs
Sims Dearing &
Robert H. McManus } Justices

Ordered that Court be adjourned untill Court in Course

Test
N. Oldham, Clk.

David Snodgrass
Sims Dearing
Rob't H. McManus

State of Tennessee

At a Court began and held for the County of White and State aforesaid in the courthouse in the town of Sparta before the Justices of said Court on the first Monday being the first day of March in the year of our Lord one thousand eight hundred and Forty one, And of the Independence of the United States the sixty fifth year

Present the Worshipful

	David Snodgrass	)	
Green to be	Sims Dearing &	)	Esquires
paid instead	William Green in	)	
of McManus	place of R. H. McManus	)	Justices

This day William R. Tucker appeared in open Court and produced a Commission autherising him to discharge the duties of Justice of the peace for the County of White and took the oath to support the Constitution of the United States and of the State of Tennessee and the several oaths prescribed by law who thereupon entered upon the discharge of the duties of his office

This day Anthony Dibrell the administrator of the estate of the estate of William Lyda Deceased returned upon oath an additional account of sales of the estate of the deceased which is ordered to be recorded.

(P-437) Monday 1st March A.D. 1841

Issd Ordered by Court that Lewis Bohannon be released from the payment of one half the appraised value of an Estray steer taken up by him and appraised to five dollars - the same having escaped from him. -

This day the Commissioners heretofore appointed by this Court to lay off and set apart one years provisions for the support and maintainance of the widow and family of Jesse H. Vermillion Deceased returned their report upon oath which is ordered to be recorded.

This day Elizabeth Vermillion Adm'x of the Estate of Jesse H. Vermillion Deceased returned upon oath an Inventory of the property of the Estate of the Deceased which is ordered to be recorded.

This day Elizabeth Vermillion adm'x of the estate of Jesse H. Vermillion Deceased returned upon an account of the sales of the property of the Estate of the Deceased - which is ordered to be recorded.

Issd Ordered by Court that Andrew Goodson be appointed Overseer of the road from James McGowens to Franks ferry being a road of the second Class and keep the same in repair as the law requires and that the list and bounds of hands that worked under William W. Knowles late Overseer thereof be assigned to work thereon. -

For reasons appearing to the satisfaction of the Court it is ordered that Joseph Herd, Thomas Robertson and Peter Burum who were heretofore appointed to assign provisions to the widow and family of James McGowen for their support for one year be permitted to correct their report in order to make a more liberal allowance and report thereof to the next term of this Court.

Issd It appearing to the satisfaction of the Court upon the oath of Thomas Nicholas that heretofore the said Thomas Nicholas filed in the Trustees Office of White County on the 18th day of October 1836 - a Jury ticket numbered 56 for the sum of five dollars - has been lost or so mislaid that it cannot be found and that the same is due and unpaid whereupon it is ordered by the Court that the Trustee of White County pay the same and take his receipt therefore - -

Issd. Ordered by Court that Sims Dearing Esquire be appointed Commissioner to apportion lists and bounds of hands between the diffrent Overseers of the road in his neighborhood having due regard to the grades of the diffrent roads.

Issd Ordered by Court that the Sherriff of White County bring immediatly into open Court 2 certain orphan boys one named Thomas Howard the other named Joseph Lamb to be dealt by according to law.

(P-438) Monday 1st March A.D. 1841

This day Thomas Howard an orphan boy aged Eleven years on the 10th day of September 1840 was bound unto Edward M. Murray to serve him after the manner of an apprentice to the saddlers trade untill he arrives at the age of 21 years and for the faithful performance of his covenant entered into bond with James Scott his security conditioned &c.

This day Joseph Lamb an orphan boy aged fourteen years the first day of October 1840 was bound to William Clayton to serve him after the manner of an apprentice to learn the art of Printing untill he arrives at the age of twenty one years and for the faithful performance of his Covenant entered into and acknowledged bond with Anthony Dibrell his security conditioned &c.

Issd This day Jacob Stipe appeared in open Court and produced an account against John Gillentine guardian to William F. Carter amounting to the sum of Forty seven dollars for board of said Carter and his horse whereupon it is ordered by the Court that said John Gillentine guardian as aforesaid pay unto the said Jacob Stipe the aforesaid sum of Forty seven dollars out of the funds of his said ward which shall be a sufficent voucher in the settlement of his accounts. -

This day David Little appeared in open Court and resigned his office of Constable in the 13th District of White County which is ordered to be recorded.

For reasons appearing to the Court it is ordered that John Haston who is before the Court in custody of the Sherriff be confined in the Common Jail of White County untill tomorrow morning 10 O'clock for contempt offered this worshipful Court.

This day James Graham appeared in open Court and resigned his office of constable in the 2nd District of White County which is ordered to be recorded - .

Ordered by Court that Samuel V. Carrick, William Simpson and John L. Prise be appointed Commissioners to assign and set apart one years provision out of the Estate of Robert Hewett Deceased for the support and maintainance of the widow and family of the Deceased and report thereof to the next term of this Court.

Issd Ordered by Court that David Mansell be released from the payment of the sum of one dollar seventy two and a half cents the tax of the 1840 he being overcharged that much and that the Sherriff of White County have a credit therefor in settlement of his accounts with the Trustee.

(P-439) Monday 1 March A.D. 1841

Issd Ordered by Court that Green Templeton, Levi Jarvis, Joseph Glenn, Robert Glenn and James Knowles freeholders, be appointed a Jury of view to examine lay off and mark the change of the shippingport road as proposed by Vashti Glenn and report thereof at the next term of this Court.

This day Mrs. Tabitha Fox appeared in open Court and renounced her right to adminester on the estate of Joshua Fox her deceased husband Whereupon Sims Dearing appeared in open Court and was appointed adminestrator of all and singular the goods and chattles, rights and credits of the said Joshua Fox deceased late of the County of White who died intestate thereupon took the oath prescribed by law and together with Joseph Herd and Nathan Earls, Jr., entered into and acknowledged bond in the sum of two thousand five hundred dollars conditioned as the law requires.

Issd Ordered by Court that David Snodgrass, Lewis Bohannon and Jesse Pendegrass be appointed Commissioners to assign and set apart one years provision for the support and maintainance of the widow and family of Joshua Fox Deceased out of his Estate and report thereof to the next term of this Court.

Issd This day David G. Wilson produced in open Court a writing purporting to be the last will and testament of Hartewell B. Wilson late of the County of White Deceased and thereupon the due execution and publication thereof as such was proved in open Court by oath of Andrew Lowell and John Baker two of the subscribing witnesses thereto for the purposes therein contained and at the same time made oath that the said Hartewell B. Wilson at that date of the execution and publication thereof as such was of sound and disposing mind and memory which is ordered to be recorded - .
And the said David G. Wilson the executor appointed by the last will and testament of the said Hartwell B. Wilson, Deceased being present in open Court agrees to take upon himself the burden of the execution of the said will and testament of the said Hartewell B. Wilson, deceased and thereupon took the oath required by law and together with Andrew Lowell and John Baker entered into and acknowledged bond in the sum of two thousand five hundred dollars conditioned as the law requires - .

Ordered by Court that the order of last term requiring the Commissioners heretofore appointed by this Court set apart to the widow and family of George Pertle, deceased an additional supply of provision for their support for one year be set aside and for nothing esteemed.

(P-440) Monday 1 March A.D. 1841

Issd Ordered by Court that Archebald Conner, Joseph McDaniel, Thomas Robertson, Indemon B. Moore, and Samuel A. Moore, Jr. freeholders be appointed a jury of view to lay off and mark a road of the second class leaving the Rockisland or Kentucky road at Joseph McDaniels or at some other suitable point thereto run the nearest and best way to Dillons Bridge across the Caney fork and report thereof to the next term of this Court.

It appearing fully to the satisfaction of the Court that the bond of James Knowles who is adminestrator of the estate of George Pertle Deceased is not sufficiently large to cover the effects of the estate of the deceased it is therefore considered by the Court that said James Knowles adminestrator as aforesaid (who being present before the Court) shall appear at the next term of this Court and enter into Bond and good security in the sum of six thousand Dollars and the said James Knowles agrees to do so.

Issd For reasons appearing to the satisfaction of the Court upon the information of William G. Sims it is ordered by the Court that the Sherriff bring before the Court the next term thereof all the minor orphan children of a certain Elizabeth White living on Cherry Creek - to be dealt by as may seem to the Court right and according to law. -

Issd Ordered by Court that James Williams be released from the payment of the sum of six dollars twenty nine and one fourth cents of the tax of the year 1840 he being overcharged - and that the Sherriff of White County have a credit for that sum in the settlement of his accounts with the Trustee of White County for the year 1840 - .

For reasons appearing to the satisfaction of the Court that the sherriff of White County forthwith release from the Common Jail of White County a certain John Harlow who was this day ordered therein to be confined - the remainder of his punishment to be remitted.

This day Samuel Usrey admr. of Wm. G. Usrey Deceased produced into open Court upon oath an Inventory of the Estate of the Deceased which is ordered to be recorded.

Ordered that Court be adjourned untill tomorrow 10 O'clock

David Snodgrass
Sims Dearing
William Green

(P-441) Tuesday morning 2nd March A.D. 1841 Court met pursuant to adjournment. Present the worshipful

David Snodgrass, Sims Dearing } Esquire
William Green in place of }
R. H. McManus } Justices

Ordered that Court be adjourned untill Court in Course

Test
N. Oldham, Clk.

David Snodgrass
Sims Dearing
William Green

(P-442)

State of Tennessee

At a County Court began and held for the County of White in the State aforesaid in the Court house in the town of Sparta before the Justices of said Court on the first Monday being the fifth day of April in the year of our Lord One thousand eight hundred and forty one and of the Independance of the United States of America the Sixty fifty year

Present the worshipful

Thomas Eastland, Esq. Chairman
David Snodgrass, William Glenn,
Sims Dearing, Thomas Jones,
William Knowles, Samuel Lance,
Elijah Frost, Thomas Green,
Robert H. McManus, William R. Tucker,
William Little, Matthias Hutson,
Asa Certain, John Pennington,
William Hitchcock, James Allison,
James Knowles.

This day Sims Dearing adminestrator of the estate of Joshua Fox deceased returned upon oath an Inventory and account of the sales of said Estate which is ordered to be recorded - .

This day the clerk of this Court exhibited in open Court the report of a settlement made by him with Benjamin Lewis, adminestrator with the will annexed of William Lewis, Deceased which is received and confirmed by the Court in all its parts which is ordered to be recorded - .

For reasons appearing to the satisfaction of the Court William Simpson is permitted to adminestrator on the Estate of Thomas Storm, Deceased so far as to the Collection and settlement of certain Debts in which the said Simpson is entestated and no farther, and the said William Simpson being present in open Court took the oath required by law and together with Richard Nelson and John Young entered into and acknowledged bond in the sum of four hundred dollars conditioned as the law requires.

Isad Ordered by Court that William Usrey be appointed Overseer of the Streets and roads in the town of Sparta except the street leading from the public square northward to the ford of the Calf Killer below Andersons salt well also on that portion of the Nashville road leading from the Sparta Bridge to the fork where the Carthage road Turns off being a road of the first Class and keep the whole in repair as required by law for roads of the first Class and that William Little, William R. Tucker and Robert H. McManus Esq appointed lists of hands between him and the other Overseer of said town to work thereon.

(P-443) Monday 5th April A.D. 1841

For reasons appearing to the satisfaction of the Court it is ordered by the Court that the Trustee of White County pay unto Daniel Clark the contractor for paving the public square in the town of Sparta the sum of Four hundred dollars the amount which the County Court appropriated to that object to be paid out of the tax laid for that purpose in 1840 provided the said Daniel Clark will enter into Bond and good security in the sum of eight hundred dollars conditioned that the said Daniel Clark shall on or before the first day of November 1841 fully comply with his contract in McAdamizing the public square in Sparta in such manner that the size of the stone thereon shall not exceed the size contemplated on and agreed to by the Commissioners who were authorized to contract therefor and agreeably to the understanding of this Court, otherwise that he will immediately refund the aforesaid sum of four hundred dollars to the County of White with interest thereon that said bond be executed before this order issue - .

Ordered by Court that the Treasure of the poor house of White County pay to Allen L. Mitchell Keeper of the poorhouse of said County for services for the year 1841 the sum of two hundred dollars to be paid in quarterly payments of fifty dollars each out of the poor tax of said County of White - .

William Glenn
to
Canada Rigsby } Bond for title of 74 acres land

This day personally appeared in open Court Martin B. Angel the only subscribing witness to the within Bond (the same having been executed when one witness was sufficient) who being first sworn deposed and said he saw William Glenn sign seal and execute the within Bond for the purpose therein contained which is deemed by the Court sufficiently proved which is ordered to be recorded and Registered in the Registers office of White County.

Isad Ordered by Court unanimously that Nicholas Oldham Clerk of this Court be allowed the sum of two dollars and fifty cents for recording and Registering the report and plott of survey of the line between the County of White and Van Buren - also the sum of thirty eight dollars and ninety four cents for money expended for Blank record Books for the use of the County Court amounting in all to the sum of forty one dollars and forty four cents to be paid by the Trustee of White County out of the tax of the year 1841

Ordered by Court that Nicholas Oldham Clerk of White County Court be allowed the sum of twenty dollars per year for (P-444) three years services relative to the Common Schools of White being up to this day amounting in all to the sum of sixty dollars to be paid by the Trustee of White County out of any monies not otherwise appropriated

This day John H. Dale produced in open Court the certificate of his Election to the office of Constable in the 2nd District of White County to fill the vacancy occasioned by the resignation of James Graham who being present in open Court took an oath to support the Constitution of the United States and of the State of Tennessee and the several oaths prescribed by law and together with Turner Lane, John White, Sr., and John White, Jr., entered into and acknowledged bond in the sum of six thousand dollars conditioned as the law requires. -

This day James Bradley produced in open Court the certificate of the Sherriff of White County of his election to the office of Constable in the 13th District of White County to fill the vacancy occasioned by the resignation of David Little - Who being present in open Court took an oath to support the Constitution of the United States and of the State of Tennessee and the several oaths prescribed by law and together with Daniel McClain, James Lowry, James Thomas and Samuel Lance entered into bond and Security in the sum of six thousand dollars conditioned as the law requires - .

Issd Ordered by Court that James A. Knowles be appointed Overseer of the road from the fork to William Knowles on the Kentucky road being a road of the second Class and keep the same in repair as the law requires and that the same list and bounds of hands that worked under Moses Grisson late Overseer thereof be assigned to work thereon - .

Issd Ordered by Court unanimously that William G. Sims Esq. Clerk of White Circuit Court be allowed the sum of Ten dollars and fifty Cents for one Blank record Book furnished for the office of said Court to be paid by the Trustee of White County out of the tax of the year 1841

Issd Ordered by Court that William Simpson be allowed the sum of One hundred dollars for keeping the Bridge across the Calf Killer at Sparta in repair agreeable to his contract during the year 1841 to be paid by the Trustee of White County out of the tax of the year 1841 levied for that purpose

This day the Com'r heretofore appointed to set apart one years provisions to the widow and family of George Pertle Dec'd returned their report which is ordered to be recorded.

(P-445) Monday 5 April A.D. 1841

Ordered by Court unanimously that the following persons be allowed the following sums as fees in the following State cases which came from the Circuit Court of White County for allowance which have been examined by Samuel Turney, Esq. the attorney of this Court as correctly taxed and properly chargeable to the county of White to wit;

In the case the state against Ann Sparkman Clerk W. G. Sims $3.37½ D.Shff N. H. Bradley 75 Shff S. J. Walling $1 - D.Shff John England 50 cents

The State vs Lindsey Brown Clerk W. G. Sims $4.25 Clerk A. Dibrell 2.12½ Shff D. L. Mitchell $3.04 witness per State S. Evans $2.50 Wm. Glenn 2.50 atto Gen. J. B. McCormick $5.00 - The State vs John H. Montgomery Clerk Sims $10.49½ - Shff J. T. Bradley $1.12½ D. Shff John England $3.37½ The State vs Hampton Ramsey Clerk W. G. Sims 10.56¼ - D.Shff Jno. England $3. - Shff J. T. Bradley $2.25 - D.Shff N. H. Bradley $1.50 witness for State Thomas Price $0.75 The State Wm. Sparkman & Henry Crawley Clerk W. G. Sims $6.31¼ Shff J. T. Bradley $0.75 John England 25 cents - D. Shff Hayes Arnold 25 cents - D. Shff S. J. Walling 12½ cents - D. Shff A. Norriss 12½ cents The State vs William Whitley Clerk W. G. Sims $2.37½ cents - D. Shff Jno England $0.62½ - D. Shff S. J. Walling $1.25 D. Shff James Graham $0.75 - The State vs Jesse Walling Clerk W. G. Sims 5.75 D. Shff Jno England 91 1/3 D. Shff. S. J. Walling $1.50 - Witness John Rasco 75 cents - The State vs Cason Swindle Clerk W. G. Sims 2.75 D. Shff S. J. Walling 1.25 The State vs Ellerson Lowry Clerk W. G. Sims $8.12½ D. Shff Jno England 50 cents D. Shff S. J. Walling 2.12½ Justice William Little 50 cents Constable Hayes Arnold 50 cents - The State vs Michael Corbet Clerk W. G. Sims 4.25 Clerk A. Dibrell $2.12½ Shff D. L. Mitchell 2.41½ D. Shff W. G. Sims 62½ cents witness S. Evans $2.50 W. Glenn $2.50 Attorney Genl. John B. McCormick $5.00 - The State vs Zachariah Hagen, Sarah Hagen, Nancy Hagen and Elizabeth Hagen Clerk W. G. Sims $10.00 D. Shff S. J. Walling 1.75 - Shff J. T. Bradley 79 - Jailor Robert H. McManus $20.68¾ Witness Matthias Hutson 6.25 - Miram Moore $8.58 Margarett Crawley $8.58 - Henry Crawley $5.79 - Justice M. Haston trying cause &c 50 cents Const. W. B. Haston 3.25 Atto Genl. Wm. Cullom $5.00 The State vs Michael Corbet clerk W. G. Sims 7.81¼ D. Shff John England 75 cents D. Shff S. J. Walling 75 - Shff J. T. Bradley 66½ Justice William Bruster .50 cents Charles Meek Const $1.25 Eliza Cook witness 1.75 Atto Genl. Wm. Cullom $5.00 - Jailor R. H. McManus 52.12½ amounting in all to the sum of two hundred and fifty seven dollars and seventeen cents to be paid by the Trustee of White County out of any money not otherwise appropriated.

Issd Ordered by Court that Elijah Pertle, William Cantrell, James Knowles, John Knowles and Thomas T. Crowder freeholders be appointed a Jury of view to lay off and mark a change in the shipping point road passing the plantation of Isham Cook being a road of the 2nd Class and report thereof to the next quarterly

(P-446) Monday 5 April 1841

Issd This day Susannah Watson late widow of James Walling Deceased exhibited her account in open Court upon oath against the minor heirs of James Walling Deceased to wit - for Board and cloathing Ruthy nine months for nine dollars for board cloathing &c of Elizabeth for nine months nine dollars. For boarding & cloathing Joseph nine months thirteen dollars fifty cents - for boarding and cloathing Sarah nine months eighteen dollars - For boarding and cloathing Nancy nine months eighteen dollars - For boarding and cloathing Isham nine months eighteen dollars amounting in all to the sum of eighty five dollars and fifty cents which is allowed by the Court and ordered to be paid to the said Susannah Watson by Anderson S. Rogers, guardian to the said Children out of the Estate of the said wards respectively - .

This day Mary Hutchens the widow of Webster Hutchens deceased exhibited in open Court upon oath her account against five of the youngest minor heirs of the said dec'd to wit: Jefferson, Nancy, Charles, Dillard and Albert G. L. Hutchens amounting to the sum of forty four dollars being for boarding and cloathing and tuition for the twelve months ending this date which is allowed by the Court and ordered to be paid to the said Mary Hutchens by Joseph Herd guardian out of the Estate of said wards Respectively - .

This day Hannah G. Farris the widow of Limas B. Farris Deceased exhibited her account upon oath in open Court for boarding cloathing and schooling the five minor heirs of said Deceased from the 27 November 1839 up to this date the sum of two hundred and fifty one dollars which is allowed by the Court and ordered to be paid to the said Hannah G. Farris by William G. Sims guardian to said minors out of their estates respectively.

Ordered by Court unanimously the Robert H. McManus, Anderson S. Rogers, Jesse Walling, Matthias Hutson, William Knowles Thomas Jones, William Hitchcock, William Glenn, John Pennington, James Bartlett, Sims Dearing, Samuel Lance and Elijah Frost Esqrs Commissioners of the Revenue for White County for the year 1841 be allowed the sum of Ten dollars each for taking the list of taxable property & polls in said County in their respective Districts for said year to be paid by the Trustee of White County out of the tax for the year 1841

This day the Commissioners heretofore appointed by this Court to set apart one years provisions out of the Estate of Joshua Fox Dec'd for the support of the widow and family of the deceased made their report upon oath which is ordered to be recorded - .

(P-447) Monday 5 April 1841

For reasons appearing to the satisfaction of the Court it is ordered by the Court that the order of this Court made at its October term 1840 requiring Elsa England to appear in open Court and give other good and sufficient security in order that Anthony Dibrell, James Scott and Samuel Johnson her securities may be released from all further and future liabilities therein as such be renewed and that a subpoena issue returnable to the next term of this Court.

Ordered by Court that the following named persons to wit: James Williams, James Hudgins, Dan Griffith, Anderson S. Rogers, William M. Bryan, Jr., Charles Smith, Edward Anderson, Elijah Denton, Jr., Christopher Swindle, Joseph Glenn, Harmon Little, Eli Sims, John Taylor, Sr., George Welch, William Hitchcock, William Glenn, Asa Certain, Jesse A. Bounds, John Pennington, James Bartlett, Alexander Officer, Thomas Broyles, Samuel Lance, David Snodgrass, John L. Smith & Nathaniel C. Davis as Jurors and Hayes Arnold and Charles Meeks as Constables good and lawful men Citizens of the County of White be appointed to serve as Jurors and Constables at the July term A.D. 1841 of the Circuit Court of White County and that a writ of Venirifacias issue directed &c.

For reasons appearing to the satisfaction of the Court it is ordered by the Court that the further consideration of the matter of the application of David Snodgrass administrator of David L. Mitchell Deceased for an allowance for services rendered by the said David L. Mitchell in his life time settling the estate of James Isham Deceased as administrator of the Estate of the said Deceased be postponed untill the next quarterly term of this Court and that a subpoena issue requiring that James Randols, Sr., appear at said Court and give testimony therein - at which day defendant by his attorney agrees that the matter shall be decided.

This day James Knowles administrator of the Estate of George Pertle Deceased appeared in open Court as he was required to do by an order of the last term of this Court and utterly refused to comply with the requirements of said order by entering into larger bond and additional security as therein required which is ordered to be recorded and that the said James Knowles in all time to come desist from acting as such adm'r aforesaid

Whereupon the Court then appointed Jacob L. Pertle administrator of all and singular the goods and chattles, rights and credits of the said George Pertle Deceased who being present in open Court took the oath required by law and together with Asa Certain, Green Templeton, Joseph Herd, Edward V. Pollard and Thomas Walling entered into and acknowledged bond in the sum of six thousand Dollars conditioned as the law requires

(P-448) Monday 5th April 1841

This day Jonathan T. Bradley, Esq. sherriff of White County appeared in open Court and undertook the collection of the public taxes of the County of White for the year 1841 and took the oath required by law and together with Richard Nelson, Asa Certain, James C. Kelly, James Thomas, Joshua Mason, Thomas Walling, Smith J. Walling & Samuel Turney entered into and acknowledged bond in the sum of Five Thousand dollars conditioned as the law requires.

BOND

Know all men by these presents that we Jonathan T. Bradley, Richard Nelson, Asa Certain, James C. Kelly, James Thomas, Joshua Mason, Thomas Walling, Smith J. Walling, Samuel Turney, all of the County of White and State of Tennessee are held and firmly bound unto Thomas Eastland, Esq. Chairman of the County Court of White County and his successors in office in the sum of five Thousand dollars current money which payment well and truly to be made and done, we bind ourselves and each and every of our heirs, Executors &c. jointly and severally, firmly by these presents sealed with our seals and dated the 5th day of April A.D. 1841

The Condition of the above obligation is such that whereas the said Jonathan T. Bradley Sherriff of White County hath been by White County Court appointed Collector of the public Taxes of said County of White for the year 1841 Now if the above bound Jonathan T. Bradley shall well and truly and faithfully collect all the taxes which shall be assessed and levied by said County for the year 1841.

To wit the County tax, Jury tax, Poor tax and Sparta Bridge tax for the use of said County of White, and pay the monies so collected over to the proper offices of said County (according to law) who are authorised to receive the same - then the above obligation to be null and void, else remain in full force and vertue.

Test
N. Oldham, Clk.

J. T. Bradley (seal)
R. Nelson (seal)
Asa Certain (seal)
J. C. Kelly (seal)
James Thomas (seal)
Joshua Mason (seal)
Thomas Walling (seal)
S. J. Walling (seal)
Sam'l Turney (seal)

Issd Ordered by Court that George Elmore, Avery Bussell, Adam Massa, John Massa and John Bussell freeholders be appointed a Jury of view to lay and mark a road of the third Class from Danagans Iron Works or Cain Creek passing Henry Colliers to the mouth of Glade Creek thence the nearest and best way to John Bussells still house, thence the nearest and best way (P-449) to entersect the Sparta road at some convenient point between Joshua Hickeys and Richard England and report thereof to the next quarterly term of this Court.

Issd Ordered by Court that Green Templeton, Levi Jarvis, Joseph Glenn, Robert Glenn, and James Knowles freeholders be appointed a Jury of view to lay off and mark a change in the Shippingport road as proposed by Vashti Glenn and report thereof to the next quarterly term of this Court.

Issd For reasons appearing to the satisfaction of the Court founded on the information of Joseph W. Bell, it is ordered by the Court that the Sherriff of White County take forthwith into his custody and bring into Court William Jones, Jonathan Jones, Arnold Jones, Bluford Jones and Mary Jones Children of the widow Jones of Sparta who are represented to be in a suffering condition to the end that the Court may have such action thereon, that the nature of the case may seem to demand according to law, and that process issue to bring said children instantly before the Court

Whereas it appearing to the satisfaction of the Court by the records of this Court that at the October term 1839 thereof a certain John Gillentine, Esquire then a Justice of the peace in and for said County and also a citizen thereof was by the said Court at said term appointed Commissioner of the revenue in the 15th District of said County the year 1840 for the purpose of taking a complete list of the taxable property and polls of said District for the year 1840 and return the same as required by law - and whereas also the said John Gillentine, Esq., Commissioner as afore said hath utterly failed, refused and neglected to take and return a full and complete list of the taxable property and polls for said District for the year 1840 as by law he was bound to do - Where upon it is considered by the Court and so ordered that the said John Gillentine, Esq., Commissioner aforesaid do make his personal appearance before the Justices of our next quarterly Court to be held for the County of White on the Court house in the town of Sparta on the first Monday of July next then and there to shew cause if any he have or can why the penalties of the second section Chapter fourteen of the act of the General Assembly of the State of Tennessee passed in the year 1835 should not be enforced against him for so failing, refusing and neglecting the duties aforesaid imposed on him by law as commissioner aforesaid - that a writ of Scairifacias issue directed &c.

Monday evening April 5th A.D. 1841

Ordered that Court (P-450) be adjourned untill tomorrow morning at 10 by the Clock

Thomas Eastland
Robert H. McManus
W. R. Tucker

Tuesday morning 6th day of April A.D. 1841 Court met pursuant to adjournment Present the worshipful

Thomas Eastland, Esq. Chairman
Robert H. McManus }
W. R. Tucker } Esqrs. Justices

This day Daniel Clark personally appeared in open Court and together with Nicholas Oldham, Richard Nelson, William G. Sims and Smith J. Walling entered into and acknowledged bond in the sum of Eight hundred dollars as the law requires

Ordered by the Court that the order made yesterday requiring the sherriff to bring into Court William Jones, Jonathan Jones, Arnold Jones, and Mary Jones Children of the widow Jones of Sparta to be dealt by as the law requires be renewed returnable to the next term of this Court - .

Ordered by Court that the following boundary of hands be assigned to work on that portion of the road on which George Ogden* Glenns corner on the public square in Sparta Northwardly to the River at Andersons old salt well from thence from the begining Eastwardly including the Hewetts as the road runs thence Northwardly to the top of the spur of the mountain and with the same oposite to Andersons old salt well including all the hands in said Bounds (excluding W. Usrey and his hands)

Ordered that Court be adjourned untill court in course

Test
N. Oldham, Clk.

Thos Eastland
Robert H. McManus
W. R. Tucker

* is overseer to wit: from

(P-451) State of Tennessee

At a quorum Court began and held for the County of White in the Courthouse in the town of Sparta before the Justice of said Court on the first Monday being the third day of May in the year of our Lord One thousand eight hundred and forty one And of the Independence of the United States the sixty fifth year

Present the worshipful

David Snodgrass	)	Esqs
Sims Dearing	)	
Robert H. McManus	)	Justices

Issd Ordered by Court that the order of last Court requiring Elsa England guardian to the minor heirs of Elijah England Deceased to appear at this term of said Court and enter into other good and sufficient Security relative to her said appointment as guardian in order that her securities should be released from future liabilities therein be renewed returnable to the next term of this Court.

Issd Ordered by Court that William P. Campbell be released from the payment of a poll tax for two years to wit for the years 1834 and 1840 in the 14th District of White County he being overcharged and that the Sherriff of White County have a credit therefor in the settlement of his accounts with the Trustee of White County

Issd For reasons appearing to the satisfaction of the Court upon the application of Samuel Johnson and John Robertson through a certain Henry B. Johnson it ordered that Leah Robertson adminestratrix of the Estate of James T. Robertson with his will annexed appear at the next term of this Court and enter into other good and sufficient security for the faithful performance of said adminestration so as to release the said Samuel Johnson and John Robertson her securities and that Subpoena issue directed &c

Ordered by Court that Legrand C. Love be released from working on road and Street in the Courty of White his residence being only temporary in Sparta and belonging also to the milk sick hills and works regularly under John Wallace Overseer thereof -

Issd Ordered by Court that Robert C. Betty be appointed overseer of the road from the Blue Spring branch to the Crossing of the Branch near James H. Nelson (now Dettys) being a road of the second class and keep the same in repair as the law requires and that the same list and bounds of hands to work thereon that worked under Jesse M. Sullivan late Overseer thereof

(P-452) Monday 3 May 1841

This day William J. Russell one of the adminestrators of John M. Little Deceased returned two Inventories of the Estate of the deceased upon oath which is ordered to be recorded -

This day William J. Russell one of the adminestrators of John M. Little Dec'd returned upon oath two accounts of sales of the Estate of the deceased which is ordered to be recorded.

This day William Hudson guardian to the minor heirs of William Durham Deceased returned his report upon oath which is ordered to be recorded -

Issd Ordered by Court that Andrew J. Holder be appointed Overseer of the road from Paynes Bridge across the Caney Fork unto a point to be designated by Thomas Green and Lewis Pettett Esquires being a road of the second Class and keep the same in repair as the law requires and that Thomas Green and Lewis Pettett Esqs sign a list and bounds of hands to work thereon between him and Forrister Fifer -

This day William Glenn one of the adminestrators of John R. Glenn deceased returned upon oath an additional account of sales of the property of said Estate which is ordered to be recorded.

This day Jonathan T. Bradley Esquire Sherriff of White County appeared in open Court and appointed William G. Green his Deputy in place of Colo. John England who being present in open Court took an oath to support the Constitution of the United States and of the State of Tennessee and the oath of Deputy Sherriff of said County and thereupon entered upon the discharge of his duties - .

Ordered by Court that Robert B. Glenn be released from the payment of fifty six and a fourth cents the amount of a poll tax for the year 1831 and that the Estate of David L. Mitchell Deceased have a credit therefor in the settlement of his accounts with the Trustee of White County-.

This day Anson Gibbs guardian to Sylvester C. Gibbs returned his report upon oath which is ordered to be recorded.

Ordered that Court be adjourned untill Court in Course

Test
N. Oldham, Clk.

David Snodgrass
Sims Dearing
Robert H. McManus

(P-453) State of Tennessee

At a Quorum Court began and held for the County of White in the State aforesaid in the Court house in the town of Sparta before the Justices of said Court on the first Mondy being the Seventh day of June in the year 1841 And of the Independence of the United States of America the sixty fifth year

Present the worshipful

Glenn	David Snodgrass	
in place	Robert H. McManus	Esquires
of	William Glenn, Jr.	
S. Dearing	Edmund Stamps	Justices

Issd Ordered by Court that Elijah Denton be appointed Overseer of the road from John Haltermans to the Kentucky road being a road of the first class and keep the same in repair as the law requires And that the same list and bounds of hands that worked under Jesse Franks late overseer thereof be assigned to work thereon.

Issd Ordered by Court that Pleasant Anderson be appointed Overseer of the road from John Haltermans to Lewis Phillips being a road of the first Class and keep the same in repair as the law requires and that the same list and bounds of hands that worked under Spencer Holder, Jr. late overseer thereof be assigned to work thereon.

Issd Ordered by Court that James W. Denton be appointed Overseer of the road from Hills branch to a post oposite to Lewis Phillips being a road of the first Class and keep the same in repair as the law requires and that the same list and bounds of hands that worked under Levi Kerr late Overseer thereof be assigned to work thereon - .

Issd Ordered by Court that John W. Cope be appointed Overseer of the road from Melton Grosses to the middle of the Carter, old field being a road of the first class and keep the same in repair as the law requires and that the same list and bounds of hands that worked under Larkin W. Stuart late Overseer thereof be assigned to work thereon -

Ordered by Court that John Warren be appointed Overseer of the road from the Corporation of the town of Sparta to the Bridge at the Harriot Iron works being a road of the first class and keep the same in repair as the law requires. And that the same list and bounds of hands that worked under Robert Wadkins late overseer thereof be assigned to work thereon - .

Issd Ordered by Court that Daniel Jones be appointed Overseer of the road from the top of Gum spring Mountain to McGowens old place (P-454) being a road of the second Class and keep the same in repair as the law requires and that the same list and bounds of hands that worked under John H. Jones late Overseer thereof be assigned to work thereon.

Issd Ordered by Court that Ransom Gun be appointed Overseer of the road from Post Oak Creek to Robert Howards being a road of the second Class and keep the same in repair as the law requires and that the same list and bounds of hands that worked under Benjamin Wilhite late Overseer thereof be assigned to work thereon.

Isd Ordered by Court that Thomas T. Watson be appointed Overseer of the road from the ford of Little Caney fork to Post oak Creek being a road of the second Class and keep the same in repair as the law requires and that the same list and bounds of hands that worked under Washington F. Williams late Overseer thereof be assigned to work thereon.

Isd Ordered by Court that John D. Erwin be appointed Overseer of the road from the pole Bridge on the Lisk road to the Peeledchesnut being a road of the second Class and keep the same in repair as the law requires. And that the same list and bounds of hands that worked under William H. Baker late Overseer thereof be assigned to work thereon - .

Isd Ordered by Court that Elihu Vandiver be appointed Overseer of the road from the flat rock on the mountain to the entersection of the Turnpike road near James Simpsons on the Mountain being a road of the second Class and keep the same in repair as the law requires and that the same list and bounds of hands that worked under James Beckwith late Overseer thereof be assigned to work thereon.

Isd Ordered by Court that Moses Netherton be appointed Overseer of the road from the mouth of Mill Creek to the 19th mile post being a road of the second Class and keep the same in repair as the law requires and that the same list and bounds of hands that worked under Thomas L. Elms late Overseer thereof be assigned to work thereon.

Isd Ordered by Court that William Waller be appointed Overseer of the milk sick Hills and flats near John W. Simpsons and that the same hands that worked under Laban Wallace late Overseer thereof who has this day resigned, be assigned to work thereon - .

This day Joseph Glenn adminestrators of Robert Glenn Deceased returned into open Court upon oath an additional Inventory of the property of the deceased which is ordered to be recorded.

(P-455) Monday 7th June A.D. 1841

This day Harman Little and William J. Russell adminestrators of the Estate of John M. Little Deceased returned upon oath into open Court an additional Inventory and account of the sales of the property of the Deceased which is ordered to be recorded.

This day the Commissioners heretofore appointed lay off and set apart one years provisions for the support and maintainance of the widow and family of Robert Hewett Dec'd out of his Estate made their report which is received and ordered to be recorded

Ordered by Court that the road leading from the fork of the road above Sparta passing Littles Bridge to the intersection of the Calf Killer road near Wm. McKennys be raised from a third Class road to a road of the second Class. And that the same be so recognised and established and that John Kitchenside be appointed Overseer thereof from the fork to Littles Bridge to its intersection and Richard Bradley be appointed Overseer from Littles Bridge to its intersection and that they respectively keep the same in repair as the law requires And that David Snodgrass and Sims Dearing Esqs be appointed to assign them lists and bounds of hands to work thereon respectively - .

Ordered by Court that Edmund Stamps Esquire be appointed to assign lists and bounds of hands between Thomas S. Elms and the diffrent Overseers of the roads in the neighbourhood having due regard to the dignity of said roads respectively -

Issd This day the death of John Cooley late of the County of White was suggested in open Court and that he departed this life intestate whereupon Elizabeth Cooley appeared in open Court and was appointed administratrix of all and singular the goods and chattles rights and credits of the said Deceased and thereupon took the oath prescribed by law and together with William Glenn, Jr., and Larkin M. Stuart entered into and acknowledged bond in the sum of one hundred dollars conditioned as the law requires - .

Issd Ordered by Court that William Glenn, Jr., Melton Gross, and Walker Bennett be appointed Commissioners to lay off assign and set apart to the widow and family of John Cooley dec'd one years provision for the maintainance out of the Estate of the deceased and report thereof to the next term of this Court.

From reasons appearing fully to the satisfaction of the Court from testimony produced before them, It is considered and so ordered that the Covenant of Indenture of a certain Joseph Lamb to a certain William Clayton Printer be cancelled, set aside, made void and for nothing esteemed that the said Clayton be released and forever discharged from all liabilities therein and that the said Joseph Lamb be set at liberty.

(P-456) Monday 7th June A.D. 1841

Issd This day the death of William Crook late of the County of White was suggested in open Court and that he departed this life intestate, whereupon Allen Crook appeared in open court and was appointed adminestrator of all and singular the goods and chattles rights and credits of the Deceased and thereupon took the oath prescribed by law and together with Levi L. Murphy, John Crook and Charles Crook intered into and acknowledged bond in the sum of seven hundred and fifty dollars conditioned as the law requires - .

Issd This day the death of William Snodgrass late of the County of White was suggested in open Court and that he departed this life intestate whereupon James Snodgrass and William G. Sims were appointed adminestrators of all and singular the goods and chattles rights and credits of the deceased, and thereupon being present in open Court took the oath prescribed by law and together with David Snodgrass, John Brown, James McKenny and Thomas Snodgrass entered into and acknowledged bond in the sum of Twenty Thousand Dollars conditioned as the law requires. And that said adm'rs have untill December term to return Inventory and sales - .

Whereas by the last will and Testament of Thomas Little Deceased a certain Brice Little, David Little and William Snodgrass were appointed and qualified Executors, and that William Snodgrass one of the said Executors has since died and a certain James Snodgrass and William G. Sims have been appointed and qualified administrator of the said William Snodgrass Deceased, which administrators are desirous to be released and discharged from any and all duties that might devolve upon them as the immediate representatives of the said Wm. Snodgrass one of the Executors of the said Thomas Little Deceased - And the Court for satisfactory reasons beleiving the said Brice Little and David Little the surviving Executors of the said Thomas Little deceased are fully capable and competent to the final settlement of said estate therefore it is considered by the Court and so ordered, that the surviving Executors of Thomas Little deceased and the administrators of William Snodgrass deceased late one of the Exer of Thomas Little deceased serve so that each shall be disconnected from the other in the future prosecution of either of said Estates to final settlement - .

Ordered by Court that the adminestrators of Robert Hewett Deceased have leave untill the next term of this Court to return the Inventory and account of sales of said Estate -

This day personally appeared in open Court Mary Ann Hayes and Reubin P. Hayes two of the minor heirs of James T. Hayes Deceased who being over the age of fourteen years and selected and made choice of Richard Crowder as their guardian and at the same time the Court appointed Richard Crowder guardian to James P. Hayes, Richard Hayes, (P-457) Sarah Hayes, Eliza Hayes, William Hayes and John Hayes, six other minor heirs of the said Deceased under the age of fourteen years, who being present in open Court took the oath required by law and together with Asa Certain and Richard Nelson Entered into and acknowledged bond in the sum of Three Hundred dollars conditioned as the law requires

This day Leah Robinson administratrix of James T. Robinson Deceased with his will annexed, in obedience to a subpoena issue from the last term of this Court appeared in open Court and thereupon with John Robinson, Edward Elms and John H. Carmachael entered into and acknowledged Bond in the sum of Ten Thousand Dollars conditioned as the law requires. And it is considered and so ordered by the Court that Samuel Johnson one of her late securities for her said adminestration from all further and future liabilities therein as such be released and forever discharged.

This day Winkfield Hill guardian to Elizabeth Hill late Elizabeth Pinner and one of the heirs of Dempsey Pinner deceased produced in open Court a receipt of his ward in full which at his request is ordered to be recorded. -

Ordered that court be adjourned untill 9 O'clock tomorrow morning

David Snodgrass
A. S. Rogers
James Bartlett

Tuesday morning 8th June A.D. 1841 Court met pursuant to adjournment
Present the Worshipful

David Snodgrass) Esquires
James Bartlett)
Anderson S. Rogers) Justices

Isad Ordered by Court that Samuel Lance Esquire be appointed to apportion a list and bounds of hands to Elihu Vandiver Overseer of the road on the mountain -

This day Nicholas Oldham the clerk of this Court produced in open Court a report of a settlement with Richard Crowder administrator of Andrew Clouse Deceased which is received by the Court and confirmed which is ordered to be recorded.

(P-458) Tuesday Morning 8th June 1841

The State of Tennessee vs Issd James Scott } Bastardy Elizabeth Savage Pros'x

This day came the prosecutrix by her Attorney Richard G. Roberts Esq and moved the Court for execution against the Defendant and securities for the payment of the sum of forty dollars rendered at a former term of this Court whereupon it is considered by the Court and so ordered that a fairi facias issue in the above cause according to law -

Ordered that Court be adjourned untill Court in course

David Snodgrass
Anderson S. Rogers
James Bartlett

Test

N. Oldham, Clk.

www.ingramcontent.com/pod-product-compliance
Lightning Source LLC
Chambersburg PA
CBHW021842020426
42334CB00013B/152

* 9 7 8 0 8 9 3 0 8 4 5 4 7 *